D1498475

Sociology of Health and Wellness

Bassim Hamadeh, CEO and Publisher
John Remington, Senior Field Acquisitions Editor
Tony Paese, Project Editor
Alia Bales, Production Editor
Miguel Macias, Senior Graphic Designer
Danielle Gradisher, Licensing Associate
Don Kesner, Interior Designer
Natalie Piccotti, Senior Marketing Manager
Kassie Graves, Vice President of Editorial
Jamie Giganti, Director of Academic Publishing

Cover images:
  Copyright © 2017 iStockphoto LP/Rawpixel.
  Copyright © 2017 iStockphoto LP/Tinpixels.
  Copyright © 2017 iStockphoto LP/Rawpixel.
  Copyright © 2017 iStockphoto LP/PeopleImages.
  Copyright © 2017 iStockphoto LP/gorodenkoff.

Printed in the United States of America.

ISBN: 978-1-5165-2550-8 (pbk) / 978-1-5165-2551-5 (br)

Sociology of Health and Wellness

AN APPLIED APPROACH

FIRST EDITION

Edited by Jacquelyn Cheun and Nichola Driver

Table of Contents

Preface

Sociology of Health and Wellness: An Applied Approach was designed as a supplemental reader. Over the years, we used various textbooks to help teach medical sociology. However, I (Dr. Cheun) realized that the textbooks were lacking current research and depth in covering a topic. Coming from the health care field (with more than ten years of experience) I found this to be very unnerving. I decided to create a reader to help supplement current textbooks available. I approached Dr. Driver to be co-author because of her experience in the health field and teaching sociology.

In this reader, we have chosen specific research articles about issues we found fundamental in the medical sociology curriculum such as upstream factors and the social and cultural meaning of illness. We also looked for more current issues facing the health care industry. We examined the increased use of technology and how this is changing health care. For instance, is technology turning patients into consumers? Or is it shrinking physicians' autonomy? We also, selected articles about health policy to show the downstream effects of policy on the population. The Patient Protection and Affordable Care Act of 2010 (ACA) has been in full effect since 2012, yet this policy is not widely mentioned in current texts. In this text, we look at the success (or lack thereof) of the ACA and ask the question: Did it lower United States' health disparities?

Our goal in creating this book is to show students the application of the medical sociology in today's society. We hope it gives teachers extra resources in the classroom to improve their students' ability to critically think about current social issues.

We hope you enjoy this textbook.

PART I

Upstream Thinking about Health

Health is a state that varies from person to person. Some people are very healthy, some people are very unhealthy, and most people lie somewhere between these two extremes, with occasional bouts of sickness. If we compare across communities, we see that some communities are healthier than others. If we compare across states or countries, we see similar variations. If we then try to think about what creates these disparities, or what makes some people healthy and some people unhealthy, what thoughts come to mind? You may think it has something to do with exposure to germs or viruses or the biological processes in the body that determine your state of physical health. You might think about the importance of an individual's genetic predisposition to certain diseases, such as cancer and heart disease. You will probably also think

1

about an individual's lifestyle choices or health behaviors, such as smoking, exercise, or eating right. All of these things play a role in whether a person develops a disease or struggles with poor health status.

Medical sociologists recognize the role that these biological and individual factors play in a person's health. For example, they recognize the need to educate individuals on the risks of alcohol and drugs and the importance of programs that help people stop smoking and eat a more balanced diet. However, medical sociologists also have a more "upstream" perspective to health. This means that they recognize the importance of social factors as determinants of health, in addition to individual factors. What do we mean by social factors that determine health (also known as the "social determinants of health")? These are characteristics of the social structure in which people live that influence the individual behaviors, lifestyle choices, exposure to germs and viruses, and so on. An individual's societal circumstances, such as income, education, occupation, race/ethnicity, cultural assimilation, gender, age, housing, neighborhood, stress levels, among other things, can determine his/her health outcomes. In their research, medical sociologists often study health patterns that emerge based on these social characteristics. For example, studies show that, even in the most affluent countries, the poor have substantially shorter life expectancies and more illnesses than the rich. In the first reading in this book, Iceland mentions that "only 30 percent of people who graduated from college report that their health is not excellent or very good, compared to 77 percent of those who did not finish high school. Disability is likewise less prevalent among those with a college degree, as are obesity, diabetes, and infant mortality." Similarly, lower levels of education are linked with a higher likelihood of smoking and shorter life expectancy (Marmot et al. 2008). Furthermore, children born into poor families are more likely to live in unsafe neighborhoods, be exposed to garbage and litter, and have poor and/or dilapidated housing. They are also less likely to have sidewalks, parks, or playgrounds to use for exercise (Singh, Siahpush, and Kogan 2010). Given the rate of residential segregation that persists in our communities, racial and ethnic minorities are more likely to experience burden of living in these unsafe and unhealthy neighborhoods.

Patients, health care providers, and policymakers often believe that medical care, including advanced medical technology and prescription drugs, is the answer to health ailments. We like to order more tests and try out new drugs or new technologies. Providers and patients alike have a hard time believing that something as simple as the way we live could make such a powerful difference. Yet, if a person's ailments are rooted in day-to-day repetition of things like hard physical labor, a lack of nutritious food, or exposure to environmental hazards, the treatment may be social in nature, not medical. Medical sociologists and public health professionals recognize the importance of good housing, public infrastructure, access to healthy food, access to green space or safe places to exercise, and good jobs in determining the health of a population. Our country has a health care system that does little to address these root problems. Instead, we spend an astronomical amount of money on managing the symptoms of a disease. We spend almost twice as much on health care in the United States as any other country in the world. Most of this money goes toward intervention in established disease, even when the disease itself is lifestyle related or social in nature and may be preventable. Ultimately, improving population health and achieving health equity will require unique and holistic approaches to health care that address social, economic, and environmental factors.

Once we understand the problems, how can we address them? We, the authors, encourage budding medical sociologists to take an applied approach to addressing the social determinants of health. Integrating an upstream perspective to health care is key to achieving greater health equity, and can result in dramatic cost savings to the public. For example, by placing individuals in housing and coordinating care across homeless service providers, health centers, and hospitals, the 10th Decile Project in Los Angeles saw a 72 percent reduction in total health care costs for their most frequent emergency department users. The program's homeless service providers work to break the cycle of chronically homeless individuals using emergency room care (Robert Wood Johnson Foundation 2014).

Camden, New Jersey, provides another example of an applied, upstream approach to health. A high poverty city, Camden residents often had difficulties accessing primary care providers (Heiman and Artiga 2015). Thus, some sought emergency room treatment for nonemergency conditions, inflating hospital costs to more than $100 million every year (with 30 percent of those costs coming from 1 percent of patients) (Robert Wood Johnson Foundation 2014). In an attempt to address barriers in access, the Camden Coalition of Health Care Providers created a care management system that connected these frequent users with primary care providers and social workers (Heiman and Artiga 2015). The main goal of the care management system, called Link2Care, was to help identify and address both their medical and social needs. Those enrolled in the initiative saw a significant decline in their average hospital admissions in the six months after enrollment (Robert Wood Johnson Foundation 2014).

Historically, we have numerous examples of the impact of addressing social determinants of health. Throughout history, infectious diseases were a common cause of death, especially among children. Even as recent as the early 1900s, common causes of death included pneumonia, influenza, tuberculosis, typhoid fever, or one of the various forms of dysentery (Yet, over the past 100 years, the United States and other western nations experienced an epidemiological transition, where deaths due to infectious diseases declined dramatically (Conrad and Leiter 2013). Today, chronic diseases are the major causes of mortality in the United States, including heart disease, cancer, and stroke (Murphy et al. 2017). Rene Dubos (1959) and Thomas McKeown (1971) were among the first to recognize that advances in clinical medicine were not the reason for this change. Rather, the change was brought on primarily by social and environmental factors, including improved sanitation, housing, nutrition, and standard of living. Thus, addressing social determinants of health and improving social conditions has changed the world as we know it today, including the average life expectancy in the United States.

The readings in the first part of this book, entitled Part I: Upstream Thinking about Health, provide you with important information on the social determinants of health, including explanations of how each works to influence health status and outcomes. In "Health and Mortality," Iceland gives a broad overview of health trends in the United States. He emphasizes that although life expectancy is improving and infant mortality has declined, these outcomes differ across socioeconomic and racial/ethnic groups. He provides the general mechanisms through which these disparities exist, including an explanation about the influence of education, residential segregation, and discrimination. He concludes with a discussion on the differences in health outcomes and spending across other developed nations, and the role that access to care, individual behaviors, and social factors play in these disparities.

In "Understanding Gender and Health: Old Patterns, New Trends, and Future Directions," Rieker, Bird, and Lang discuss gender differences across a variety of diseases, as well as the pathways and mechanisms that underlie these differences. They describe health behaviors as a primary reason for these differences, but they also emphasize the importance of gender norms in proscribing these health behaviors. They also offer the constrained-choice model as an explanation for socially patterned health for men and women.

In "The Relationship between Socioeconomic Status and Health, or, They Call It 'Poor Health' for a Reason," Barr speaks about perhaps the most fundamental of social determinants of health: socioeconomic status. He outlines the explanations for this pattern, including a possible difference in time preference between higher and lower social classes. In "Social Capital and Health" and "Does Your Neighborhood Make You Fat?" Kawachi and Guthman expand on additional social determinants of health, explaining how interactions with one's environment play a role in health status. Each gives important policy implications for addressing these determinants as well as encourages unique perspectives to these areas of interest. For example, Kawachi stresses the importance of policymakers distinguishing between bonding and bridging social capital, in order to connect disadvantaged community members to important resources without tapping into the help of already-strained disadvantaged neighbors and family members. Likewise, Guthman recommends policymakers use caution when linking the built environment to obesity, without recognizing the importance of social class.

In "Health Social Movements: History, Current Work, and Future Directions," Brown and colleagues discuss how health social movements routinely address the issues that medical sociologists write about. Like sociologists, social activists try to understand how the social structure plays a role in negative health outcomes and criticize the systemic injustices or patterns of inequality that exist. We include this article to further encourage new scholars to not only think critically about the health problems, but also think critically about solutions.

Finally, in "The Effect of Social Support on State Anxiety Levels During Pregnancy," Duman and Kocak provide an example of a social research study in the realm of medical sociology. The article explores the influence of one social determinant of health, social support, on women's anxiety levels during pregnancy. The authors provide a basic example of the process and craft of research through their description of their hypotheses, methods, and findings. Ultimately, the findings demonstrate a specific example of the power of social components on physical and mental health.

REFERENCES

Conrad, Peter, and Valerie Leiter. 2012. *Sociology of Health and Illness.* New York: Worth Publishers.

Dubos, René J. 1959. *Mirage of Health: Utopias, Progress, and Biological Change.* New Brunswick, NJ: Rutgers University Press.

Heiman, Harry J., and Samantha Artiga. 2015. *Beyond Health Care: The Role of Social Determinants in Promoting Health and Health Equity.* The Kaiser Family Foundation Issue Brief. November 2015. https://www.kff.org/disparities-policy/issue-brief/beyond-health-care-the-role-of-social-determinants-in-promoting-health-and-health-equity/.

Marmot, Michael, Sharon Friel, Ruth Bell, Tanja AJ Houweling, Sebastian Taylor, and Commission on Social Determinants of Health. "Closing the gap in a generation: health equity through action on the social determinants of health." *The Lancet* 372, no. 9650 (2008): 1661–1669.

McKeown, Thomas. 1971. "A Historical Appraisal of the Medical Task." In *Medical History and Medical Care: A Symposium of Perspectives*, edited by Gordon McLachlan and Thomas McKeown. New York: Oxford University Press.

Murphy, Sherry L., Jiaquan Xu, Kenneth D. Kochanek, Sally C. Curtin, and Elizabeth Arias. "Deaths: Final data for 2015." National Vital Statistics Report. (2017). Robert Wood Johnson Foundation. 2014. *A Coalition Creates a Citywide Care Management System*. Program Results Report. June 13, 2014.

Singh, Gopal K., Mohammad Siahpush, and Michael D. Kogan. 2010. "Neighborhood Socioeconomic Conditions, Built Environments, and Childhood Obesity," *Health Affairs* 29(3): 503–12.

Health and Mortality

John Iceland

Few issues have been more contentious than the state of our nation's health and health care system. People differ in their views on how to best deliver quality care while containing health care costs that threaten to overwhelm federal and state budgets. As a way of providing a firm factual footing for these discussions, the National Academies convened an expert panel of researchers to report on the health of Americans in comparison with people in a number of peer countries. The report, released in 2013, was ominously titled *U.S. Health in International Perspective: Shorter Lives, Poorer Health.* Indeed, the panel concluded: "The United States is among the wealthiest nations in the world, but it is far from the healthiest. Although life expectancy and survival rates in the United States have improved dramatically over the past century, Americans live shorter lives and experience more injuries and illnesses than people in other high-income countries."[1]

The findings were widely reported in the press, and naturally the public weighed in with their opinions on why the United States fares so poorly. Some pointed to the health care system. One tweet sent in to CNN read: "America has made healthcare most difficult to access even for the middle class. Imagine the poor. That's what greed does!" Others pointed to obesity and the environment: "We invented the term #supersize" and "I moved from Europe to the U.S. about six months ago. First observation after a visit to the supermarket: fruits and vegetables way too expensive; cheap products stuffed with fats and sugars. In short, if you want to kill off a whole population, slow but sure, I couldn't come up with a better strategy." CNN commentator Steve Cray added, "They [the National Academies panel] needed 18 months to determine the problem! It will take me less than a minute: obesity, sedentary lifestyle, a for-profit healthcare system controlled by insurance and pill-pushing pharmaceutical companies that try to limit preventative healthcare."[2]

Many of these observations hold at least some truth. There is no single reason why health in the United States is worse than in other countries; rather, it is a confluence of factors, including disparities in people's access to health care, individual health behaviors, and the physical and social environment.[3] The rest of this chapter provides an in-depth discussion of these and related issues. First, I document recent patterns and trends in health and mortality in the United States. I review evidence on health disparities by gender, race, and socioeconomic status and describe their origins. I discuss the aging of the American population and the strains this puts on the health care system and the U.S. budget. I end by systematically describing why the health of Americans lags behind their peers in other developed countries.

John Iceland, "Health and Mortality," A Portrait of America: The Demographic Perspective, pp. 188-206, 227-229. Copyright © 2014 by University of California Press. Reprinted with permission.

FIGURE 1.1 Life expectancy at birth, by sex, 1970–2010.

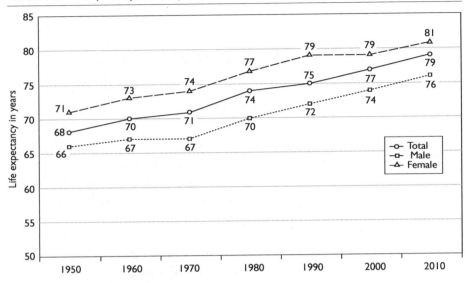

Source: Centers for Disease Control and Prevention 2011.

PATTERNS AND TRENDS IN HEALTH AND MORTALITY

Let's start with the good news. In many important respects the health of Americans has improved. Figure 1.1 shows that life expectancy at birth grew from 66 years in 1950 to 76 in 2010 for men and from 71 to 81 for women. This kind of gradual health improvement shows up in other ways. In 1970, the infant mortality rate was 20 (indicating that 20 infants out of 1,000 died before their first birthday). By 2011, this figure was less than a third as large, at 6.[4] As a National Center for Health Statistics reported in an examination of mortality patterns over the 1935 to 2010 period, "Although there were year to year exceptions, the last 75 years witnessed sustained declines in the risk of dying in the United States."[5] Decreases in death rates occurred for men and women, all age groups, and for all racial and ethnic groups. The number of Americans living to see their hundredth birthday has risen from 32,000 to 53,000 from 1980 to 2010. The centenarian population increased by a

greater percentage (66 percent) than the increase in the population as a whole (36 percent).[6]

Why women live longer than men is not fully understood, but part of the reason may be biological (the female advantage in life expectancy is found among a majority of animals), and part is due to environmental and behavioral factors. Men consume more tobacco, alcohol, and drugs than women, and they are more likely to die from accidents and intentional injuries (homicides, suicides, and in war). The slight narrowing of the gender gap in life expectancy in the United States and other developed countries since the 1970s is likely a function of a reduction in lifestyle differences. Women, for example, are more likely to smoke than they used to be, and this has contributed to a decline in the gender mortality gap.[7]

Health outcomes vary considerably by race and Hispanic origin. The life expectancy among whites was 79 in 2010, four years more than the life expectancy among blacks (75). This gap, however, is narrower than in the past, especially since 1990 (see figure 1.2).[8] This trend applies to both men and

FIGURE 1.2 Life expectancy at birth, by race and Hispanic origin, 1950–2010. Note: The Centers for Disease Control and Prevention time series for Hispanic life expectancy does not begin until 2006.

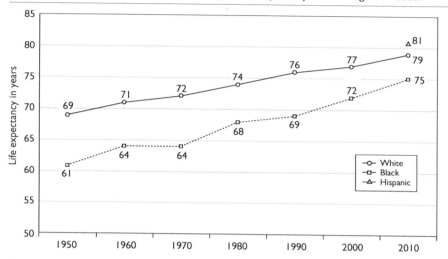

Source: Centers for Disease Control and Prevention 2011.

women, though the black-white gap among women (3 years) is narrower than among men (5 years).[9] The persistence of significant health disparities between blacks and whites—but the narrowing of the gap in recent years—shows up in other ways, including age-adjusted death rates, cause-specific death rates, infant mortality, and disability.[10] The higher rates of disease and death among blacks compared with whites reflect the earlier onset of illness, the greater severity of diseases, and lower rates of survival.[11] A final finding of note in the figure is that, contrary to what one might expect given socioeconomic differentials across groups […], Hispanics have a higher life expectancy (81) than both blacks and whites. This "Hispanic health paradox" is discussed in more detail shortly. The Centers for Disease Control do not publish life expectancy figures for Asians, but other data indicate that Asians are not disadvantaged when it comes to health outcomes and in fact often fare better than whites.[12] For example, the infant mortality rate for babies born to Asian mothers (4.5 per 1,000 live births) is lower than among non-Hispanic whites (5.5). Finally, it should be noted that statistics for pan-ethnic groups mask some variation across origins within a given group. For example, regarding Hispanics, the infant mortality rate among Puerto Ricans (7.3) is higher than among Mexicans (5.6) and Cubans (4.9).[13]

Health and mortality are strongly associated with socioeconomic status. Figure 1.3 shows the differences in health outcomes by levels of education. (These patterns are also observed across income groups.) Only 30 percent of people who graduated from college report that their health is not excellent or very good, compared with 77 percent of those who did not finish high school. Disability is likewise less prevalent among those with a college degree, as are obesity, diabetes, and infant mortality.[14] Socioeconomic status has also been linked to an even wider array of health problems, including low birth weight, cardiovascular disease, hypertension, arthritis, cancer, and

FIGURE 1.3 Health, by educational attainment, 2000s. Note: The percentage of those without excellent or very good health refers to self-reported health among respondents ages 25 to 74; activity limitation refers to respondents age 25 and over; the percentage of obese respondents refers to those age 20 and over with a body mass index greater than or equal to 30 kg.

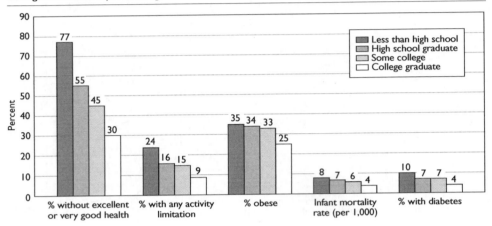

Source: Braveman et al. 2010, table 2.

depression.[15] Contrary to the narrowing of the racial health gap, the strength of the relationship between socioeconomic status and health has increased in recent decades, with growing gaps in mortality, life expectancies, and the prevalence of disabilities by educational attainment.[16]

What explains these socioeconomic health disparities? Education, income, and occupational status can all affect one's health. Better-educated people tend to have greater access to information and resources that promote health—no small matter when considering the complexity of diagnosing and treating health problems and navigating through our health care system. People with higher levels of education also tend to have a greater sense of control over their lives, are more likely to plan ahead, and are better able to draw upon useful social networks that can provide advice and assistance during difficult times.[17] Obtaining a higher level of education also increases one's earning power and probability of landing a high-status, stable job, which in turn also lead to better health and lower mortality.

With regard to income, people with fewer resources may not have the means to purchase health care insurance that provides access to better health services. More than 60 percent of the uninsured are in low-income families. Although many poor individuals may be eligible for Medicaid, many do not end up enrolling. As a result, low-income individuals are less likely to see a physician and get preventative screening.[18] In addition, lower-income families may not have the resources to access quality housing, schooling, recreation, and nutrition that can enhance health. For example, poorer neighborhoods are more likely to be located near highways, industrial areas, and toxic waste sites, since land is cheaper in those areas. Families of low socioeconomic status (SES) are more likely to live in crowded and noisy environments, which can lead to, among other conditions, hypertension. The struggle to get by can be stressful, and this can affect both physical and mental health.

Similarly, people employed in lower-status occupations often have jobs that expose them to greater physical risk. For example, some blue-collar jobs involve exposure to toxic substances or to physical activity that can lead to injury and disability.[19] In contrast, people in higher-status professions have more control over their own working environment and are generally less likely to lose their job.[20]

In addition to the direct ways in which SES may contribute to poorer health, a number of indirect pathways have also been identified, including behavior and lifestyle, which might account for half of the earlier mortality among lower-SES individuals. Those with less education and income are more likely to smoke and drink heavily, are less likely to exercise and eat nutritiously, and are thus more likely to be overweight. Low-income individuals and their children have less access to safe, well-lit places to walk, bike, and play, and these all contribute to less healthy living.[21]

The following story on the growing poverty in the United States in the wake of the Great Recession illustrates the health challenges faced by poor individuals:

> Millions of workers and their families are similarly vulnerable to such mundane changes as a slight decline in the number of hours per workweek or an extra few cents per gallon in the cost of gasoline. ... One such person is 67-year-old Mary Vasquez, whose Social Security check is $600 and whose rent is $500. A tiny woman, her health broken by cancer, heart attacks, diabetes, high blood pressure and a multitude of other ailments, Vasquez works as a phone operator at a Walmart on the outskirts of Dallas. ... A large part of her salary went for medical expenses not covered by Medicare or her Walmart healthcare plan; much of the rest went to pay down usurious payday loans she'd accumulated in recent years as her health declined. Sitting in a union hall in the suburb of Grapevine, Vasquez (one of

a handful of employees working to unionize her workplace) explains that she skips "mostly breakfast and sometimes lunch." As a diabetic, she is supposed to eat fresh produce. Instead, she says, "a lot of times I buy a TV dinner; we have them on sale for 88 cents. A lot of times, food, I can't pay for."

> Another American who struggles to put food on the table is Jorge, a 57-year-old who migrated to the United States from Mexico in 1982. Jorge (who doesn't want his last name used) lives with his wife in the large Chaparral *colonia,* an informal settlement of trailers, small houses and shanties near Las Cruces, New Mexico. ... "There's a lot of deterioration of the trailers," Jorge says in Spanish. "In winter, pipes explode because of the freeze. I don't have water right now. Heating is so expensive, with propane gas. Those who have little children, they have to use it, but it's so expensive." A volunteer firefighter, he adds, "We see a lot of accidents with water heaters and explosions with the propane tanks."[22]

These stories illustrate the many factors contributing to the poor health of low-income Americans, including the challenge of paying for health care, the propensity to purchase low-cost and often high-caloric food of dubious nutritional value, and problems with housing conditions that can lead to accidents and poor health.

Regarding racial disparities, the health disadvantage among blacks stems not only from their disadvantaged socioeconomic position but also from racism and residential segregation. Differences in their health outcomes cannot be attributed entirely to SES, because blacks are more disadvantaged than whites even when compared with those in the same income brackets and at the same educational levels. Simple comparisons overlook the multiple SES disadvantages that blacks often face. Blacks have less income and wealth than whites of the same educational backgrounds, and they also live in worse neighborhoods with higher poverty. The differences in the residential circumstances of blacks and whites, rooted in residential segregation, ensure that blacks are more likely to live in neighborhoods with greater social disorder and isolation. These differences reflect the historical legacy of institutional discrimination as well as contemporary racism. Experiences of discrimination can increase stress and hypertension and are predictive of an increased risk of substance abuse to cope with the extra stress.[23]

Given what we know about the association among socioeconomic status, race, and health, why do Hispanics have a higher life expectancy and lower levels of fatal chronic diseases, such as heart disease, cancer, lung disease, and stroke, than both blacks and whites?[24] This unexpected finding has been termed the *Hispanic paradox*. Further deepening the puzzle, immigrants' risk of disability and chronic disease increases with increasing length of residence in the United States, and native-born Hispanics have worse health and lower life expectancies than Hispanic immigrants. A number of explanations have been offered to explain these patterns. Some believe that cultural factors, such as better health habits and strong networks of social support in Hispanic communities help explain it. Thus, according to this view, as Hispanic immigrants and their children acculturate to the poor eating habits of the native population, their health outcomes worsen and their life expectancy declines.[25] Certainly, anecdotal evidence supports the view that Hispanic health behaviors become unhealthier in the United States. As one story in the news described it:

> Becoming an American can be bad for your health. ... For the recently arrived, the quantity and accessibility of food speaks to the boundless promise of the United States. Esther Angeles remembers being amazed at the size of hamburgers—as big as dinner plates—when she first came to the United States from Mexico 15 years ago. "I thought, this is really a country of opportunity," she said. "Look at the size of the food!"
>
> Fast-food fare not only tasted good, but was also a sign of success, a family treat that new earnings put in reach. "The crispiness was delicious," said Juan Muniz, 62, recalling his first visit to Church's Chicken with his family in the late 1970s. "I was proud and excited to eat out. I'd tell them: 'Let's go eat. We can afford it now.'"
>
> For others, supersize deals appealed. "You work so hard, you want to use your money in a smart way," said Aris Ramirez, a community health worker in Brownsville, explaining the thinking. "So when they hear 'twice the fries for an extra 49 cents,' people think, 'That's economical.'"
>
> For Ms. Angeles, the excitement of big food eventually wore off, and the frantic pace of the modern American workplace took over. She found herself eating hamburgers more because they were convenient and she was busy in her 78-hour-a-week job as a housekeeper. What is more, she lost control over her daughter's diet because, as a single mother, she was rarely with her at mealtimes.[26]

While these stories seem compelling, there is danger in relying too much on anecdotes, as the evidence supporting the notion that migration to the United States is wholly responsible for causing increasing obesity is actually not overwhelming. Notably, important shifts in nutritional patterns and trends toward inactivity have occurred in countries around the globe in recent years. Barry

Popkin, who has written extensively about this *nutritional transition,* notes: "The diet of poor people in rural or urban settings in Asia during the 1960s was simple and rather monotonous: rice with a small amount of vegetables, beans or fish. Today, their eating is transformed. It is common for people in these settings to regularly consume complex meals at any number of away-from-home food outlets—western or indigenous. The overall composition of diets in the developing world is shifting rapidly, particularly with respect to fat, caloric sweeteners, and animal-source foods."[27]

The prevalence of obesity has increased so rapidly in Mexico that the obesity rate there now surpasses the rate in the United States—making Mexico the most obese country in the hemisphere.[28] This suggests that immigrants and their children who are eating less nutritional foods now in the United States would be doing so regardless of whether they had migrated to the United States or not. As one commentator on growing obesity in Mexico put it, "The speed at which Mexicans have made the change from a diet dominated by maize and beans to one that bursts at the seams with processed fats and sugars poses one of the greatest challenges to public health officials."[29]

Factors that have contributed to growing obesity in Mexico and other developing countries include globalization and lifestyle changes. Some of these changes are cultural, in that patterns of food consumption associated with Western countries (the United States in particular) are being diffused throughout the world. Migration networks may have helped diffuse these eating patterns to Mexican communities,[30] but they may have occurred eventually anyway given their rise in countries around the globe. International food trade, commercialization, and marketing have made many new high-calorie foods and beverages with little nutritional value widely available at a relatively low cost. Such foods were initially mainly accessible to wealthier families in urban areas in developing countries, but they are increasingly available to poor families in rural areas as well.[31] Lifestyle changes stem from urbanization and the decline in physical activity in many occupations, both in the United States and abroad. Mechanization at work and in the household has reduced the need for strenuous labor. Many fewer people are employed in physically intensive activities such as farming, mining, and forestry, and an increasing number in the service sector are employed to perform sedentary activities, such as sitting in front of a computer terminal (much as I am as I write this).[32]

A growing consensus suggests that the issue of the Hispanic advantage in life expectancy in the United States is primarily related to *migration.* Specifically, Hispanics who migrate to the United States tend to be healthier than those who stay behind (in other words, immigrants are positively selected for their good health), and immigrants who leave the United States to return to home often do so when their health worsens. Indeed, studies have found that foreign-born Hispanics who left the United States had higher mortality levels than those who remained, and returnees to Mexico were more than three times more likely to rate their health as fair or poor than those who remained in the United States.[33] The Hispanic paradox has thus sometime been referred to as the immigrant paradox, as immigrants from a wide range of countries have longer life expectancies than do native-born Americans, and much of this has been attributed to the selectivity of immigrants more generally.[34] This issue is not fully settled, as it is not clear if migration fully explains the Hispanic health advantage. Research continues on the potentially protective roles that immigrant communities and health behaviors play.[35]

FIGURE 1.4 Age distribution and median age of the U.S. population, 1960–2010.

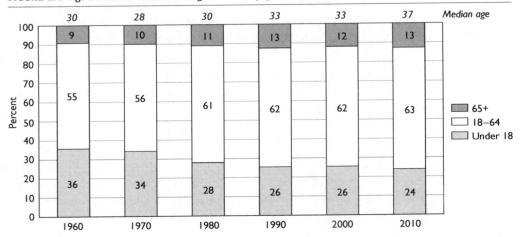

Source: Howden and Meyer 2011, figure 4.

THE AGING OF THE AMERICAN POPULATION AND HEALTH CARE COSTS

Like the population of most developed countries around the world, the U.S. population is gradually aging. This is a function of declining fertility rates, the aging of the relatively large baby boom generation, and declining mortality. Figure 1.4 shows that the median age of the U.S. population dipped slightly from 30 to 28 between 1960 and 1970 because of the lingering effects of the baby boom, before increasing to 37 by 2010. Likewise, the percentage of the population over the age of 65 increased from 9 percent in 1960 to 13 percent in 2010. This is expected to rise to 20 percent by the year 2050. The percentage of the population that is over the age of 65 is lower in the United States than in other countries with low fertility, such as Japan, Germany, and Italy (all of whose percentage over the age of 65 already exceeds 20 percent), but considerably higher than the corresponding percentages in rapidly growing developing countries such as Uganda and Egypt, where 2 percent and 5 percent of the population are over the age of 65, respectively.[36]

The composition of the older population varies by gender and race/ethnicity. Because of women's longer life expectancies, women made up well over half of the elderly population (57 percent) in 2010, though the narrowing of the male-female life expectancy gap in recent years has reduced the percentage of the older population that is female. (Women made up 59 percent of the elderly population in 2000.)[37] Whites currently constitute about 80 percent of the elderly population, but they make up just 63 percent of the total population. Moreover, only about 54 percent of all births in 2011 were to white women, indicative of the very different racial and ethnic composition of the American population by age. By 2030, the projection is that about a third of the elderly population will be ethnic minority group members.[38]

The leading causes of death vary across the life course. [...] described how the five leading causes of death for the population as a whole in 2010 were heart disease, cancer, chronic lower respiratory disease, stroke, and accidents. However, as shown in figure 1.5, among children and young adults of ages 1 to 24, the leading causes of death were accidents (unintentional injuries), homicides,

FIGURE 1.5 Percentage distribution of five leading causes of death, by age group, in the United States, 2010.

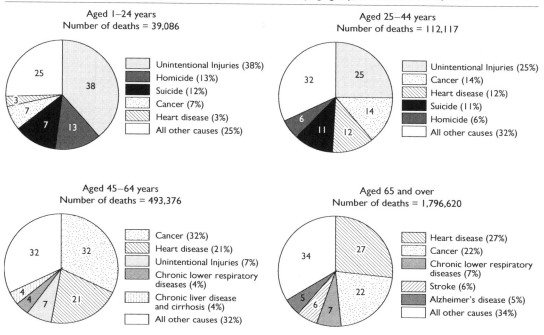

Source: Minino and Murphy 2012, 4.

and suicides, followed by cancer and heart disease, while among those age 65 and over, the leading causes nearly mirrored the totals for the population as a whole (reflecting the concentration of deaths in this age group): heart disease, cancer, chronic lower respiratory diseases, stroke, and Alzheimer's. Accidents top the list for those age 25 to 44, while cancer was the top killer among people age 45 to 64.[39] Health and mortality vary across states. Life expectancy is longer and health is better in states such as Hawaii, Florida, and Connecticut, and worse in many states of the South, such as Mississippi, Kentucky, and West Virginia, where rates of obesity, diabetes, heart disease, and smoking are relatively high.[40]

One general concern about an aging population is that it can strain government budgets. While the elderly often amass savings during their lifetime in the form of pension plans, savings accounts, mutual funds, and equity in their homes—and they often

continue to work even after the age of 65—they are nevertheless often economically dependent on the working-age population. The two main programs that serve the elderly—and whose growth has been met with alarm—are Social Security and Medicare. These two programs cost the federal government $1.3 trillion in 2012, accounting for about 37 percent of federal spending.[41] As many understand it, people contribute payroll taxes during their working years and then, when they retire, receive in benefits what they paid in. However, the way the program is structured, people who are currently employed pay for current retirees. While a Social Security trust fund was set up to cover future needs, some of these funds have been used to help finance other government programs. In short, because the U.S. population is aging and the number of elderly is swelling compared with the size of the working-age population, the Social Security trust fund is projected to run out of revenue at some point in the next couple of decades (in 2033, according to a recent estimate).[42]

Likewise, the elderly require, on average, much more medical attention than younger people, and health care costs have been soaring well beyond inflation in recent years. The hospital component of Medicare, which accounts for about half of Medicare spending, is financed much like Social Security, through payroll taxes. This trust fund is expected to be depleted by about 2026.[43] Making structural changes to these programs is difficult because they are generally popular and actually quite effective, as Social Security significantly reduces poverty, and Medicare helps provide access to much-needed health care services. Medicare is in fact often better at controlling costs than other kinds of health insurance, as it is able to bargain with doctors and hospitals for lower prices because of the number of people it represents.[44]

While an aging population has put some stress on health care spending, it is important to note that the problem is considerably broader. Our health care system is not well designed to provide efficient care to either young or old Americans. In just the ten years between 1999 and 2009, the average annual premium for employer-sponsored family insurance coverage rose from $5,800 to $13,400, and the average cost per Medicare beneficiary went from $5,500 to $11,900.[45] Our medical spending is high and increasing for many reasons. Part of it has to do with the fact that doctors and hospitals are paid for the tests and procedures they conduct rather than for results (health outcomes). Thus, the incentive is to prescribe many such tests and procedures. Moreover, prices are often vastly inflated and arbitrary. *Time* magazine ran a series of articles on health care costs run amok in the United States:

When Sean Recchi, a 42-year-old from Lancaster, Ohio, was told last March that

he had non-Hodgkin's lymphoma, his wife Stephanie knew she had to get him to MD Anderson Cancer Center in Houston. Stephanie's father had been treated there 10 years earlier, and she and her family credited the doctors and nurses at MD Anderson with extending his life by at least eight years.

Because Stephanie and her husband had recently started their own small technology business, they were unable to buy comprehensive health insurance. For $469 a month, or about 20% of their income, they had been able to get only a policy that covered just $2,000 per day of any hospital costs. "We don't take that kind of discount insurance," said the woman at MD Anderson when Stephanie called to make an appointment for Sean. … The total cost, in advance, for Sean to get his treatment plan and initial doses of chemotherapy was $83,900.

Why? The first of the 344 lines printed out across eight pages of his hospital bill—filled with indecipherable numerical codes and acronyms—seemed innocuous. But it set the tone for all that followed. It read, "1 ACETAMINOPHEN TABS 325 mg." The charge was only $1.50, but it was for a generic version of a Tylenol pill. You can buy 100 of them on Amazon for $1.49 even without a hospital's purchasing power.

Dozens of midpriced items were embedded with similarly aggressive markups, like $283.00 for a "CHEST, PA AND LAT 71020." That's a simple chest X-ray, for which MD Anderson is routinely paid $20.44 when it treats a patient on Medicare, the government health care program for the elderly. Every time a nurse drew blood, a "ROUTINE VENIPUNCTURE" charge of $36.00 appeared, accompanied by charges of $23 to $78 for each of a dozen or more lab analyses performed on the blood sample. In all, the charges for blood and other lab tests done on Recchi amounted to more than $15,000. Had Recchi been old enough for Medicare, MD Anderson would have been paid a few hundred dollars for all those tests. By law, Medicare's payments approximate a hospital's cost of providing a service, including overhead, equipment and salaries.[46]

This story helps provide an inkling as to why the health of Americans compares poorly with that of people in other rich countries—the topic to which I now turn.

INTERNATIONAL COMPARISONS

Among the many indicators of relatively poor health in the United States is life expectancy at birth. As shown in figure 1.6, the U.S. life expectancy, at 79, is slightly below the OECD average (80), and below that of all western European countries, such as France, Sweden, the United Kingdom,

and Germany. The United States fares slightly better than OECD countries that have considerably lower GDPs than that of the United States, such as the Czech Republic, Poland, Turkey, and Mexico. Granted, all of these countries fare well compared with truly poor or war-torn developing nations, such as Zimbabwe, Somalia, and Afghanistan, where the life expectancy for women at birth ranges from 49 to 53. Nevertheless, the United States surprisingly falls behind other non-OECD countries not shown in figure 1.6, including Cuba and Costa Rica, and not far ahead of others, such as Albania and Uruguay.[47] As a result, the life expectancy gap between Mexico and the United States (a 1.8-year U.S. advantage) is smaller than the gap between the United States and Canada (a 2.5-year Canadian advantage).[48]

Unfortunately, the United States has become more disadvantaged relative to other developed countries over time. For example, while female life expectancy had been near the median among sixteen of its peers in 1979, by 2006 it ranked last among these countries, according the National Academies report mentioned at the beginning of

FIGURE 1.6 Life expectancy at birth in selected OECD countries, 2011.

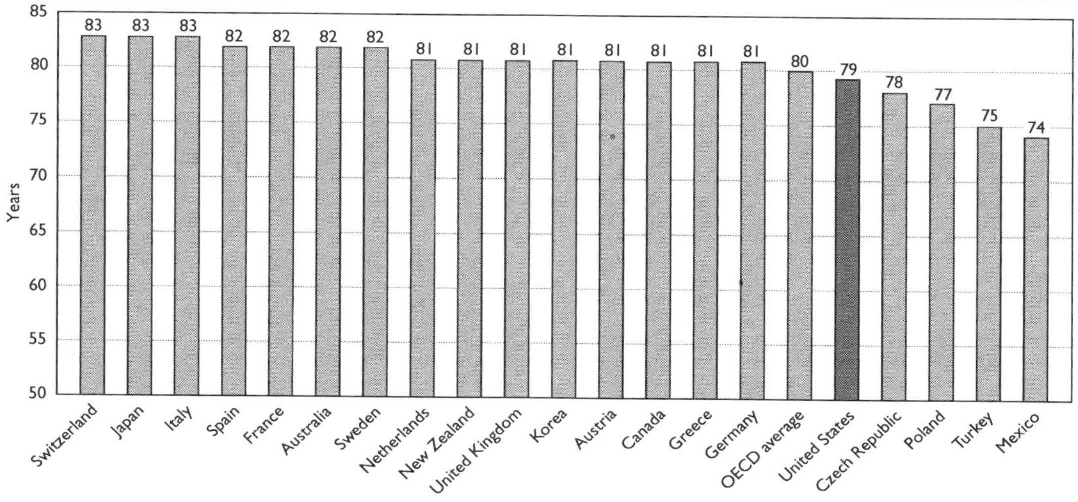

Source: OECD 2013c.

this chapter. The United States also fares poorly across a number of indicators, including age-specific death rates and infant mortality. The infant mortality rate in the United States in the 2005–9 period was 6.7, well above the rates in the other sixteen countries. Sweden and Japan had the lowest infant mortality rates, at 2.5 and 2.6, respectively. The three most important reasons for extra years of life lost in the United States among men under the age of 50 (accounting for 57 percent of the deficit) include homicides, motor vehicle accidents, and accidents and injuries due to other causes. Noncommunicable diseases also play an important role, especially among women. The U.S. mortality disadvantage is accompanied by worse health along a number of indicators, including relatively high levels of child and adult obesity, diabetes, heart disease, and disability. The adolescent birthrate is also relatively high in the United States, as are sexually transmitted infections, HIV and AIDS, and drug-related mortality.[49]

The disparities in health and mortality are likely caused by differences in access to health care, individual behaviors, social factors, physical and environmental factors, and political and social values. Regarding the first, access to health care, the National Academies panel was careful to note that definitively assessing the magnitude of the impact of health care systems on health is difficult. It does note, however, that access to health care in the United States is more dependent on family resources than in other rich countries. For example, a higher percentage of Americans report having difficulty paying for medical bills (27 percent) than in ten other countries in the study, which ranged from a low of 1 percent in the United Kingdom to 14 percent in the Netherlands. Similarly, 29 percent of Americans reported not visiting a doctor when having a medical problem because of cost issues, compared with 6 to 18 percent of respondents in the other countries.[50]

Individual behaviors might help explain some of the cross-national differences, though again better data and more research are needed to definitively show how individual behaviors vary across countries. While Americans are currently less likely to smoke than people in many other countries, they used to have the highest rates of tobacco consumption. These previously high rates, combined with the lagged effect between smoking and disease, may contribute to some of the relatively high mortality among Americans today.[51] In addition, the diets of Americans are less healthy and the U.S. population tends to be more sedentary than its peers in many other countries. This would help explain higher rates of obesity and diabetes in the United States—conditions that can later contribute to heart disease. Likewise, the greater incidence of accidents and homicides in the United States is likely a function of the greater prevalence of drug abuse and firearms, as well riskier behaviors more generally.[52] For example, the proportion of drivers wearing seatbelts is lower in the United States than all but one of fifteen peer countries in one study; in addition, the percentage of road traffic deaths attributable to alcohol is higher in the United States than in all of the other countries. There are 89 firearms per 100 people in the United States—about double the number in the country with the second highest level of gun ownership (Switzerland, at 46 per 100) among the fifteen countries compared, not to mention many orders of magnitude greater than the country with the lowest level (Japan, at fewer than 1 per 100).[53]

In terms of social conditions, the rise in income inequality, child poverty, single-parent households, and incarceration—problems that are worse in the United States than in other countries—may also contribute to the American health disadvantage. Similarly, environmental factors, in the form of low-density housing and dependence on cars, the wide availability of unhealthy foods, and racial and economic segregation, may all contribute to poor health and mortality in the United States. Finally, political and social values can affect health disparities, as there is relatively less public support for policies that redistribute income and resources to alleviate poverty, health, and other inequalities in the United States than in many other welfare states.[54] These factors collectively help explain worse health outcomes among Americans than among people in other rich countries.

CONCLUSION

Life expectancies in the United States have continued to increase over the last several decades. Infant mortality is down, other age-specific death rates are also down, and mortality from curable diseases has also declined. Nevertheless, significant disparities in health and mortality by ethnicity and socioeconomic status remain. Blacks live shorter lives on average and are more likely to suffer from a number of health conditions than whites. People with relatively low levels of education and income and those who work in low-status occupations likewise suffer from health deficits. However, ethnic disparities have slowly declined in recent years, and socioeconomic ones have significantly increased—consistent with broader trends in ethnic and socioeconomic inequality in the United States.

Those with higher levels of education have more information about healthy living and the ability to navigate through our complex health care system, those with higher income have greater access to health care services and healthy homes and neighborhood environments, and those in high-status occupations are less exposed to risky working conditions. Some of the ethnic disparity in health is explained by socioeconomic disparities associated with ethnicity, but minority—especially black—individuals also contend with residential segregation that exacerbates social and health inequality and with discrimination that increases stress and hypertension. Notably, Hispanics have higher life expectancies than both blacks and whites, though at least a significant portion of this health advantage is a function of the selectivity of relatively healthy immigrants who come to the United States (compared with those who stay behind), as well as the selective migration back home of immigrants with worsening health.

With relatively low fertility, declining mortality, and the aging of the relatively large baby boom generation, a growing proportion of the American population is over the age of sixty-five. This has led to greater expenditures on popular and effective programs such as Social Security and Medicare, which has in turn put a greater stress on government budgets. Health expenditures are very high in the United States for a variety of reasons, including the absence of incentives to reduce the number of tests and procedures prescribed by doctors as well as the high cost of these procedures.

Despite the large amount of money spent on health care, Americans suffer from high mortality and worse health than people in other rich countries. The U.S. life expectancy, for example, is below the OECD average even though the United States has a higher GDP per capita than nearly all of the other countries. While the causes of this health deficit are difficult to pinpoint, they are likely rooted in differences in health care accessibility, individual behaviors, social factors, physical and environmental factors, and political and social values across countries.

The National Academies report on these issues offers recommendations for improving health outcomes in the United States, such as setting specific national health objectives. The report provides a concrete list of such objectives, ranging from improving the quality of air, land, and water to expanding community-based preventative services. It also recommends alerting the public about the U.S. health disadvantage to spark a national discussion on these issues, which might help promote a broader campaign on healthy living.[55] Thus, even though the health of Americans currently lags behind that of their peers, many positive steps can be taken to improve health and well-being in the future.

NOTES

1 National Research Council and Institute of Medicine 2013, 1.

2 J. Wilson 2013.

3 National Research Council and Institute of Medicine 2013, 4–6.

4 World Bank 2012.

5 Hoyert 2012, 2.

6 Meyer 2012.

7 Thorslund et al. 2013, 2–3; Preston and Wang 2006, 631.

8 Race and Hispanic origin information is collected from two separate questions. Hispanics can be of any race.

9 Centers for Disease Control and Prevention 2011.

10 Hoyert 2012, 5; MacDorman, Hoyert, and Mathews 2013; Schoeni, Freedman, and Martin 2009.

11 D. R. Williams et al. 2010.

12 Centers for Disease Control and Prevention 2012b, 5–6.

13 Centers for Disease Control and Prevention 2012c.

14 Braveman et al. 2010, table 2.

15 Adler and Newman 2002; Gallup 2012.

16 Hummer and Lariscy 2011, 254; Masters, Hummer, and Powers 2012; Miech et al. 2011; Montez et al. 2011; Olshansky et al. 2012, 1806; Schoeni, Freedman, and Martin 2009.

17 Hummer and Lariscy 2011, 243–45.

18 Peckham and Wyn 2009.

19 Adler and Newman 2002, 61–68; Williams and Mohammed 2008, 136.

20 Hummer and Lariscy 2011, 245.

21 Adler and Newman 2002, 68–69; Hummer and Lariscy 2011, 243.

22 Abramsky 2012.

23 D. R. Williams and Sternthal 2010, S20–S21.

24 Zhang, Hayward, and Lu 2012.

25 Singh and Miller 2004; Osypuk et al. 2009; see also Population Reference Bureau 2013 for a concise discussion of the Hispanic paradox.

26 Tavernise 2013.

27 Popkin 2004, 38.

28 Food and Agriculture Organization of the United Nations 2013, annex table.

29 Lakhani 2013.

30 Riosmena et al. 2012.

31 Popkin, Adair, and Ng 2012.

32 Popkin 2004, 39.

33 Palloni and Arias 2004; Turra and Elo 2008; Riosmena, Wong, and Palloni 2013.

34 Markides and Eschbach 2011, 227; Singh and Miller 2004.

35 Markides and Eschbach 2011, 237.

36 Jacobsen et al. 2011, 3.

37 Werner 2011, 2.

38 Jacobsen et al. 2011, 4–5; Motel and Patten 2013, tables 1 and 11.

39 Minino and Murphy 2012, 2–4.

40 Centers for Disease Control and Prevention 2013.

41 Holzer and Sawhill 2013.

42 Board of Trustees, Federal Old-Age and Survivors Insurance and Federal Disability Trust Funds 2013.

43 Board of Trustees, Federal Old-Age and Survivors Insurance and Federal Disability Trust Funds 2013.

44 Isaacs et al. 2012.

45 Gawande 2009.

46 Brill 2013.

47 United Nations 2012.

48 Caselli et al. 2013, 5.

49 National Research Council and Institute of Medicine 2013, 27–88.

50 Schoen et al. 2011, exhibit 1.

51 National Research Council and Institute of Medicine 2013, 190–238; Preston and Wang 2006; Pampel 2005.

52 National Research Council and Institute of Medicine 2013, 190–238.

53 National Research Council and Institute of Medicine 2013, 155–58.

54 National Research Council and Institute of Medicine 2013, 159.

55 National Research Council and Institute of Medicine 2013, 347–74.

Understanding Gender and Health

Old Patterns, New Trends, and Future Directions

Patricia P. Rieker, Chloe E. Bird, and Martha E. Lang

A central feature of mortality trends throughout the twentieth century is the sex/gender difference in life expectancy: in the United States, women live on average 5.2 years longer than men do (NCHS 2009). Women have not always held a mortality advantage (Berin, Stolnitz, and Tenenbein 1990) and it may not continue. In fact, the age-adjusted gender gap in longevity appears to widen and narrow due to environmental/behavioral risk and protective factors, as well as genetic, biological, and hormonal processes (Annandale 2009). Biomedical and social science researchers who have pursued the causes of men's and women's differential mortality seldom agree on explanations, partly because, as Nathanson (1984, 196) stated in her discussion of the literature on differences in men's and women's health, "investigators' disciplinary orientations are reflected in specification of what is to be explained ... in their choice of potential explanatory variables, and in the methods they employ; ... the biologist sees hormones; the epidemiologist, risk factors; and the sociologist, social roles and structural constraints."

Even sociologists' understanding of the differences and similarities in men's and women's physical and mental health has changed dramatically over the past twenty-five years. Reviews of this literature indicate that researchers have often asked the wrong questions. For example, "Which is the weaker sex?" is framed in the binary language of biological advantage of one sex over the other and "Which gender is more advantaged?" assumes social advantage of one gender over the other. Even if there are real circumstances where biological superiority and social inequality can be observed, the framing of such questions implies that biological differences or social positions and roles can be summed up to determine which sex is the fittest or which gender is the most privileged. At best, this approach produces oversimplified models of the complex patterns of gender differences in health with little thought given to similarities.

A binary approach has the additional limitation of treating men and women as distinct homogenous groups, whereas gender differences in health vary substantially by age, race/ethnicity, and socioeconomic status. The dichotomy also ignores the wide array of gender identities and sexualities. Although men and women do seem to have on average some unique biological advantages and disadvantages over each other, substantial variation occurs among women and among men, and these differences seem to vary with certain social conditions (Fausto-Sterling 2005, 2008). It is still the case that much of clinical research tends to minimize or ignore the social and environmental processes that can influence health differentially and to reify biomedical models that portray men's

Patricia P. Rieker, Chloe E. Bird and Martha E. Lang, "Understanding Gender and Health: Old Patterns, New Trends, and Future Directions," Handbook of Medical Sociology, pp. 52-74. Copyright © 2010 by Vanderbilt University Press. Reprinted with permission.

and women's health disparities as inherently biological or genetic.

In recent years, a growing number of clinical researchers has come to recognize that social and biological factors interact in complex ways, and that this explains not only health or illness at the individual level but also population health and the observed patterns of men's and women's health and longevity in general. Yet relatively few biomedical or sociological studies examine both sets of factors (Institute of Medicine 2001a, b), highlighting the need to move beyond the binary in thinking and research, as ultimately integrating them will contribute to better science. Biological "sex" and social "gender" processes can interact and may be confounded. In acknowledgement of this, we use the term "gender" to refer to observed differences in men's and women's lives, morbidity, and mortality.

In this chapter, we briefly review gender differences in longevity and health in the United States and cross nationally, examine U.S. disease patterns for four specific conditions to illustrate gender disparities, review recent findings on the relationship between mental and physical health and its possible connection to gender differences in health, and consider limitations of current approaches to understanding men's and women's health. We suggest that in contrast to prevailing models of inequality, our integrative framework of constrained choice describes how decisions made and actions taken at the levels of family, work, community, and government shape men's and women's opportunities to pursue health and contribute to observed disparities. The constrained-choice model and gender-based analysis provide a new direction for discourse, research, and policy. We close with suggestions of interesting questions and issues for researchers to consider.

GENDER GAPS IN HEALTH AND

LONGEVITY: PUZZLE OR PARADOX?

For decades differences in men's and women's longevity and physical health have been considered paradoxical, although some challenge the conception of a "gender paradox" (Hunt and Annandale 1999). In the United States, as in most industrialized countries, men live shorter lives than women do, yet women have higher morbidity rates and in later years a diminished quality of life. The gender gap in longevity in the United States has been decreasing, from 7.8 years in 1970 to 5.2 years in 2006 (NCHS 2009). U.S. women's life expectancy has exceeded that of men since 1900, with women experiencing lower mortality rates in every age group and for most causes of death. Even though the female advantage is persistent and life expectancy has been increasing for both men and women, the gender gap in longevity has been closing in the United States and other countries. For example, Annandale (2009, 128) shows that between 1969 and 2007 in the United Kingdom men gained 9.0 years compared to women's 6.7 years. The same decreasing gender gap prevails in most industrialized countries, including Sweden, Finland, and Australia.

This female longevity advantage pattern holds worldwide except in the poorest countries, where life expectancy is low for both men and women (WHO 2006). However, the causes of death and gender difference in mortality rates vary substantially across age groups, as do the leading contributing factors (WHO 2008). For example, the higher infant mortality rates among boys compared to girls in the United States and other developed countries may have largely biological causes, such as congenital abnormalities and X-chromosome immune-related disorders (Abramowicz and Barnett 1970; Waldron 1998), while the gender gap among young adults between the ages of nineteen and twenty-two years may have primarily behavioral causes, such as motor vehicle accidents and homicide. Similarly, the gender gap in mental health is both age- and disorder-specific, with women experiencing higher rates of depression and anxiety, and men experiencing higher rates of alcoholism, other substance abuse, and antisocial behaviors (Bird and Rieker 2008; Kessler, Barker, et al. 2003; Kessler, Berglund, et al. 2003).

Life Expectancy Cross-Nationally

When we consider data on cross-national gender differences in life expectancy, the paradox becomes even greater. The comparative life expectancy rates listed in Table 2.1 help capture these differences, showing that both the size of the gender gap and the pattern of longevity vary considerably by country and by national wealth (United Nations 2005). As one would expect, the gap in life expectancy at birth between the thirty countries with the highest life expectancy and the thirty with the lowest life expectancy is dramatic, ranging from 82.3 years in Japan to 40.5 years in Zambia and 40.9 years in Zimbabwe.

The countries with the lowest life expectancy, with few exceptions, are mainly poor countries in Southeast Asia and sub-Saharan Africa. However, a country's wealth does not necessarily guarantee higher average longevity. For example, Japan ranks first in overall life expectancy (82.3) but sixteenth in its gross domestic product (GDP) per capita ($31,267). Luxembourg ranks first in GDP per capita ($60,228) but twenty-fourth in life expectancy (78.4 years). In fact, none of the four wealthiest countries (Ireland, United States, Luxembourg, and Norway) rank among the top five countries in terms of overall life expectancy.

Another interesting aspect of the information in Table 2.1 is that the variation in the gender gap in life expectancy itself is greater in the thirty wealthier countries (with higher overall life expectancy) than in the thirty poor countries (with lower

life expectancy). The gap ranges from 3.2 to 7.5 years in the wealthier countries and −1.8 to 4 years in the poorer countries, with some exceptions. Pinnelli (1997), a demographer, has discussed "male supermortality" and suggests that a five-year life-expectancy gender gap favoring women might be normal. She also contends that a greater difference indicates that men may be disadvantaged, in part because of their aggressive and risky health behaviors, while a smaller gap indicates that women may be disadvantaged regarding access to medical care, diet, and restricted labor-force participation. One clear example of this is the overall decline in life expectancy in the Russian Federation (not shown in the table) with a thirteen-year gap between men and women (fifty-nine vs. seventy-two), which generally is attributed to men's excessive alcohol use and greater smoking, suicide, and homicide rates (Kalben 2002). While it is debatable whether a five-year gap reflects a normal or biologically driven gender difference in life expectancy, changing environmental hazards, such as pandemics or civil wars, might alter this interpretation by shifting the balance one way or the other. However, we generally agree that the current data tend to support Pinnelli's interpretation.

In contrast to the worldwide pattern of women outliving men, the difference disappears and is even reversed in several of the poorer countries, with women outliving men by one year or less, if at all (e.g., Zimbabwe, Zambia, and Malawi). The lower overall life span and the minimal gender gap in these countries illustrates the extent to which extreme poverty, political disruption, and disease-specific mortality patterns (such as AIDS, malaria, and other infectious diseases) diminish life expectancy for both men and women (Andoh et al. 2006; Rao, Lopez, and Hemed 2006). These data also suggest that if women do indeed have some biological advantages that contribute to greater life

TABLE 2.1 Countries with Highest and Lowest Life Expectancy, with GDP per Capita

| Countries with Highest Life Expectancy | | | | | | Countries with Lowest Life Expectancy | | | | | |
Country	Life Expectancy at Birth	Women	Men	Difference	GDP per Capita	Country	Life Expectancy at Birth	Women	Men	Difference	GDP per Capita
Japan	82.3	85.7	78.7	7.0	31,267	Senegal	62.3	64.4	60.4	4.0	1,792
Hong Kong, China (SAR)	81.9	84.9	79.1	5.8	34,833	Yemen	61.5	63.1	60.0	3.1	930
Iceland	81.5	83.1	79.9	3.2	36,510	Timor-Leste	59.7	60.5	58.9	1.6	N/A
Switzerland	81.3	83.7	78.5	5.2	35,633	Gambia	58.8	59.9	57.7	2.2	1,921
Australia	80.9	83.3	78.5	4.8	31,794	Togo	57.8	59.6	56.0	3.6	1,506
Sweden	80.5	82.7	78.3	4.4	32,525	Eritrea	56.6	59.0	54.0	5.0	1,109
Spain	80.5	83.8	77.2	6.6	27,169	Niger	55.8	54.9	56.7	-1.8	781
Canada	80.3	82.6	77.9	4.7	33,375	Benin	55.4	56.5	54.1	2.4	1,141
Italy	80.3	83.2	77.2	6.0	28,529	Guinea	54.8	56.4	53.2	3.2	2,316
Israel	80.3	82.3	78.1	4.2	25,864	Djibouti	53.9	55.2	52.6	2.6	2,178
France	80.2	83.7	76.6	7.1	30,386	Mali	53.1	55.3	50.8	4.5	1,033
Norway	79.8	82.2	77.3	4.9	41,420	Kenya	52.1	53.1	51.1	2.0	1,240
New Zealand	79.8	81.8	77.7	4.1	24,996	Ethiopia	51.8	53.1	50.5	2.6	1,055
Austria	79.4	82.2	76.5	5.7	33,700	Burkina Faso	51.4	52.9	49.8	3.1	1,213
Singapore	79.4	81.4	77.5	3.9	29,663	Tanzania	51.0	52.0	50.0	2.0	744
Netherlands	79.2	81.4	76.9	4.5	32,684	Chad	50.4	51.8	49.0	2.8	1,427
Germany	79.1	81.8	76.2	5.6	29,461	Uganda	49.7	50.2	49.1	1.1	1,454
United Kingdom	79.0	81.2	76.7	4.5	33,238	Burundi	48.5	49.8	47.1	2.7	699
Cyprus	79.0	81.5	76.6	4.9	22,699	Cote d'Ivoire	47.4	48.3	46.5	1.8	1,648
Finland	78.9	82.0	75.6	6.4	32,153	Nigeria	46.5	47.1	46.0	1.1	1,128
Greece	78.9	80.9	76.7	4.2	23,381	Malawi	46.3	46.7	46.0	0.7	667
Belgium	78.8	81.8	75.8	6.0	32,119	Congo	45.8	47.1	44.4	2.7	714
Ireland	78.4	80.9	76.0	4.9	38,505	Guinea-Bissau	45.8	47.5	44.2	3.3	827
Luxembourg	78.4	81.4	75.4	6.0	60,228	Rwanda	45.2	46.7	43.6	3.1	1,206
United States	77.9	80.4	75.2	5.2	41,890	Central African Republic	43.7	45.0	42.3	2.7	1,224
Denmark	77.9	80.1	75.5	4.6	33,973	Mozambique	42.8	43.6	42.0	1.6	1,242
Korea (Republic of)	77.9	81.5	74.3	7.2	22,029	Sierra Leone	41.8	43.4	40.2	3.2	806
Portugal	77.7	80.9	74.5	6.4	20,410	Angola	41.7	43.3	40.1	3.2	2,335
Slovenia	77.4	81.1	73.6	7.5	22,273	Zimbabwe	40.9	40.2	41.4	-1.2	2,038
Brunei Darussalam	76.7	79.3	74.6	4.7	28,161	Zambia	40.5	40.6	40.3	0.3	1,023

Source: United Nations 2005

expectancy, they can be attenuated by harsh social conditions and restrictive gender roles. Although a country's wealth (as measured by GDP) can contribute to population health, it does not appear to be the main factor affecting the gender gap in life expectancy among relatively wealthy countries; but a specific wealth threshold may be more critical in poor countries.

The variability in the gender gap highlights the impact of differences in life circumstances overall, as well as between men and women. Having considered the variation in life expectancy across countries, we need also to consider how the causes of death differ geographically and by gender. In some parts of the world, adults typically die relatively young and most often from infectious disease (particularly Southeast Asia and sub-Saharan Africa). Yet even in these societies, the factors that contribute to early mortality differ somewhat for men and women. And the variation is not only by gender. For example, in countries with high rates of abject poverty such as Zambia and Zimbabwe, there are also geographic patterns to the leading causes of death both among men and among women. In Zambia (40.3 vs. 40.6) and Zimbabwe (41.4 vs. 40.2) there is little gender difference in life expectancy, which has been declining for both men and women due in large part to political turmoil and the countries' inability to control infectious diseases. In fact, a review of the data on the ten countries with the highest seropositivity rates over the past fifteen years shows that the female gender advantage decreases as HIV prevalence increases, a further reminder that neither the trends nor the gaps in life expectancy will remain constant over time, particularly as the leading causes of death vary with changing social and environmental circumstances (Velkoff and Kowal 2007).

Thus, it is clear that biological sex differences between men and women are not equally advantageous (or disadvantageous) in all circumstances;

consequently the gender differences in mortality are dynamic. This insight is not new. Kalben (2002, 2) quotes a 1974 report by the Committee on Ordinary Issuance and Annuities that noted that differences in the leading causes of death "strongly suggest that sex differentials in mortality are due to biological as well as environmental factors and that the relative importance of the biological components varies by sex and social circumstances."

There is little precise understanding of the biological and social factors or pathways between them that can or do widen or narrow the gender gap in both longevity and general health. Although many reasons for the variation have been identified, biological or social factors alone are not considered a sufficient explanation for the cross-national gender differences (Kalben 2002; Krieger 2003; Yin 2007). Some social scientists argue that health status differences among individuals and groups within a country are due to income inequalities or other fundamental social causes (Phelan et al. 2004), while others contend it is the status syndrome associated with positions in the social hierarchy that explains such phenomena (Marmot 2004, 2005). Cross-national differences in life expectancy are often linked to a country's wealth (Kawachi and Kennedy 2006) or to the distribution of income within a country (Wilkinson 1996). Moreover, when Krieger and colleagues (2008) examined inequities in premature mortality rates in the United States between 1960 and 2002, they found that as population health improves the magnitude of health inequalities can either rise or fall, and the reasons for the observed trends are largely unknown. For the most part, the general explanations of population health disparities are not focused on gender differences or the gender gap, so they don't provide a comprehensive understanding of these complexities.

However, some evidence of what contributes to the gender gap is provided by biomedical studies of sex-related changes in mortality rates in cardiovascular diseases and other specific diseases. In an influential article, Verbrugge and Wingard (1987) explained the paradox of men's higher mortality and lower morbidity compared to women's on the basis of gender differences in the patterns of disease. Unlike others who advanced the prevailing paradigm of focusing on men's premature mortality, Verbrugge and Wingard also called for researchers and clinicians to move beyond the focus on men's higher cardiovascular disease (CVD) mortality toward a more nuanced view of the gender differences in disease patterns over the life course. They also offered more complex explanations of the implications of gender differences in disease prevalence, including women's increased risk for CVD after menopause and their greater morbidity from debilitating illnesses such as rheumatoid arthritis. But a knowledge gap remains in understanding the sex-specific differences in the epidemiology of many specific diseases, and most notably cardiovascular diseases.

Disease Patterns in the United States

Our examination here of four conditions that vary considerably by gender—CVD and immune function disorders for physical health, and depression and substance abuse for mental health—is not intended to be exhaustive; rather we seek to provide a more complex portrait of specific patterns of gender difference in mental and physical health that extends beyond the life expectancy and mortality difference. We contend that this more nuanced picture also requires more multifaceted explanations than are typically articulated in a summary of gender differences in health.

Cardiovascular Disease (CVD)

CVD is the world's leading cause of death, causing one-third of all deaths globally, and the single largest cause of death among both men and women

worldwide. In the United States, 8.4 percent of men and 5.6 percent of women report a diagnosis of CVD (Thom et al. 2006). Historically, men have greater prevalence and age-adjusted CVD mortality rates than women, a consistent finding across most developed countries (WHO 2006). While men outnumber women three or four to one in mortality from coronary heart disease (CHD) before age seventy-five, the gender difference in prevalence and incidence narrows at older ages (Verbrugge and Wingard 1987). A growing body of research indicates that despite later onset in women, risk factors such as smoking, family history, depression, diabetes, and inflammation (measured using C-reactive protein) may have a more negative influence on CVD in women than in men (Bassuk and Manson 2004; Pai et al. 2004; Thorand et al. 2007).

Due in part to earlier onset among men than among women, CVD also contributes substantially to gender differences in the number of years lived with and without CVD and related conditions (Crimmins, Kim, and Hagedorn 2002). For example, Crimmins and colleagues indicate that a cohort of women in the United States will experience 70 percent more years of life after age sixty-five with hypertension than a similar-sized birth cohort of men. Today, the patient undergoing treatment for CVD and hypertension is likely to be a woman beyond middle age. Yet until recently, scientists and clinicians focused on explaining and addressing the earlier onset of CVD in men, whereas the role of biological mechanisms in women's greater lifetime risk remained largely unexplored.[1] Ultimately women's increased inclusion in research led to a dramatic shift in knowledge and understanding regarding women's CVD risk (see Bird and Rieker 2008 for details on the Women's Health Initiative and this shift in research). However, this shift is only beginning to produce insights into the antecedents of gender differences in risk and life expectancy differences. For example, Shetty and colleagues (2009) took advantage of the sharp drop in women's use of Hormone Replacement Therapy (HRT) following the negative findings reported in 2002 regarding HRT and CVD to conduct an observational study of the relationship between HRT use and cardiovascular outcomes in the entire U.S. population. They found that the decreased use of HRT was associated with a decreased acute myocardial infarction rate among women but not with a reduced stroke rate.

Immune Function and Disorders

Researchers and clinicians are challenged and perplexed by the sex-linked patterns of immune function and disorders. The sex ratios in immune function also contribute to substantial differences in men's and women's disease risks and longevity. Although men and women tend to develop different disorders, women still have a greater risk than men of autoimmune rheumatic disorders and a higher risk of genetic immune suppression disorders (Jacobson et al. 1997; Lockshin 2001; Walsh and Rau 2000). Although the incidence of female/male ratios varies, the severity of the disease does not. For example, the female-to-male ratio of lupus, Graves', and Sjögren's is 7–10:1; that of rheumatoid arthritis, scleroderma, and multiple sclerosis is 2–3:1; while Type 1 diabetes and inflammatory bowel disease have equal sex frequencies (Lockshin 2006). Much of the disability men and women experience from rheumatologic and thyroid disorders, especially from middle age on, can be attributed to autoimmune disease. However, the differences in incidence in the most common disorders contribute to women's greater morbidity.

Since Selye's original work (1956) delineating physiological responses to stress, transdisciplinary research has greatly expanded our knowledge of human physiology and the ways that it can be influenced by social psychological phenomena (see Dedovic et al. 2009 for a review of gender socialization and stress reactivity). A growing body of evidence indicates that a variety of psychosocial factors can affect physiologic processes with implications for immune function. Researchers have described various possible pathways through which psychological factors impact immune function (Kiecolt-Glaser et al. 2002a, b). For example, some researchers and physicians argue that gender differences in men's and women's exposure to environmental substances and experiences of stress also contribute to gender differences in autoimmune disease incidence and severity (Legato 2002; Lockshin et al. 1999). Moreover, there is considerable debate about whether sex hormones, including estrogen and testosterone, affect inflammatory and immune responses (Begg and Taylor 2006; Lockshin 2006; Lockshin, forthcoming).

Mental Health

Although the overall rate of mental health disorders in the United States is similar for men and women, researchers, clinicians, and even women's rights advocates believed until the early 1990s that women suffer from higher rates of mental illness than do men (Chodorow 1978; Cleary, Mechanic, and Greenly 1982; Dohrenwend and Dohrenwend 1976, 1977; Gove and Tudor 1973). This assumption was based largely on the higher prevalence of depression among women and the fact that more women than men sought care for mental health problems. In addition, clinical studies suggested that the gender differences in depression had a hormonal basis and were at least partly biological, while sociologists contended that the differences were due to gender inequalities and restricted social roles.

However, findings based on the 1991 Epidemiologic Catchment Area Data (ECA) revealed that there are no large gender differences in the overall prevalence of major psychological disorders, whether one compares prevalence rates for one month, six months, a year, or a lifetime (Kessler, McGonagle, Zhao, et al. 1994; Regier and Robins 1991; Regier et al. 1993). Ten years later, the first nationally representative mental health study, the National Comorbidity Survey (NCS 1), confirmed these findings (Kessler and Walters 2002; Narrow et al. 2002).

The discrepancy with respect to prior findings is partly the result of the development of more rigorous research methods and of previous studies' focus on rates of depressive and anxiety disorders, which are higher among women; the ECA and the NCS included substance abuse, which is more common among men. The interpretation of the overall gender differences in mental health changed radically in light of new information on the full range of mental health disorders from these population-based studies. The new insights into men's and women's mental health reflected a typical pattern of scientific progress resulting from challenges to prior findings along with the application of more rigorous methods to answer both old and new questions.

In our discussion of gender differences in mental health, we focus on depression and substance abuse because they represent disorders with substantially different prevalence rates among men and women and because they create an enormous health burden (Kessler, Barker, et al. 2003). The World Health Organization (WHO) ranks major depression and substance abuse among the most burdensome diseases in the world (WHO 2002). Moreover, a growing body of research links depression and serious psychological distress with physical health (Pratt 2009; Whang et al. 2009), further illustrating the need to consider the interaction between physical and mental health in unraveling the puzzle of gender differences in health.

Depressive Disorders

Women's rates of depressive disorders are 50 to 100 percent higher than men's (Gove and Tudor 1973; Kessler, Barker, et al. 2003; Kessler, Berglund, et al. 2003; Mirowsky and Ross 2003). Until the recent men's health movement, women's disproportionately high depression rates generated the erroneous impression that men were comparatively immune to depression (Courtenay 2000a, b). Clinicians' underdiagnosis of men's depression has been linked to a combination of gender differences in the causes and symptoms of depression, men's unwillingness to seek help for such feelings, as well as men's tendency to cope with sadness and loss through drinking and drug use and through acting-out and risk-taking behaviors (Bird and Rieker 2008; Chino and Funabaki 1984; Courtenay 2000a, b; Nolen-Hoeksema 1987, 1990). When symptoms of depression are acknowledged and diagnosed, men as well as women appear to seek treatment (Nazroo, Edwards, and Brown 1998; Rhodes et al. 2002).

Although men and women do differ in the age and rates of onset of depression (young males have higher rates until early adolescence), the gender gap appears to be greatest during the reproductive years (Bebbington 1996; Piccinelli and Wilkinson 2000). Moreover, while cross-sectional studies indicate that once major depression develops, the course is similar for both genders (Kessler, McGonagle, Swartz et al. 1993; Wilhelm, Parker, and Hadzi-Pavlovic 1997), several longitudinal studies have reported that girls and women have longer episodes and higher rates of recurrent and chronic depression (Aneshensel 1985; Ernst and Angst 1992; Keitner et al. 1991; Kornstein et al. 2000; Sargeant et al. 1990; Winokur et al. 1993). What is clear is that women have consistently higher lifetime prevalence rates for depression, and that depressed women are more likely than are men to have comorbid anxiety (Gregory and Endicott 1999; Kessler, Berglund et al. 2003), while men are more likely to have comorbid substance abuse or dependence (Endicott 1998; Kessler, Berglund et al. 2003). However the determinants of these gender differences and how they are related to substance abuse and other mental health disorders is unclear (Piccinelli and Wilkinson 2000).

Substance Abuse Disorders

Men have significantly higher rates of alcohol and drug use, abuse, and dependence, as well as anti-social behavior disorders, than do women (Kessler, McGonagle, Zhao et al. 1994; Regier et al. 1993). In fact, the prevalence of substance abuse disorders in men and women is the reverse of that seen for depression. The gender difference in prevalence of substance use is smallest among adolescents, increases with age, and varies by type and level of drug use (Kandel, Warner, and Kessler 1998).

Although those who initiate substance use earlier in life are more likely to continue using and to become dependent, not all users in any age group become dependent (even with highly addictive substances). With the exception of tobacco, lifetime dependence rates are considerably higher for men than for women (Kessler, Crum et al. 1997; Kessler, McGonagle, Zhao et al. 1994; Kessler, Nelson et al. 1996). It is unclear whether the gendered patterns in dependence among users are due to greater use of alcohol by men and of psychotherapeutics by women, or to other biological and environmental factors that vary by drug type (see Pescosolido et al. 2008 for a detailed and nuanced analysis of the pathway to alcohol dependence in men and women and the complex interplay between social and genetic influences). However, extensive comorbidity exists between drug and alcohol disorders, as well as with other psychiatric disorders in both men and women, especially in those with a major depressive disorder (Kessler, Berglund et al. 2003; Kessler, Nelson et al. 1996).

The emerging field of men's studies recognizes that while gender roles advantage men in some ways, they disadvantage them in others, and that not all men are equally advantaged nor are all women equally disadvantaged (Cameron and Bernardes 1998; Harrison 1978; Kimmel and Messner 1993; Pleck 1983, 1984; Pleck and Brannon 1978; Rieker and Bird 2000, 2005; Sabo and Gordon 1995). Work by Courtenay (2000a, b) and others has also begun to reexamine the role of masculine identities in the development of men's unhealthy and risky behaviors and subsequent mental and physical health problems. Other research has focused on stressors to which men are either more exposed or potentially more vulnerable, such as those in the workplace and in the military (Connell 1987; Jaycox 2008; Levant and Pollack 1995; Sabo and Gordon 1995). For instance, combat duty, which continues to be more common for men, puts soldiers at risk for post-traumatic stress disorder (PTSD), whereas physical and sexual abuse remains the most likely PTSD risk factor for women (Rieker and Carmen 1984).[2] In contrast, the stress associated with being unemployed can differ depending on one's options and constraints: unemployed women frequently have access to more socially acceptable roles than men do, including caregiver and housewife, which are more highly stigmatized for men and may therefore lead to greater stress or simply deter men from considering or accepting these roles (Lennon 2006). The high rates of combat duty in recent and ongoing wars and conflicts, along with the high current rates of unemployment, provide an important opportunity for much-needed research to better understand vulnerability to depression and PTSD and to learn more about how to provide better care to men and women afflicted with these debilitating disorders. Such research can also inform theories that explain both male and female psychological health and illness and the ways these gender patterns vary across race, class, and ethnicity.

PATHWAYS AND MECHANISMS UNDERLYING GENDER DIFFERENCES

Although social and biological pathways to illness and the mechanisms connecting them with gender differences in health are relatively unexplored, we would like to suggest some topics that warrant attention. For example, a growing body of research demonstrates that mental and physical health are deeply intertwined. Thus, not only can physical health problems cause symptoms that appear to be attributable to one's mental health or current mental state (such as fatigue, hopelessness), but also mental health conditions can exacerbate physical health problems, and serious or chronic physical health problems can lead to depression or anxiety. Understanding relationships between physical and mental health is relevant to researching and explaining health trajectories, identifying opportunities for intervention, and recognizing the full benefits of such interventions in terms of reduced morbidity and mortality.

Impact of Health Behaviors on Physical and Mental Health

Health behaviors are a primary pathway through which psychological distress and depression impact health. For example, a longitudinal study of patients with stable cardiovascular disease found that the association between depressive symptoms and subsequent cardiovascular events was explained in part by differences in health behaviors, including smoking, alcohol use, and level of physical activity (Whooley et al. 2008). Individuals with more depressive symptoms at baseline engaged in fewer positive and more negative health behaviors and consequently faced an increased risk of cardiovascular events.

Gender differences in both mental health and self-care may exacerbate the problem of negative effects of psychological distress and depression on specific health behaviors. In particular, although women engage more often in self-care behaviors than men do, they are somewhat less likely to engage in regular physical activity. Moreover, depressed mood may reduce any female advantage in health behaviors, as women typically begin to drop self-care behaviors before decreasing their caring for others (Rosenfield 1999). Depressed mood and other mental health problems may similarly affect men and women by reducing positive health behaviors, even though men and women engage on average in somewhat different positive behaviors (Reeves and Rafferty 2005; Whooley et al. 2008).

Recent research also suggests that some negative health behaviors play a central role in gender differences in health. For example, Grundtvig and colleagues (2009) examined data from 1,784 patients admitted for a first heart attack at a hospital in Lillehammer, Norway. Their retrospective study found that on average men had their first heart attack at age seventy-two if they didn't smoke, and at sixty-four if they did. In contrast, women in the study had their first heart attack at age eighty-one if they didn't smoke, and at age sixty-six if they did. If supported by prospective studies, their data suggest that smoking drastically reduces gender differences in age at first heart attack, narrowing women's advantage from nine to merely two years. Grundtvig speculated that smoking may lead to earlier onset of menopause in women, reducing the length of women's premenopausal protection from heart disease. Thus smoking represents a negative health behavior that is frequently used in part as a means of coping with stress, but that also interacts differently with men's and women's biology to increase their health risks. Other health conditions related to health behavior and cardiovascular disease have also been found to have a greater negative effect on women's health than men's. For example, diabetes in particular has been found to outweigh (and even eliminate) women's otherwise lower cardiovascular risk prior to menopause (Kannel and Wilson 1995; Sowers 1998). In regard to diabetes, Lutfey and Freese (2005) use ethnographic data to provide an in-depth analysis of the mechanisms that perpetuate disparities in diabetes treatment regimens, including some differences between men and women.

Social Norms, Biology, and Gendered Behaviors

As West and Zimmerman (1987) argued, a cost and consequence of living in a social world is the ongoing process of *doing gender*. Specifically, individuals are expected in innumerable social circumstances to express themselves in gender-appropriate ways (Ridgeway and Smith-Lovin 1999; Taylor et al. 2000). While gender roles have become far less circumscribed over time, gender scripts remain and are obvious even in fitness recommendations (Dworkin and Wachs 2009). Moreover, behaving and communicating in ways that are seen as gender appropriate are rewarded in subtle ways.

Recent work suggests that men and women also have some physiologic differences that may complement the social norms to behave in gender-appropriate ways. Partly in response to the extensive literature on the fight-or-flight response, most of which was theorized and studied in males (including animal studies), Taylor and colleagues (2000) began to study and write about the "tend or befriend" stress response, which they contend is supported by a hormonal response present only in females. They do not suggest that males are prevented from responding to stress with the same hypervigilance aimed at protecting and caring for others they found in females, but that in females, oxytocin encourages these specific behaviors.

Compared to men, women tend to engage in more nurturant activities designed to protect the self and others that in turn promote safety and reduce distress. Women also tend to create and maintain social networks that may aid in this process. This gendered response to stress is encouraged and supported both socially and biologically (Ridgeway and Smith-Lovin 1999; Taylor et al. 2000). Unlike the fight-or-flight response, which is hormonally present in both men and women, oxytocin in conjunction with female reproductive hormones and endogenous opioid peptide mechanisms supports the "tend and befriend" stress regulatory mechanism. Taylor and colleagues proposed that the attachment-caregiving system forms the biobehavioral underpinnings of tending and befriending in response to stress. These in turn may contribute to differences in men's and women's CVD risk and mortality.

Pescosolido and colleagues (2008) provide another example in their study of how gendered stress reactions become part of the pathway to alcohol dependence. In their provocative findings, they explicate the causal pathway through which the gene GABRA2 interacts with social factors to produce gender differences in alcohol dependence. Specifically, they conclude that "genetic predisposition to alcohol dependence on GABRA2 is operative in men but not in women" (S192). The genetic inheritance of GABRA2 can become triggered or suppressed through social patterns. Daily hassles, past stressors, and the coping response differentiate men and women regarding their propensity to engage in "escapist drinking." The researchers contend that drinking to excess in public is also more acceptable for men and that such behavior sets men up for greater alcohol dependence, which then can be attenuated or exacerbated by early childhood deprivation and family-based social support.

Thus social processes and biological mechanisms can interact in complex ways to produce observed differences in men's and women's health. Earlier explanations of women's higher morbidity hinged largely or exclusively on the negative consequences of female social and economic disadvantages (for a review, see Wingard 1984), whereas the explanations of women's greater longevity focused solely on the hypothesized biological advantages of hormones (see Ramey 1982). Yet each explanation applied to only a narrow portion of the complex differences in men's and women's health. As we have argued elsewhere, what is needed to advance research and understanding of gender differences in morbidity and mortality is a synthesis of social and biological theories and evidence. To begin to address this conundrum, we introduced a model of constrained choice as a promising direction for understanding and researching gender differences and other health disparities (Rieker and Bird 2005).

CONSTRAINED CHOICE: A DIFFERENT WAY TO VIEW HEALTH DISPARITIES

Much of the recent work on health disparities focuses primarily on the contribution of socioeconomic status. We take a broader perspective on the range of factors that pattern individual lives. In so doing, we identify additional potential levers for addressing gender, racial/ethnic, and socioeconomic disparities in health. While population health and the health of disadvantaged subgroups are in part functions of the income distribution in a society, it does not necessarily follow that income redistribution is the most feasible and effective way to address such disparities. Nor is it clear that such efforts would address gender differences in health or effectively resolve disparities among men and among women (James et al. 2009; Murray et al. 2006). While other countries (notably, the Nordic countries) have instituted a multifaceted series of policies affecting the distribution of income, such policies are unlikely in the United States in the foreseeable future.

We offer constrained choice as an alternative framework that recognizes a wider range of contributing factors and thus identifies additional research foci and intervention points for improving individual and population health. Our approach is not intended to minimize the role of social inequalities in health or to emphasize individual behaviors over structural factors. To the contrary, we developed a framework that shows how structural constraints narrow the opportunities and choices available to individuals in both absolute and relative ways. In the extreme case, structural inequalities socially pattern health, creating or exacerbating particular gender, racial/ethnic, and socioeconomic disparities in health; for example, when discrimination creates differential opportunities for specific groups, it enhances or protects the range of opportunities for some while constraining them for others. But discrimination is not the only factor that socially patterns the constraints that men and women (as a group or individually) experience in their everyday lives and that also affect their health. While the impact of gender roles may be obvious—including differences in the distribution and nature of caregiving and other relationships at the level of family—the indirect health impact of decisions at the levels of community and social policy have received far less attention in research to date.

In *Gender and Health* (Bird and Rieker 2008), we presented the constrained-choice model to address these gaps. The multilevel model explains how decisions made and actions taken at the family, work, community, and government levels contribute to differences in individuals' opportunities to incorporate health into a broad array of everyday choices. We argue that the unintentional and cumulative consequences of constrained choice socially pattern women's and men's lives in differential ways that impact their exposure to stressors, their health behaviors, and their physiology. Therefore, we conclude that health is not only an individual responsibility but one shared by decision makers at multiple levels.

Levels and Processes of Constrained Choice

Individuals make everyday choices that create health outcomes. Furthermore, they make these choices in the context of family, employment settings, and community. For example, many young families must negotiate ongoing decisions on where to live, how to balance career with family life, child rearing, child care, and financial management. When attempting to meet these explicit priorities every day, young families may make immediate choices that are not health promoting. Consider a dual income family: over the course of a day a parent may choose to skip breakfast to ensure being able to drop a child off at daycare and get to work on time. A parent may bring home a fast-food dinner in order to spend time with family rather than spend time cooking, or simply to get food on the table quickly to feed a hungry family. Similarly, a parent may choose to sleep less in order to spend time with children, manage the household, or complete work-related tasks. None of these actions are necessarily gender-specific nor may any of them as discreet, individual actions result in major health consequences. Yet when the wider context shapes and constrains opportunities and choices, as it does in everyone's life to varying degrees, such trade-offs can have cumulative effects on health. These choices occur and play out in gendered ways, as men's and women's everyday decisions and priorities differ somewhat on average, due in part to differences in their social roles. Moreover, the

FIGURE 2.1 Conceptualization of Constrained Choice

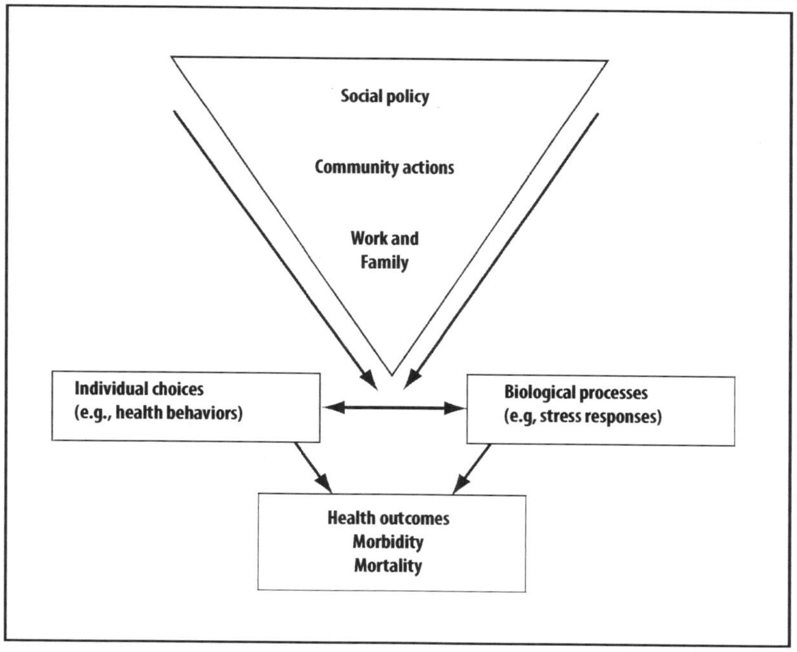

Source: Bird, C.E., & Rieker, P.P. (2008). *Gender and health: The effects of constrained choices and social policies.* New York: Cambridge University Press.

consequences of such everyday actions cumulatively affect health, and their impact depends in part on innate and acquired differences in men's and women's biology or genetic predisposition.

Our model of constrained choice includes three levels of organizational context that can influence men's and women's health outcomes: social policy, community actions, and work and family (see Figure 2.1). The model demonstrates how decisions made within these organizational contexts can limit the opportunities that individuals have to choose healthy behaviors. Two recent reports on racial and ethnic disparities in women's health across the United States demonstrate clearly such constraints (James et al. 2009; Rustgi, Doty, and Collins 2009). The model also acknowledges how the interplay between gendered health choices and sex-specific biological patterns and responses can shape morbidity and mortality outcomes.

Work and Family

Many of the differences in men's and women's lives are rooted in their work and family roles. Men and women are exposed to different kinds of work, as well as differences in pay and other benefits. Occupations and social roles carry expectations, create routines of daily life, and establish norms of social interaction, all of which contribute to stress levels, health-related behaviors, and coping styles. For example, a role such as single parent or caregiver to aging parents or to children with special health-care needs can be time consuming and stressful, and these roles are more often performed by women. Moreover, both work and family roles include flexible or inflexible demands (such as urgent situations that require immediate attention) or routines that may not easily be combined with other obligations. Even for those who do not work from home, the boundaries between work and home life have become increasingly blurred as technology makes us always available. While in

theory this flexibility increases the possibilities for managing conflicting demands, it also reduces the physical and temporal boundaries between work and home life for both singles and couples.

Even though differences in men's and women's roles have diminished over time, the lingering differences have cumulative effects on health and on the ways in which family decisions impact health. For example, compared to men, women typically acquire more health information and take a larger role in the health of their families. Clearly men and women continue to be differentially distributed across industries and workplaces, with more women in service occupations and men more concentrated in manufacturing, transportation, and military work. Occupations and work environments differ substantially in both the demands placed on workers and the level of control individuals have over the speed and content of their work. Whereas some occupations and work environments provide manageable demands and healthy and supportive environments, others place substantial physical or emotional demands on employees. High-demand and low-control work has been shown to be particularly stressful in ways that impact health (Theorell and Karasek 1996). Workplaces also differ in the extent to which they provide work-life programs and policies that facilitate or even encourage positive health behaviors such as physical activity and healthy eating.

Some workplaces or work arrangements may indirectly promote destructive behaviors such as smoking, poor diet, or even excess alcohol consumption. For example, a British study demonstrated that working very long hours was negatively associated with women's, but not men's, health behaviors; among those who worked long hours, the women consumed more high-fat and high-sugar snacks, exercised less, and, if smokers, smoked more (O'Connor et al. 2005). There is generally less understanding about how men experience structural constraints, formulate their priorities, or respond to work and family stress, or about when and how, for example, they learn to turn to alcohol and drugs as forms of coping or self-care. Such information is essential to designing gender-appropriate interventions to improve men's and women's health.

Norms of long work hours can affect the costs and consequences of achieving success at work by reducing the possibility of balancing work, family, and time for exercise and other positive self-care activities. In their insightful critique of the media's role in selling the desire for perfect bodies rather than health and healthy behaviors, Dworkin and Wachs (2009) describe the different priorities and time constraints on men's and women's health behavior and self-care. In describing the barriers women face after pregnancy and childbirth, they characterize paid work as the first shift, work in the home (child care, feeding oneself and the family, paying bills, and otherwise maintaining a household) as the second shift, and the time spent pursuing health and fitness regimens that allow for adherence to the latest bodily requirements as promoted in the media as the third shift (see also Dworkin 2001; Dworkin and Messner 1999). Individuals, particularly those with long work hours or family caregiving responsibilities, typically fit exercise and other activities they view as health promoting into their schedules after addressing these other tasks and responsibilities. Thus, both theory and evidence suggest that women are more likely than men to minimize or forgo such self-care in response to the competing demands on their time and energy.

Community Actions

In the constrained-choice model, "community" refers to both social networks of relationships with family, friends, and acquaintances at home and at work and the physical environment in which one lives. Thus one can imagine these communities distributed on a continuum from supportive to draining, negating the effects of stress or exacerbating them or enlarging or diminishing options of many types. These social and physical environments affect the ease or difficulty of men and women in meeting the demands of specific roles. However, the impact of living in a community at a given point along this continuum would on average differ somewhat for men versus women, as they are differentially exposed to and impacted by available resources and stressors. For example, as noted earlier, men and women differ in their exposure to specific daily stressors, which in turn affect their stress levels and responses due in part to gender differences in role activity and role expectations. At the community level, gender roles and responsibilities interact with resources and barriers such as employment opportunities or security, the provision of child care and elder care (both as givers and recipients of each), mass transit, and public safety.

The study of the impact of community or neighborhood on health is a rapidly growing transdisciplinary field of research. Yet research focused on assessing and explaining gender differences in the links between neighborhood factors and mortality is just emerging. For example, Grafova and colleagues (2008) found that economic and social environment aspects were important for men's risk of obesity, whereas aspects of the built environment were more important for women's. Similarly, Anderson and colleagues (1997) reported that the relationship between neighborhood socioeconomic status and mortality varied by age, gender, and race/ethnicity. Men and women typically live in the same neighborhoods, so unlike workplace effect, residential place effects are not related to gender segregation. Also, many studies have found gender differences in the link between neighborhood deprivation—an index generally based on unemployment, income, educational attainment, and utilization of public assistance—and health and mortality (Berke et al. 2007; Ross et al. 2007). Winkleby, Sundquist, and Cubbin (2007) found an association between higher neighborhood-level deprivation and both incident coronary heart disease and one-year case fatality for Swedish adults, with slightly stronger effects among women.

While such studies show that neighborhood effects contribute to gender differences in health, it remains unclear how neighborhood effects get under the skin. Men and women may differ in their physiological responses to particular neighborhood features partly through the possible impact on health behaviors. For example, Ross and colleagues (2007) found metropolitan sprawl was associated with higher body mass index (BMI) for men, but the effect was not significant for women. This finding may be explained by research showing that men and women use neighborhood features such as parks differently and that neighborhood walkability is more strongly associated with men's walking (Cohen et al. 2006; Morenoff and Sampson 1997). Other research has shown gender differences in how men and women incorporate social support and social networks. For men, such influences are often more place based. For women, place of residence may not be as strong an influence as work, family, and other social and role-related influences in their lives. Taken together, this work suggests that men's health behaviors may be more strongly affected by characteristics of their residential environment.

Social Policy

Finally, the constrained-choice framework includes the impact of social policy, including federal, state, and local government decisions and policies. To illustrate this at the federal level, we explored the proposition that different types of policy regimes formulate policies and regulations that directly

and indirectly affect gender differences in health. We used cross-national differences in longevity and the gender gap in health behaviors to show how these policies could differentially increase the options and opportunities to for men and women to pursue health (see Bird and Rieker 2008, chapters 3 and 6). Obvious examples of social policies that affect health are universal day care, universal access to education, and retirement benefits not tied to employment or retirement benefits that affect continued employment. Such policies provide an economic safety net through a variety of public and private mechanisms and assure at least a minimum level of income and health-care access for a country's citizens. In addition, for a more general discussion emphasizing the value of integrating and the need to integrate medical sociology and social welfare theory, see Olafsdottir and Beckfield 2009.

These policies can have intended and unintended differential effects on men's and women's lives regardless of whether policy makers assume the genders are the same or different. However, the more critical issue is how much responsibility the state assumes for protective public health regulations and especially for family well-being and child care, and how much remains the responsibility of individuals and families. For example, in social democratic regimes such as the Nordic countries, where the state has more responsibility, both longevity and health status are better than in liberal regimes such as the United States and Australia, where social policies rely on the market and where health care is tied to employment. Other examples concern antismoking and alcohol regulations enacted at the country or state level and the demonstrable effects these have had on declines in smoking rates and alcohol abuse (see Bird and Rieker 2008, chapter 6).

Consider also, for example, how in the United States the current recession has had a far greater effect on men's employment to date than on women's, due largely to the job losses in manufacturing (U.S. Department of Labor 2009a, b, c), resulting in the highest gender gap in unemployment in U.S. history (10 percent for men vs. 7.6 percent for women in April 2009). However, women are more highly represented in the part-time work force, which offers fewer benefits; thus a combination of recent economic trends and employment policies differentially affect men's and women's exposure to job and income loss and the related risk of loss of health insurance. Ironically perhaps, within families, higher rates of unemployment among men increase pressure on women to fill the role of breadwinner, despite their lower average incomes and differences in average work hours and benefits (Hartmann 2008; Lorber 1995; Risman 1998). Moreover as Heidi Hartmann (2008) noted in her congressional testimony on the impact of the current economic downturn on women: "A recession or weak job growth will only exacerbate the problems that face mothers who want and need to work but must find work that is compatible with their families' needs."

Loue (2008) notes that our cross-national comparison of health and economic indicators "underscores the irony of the position of the United States: even as we emphasize individual choice and responsibility for health, we fail as a nation to address and rectify the larger constraints that constitute barriers to opportunities and impediments to choice." Thus while our work to date has focused on the ways in which the social organization of men's and women's lives contributes to gender differences in health, our constrained-choice model clearly applies to racial/ethnic and socioeconomic health disparities as well. For example, differences in opportunities shape the trade-offs and choices made by racial and ethnic minorities—from where to live and what job to take, to who is responsible for caring for children

and the elderly (Bird and Rieker 2008). Thus, we argue that the constrained-choice framework is also relevant to understanding and intervening on racial/ethnic disparities in health. An explanation of the complex link between gender and health behaviors cannot be complete without addressing the relationship of SES to healthy lifestyles and to health over the life course, but that broader discussion is beyond the scope of this chapter.

FUTURE RESEARCH QUESTIONS AND ISSUES TO CONSIDER

The idea that decisions and policies at multiple levels affect health is not new. Researchers, employers, public health officials, and policy makers use both implicit and explicit ecological models to understand and estimate the health effects of specific decisions and to identify individual, environmental, and population-based ways to reduce risk and unsafe behaviors. However, such models and health improvement efforts seldom focus on whether and how pathways and effects may differ by gender.

What do constrained-choice and gender-based analysis have to contribute to the study of health disparities and ultimately to population health? They can provide an understanding of how decisions made and actions taken at the family, work, community, and government levels differentially shape women's and men's health-related priorities, opportunities, and choices. This is not to suggest that individual health and behavior are fully determined by external forces, but that priorities and decisions beyond the level of the individual can reduce the latitude or sense of agency individuals have and the options they perceive in everyday life to pursue health. Clearly, many regulatory measures such as protecting and improving air quality and assuring a clean water supply or the safety of food and other products are largely beyond the reach of most individuals. Thus, we view constrained choice as a platform for prevention where the intention is to create a different kind of health consciousness, one that recognizes the role of differential gender constraints as an additional means for improving population health, both among individuals and decision makers at all levels. Moreover this model includes consideration of how racial/ethnic and socioeconomic constraints interact with sex and gender to produce health disparities among men and among women. As a research framework, it calls for transdisciplinary and comparative approaches at a variety of levels, and for studies that take into account the longer-term costs of policies that damage or undermine health, as well as the benefits of policies that foster health.

Recognizing the contributions to both individual and population health and to health disparities of decisions made at multiple levels beyond the individual raises key questions for researchers, clinicians, and policy makers. For example: Whose responsibility is health? Are protective measures, preventive behaviors, and the costs and consequences of poor health practices the province of individuals, families, the workplace, communities, states, or some combination of these? How such questions are answered has ramifications for improving population health and studying gender and health (see for example Walter and Neumann 2009 on how advances in gender sensitivity and analysis can affect health).

Other key questions seldom raised are: How can we measure the contribution of social, political, and economic policies to gender differences in health? How important are nonhealth policies for improving population health and preventing illness? How do we account for health-care access and quality within a constrained-choice framework (see Banks et al. 2006 and Schoeni et al. 2008 for an elaboration of some of these issues)?

How do such policies interact with advances in biomedical science and technology to produce health? Although not focused on gender, others have been thinking about these topics as well. For example, Phelan and Link (2005) address the bidirectionality of biomedical processes and social phenomena in a way that resonates with our model. They argue that over the past century biomedical science and technology advances have made it possible for individuals to avoid some diseases and live longer, thereby transforming disease patterns and increasing human control over health. The added control makes understanding social factors even more important for improving population health through a "social shaping" approach (Link 2008). Link also notes that "when humans have control, it is their policies, their knowledge, and their behaviors that shape the consequences of biomedical accomplishments and thereby extant patterns of disease and death" (36).

We contend that constrained choice along with gender-based research can lead to better science. This approach provides an opportunity to explore biological and social pathways and mechanisms together as gender opens a window into biological processes, which is not the case with race/ethnicity and SES. However, if we start with gender and examine the intersectionalities with race/ethnicity and SES, then constrained choice can provide a glimpse of the pathways and mechanisms that create gendered health behaviors and outcomes (see Loue 2006 for a discussion of methods and measurement issues in such sex/gender research). Moreover there are a variety of ways and levels at which gender differences can be addressed. Briefly, research can be focused on: disease patterns; a specific disease or biological and genetic predispositions; health behaviors; comparative social regimes and health status; employment patterns; differential stress exposure and responses; and social networks. These topics can be studied as variations within a country, as cross-national comparisons, or as some combination of these.

Research such as what we are advocating is already under way. There is considerable momentum to include both biological and social factors in health studies, a trend observable in both research and policy domains where gender-based analysis is promoted (see for example Fausto-Sterling 2008, 2005; Johnson, Greaves, and Repta 2007, 2009; Klinge 2007; Lohan 2007; Spitzer 2005). These efforts will substantially advance understanding of the biological and social circumstances and identify pathways and mechanisms that expose men and women to harmful stress levels or that place them at risk for adopting unsafe health behaviors that contribute to differential outcomes. Pescosolido and colleagues' (2008) analysis of the intersecting biological and social pathways to gender differences in alcohol dependence provides one very promising example. These authors not only examine the genetic and social interaction empirically but also address the implications of the findings for sociological theories. Extending this thinking to gender-based analysis and theories would advance our knowledge of these phenomena.

If sociologists seek to improve population health and reduce health disparities by influencing the broad range of decisions that occur beyond the level of the individual but affect opportunities to pursue a healthy life, there is much work to be done. The next phase of gender and health comparison work should include the application of the constrained-choice framework to various research agendas. Decision makers at all levels need actionable evidence from gender-focused, generalizable studies on the health benefits or costs of specific choices and policies. This approach requires analyses of the health effects of particular policies that provide clear directives for action beyond the provision of and access to health care. For example, where work to date has typically sought to capture the short-term, and in some cases longer-term, economic costs of policies as diverse as education, employment, and transportation, constrained choice suggests that assessing and reporting the probable health impacts would allow policy makers to take population health effects into account and to value health in considering the trade-offs among policy options (Schoeni et al. 2008). In a society where future prosperity depends on the health and well-being of the population, researchers have tremendous new opportunities to inform policy decisions and a responsibility to take into account whether and how specific policies will affect population health. Attention to the differences in men's and women's lives can further assure that policies will not inadvertently exacerbate these differences or contribute to health disparities among men or among women.

NOTES

1   The *Canadian Medical Association Journal* devoted a special issue (March 13, 2007) to the knowledge gap in understanding the sex-specific differences in the epidemiology of CVD. For example, in one article Pilote and colleagues (2007) conclude that the knowledge gap might explain why cardiovascular health is not improving as rapidly among women as it is in men, and that the regional/country gender differences in CVD incidence may result from an interaction between sex- and gender-related factors.

2   Although both combat duty and exposure to sexual abuse are PTSD risk factors for both men and women, their exposure rates differ by gender. However, women's increasing presence in combat roles and a growing recognition of the prevalence of sexual abuse of boys by clergy members may be narrowing these long-standing differences.

REFERENCES

Abramowicz, Mark, and Henry L. Barnett. 1970. "Sex Ratio of Infant Mortality." *American Journal of Diseases of Children* 119(4): 314–15.

Anderson, Roger T., Paul Sorlie, Eric Backlund, Norman Johnson, and George A. Kaplan. 1997. "Mortality Effects of Community Socioeconomic Status." *Epidemiology* 8(1): 42–47.

Andoh, S. Y., M. Umezaki, K. Nakamura, M. Kizuki, and Takehito Takano. 2006. "Correlation between National Income, HIV/AIDS and Political Status and Mortalities in African Countries." *Public Health* 120(7): 624–33.

Aneshensel, Carol S. 1985. "The Natural History of Depressive Symptoms." *Research in Community and Mental Health* 5:45–74.

Annandale, Ellen. 2009. *Women's Health and Social Change.* London: Routledge.

Banks, James, Michael Marmot, Zoe Oldfield, and James P. Smith. 2006. "Disease and Disadvantage in the United States and in England." *Journal of the American Medical Association* 295(17): 2037–45.

Bassuk, Shari S., and JoAnn E. Manson. 2004. "Gender and Its Impact on Risk Factors for Cardiovascular Disease." In *Principles of Gender Specific Medicine*, ed. M. J. Legato, 193–213. London: Elsevier Academic Press.

Bebbington, Paul. 1996. "The Origins of Sex Differences in Depressive Disorder: Bridging the Gap." *International Review of Psychiatry* 8(4): 295–332.

Begg, Lisa, and Christopher E. Taylor. 2006. "Regulation of Inflammatory Responses: Influence of Sex and Gender: Workshop Summary." In *NIH Workshop: Regulation of Inflammatory Responses: Influence of Sex and Gender.* Bethesda, Md.: Office of Research on Women's Health.

Berin, Barnet N., George L. Stolnitz, and Aaron Tenenbein. 1989. "Mortality Trends of Males and Females over the Ages." *Transactions of Society of Actuaries* 41(1): 9–32.

Berke, Ethan M., Laura M. Gottlieb, Anne V. Moudon, and Eric B. Larson. 2007. "Protective Association between Neighborhood Walkability and Depression in Older Men." *Journal of the American Geriatrics Society* 55(4): 526–33.

Bird, Chloe E., and Patricia P. Rieker. 2008. *Gender and Health: The Effects of Constrained Choices and Social Policies.* New York: Cambridge University Press.

Cameron, Elaine, and Jon Bernardes. 1998. "Gender and Disadvantage in Health: Men's Health for a Change." *Sociology of Health and Illness* 20(5): 673–93.

Chino, Allan F., and Dean Funabaki. 1984. "A Cross-Validation of Sex Differences in the Expression of Depression." *Sex Roles* 11(3–4): 175–87.

Chodorow, Nancy J. 1978. *The Reproduction of Mothering.* Berkeley: University of California Press.

Cleary, Paul D., David Mechanic, and James R. Greenly. 1982. "Sex Differences in Medical Care Utilization: An Empirical Investigation." *Journal of Health and Social Behavior* 23(2): 106–19.

Cohen, Deborah A., Amber Sehgal, Stephanie Williamson, Ronald Sturm, Thomas L. McKenzie, Rosa Lara, and Nicole Lurie. 2006. "Park Use and Physical Activity in a Sample of Public Parks in the City of Los Angeles." Santa Monica, Calif.: RAND Corporation.

Connell, Robert W. 1987. *Gender and Power.* Stanford, Calif.: Stanford University Press.

Courtenay, Will H. 2000a. "Behavioral Factors Associated with Disease, Injury, and Death among Men: Evidence and Implications for Prevention." *Journal of Men's Studies* 9(1): 81–142.

———. 2000b. "Constructions of Masculinity and Their Influence on Men's Well-Being: A Theory of Gender and Health." *Social Science and Medicine* 50(10): 1385–1401.

Crimmins, Eileen M., Jung K. Kim, and Aaron Hagedorn. 2002. "Life with and without Disease: Women Experience More of Both." *Journal of Women and Aging* 14(1–2): 47–59.

Dedovic, Katarina, Mehereen Wadiwalla, Veronica Engert, and Jens C. Pruessner. 2009. "The Role of Sex and Gender Socialization in Stress Reactivity." *Developmental Psychology* 45(1): 45–55.

Dohrenwend, Bruce P., and Barbara S. Dohrenwend. 1976. "Sex Differences and Psychiatric Disorders." *American Journal of Sociology* 81(6): 1147–54.

———. 1977. "Reply to Gove and Tudor's Comment on 'Sex Differences and Psychiatric Disorders.'" *American Journal of Sociology* 82(6): 1336–45.

Dworkin, Shari L. 2001. "'Holding Back': Negotiating a Glass Ceiling on Women's Strength." *Sociological Perspectives* 44(3): 333–50.

Dworkin, Shari L., and Michael A. Messner. 1999. "Just Do What? Sport, Bodies, Gender." In *Revisioning Gender*, ed. M. M. Ferree, J. Lorber, and B. B. Hess, 341–61. Thousand Oaks, Calif.: Sage Publications.

Dworkin, Shari L., and Faye L. Wachs. 2009. *Body Panic: Gender, Health, and the Selling of Fitness.* New York: New York University Press.

Endicott, Jean. 1998. "Gender Similarities and Differences in the Course of Depression." *Journal of Gender-Specific Medicine* 1(3): 40–43.

Ernst, Cecille, and Jules Angst. 1992. "The Zurich Study, XII: Sex Differences in Depression: Evidence from Longitudinal Epidemiological Data." *European Archives of Psychiatry and Clinical Neuroscience* 241(4): 222–30.

Fausto-Sterling, Anne. 2005. "The Bare Bones of Sex: Part 1—Sex and Gender." *Signs* 30(5): 1491–1526.

———. 2008. "The Bare Bones of Race." *Social Studies of Science* 38(5): 657–94.

Gove, Walter R., and Jeannette F. Tudor. 1973. "Adult Sex Roles and Mental Illness." *American Journal of Sociology* 78(4): 812–35.

Grafova, Irina B., Vicki A. Freedman, Rizie Kumar, and Jeannette Rogowski. 2008. "Neighborhoods and Obesity in Later Life." *American Journal of Public Health* 98(11): 2065–71.

Gregory, Tanya, and Jean Endicott. 1999. "Understanding Depression in Women." *Patient Care* 33(19): 19–20.

Grundtvig, Morten, Terje P. Hagen, Mikael German, and Asmund Reikvam. 2009. "Sex-Based Differences in Premature First Myocardial Infarction Caused by Smoking: Twice as Many Years Lost by Women as Men." *European Journal of Cardiovascular Prevention and Rehabilitation* 16(2): 174–79.

Harrison, James. 1978. "Warning: The Male Sex Role May Be Dangerous to Your Health." *Journal of Social Issues* 34(1): 65–86.

Hartmann, Heidi. 2008. "The Impact of the Current Economic Downturn on Women (Testimony Presented to the Joint Economic Committee)." Washington, D.C.: Institute for Women's Policy Research.

Hunt, Kate, and Ellen Annandale. 1999. "Relocating Gender and Morbidity: Examining Men's and Women's Health in Contemporary Western Societies. Introduction to Special Issue on Gender and Health." *Social Science and Medicine* 48(1): 1–5.

Institute of Medicine. 2001a. *Exploring the Biological Contributions to Human Health: Does Sex Matter?* ed. T. M. Wizemann and M. L. Pardue. Washington, D.C.: National Academies Press.

———. 2001b. *Health and Behavior: The Interplay of Biological, Behavioral and Societal Influences*. Washington, D.C.: National Academies Press.

Jacobson, Denise L., Stephen J. Gange, Noel R. Rose, and Neil M. Graham. 1997. "Epidemiology and Estimated Population Burden of Selected Autoimmune Diseases in the United States." *Clinical Immunology and Immunopathology* 84(3): 223–43.

James, Cara V., Alina Salganicoff, Megan Thomas, Usha Ranji, Marsha Lillie-Blanton, and Roberta Wyn. 2009. *Putting Women's Health Care Disparities on the Map: Examining Racial and Ethnic Disparities at the State Level*. Menlo Park, Calif.: Henry J. Kaiser Family Foundation.

Jaycox, Lisa H. 2008. "Invisible Wounds of War: Summary of Key Findings on Psychological and Cognitive Injuries." Santa Monica, Calif.: RAND Corporation.

Johnson, Joy L., Lorraine Greaves, and Robin Repta. 2007. *Better Science with Sex and Gender: A Primer for Health Research*. Vancouver, B.C.: Women's Health Research Network.

———. 2009. "Better Science with Sex and Gender: Facilitating the Use of a Sex and Gender-Based Analysis in Health Research." *International Journal for Equity in Health* 8(1): 14.

Kalben, Barbara B. 2002. *Why Men Die Younger: Causes of Mortality Differences by Sex*. SOA Monograph M-L101–1. Schamburg, Ill.: Society of Actuaries.

Kandel, Denise B., Lynn A. Warner, and Ronald C. Kessler. 1998. "The Epidemiology of Substance Use and Dependence among Women." In *Drug Addiction Research and the Health of Women*, ed. C. L. Wetherington and A. B. Roman, 105–30. NIDA Research Monograph. Rockville, Md.: National Institute of Drug Abuse.

Kannel, William B., and Peter W. Wilson. 1995. "Risk Factors That Attenuate the Female Coronary Disease Advantage." *Archives of Internal Medicine* 155(1): 57–61.

Kawachi, Ichiro, and Bruce Kennedy. 2006. *The Health of Nations: Why Inequality Is Harmful to Your Health*. New York: New Press.

Keitner, Gabor I., Christine E. Ryan, Ivan W. Miller, Robert Kohn, and Nathan B. Epstein. 1991. "12-Month Outcome of Patients with Major Depression and Comorbid Psychiatric or Medical Illness (Compound Depression)." *American Journal of Psychiatry* 148(3): 345–50.

Kessler, Ronald C., Peggy R. Barker, Lisa J. Colpe, Joan F. Epstein, Joseph C. Gfroerer, Eva Hiripi, Mary J. Howes, Sharon-Lise T. Normand, Ronald W. Manderscheid, Ellen E. Walters, and Alan M. Zaslavsky. 2003. "Screening for Serious Mental Illness in the General Population." *Archives of General Psychiatry* 60(2): 184–89.

Kessler, Ronald C., Patricia Berglund, Olga Demler, Robert Jin, Doreen Koretz, Kathleen R. Merikangas, A. John

Rush, Ellen E. Walters, and Philip Wang. 2003. "The Epidemiology of Major Depressive Disorder: Results from the National Comorbidity Survey Replication (Ncs-R)." *Journal of the American Medical Association* 289(23): 3095–3105.

Kessler, Ronald C., Rosa M. Crum, Lynn A. Warner, Christopher B. Nelson, John Schulenberg, and James C. Anthony. 1997. "Lifetime Co-Occurrence of DSM-III-R Alcohol Abuse and Dependence with Other Psychiatric Disorders in the National Comorbidity Survey." *Archives of General Psychiatry* 54(4): 313–21.

Kessler, Ronald C., Katherine A. McGonagle, Marvin Swartz, Dan G. Blazer, and Christopher B. Nelson. 1993. "Sex and Depression in the National Comorbidity Survey 1: Lifetime Prevalence, Chronicity and Recurrence." *Journal of Affective Disorders* 29(2–3): 85–96.

Kessler, Ronald C., Katherine A. McGonagle, Shanyang Zhao, Christopher B. Nelson, Michael Hughes, Suzann Eshleman, Hans-Ulrich Wittchen, and Kenneth S. Kendler. 1994. "Lifetime and 12-Month Prevalence of DSM-III-R Psychiatric Disorders in the United States: Results from the National Comorbidity Survey." *Archives of General Psychiatry* 51(1): 8–19.

Kessler, Ronald C., Christopher B. Nelson, Katherine A. McGonagle, J. Liu, Marvin Swartz, and Dan G. Blazer. 1996. "Comorbidity of DSM-III-R Major Depressive Disorder in the General Population: Results from the U.S. National Comorbidity Survey." *British Journal of Psychiatry* 168, suppl. 30:17–30.

Kessler, Ronald C., and Ellen E. Walters. 2002. "The National Comorbidity Survey." In *Textbook in Psychiatric Epidemiology*, ed. M. T. Tsuang and M. Tohen, 243–62. New York: John Wiley and Sons.

Kiecolt-Glaser, Janice K., Lynanne McGuire, Theodore F. Robles, and Ronald Glaser. 2002a. "Emotions, Morbidity, and Mortality: New Perspectives from Psychoneuroimmunology." *Annual Review of Psychology* 53:83–107.

———. 2002b. "Psychoneuroimmunology: Psychological Influences on Immune Function and Health." *Journal of Consulting and Clinical Psychology* 70(3): 537–47.

Kimmel, Michael S., and Michael A. Messner. 1993. *Men's Lives*. New York: Macmillan.

Klinge, Ineke. 2007. "Bringing Gender Expertise to Biomedical and Health-Related Research." *Gender Medicine* 4, suppl. 2:S59–63.

Kornstein, Susan G., Alan F. Schatzberg, Michael E. Thase, Kimberly A. Yonkers, James P. McCullough, Gabor I. Keitner, Alan J. Gelenberg, C. E. Ryan, A. L. Hess, Wilma Harrison, Sonia M. Davis, and Martin B. Keller. 2000. "Gender Differences in Chronic Major and Double Depression." *Journal of Affective Disorders* 60(1): 1–11.

Krieger, Nancy. 2003. "Genders, Sexes, and Health: What Are the Connections—and Why Does It Matter?" *International Journal of Epidemiology* 32(4): 652–57.

Krieger, Nancy, David H. Rehkopf, Jarvis T. Chen, Pamela D. Waterman, Enrico Marcelli, and Malinda Kennedy. 2008. "The Fall and Rise of U.S. Inequalities in Premature Mortality: 1960–2002." *PLoS Medicine* 5(2): e46.

Legato, Marianne J. 2002. *Eve's Rib: The Groundbreaking Guide to Women's Health*. New York: Three Rivers Press.

Lennon, Mary C. 2006. "Women, Work and Depression: Conceptual and Policy Issues." In *The Handbook for the Study of Women and Depression*, ed. C. L. M. Keyes and S. H. Goodman, 309–27. New York: Cambridge University Press.

Levant, Ronald F. and William S. Pollack. 1995. *A New Psychology of Men*. New York: Basic Books.

Link, Bruce G. 2008. "Epidemiological Sociology and the Social Shaping of Population Health." *Journal of Health and Social Behavior* 49(4): 367–84.

Lockshin, Michael D. 2001. "Genome and Hormones: Gender Differences in Physiology: Invited Review: Sex Ratio and Rheumatic Disease." *Journal of Applied Physiology* 91(5): 2366–73.

———. 2006. "Sex Differences in Autoimmune Disease." *Lupus* 15(11): 753–56.

———. Forthcoming. "Non-Hormonal Explanations for Sex Discrepancy in Human Illness."

Lockshin, Michael D., Sherine Gabriel, Zahra Zakeri, and Richard A. Lockshin. 1999. "Gender, Biology and Human Disease: Report of a Conference." *Lupus* 8(5): 335–38.

Lohan, Maria. 2007. "How Might We Understand Men's Health Better? Integrating Explanations from Critical Studies on Men and Inequalities in Health." *Social Science and Medicine* 65(3): 495–504.

Lorber, Judith. 1995. *Paradoxes of Gender*. New Haven, Conn.: Yale University Press.

Loue, Sana. 2006. *Assessing Race, Ethnicity and Gender in Health*. New York: Springer.

———. 2008. "Gender and Health: The Effects of Constrained Choices and Social Policies." *New England Journal of Medicine* 359(11): 1187.

Lutfey, Karen, and Jeremy Freese. 2005. "Toward Some Fundamentals of Fundamental Causality: Socioeconomic Status and Health in the Routine Clinic Visit for Diabetes." *American Journal of Sociology* 110(5): 1326–72.

Marmot, Michael. 2004. *The Status Syndrome: How Social Standing Affects Our Health and Longevity*. New York: Henry Holt.

———. 2005. "Social Determinants of Health Inequalities." *Lancet* 365(9464): 1099–1104.

Mirowsky, J., and K. Ross. 2003. *Education, Social Status, and Health*. Hawthorne, N.Y.: Aldine De Gruyter.

Morenoff, Jeffrey D., and Robert J. Sampson. 1997. "Violent Crime and the Spatial Dynamics of Neighborhood Transition: Chicago, 1970–1990." *Social Forces* 76(1): 31–64.

Murray, Christopher J., Sandeep C. Kulkarni, Catherine Michaud, Niels Tomijima, Maria T. Bulzacchelli, Terrell J. Iandiorio, and Majid Ezzati. 2006. "Eight Americas: Investigating Mortality Disparities across Races, Counties and Race-Counties in the United States." *PLoS Medicine* 3(9): e260.

Narrow, William E., Donald S. Rae, Lee N. Robins, and Darrel A. Regier. 2002. "Revised Prevalence Estimates of Mental Disorders in the United States." *Archives of General Psychiatry* 59(2): 115–130.

Nathanson, Constance A. 1984. "Sex Differences in Mortality." *Annual Review of Sociology* 10:191–213.

National Center for Health Statistics (NCHS). 2009. *Health, United States, 2008, with Chartbook*. Hyattsville, Md.: NCHS.

Nazroo, James Y., Angela C. Edwards, and George W. Brown. 1998. "Gender Differences in the Prevalence of Depression: Artefact, Alternative Disorders, Biology or Roles?" *Sociology of Health and Illness* 20(3): 312–30.

Nolen-Hoeksema, Susan. 1987. "Sex Differences in Unipolar Depression: Evidence and Theory." *Psychological Bulletin* 101(2): 259–82.

———. 1990. *Sex Differences in Depression*. Stanford, Calif.: Stanford University Press.

O'Connor, Daryl B., Mark T. Conner, and Fiona Jones. 2005. "Effects of Stress on Eating Behaviour: An Integrated Approach." Swindon, UK: Economic and Social Research Council.

Olafsdottir, Sigrun, and Jason Beckfield. 2009. "Health and the Social Rights of Citizenship: Integrating Welfare State Theory and Medical Sociology." In *Handbook of Sociology of Health, Illness, and Healing*, ed. B. A.

Pescosolido, J. K. Martin, J. D. McLeod, and A. Rogers. New York: Springer.

Pai, Jennifer K., Tobias Pischon, Jing Ma, JoAnn E. Manson, Susan E. Hankinson, Kaumudi Joshipura, Gary C. Curhan, Nader Rifai, Carolyn C. Cannuscio, Meir J. Stampfer, and Eric B. Rimm. 2004. "Inflammatory Markers and the Risk of Coronary Heart Disease in Men and Women." *New England Journal of Medicine* 351(25): 2599–2610.

Pescosolido, Bernice A., Brea L. Perry, J. Scott Long, Jack K. Martin, John I. Nurnberger Jr., and Victor Hesselbrock. 2008. "Under the Influence of Genetics: How Transdisciplinarity Leads Us to Rethink Social Pathways to Illness." *American Journal of Sociology* 114, suppl. 1:S171–201.

Phelan, Jo C., Bruce G. Link, Ana Diez-Roux, Ichiro Kawachi, and Bruce Levin. 2004. "'Fundamental Causes' of Social Inequalities in Mortality: A Test of the Theory." *Journal of Health and Social Behavior* 45(3): 265–85.

Phelan, Jo C., and Bruce G. Link. 2005. "Controlling Disease and Creating Disparities: A Fundamental Cause Perspective." *The Journals of Gerontology Series B: Psychological Sciences and Social Sciences* 60(2): S27–33.

Piccinelli, Marco, and Greg Wilkinson. 2000. "Gender Differences in Depression: Critical Review." *British Journal of Psychiatry* 177:486–92.

Pilote, Louise, Kaberi Dasgupta, Veena Guru, Karin H. Humphries, Jennifer McGrath, Colleen Norris, Doreen Rabi, Johanne Tremblay, Arsham Alamian, Tracie Barnett, Jafna Cox, William A. Ghali, Sherry Grace, Pavel Hamet, Teresa Ho, Susan Kirkland, Marie Lambert, Danielle Libersan, Jennifer O'Loughlin, Gilles Paradis, Milan Petrovich, and Vicky Tagalakis. 2007. "A Comprehensive View of Sex-Specific Issues Related to Cardiovascular Disease." *Canadian Medical Association Journal* 176(6): S1–44.

Pinnelli, Antonella. 1997. "Gender and Demography." In *Démographie: Analyse et synthèse: Causes et conséquences des évolutions démographiques: Actes du Séminaire "Population et démographie: Problèmes et politiques."* San Miniato. Vol 1. Rome: Universita' La Sapienza, Dipartimento di Scienze.

Pleck, Joseph H. 1983. *The Myth of Masculinity*. Cambridge, Mass.: MIT Press.

———. 1984. "Men's Power with Women, Other Men, and Society: A Men's Movement Analysis." In *The Gender Gap in Psychotherapy: Social Realities in Psychological Processes*, ed. P. P. Rieker and E. H. Carmen, 79–90. New York: Plenum Press.

Pleck, Joseph H., and Robert Brannon. 1978. "Male Roles and the Male Experience: Introduction." *Journal of Social Issues* 34(1): 1–4.

Pratt, Laura A. 2009. "Serious Psychological Distress, as Measured by the K6, and Mortality." *Annals of Epidemiology* 19(3): 202–9.

Ramey, Estelle R. 1982. "The Natural Capacity for Health in Women." In *Women: A Developmental Perspective*, ed. P. W. Berman and E. R. Ramey, 3–12. NIH Publication No. 82–2298. Washington, D.C.: U.S. Department of Health and Human Services.

Rao, Chalapati, Alan D. Lopez, and Yusuf Hemed. 2006. "Causes of Death." In *Disease and Mortality in Sub-Saharan Africa*, 2d ed., ed. D. T. Jamison, R. G. Feachem, M. W. Makgoba, E. R. Bos, F. K. Baingana, K. J. Hofman, and K. O. Rogo, 43–58. Washington, D.C.: World Bank Publications.

Reeves, Mathew J., and Ann P. Rafferty. 2005. "Healthy Lifestyle Characteristics among Adults in the United States, 2000." *Archives of Internal Medicine* 165(8): 854–57.

Regier, Darrel A., William E. Narrow, Donald S. Rae, Ronald W. Manderscheid, B. Z. Locke, and F. K. Goodwin. 1993. "The De Facto U.S. Mental and Addictive Disorders Service System: Epidemiological Catchment Area 1-Year Prevalence Rates of Disorders and Services." *Archives of General Psychiatry* 50(2): 85–94.

Regier, Darrel A., and Lee N. Robins. 1991. *Psychiatric Disorders in America: The Epidemiologic Catchment Area Study*. New York: Free Press.

Rhodes, Anne E., Paula N. Goering, Teresa To, and J. Ivan Williams. 2002. "Gender and Outpatient Mental Health Service Use." *Social Science and Medicine* 54(1): 1–10.

Ridgeway, Cecilia L., and Lynn Smith-Lovin. 1999. "The Gender System and Interaction." *Annual Review of Sociology* 25:191–216.

Rieker, Patricia P., and Chloe E. Bird. 2000. "Sociological Explanations of Gender Differences in Mental and Physical Health." In *The Handbook of Medical Sociology*, 5th ed., ed. C. E. Bird, P. Conrad, and A. M. Fremont, 98–113. Englewood Cliffs, N.J.: Prentice Hall.

———. 2005. "Rethinking Gender Differences in Health: Why We Need to Integrate Social and Biological Perspectives." *Journals of Gerontology Series B: Psychological Sciences and Social Sciences* 60(2): S40–47.

Rieker, Patricia P., and Elaine H. Carmen. 1984. *The Gender Gap in Psychotherapy: Social Realities in Psychological Processes*. New York: Plenum Press.

Risman, Barbara J. 1998. *Gender Vertigo: American Families in Transition*. New Haven, Conn.: Yale University Press.

Rosenfield, Sarah. 1999. "Gender and Mental Health: Do Women Have More Psychopathology, Men More, or Both the Same (and Why)?" In *The Sociology of Mental Health and Illness*, ed. A. Horwitz and T. Sheid, 348–60. New York: Cambridge University Press.

Ross, Nancy A., Stephane Tremblay, Saeeda Khan, Daniel Crouse, Mark Tremblay, and Jean-Marie Berthelot. 2007. "Body Mass Index in Urban Canada: Neighborhood and Metropolitan Area Effects." *American Journal of Public Health* 97(3): 500–508.

Rustgi, Sheila D., Michelle M. Doty, and Sara R. Collins. 2009. *Women at Risk: Why Many Women Are Forgoing Needed Health Care—Analysis from the Commonwealth Fund 2007; Biennial Health Insurance Survey*. New York: Commonwealth Fund.

Sabo, Don, and David F. Gordon. 1995. "Rethinking Men's Health and Illness." In *Men's Health and Illness: Gender, Power and the Body*, ed. D. Sabo and D. F. Gordon, 1–21. Thousand Oaks, Calif.: Sage.

Sargeant, J. Kent, Martha L. Bruce, Louis P. Florio, and Myrna M. Weissman. 1990. "Factors Associated with 1-Year Outcome of Major Depression in the Community." *Archives of General Psychiatry* 47(6): 519–26.

Schoeni, Robert F., James S. House, George A. Kaplan, and Harold Pollack. 2008. *Making Americans Healthier: Social and Economic Policy as Health Policy*. New York: Russell Sage Foundation.

Selye, Hans. 1956. *The Stress of Life*. New York: McGraw-Hall.

Shetty, Kanaka D., William B. Vogt, and Jayanta Bhattacharya. 2009. "Hormone Replacement Therapy and Cardiovascular Health in the United States." *Medical Care* 47(5): 600–606.

Sowers, James R. 1998. "Diabetes Mellitus and Cardiovascular Disease in Women." *Archives of Internal Medicine* 158(6): 617–21.

Spitzer, Denise. 2005. "Engendering Health Disparities (Commentary)." *Canadian Journal of Public Health* 96, suppl. 2: S78–S96.

Taylor, Shelley E., Laura C. Klein, Brian P. Lewis, Tara L. Gruenewald, Regan A. Gurung, and John A. Updegraff. 2000. "Biobehavioral Responses to Stress in Females: Tend-and-Befriend, Not Fight-or-Flight." *Psychological Review* 107(3): 411–29.

Theorell, Tores, and Robert A. Karasek. 1996. "Current Issues Relating to Psychosocial Job Strain and

Cardiovascular Disease Research." *Journal of Occupational Health Psychology* 1(1): 9–26.

Thom, Thomas, Nancy Haase, Wayne Rosamond, Virginia J. Howard, John Rumsfeld, Teri Manolio, Zhi-Jie Zheng, Katherine Flegal, Christopher O'Donnell, Steven Kittner, Donald Lloyd-Jones, David C. Goff Jr., Yuling Hong, Robert Adams, Gary Friday, Karen Furie, Philip Gorelick, Brett Kissela, John Marler, James Meigs, Veronique Roger, Stephen Sidney, Paul Sorlie, Julia Steinberger, Sylvia Wasserthiel-Smoller, Matthew Wilson, Philip Wolf, and American Heart Association Statistics Committee and Stroke Statistics Subcommittee. 2006. "Heart Disease and Stroke Statistics—2006 Update: A Report from the American Heart Association Statistics Committee and Stroke Statistics Subcommittee." *Circulation* 113(6): e85–151.

Thorand, Barbara, Jens Baumert, Hubert Kolb, Christa Meisinger, Lloyd Chambless, Wolfgang Koenig, and Chris tian Herder. 2007. "Sex Differences in the Prediction of Type 2 Diabetes by Inflammatory Markers: Results from the Monica/Kora Augsburg Case-Cohort Study, 1984–2002." *Diabetes Care* 30(4): 854–60.

United Nations. 2005. "The World's Women 2005: Trends and Statistics." New York: United Nations.

U.S. Department of Labor. Bureau of Labor Statistics. 2009a. "Employed Persons by Occupation, Sex, and Age." May 29. bls.gov/cps/cpsaat9.pdf.

———. 2009b. "Extended Mass Layoffs." May 29. bls.gov/news.release/pdf/mslo.pdf.

———. 2009c. "News: The Employment Situation; April 2009." May 29. bls.gov/news.release/pdf/empsit.pdf.

Velkoff, Victoria A., and Paul R. Kowal. 2007. *Current Population Reports, P95/07–1 Population Aging in Sub-Saharan Africa: Demographic Dimensions 2006.* Washington, D.C.: U.S. Department of Health and Human Services, U.S. Department of Commerce.

Verbrugge, Lois M., and Deborah L. Wingard. 1987. "Sex Differentials in Health and Mortality." *Women and Health* 12(2): 103–45.

Waldron, Ingrid. 1998. "Sex Differences in Infant and Early Childhood Mortality: Major Causes of Death and Possible Biological Causes." In *Too Young to Die: Genes or Gender?* Department of Economic and Social Affairs, Population Division, 64–83. New York: United Nations.

Walsh, Stephen J., and Laurie M. Rau. 2000. "Autoimmune Diseases: A Leading Cause of Death among Young and Middle-Aged Women in the United States." *American Journal of Public Health* 90(9): 1463–66.

Walter, Ulla, and Brigitte Neumann. 2009. *Gender in Prevention and Health Promotion: Policy Research Practice.* New York: Springer.

West, Candace, and Don H. Zimmerman. 1987. "Doing Gender." *Gender and Society* 1(2): 125–51.

Whang, William, Laura D. Kubzansky, Ichiro Kawachi, Kathryn M. Rexrode, Candyce H. Kroenke, Robert J. Glynn, Hasan Garan, and Christine M. Albert. 2009. "Depression and Risk of Sudden Cardiac Death and Coronary Heart Disease in Women: Results from the Nurses' Health Study." *Journal of the American College of Cardiology* 53(11): 950–58.

Whooley, Mary A., Peter de Jonge, Eric Vittinghoff, Chris tian Otte, Rudolf Moos, Robert M. Carney, Sadia Ali, Sunaina Dowray, Beeya Na, Mitchell D. Feldman, Nelson B. Schiller, and Warren S. Browner. 2008. "Depressive Symptoms, Health Behaviors, and Risk of Cardiovascular Events in Patients with Coronary Heart Disease." *Journal of the American Medical Association* 300(20): 2379–88.

Wilhelm, Kay, Gordon Parker, and Dusan Hadzi-Pavlovic. 1997. "Fifteen Years On: Evolving Ideas in Researching Sex Differences in Depression." *Psychological Medicine* 27(4): 875–83.

Wilkinson, Richard. 1996. *Unhealthy Societies: The Afflictions of Inequality.* London: Routledge.

Wingard, Deborah L. 1984. "The Sex Differential in Morbidity, Mortality, and Lifestyle." *Annual Review of Public Health* 5:433–58.

Winkleby, Marilyn, Kristina Sundquist, and Catherine Cubbin. 2007. "Inequities in CHD Incidence and Case Fatality by Neighborhood Deprivation." *American Journal of Preventive Medicine* 32(2): 97–106.

Winokur, George, William Coryell, Martin Keller, Jean Endicott, and Hagop Akiskal. 1993. "A Prospective Follow-Up of Patients with Bipolar and Primary Unipolar

Affective Disorder." *Archives of General Psychiatry* 50(6): 457–65.

WHO [World Health Organization]. 2002. "The World Health Report: Reducing Risks, Promoting Healthy Life." Geneva: World Health Organization.

———. 2006. "World Health Statistics 2006." February 18. who.int/whosis/whostat2006.pdf.

———. 2008. "Primary Health Care: Now More Than Ever." May 29. who.int/whr/2008/summary/en/index. html.

Yin, Sandra. 2007. "Gender Disparities in Health and Mortality 2007. Population Reference Bureau." February 16. prb.org/Articles/2007/genderdisparities.aspx?p=1.

READING 3

The Relationship between Socioeconomic Status and Health, or, "They Call It 'Poor Health' for a Reason"

Donald A. Barr

In 1997 the *New York Times* published an article by Richard Shweder reporting on his research into the health of the U.S. public. The subtitle for this chapter is taken from the title of that article. Shweder looked at a variety of diseases and conditions, and concluded that "lower-middle-class Americans are more mortal, morbid, symptomatic and disabled than upper-middle-class Americans. With each little step down on the educational, occupational, and income ladders comes an increased risk of headaches, varicose veins, hypertension, sleepless nights, emotional distress, heart disease, schizophrenia, and an early visit to the grave."

[…] We considered the fictional lives of Mimi, the poor seamstress in *La Boheme,* and Hans Castorp, the son of a well-to-do family in *Magic Mountain.* Each had tuberculosis; Mimi died, Hans survived. This pattern has been the same throughout history. When the plague swept through Europe in the Middle Ages, commoners were more likely to die from it than aristocrats. When world wars ravaged the twentieth century,

sergeants were more likely than generals to die on the battlefield from wounds and to die in the barracks from a heart attack.

From the Whitehall study […], we saw that blue-collar workers in the British Civil Service are more likely than white-collar workers to die from a variety of causes. The Black Report—a government-financed study that examined the health status of a full range of social classes in England and Wales, using occupation as a marker for social class (London Department of Health and Social Security 1980)—also found consistent differences in health status that were associated with one's position on the hierarchy of occupational status. Both the Black Report and the Whitehall study were in a country that had health care available to all under the British National Health Service. The consistent differences in health status could not be attributed to differences in access to health care.

On October 29, 2012, Hurricane Sandy struck coastal areas of New York, New Jersey, and surrounding areas. The Red Cross reported that 117

Donald A. Barr, "The Relationship between Socioeconomic Status and Health, or, "They Call It 'Poor Health" for a Reason'," Health Disparities in the United States: Social Class, Race, Ethnicity, and Health, pp. 36-57. Copyright © 2014 by Johns Hopkins University Press. Reprinted with permission.

47

people died from the storm. Of those who died, half were over the age of 55, with drowning as the most common cause of death (U.S. Department of Health and Human Services 2013).

We saw similar patterns in 2005, when Hurricane Katrina, characterized by the U.S. Centers for Disease Control and Prevention as, "one of the strongest hurricanes to strike the United States during the past 100 years and was likely the nation's costliest natural disaster to date" (U.S. Department of Health and Human Services 2006, p. 240), destroyed much of the city of New Orleans and surrounding areas. Thousands of people were treated for illnesses and injuries caused by the storm, and nearly 1,000 people died (U.S. Department of Health and Human Services, Centers for Disease Control and Prevention 2006).

Might we expect illnesses and deaths due to natural disasters such as hurricanes to follow the same pattern as tuberculosis in the nineteenth century and the plague throughout history?

Grennough and colleagues (2008) surveyed a random sample of evacuees from Katrina who were staying in Red Cross shelters. They found that, prior to the storm, those being housed at shelters were disproportionately unemployed or underemployed, low-income, unmarried, with chronic medical problems, yet lacking health insurance. Brunkard and colleagues (2008) examined the death records of those who died from the storm in Louisiana, finding half of them to be older than 75, with drowning once again the most common cause of death. While the racial distribution of those who died and those being housed at shelters largely matched the racial distribution of the local population, for those coming from Orleans Parish, the hardest hit section of New Orleans, the death rate of blacks over the age of 18 was consistently higher than for whites, with the black/white ratio for different age groups ranging from 1.7:1 to 4:1.

Heat waves are another form of natural disasters. In July 1995 Chicago and the surrounding areas experienced a severe, intense heat wave. The temperature climbed above 100 degrees and stayed there for several days. The rise in temperature was soon followed by a sharp rise in the number of deaths due either to the heat alone or due to cardiovascular disease made worse by the heat. More than 700 people in Chicago died from heat-related causes.

Semenza and colleagues (1996) reported on a detailed analysis of the nature of the deaths in Chicago that were a result of the heat wave and of the social and demographic characteristics of those who died. They were able to identify a series of factors that were associated with an increased likelihood of dying during the heat wave:

- people with known medical problems who were confined to bed
- people who did not leave home each day
- people who lived alone
- people who lived on the top floor of a building
- people with few regular social contacts
- people with no working air conditioner
- people with no access to transportation
- people who had nailed their windows shut for safety

As we might expect, people with known medical problems who were confined to bed were more likely to die from the heat. We might expect frail elderly people to be more susceptible to the heat. But the pattern does not stop there. Two general categories of risk factor emerge from the analysis.

1. *Those with few social contacts.* Those who lived alone and did not leave home at least daily were more likely to die, as were those with few social contacts with friends and family. […] We will see

evidence that weak social networks are associated with a variety of health risks.

2. *Those with evidence of low income.* In many neighborhoods in Chicago, in which the buildings are not air conditioned and many do not have elevators, the rent for apartments on the top floor will be less than for those on lower floors. Those who rent these apartments are also less likely to be able to afford the cost of having their own air conditioner or to have access to their own means of transportation. It should also be clear that those who find it necessary to nail their windows shut for safety will be living in lower-income neighborhoods than those who leave their windows operable (and thus available to create a cooling cross-draft).

In a heat wave, people are more likely to die if they are sick, are poor, and have few social contacts. In a hurricane, similar patterns emerge. As with the infectious diseases from centuries past, those today with lower income or other forms of socioeconomic disadvantage are more likely to die from natural disasters such as heat waves or hurricanes.

TERMINOLOGY: SOCIOECONOMIC STATUS OR SOCIOECONOMIC POSITION?

As reflected in the title of this chapter, I refer to a person's place on the hierarchy of social and economic attainment as their "socioeconomic status." This is a term that has been used commonly by social scientists for quite some time. Nancy Krieger and colleagues have suggested that a more appropriate term to describe this hierarchy might be "socioeconomic position," which they define as "an aggregate measure that includes both resource-based and prestige-based measures … [that] refer to individual's rank or status in a social hierarchy" (1997, p. 345). They go on to suggest that "'socioeconomic status' blurs the distinction between two different aspects of socioeconomic position:

(a) actual resources, and (b) status, meaning prestige- or rank-related characteristics" (p. 346).

In the literature on health disparities, one commonly encounters both phrases. To explore the differences in the intended meaning of these two terms, I consulted the Oxford English Dictionary. The OED defines the word "status" as "social or professional rank, position, or standing; a person's relative importance." It defines "position" as "a person's circumstances, condition, or situation, esp. as affecting his or her influence, role, or power to act."

Both terms seem to reflect common perceptions of a rank-ordered hierarchy. For example, when I was a Boy Scout, I was fully aware that an Eagle Scout was in a position of higher status, that is, higher respect and influence, than was a mere First Class Scout. Does "status" also subsume the level of one's resources, whether economic or otherwise? To me it does. Accordingly, I use the term "socioeconomic status" to refer both to one's access to resources as well as to one's place in a hierarchy of influence and prestige.

WHAT IS SOCIOECONOMIC STATUS? HOW SHOULD WE MEASURE IT?

So far I have been talking principally about the association between income and health status. Those with lower levels of income tend to have lower health status than those who have higher levels of income. I have been using income as a measure of socioeconomic status—which I refer to from here on simply as SES. Sometimes I use the income earned by an individual; sometimes, the total income earned by all the people in the house hold of which the individual is a member.

However, we also saw from the Whitehall study and the Black Report from the United Kingdom that the relative status of one's occupation is also strongly associated with health status over time. For these studies, occupational status was used as a

FIGURE 3.1 Mean annual earnings for individuals in 2012, by highest level of education.

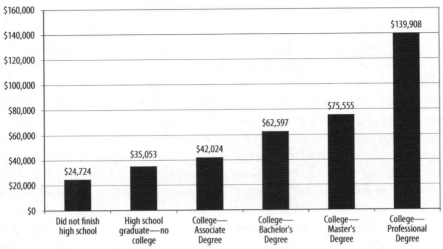

Source: U.S. Census Bureau, Current Population Survey, 2012.

measure of SES. We would certainly expect those with higher-status occupations also to enjoy higher incomes. In fact, the median or average income associated with a certain type of occupation often serves as the metric for assigning the place of an occupation on the scale of occupational status.

Beyond income and occupational status, the level of education one has completed is a third way in which SES is often measured and reported. Those with higher levels of education will typically enjoy better health. By means of example, Montez and Zajacova (2013) looked at the change in mortality rates among white women in the United States between the ages of 45 and 84, comparing women of differing levels of education. They found that mortality rates decreased for college educated women, remained fairly constant for high school graduates without a bachelor's degree, and increased for women who did not graduate from high school. The end result was widening disparities in mortality rates based on education.

While the level of education attained is strongly associated with death rates and other aspects of health inequality, perhaps not surprisingly, those

with higher levels of education will also tend to have higher levels of income, and they will tend to occupy occupations with higher levels of occupational status. This association is illustrated in Figure 3.1.

Using data for 2011 gathered by the U.S. Census Bureau, we are able to see the average yearly income for all working adults in the United States who are 25 years old or older, sorted by level of education. With each step up the educational ladder, income goes up. The incremental increase is largest for those with a college degree and various levels of graduate or professional education after college. Thus, we should view income and education as two sides of the same SES coin. Both income and education will in turn be closely associated with occupational status.

McDonough and colleagues (1997) published an earlier analysis of the association between household income and the odds of dying from any cause. Using data from the period 1972–89, they identified a strong stepwise association, as shown in Figure 3.2. Using as a point of reference the death rates of those households with an income greater

FIGURE 3.2 Adjusted odds ratio for all-cause mortality, based on annual household income. Data from 1972-89; income is indexed to 1993 dollars. >$70,000 = 1.00.

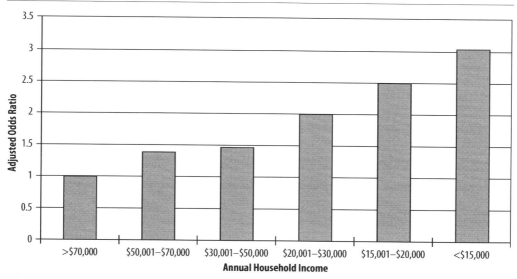

Source: Based on McDonough et al. (1997).

FIGURE 3.3 Additional life expectancy at age 25, United States 2006, by sex and education level.

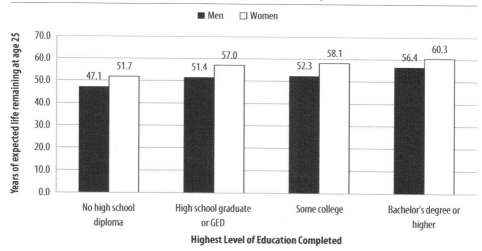

Source: National Center for Health Statistics, Health, United States, 2011.

than $70,000 (measured in 1993 dollars), it should be apparent that, for every step down the income ladder, the odds of dying go up.

Using data from 2006, the relationship between education as a measure of SES and the life expectancy at age 25 is illustrated in Figure 3.3. The chart shows how many more years, on average, a

25-year-old man or woman could expect to live, based on the highest level of education completed. For those aged 25, each step up the educational ladder brings with it the expectation of additional years of life.

Confirming the association between education, income, and health status, the U.S. Congressional Budget Office (2008) looked at changes in life expectancy in the United States, and concluded that overall life expectancy had steadily increased between 1950 and 2004. "Accompanying the recent increases, however, is a growing disparity in life expectancy between individuals with high and low income and between those with more or less education. The difference in life expectancy across socioeconomic groups is significantly larger now than in 1980 or 1990" (p. 1).

Isaacs and Schroeder (2004) published a discussion of these associations in a paper entitled "Class: The Ignored Determinant of the Nation's Health." They note the tremendous advances medicine made over the course of the twentieth century, citing an Institute of Medicine report and stating that "Americans today, as compared with those in 1900, 'are healthier, live longer, and enjoy lives that are less likely to be marked by injuries, ill health, or premature death.'" However, the authors go on to acknowledge that, "any celebration of these victories must be tempered by the realization that these gains are not shared fairly by all members of our society. People in upper classes—those who have a good education, hold high-paying jobs, and live in comfortable neighborhoods—live longer and healthier lives than do people in lower classes, many of whom are black or members of ethnic minorities. And the gap is widening" (p. 1137).

The association between SES as measured by educational attainment and death rates has been found consistently in studies of other developed countries. Marmot and colleagues (1995) summarized the results of studies done in Hungary,

Finland, Denmark, Sweden, and Norway in addition to England and Wales. For all these studies, the age-standardized death rate falls continuously with increasing years of education. Similarly, Semyonov and colleagues (2013) examined the association between wealth (as opposed to income) and health in the United States and in 15 European countries. They found that in all these countries, "rich persons tend to be healthier than poor persons," and that "the positive association between wealth and health holds even after controlling for socio-demographic attributes and household income" (p. 10).

Martinson (2012) made a direct comparison between the United States and England, comparing the income gradient in health across a range of conditions such as diabetes, hypertension, heart disease, and stroke. Despite the fact that the English population exhibits better overall health and has universal health insurance through the British National Health Service, "inequality in health by income was quite similar" in both countries (p. 2054).

IS RACE A MEASURE OF SES INDEPENDENT OF EDUCATION, INCOME, AND OCCUPATION?

[…] There is a complex relationship among race, SES, and health. Using data for 2010, Table 3.1 shows age-adjusted death rates in the United States broken down by race and gender. For both men and women, black Americans have death rates that are substantially higher than those of white Americans. The death rate of black men is 26 percent higher than that of white men. For black women the death rate is 19 percent higher than that of white women.

FIGURE 3.4 Educational attainment of the adults 25 years and over, by race and gender, 2012.

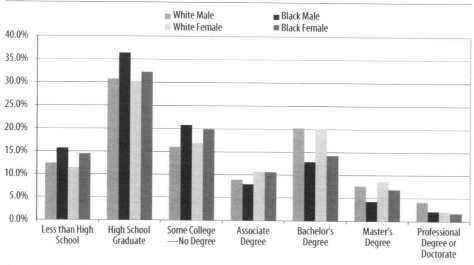

Source: U.S. Census Bureau.

TABLE 3.1 U.S. Age-Adjusted Death Rate per 100,000 Person-Years, by Race and Gender, 2010

	Male	Female
Black	1,104	753
White	879	631

Source: Murphy SL, Xu J, Kochanek KD. Deaths: Final Data for 2010. 2013. National Vital Statistics Reports. May 8, 61(4) http://www.cdc.gov/nchs/data/nvsr/nvsr61/nvsr61_04.pdf.

One possible explanation for these disparities in age-adjusted death rates is the level of educational attainment for black and white Americans. Figure 3.4 compares the educational attainment of whites and blacks in the United States, sorted by gender.

From Figure 3.4, we see that blacks in the United States are more likely than whites

- never to graduate from high school
- to graduate from high school but not go on to college

At the other end of the educational spectrum, substantially more whites

- finish college
- obtain a master's degree
- obtain a doctorate or professional degree

With education as a principal measure of SES, and lower average educational attainment among blacks as compared to whites, we might expect higher death rates among the black community.

When we compare the median level of earnings for blacks and whites broken down by educational attainment and by gender, we find that at all levels of educational attainment, black men and women earn lower incomes than white men and women with the same level of education. These data are shown in Figure 3.5.

Even for those who stop with a high school education and for those who never finish high school, white men earn more than black men. In this case we find that educational attainment does indeed predict income, but it does so differently for blacks and whites. This might lead us to ask whether we will also see differences in health status of blacks and whites at the same level of SES.

FIGURE 3.5 Earnings by educational attainment of workers 18 years and over, by race and gender, 2011 (* indicates that this group was too small for comparison).

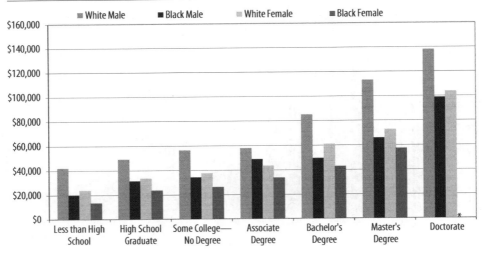

Source: U.S. Census Bureau.

TABLE 3.2 Average Annual Age-Adjusted Rates of Death from Heart Disease among Persons 25 to 64 Years Old, 1979–89

	Men			Women		
Annual Income	White	Black	Ratio of Black Men to White Men	White	Black	Ratio of Black Women to White Women
	No. of deaths/100,000 person-years					
<$10,000	324.1	390.8	1.21	112.2	184.7	1.65
$10,000–$14,999	255.4	292.8	1.15	71.3	119.2	1.67
$15,000–$24,999	136.9	142.2	1.04	43.7	64.8	1.48
Ratio of lowest to highest income	2.4	2.7	—	2.6	2.9	—

Source: S. L. Isaacs and S. A. Schroeder, "Class: The Ignored Determinant of the Nation's Health," *New England Journal of Medicine* 351 (2004):1137–42. Copyright © 2004 Massachusetts Medical Society. All rights reserved.

Note: Data on income ranges (in 1980 dollars) and ratios of black men to white men and black women to white women are from Williams (2001, p. 69).

Table 3.2 provides data from Isaacs and Schroeder (2004) that confirm per sis tent racial differences in health even when we compare those with similar levels of income. Using income reported in 1980 dollars, we see a dual relationship:

- Those with lower incomes have higher death rates than those with higher incomes, with the ratio in the death rate of lowest income to highest income ranging from 2.4 to 2.9.
- At a given level of income, blacks die at a higher rate than whites, with the ratio ranging from 1.04 for higher-income men to 1.65–1.67 in lower- and middle-income women.

(Note: To compare 1980 dollars with more current data: in 1980 the median house hold income in the United States was $17,710; in 2011 it was $50,054.)

Even when we look at individuals with the same level of SES (in this case measured by income), we see persisting differences in death rates, with blacks dying more often than whites. This raises the question as to whether being a member of a minority racial or ethnic group that has experienced discrimination in the past might constitute another form of SES. […]

DEVELOPING A MODEL OF THE VARIOUS MEASURES OF SES

It may be useful at this point to summarize our understanding of the association between SES and health. So far we have determined:

- The association between SES and health is not due to a threshold effect, with all those above the threshold enjoying equal levels of health. Rather, the association between SES and health appears to be continuous, with health status increasing with each increment in SES.
- The association between SES and health has to do with more than simply a person's position in the hierarchy of income distribution. That association reflects multiple forms of the social hierarchy, including the hierarchies of education and occupation, and possibly an additional hierarchy of race.

It is important to keep in mind a fundamental principle of statistical analysis. For any two variables (let us call them a and b), stating that "a is associated with b" does not in itself prove that "a is the cause of b." There are three possible explanations for this association:

- a is the cause of b (often illustrated as $a \rightarrow b$)
- b is the cause of a (often illustrated as $b \rightarrow a$)
- Some missing third factor is the cause of both a and b, often illustrated as:

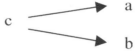

It is possible to consider various possibilities for the missing third factor c in this model. These include time preference, self-efficiency, and social anomie and a loss of trust in society.

Time Preference

It is possible that one's position in the hierarchy of a social system leads to an individual's having a sense of time preference that differs from the time preference of others in a different position. To be successful in obtaining an education, especially an education that includes a college or graduate degree, one must be willing to postpone the payoff for one's investment of time and effort. Similarly, to take seriously the warnings of the dangerous health outcomes caused by smoking cigarettes, one must have a clear perception that it is worthwhile to forgo the immediate satisfaction gained by smoking to avoid the health consequences that will likely not appear for years, if not de cades. Those who find it difficult to forgo satisfaction in the present in order to obtain even greater satisfaction in the future may also find it difficult to stop smoking or to persist in their education.

Mischel and colleagues (1988) and Shoda and colleagues (1990) demonstrated the effects of differences in time preference and the ability to delay gratification in a study of four- and five-year-olds from a reasonably affluent university community. These children were shown two possible reward objects—for example, a plate with one marshmallow and a second plate with two marshmallows—and were asked which they preferred. Not surprisingly, most children preferred two marshmallows to one. The child was then told that she or he could have the preferred reward, so long as she or he would wait while the researcher stepped outside of the room for a while, with the promise of returning soon. However, the child was also given the option of ringing a bell, which would bring the researcher back into the room right away. The reward system was fairly straightforward. If the child waited for the researcher to return without ringing the bell, she or he would get the two marshmallows. If she or he rang the bell to bring the researcher back sooner, the child would get one marshmallow.

Some children were able to wait for the researcher to return, thus gaining the increased reward by delaying that reward. Others found that too difficult, and chose instead to accept the smaller reward without the required wait. Some were able to delay gratification in return for a greater reward; others had difficulty delaying gratification.

The fascinating part of this study came several years later, when the researchers tracked these study subjects into adolescence. They compared the two groups of children—the delayed gratifiers with the immediate gratifiers—on a number of scales that might predict future SES. They found consistent differences, in that the delayed gratifiers as adolescents demonstrated better academic and cognitive abilities, better verbal fluency, better ability to plan and attend to detail, and a better ability to deal with frustration and stress. As described in a *New York Times* op-ed about these studies,

> The children who waited longer went on to get higher SAT scores. They got into better colleges and had, on average, better adult outcomes. The children who rang the bell quickest were more likely to become bullies. They received worse teacher and parental evaluations 10 years on and were more likely to have drug problems at age 32. … The Mischel experiments, along with everyday experience, tell us that self-control is essential. Young people who can delay gratification can sit through sometimes boring classes to get a degree. They can perform rote tasks in order to, say, master a language. They can avoid drugs and alcohol. (Brooks 2006)

Psychologists have delved more deeply into the issue of time perspective. Zimbardo and Boyd (1999) were able to assess a person's time perspective based on their answers to a series of questions. They identified forms an individual's time perspective might take, including:

- Future—"Characterized by planning for and achievement of future goals … with consideration of future consequences, conscientiousness, preference for consistency, and reward dependence, along with low levels of novelty and sensation seeking"
- Present—Fatalistic—"reveals a belief that the future is predestined and uninfluenced by individual actions, whereas the present must be borne with resignation because

humans are at the whimsical mercy of 'fate'"

- Present—Hedonistic—"orientation toward present enjoyment, plea sure, and excitement, without sacrifices today for rewards tomorrow … a lack of consideration of future consequences … low ego or impulse control"

Zimbardo and Boyd used these scales in a study of more than 500 college students in California, and were able to determine a series of significant correlations between their scales of time perspective and an individual's personal characteristics and academic performance. Students who demonstrated a "Future" perspective had higher grades in college and spent more hours per week studying. They were also less likely to exhibit aggressive tendencies or to lack impulse control. By contrast, those students who demonstrated a "Present—Fatalistic" perspective showed more aggression and more impulsive behavior, and had lower grades.

These results are strikingly similar to the results of the Mischel study, when they followed their subjects into high school. Might it be that, at the age of four, children have already adopted their own perspective on time, and that this time perspective stays with them as they enter and subsequently move through school?

Will the time perspective adopted in childhood persist into the adult years? In 2009, Guthrie and colleagues used the Zimbardo scales of "Time Perspective" in a study of more than 500 adults recruited from hair salons and barber shops in a suburb of Washington, DC. They found that those adults who exhibited a "Future" perspective tended to be more highly educated, and as a consequence more likely to be in a professional occupation. By contrast, those with a "Present—Fatalistic" perspective had the reverse—tending to

be less educated and less likely to be in a professional occupation. They did not find an association between the "Present—Hedonistic" perspective and either education or occupation.

Time perspective, whether measured as a child, as a college student, or as an adult, seems to be an important predictor of educational and occupational attainment. We know also that these outcomes are strongly associated with one's health status as an adult.

Self-Efficiency

Based on differences in childhood experience and family dynamics, some individuals may grow into adulthood with strikingly different perceptions of their own ability to direct their own life and influence their own existence. If a person has a sense that he is free to choose from alternative actions and is principally responsible for his own successes and failures, it may be much easier to pursue long-term goals such as higher education. By contrast, a person who has developed the sense that his life will be directed by forces outside his control may be more likely to approach choices as if they were up to luck or fate, and correspondingly may be less likely to invest in longer-term outcomes such as education or the positive health consequences of avoiding harmful behavior such as smoking. Recall […] that I distinguished between attaching responsibility to an individual for his unhealthy behaviors and attaching blame. Blame carries with it the connotation of personal weakness and failure. If a person has never developed the sense that he is actually in charge of his own life, it would not be appropriate to assign to him the negative connotations of blame for unhealthy behaviors that he may view as out of his own control.

SOCIAL ANOMIE AND A LOSS

OF TRUST IN SOCIETY

Sociologist Emil Durkheim (1897) spoke of the deleterious effects that develop when an individual loses faith that the norms of the society in which he lives will treat him fairly and equally with others. When society appears to hold out one normative message, yet reacts with another, an individual may come to distrust society and its system of norms. In the face of a loss of normative faith, one tends to become isolated and alienated from the norms of society. In the face of such "social anomie," it may be extremely difficult for a person born into a position of disadvantage (whether it be economic, social, or racial) to adhere to the behaviors identified by the norms of that society as leading to healthy outcomes.

Taking a step back from the individual associations of income, education, occupation, and race with health status, it is possible to envision a relationship in which all of these markers of SES are in turn caused by being born into and/or growing up in a position of general social disadvantage. It is being a member of this disadvantaged "class" that makes one substantially more likely to experience the sense of isolation, powerlessness, alienation, and foreshortened time preference that leads directly to lower levels of education, with resultant lower occupational status and lower income. Graham (2004) refers to this causal cascade as the "social determinants of health," as illustrated in Figure 3.6.

FIGURE 3.6 The causal cascade of the social determinants of health.

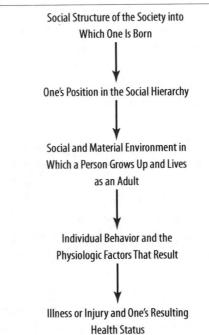

Social Structure of the Society into Which One Is Born

↓

One's Position in the Social Hierarchy

↓

Social and Material Environment in Which a Person Grows Up and Lives as an Adult

↓

Individual Behavior and the Physiologic Factors That Result

↓

Illness or Injury and One's Resulting Health Status

Source: Based on Graham (2004).

UNDERSTANDING THE NATURE OF A SOCIAL HIERARCHY

In the preceding section I considered the possibility that a missing factor caused individuals to have both low SES and poor health. I then considered certain psychological and behavioral characteristics that may devolve over time as a result of a person being born into or growing up in a position of relatively low social position. It is the long-term effects of occupying a low position in the overall social hierarchy that eventually leads both to low SES and to poor health outcomes. In addition, this association between social position and social outcomes is a continuous one that spans all levels of social status. Marmot and colleagues (1995) described research that illustrates these points. They looked at the mortality rate of men in England and Wales for the period 1976–81. Recognizing the differing rates of death within different age groups, they separated the men into three age groups: 15–64, 65–74, and 75 or older. They then considered the following characteristics of the men under study:

- Did they own a car?
- Did they own their dwelling, or rent it?
- Did their principal occupation involve manual labor or nonmanual labor?

Within each age group they broke their subjects down sequentially by these three dichotomies. They first divided the subjects by car ownership: owning a car or not owning a car. They then broke each of these groups down by type of housing: owner-occupied or rental. These groups were further broken down by type of occupation: nonmanual or manual. The authors then graphed the mortality rate for these men according to which of the eight possible groups they fell into. They found a consistent pattern:

- Those who owned a car had lower rates of mortality than those who did not own a car.
- Within both categories of car ownership, those who owned their home had lower mortality than those who rented their home.
- Within both categories of car ownership, and further within both categories of home ownership, those with nonmanual occupations had lower mortality than those with manual occupations.

Mortality rates generally increased in stepwise fashion from those who owned a car, owned their home, and worked in a nonmanual occupation (with the lowest mortality) to those who did not own a car, rented their home, and worked in a manual occupation (with the highest mortality).

Each of the three dichotomies in this study describes a position of social advantage/ disadvantage. The study illustrates the following principle: the more forms of social advantage a person has, the lower the chances of death over time.

If having several markers of low status is associated with poor health, does it matter how long one experiences the resulting social disadvantage? Will those who are able to move out of a position of disadvantage over time have better health than those who remain disadvantaged over time? This was the question addressed by a long-term study conducted not in England and Wales, but in Alameda County, situated in California across the bay from San Francisco. Alameda County has some sections that are quite well-to-do and other sections that have high concentrations of poverty and inadequate housing.

The Alameda County study is one of the longest running health studies that has followed a single cohort of subjects over time. It initially gathered data on nearly 7,000 adults who were representative of the overall population of the county. There have been numerous publications from the study describing a wide range of psychological and behavioral factors and measuring health outcomes in terms of both death rates and a range of other measures of illness and disability.

Lynch and colleagues (1997) looked at the health histories of nearly 1,100 adults who had been followed from 1965 through 1994. In 1994 the median age of these subjects was 65 years. The authors recorded the subjects' reported income at three times—1965, 1974, and 1983—determining whether that income fell below or above a figure that represented twice the federal poverty line.

The federal government publishes annually the amount of money a family of a given size requires each year to pay for the basic necessities such as food, clothing, and shelter. Those who fall below this poverty line are officially deemed to be living in poverty. Those with incomes marginally above

FIGURE 3.7 Effect of sustained poverty on odds of reporting health problems. Shows odds ratio based on the number of times subjects reported being in poverty.

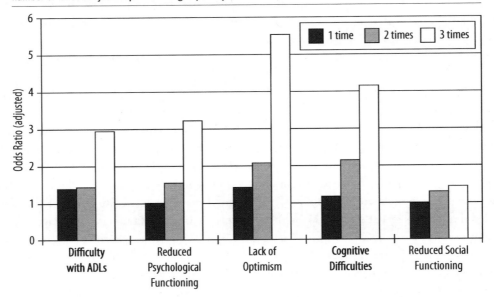

Source: Based on Lynch et al. (1997).

this poverty level are not impoverished, but are in a position of relatively low income. Thus, those with up to twice the poverty line in the study group include working individuals and families as well as poor individuals and families. However, all are in a position of relative economic disadvantage described by the authors as "economic hardship." The authors measured how many times over the study period subjects reported experiencing this economic hardship. The maximum number of times was three. They then compared a variety of health measures for those reporting economic hardship one, two, or three times to those never reporting economic hardship. The results are shown in Figure 3.7.

Those reporting economic hardship only once during the 18-year study period had health outcomes that were nearly identical to those never experiencing economic hardship. For those reporting two episodes of hardship, the odds of experiencing poor health outcomes were up to

two times greater than those of people with no experience of hardship. For those reporting three episodes of economic hardship, suggesting that they had experienced continuous hardship for 18 years, the odds of experiencing a poor health outcome were typically three to five times greater than for those with no hardship. Not only does economic hardship expose one to the risk of poor health outcomes, but also the longer one is in a disadvantaged economic state, the greater one's chances of having a poor health outcome.

Frank and colleagues (2003) reported on a fourth follow-up episode for the Alameda County study. They examined data from subjects responding in all four surveys between 1965 and 1994, focusing on the presence of the following conditions:

- high blood pressure
- perceived health
- depression
- heart trouble

- trouble breathing
- trouble feeding
- sick days

The authors found substantial consistency in the pattern of the data. They sorted subjects according to which percentile of family income they fell into in 1965. Using this rank ordering of individual subjects by income, they then compared subjects on the percentage reporting one of the above problems. To rule out gender effects, they examined this relationship between baseline income percentile and health outcomes separately for men and women.

There is a consistent downward gradient for the relationship between income percentile and the percentage reporting poor or fair health. For women this association is nearly linear, while for men it is somewhat curvilinear. The same general pattern is true for all of the outcomes studied. In Alameda County, California, the lower the income you start with and the longer you face the social disadvantage coincident with economic hardship, the worse your health will be on a variety of different measures that capture all three general aspects of health […].

One can look at any of the major causes of death in this country and find similar social gradients in mortality rates, including:

- lung cancer
- other cancers
- coronary heart disease
- strokes
- other cardiovascular disease
- chronic bronchitis and other respiratory disease
- gastrointestinal disease
- genitourinary disease
- accidents and violence

Galea and colleagues (2011) reviewed nearly 30 years of published research addressing how various forms of social inequality are associated with increased rates of illness and mortality. Based on a mathematical model they developed based on this research, they estimated the number of deaths that take place each year in the United States that are attributable to social factors such as these. Of the approximately 2.3 million deaths that occurred in 2000 in the United States, they reported that approximately 873,000 (38%) were due the effects of various forms of social inequality, principally low levels of education, residential racial segregation, poverty, and low levels of social support.

As summarized by Frank and colleagues, "Among health researchers, there is widespread consensus that 'something' about SES, as indicated by readily available markers such as income or education, is a fundamental determinant of human health. But there is no agreement on what that something is. However, the shape of SES-health gradients may hold clues as to the key mechanisms by which gradients are created and maintained over the life-course" (p. 2306). They go on to suggest two broad categories of factors, each of which is a core aspect of overall social structure that may be this "something." These are:

1. material deprivation
2. the perception of relatively less privilege, which then may lead to "psycho-neuro-endocrinological/immunological cascades" that have clinical health effects

[…]

THE ASSOCIATION OF TRANSITION AMONG SES CATEGORIES AND HEALTH OUTCOMES

Until now I have been speaking of SES as if it were fixed, with little opportunity for an individual or a family to transition up or down the

SES spectrum over time. This, of course, is not an accurate reflection of American society. One of the core historical values of American culture has been the opportunity, often through education, for someone from a lower stratum of SES to be able to move into a higher stratum.

Similarly, it is possible for one to move down the SES ladder. Often illness or disability will impair one's ability to function at a high level, and over time one's SES may decline. Given the opportunity to move up in SES, or to move down, how would we expect such transitions to affect health status? If they do indeed affect health status, will the effect of a transition up be similar in magnitude to a transition down?

Pensola and Martikainen (2003) addressed this question in a study of more than 110,000 men born in Finland between 1956 and 1960. They followed these men, recording how many of them died as young adults in the period 1991–98. They placed each subject in the study in one of two SES categories at the time of their birth and again at the time of their death. The SES at birth was determined by whether the head of the child's household at the time of birth was engaged in a manual-labor occupation (lower SES) or a non-manual labor occupation (higher SES). The SES in the 1991–98 study period was determined by the occupation of the subject himself, using the same SES dichotomy. Occupational data were obtained from the Finnish census.

Thus, these subjects could fall into one of three categories:

1. The subject was low SES at both birth and as an adult
2. The subject was high SES at both birth and as an adult
3. The subject had changed SES categories between birth and adulthood

This third category could be further subdivided into

3a. Those who were low SES at birth and high SES as an adult
3b. Those who were high SES at birth and low SES as an adult

The researchers found that the mortality rate is nearly three times as high for the men born into lower SES and remaining in lower SES, when compared to men who were born into and remained in higher SES. By contrast, the mortality rate for those men who transitioned from one SES category to another between childhood and adulthood had a mortality rate that was midway between the rates for the constant SES categories.

These findings mirror those from the Alameda County study, described above. The longer one stays in a lower SES position, the more that person's health declines. This study is able to address a question the Alameda County study did not. Are the health effects different if you transition over time from low SES to high SES, as compared to transitioning from high SES to low SES? Among those subjects experiencing a transition between SES groups, substantially more subjects experienced an upward transition between childhood and adulthood than experienced a downward transition. Those who made the upward transition had a mortality rate as young adults that was nearly as low as the rate for those who were both born into and remained in the high SES category. By contrast, those who were born into high SES but ended in low SES as adults had a mortality rate that was indistinguishable from that experienced by those who both were born into and remained in low SES. Thus, these data suggest the following:

• Those who remain in a low SES category between birth and adulthood will have substantially worse health as adults than those who are born into and remain in a high SES category.

- For those who transition between SES categories, the SES into which they were born and spent their childhood has less predictive power for their health as an adult than does their SES category as an adult.

THE SOCIAL ROOTS OF HEALTH INEQUALITY: "THE STATUS SYNDROME"

In this chapter we have seen that SES is associated with health across the full spectrum of SES—from the least well-off to the most well-off. SES can be approached in a variety of ways, but the association with health status seems fairly constant. A person can improve her or his chances of enjoying better health by moving up the SES ladder through education, but the longer one remains in a position of disadvantaged SES, the worse one's health tends to be. In addition, there seems to be a lingering effect on health of the SES circumstances into which one is born and spends one's childhood.

We can appreciate how growing up under impoverished circumstances will lead to a deterioration of health over time. Crowding, inadequate sanitation, and nutritional shortages all weaken the body and contribute to illness. How, though, are we to explain why a fully employed administrative worker tends to have better health than a fully employed professional worker? Or, in the words of Michael Marmot, "Why should someone with a master's degree have a longer life expectancy than someone with a bachelor's?" He offers the following explanation: "Socioeconomic differences in health are not confined to poor health for those at the bottom and good health for everyone else. Rather, there is a social gradient in health in individuals who are not poor: the higher the social position, the better the health. I have labeled this 'the status syndrome'" (Marmot 2006, p. 1304).

Marmot has written further about this syndrome: "For people above a threshold of material well-being, another kind of well-being is central. Autonomy—how much control you have over your life—and the opportunities you have for full social engagement and participation are crucial for health, well-being, and longevity. It is inequality in these that plays a big part in producing the social gradients in health. Degrees of control and participation underlie the status syndrome" (Marmot 2004, p. 2).

How does social status in its many forms impact health across the life course and across the spectrum of status? Developing an understanding of the possible mechanisms that explain this relationship is key to understanding the social roots of health disparities. We have identified as an important contributor the material benefits that go along with increasing social status, such as sanitation and nutrition. However, it is difficult to see how better material benefits might explain health differences for those at the upper ends of the SES distribution who have more than adequate material comforts. Alternative explanations include individual behaviors. Differences in time preferences and the ability to delay gratification may explain such things as the striking gradients we see in the rate of cigarette smoking across social strata. We might also expect differences in the physical environment that follow the social status hierarchy also to contribute to health disparities. Those who live in more crowded conditions may also be exposed to more environmental pollutants over time, with resultant health effects.

What, though, about Marmot's suggestion that there may be important psychological differences that track social status? Might there be psychological effects of living in a higher- (or lower-) status condition, such as perceptions of autonomy and control, which will also affect health over time? These are the questions I address […], in which I attempt to build a theoretical model of the many ways that being in a disadvantaged social position, whether it be socioeconomic, socioenvironmental, or sociopsychological, can affect health over one's lifetime.

Social Capital and Health

Ichiro Kawachi

Social capital has been hailed as one of the most popular exports from sociology into the field of population health. At the same time, the application of the concept to explain variations in population health has been greeted with spirited debate and controversy (Kawachi et al. 2004). The debates have ranged from the very definition of social capital—whether it ought to be understood as an individual-level attribute or as a property of the collective—to skepticism about the utility of applying the concept to the health field as a health promotion strategy (Pearce and Davey Smith 2003; Navarro 2004). As Szreter and Woolcock (2004) noted, social capital has become one of the "essentially contested concepts" in the social sciences, like class, race, and gender.

DEFINITIONS OF SOCIAL CAPITAL

In modern sociology, the origins of social capital are most closely identified with the writings of Pierre Bourdieu and James Coleman. Bourdieu defined social capital as "the aggregate of actual or potential resources linked to possession of a durable network" (1986, 248). Coleman defined the concept via a more functionalist approach, as in: "Social capital is defined by its function. It is not a single entity, but a variety of different entities having two characteristics in common: They all consist of some aspect of social structure, and

they facilitate certain actions of individuals who are within the structure" (1990, 302). As examples of the forms that social capital could take, Coleman cited the trustworthiness of social environment, which makes possible reciprocity exchanges; information channels; norms and effective sanctions; and "appropriable" social organizations, that is, associations established for a specific purpose (for example, a neighborhood block group established to fight crime) that can later be appropriated for broader uses (304–12).

Following these contrasting definitions set forth by Bourdieu and Coleman, the empirical literature on social capital has been split according to those who treat the concept from a network perspective (à la Bourdieu) and those who define the concept from a social cohesion perspective (i.e., emphasizing the forms of social capital highlighted by Coleman such as trust, reciprocity exchanges, norms, and sanctions). Within the field of population health, the social cohesion school has been so far dominant—and has been criticized for paying insufficient attention to network-based definitions of social capital (Moore et al. 2005; Carpiano 2008).[1] According to Carpiano (2008), Bourdieu's network approach to social capital offers a couple of nuances that are not highlighted in the social cohesion-based approaches. First, by conceptualizing social capital as "the resources available through social networks," the approach explicitly recognizes

Ichiro Kawachi, "Social Capital and Health," Handbook of Medical Sociology, pp. 18-32. Copyright © 2010 by Vanderbilt University Press. Reprinted with permission.

that inequalities can arise in between-individual and between-group access to social capital, since networks are not all the same—some networks are more powerful than others by virtue of the stocks of material and symbolic resources available to their members. Second, the network perspective opens the way to begin considering the negative effects (the "dark side") of social capital, which critics point out have tended to be neglected in the social cohesion literature.

A further critical distinction in the literature lies between those who consider social capital a characteristic of individuals and those who treat social capital as a characteristic of the collective (such as residential neighborhoods or workplaces). Methodological individualists tend to view individual actors within a social structure as either possessing or lacking the ability to secure benefits by virtue of their membership in networks. For example, Nan Lin's (2001) Position Generator is an example of a measurement approach to social capital that inquires about the individual's ability to access resources through personal connections to others with valued occupational positions, such as lawyers, physicians, or bank managers. By contrast, the practice of treating social capital as a collective characteristic treats it as an extraindividual, contextual influence on health outcomes. This practice is in turn reflected by measurement approaches that emphasize the degree to which social cohesion exists within a group (or alternatively, if one hews to the network-based definition of social capital, by attempts to describe group characteristics through whole network analysis). As Coleman noted, the "social" aspect of social capital is aptly chosen because "as an attribute of the social structure in which a person is embedded, social capital is not the private property of any of the persons who benefit from it" (1990, 315).

The main reason population health researchers tend to treat social capital as a group characteristic is that a rich empirical tradition already exists within the field of investigating individual-level access to social support as an influence on health outcomes (Berkman and Glass 2000). In other words, it seems redundant to replace an existing term ("an individual's access to instrumental and emotional social support") with another, albeit fancier term ("social capital").

MECHANISMS THROUGH WHICH SOCIAL CAPITAL INFLUENCES HEALTH OUTCOMES

Social capital, considered as a group-level construct, is hypothesized to influence population health outcomes through at least four distinct mechanisms (Kawachi and Berkman 2000). First, more cohesive groups are better equipped to undertake collective action. Examples relevant to population health include the ability of a community to organize to protest the closure of a local hospital, the passage of local ordinances to restrict smoking in public places, or the use of zoning restrictions to prevent the incursion of fast-food outlets. The residents' perceived ability to mobilize to undertake collectively desired actions is referred to as "collective efficacy," and validated survey instruments have been developed to tap this form of social capital, for example, in the Project on Human Development in Chicago Neighborhoods (Sampson, Raudenbush, and Earls 1997).

A second pathway through which social capital influences health consists of the ability of the group to enforce and maintain social norms. For example, when adults within a community feel empowered to step in to intervene when they observe instances of deviant behavior by adolescents (such as underage smoking and drinking), it is referred to as "informal social control." The power of informal social control consists in the ability of the community to enforce desired norms without resort to the police or schoolteachers. It is a collective characteristic in the sense that the parents of the offending minors need not be involved; instead their neighbors can be relied upon to step in to admonish the offenders on their behalf. Groups with a strong sense of informal social control are often characterized by high degrees of "network closure"—another form of social capital cited by Coleman (1990). Network closure occurs when not only children A and B are connected via friendship, but also their parents are in close contact. An instance of such network closure used to be found in Japan, where parents (primarily mothers) were connected to each other through volunteering in local PTAs. Adolescent smoking in Japanese society remained fairly uncommon (by Western standards) until the 1980s despite the ubiquitous presence of cigarette-vending machines on virtually every street corner. One reason Japanese schoolchildren observed the legal prohibition of smoking under the age of twenty was because if any child surreptitiously bought and smoked a cigarette on the way home from school, his mother was likely to learn about it from a neighbor before he reached home.[2] As network closure has declined with the retreat of PTA membership in urban Japanese communities, the rate of adolescent smoking has climbed in tandem.

A third mechanism through which social capital influences health is via reciprocity exchanges between members of a network. As Coleman (1990) pointed out, norms of reciprocity are established when actor A does a favor for actor B and trusts that the recipient will return the favor at a later point in time. A's expectation that B will repay the debt creates an obligation on the part of B to keep the trust. As these "credit slips" begin to multiply and to extend to other members of the network, the result is a community where people are constantly helping each other out. An instance of such a system of reciprocity exchanges is described in Hideo Okuda's 2005 novel *Southbound* about an island community in Okinawa, where the locals use the term *yuima̅ru* to describe the norms of mutual aid. When a new family arrives on the island, a steady procession of neighbors gathers on their doorstep to help the newcomers refurbish their dwelling, lend them farming equipment, and donate food.[3] The maintenance of reciprocity exchanges in turn depends upon two key elements: the trustworthiness of the social environment, and the ability of the group to enforce sanctions against free riders.

Finally, social capital is linked to health through the diffusion of innovations via information channels that exist within network structures. As Granovetter (1973) pointed out in his influential paper on "the strength of weak ties," the diffusion of information need not occur through close social contacts. Indeed, the potential to glean new information from intimate relationships is often low, because by definition such people are likely to share the same information. In Granovetter's study of job seekers, individuals were more likely to find out about jobs from friends of friends. In other words, the diffusion of information and other resources from the outside into the network depends upon the presence of network bridges, individuals who serve as channels that connect disparate, unconnected groups of actors (Lakon, Godette, and Hipp 2008). The diffusion of innovations via "connectors," "mavens," and "salesmen" was popularized by Malcolm Gladwell's *The Tipping Point* (2000). For a more formal treatment of sociometric approaches to investigate the spread of health-related innovations, see Valente, Gallaher, and Mouttapa 2004.

Although the discussion of the mechanisms linking social capital to health so far has focused on the positive (i.e., benign and beneficial) aspects of social capital, each mechanism described is equally applicable to the so-called downsides of social capital. Thus, a community with high levels of collective efficacy could just as easily use those resources to oppress and discriminate against outsiders (the South Boston riots during the busing and forced desegregation of schools during the 1960s come to mind). The flip side of informal social control is a community that is often controlling and intolerant of diversity, with restrictions on individual freedom that nonconformists might chafe at. A dense system of reciprocity exchanges is often associated with excessive obligations on the part of group members who are called upon to provide aid to others, sometimes at high personal cost. And not all information that diffuses through a dense social network is good or beneficial. The spread of malicious rumors via social networking sites (cyber-bullying) is a case in point.

Finally, social capital researchers—particularly those who hew to the social cohesion school—have been accused of yearning for a romanticized vision of "community" as it existed in a bygone era, or perhaps only in the imagination (Muntaner, Lynch, and Davey Smith 2001). This is a strawman argument—the aim of social capital studies is not to turn the clock back or to advocate the transformation of American suburbia into Okinawan society, but to attempt to identify resources within social relations that can be practicably mobilized in contemporary settings to promote health; as well as to understand and manage the situations in which social cohesion can lead to deleterious consequences (such as the spread of misinformation and rumors).

THE MEASUREMENT OF SOCIAL CAPITAL

The measurement of social capital hinges on the way in which the investigator defines the concept—as an individual attribute or a collective attribute, or from a network-based perspective or a cohesion-based perspective. Four broad approaches to measurement have been applied: surveys of individuals or groups, sociometric methods, experimental elicitation of trust and cooperation, and qualitative approaches.

Surveys

Survey-based approaches are the commonest method encountered in the field of population health for assessing social capital either at the individual or the collective level. At the individual level, Lin's Position Generator (2001) is an instrument that inquires about whether the respondent has access to people with high-prestige occupations (e.g., doctor, lawyer). The assumption is that knowing people with high-prestige occupations correlates with the ability of the individual to access a variety of resources, such as instrumental support, information and advice, or symbolic status. Responses to the instrument can be then used to generate measures of social capital such as the highest level of accessed prestige ("upper reach-ability") or the range in accessed prestige (the difference in prestige between the highest and lowest occupations accessed). Upper reachability is akin to the concept of linking social capital, which refers to resources accessed across socio-economic gradients—as contrasted with bonding social capital, which describes resources accessed within groups that are similar with respect to class, race, and ethnicity (Szreter and Woolcock 2004).

As is evident from its emphasis on occupational prestige, the Position Generator has been used to examine the instrumental uses of social capital—how individuals can use their social connections to get ahead in society. When it comes to studying the potential influence of social capital on health outcomes, the Position Generator has some limitations. For example, accessing occupational prestige is not relevant for all types of resources—receiving emotional support from a surgeon is not necessarily better than receiving it from a priest. Likewise, some positions are not assigned official job prestige, such as homemakers, yet they provide valued resources from a health perspective (van der Gaag and Webber 2008).

An alternative approach to measuring individual social capital is exemplified by van der Gaag and Snijders's Resource Generator (2005). This validated instrument provides a checklist of different kinds of social resources that respondents can potentially access through their networks. Items are phrased in the form: "Do you know anyone who ___," with examples of resources such as "can repair a car," "owns a car," "has knowledge about financial matters," "can baby sit for your children." As is evident from the foregoing description, the Resource Generator closely parallels the survey instruments already used in the public health literature to tap into individual access to social support. The Resource Generator has been reported to correlate well with health outcomes (e.g., Webber and Huxley 2007), which might be expected given the resemblance of the instrument to measures of social support, and the well-established associations of social support with health outcomes.

From a social cohesion perspective, researchers have sought to measure social capital through surveys inquiring about what people feel (their values and perceptions), as well as what people do (participation in formal and informal contacts) (Harpham 2008). The responses to such surveys can be then analyzed at the individual level (as in residents' perceptions of the cohesiveness of their neighborhood) or aggregated up to the group level and analyzed as a contextual influence on individual health outcomes. Table 4.1 illustrates these distinctions.

TABLE 4.1 Typology of measurement approaches to social capital

Definition of Social Capital	Level of Analysis	
	Individual	Group
Network based	Position generator, resource generator	Whole social network analysis
Cohesion based	Individual perceptions (e.g., trustworthiness of neighbors) and behaviors (e.g., participation in civic associations)	Survey responses aggregated to the group level

Community surveys have been the mainstay in health research to assess neighborhood characteristics such as social cohesion, collective efficacy, and informal social control. For example, instruments that measure social cohesion typically consist of multi-item scales that inquire about the trustworthiness of neighbors, norms of reciprocity and mutual aid, and the extent to which residents share the same values. A number of psychometrically validated instruments have been developed for use in field studies (see Harpham 2008).

A frequent criticism leveled at survey instruments is that they often include elements that are not properly part of social capital, but rather are antecedents or consequences of it (Harpham 2008; De Silva 2006). Examples include residents' satisfaction with their neighborhood or perceptions of safety from crime. On occasion, when survey data are lacking, researchers have resorted to the use of proxies such as crime rates obtained from Justice Department statistics or voting participation. The problems with these approaches are that they lay the practice open to charges of "conceptual stretching," where social capital begins to lose meaning, and that they conflate the consequences of social capital with its measurement, which risks tautology ("a community with low crime rates must have high social capital because it has low crime rates") (Portes 1998).

Social Network Analysis

An altogether different approach to measuring social capital is via whole network (sociometric) analysis. Within the public health literature it is quite common to see social networks assessed from the individual (egocentric) perspective (e.g., "How many friends do you have, and how often do you see them?") (Berkman and Glass 2000). In contrast to the ego-centered network assessment approach, the sociometric approach seeks to characterize the whole network by interviewing all the alters nominated by the ego and, in turn, all of their alters, until saturation is reached. As the description makes clear, the limiting step for initiating such studies is establishing the boundary of the network. While boundaries are readily identifiable in settings like schools or companies or within subcultures such as injection drug users, they are less straightforward in contexts like neighborhoods, which may explain why few studies so far have applied sociometric network analysis to the investigation of social capital and health. However, as Lakon, Godette, and Hipp (2008) illustrate, several measures derived from sociometric analysis have direct relevance for the concept of social capital, including network-based analogs of cohesion, bonding, and bridging social capital (more about this later).

Experimental Approaches

Experimental approaches to measure constructs related to social capital (such as trust and cooperation) have been advocated by economists who inherently distrust survey responses to questions inquiring about perceptions, opinions, and attitudes. For example, Glaeser and colleagues (2000) have suggested that instead of relying on survey-based measures of trust, researchers should attempt to directly elicit observable behavioral measures of trust such as the envelope drop. In this approach, subjects are told that the experimenter will intentionally drop a money-filled envelope addressed to the sender, say, in the middle of Harvard Square. If the subject places a high value on the dropped envelope, the economist infers that the subject is more likely to trust the anonymous stranger who will find the envelope and mail it.

Another experimental approach to studying trust and cooperation is the trust game, in which subject A is given a sum of money and offered the opportunity to pass some, all, or none of it to partner B. The experimenter then increases the transferred amount by some multiple before passing it on to B. Finally, B has the opportunity to return some, none, or all of the money to A. In this experiment, the amount initially transferred by A is interpreted as a measure of trusting behavior. Anderson and Mellor (2008) describe other versions of the trust experiment, including the public-goods game, a version of the prisoner's dilemma. Some of these experiments have found that individuals who self-report greater trust of others or higher participation in voluntary groups (two survey-based indicators of social capital) are also more likely to exhibit trusting and cooperative behaviors in experimental situations (Anderson, Mellor, and Milyo, 2004), thereby suggesting convergent validity between survey-based and experimental measures of social capital.

Qualitative Approaches

Finally, qualitative approaches to investigating social capital have yielded important insights into the complexity and nuances of the links between social capital and health that quantitative studies do not reveal. In a systematic review of qualitative studies, Whitley (2008) concluded that they had been instrumental in drawing attention to the downsides of social capital, as well as in reminding us of the existence of broader historical and structural forces that shape the health of community residents.

EMPIRICAL EVIDENCE LINKING SOCIAL CAPITAL TO HEALTH

The relationship between social capital and health has been investigated through a variety of study designs, including ecological, individual-level, multilevel, and qualitative approaches. As mentioned earlier, the majority of studies in the population health realm have focused on the health effects of social cohesion. From the perspective of social capital as a contextual influence on health, the most convincing design is the multilevel study in which relationships of social capital to individual health can be examined after controlling for potential confounding by individual-level compositional variables. In other words, the merit of the multilevel study is being able to test the counterfactual question, "If two individuals with exchangeable characteristics (i.e., the same sociodemographic characteristics, occupying the same socioeconomic position, with the same level of social ties and trust of others) were observed in a high social capital community and in a low social capital community, would their health outcomes differ, all other things equal?" The limitation of ecological studies is that any difference observed in average health status across communities with different levels of social capital could be confounded by the characteristics of residents who belong to each place. Controlling for the aggregated characteristics of residents will not solve the problem, since in an ecological study, by definition, we do not know the distribution of confounders (the common prior causes of social capital and health) among individual residents.

When we turn to individual-level studies of social capital and health, they tend to be limited by common method bias: individuals' perceptions of the trustworthiness of their neighbors are potentially contaminated by unobserved characteristics such as personality and negative affectivity that simultaneously influence health status. This problem is particularly salient in studies that have used self-reported health outcome measures as the endpoint of interest. Similarly, an association between individual-level participation in associational activity and health outcomes is likely to suffer from endogeneity bias. The direction of the bias can theoretically cut in both directions—either healthier people are more likely to volunteer in groups (positive selection) or sick people are more likely to join some groups (adverse selection). This bias may partly account for the contradictory findings in the literature when social participation is used as an indicator of social cohesion (Ellaway and Macintyre 2007).

With these caveats in mind, we find that systematic reviews of social capital and health have identified fairly consistent evidence of associations between markers of social cohesion and health outcomes, including physical health (e.g., mortality and self-rated health; Kim, Subramanian, and Kawachi 2008), mental health (e.g., depressive symptoms; Almedom and Glandon 2008), and health-related behaviors (smoking, drinking, high-risk sexual behavior; Lindstrom 2008b).

The preponderance of evidence suggests that there is something there, although strong causal claims are premature due to the number of gaps in the existing literature, as noted by the systematic reviews. These include: (a) the cross-sectional design of most studies so that temporal ordering cannot be established; (b) the reliance of many studies on secondary analyses of survey data that were not specifically designed to measure social capital (De Silva 2006); (c) the reliance of many studies on single indicators of social capital (often a single item on social trust, at that); (d) residual confounding by omitted variables such as personality and negative affectivity in studies that examined correlations between individual-level perceptions of trust and reciprocity and self-reported health outcomes; and (e) the preponderance of evidence from Western countries (North America and Europe) and the sparseness of studies conducted in other cultural contexts.

A major source of heterogeneity across studies arises in the choice of scale for examining the effects of social capital on health, which ranges from cross-national comparisons (e.g., Lynch et al. 2001) to U.S. state-level analyses (Kawachi et al. 1997) to municipalities (Islam et al. 2006a) and neighborhoods (e.g., within Chicago, see Lochner et al. 2003). Critics have complained that this breadth of application illustrates another instance of "conceptual stretching" (Portes 1998), although from a social cohesion perspective, plausible arguments could be raised in defense of theorizing that whole societies as well as neighborhoods can be characterized as cohesive (or not). Nonetheless, as a general principle, the further the researcher moves away from proximal processes linking exposures to health outcomes, the greater the number of plausible confounders, and the higher the likelihood that we lose our grasp of the causal steps linking the "exposure" variables to the outcomes of interest (Zimmerman 2008).

A further pattern remarked in the literature is that the associations between social cohesion and health outcomes seem stronger and more consistently observed in less egalitarian societies (e.g., with high levels of economic inequality) compared to more egalitarian societies marked by the presence of strong welfare states and safety-net provisions (Islam et al. 2006b). Thus, for example, the intraclass correlation (ICC, corresponding to the percent of variation in outcomes explained

at the area level) was considerably higher in a U.S. study of neighborhood influences on violent crime and homicide (7.5 percent) than the corresponding ICCs observed in studies from Sweden and Canada (0–2 percent) (Islam et al. 2006b). This pattern seems to argue against the strand of political theory that posits that strong welfare states tend to crowd out associational activities and norms of mutual assistance. If anything, social cohesion would appear to be even more salient in explaining the health variations among citizens belonging to societies with weak safety-net provisions, for example, in health care, public education, and unemployment protections (Rostila 2007).

With regard to the potential diversity of settings in which social cohesion could be observed and assessed, the systematic reviews reveal that the bulk of studies to date—whether quantitative or qualitative—have focused on residential neighborhoods. This is understandable given the burgeoning interest in neighborhood influences in population health (Kawachi and Berkman 2003). However, social capital can be transported to other settings such as schools or workplaces. A recent example is a prospective study of more than thirty-three thousand Finnish public-sector employees that sought to examine the relationships between workplace social cohesion and the risk of incident depression (Kouvonen et al. 2008). Workplace social capital was measured by a scale developed by the authors that inquired about cohesion (trust and cooperation) between employees, as well as relations between employees and supervisors. The eight-item scale had good internal consistency reliability (Cronbach alpha = 0.87) (Kouvonen et al. 2006). While lower individual-level perceptions of workplace social capital was associated with a 20–50 percent higher risk of depression during follow-up, the study found no association in multilevel analyses between aggregate workplace social cohesion and depression. Thus the study did not find a significant contextual influence of workplace social capital on the risk of depression, and even the individual-level findings could have been artifacts of reverse causation (i.e., negative emotions leading to lower perceptions of workplace social cohesion). Nevertheless, the study points to a novel direction for empirical studies of social capital and health, especially since workplaces (as compared to neighborhoods) are where people in midlife spend an increasing part of their time engaged in social interactions. In a thoughtful commentary accompanying the Finnish study, Lindstrom (2008a) suggested additional directions in which research on workplace social capital could be advanced, including: (a) drawing the distinction between so-called horizontal social capital (cohesion between employees occupying similar levels of employment grade) and vertical social capital (cohesion between workers and their supervisors); and (b) examining the interactions between social capital in the workplace and social capital outside the workplace. In other words, as workers seek to maintain work/family balance, their health is likely to be shaped by the simultaneous and interactive influences of workplace, family, and neighborhood social environments. Extensions of the multilevel approach—so-called cross-classified models—are well equipped to handle such analytical complexity (Subramanian, Jones, and Duncan 2003).

Lastly, a relatively underexplored dimension of social cohesion and health is the potential for cross-level interactions between aggregate-level cohesion and individual characteristics. Multilevel analysis permits the explicit testing of such cross-level interactions. For example, Subramanian, Kim, and Kawachi (2002) found in an analysis of the U.S. Social Capital Benchmark Survey that community levels of social cohesion (as proxied by aggregate levels of trust) were not statistically significantly associated with residents' self-rated health after controlling for individual-level compositional characteristics, including individual reports of trust in others. However, in the same study the authors found evidence of a significant cross-level interaction whereby individuals reporting high levels of trust report better health when their neighbors were also trusting. On the other hand, individuals reporting low levels of trust tended to fare worse when they were surrounded by more-trusting neighbors. This result echoes the observations made in qualitative studies that social capital does not uniformly affect the health of all individuals within the same community (Whitley 2008). While social capital can be beneficial for some individuals, it may harm others.

FUTURE DIRECTIONS IN SOCIAL CAPITAL RESEARCH

While the use of multilevel analysis has become fairly standard in investigations of the health effects of social capital, this is in one sense only the starting point of methodological sophistication required for strengthening causal inference. Aside from the need for more prospective data, as well as the application of network-based approaches to studying social capital already alluded to, future research needs to engage more seriously with thornier issues such as unobserved heterogeneity and endogeneity. Multilevel analysis is quite good at dealing with compositional confounding and partitioning the variance in health outcomes at different levels of influence (individual versus the community). However, additional approaches are called for to deal with issues such as the selective sorting of different individuals into different contexts, as well as the reciprocal and dynamic relationships among social cohesion, individual social interactions, and health.

The problem of nonrandom sorting of residents into different types of residential areas is already familiar to researchers who study neighborhood effects on health (Oakes 2004; Subramanian, Glymour, and Kawachi 2007). Suppose we demonstrate in a multilevel analysis that more cohesive neighborhoods are associated with better health outcomes for individual residents even after controlling for individual-level characteristics (such as SES); this still does not prove causation. If trusting and sociable individuals selectively move into areas where they are surrounded by neighbors who share the same preferences, an association between social cohesion and health merely proves that cohesive neighborhoods have more sociable residents who are healthier by virtue of their proclivities. It does not necessarily follow that if we relocate a socially isolated individual from a less cohesive to a more cohesive neighborhood, her health status will improve. This type of confounding could be controlled by adjusting for those individual characteristics (e.g., sociability, trust). However, such data may not be available, and life is too short (as well as resources finite) to keep going back to the study sample to measure and control for every unobserved characteristic. In this type of situation, it has been suggested that techniques such as instrumental variable (IV) estimation could improve causal inference (Glymour 2006).

The idea of instruments is to find variables that cause exogenous variation in the treatment (or exposure) of interest—in this instance, neighborhood social cohesion—without directly affecting the values of the outcome variable (individual health status). In other words, instruments are natural experiments that randomly assign individuals into different social contexts, for instance, neighborhoods with high or low social cohesion. High population density, high immigrant concentration, and income polarization are each plausible instruments for social cohesion within a community (e.g., Alesina et al. 2003). Provided that these variables are not independently associated

with differences in individual health status, they may serve as instruments to identify the causal effect of social cohesion on health.[4] For example, an individual residing in an area with high immigrant concentration will be more likely to find himself in a low-cohesion environment (this can be checked empirically within the data). Provided that immigrant concentration does not predict health status—other than through its influence on levels of social cohesion—the causal effect of social capital can be obtained by comparing the difference in health status of individuals who reside within high- versus low-cohesion neighborhoods induced by the fact that they "happen" to be living in areas with high or low immigrant concentration.[5] Although clearly not a panacea for solving the thorny issues of causal inference, instruments represent a hitherto underutilized approach (at least within the field of social capital and health) for squeezing more out of observational data without going to the extent of launching a randomized controlled trial.

A more direct approach to utilize natural experiments would be to observe real-life scenarios such as the evacuation and resettlement of residents into different neighborhoods following a natural disaster—such as Hurricane Katrina—or to examine changes in the health status of residents who happen to live near a newly opened community center where people can congregate. Taking advantage of such scenarios relies upon serendipity, foresight (i.e., the measurement of the health of residents both at baseline as well as following the natural experiment), or both. In the example of Hurricane Katrina, the opportunity to study the natural experiment (residents from the same neighborhoods in New Orleans being relocated to neighborhoods with different levels of social capital) was unfortunately lost because the Federal Emergency Management Agency failed to keep records of the addresses to which people were evacuated. In the example of the opening of a new community center, the natural experiment would not work if the decision to locate the center in a particular neighborhood was influenced by lobbying by the residents, or if residents deliberately moved into the neighborhood to be closer to the new facility. These caveats notwithstanding, it seems likely that such natural experiments are being repeated on a regular basis throughout the social world, and causal inference would be strengthened by taking advantage of them.

The gold standard of causal inference is to directly manipulate the treatment—either through cluster-randomized community trials (e.g., opening senior centers in one set of randomly selected communities, and rolling out the same intervention at a later time in a control set of communities), or by randomizing residents to move into different communities, such as happened in HUD's Moving to Opportunity (MTO) Demonstration Project (Lieberman, Katz, and Kling 2004).

A separate set of challenges to causal inference is posed by studies in which individual-level measures of social capital (such as perceptions about the trustworthiness of neighbors, or the perceived availability of resources within one's network) are linked to self-reported health outcomes, such as mental health. Two kinds of biases are possible: (a) common method bias, where unmeasured individual characteristics such as negative affectivity may influence individuals' ratings of social capital as well as their reported health status; and (b) confounding by omitted variables such as early life circumstances or genetic factors, which may predispose an individual to being hostile, mistrusting, and unhealthy. That is, variations in individual characteristics such as attachment styles, sociable personality, and trusting attitudes are likely to be shaped by early family experiences. In the absence of data that permit the investigator to control for these characteristics, studies among twins can help

to mitigate these concerns. Not only do twins share genetic and perinatal factors, but also often their family environment during childhood. In the twin fixed-effects design, the investigator is able to examine health differences between twin pairs who are discordant with respect to their reported perceptions of social capital, thereby canceling the potential confounding influences of the unmeasured genetic and personality traits, as well as shared early life circumstances.

In an analysis of 944 adult twin pairs (37 percent monozygotic and 63 percent dizygotic) enrolled in the National Survey of Midlife Development in the U.S., Fujiwara and Kawachi (2008) examined the associations between individual-level perceptions of social capital (trust of neighbors and neighborhood cohesion) and self-reported behavioral indicators of community participation and voluntarism, in relation to a set of health outcomes that included perceived physical and mental health, depressive symptoms, and physician-diagnosed major depression. When the analyses were carried out ignoring the discordant twin design, each indicator of social capital was significantly associated with health outcomes in the expected direction (e.g., more community participation = lower risk of major depression). However, when the analyses were repeated using the twin fixed-effects design, most of the associations became statistically non-significant. Only the association between trust of neighbors remained strongly associated with perceived physical health among both monozygotic and dizygotic twins. Notably, no associations remained between any of the measures of social capital and the diagnosis of major depression.

In summary, much work remains to be carried out in shoring up the empirical evidence base linking social capital to health outcomes. There is a need to improve the measurement of social capital by applying reliable and valid survey instruments, or by attempting whole network–based approaches.

Panel data, objective assessment of health status, and multilevel analysis are good starting points for methodological rigor, but in addition, research needs to strengthen causal inference by incorporating more rigorous study designs and analytical methods, such as propensity score matching, instrumental variable approaches, and the use of natural experiments (Subramanian, Glymour, and Kawachi 2007).

POLICY IMPLICATIONS OF SOCIAL CAPITAL FOR HEALTH PROMOTION

Critics of social capital have voiced skepticism about the utility of applying the concept as a health promotion strategy (Pearce and Davey Smith 2003). They point out that: (a) social capital is an unwarranted distraction from more pressing policy agendas such as the elimination of poverty;[6] (b) attributing the poor health status of disadvantaged communities to the lack of social capital only serves to blame the victims for their unfortunate predicament (Muntaner, Lynch, and Davey Smith 2001); and (c) even if interventions could be mounted to successfully build social capital, the results might be counterproductive to health because of the unintended side effects of social cohesion, which tend to be ignored or downplayed by overenthusiastic advocates.

These are all cogent arguments that dictate caution in how social capital should be exported and adapted to the population health realm. As Szreter and Woolcock (2004) point out, the discourse on social capital in the policy realm needs to be more productively directed toward how to optimize community cohesion and network-based resources under specific circumstances to improve health, rather than focusing on mindless calls to citizens to behave more nicely toward each other. These considerations tend to rule out mass media campaigns based on generic slogans that exhort citizens to "practice random acts of kindness," as well as spraying oxytocin from overhead helicopters to promote trust among strangers.

For social capital to contribute usefully to population health improvement, two questions need to be answered: (1) Can interventions effectively build social capital? and (2) If we strengthen social capital, will health improve? Regarding the first question, suggestions abound but demonstrations remain sparse. The political scientist Robert Putnam (2000), who has been more effective than any other academic in popularizing the concept of social capital, suggests several directions for such efforts, including expanding funding for community service programs, providing incentives to private sector employers to introduce flexible work arrangements that facilitate employees to invest in the social capital of their families and communities, and incorporating Social Capital Impact Assessments (modeled after Health Impact Assessments) to forecast the consequences of social policies for levels of social capital within society. While each of these prescriptions has the merit of plausibility, they remain somewhat generic and several steps removed from influencing the health outcomes of individuals.

A more concrete demonstration of building social capital is provided by the Experience Corps, originally piloted as a randomized trial in Baltimore, Maryland, but subsequently scaled up across communities in the United States (Glass et al. 2004; Fried et al. 2004). The program places older volunteers in public elementary schools in roles designed to meet the schools' needs and to increase the social, physical, and cognitive activity of the volunteers. In other words, the program builds intergenerational social capital, and it has been described as providing a win/win outcome for the seniors whose functional abilities are improved through social engagement, physical activity, and cognitive stimulation, as well as for the pupils (who are primarily in resource-scarce public school settings) for whom academic performance is improved.

Additional grassroots-based ideas for boosting community social capital have been suggested by advocacy groups such as the Saguaro Seminar of the Kennedy School of Government at Harvard University (Sander and Lowney 2005). The Saguaro Seminar advocates making a series of so-called smart bets based upon established principles of community organizing, such as encouraging the formation of neighborhood associations. However, it remains to be proven through rigorous evaluation whether organizing neighborhood associations, book clubs, or carpooling (all examples cited in the Seminar's "Toolkit") can boost social capital in a sustainable manner. More importantly, before rushing off to organize a block party, it is critical to reflect that it is not only the overall level of social capital that matters, but also the *type* of social capital that matters for different purposes. For example, widely scattered weak ties are more effective at disseminating information, whereas strong and dense connections are more effective for collective action (Chwe 1999). As Sobel (2002, 151) cautions: "People apply the notion of social capital to both types of situation. Knowing what types of networks are best for generating social capital requires that one be specific about what the social capital is going to be used to do." For example, it would not be sufficient (and possibly counterproductive) to encourage reciprocity between residents of a highly disadvantaged community. Residents of disadvantaged communities are often already maxed out on assisting each other as a survival strategy, and launching a campaign to encourage stronger bonding ties within such a setting might only add to that strain. The type of social capital called for in such a situation would be of the bridging kind, which connects disadvantaged residents

with credit counselors, employment agencies, or loan officers.

As the foregoing example illustrates, there is a critical distinction to be drawn between so-called bonding social capital and bridging social capital (Gittell and Vidal 1998; Szreter and Woolcock 2004; Kawachi 2006). Bonding capital refers to resources that are accessed within social groups whose members are alike (homophilous) in terms of their social identity, such as class or race. By contrast, bridging capital refers to the resources accessed by individuals and groups through connections that cross class, race/ethnicity, and other boundaries of social identity. Although few empirical studies to date have gone to the trouble of distinguishing between these two types of capital, growing evidence suggests that a deeper understanding of the consequences of each form of capital may prove to be helpful in avoiding some of the downsides of social cohesion. Hence, bonding capital represents part of the day-to-day survival strategy for residents of disadvantaged communities. As documented in Carol Stack's (1974) ethnographic study of a poor African American community, the mutual exchange of resources through kinship networks is the primary mechanism for getting by in such communities. At the same time, bonding capital extracts a cost from the network members in the mental and financial strain associated with providing support for others in need. Consistent with this notion, Mitchell and LaGory (2002) found that in a small study of a disadvantaged minority community in Birmingham, Alabama, high levels of bonding social capital (measured by the strength of trust and associational ties with others of a similar racial and educational background as the respondent) were paradoxically associated with higher levels of mental distress. By contrast, individuals in the same study who reported access to high levels of bridging social capital (ties to others who were unlike them with respect to race and class) were less likely to experience mental distress.

Yet another instance of the importance of distinguishing between bonding and bridging social capital is illustrated by Ashutosh Varshney's (2002) study of sectarian violence across cities of India. According to Varshney, cities in India are characterized by marked variations in the outbreak of violence between Hindus and Muslims, even though they superficially resemble each other in terms of ethnic makeup. The difference between peaceful and violence-wracked localities, according to Varshney, can be attributed to the presence of bridging social capital in the former. In cities that are able to maintain the peace, bridging capital takes the form of integrated civic organizations—business groups, trade unions, and even reading circles based in local libraries—that include both Muslims and Hindus among their members. Such organizations, Varshney maintains, have proved extremely effective both at preventing the outbreak of violence by maintaining channels of communication across ethnic groups, and at quelling rumors that troublemakers often initiate within a community to incite riots.

Distinguishing between bonding and bridging forms of social capital may thus assist in answering the second question posed at the beginning of this section: If you build social capital, will it improve health? Social capital, like any form of capital (e.g., financial capital), can be deployed for both good ends and bad ends, and bonding capital may be particularly susceptible to both uses. For example, in India, belonging to the local branch of the Bharatiya Janata Party promotes a member's sense of Hindu nationalism, while belonging to the Muslim League promotes the sense of Muslim nationalism. Both are forms of bonding capital. A generic, one-size-fits-all prescription to boost social capital by encouraging membership in local organizations may not end up promoting the greater good if it simply drives people to join these highly bonding but divisive manifestations of social cohesion.

Social capital has been an active topic of research throughout the social sciences for some time, including in mainstream sociology, economics, and political science. Population health is a relative newcomer to the field, with the first study linking social capital to health outcomes appearing circa 1997 (Kawachi et al. 1997). Social capital serves to remind us that population health is determined by more than access to health care, genetics, lifestyles, money, and schooling. The social world also matters a great deal, and our ties to family, friends, coworkers, and neighbors constitute a credit bank—a form of capital—that we can rely upon to promote health. And even though much work remains to be carried out in filling in both the theories and empirical evidence linking social capital to population health outcomes, few would deny the intuitive appeal of the concept in bringing together diverse fields of inquiry in medical sociology, including studies of social relationships and networks, social stratification, and health disparities, as well as neighborhood and other contextual influences on health.

NOTES

1 According to Moore et al. (2005), the public health literature on social capital has tended to exhibit an uncritical acceptance of the definition offered by the political scientist Robert Putnam (1993, 2000), who defined social capital as "the features of social organization, such as trust, norms, and networks, that can improve the efficiency of society by facilitating coordinated actions" (Putnam 1993, 167). Interestingly, Putnam himself cites his source as Coleman, not Bourdieu.

2 By contrast, smoking prevalence among Japanese males jumps to over 30 percent as soon as they reach the legal age. Indeed, twenty years ago, it was not uncommon for free cigarettes to be distributed at local town halls across the nation on Adults' Day, where fresh batches of twenty-year-olds were formally inducted into adulthood by local functionaries.

3 Okinawa was—at least until comparatively recently—renowned as the prefecture with the highest average life expectancy in Japan, a nation with notably high longevity. According to the researchers of the Okinawa Centenarian Study, a major key to the islanders' longevity is their diet, followed by their close family ties (Wilcox, Wilcox, and Suzuki 2001). A social epidemiologist would switch the order of the emphasis on these factors. A similar literary example of community mutual aid can be found in Flora Thompson's *Lark Rise to Candleford* (1939, 2000), about a rural Oxfordshire village in early twentieth-century England.

4 On the other hand, if the proposed instruments are, in fact, associated with the outcomes of interest, they will fail. For instance, income polarization has been proposed as an independent determinant of health, although the hypothesis is controversial (Subramanian and Kawachi, 2004). However, in empirical studies, income inequality is more consistently associated with health outcomes at larger levels of spatial aggregation such as states, and much less at lower levels of aggregation such as neighborhoods. If this is true, income polarization may still serve as an instrument for studies of social cohesion at the neighborhood level. One of the downsides of the IV approach is that the validity of the instrument is often untestable and must rest on prior knowledge and theory.

5 In regression, this is accomplished by a two-stage least squares procedure.

6 The apparent cooption of social capital by third-way politicians as a cheap way to solve the problems of poverty is often cited as an instance of distracting the gullible public (Fine 2001; Muntaner, Lynch, and Davey Smith 2001; Navarro 2002).

REFERENCES

Alesina, A., A. Devleeschauwer, W. Easterly, S. Kurlat, and R. Wacziarg. 2003. "Fractionalization." *Journal of Economic Growth* 8:155–94.

Almedom, Astier M., and Douglas Glandon. 2008. "Social Capital and Mental Health: An Updated Interdisciplinary Review of Primary Evidence." In *Social Capital and Health*, ed. Ichiro Kawachi, S. V. Subramanian, and Daniel Kim, 191–244. New York: Springer.

Anderson, Lisa R., Jennifer M. Mellor, and Jeffrey Milyo. 2004. "Social Capital and Contributions in a Public Goods Experiment." *American Economic Review Papers and Proceedings* 94(2): 373–76.

Anderson, Lisa R., and Jennifer M. Mellor. 2008. "The Economic Approach to Cooperation and Trust: Lessons for the Study of Social Capital and Health." In *Social Capital and Health*, ed. Ichiro Kawachi, S. V. Subraminian, and Daniel Kim, 117–36. New York: Springer.

Berkman, Lisa F., and Thomas Glass. 2000. "Social Integration, Social Networks, Social Support, and Health." In *Social Epidemiology*, ed. Lisa F. Berkman and Ichiro Kawachi, 137–73. New York: Oxford University Press.

Bourdieu, Pierre. 1986. "The Forms of Capital." In *The Handbook of Theory: Research for the Sociology of Education*, ed. J. G. Richardson, 241–58. New York: Greenwood Press.

Carpiano, Richard M. 2008. "Actual or Potential Neighborhood Resources for Health: What Can Bourdieu Offer for Understanding Mechanisms Linking Social Capital to Health?" In *Social Capital and Health*, ed. Ichiro Kawachi, S. V. Subramanian, and Daniel Kim, 83–93. New York: Springer.

Chwe, M. S. 1999. "Structure and Strategy in Collective Action." *American Journal of Sociology* 105:128–56.

Coleman, James S. 1990. *Foundations of Social Theory*. Cambridge, Mass.: Harvard University Press.

De Silva, Mary. 2006. "A Systematic Review of the Methods Used in Studies of Social Capital and Mental Health." In *Social Capital and Mental Health*, ed. Kwame McKenzie and Trudy Harpham, 39–67. London: Jessica Kingsley.

Ellaway, Anne, and Sally Macintyre. 2007. "Is Social Participation Associated with Cardiovascular Disease Risk Factors?" *Social Science and Medicine* 64(7): 1384–91.

Fine, Ben. 2001. *Social Capital versus Social Theory: Political Economy and Social Science at the Turn of the Millennium*. London: Routledge.

Fried, L. P., M. C. Carlson, M. Freedman, K. D. Frick, T. A. Glass, J. Hill, S. McGill, G. W. Rebok, T. S. Seeman, J. Tielsch, B. A. Wasik, and S. Zeger. 2004. "A Social Model for Health Promotion for an Aging Population: Initial Evidence on the Experience Corps Model." *Journal of Urban Health* 81(1): 64–78.

Fujiwara, Takeo, and Ichiro Kawachi. 2008. "Social Capital and Health: A Study of Adult Twins in the U.S." *American Journal of Preventive Medicine* 35(2): 139–44.

Gittell, Ross J., and Avis Vidal. 1998. *Community Organizing: Building Social Capital as a Development Strategy*. Thousand Oaks, Calif.: Sage.

Gladwell, Malcolm. 2000. *The Tipping Point*. Boston: Little, Brown.

Glaeser, E. L., D. I. Laibson, J. A. Scheinkman, and C. L. Soutter. 2000. "Measuring Trust." *Quarterly Journal of Economics* 115(3): 811–46.

Glass, T. A., M. Carlson, M. Freedman, et al. 2004. "Experience Corps: Design of an Intergenerational Health Promotion Program to Boost Social Capital." *Journal of Urban Health* 81(1): 79–93.

Glymour, Maria M. 2006. "Natural Experiments and Instrumental Variable Analyses in Social Epidemiology." In *Methods in Social Epidemiology*, ed. J. Michael Oakes and Jay S. Kaufman, 429–60. San Francisco: Jossey-Bass.

Granovetter, Mark S. 1973. "The Strength of Weak Ties." *American Journal of Sociology* 78(6): 1360–80.

Harpham, Trudy. 2008. "The Measurement of Community Social Capital through Surveys." In *Social Capital and Health*, ed. Ichiro Kawachi, S. V. Subramanian, and Daniel Kim, 51–62. New York: Springer.

Islam, M. K., J. Merlo, I. Kawachi, M. Lindstrom, K. Burstrom, and U-G. Gerdtham. 2006a. "Does it Really Matter Where You Live? A Panel Data Multilevel Analysis of Swedish Municipality-Level Social Capital on Individual Health-Related Quality of Life." *Health Economics, Policy and Law* 1 (Pt 3): 209–35.

Islam, M. K., J. Merlo, I. Kawachi, M. Lindstrom, and U-G. Gerdtham. 2006b. "Social Capital and Health: Does Egalitarianism Matter? A Literature Review." *International Journal of Equity in Health* 5(1): 3.

Kawachi, I. 2006. "Commentary: Social Capital and Health—Making the Connections One Step at a Time." *International Journal of Epidemiology* 35(4): 989–93.

Kawachi, I., and L. F. Berkman. 2000. "Social Cohesion, Social Capital, and Health." In *Social Epidemiology*, ed. Lisa F. Berkman and Ichiro Kawachi, 174–90. New York: Oxford University Press.

———, eds. 2003. *Neighborhoods and Health*. New York: Oxford University Press.

Kawachi, I., B. P. Kennedy, K. Lochner, and D. Prothrow-Stith. 1997. "Social Capital, Income Inequality, and Mortality." *American Journal of Public Health* 87:1491–98.

Kawachi, I., D. J. Kim, A. Coutts, and S. V. Subramanian. 2004. "Reconciling the Three Accounts of Social Capital." *International Journal of Epidemiology* 33(4): 682–90.

Kawachi, I., S. V. Subramanian, and D. Kim, eds. 2008. *Social Capital and Health*. New York: Springer.

Kim, Daniel, S. V. Subramanian, and Ichiro Kawachi. 2008. "Social Capital and Physical Health: A Systematic Review of the Literature." In *Social Capital and Health*, ed. Ichiro Kawachi, S. V. Subramanian, and Daniel Kim, 139–90. New York: Springer.

Kouvonen, A., M. Kivimäki, J. Vahtera, et al. 2006. "Psychometric Evaluation of a Short Measure of Social Capital at Work." *BMC Public Health* 6:251.

Kouvonen, A., T. Oksanen, J. Vahtera, M. Stafford, R. Wilkinson, J. Schneider, A. Väänänen, M. Virtanen, S. J. Cox, J. Pentti, M. Elovainio, and M. Kivimäki. 2008. "Low Workplace Social Capital as a Predictor of Depression: The Finnish Public Sector Study." *American Journal of Epidemiology* 167(10): 1143–51.

Lakon, Cynthia M., Dionne C. Godette, and John R. Hipp. 2008. "Network-Based Approaches for Measuring Social Capital." In *Social Capital and Health*, ed. Ichiro Kawachi. S. V. Subramanian, and Daniel Kim, 63–81. New York: Springer.

Lieberman, Jeffrey B., Lawrence F. Katz, and Jeffrey R. Kling. 2004. *Beyond Treatment Effects: Estimating the Relationship between Neighborhood Poverty and Individual Outcomes in the MTO Experiment*. Princeton, N.J.: Princeton Industrial Relations Section.

Lin, Nan. 2001. *Social Capital: Theory and Research*. New York: Aldine de Gruyter.

Lindstrom, Martin. 2008a. "Invited Commentary: Social Capital, Social Contexts, and Depression." *American Journal of Epidemiology* 167(10): 1152–54.

———. 2008b. "Social Capital and Health-Related Behaviors." In *Social Capital and Health*, ed. Ichiro Kawachi, S. V. Subramanian, and Daniel Kim, 215–38. New York: Springer.

Lochner, K., I. Kawachi, R. T. Brennan, and S. L. Buka. 2003. "Social Capital and Neighborhood Mortality Rates in Chicago." *Social Science and Medicine* 56(8): 1797–1805.

Lynch, J. W., G. Davey Smith, M. M. Hillemeier, M. Shaw, T. Raghunathan, and G. A. Kaplan. 2001. "Income Inequality, the Psychosocial Environment, and Health: Comparisons of Wealthy Nations." *Lancet* 358:194–200.

Mitchell, C. U., and M. LaGory. 2002. "Social Capital and Mental Distress in an Impoverished Community." *City and Community* 1:195–215.

Moore, S., A. Shiell, P. Hawe, and V. A. Haines. 2005. "The Privileging of Communitarian Ideas: Citation Practices and the Translation of Social Capital into Public Health Research." *American Journal of Public Health* 95:1330–37.

Muntaner, C., J. Lynch, and G. Davey Smith. 2001. "Social Capital, Disorganized Communities, and the Third Way: Understanding the Retreat from Structural Inequalities in Epidemiology and Public Health." *International Journal of Health Services* 31(2): 213–37.

Navarro, V. 2002. "A Critique of Social Capital." *International Journal of Health Services* 32(3): 423–43.

———. 2004. "Commentary: Is Capital the Solution or the Problem?" *International Journal of Epidemiology* 33:672–74.

Oakes, J. M. 2004. "The (Mis)estimation of Neighborhood Effects: Causal Inference for a Practicable Social Epidemiology." *Social Science and Medicine* 58:1929–52.

Okuda, Hideo. 2005. *Southbound* (in Japanese). Tokyo: Kadokawa.

Pearce, N., and G. Davey Smith. 2003. "Is Social Capital the Key to Inequalities in Health?" *American Journal of Public Health* 93(1): 122–29.

Portes, Alejandro. 1998. "Social Capital: Its Origins and Application in Modern Sociology." *Annual Reviews of Sociology* 24:1–24.

Putnam, Robert D. 1993. *Making Democracy Work: Civic Traditions in Modern Italy.* Princeton, N.J.: Princeton University Press.

———. 2000. *Bowling Alone: The Collapse and Revival of American Community.* New York: Simon and Schuster.

Rostila, Mikael. 2007. "Social Capital and Health in the Swedish Welfare State." In *Health Inequalities and Welfare Resources: Continuity and Change in Sweden*, ed.

Johan Fritzell and Olle Lundberg, 157–77. Bristol: Policy Press.

Sampson, R. J., S. W. Raudenbush, and F. Earls. 1997. "Neighborhoods and Violent Crime: A Multilevel Study of Collective Efficacy." *Science* 277:918–24.

Sander, Thomas H., and Kathleen Lowney. 2005. "Social Capital Building Toolkit, Version 1.1." Cambridge, Mass.: Harvard University John F. Kennedy School of Government. ksg.harvard.edu/saguaro/pdfs/skbuildingtoolkitversion1.1.pdf.

Sobel, J. 2002. "Can We Trust Social Capital?" *Journal of Economic Literature* 40:139–54.

Stack, Carol B. 1974. *All Our Kin: Strategies for Survival in a Black Community.* New York: Harper and Row.

Subramanian, S. V., Maria M. Glymour, and Ichiro Kawachi. 2007. "Identifying Causal Ecological Effects on Health: A Methodological Assessment." In *Macrosocial Determinants of Population Health*, ed. Sandro Galea, 301–31. New York: Springer.

Subramanian, S. V., Kelvyn Jones, and Craig Duncan. 2003. "Multilevel Methods for Public Health Research." In *Neighborhoods and Health*, ed. Ichiro Kawachi and Lisa F. Berkman, 65–111. New York: Oxford University Press.

Subramanian, S. V., and I. Kawachi. 2004. "Income Inequality and Health: What Have We Learned So Far." *Epidemiologic Reviews* 26:78–91.

Subramanian, S. V., D. J. Kim, and I. Kawachi. 2002. "Social Trust and Self-Rated Health in U.S. Communities: Multilevel Analysis." *Journal of Urban Health* 79(4), Suppl. 1: S21–34.

Szreter, S., and M. Woolcock. 2004. "Health by Association? Social Capital, Social Theory, and the Political Economy of Public Health." *International Journal of Epidemiology* 33(4): 650–67.

Thompson, Flora. 1939 (2000). *Lark Rise to Candleford.* London: Penguin Modern Classics.

Valente, T. W., P. Gallaher, and P. Mouttapa. 2004. "Using Social Networks to Understand and Prevent Substance Use: A Transdisciplinary Perspective." *Substance Use and Misuse* 39:1685–1712.

Van der Gaag, M., and T. A. B. Snijders. 2005. "The Resource Generator: Measurement of Individual Social Capital with Concrete Items." *Social Networks* 27:1–29.

Van der Gaag, M., and M. Webber. 2008. "Measurement of Individual Social Capital. Questions, Instruments, and Measures." In *Social Capital and Health*, ed. Ichiro Kawachi, S. V. Subramanian, and Daniel Kim, 29–49. New York: Springer.

Varshney, Ashutosh. 2002. *Ethnic Conflict and Civic Life: Hindus and Muslims in India.* New Haven, Conn.: Yale University Press.

Webber, M. P., and P. J. Huxley. 2007. "Measuring Access to Social Capital: The Validity and Reliability of the Resource Generator-UK and Its Association with Common Mental Disorder." *Social Science and Medicine.* 65(3): 481–92.

Whitley, Rob. 2008. "Social Capital and Health: Qualitative and Ethnographic Approaches." In *Social Capital and Health*, ed. Ichiro Kawachi, S. V. Subramanian, and Daniel Kim, 95–115. New York: Springer.

Wilcox, Bradley J., Craig D. Wilcox, and Makoto Suzuki. 2001. *The Okinawa Program: How the World's Longest-Lived People Achieve Everlasting Health—and How You Can Too.* New York: Clarkson Potter.

Zimmerman, F. J. 2008. "A Commentary on 'Neomaterialist Theory and the Temporal Relationship between Income Inequality and Longevity Change.'" *Social Science and Medicine* 66:1882–94.

Does Your Neighborhood Make You Fat?

Julie Guthman

"Data Show Manhattan Is Svelte and the Bronx Is Chubby, Chubby" read a headline in a July 2009 edition of the *New York Times*. The story reported on a study that had just been released that had compared obesity rates in the Bronx and Manhattan boroughs of New York City (Chan 2009). As might be expected, Manhattan's rates of overweight and obesity were far lower than those in the Bronx, and "the prosperous swath of Manhattan from the Upper East Side down to Gramercy Park had the lowest obesity rate (less than 15 percent) in the city." As reported by the *Times,* the head researcher, Andrew Rundle, noted that at the neighborhood level, socioeconomic and demographic factors were the strongest predictors of obesity rates. He then equivocated, stating that even when adjusting for poverty and race, at least three factors are associated with reduced obesity: proximity to supermarkets and groceries where fresh produce is sold; proximity to parks; and access to public transportation, which reduces reliance on cars. The article thus concluded that increasing the number of produce markets and making neighborhoods easier to walk in might reduce obesity rates.

This study is one of dozens, and possibly hundreds, of studies completed in the past decade or so that test the thesis that people are fat because they are surrounded by cheap, fast, nutritionally inferior food and a built environment that discourages physical activity. This theory was first formalized in the academic literature as the "obesogenic environment" (Swinburn, Egger, and Raza 1999; Hill and Peters 1998). According to Hill and Peters (1998: 1371), "our current environment is characterized by an essentially unlimited supply of convenient, relatively inexpensive, highly palatable, energy-dense foods, coupled with a lifestyle requiring only low levels of physical activity for subsistence. Such an environment promotes high energy intake and low energy expenditure." Importantly, the part of the thesis that speaks to the food environment articulates with a major approach in food systems research which has focused on questions of spatial access to healthy food and the way food retailing practices entice people to buy the wrong food (Winson 2004).

Along with generating research, the thesis has animated various planning, advocacy, and educational interventions to address these obesogenic qualities of the built environment. These have included creating outlets for fresh fruits and vegetables in urban "food deserts," redesigning (or remarketing) public spaces to encourage walking and bicycle riding, or city-sponsored educational campaigns to achieve obesity reduction (Herrick

Julie Guthman, "Does Your Neighborhood Make You Fat?," Weighing In: Obesity, Food Justice, and the Limits of Capitalism, pp. 66-90, 198. Copyright © 2011 by University of California Press. Reprinted with permission.

2007). The last has been a favorite of cities pinned as being some of the country's fattest, such as Houston, which topped a list created by *Men's Fitness* magazine several years in a row.

The focus on the built environment in explaining and attempting to prevent obesity is in many ways salutary. Deemphasizing individual behaviors would seem to diminish the moral scrutiny and invocations of personal responsibility that typically accompany discussions of obesity's causes. Moreover, it brings some needed focus to food industry and regional planning practices, which potentially assigns culpability to powerful and malignant actors. So I don't want to dismiss this line of argument altogether. However, these so-called environmental explanations of obesity are flawed in a number of respects. A key one is that the studies designed to test the thesis are based on entrenched assumptions about the causes of obesity, leading to the kind of equivocation mentioned earlier. Apropos to the Bronx-Manhattan study, the existing assumptions also neglect, or at least downplay, the salience of race and class in explaining spatial patterning of obesity and defining what constitutes a healthy environment. As such, the obesogenic environment thesis and efforts to study and fix it tend to reinforce healthism, ironically so. That is because environments that are characterized as obesogenic tend to have features that, when juxtaposed to ideal, let's call them "leptogenic" (after the Latin for thinness) environments, reveal important, unstated preferences for certain types of places and their attendant lifestyles. And these preferences may, ironically, worsen wealth disparities among different environments.

This chapter will discuss these arguments in detail. In addition, it will introduce findings from a study I conducted that did not presuppose how built environments affect obesity. On the contrary, unlike the deductive approach of the quantitative spatial studies I discuss, this study was entirely inductive, designed to explore how people who live in so-called obesogenic environments mediate these environments in their own terms. First, though, I want to introduce the more typical ways researchers approach the obesogenic environment.

COPRODUCING THE OBESOGENIC ENVIRONMENT

To the extent that the Bronx-Manhattan study found that lack of proximity to grocery stores and parks and lack of access to public transportation "predict" obesity, researchers were testing those as variables in the models they used. This approach to formulating and studying the obesogenic environment exemplifies what those in science studies call coproduction. Coproduction refers to assumptions about a scientific object's causes and character being built into models of examining it (Jasanoff 2004). The obesogenic environment thesis internalizes two critical presumptions, only one of which is explicit. *Explicitly*, it assumes the energy balance model, which holds that obesity results from an excess of calories in relative to those expended. To the extent to which it black boxes questions about human behavior, specifically how humans negotiate their environments, it *implicitly* assumes that the environment simply acts on people, so that people are objects, not agents, in these environments.

The energy balance model is taken for granted in virtually all discussions of obesity, yet, […], it is not indubitable. Nevertheless, rather than testing this assumption, studies of the obesogenic environment embed it in ways that can render these studies circular. For a particularly marked example of this, consider how *Men's Fitness* calculates America's fattest cities. In making their calculation, they do not even begin with those cities with the highest BMI per capita. Rather, they use a range of indicators, not all of which are controllable, including statistics on total number of clubs, gyms, and sporting goods stores; fruit and vegetable consumption; alcohol and tobacco use; air and water quality; and parks and recreation facilities. (In determining the worst cities they give good grades to cities that have qualities associated with good health and give poor grades to cities that have qualities associated with bad health, such as bad air quality.) In other words, they include measures that they *assume cause* obesity in measures *of* obesity—a clear instance of coproduction.[1]

The concept of coproduction is also meant to elucidate how science helps produce the social worlds it is intended to explain. The obesogenic environment thesis does this in multiple ways. First, the idea that the environment acts on people in unmediated ways is in some sense a by-product of the thesis itself, yet it leaves the impression of unthinking behavior in regard to these environments. Second, by making judgments about what constitutes a leptogenic environment (e.g., air quality in the *Men's Fitness* study), it contributes to the economic and cultural valuation of the places it describes. Third, by incorporating factors such as proximity to grocery stores and parks in its measurements, it effectively validates a policy approach that emphasizes supply-oriented issues of availability and proximity rather than demand-oriented ones of, say, affordability and need.

The Bronx-Manhattan study nevertheless differs in emphasis from many others. First, it nods to the importance of studying thinness as well as fatness (i.e., to make any claims about neighborhood effects on obesity we have to show neighborhood effects on thinness). Second, it acknowledges that class and race have a role in explaining neighborhood differences in obesity rates. This point, alone, does not negate the assumptions of the thesis; indeed, it is perfectly compatible with the supposition that race and class differences in BMI

are a consequence of differences in energy intake and expenditure. But it does suggest the existence of factors independent of the built environment and even leaves open the possibility that race and class variations in obesity rates are unrelated to energy balance. Where it falls into the same trap as the *Men's Fitness* study is in assuming that the problem features of the built environment are independent of who lives there. I argue, instead, that the relationship among the built environment, spatial variation of obesity, and spatial variation in race and class are all of a piece that cannot be dissected and made amenable to various supply-oriented interventions. Gentrified urban cores such as Gramercy Park are thin and wealthy, and it is unclear which begets which. Conversely, features associated with obesogeneity are precisely what make the Bronx affordable and thus available to those whose class status may exist by virtue of their being big. Yet, the quantitative spatial research that attempts to demonstrate the relationship between the built environment and obesity cannot account for this inseparability, leading to the reductionist—and simplistic—conclusion that more grocery stores will reduce obesity.

OBESOGENIC ENVIRONMENTS: STUDYING THE STUDIES

It is worth considering how researchers might go about trying to prove a relationship between obesity and features of the built environment. Some might simply observe that people seem fat in a particular place and then look around and try to ascertain what's different about that environment. Those who assert that Europeans are thinner because they walk a lot are basically relying on this sort of casual observation. But if they tried to publish these "findings" in a scholarly journal, they might not be taken seriously. So instead they turn to more established scientific methods for establishing relationships between health outcomes and place: geographic information systems (GIS) and spatial analysis. Basically, these involve the use of spatial statistics and mapping to demonstrate correlative relationships between places with higher obesity prevalence and environmental features that might contribute to obesity. Fair enough. But what assumptions go into the data selection? What data are available to make these correlations and what kind of explanations might be left out because of lack of data? And what does statistical analysis imply about human behavior? My argument here is that it is in the effort to operationalize the thesis that the simplifications become manifest.

First, researchers would need to ascertain variations in prevalence of obesity across space to establish that some neighborhoods, places, or regions have higher obesity prevalence than others. They would tend to use BMI as a measure of obesity, since height and weight are the size measurements collected for large numbers of people. At the national level these are collected through the National Health and Nutrition Examination Survey (NHANES) and the Behavioral Risk Factor Surveillance System (BFRSS). BFRSS samples many more people, but NHANES is considered more accurate because it includes in-person interviews and medical examinations—and collects more detailed (and longitudinal) data about socioeconomic status and behaviors that can be used as variables in an analysis. Thus, the choice of which survey to use would influence the depth and breadth of findings. To show that BMI values vary across space, researchers would need to sort individual BMI values by geocodes—codes that identify the individual with a particular state, county, zip code, or census tract. To measure neighborhood environmental influences, researchers would want these codes to be available at fine-grained scales, but they might find that due to sampling issues in health surveys (especially detailed ones such

as NHANES), it is difficult to obtain statistically reliable measures of BMI at finer-grained scales than the state, metropolitan area, or county.

They might then map this variation to identify pockets of high obesity prevalence. The maps put out by the CDC that show obesity rates by state and county illustrate the differences in what the scale of analysis—as well as researcher assumptions—may lead the researcher to hypothesize. The state map (figure 5.1) might draw your attention to the "thin" Rocky Mountain west and suggest that obesity has something to do with exercise and spending time outdoors. Alternatively, you might look at the map that selects for whites only (figure 5.2) and see that West Virginia is the fattest state, and consider that obesity has something to do with economic decline. The more fine-grained county map (figure 5.3) might draw your attention to lower rates of obesity around cosmopolitan coastal cities and university towns—or higher rates of obesity in areas with high populations of African Americans and Native Americans. Whether by state or by county, these maps, which visualize *rates* of obesity per geocode rather than, say, *average BMI* per geocode, might give the impression of dramatic differences among different regions. Using the latter would tend to produce finer gradations of difference among places and might lead you to question whether obesity "clusters" much. Of course, how the maps were color-coded would also affect the visualization, since colors close in tone suggest more graded difference than colors different in hue. And red almost always calls out for alarm.

Thus far, however, the analysis would only have identified geographic variation in obesity—or, perhaps, clusters of obesity. In any case, many researchers do not start with the map; instead, they identify a place or region they wish to study for its obesogeneity—or compare two places in

FIGURE 5.1 Obesity rates by state, 2007 *(percentage of adults with BMI ≥ 30)*

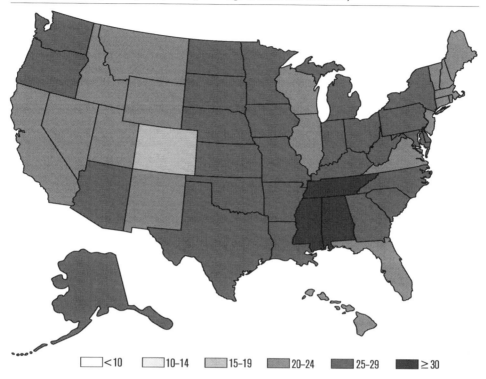

☐ <10   ☐ 10–14   ☐ 15–19   ☐ 20–24   ☐ 25–29   ☐ ≥ 30

Source: Behavioral Risk Factor Surveillance System, CDC.

close proximity, as in the New York study. Either way, the next step would be to identify statistical associations between higher obesity rates and environmental features. Naturally, to show that these statistics are robust as geographic phenomena, they would want their models to incorporate spatial dimensions such as proximity to or density of various features, regardless of whether or in what way proximity or density is a deciding factor in peoples' decisions.

To demonstrate relationships between features of the built environment and BMI variation, the researchers would need to hypothesize what features might actually contribute to obesity and turn them into variables. If they were testing the obesogenic environment thesis, they would want to ascertain differences in (junk) food availability and opportunities for or obstacles to physical activity. On the food side, researchers might be interested in the availability and mix of grocery stores, fast-food restaurants, big-box stores, and so forth. Interestingly, though, researchers might assume different things about the roles these play. For instance, many might assume that big-box stores are a feature of the obesogenic environment based on the supposition that they encourage people to buy more food than they need for the week. One research team went against the grain, however, to hypothesize that big-box stores allow people to purchase more fruits and vegetables at lower cost (Courtemanche and Carden 2010). On the physical activity side, researchers would most definitely consider suburban sprawl, which figures prominently in notions of obesogeneity.

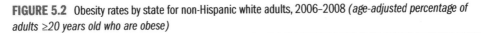

FIGURE 5.2 Obesity rates by state for non-Hispanic white adults, 2006–2008 *(age-adjusted percentage of adults ≥20 years old who are obese)*

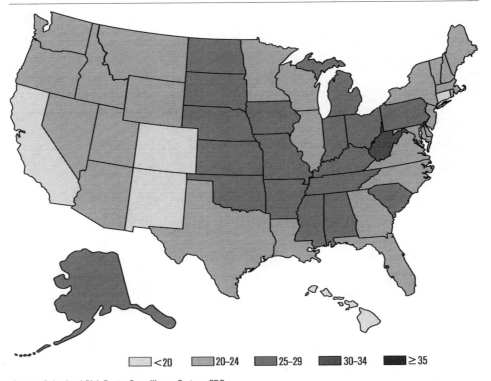

<20   20–24   25–29   30–34   ≥ 35

Source: Behavioral Risk Factor Surveillance System, CDC.

One research team, Plantinga and Bernell (2005), suggested several ways in which low-density residential areas have contributed to obesity: the poor connectivity of street networks that increases trip distances, suburban layouts that make walking and cycling impractical and unsafe, the reduced viability of public transportation, and the insufficiency of park development. And although many seem to agree that low-income urban neighborhoods are a problem because of their density of convenience and liquor stores and dearth of good grocery stores (so-called food deserts), researchers' suppositions are more mixed about the impact of these neighborhoods on physical activity. Some have hypothesized that low-income, dense, urban neighborhoods inhibit physical activity, based on

the supposition that people might fear walking in their neighborhoods (Lee 2006). Others have suggested that the fear of walking might be offset by the necessity of walking among carless residents (Poortinga 2006).

But it would not be enough to conceptualize features of the built environment that contribute to obesity. The researchers would need to find data to approximate those features. But what kinds of data are available? They would likely turn to business censuses to obtain data on things such as the number of restaurants, gyms, and big-box stores found in a geocode, remote-sensing technologies to find operational measures of urban density, and health surveys to obtain data on drive-to-work times. Researchers might also do their own

FIGURE 5.3 Obesity rates by county, 2007 *(age-adjusted percentage of adults ≥20 years old who are obese)*

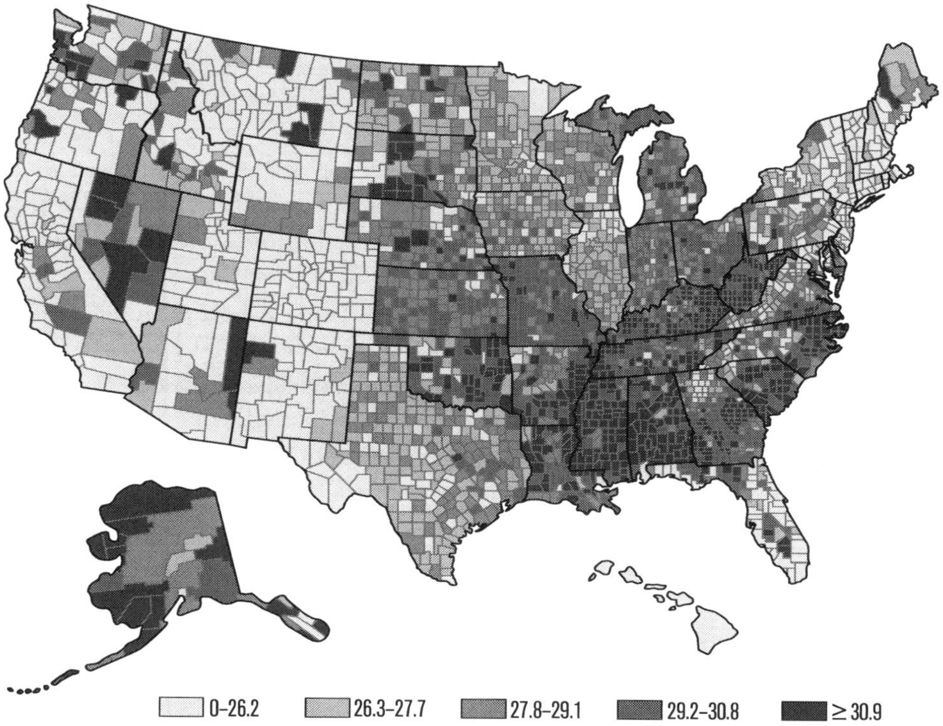

| | 0–26.2 | | 26.3–27.7 | | 27.8–29.1 | | 29.2–30.8 | | ≥ 30.9 |

Source: Behavioral Risk Factor Surveillance System, CDC.

surveying, perhaps walking and driving to estimate travel times to different sorts of businesses. These are typically the sources of data most published studies have used to measure variables such as housing density, vehicle miles traveled, distance to grocery stores, density of fast-food restaurants and convenience stores, and the presence of big-box retailers (Papas et al. 2007). Some have tried to be more creative: one study looked at the number of interstate highway exits in a county as an "instrumental variable" for fast-food availability (Dunn 2008), but a second study directly challenged these conclusions on methodological grounds (Anderson and Matsa 2009).

Finding data would not be the only challenge researchers face. They would also have to make their data geographically commensurate, which might entail aggregating all of their data, including their BMI data, to the largest geographic scale used. Too coarse a scale, though, provides very little information. A demonstrated relationship between the density of fast-food restaurants per square mile and rates of obesity on statewide levels (Maddock 2004) doesn't seem all that convincing. To get that finer-grained analysis, researchers might make compromises in other dimensions of the research. For example, the North American Industry Classification System used in the business census does not differentiate fine dining from family-oriented chain restaurants in the "full-service restaurant" category. Whether that restaurant is Denny's or upscale Charlie Trotter's in Chicago would seem to matter greatly. A study in Erie County, New York, which found a statistically positive relationship between women's BMI and diverse land use, especially when restaurants dominated nonresidential land use, was not able to identify the type of restaurant that predicted higher BMIs (Raja et al. 2010). In the absence of fine-grained data, researchers might be tempted to assume the relationship between features of the built environment and obesity based on a third factor. One study, for example, attempted to look at the relationship between convenient access to fast food and the prevalence of obesity among black and low-income populations focusing on Orleans Parish, Louisiana (Block, Scribner, and DeSalvo 2004). The researchers found that fast-food restaurants were associated with predominately black and low-income neighborhoods, but without equivalent ecologic measures of obesity, they were only able to assert the relationship.

These are just some of the constraints of quantitative models, and it appears that data availability has driven much of the research. Yet, as a result of these constraints, many possible explanations of geographic variation in obesity are not explored, whether cultural, economic, or environmental. Data on, say, cultural attitudes toward appropriate body sizes are hard to quantify, much less collect on a zip code basis. Conversely, data that *are* available at the ecologic level go underutilized in these studies, perhaps because they don't fit existing assumptions about what causes obesity. To my knowledge, no studies have looked at, for example, unemployment rates, housing prices, proximity to cultural centers and institutions of higher learning, or, for that matter, proximity to toxic waste dumps and exposure to pesticide drift. To what extent does this exclusive focus on the supply side of food and physical activity also incorporate existing assumptions about how the problem could be solved?

While the data are in part constrained by existing assumptions about the biological causes of obesity, the method helps reproduce assumptions about the behavioral causes of obesity. Spatial analysis, like epidemiology, can only demonstrate association. These studies pay scant attention to human behavior, because they are methodologically incapable of doing so (Brown and Duncan 2002; Kearns and Moon 2002). In leaving questions of behavior untouched, however, they can easily give the impression that the environment simply acts on people in unmediated ways, as if once you find yourself living in the sprawling suburbs the fat will pile on. Surely, the idea that merely the presence of bad food makes people fat is well circulated. It is fairly explicit in Michael Pollan's (2006: 102) claim, "When food is abundant and cheap, people will eat more of it and get fat." Jane Goodall, Gary McAvoy, and Gail Hudson (1995: 240) make a similar leap when they write, "there is no mechanism that turns off the desire—instinct, really—to eat food when it is available." Since not everyone is in fact fat, and since these writers make great efforts to educate people to the quality of food to encourage informed decisions, they are in effect betraying their healthist sensibilities, suggesting that those who manage to exercise restraint in such environments (or avoid them altogether) must have greater disciplinary powers, taste, and knowledge.

Some researchers let their own interpretations stand in for these unexamined behavioral explanations. Lopez (2004), for example, asked whether some people might choose to live in areas of sprawl in order to avoid walking, but then dismissed that possibility as being unreasonable. Plantinga and Bernell (2005: 490) suggested that consumers make a tradeoff between weight gain and low-price housing. Specifically, they claimed that people who choose low-density suburbs do so to maximize price utility, whereas those who "have a stronger aversion to weight" seek out "healthier locations" (p. 490). And Rosenberger,

Sneh, and Phipps (2005) wondered if areas rich in natural amenities and recreation would attract what they call "healthier migrating populations." So whereas in some spatial analytic studies, subjects are simply treated as objects; in others, people are treated as rational, utility-maximizing actors, with little constraints on their decisions other than, perhaps, income.

As a whole, the results of these studies have been fairly inconclusive. Studies of food environments yield particularly mixed results. The most robust results seem to be in the association of sprawl and obesity. Lopez, for example, used individual-level data from BFRSS with an index of urban sprawl for various metropolitan areas and found modest but significant correlations between sprawl and overweight/obesity after controlling for variables such as gender, age, race or ethnicity, income, education, and diet. Yet, another variant of the physical activity argument produced less robust results. Rosenberger, Sneh, and Phipps (2005) examined the relationship between recreation supply and obesity in West Virginia (one of the fattest states in the country) and found no statistically significant relationship between the quantity of recreation opportunities and rates of obesity across various counties, although they did find a relationship between the quantity of recreation opportunities and rates of physical activity—which they then *presumed* would triangulate to rates of obesity. Notably, however, a study of parks in New York City was able to link access to safe parks, physical activity, and lower BMI (Quinn et al. 2007).

Alas, though, the same questions remain begged: is it really *access* to parks that predicts obesity or is it class/race clustering and segregation across New York City that makes these correlations robust? Likewise, is it really about the *layout* of the suburbs or the situations and characteristics

of people who live in the suburbs? And is it really about all suburbs or particular kinds of suburbs?

A DIFFERENT APPROACH

With these concerns and questions in mind, I set out to ask people who live in so-called obesogenic environments about how their daily practices are affected by their surroundings in ways that most research presumes to affect body size. I was particularly interested in white women, in light of well-documented inverse correlations between socioeconomic status and BMI among this particular group (Chang and Christakis 2005; Lee 2006; Zhang and Wang 2004). Let me be clear on this point: women in all racial groups vary much more in BMI than men do, and white women show greater variation in BMI than any other racial group. So it seemed to me if there was something to be discovered about how the built environment affects obesity, it would be among those whose bodies seem most prone to social influences.

I conducted a small study in 2009–2010 in two different former farming towns in California: Tracy and Fresno. Tracy is located in San Joaquin County, which, as shown in table 5.1, has high rates of obesity in comparison with both state-wide figures and California's thinnest counties, Marin and San Francisco, which are arguably "leptogenic" environments. Although Tracy is a relatively old town in California's Central Valley, it has grown quickly in the past twenty years, primarily because it is within commuting distance of the San Francisco Bay Area, and the high-tech industries of Silicon Valley in particular. It has many of the characteristics that are typically quantified in studies of obesogenic environments: long commute times, sprawling residential housing without walking linkages to public spaces, a dearth of nearby sites for outdoor recreation, and new, auto-oriented retail districts of big-box stores,

TABLE 5.1 Percentage of adults obese or overweight by county, 2007

	San Joaquin	Fresno	Marin	San Francisco	Statewide
Percentage of adults obese	28.9	28.7	13.6	11.8	22.7
Percentage of adults overweight or obese	65.0	63.6	41.9	42.9	57.1
Percentage of white women obese	21.1	19.6	11.8	9.5	18.4
Percentage of white women overweight or obese	58.4	46.2	30.3	30.4	45.4
Median home price (in dollars), Dec. 2008	253,500[a]	157,499	704,545	638,888	

[a]For town of Tracy only

Sources: Overweight and obesity rates: California Health Interview Survey (2007), http://www.chis.ucla.edu/. Median home prices: California Association of Realtors, http://www.car.org/3550/pdf/econpdfs/County_Sales___Price_Statis8.pdf; Median Price of Existing Single-Family Homes; California Association of Realtors, December 2008 Median Prices, http://www.car.org/marketdata/historicalprices/2008medianprices/dec2008medianprices/.

malls, and fast-food and chain restaurants. Fresno, in Fresno County (which also has comparatively high rates of obesity), is an older and larger valley town that has become a city in the past thirty or so years. The most significant difference with Tracy is that residents tend to work in the area rather than commute. Still, it is known for large strips of retail stores and fast-food restaurants. And although the oldest parts of the city are built on a grid with shady streets and sidewalks (typical of older valley towns), the vast majority of space in Fresno is sprawl. For recreational amenities, residents look to the nearby Sierra Nevada foothills for boating and the famous national parks—Yosemite, King's Canyon, and Sequoia—for hiking, climbing, and skiing—all of which are at least a 1.5 hour drive away.

The study involved intensive interviews with middle-aged (35–60) white women, the population with BMIs that vary the most in relation to class and, apparently, location.[2] The percentages of white women considered obese in these two towns are nearly double those in the two thinnest counties, Marin and San Francisco, as shown in table 5.1. Not incidentally, these latter counties are two of the wealthiest, here demonstrated through median

home prices, which were the two highest in the state at the county level in 2008. In selecting twelve women for intensive interviews, I was aiming for maximum variation (in their size and socioeconomic status), in keeping with recommendations of methodologists of small-sample qualitative research (Seidman 2006). Frequency is not a goal of this sort of qualitative research, but depth and cohesion are, and saturation is reached when you find the gem that puts everything in perspective (Morse 1995). Interviews were conducted by my graduate research assistant, who made a best (eyeball) guess whether interviewees fell into "normal," "overweight," "obese," or "morbidly obese" ranges of BMI. (Several interviewees volunteered that information without prompts.)

These interviews revealed quite a bit about the obesogenic environment thesis, namely, that the ideas embedded in the thesis are well enough circulated to have affected how these women felt about where they live. It appears, however, that other aspects of their lives were more salient in affecting their behavior. And, in defiance of the energy balance model, their behavior did not easily map onto their body sizes. In what follows, I draw on interviews to demonstrate these claims. Interviewees' names are fictionalized to protect confidentiality.

The women interviewed were well aware of the ways that their environments are supposed to—and sometimes do—affect behavior. Several interviewees complained about the ubiquity of chain and fast-food restaurants, although women in Fresno, which housed a Whole Foods supermarket and Trader Joe's, were generally more satisfied with options for grocery shopping. (Remarkably, both stores were uniformly associated with healthful eating, as was vegetarianism, despite that much of what is carried at Trader Joe's is snack food and ready-made meals, glorified by labels of "natural" and "organic.") They also spoke approvingly of the farmers markets in each town. Regarding opportunities for physical activity, women in Fresno spoke about traffic and heat as obstacles to walking, while those in Tracy focused on commute times that cut into exercise opportunities. In both places, women mentioned the need to drive long distances to take advantage of outdoor recreation amenities but also noted the existence of plenty of gyms in town, for those who *like* to use them.

Cynthia, an obese, moderate-income woman in her late forties, discussed how several aspects of the obesogenic environment concatenate in Tracy:

> The problem with Tracy is that it's primarily a commuter community. We have a lot of people in Tracy that have moved here to try and get away from high prices and find family life. But they commute. So they leave at 4, 5:30, or 6 in the morning and they don't get home until 6:30, 7 o'clock at night so there's lots of picking up food on the way home. Their kids are involved in sports so they're helping their kids chasing all their sports but a lot of times that involves late . . . eating fast food . . . eating Taco Bell: that kind of stuff on the way to the game,

on the way to practice, or whatever else is going on. So unless you really live and work in Tracy, it's hard to stay in a healthy regime because of your lifestyle.

Beth, a middle-class (moderate-income, homeowner) "obese" woman in her early fifties from Fresno, made an explicit comparison with a "healthier" environment, in this case, Lake Tahoe. According to Beth, who had grown up in the Central Valley, but had also lived in Lake Tahoe,

> The food options in Fresno suck. They totally suck. Like in Tahoe if you stopped off at the coffee place you could get a healthy something to eat. Even their cookie was healthy and then in Fresno you drive back and it's all fast food, it's all processed. You can't even get anything good to eat here. It's all chains. It's sad. It really is sad.

Beth also compared Fresno to Tahoe in terms of walkability. She said she used to walk in Tahoe, but didn't like to walk in Fresno because she gets "hot, sweaty and ugly."

Indeed, almost all of the women disliked where they lived—and thought they'd be different, thinner, if they lived elsewhere. Those in Tracy complained about the lack of proximity to places they wanted to go and the disappearance or absence of community. People in both towns looked to other places— often the coast or mountains—as places where they could live the lives they really wanted and, for that matter, enjoy the food and exercise opportunities that these towns lack. Despite her professed love for Fresno, including the smells and "the earthy feel of the farm community," Susan, who was mildly obese and who had been big as a child, preferred to eat out on the coast, and also commented that she did more walking on the coast, which she visited regularly. Janine, who was very big (and had always been so) even though she belonged to a community-supported agriculture program and was delighted to cook homemade meals with the local, fresh produce, spoke wistfully about her days living in Santa Rosa, where there was nice scenery for walking and biking and not just the mall or gyms. Most strikingly, Rachel, who had become morbidly obese in her adult life, had traveled a lot and lived in Sweden and associated her time in Sweden with better health, even though the food was fatty ("mayo and cheese") and even though she couldn't exercise in the cold winters. Living there was "more inspiring to her artistic side," while Fresno made her feel "dull and bored and frustrated." Then she stated quite explicitly that she'd be thinner if she lived elsewhere—not only because she'd eat healthier food but also because she'd lead a more enchanted, less stressed-out life.

By the same token, several women expressed relief that these places allowed them an opportunity to let go of difficult-to-attain bodily norms. This sense of comfort reflects a variant of the obesogenic environment thesis, albeit one that is often applied to African Americans. To wit, studies that have sought to test whether BMI values are higher in African American communities hypothesize that shared norms, values, and beliefs shape notions of acceptable body sizes (Boardman et al. 2005; Robert and Reither 2004). Several of these women stated that they felt comfortable in Fresno or Tracy precisely because of the way they looked relative to those around them. Beth noted that she felt better about her body than she did when she was eighteen and stuck out for being fat; now, "I feel like a lot of people look like me so yeah it's much easier." Susan also noted a climate of body acceptability in Fresno, as demonstrated by the lack of high-end stores and the prevalence of what she called "industrial clothes." Janine's fond remembrances of Santa Rosa were tempered by having "to worry

about size 00 walking by you." As she said about Fresno, "Yeah we're just not like a couture area. We're just not on that cutting edge of Fashion Week and this and that and it's just not, you're not on display here; it's not like, oh the beautiful people live in LA or they live in NY or in Hawaii or whatever." In other words, there was something about the social context of Fresno and Tracy that allowed for bigger bodies—and they noticed it.

The Experience of Class

To the extent that interviewees felt their lives constrained by their environments, in discussing their daily lives, it appears that other aspects, particularly those related to class, were much more salient in affecting their eating and exercise behaviors. Many women mentioned the cost of Whole Foods, and the less financially secure women most definitely shopped at discount grocers and stores where they could buy generic food in bulk. A couple claimed they sought out cheap fast food because they could get a lot for little money. One of the thinnest women interviewed, by the way, was also the least financially secure. Cathy had lived in Fresno her entire life and because of her limited budget ate from fast-food restaurants, big-box stores, and wholesale groceries, and always bought the cheapest food, careful not to buy name brands because of the extra cost. Even then, the cost of food was not necessarily the most determinate factor in affecting what and how they ate; some did not have partners to help shop for and prepare food. And some noted that it was their male partners who preferred buying at the cheaper places and cooking with more meat. Strikingly, a couple of the larger women talked about their lack of interest and talent in preparing food, one to the point of rancor. They would buy fresh vegetables that "would just rot in the fridge." For Rachel, it came down to a matter of time.

I would have a chef who would make healthy meals. Like, I like healthy meals, when I go eat, like, vegetarian (I was a vegetarian for a year, I just wasn't able to sustain it). You know I love healthy stuff when it's cooked well; I just don't want to do it myself. It just takes too much time and I'm not that interested in food preparation. But I can appreciate it, you know, and I love to eat a good healthy meal when someone else makes it. Maybe that's laziness but again, time.

Not only time, but also issues with child care, and especially stress, made a couple of interviewees quite adamant. Beth, for example, who detested the Fresno environment, attributed having reached two hundred pounds by the time she was eighteen, not to the environment per se, but to stress:

I would start off every year, school year, lost weight during the summer (would really focus on it) and then would always gain ten or so pounds during the year because I was so stressed out raising my daughter by myself. Her dad only took her two weekends a month so I took her the rest, I had all the responsibility. And then starting the teaching career there's so much stress on being wonderful. And I don't know, there was a point when I hit like pre-menopause about 40, where I just put on 20 pounds and couldn't wear any of my clothes so I'd wear the same crappy things, like 5 things. I don't know, I went through this weird period where I just put on a lot of weight and got really stressed out and pulled back. And I don't know if I ever really came out of it. … I used to just say, just flat out, "I'm bitter. I'm very bitter."

And Jackie, a single mom whose former husband had died and who was in a pretty tenuous economic situation, noted several ways in which her situation affected her ability to maintain supposedly healthy practices. For example, she didn't particularly like fast food but her son loved it. She also said she couldn't afford Whole Foods. She reported having hardly any time to herself and sleeping three hours a night. She didn't use the weight room in her apartment building because she couldn't bring her son. She wouldn't have minded walking but had no one to take care of her son while she was out. Basically, she was at her wit's end:

I'm obviously obese. I need to lose weight. I know that I should. Yeah so, I mean, it's funny because in college I was a runner and I was half my size, you know, so I know what it's like to be thin and feeling good and being buff. But, especially since I've moved to Fresno, I've had a lot, a lot of stress, and when I am stressed I eat. And I've had more stress than you can even imagine.

It is worth noting here that several recent studies have found connections between stress and obesity, specifically the kind of stress that affects those whose work situations afford them little control or autonomy. And it is not necessarily stress eating that accounts for increased weight, suggesting that other biological mechanisms are at work (cf. Berlant 2007). Rather, elevated cortisol, the stress hormone, is strongly associated with visceral fat accumulation and metabolic syndrome (Björntorp 2001; Rosmond 2005). To the extent that these aspects of class do potentially affect size, they are not incorporated into models of obesogenic environments that focus on proximity and affordability.

Nevertheless, it *is* class that appears to prevent these women from living where they might want. Virtually all of the interviewees lived in Fresno and Tracy because of affordability, where, as shown in table 5.1, median housing prices are far below those in the more desirable places of Marin and San Francisco. Either they never had the opportunity to leave or they moved there, especially Tracy, because they could afford to buy a home. Cynthia, a Tracy interviewee, moved to Tracy when "prices in San Jose went off the charts." But when asked where she'd most like to live, she said Santa Cruz, where she had grown up. Likewise, Mary moved to Tracy expecting to stay there for only five years. Rachel was quite explicit that she never intended to stay in Fresno but that finances had gotten in the way of moving. With class so salient in their clearly constrained choices to live in these places, it wouldn't seem farfetched to argue that it is class that explains the prevalence of obesity rates in these towns, more than the built environment per se. Consider the following.

The Place of Class

Contemporary geographers emphasize that spatial patterns in housing, commercial development, and public-land access are a reflection of social relations of race and class rather than a producer of them (Schein 2006). These spatialized patterns of race and class have accentuated in an era when many economic development opportunities stem from the buying power and tax-ability of local residents (Massey and Denton 1998). Consider the origins of two of the kinds of urban environments associated with obesogeneity. One is the so-called food desert, a term used to describe low-income urban neighborhoods, generally inhabited by people of color, with a paucity of supermarkets and other venues to purchase healthful fruits, vegetables, meats, and grain products, often coupled with an abundance of liquor and convenience stores where

only snack food and highly processed ready-to-eat meals can be purchased (Cummins and Macintyre 2002). The existence of such neighborhoods is rooted in racist insurance and lending practices (redlining), which have historically made it difficult to develop and sustain businesses in certain areas (Eisenhauer 2001). Importantly, the food desert phenomenon is also attributed to white flight and the net loss of supermarkets to suburbs with larger sites, fewer zoning impediments, and customers with greater purchasing power (Alwitt and Donley 1997; Cotterill and Franklin 1995). These are the urban ghettos conceived as too scary for walking.

Juxtaposed with the investment-starved urban ghetto and landscapes of dearth, the other problem landscape is one of new investment and excess, albeit the cheap kind. These expansive working- and middle-class suburbs owe much to new waves of regional economic development in the form of big-box stores, malls, and outlet centers—as well as the white flight that created food deserts in the urban cores. Much of this was driven by localities starved for tax revenue that encouraged such retail development to generate sales tax revenue. As the foreclosure crisis has taught, much contemporary suburban sprawl has also been driven by developers and mortgage bankers encouraging a struggling, debt-ridden middle class to move far from the urban core to take advantage of cheap housing in areas with lower land values. In other words, to the extent that some places have many features that are supposedly obesogenic, it reflects the financial resources of those who inhabit such places and the waves of investment and disinvestment that have produced such environments. Therefore, what may be "predicting" the prevalence of obesity in certain places is, in fact, race and class (putting aside for now what produces variation in size relative to race and class), with features of the built environment being an effect of that spatial patterning rather than a cause.

That brings me to Diane from Fresno, the exception that possibly proves the rule. Diane was an educated, solidly middle-class woman with a long marriage and adult children. Although she claimed she had a "weight problem" as a teenager, she was thin at the time of the interview, possibly below the normal range of BMI. Diane admitted to being price conscious, especially since her family had hit some hard times. For example, she said she had a hard time justifying buying apples at Whole Foods for her own family. Diane also recognized that living in Fresno limited her exercise opportunities because "the air quality sucks" and it is intensely hot in the summer—both of which, she acknowledged, got in the way of outdoor activity, as does the long drive to the national parks. Diane never imagined she would have stayed in Fresno. And yet, Diane attributed the family's staying in Fresno precisely to their financial situation. When discussing the air quality, she said: "That's one of the weird things about Fresno. We live here. Obviously you financially can't just pick up and move. We deal with it."

Still, Diane managed to negotiate much of this environment, which for her depended on time possibly even more than money. Rather than worrying too much about food, she managed to run two miles a day, despite the heat and smog, or work out at the gym, noting at several junctures "the privilege of time."

> I realize I have to take personal responsibility for me, knowing that I don't have the freedom to walk in a climate that's limiting. Like I said, transitional months (fall and spring) are great. I realize that I have the luxury of being able to run in the morning. I'm not a single mom. I don't have to get on the bus to go to a job. We have the luxury of belonging to this little health club, you know, where we can stop in there and swim

if we want or use the weights. That's a luxury. I realize that. If I was working full-time, single mom, had to come home and do the second shift with my children. If I was on a limited income and your question before, "*When you go shopping are you cost conscious?*" hell no, I wouldn't be, we wouldn't be able to really eat the way we do now.

Yet, it was Diane's remarks on her love-hate relationship with Fresno that was the gem that put everything in perspective. She was quite excited about the emerging arts scene in Fresno and how that was affecting the cultural value of Fresno:

> Well, it's interesting that Fresno has always been the butt of a lot of jokes culturally when I was growing up but it's really gone through a lot of cool changes. I told you we were coming from downtown art hop open studio night. There's a great theater here. There's a lot of interesting revitalization downtown. There's the university has great things to do as well.

This quotation, along with several nods to "personal responsibility," suggests that Diane had taken on norms of body management that are associated with higher-status people—and higher-status places. As she put it, "So for me and my needs to stay healthy, I'd have to not blame it on Fresno and I'd have to just be creative."

OBESOGENIC SPACES AND IDEAL PLACES

Diane's comments, along with those of several other interviewees, suggest a perceived disjuncture between healthy lifestyles and places like Fresno. If Fresno's environment is so problematic, what does a healthy, or leptogenic, environment look like and, more important, who can afford to live there? What I am suggesting is that the concept of the obesogenic environment reveals unstated preferences for places with the amenities often associated with urbane, privileged environments, including university towns, artsy enclaves, gentrified urban cores, and even older well-heeled suburbs. By lauding environments unobtainable to most, we begin to see how the obesogenic environment thesis might help produce a social geography.

On the food side, it is surely striking that the distinction between food deserts and food cornucopia is confusing. Is the problem dearth or ubiquity? When you separate the wheat from the chaff of the claims, it becomes clear that the critique is really not about ubiquity and more about the availability of too much of the wrong food (fast and junky) relative to the right food (fresh and wholesome). The case in point is an emerging discourse that characterizes endless strip malls of chain restaurants and fast-food joints as food deserts because they lack "real food" (Breitbach 2007). Those who tout the obesogenic environment thesis would hardly characterize ubiquitous farmers markets and gourmet market halls, upscale restaurants, and natural food stores as a problem.

The distinction between the damned and the preferred is even odder but equally pronounced on the physical activity side. The problem of suburban sprawl is not only the absence of sidewalks and the presence of freeways but, it seems, the absence of unique character or interesting form (Ritzer 1993). Curiously, though, since some suburbs are not known or tested as obesogenic, they seem to escape this critique. This would include the elite older suburbs of New York, Boston, Philadelphia, and Chicago, or, here in California, the exurbs of Marin County, again one of the thinnest places in the state. Marin County, for instance, would by several measures count as an obesogenic environment, with its low housing density, long commute times, and large malls and strips replete with fast food,

although some would note the upscale restaurants and markets and the beautiful recreational amenities alongside those "obesogenic" features (but again, would a spatial model capture this mix?). Equally confusing is the finding that mixed-use areas have lower rates of obesity than residential ones (Lopez 2004). This would not be surprising to anyone who has traipsed through the Upper West Side of Manhattan or San Francisco's Noe Valley. And yet, the Bronx and South Side of Chicago are also "mixed use" but are apparently obesogenic nevertheless. Studies that speak to fear of walking (Lee 2006) or lack of "safe" parks (Quinn et al. 2007) raise further doubts that the issue is really just a matter of spatial layout.

Furthermore, for a thesis that aspires to name structural and environmental causes it actually returns a great deal of responsibility—or lack thereof—to individuals (Kirkland 2010). Too much food and too little sidewalk translate into too much eating and too little exercise, where the environment plays a mediating role, at best. And yet, since the thesis doesn't allow much for the agency of people who inhabit these environments, it reinforces the idea that they are unthinking dupes, without personal responsibility. Only those who manage to escape these environments or mediate them well, such as Diane, are endowed with agency. So the thesis also reveals unstated preferences for certain lifestyles associated with self-efficacy, personal responsibility, and, apparently, a good deal of time and money to take advantage of the amenities the favored environments offer.

In short, the thesis takes the tenets of healthism and lifestylism and projects them onto the built environment. Just as healthism tends to laud the lifestyles of those with class and race privilege, this spatialized healthism tends to laud spaces made by class and race privilege. The problem is that if the idealized "leptogenic" environment is one of privilege, there are limits to how much we can redress the obesogenic environment without confronting class and racial inequality.

BEYOND THE BUILT ENVIRONMENT AND THE SUPPLY SIDE

The obesogenic environment thesis, with its focus on access and proximity to grocery stores, restaurants, parks, gyms, and public transportation, leads to the conclusion that if these conditions are changed, behaviors will follow. It thus draws forth a set of interventions that are strongly supply-sided. Arguably, that is the reason that public health professionals and food system advocates have embraced the thesis. Supply-side interventions are reasonably palatable politically and provide clarity about what to do. Accordingly, public health advocates have put a good deal of effort into soda bans in schools or good neighbor agreements that ask corner liquor stores to sell fruits and vegetables, or even creating more walkable public space in new suburbs.

And those who endorse such efforts often do so in the name of combating racial and class inequality. Yet, if these obesogenic environments are as inseparable from race and class as I contend they are, picking out particular features of the built environment and making them more leptogenic isn't likely to cut it as a body-size-altering strategy—and may have unintended consequences. It effaces the problem that the very conditions and amenities that make certain places sites of "the good life" make them unobtainable to most. It must be remembered that elite suburbs themselves came into being in escape from the "dangerous classes" of the city in an earlier historical period (Szasz 2007). And these gentrified urban cores that allow rarified eating and walking in public space are themselves products of particular economic development strategies to attract capital,

which in doing so displace those with fewer means (Smith 1996).

Towns and cities with artistic, independent, and healthful restaurants, beautiful outdoor amenities, vibrant public spaces, and unique character are "leptogenic," to be sure. But they are leptogenic not only because of the food choices and physical activity opportunities they offer. They are leptogenic because wealth has made them into even more pleasant (but costly places). That is because places with wealth both attract businesses to meet the food tastes of residents and generate the taxes to improve and maintain those enjoyable public spaces. Yet the more wealth they attract, the more they become inaccessible to many, as home prices follow. Thin real estate is expensive.

On that note, I have continued to skirt the question of the relationship between socioeconomic status and body size. Most people assume that it derives directly from energy intake relative to expenditure, and therefore that the wealthy white women who differ from their poorer peers must eat much less and exercise much more. Chang and Christakis (2005) suggest that the importance of thinness as a means to maintain and display class status makes high-income white women work harder at it. Others have argued that body size is a cause of class status rather than the inverse (Julier 2008; Kirkland 2010). This is based on the many studies that have demonstrated how weight bias affects people across the course of their lives, including student-teacher relations, college admissions, marital prospects, and job advancement. Kirkland and Julier's point is not that thinness guarantees you high status, although a thin body and a beautiful face do seem to be a vehicle for upward mobility for some women (through, for example, marriage, the beauty professions, and to some extent the sex trade); it is that fatness pretty much guarantees that you will not have high status. The question of what begets which is far from settled, [...]. Suffice it to say that just as living in Fresno and Tracy relaxes pressures to be thin, living in wealthy areas seems to intensify pressures to be thin. By the same token, the features and resources available in thin and fat places affect the possibilities for self-management in such places, so the relationship between size and place seems profoundly iterative.

No matter what, to replicate features of the leptogenic environment to make people thin is unlikely to be efficacious. Kirkland (2010) likens efforts to get people to lose weight in order to make them higher status to programs to promote marriage among the poor because married people are healthier and wealthier. Such programs miss the point. Analogously, so might programs to make people thin by replicating the environments of wealthy people. But these programs are not just missing the point. Trying to make environments more like those of the wealthy upholds an economic differentiation of urban landscape that could have perverse social justice ramifications. Already efforts to redress the supply-side problems, such as community gardens, farmers markets, and spruced-up parks, have led to gentrification, which is why people in low-income areas are beginning to reject such projects (Quastel 2009).

So when the food and health writers glorify certain places for the qualities they have (e.g., gentrified urban cores) and devalue others for their dearth (e.g., food deserts), they actually contribute to the problem. It is precisely this simultaneously cultural and economic valuation process that George Lipsitz describes in *The Possessive Investment in Whiteness* (1998), in which he shows how the legacies of racist housing policy actually produced wealth for whites in the suburbs in inverse relationship to African Americans in the inner cities. Bringing wealth and investment to certain places and leaving others behind are causally linked processes (Szasz 2007). So even if you could prove that the built environment matters in terms of contributing to obesity through practices of the self that they encourage or discourage, you can't address the problem without addressing class cultures, class inequalities, and the policies that continue to heighten or exacerbate them. And yet [...], it is not so clear that it is only self-practices that are contributing to changes and variation in size, which, among other things, further complicates the presumed relationship between class and socioeconomic status.

NOTES

1   In truth, the *Men's Fitness* methodology is hopelessly flawed. Not only does it mix indicators of health conditions with city characteristics and policy initiatives, it weighs these indicators in nontransparent ways. If you dig around a little, it becomes apparent that the editors choose in advance what cities they want to promote—or disparage—and then find measures to make their case. In a funny way, it is a textbook example of coproduction.

2   Although I prioritized this group, the study ended up including one Latina and one woman of mixed race (Asian/white) because I did not want to be exclusive in a snowball sample.

READING 6

Health Social Movements

History, Current Work, and Future Directions

Phil Brown, Crystal Adams, Rachel Morello-Frosch, Laura Senier, and Ruth Simpson

The last several decades have seen a burgeoning movement in health activism in which patients, consumers, and other lay people, sometimes in conjunction with scientists and health-care professionals, have lobbied for a more active role in defining and finding solutions for health concerns. In the 1960s the women's health movement began challenging prevailing conceptions of medical authority, feminine sexuality, and reproductive rights, with consequent changes in medical research, practice, and standards. In the 1970s and 1980s mental health activists advocated for patients' rights, while AIDS activists fought to expand the funding and scope of research and treatment, as well as the role of patient-activists in research decisions. More recent health social movements have taken on issues such as medical service cutbacks, insurance restrictions, discrimination against the disabled, and, through the environmental justice movement, the unequal distribution of exposure to environmental hazards. This recent activism is noteworthy in part for the emergence of citizen-science alliances in which citizens and scientists collaborate on issues that usually have been identified by lay people. These movements have in turn spawned an increase in scholarly activity related to health activism. Over the past decade several thematic conferences and an increasing number of articles and special issues of scholarly

journals have focused attention on health social movements: special streams at the 2001 and 2003 conferences of the Society for the Social Study of Science, a workshop at the American Sociological Association's Collective Behavior and Social Movements Section Conference in 2002, a Medical Social Movements symposium in Sweden in 2003 that led to a *Social Science and Medicine* special issue on patient-based social movements in 2006, a special issue of *Annals of the American Academy of Political and Social Science* on health and the environment in 2002 (edited by Phil Brown), the *Sociology of Health and Illness* 2004 annual monograph on health social movements (later a book edited by Phil Brown and Stephen Zavestoski), and a conference on social movements and health institutions at the University of Michigan in 2007 from which a volume will shortly be published.

In their campaigns, health activists routinely address the same issues that have long concerned medical sociologists. For example, in challenging traditional roles and systems of knowledge, members of health social movements are highly attuned to how the authority of experts and social institutions—such as medical professionals, health-care organizations, and government agencies—affects the health-care process. Like sociologists of health and illness, many activists seek to understand how health problems are socially constructed, so they

Phil Brown, et al., "Health Social Movements: History, Current Work, and Future Directions," Handbook of Medical Sociology, pp. 380-394. Copyright © 2010 by Vanderbilt University Press. Reprinted with permission.

101

can better grasp the trajectories of the illness experience and can improve conditions for patients. Campaigns for health and social justice focus attention on the social determinants of health and disease and criticize systematic injustices or patterns of inequality that negatively affect health and quality of life. Health social movements and the scholarly work that focuses on them thus cut across many of the core theoretical concerns of medical sociology, such as medicalization, stratification, authority, and empowerment.

But despite the concerns that health social movements share with medical sociologists, and despite the existence of a well-developed scholarly literature about the health social movements themselves, medical sociology has traditionally not incorporated the conceptual or methodological lessons of health activism and the health social movement literature. This is surprising, given that the public health literature has actively engaged in studies of health activism, especially in terms of community-based participatory research, where community groups and individuals are involved from the beginning of a research question through the entire process of research, dissemination, and policy application. There are a number of possible reasons for this apparent disconnect between health social movements and medical sociology. Conceivably, the traditional exclusion from medical sociology of the physiological and biological dimensions of disease (Timmermans and Haas 2008) has discouraged exploration of health social movements, where patients' accounts of symptoms and their contesting of medical definitions of disease play such central roles. Perhaps the current lack of attention to health social movements owes something to the early divide described by Straus (1957) as the "the sociology *of* medicine" versus "sociology *in* medicine," a gulf that has narrowed but not disappeared (Bird, Conrad, and Fremont 2000). The degree to which health social movement

researchers work closely with activists and their goals may seem to threaten the independent critical perspective valued by those who identify as sociologists *of* medicine. Similarly, sociologists *in* medicine, already on the defensive for their collaborative work with health-care professionals and institutions, may be reluctant to add health activists to that list. Of course, the reasons for the separate lives of health social movements and medical sociology may be more mundane: the realities of academic specialization and associated professional pressures impede mutual awareness across any number of scholarly disciplines and subfields. In that sense, the disconnect between medical sociology and the health social movement literature may simply result from want of routine contact—a situation we seek to change with this chapter.

Medical sociologists may often be unaware of the importance of health social movements for the sociological analysis of health and illness and associated actors and institutions. Yet studies of health social movements—particularly citizen-science alliances and other forms of community-based participatory research—have much to offer medical sociology conceptually and methodologically. First, health social movement research directs attention to a range of actors and institutions outside the traditional focus of medical sociology that nonetheless contribute to how diseases are perceived and addressed. Second, the literature on health social movements helps illuminate the development of patient identity—a process closely linked to health social movements that has profound consequences for the ways patients will interact with the medical system. Third, the existence of citizen-science alliances in health social movements and the use of community-based participatory research in the health social movement literature affords an opportunity to bridge (or avoid) some of the divides within medical sociology and sociology as a whole, such as the gap between theory and practice. Finally, because health social movements represent actors actively engaged in questioning, challenging, and exploring the existence and causes of disease, studying health social movements offers the opportunity to engage in vibrant, cutting-edge research.

In this chapter, after a brief introduction to health social movements, we explain in detail how attention to health social movements and the health social movement literature would enhance the ways medical sociologists approach their own theoretical, methodological, and practical- and policy-related challenges. Finally, we discuss the applications of health social movement research for medical sociology and illustrate its utility through a case study.

A HISTORICAL AND CONCEPTUAL OUTLINE OF HEALTH SOCIAL MOVEMENTS

Drawing on Della Porta and Diani's definition of social movements (1998), we define health social movements as informal networks comprised of an array of formal and informal organizations, supporters, networks of cooperation, and media that mobilize specifically in response to issues of health-care policy and politics, medical research and practice, and medical and scientific belief systems. In doing so, health social movements challenge political power, professional authority, and personal and collective identity (Zavestoski et al. 2002; McCormick, Brown, and Zavestoski 2003).

Organized activism around health issues dates back to the Industrial Revolution, when activists within the settlement house movement crusaded against urban poverty and industrial hygienists sought to improve health and safety conditions for workers (Waitzkin 2000). Women led much of that early organizing and were leaders as well in the 1960s when women's health activists' challenge to medical authority significantly altered

medical conceptions of feminine behavior and sexuality, broadened reproductive rights, expanded funding and services, influenced standards of care, and changed medical research and practice (Ruzek 1978; Ruzek, Olesen, and Clarke 1997; Morgen 2002). Beginning in the 1980s, AIDS activists fought for expanded funding for research and treatment, increased appreciation for and integration of alternative treatment approaches, and won major victories in the design and execution of clinical trials (including the right of patient-activists to participate in decisions about allocation of research dollars and discussions about research design [see Epstein 1996]). Self-care and alternative care activists have broadened health professionals' awareness of people's ability to deal with health problems in ways not necessarily sanctioned by allopathic medicine (Goldstein 1999). Mental patients' rights activists obtained major reforms in mental health care, demanding recognition of basic human and civil rights of mental patients and their right to better treatment and to refuse treatment (Brown 1984). Occupational health and safety movements have brought medical and governmental attention to a wide range of ergonomic, radiation, chemical, and stress hazards in workplaces, leading to extensive regulation and the creation of the Occupational Safety and Health Administration and National Institute of Occupational Safety and Health (Rosner and Markowitz 1987).

More recently, health social movements have broadened their focus from patient rights and standards of medical care to health access and social justice inequalities, targeting health-care organizations and governmental agencies in the process. Citizens have fought against hospital closings, medical service cutbacks, and restrictions by insurers (Waitzkin 2001). Disability rights activists have won major advances in areas such as accessibility and job discrimination, and countered stigmas against people with disabilities (Shapiro 1993). Toxic waste activists have brought national attention to the health risks of chemicals, radiation, air pollution, and other hazards, helping obtain regulations and bans on toxics, and remediate many hazardous sites (Brown and Mikkelsen 1990; Brown 2007). Environmental justice activists have expanded on toxic waste activism by demonstrating the class and race inequalities of environmental burdens (Bullard 2000). Their early focus on the siting of hazardous waste facilities has expanded to show how low-income communities and communities of color also suffer from a lack of environmental amenities such as parks and open spaces (Agyeman 2005).

While many participants in health social movements have been lay people, health professionals have also formed advocacy groups around health issues. Physicians, for example, have organized to advance health care for the underserved, to seek a national health plan, and to oppose the nuclear arms race (McCally 2002).

Health Social Movements: A Typology

We can usefully categorize health social movements (HSMs) into three types according to their dominant goals (Brown et al. 2004).[1] Health access movements seek equitable access to health care and improved provision of health-care services. These include movements such as those seeking national health-care reform, increased ability to pick specialists, and coverage of the uninsured. Constituency-based health movements, such as the women's health movement, gay and lesbian health movement, and environmental justice movement, concentrate on health inequalities rooted in race, ethnicity, gender, class, sexuality, or a combination of these. They address unequal health outcomes, unequal oversight by the scientific community, and scientific findings that are weak or tainted by conflicts of interest. Embodied health movements

address disease, disability, or the experience of illness by challenging accepted scientific and medical perspectives on etiology, diagnosis, treatment, and prevention. Embodied health movements often mobilize around "contested illnesses" (Brown 2007) that are either unexplained (or even unacknowledged) by current medical science or whose purported cause is disputed (such causes are often, but by no means always, environmental). Contested illnesses require activists to organize to achieve medical recognition, treatment, and research. Embodied health movements include the breast cancer movement, the AIDS movement, and the tobacco control movement. Some established embodied health movements, such as breast cancer activism, include constituents who are not ill, but who consider themselves at risk of disease. Regardless, embodied health movements make the biological body central to social movements, primarily in terms of the embodied experience of disease-affected people, as in the disability rights movement (Fleischer and Zames 2002), and women's health movements (Morgen 2002). While the examples we include in this chapter focus on controversies in environmental health, many HSMs address nonenvironmental issues. The broader breast cancer movement, for example, works to guarantee women access to treatment and patient involvement in treatment and research. In the realm of infectious disease, Lyme disease sufferers faced challenges in getting their illness recognized and addressed by the medical establishment (Weintraub 2008).

Our interest in embodied health movements developed during a period of conflict among schools of thought within the social movements field. Our focus on embodied health movements allowed us to draw from these schools of thought rather than become enmeshed in the conflict itself. Like resource mobilization theory (e.g., Jenkins 1983; McCarthy and Zald 1977), our conceptualization of embodied health movements emphasizes the importance of the development of social movement organizations, although we reject resource mobilization theory's emphasis on rational action, as it would downplay the importance of grievance in the formation of embodied health movements. We draw on the political opportunity approach (McAdam 1982; McAdam, McCarthy, and Zald 1996; Tilly 1978) to emphasize how changing political circumstances and alliances can affect the ability of an embodied health movement to gain attention and recognition, although we extend our focus to include arenas other than state and political bodies, such as science, medicine, and the individual illness experience. The frame alignment perspective (e.g., Benford and Snow 2000; Snow et al. 1986) has been useful for understanding how those involved in embodied health movements emphasize solutions and agendas that will resonate with the personal experiences, values, and expectations of potential supporters, although such frame alignment strategies are initially viable only among illness sufferers or those closely allied with them. Finally, we share with new social movement theory the goal of understanding social movements that are not well explained by traditional models, although we have found that its dismissal of the significance of social class in postindustrial societies (Fitzgerald and Rodgers 2000) does not ring true for many embodied health movements where unequal access to housing, transportation, and economic development are tightly connected to the understanding and experience of illness (Brown et al. 2003, Morello-Frosch et al. 2006).

Citizen-Science Alliances

Embodied health movements often involve citizen-science alliances in which activists collaborate with scientists and health professionals in pursuing treatment, prevention, research, and expanded funding. Citizen-science alliances represent the willingness of citizens and scientists to go beyond an us-versus-them paradigm in order to develop innovative organizational forms that can effectively address the social determinants of health. Citizens bring insights from their personal illness experience and scientists contribute their technical skills and knowledge. These alliances contribute to new knowledge, and they also challenge—and sometimes change—scientific norms by valuing the experience and knowledge of illness sufferers. Citizen-science alliances may be citizen initiated, professionally initiated, or created through a joint affinity model in which lay and researcher interests are aligned.

Examples of citizen-science alliances include AIDS activists who have sought a place at the scientific table so that their personal illness experiences can help shape research design (Epstein 1996). Breast cancer activists have been involved in federal and state review panels, as well as in democratizing foundations' funding processes (Brown et al. 2006). Asthma activists have cooperated with scientists in projects linking air pollution to respiratory illnesses in urban neighborhoods that house bus depots and transit hubs (Shepard et al. 2002). Citizen-science alliances have also been important in the environmental breast cancer, environmental justice, and environmental health movements, which are concerned with the role of chemical and industrial exposures in human health. Participants in these movements have become involved in a new form of activism that helps generate new evidence of the omnipresent chemical assault by petrochemicals, plastics, and other industrial sectors.

Community-based participatory research (CBPR) programs are the most far-reaching example of citizen-science alliances. In CBPR programs, members of an affected community engage in the research process alongside scientists, social scientists, medical professionals, and other researchers. Drawing on their own experiences as members of the affected community, they participate in the definition of research questions and design, assist in carrying out the study, help disseminate information back to the community and the broader public, and actively help shape resulting policies. CBPR is thus inclusive of all affected parties and all potential end-users of the research, including community-based organizations, public health practitioners, and local health and social services agencies (Shepard et al. 2002; Israel et al. 1998). More comprehensive citizen involvement in research often occurs as a social problem becomes more public and the accompanying social movement gains strength and momentum.

CBPR and citizen-science alliances can expose tensions associated with merging sociological scholarship with research connected to specific policy goals. This linking of sociological research and policy action understandably raises concerns about the researcher's ability to maintain objectivity and a critical perspective on the social phenomena under study. While such tensions exist, it is possible to manage them through more intensive dialogue with community participants about research methods and by an increased focus on research methods to improve the rigor and integrity of the overall study design. As a mode of knowledge production, CBPR broadens the research process by ensuring that stakeholders have access to the process and results of knowledge production. Researchers who work on CBPR projects and in citizen-science alliances must find ways to negotiate the tensions that arise in working with multiple stakeholders. Later in this chapter, we describe some specific challenges that have arisen in designing research that meets rigorous scientific standards while also addressing the needs and concerns of community stakeholders. Ultimately, CBPR advances the public good by producing scientifically rigorous research that also has significant policy applications.

Policy Ethnography

In our research, we have come to rely on policy ethnography (Brown et al., 2010), a form of extended, multisited ethnography that studies social movements by including organizational and policy analysis alongside ethnographic observations and interviews, and that operates with a policy goal in mind (in some cases, policy ethnographers themselves engage in policy advocacy). We developed this approach when traditional ethnography proved too limited for our particular research situations. What happens in one health social movement organization is related to larger social movement networks and also involves institutions such as science and government. Therefore, one cannot separately address science, activism, and policy. Policy ethnography offers a more holistic outlook that integrates micro-, meso-, and macrolevels of society, targets the centrality of social movement interaction with science, and situates movements within large, complex fields.

In our practice, policy ethnography combines ethnographic interview and observation material, background history on the organizations we study, current and historical policy analysis, evaluation of the scientific basis for policy making and regulation, and in some cases engaging in policy advocacy through ongoing collaborations with health social movements. While a good deal of ethnography may engage in the first four elements to some extent, policy ethnography suggests that integrating sociology scholarship with the practical policy applications of CBPR can reveal the broader impacts of health social movements in reshaping regulatory science and policy making to protect community health.

HEALTH SOCIAL MOVEMENTS

AND MEDICAL SOCIOLOGY

The challenges that health social movements pose to professional and disciplinary boundaries (through embodied health movements and citizen-science alliances) and the ways health social movements connect research directly to policy formation (through community-based participatory research) mean the health social movement literature is a rich resource for any medical sociologist. Here we discuss four ways that medical sociology can benefit from attention to the health social movement literature. First, the literature has helped to identify and explore the range of nonmedical actors and institutions that are involved in the process of defining, identifying, and responding to health issues, such as activists, government agencies, and researchers; particularly important here are scientists. Second, health social movements help us track and understand the development of patient identity, which is often directly connected to the actions of health social movements, even for patients who have not become activists themselves. Third, citizen-science alliances and CBPR demonstrate how to merge theory with practice, and how to merge critical perspectives with embedded research interests. Fourth, the dynamic nature of the health social movements allows medical sociologists to do innovative research on concepts of health and disease, the roles and relationships of patients and health-care professionals, and the development and implementation of health policy.

Health Social Movements: Extending the Range of Medical Sociology

A focus on health social movements makes clear that the meaning and existence of diseases and decisions about preventive and ameliorative courses of action derive in part from institutions and actors outside the traditional focus of medical sociology. Health-care policies derive not just from health-care professionals and institutions but also from the actions of social movement activists and the scientists with whom they engage. Government and medical action on AIDS, for example, was due in part to AIDS activists engaging with the scientific enterprise to push for faster action based on better information and faster review and approval of emerging treatment regimes. Similarly, the identification of tobacco as an unhealthy substance for users and bystanders owed much to a tobacco control movement, including work by groups such as Groups Against Smoker's Pollution (GASP), which criticized science for failing to adequately pursue the dangers of primary tobacco use and secondary smoke hazards, and pushed scientists to take up more research on second-hand smoke (Wolfson 2001).

The literature on health social movements thus reveals that scientists and social movement activists, through both conflict and cooperation, play a major role in health-care policy. Fully understanding the development and implementation of health policy often requires an appreciation of how social movements work and how scientific knowledge is created and disseminated, making the sociology of science and social movements literatures deeply relevant for sociologists of medicine. Interestingly, we find a considerable number of publications on health social movements in *Science, Technology, and Human Values*, the major science studies publication. CBPR, a strong influence on the health social movement approach, is broadly informed by new theoretical approaches to citizen involvement, local democracy, environmental justice, lay knowledge, sociology of risk, and the new intersection of medical sociology, environmental sociology, science studies, and social movements that we and others (e.g., Moore and Frickel 2006) are employing. Because activists increasingly participate directly in the scientific research on the illnesses that afflict them, social scientists studying these movements need to be prepared to extend ethnographic research into the labs and field research settings of the scientists who are central to the movements being studied.

Health social movements—and especially embodied health movements—encourage researchers to pay special attention to the role that science and the scientific perspective play in medicine. Embodied health movements demonstrate the degree to which medicine has adopted a scientific approach that privileges quantitatively measurable and generalizable evidence over that which is particular to individual patients and knowable only through their accounts. Modern patients may find themselves clinically sick in the absence of any experience of disease or, alternatively, experiencing symptoms while being told that medically they show no signs of illness—one example, Lyme disease (Weintraub 2008), is now accepted by scientists and clinicians as an emerging infectious disease. This sociologically driven perspective in medicine is relatively recent and represents a break from a long medical tradition in which the patient's bodily experience of illness was the primary means of diagnosis.

Health social movements' unique interaction with science and medicine poses a radical challenge to the professional hegemony of scientific and medical authorities that adhere to the "dominant epidemiological paradigm"—a set of entrenched beliefs and practices about disease treatment and causation embedded within a network of institutions, including medicine, science, government, health charities and voluntaries, professional associations, journals, universities, and the media (Brown et al. 2006). Activists point out that scientists are often asked to weigh in on questions that are impossible to answer scientifically in the here and now—either because data do not exist, or because studies required to answer the question at hand are not feasible. When science is in flux, it is essential that scientists have a say in the discussion,

but their scientific opinions cannot be the deciding factor for the resolution of health problems, precisely because the science is inconclusive. Further, activists claim that many scientists, especially those who embrace the dominant epidemiological paradigm, inappropriately frame political, moral, or ethical questions in scientific terms. Such framing may limit participation in scientific decision making to the traditional experts and thus remove the concerned public from the process. Finally, activists point out how the dominant epidemiological paradigm delegitimizes questions that cannot be framed in scientific terms. They seek to redefine scientific problems in a way that opens up democratic avenues for public participation in science, and to redirect scientific effort to address problems of public concern (Morello-Frosch et al. 2006). For example, community advocates seeking to address high asthma rates among urban communities of color argue that scientific research has focused too exclusively on etiologic factors and lost sight of a solutions-based approach that assesses the effectiveness of social interventions that expand access to better-quality housing. In some cases, health social movements respond by marshaling resources to conduct their own research and produce their own scientific knowledge, as Corburn (2005) describes in terms of linking air pollution and asthma, and lead poisoning from bridge sanding in Williamsburg, Brooklyn. In doing so, the movements democratize the production of scientific knowledge and then use that transformed science as the basis for demanding improved research, treatment, and prevention, as well as calling for stricter and more protective policies and regulations. Movements also use that transformed science to demand structural changes in the political economy that reduce risk of the disease and facilitate research. Indeed, one of the common features of embodied health movements is that they often initiate new scientific directions in advance of medical science.

Health Social Movements and Patient Identity

The health social movement literature can also help medical sociologists better understand the development of patient identity, which in turn affects how patients come to perceive their own conditions and participate in their own care. Embodied health movements depend on the emergence of a collective identity, what we term a "politicized illness experience," as a mobilizing force. When institutions of science and medicine, correctly or incorrectly, fail to offer disease accounts that are consistent with individuals' experiences of illness, or when science and medicine offer accounts of disease that individuals are unwilling to accept, people may adopt an identity as aggrieved illness sufferers and progress to collective action.

For example, although lay perceptions of etiology may not be borne out by scientific investigation, in certain instances, hypothesized links between environmental exposures and human disease have been found to have some support, although these associations are often not immediately recognized (Gee and Stirling 2003). But even if evidence does not ultimately confirm a connection, the politicized illness experience may still be an understandable reaction to researcher or government resistance to a comprehensive research program or to public involvement in that research.

For environmental justice groups, urban asthma sufferers epitomize such a politicized illness experience (Shepard et al. 2002). Similarly, the environmental breast cancer movement has been an exceptional locale for such a politicized transformation (McCormick, Brown, and Zavestoski 2003). In both these cases, sufferers' etiologic perceptions challenged the dominant epidemiological paradigm, which focused on individual factors and downplayed or ignored environmental causation.

Patients that move from being isolated, individual sufferers to active members in a health social movement often find that their self-concept changes as well. For those diagnosed with illnesses for which there are well-established activist movements, those movements may very well shape the way patients perceive their illness and their relationship to medical institutions and health-care professionals, even without direct involvement in the health social movement. By attending to the health social movement literature, medical sociology can gain valuable insight into the roles that science and social movements play in the concepts, actors, and institutions that are central to their field, and the ways that scholars of social movements and science and technology studies are contributing to the medical sociology discourse.

Bridging Gaps via Health Social Movements

Community-based participatory research of health social movements avoids many of the divisions that exist within medical sociology (and sociology generally), variously described as the gap between theory and practice, the *of* medicine/*in* medicine divide (Straus 1957), and the different though not inevitably divergent paths of public, professional, critical, and policy sociology (Burawoy 2004). In CBPR, theory and practice are tightly linked, each informing the other. For researchers involved in the very movement they are analyzing, the disciplinary advancement of professional sociology and the service element of public sociology work together organically (and thus, strictly speaking, do not need to be bridged). Indeed, in his 2004 presidential address to the American Sociological Association, Burawoy identified CBPR studies of health social movements as having "married all four sociologies through collaboration with citizen groups around [various] illnesses" (Burawoy 2004, 16).

CBPR thus provides many examples of how to avoid the divide between theory and practice, and between our lives as professional sociologists and the action we may take in the public sphere. For example, scholars studying policy-relevant issues are likely at some point to be asked to take a stand or to provide information and expertise to community collaborators. In our experience with a toxic-contaminated community in Rhode Island, the academic partnership led to successful legislation that provided home equity loans to homeowners who could not qualify on the open market due to their homes' contamination. Our efforts were appreciated not only by the community partners, but also by federal government officials in the Environmental Protection Agency and the National Institute of Environmental Health Sciences (Senier et al. 2008). In the teaching component of our academic life, we have integrated CBPR approaches in educating students in an ongoing research group, as well as conducting service learning in undergraduate classes (Senier et al. 2006). Blending professional and public sociologies through CBPR is a beneficial community service, but also has benefits for researchers. In our own work as scholars in a larger collaboration on breast cancer and environmental justice, which has a strong component of biomonitoring and household exposure, we have learned much about sociological research, including its intersection with the promotion of environmental public health. Our CBPR work is not only a service for community groups but has also produced high-quality research that has been received well in medical sociology, as well as in environmental public health. Specifically, community groups have pointed to important contaminants for sampling and have been critical in preparing the community for research participation and in recruiting participants, aiding in research design, guiding the process of dissemination and education, and directing policy applications.

Integrating community involvement and scholarly research can challenge and benefit research design. A good example of community involvement in research design occurred in our work on the Northern California Household Exposure Study, a project that involved university researchers, Communities for a Better Environment (an environmental justice organization in Richmond, California), and Silent Spring Institute (a community-oriented nonprofit organization focusing on women's health and the environment that was founded by a breast cancer movement organization). The project entails air and dust sampling for a wide range of endocrine-disrupting chemicals and other pollutants, with an expressed purpose of providing scientific data to support Communities for a Better Environment in their efforts to stop the expansion of production activities of a nearby oil refinery. Our initial sampling protocol entailed a random sample of forty homes in Richmond. However, Communities for a Better Environment encouraged the research collaborative to accept some households as volunteers for the study, since the organization had worked hard to mobilize a base that wanted to integrate sampling data into their organizing efforts to address refinery emissions. Despite initial methodological concerns about accepting volunteers, the research collaborative revised its recruitment protocol by setting aside twenty of the forty slots for volunteers, realizing that some of the volunteers might also be among those randomly selected. Thus the research collaborative learned how democratizing the process of designing study protocols may improve the rigor, relevance, and reach of the broader research enterprise.

The CBPR literature on health social movements (e.g., Shepard et al. 2002; Corburn 2005; Agyeman 2005; Sze 2007) is similarly helpful in surmounting the diverging perspectives of "sociology of medicine" and "sociology in medicine." Because it focuses on issues and problems that the medical establishment itself has identified as important, sociology in medicine has been assessed as insufficiently critical of the actors and institutions it serves. At first glance, CBPR would seem vulnerable to the same critique, given its close affiliation with the participants inside and outside health social movements. However, health social movements (and embodied health movements in particular) are themselves engaged in challenging tradition, giving the entire enterprise an inherently critical perspective. Also, researchers are using CBPR work in multiple settings and with multiple groups, collaborating with laypeople and community groups on one side, and mainstream institutions and professionals on the other (Senier et al. 2008). This involvement with multiple interests and perspectives helps the researcher maintain a critical eye on all facets of the process, and provides a useful example of how medical sociology can pursue the research interests of specific groups while maintaining a critical perspective on the entire enterprise.

Cutting-Edge Medical Sociology

This community involvement in our own professional sociological research process demonstrates a fourth way that work on health social movements can benefit medical sociology: medical sociologists who participate in health social movements have the opportunity to be engaged not only with activism, but also with forms of science that are new and innovative to which they might not otherwise have access. Direct involvement with the actors and activities of health social movements can lead to a sociology of medicine that is especially current and dynamic in its theory, concepts, methods, and findings.

The use of policy ethnography for health social movements, for example, has led researchers into interesting and new hybrid spaces where the work of science, policy making, and social change take place. Science is increasingly being conducted outside laboratories, and policy is being devised beyond policy chambers. Social movement groups also cross multiple sector boundaries, as conveyed in concepts like boundary movements (Brown et al. 2004) and interpenetration (Wolfson 2001). Boundary movements are a combination of social movements and their constituent organizations, including some or all of the following: individual activists, outside supporters, scientists, academics, legislators, government officials, government agencies (usually parts of them), and foundations. With so many components, they blur traditional distinctions, such as those between movement and nonmovement actors and between lay people and professionals.

Five characteristics define boundary movements. First, they attempt to reconstruct the line that separates science from nonscience. They push science in new directions and participate in scientific processes as a means of bringing previously unaddressed issues to clinical and bench scientists. Second, they blur the boundary between experts and lay people. Some activists informally become experts by arming themselves with medical and scientific knowledge that can be employed in conflicts with health-care providers or environmental health regulators. Others gain a more legitimate form of expertise by collaborating with scientists and medical experts in research. Third, boundary movements often have state allies. For example, the tobacco control office of a public health department might be part of an anti-tobacco movement in tandem with a nonprofit organization or a political group (Wolfson 2001). Fourth, boundary movements transcend the traditional conceptions (i.e., boundaries) of what is or is not a social movement by moving fluidly between lay and expert identities and across organizational forms. Fifth, boundary movements use "boundary objects," which overlap social worlds and are malleable enough to be used for different purposes by different parties (Star and Griesemer 1989). For instance, a mammography machine is a diagnostic tool for science, a symbol of unequal health-care access to black activists, and for environmental breast cancer activists, a symbol of overemphasis on mammography and of the false claim that mammography is a form of disease prevention.

When studying human burdens of chemicals, Altman (2008) found herself crossing many boundaries and entering many spaces between boundaries. She observed a social movement organization's press conference at the Maine state house, watched community organizers pack glass specimen collection jars in the offices of an Alaskan environmental health and justice organization, and attended science-intensive discussions in a rural Appalachian high school auditorium. The use of policy ethnography in the health social movement literature, with its at once broad and intricate perspective, can help medical sociologists identify and explore similar hybrid spaces that shape health concepts and policies, and that may otherwise go unnoticed.

This attention to ongoing health social movements that involve multiple perspectives and actors engaged in contesting traditional sources of authority allows researchers to examine the twists and turns of policy as it happens. For example, in studying the environmental breast cancer movement, researchers sat benchside with breast cancer scientists, entered surgical suites as patients underwent mastectomies, marched alongside survivors and women living with breast cancer at public rallies, and examined how policy makers allocated money for etiological research. Such research could explain how local groups on

Long Island were more likely to link up with status quo allies, including Republican lawmakers, while more radical groups like Breast Cancer Action took direct action, engaging in demonstrations and challenging mainstream breast cancer organizations (Brown et al. 2006).

CASE STUDY: BIOMONITORING/ HOUSEHOLD EXPOSURE ACTIVISM

We illustrate how health social movement literature can contribute to the objectives of medical sociology with a brief description of a CBPR project on the use of biomonitoring in health social movements concerned with the possibilities of household exposure to chemicals. The project exemplifies the way HSMs connect to public health, in that in the absence of specific disease, personal exposure monitoring serves as the surveillance so central to public health.

Recently, environmental exposure science has evolved from measuring contaminants in outdoor environments to measuring chemicals in human bodies and the household environments in which they live (Altman et al. 2008). Biomonitoring, the study of the presence and concentration of chemicals in humans, usually by the measurement of breast milk, blood, urine or breath, has the potential to identify the links between chemical exposure and health (NAS 2006). Household exposure studies, too, are undertaken to identify chemical exposure patterns in the hopes of providing insight on the health impacts of chemical exposure. While scientists hope this empirical data will lead to scientifically valid conclusions, the immediate impacts of these techniques reach beyond the scientific realm and into the lay sphere where these studies are being conducted. Health social movements have recently begun to initiate and draw on these studies to buttress their claims that, in spite of a lack of evidence of the effects of most environmental pollutants, chemicals pose a threat to the livelihood of people and the environments in which they live, work, and play.

Organizations that integrate exposure studies into their movement activities exhibit the defining characteristics of embodied health movements: the centrality of the biological body, challenges to existing medical/scientific knowledge and practice, and citizen-science alliances. These organizations encourage the development of a proactive stance that questions and challenges parties adhere to the dominant epidemiological paradigm. Particularly among communities in the most contaminated environments, awareness of widespread chemical exposure can often lead to political engagement to confront the institutions responsible for contamination, remediation, or prevention. The "Is It in Us?" network of environmental health groups around the country that conducted human biomonitoring of 250 people in seven states is one such example (Coming Clean Network 2008). Communities for a Better Environment in California, with whom we partner, also uses household exposure work to advance their opposition to high emissions levels from a major oil refinery. These examples are part of a phenomenon we call advocacy exposure assessment.

Health social movements that are empowered to marshal scientific knowledge are born from the personal and collective realization that biological ills arise in part from social ills, and that the resolution of both lies in cooperation. When health social movements, in collaboration with their science and community partners, play a dominant role in conducting exposure studies, they infuse them with a sense of relevance for study participants, and exposure studies become avenues by which the lay public becomes empowered to adopt an activist stance. When a study participant receives results from a health social movement organization that values the right of an individual to receive their

results, a previously remote problem becomes real and deeply salient to the person. Even among environmental activists educated about environmental issues, chemical contamination is transformed from an abstract issue into a personal concern when chemical body burden or toxic trespass in the home is revealed to study participants and the broader public.

Changes in perception and action orientation toward one's household and community often accompany this altered awareness, as indicated by a quote from an environmentally conscious participant to whom we reported personal household chemical exposures in the Northern California Household Exposure Study:

> *Researcher*: So what were your thoughts or feelings the first time you read the information packet that was mailed to you?
>
> *Participant*: I was in shock. I was stunned. I mean, I was really kind of traumatized by the information because having lived in this unit for—I guess it had been three and a half years when I got that information—and proceeding the way I do trying to use non-toxic things, the number of problem chemicals from my home was just an utter shock … so, then I kind of stepped back and thought, "Ok, well, there is no real difference, probably, it's just that I had this information."

This participant's initial reaction is at the heart of the most common criticism of exposure studies: the release of results in the context of scientific uncertainty can initially surprise study participants, who become aware of the ubiquity of chemical exposures in their everyday lives. Public health practitioners who abide by a clinical ethics approach contend that a researcher has an ethical obligation to inform subjects about their personal exposure results only when action can be taken (Brody et al. 2007). Communication of exposure results that are more consistent with the CBPR paradigm assumes that research results belong to study participants themselves. These tensions over participants' right to know are especially salient when there is scientific uncertainty and the health implications of exposure results are not clear. In situations where the clinical relevance of exposures is well understood (as in the case of lead, for example) right-to-know conflicts are less likely to arise. However, in cases where the implications of exposures results are contested, scientists are more likely to withhold exposure results from participants.

Citizen-science alliances utilizing household exposure studies are emerging at a time when many are critical of the authoritative claims made by scientists. But far from challenging scientific validity, citizen-science alliances reach dual empowerment: scientists learn about personal and community impact of illness experience from affected people, and citizens learn about the state of the science. The use of biomonitoring and household exposure studies among health social movements touches on many significant topics in medical sociology, from lay-professional conflict, illness experience, and the political economy of health to privacy, confidentiality and right-to-know issues. Because of the myriad issues involved and the increasingly blurred boundaries between sectors, our policy ethnography approach has allowed us to make sense of and manage the messy dynamics of health social movement's use of exposure studies.

CONCLUSION

In sum, the multifaceted area of health social movements allows medical sociology to incorporate many of its core components. Through health social movements, medical sociologists can get a more intricate picture of the process through which diseases are defined (or dismissed). By examining health social movements, medical sociologists understand how patients perceive themselves as sufferers of specific illnesses and how they define their own relationship to the medical enterprise and medical authority. Further, health social movements turn a necessary spotlight on the role that science plays in the development of disease concepts and health policy. More fundamentally, health social movements (and particularly embodied health movements) help highlight the degree to which the epistemological assumptions of science have come to be part of the dominant epidemiological paradigm in ways that frequently go unnoticed and unexamined, until patients in embodied health movements begin to challenge them.[2]

While our biomonitoring case study focused on environmentally caused disease, contested illnesses and embodied health movements are conceptually broader categories that are also relevant to disease movements not associated explicitly with the environment. Those wrestling with any contested illness share problems of classification as they struggle to define the boundaries of an illness and show how it is distinct from established diseases. Contested illnesses of all sorts also share problems of etiology, as patients, health-care professionals, and other interested parties attempt to identify possible causes of the condition (environmental, genetic, or otherwise). By the same token, embodied health movements of all types—not merely those associated with environmental causes—involve conflicts between the individual's experience of illness and the existing scientific measures that may or may not endorse that experience (Barker 2005; Brown et al. 2001).

The health social movement literature is also unique for its strong emphasis on CBPR and use of policy ethnography. Together these research approaches can help to provide a more comprehensive account of the development of disease concepts and links to health policy. In addition, by bringing researchers from a variety of fields into direct contact with the challenges posed by health social movement activists, CBPR is a dynamic source of new perspectives and ideas for any field, medical sociology included. Finally, by blending research activities with service to health social movements, CBPR allows the researcher to blend seamlessly and rewardingly the often-separate worlds of theory and practice in ways that are beneficial to all involved. In the case of health social movements, the practical approach of community-based participatory research contributes new theoretical richness. This produces a valuable guide to how medical sociology can simultaneously serve itself and the public good, in ways that transcends the gap between "in" and "of." As an outcome, we arrive at research that pursues questions of interest to the medical establishment, but also to patients and others who interact with that establishment, and that retains always its own sociological agenda and perspective.

NOTES

1   These categories are ideal types and do not cover the universe of health social movements (Epstein 2007). Some movements fall into more than one category, such as the women's health movement, a constituency-based movement that contains elements of both access health social movements (e.g., in seeking more health services for women) and embodied health social movements (e.g., in challenging assumptions about psychiatric diagnoses for premenstrual symptoms). Similarly, environmental justice organizing motivated by the disproportionate emergence of environmentally linked illnesses among marginalized communities shares features of both embodied health social movements and constituency-based health social movements.

2   "Patients" here includes "prepatients." Health social movements often involve not only those who have been diagnosed with the illness but also those who worry, for various reasons, that they might one day be diagnosed.

REFERENCES

Agyeman, Julian. 2005. *Sustainable Communities and the Challenge of Environmental Justice.* New York: NYU Press.

Altman, Rebecca Gasior. 2008. "Chemical Body Burden and Place-Based Struggles for Environmental Health and Justice: A Multi-Sited Ethnography." Ph.D. diss., Brown University.

Altman, Rebecca Gasior, Julia Brody, Ruthann Rudel, Rachel Morello-Frosch, Phil Brown, and Mara Averick. 2008. "Pollution Comes Home and Pollution Gets Personal: Women's Experience of Household Toxic Exposure." *Journal of Health and Social Behavior* 49:417–35.

Barker, Kristen. 2005. *The Fibromyalgia Story: Medical Authority and Women's Worlds of Pain.* Philadelphia: Temple University Press.

Benford, Robert D., and David Snow. 2000. "Framing Process and Social Movements: An Overview and Assessment." *Annual Review of Sociology* 26:611–39.

Bird, Chloe, Peter Conrad, and Allen Fremont. 2000. "Medical Sociology at the Millennium." In *Handbook of Medical Sociology*, ed. Chloe Bird, Peter Conrad, and Allen Fremont, 1–10. Upper Saddle River, N.J.: Prentice Hall.

Brody, Julia Green, Rachel Morello-Frosch, Phil Brown, Ruthann A. Rudel, Rebecca Gasior Altman, Margaret Frye, Cheryl C. Osimo, Carla Perez, and Liesel M. Seryak. 2007. "Is It Safe? New Ethics for Reporting Personal Exposures to Environmental Chemicals." *American Journal of Public Health* 97:1547–54.

Brown, Phil. 1984. "The Right to Refuse Treatment and the Movement for Mental Health Reform." *Journal of Health Policy, Politics, and Law* 9:291–313.

———. 2007. *Toxic Exposures: Contested Illnesses and the Environmental Health Movement*. New York: Columbia University Press.

Brown, Phil, Sabrina McCormick, Brian Mayer, Stephen Zavestoski, Rachel Morello-Frosch, Rebecca Gasior Altman, and Laura Senier. 2006. "'A Lab of Our Own': Environmental Causation of Breast Cancer and Challenges to the Dominant Epidemiological Paradigm." *Science, Technology, and Human Values* 31:499–536.

Brown, Phil, and Edwin J. Mikkelsen. 1990. *No Safe Place: Toxic Waste, Leukemia, and Community Action*. Berkeley: University of California Press.

Brown, Phil, Rachel Morello-Frosch, Stephen Zavestoski, Laura Senier, Rebecca Altman, Elizabeth Hoover, Sabrina McCormick, Brian Mayer, and Crystal Adams. 2010. "Field Analysis and Policy Ethnography: New Directions for Studying Health Social Movements." In *Social Movements and the Development of Health Institutions*, ed. M. Zald, J. Banaszak-Holl, and S. Levitsky. New York: Oxford University Press.

Brown, Phil, Stephen Zavestoski, Theo Luebke, Joshua Mandelbaum, Sabrina McCormick, and Brian Mayer. 2003. "The Health Politics of Asthma: Environmental Justice and Collective Illness Experience in the United States." *Social Science and Medicine* 57:453–64.

Brown, Phil, Stephen Zavestoski, Sabrina McCormick, Joshua Mandelbaum, Theo Luebke, and Meadow Linder. 2001. "A Gulf of Difference: Disputes over Gulf War–Related Illnesses." *Journal of Health and Social Behavior* 42:235–57.

Brown, Phil, Stephen Zavestoski, Sabrina McCormick, Brian Mayer, Rachel Morello-Frosch, and Rebecca Gasior Altman. 2004. "Embodied Health Movements: New Approaches to Social Movements in Health." *Sociology of Health and Illness* 26:50–80.

Bullard, Robert D. 2000. *Dumping in Dixie: Race, Class, and Environmental Quality*. 3rd ed. Boulder, Colo.: Westview Press.

Burawoy, Michael. 2004. "Public Sociologies: Contradictions, Dilemmas, and Possibilities." *Social Forces* 82:1603–18.

Coming Clean Network. 2008. "Is It in Us?" isitinus.org/home.php.

Corburn, Jason. 2005. *Street Science: Community Knowledge and Environmental Health Justice*. Cambridge, Mass.: MIT Press.

Della Porta, Donatella, and Mario Diani. 1998. *Social Movements: An Introduction*. Malden, Mass.: Blackwell.

Epstein, Steven. 1996. *Impure Science: AIDS, Activism, and the Politics of Knowledge*. Berkeley: University of California Press.

———. 2007. "Patient Groups and Health Movements." In *The Handbook of Science and Technology Studies*, ed. Edward J. Hackett, Olga Amsterdamska, Michael Lynch, and Judy Wajcman, 499–539. Cambridge, Mass.: MIT Press.

Fitzgerald, Kathleen J., and Diane M. Rodgers. 2000. "Radical Social Movement Organizations: A Theoretical Model." *Sociological Quarterly* 41:573–92.

Fleischer, Doris, and Frieda Zames. 2002. *The Disability Rights Movement: From Charity to Confrontation*. Philadelphia: Temple University Press.

Gee, David, and Andrew Stirling. 2003. "Late Lessons from Early Warnings: Improving Science and Governance under Uncertainty and Ignorance." In *Precaution: Environmental Science and Preventive Public Policy*, ed. Joel Tickner, 195–214. Washington, D.C.: Island Press.

Goldstein, Michael. 1999. *Alternative Health Care: Medicine, Miracle, or Mirage?* Philadelphia: Temple University Press.

Israel, Barbara, Amy J. Schulz, Edith A. Parker, and Adam B. Becker. 1998. "Review of Community-Based Research: Assessing Partnership Approaches to Improving Public Health." *Annual Review of Public Health* 19:173–202.

Jenkins, J. Craig. 1983. "Resource Mobilization Theory." *Annual Review of Sociology* 9:527–53.

Krimsky, Sheldon. 2000. *Hormonal Chaos: The Scientific and Social Origins of the Environmental Endocrine Hypothesis*. Baltimore: Johns Hopkins University Press.

McCarthy, John D., and Mayer N. Zald. 1977. "Resource Mobilization and Social Movements." *American Journal of Sociology* 92:64–90.

McAdam, Doug. 1982. *Political Process and the Development of Black Insurgency, 1930–1970*. Chicago: University of Chicago Press.

McAdam, Doug, John D. McCarthy, and Mayer N. Zald, eds. 1996. *Comparative Perspectives on Social Movements: Political Opportunities, Mobilizing Structures, and Cultural Framings*. Cambridge: Cambridge University Press.

McCally, Michael. 2002. "Medical Activism and Environmental Health." *Annals of the American Academy of Political and Social Science* 584:145–58.

McCormick, Sabrina, Julia Brody, Phil Brown, and Ruth Polk. 2004. "Lay Involvement in Breast Cancer

Research." *International Journal of Health Services* 34:625–46.

McCormick, Sabrina, Phil Brown, and Stephen Zavestoski. 2003. "The Personal Is Scientific, the Scientific Is Political: The Public Paradigm of the Environmental Breast Cancer Movement." *Sociological Forum* 18:545–76.

Moore, Kelly, and Scott Frickel, eds. 2006. *The New Political Sociology of Science: Institutions, Networks, and Power.* Madison: University of Wisconsin Press.

Morello-Frosch, Rachel, Manuel Pastor Jr., James L. Sadd, Carlos Porras, and Michele Prichard. 2005. "Citizens, Science, and Data Judo: Leveraging Secondary Data Analysis to Build a Community-Academic Collaborative for Environmental Justice in Southern California." In *Methods in Community-Based Participatory Research for Health*, ed. Barbara A. Israel, Eugenia Eng, Amy J. Schulz, and Edith A. Parker, 371–92. San Francisco: Jossey-Bass.

Morello-Frosch, Rachel, Stephen Zavestoski, Phil Brown, Rebecca Gasior Altman, Sabrina McCormick, and Brian Mayer. 2006. "Embodied Health Movements: Responses to a 'Scientized' World." In *The New Political Sociology of Science: Institutions, Networks, and Power*, ed. Kelly Moore and Scott Frickel. Madison: University of Wisconsin Press.

Morgen, Sandra. 2002. *Into Our Own Hands: The Women's Health Movement in the United States, 1969–1990.* New Brunswick, N.J.: Rutgers University Press.

NAS [National Academy of Sciences]. 2006. *Human Biomonitoring for Environmental Chemicals.* Washington, D.C.: NAS.

Rosner, David, and Gerald Markowitz. 1987. *Dying for Work: Workers' Safety and Health in Twentieth-Century America.* Indianapolis: Indiana University Press.

Ruzek, Sheryl Burt. 1978. *The Women's Health Movement: Feminist Alternatives to Medical Control.* New York: Praeger.

Ruzek, Sheryl Burt, Virginia L. Olesen, and Adele E. Clarke, eds. 1997. *Women's Health: Complexities and Differences.* Columbus: Ohio State University Press.

Senier, Laura, Rebecca Gasior Altman, Rachel Morello-Frosch, and Phil Brown. 2006. "Research and Action for Environmental Health and Environmental Justice: A Report on the Brown University Contested Illnesses Research Group." *Collective Behavior and Social Movements Newsletter* (American Sociological Association).

Senier, Laura, Benjamin Hudson, Sarah Fort, Elizabeth Hoover, Rebecca Tillson, and Phil Brown. 2008. "Brown Superfund Basic Research Program: A Multistakeholder Partnership Addresses Real-World Problems in Contaminated Communities." *Environmental Science and Technology* 42(13): 4655–62.

Shapiro, Joseph. 1993. *No Pity: People with Disabilities Forging a New Civil Rights Movement.* New York: Random House.

Shepard, Peggy M., Mary E. Northridge, Swati Prakash, and Gabriel Stover. 2002. "Preface: Advancing Environmental Justice through Community-Based Participatory Research." *Environmental Health Perspectives* 110, suppl. 2:139–40.

Snow, David, E. Burke Rochford, Steven K. Worden, and Robert D. Benford. 1986. "Frame Alignment Processes, Micromobilization, and Movement Participation." *American Sociological Review* 51:464–81.

Star, Susan Leigh, and James R. Griesemer. 1989. "Institutional Ecology, 'Translations' and Boundary Objects: Amateurs and Professionals in Berkeley's Museum of Vertebrate Zoology, 1907–39." *Social Studies of Science* 19(3): 387–420.

Straus, Robert. 1957. "The Nature and Status of Medical Sociology." *American Sociological Review* 22(2): 200–204.

Sze, Julie. 2007. *Noxious New York: The Racial Politics of Urban Health and Environmental Justice.* Cambridge, Mass.: MIT Press.

Tilly, Charles. 1978. *From Mobilization to Revolution.* Reading, Mass.: Addison-Wesley.

Timmermans, Stefan, and Steven Haas. 2008. "Towards a Sociology of Disease." *Sociology of Health and Illness* 30(5): 659–76.

Waitzkin, Howard. 2000. *The Second Sickness: Contradictions of Capitalist Healthcare.* Updated ed. Lanham, Md.: Rowman and Littlefield.

———. 2001. *At the Front Lines of Medicine: How the Health Care System Alienates Doctors and Mistreats Patients.* Lanham, Md.: Rowman and Littlefield.

Weintraub, Pamela. 2008. *Cure Unknown: Inside the Lyme Epidemic.* New York: St. Martin's Press.

Wolfson, Mark. 2001. *The Fight against Big Tobacco: The Movement, the State, and the Public's Health.* New York: Aldine de Gruyter.

Zavestoski, Stephen, Phil Brown, Meadow Linder, Brian Mayer, and Sabrina McCormick. 2002. "Science, Policy, Activism, and War: Defining the Health of Gulf War Veterans." *Science, Technology, and Human Values* 27:171–205.

The Effect of Social Support on State Anxiety Levels during Pregnancy

Nuriye Büyükkayaci Duman and Cem Kocak

Pregnancy is a crisis or a critical period in women's lives. During this period, physical changes as well as psychological and social changes are experienced by the pregnant woman. Adaptation to the conditions created by these changes prevents negative emotions during the pregnancy and the perception of pregnancy as a crisis period. Thus, difficulty in adaptation may lead to irreversible psychological problems (Heron et al., 2004; Kelly, Russo, & Katon, 2001). It has been reported that the most common psychological problems during pregnancy are depression and anxiety disorders, and it has been suggested that increased anxiety and intense anxiety experienced during pregnancy aggravate depression and raise the risk of suicide (Heron et al., 2004; Kelly et al., 2001). As well as causing severe somatic problems, psychological symptoms may lead to miscarriage, preterm birth, or other stress-related pregnancy complications (Heron et al., 2004). Therefore, it may be said that the woman's adaptation to pregnancy is of high importance in coping with psychological problems that may occur during pregnancy.

Chou, Avant, Kuo, and Fetzer (2008) reported that psychological manifestations related to pregnancy are associated with various factors, either individually or combined. These factors are as follows: sociodemographic factors, emotional stability, attitudes towards femininity, relationships with husband and mother, cultural attitudes, preparation for motherhood, previous psychological problems, presence or absence of a child, previous abortion, and whether or not there are medically high risks in the pregnancy (Chou et al., 2008). Another factor that negatively affects coping with psychological problems during pregnancy is lack of social support. *Social support* is described *as financial or spiritual assistance given to the individuals under stress by surrounding people such as husbands, friends, or family members* (Chou, Chen, Kuo, & Tzeng, 2006; Jesse, Walcott-McQuigg, Mariella, & Swanson, 2005).

Other researchers have shown that women with poor social support experience difficulties in their adaptation to pregnancy and suffer from psychosocial problems (Jesse et al., 2005; Swallow, Lindow, Masson, & Hay, 2004). Social support during pregnancy helps eliminate emotional tensions by reducing the perceived importance of the stress-causing situations or events. The presence of supportive systems enhances self-control, and positive emotions, and makes some pregnancy-related changes seem less stressful for the pregnant woman (Chou et al., 2008; McKee, Cunningham, Jankowski, & Zayas, 2001).

Duman Nuriye Büyükkayacı and Cem Kocak, "The Effect of Social Support on State Anxiety Levels During Pregnancy," Social Behavior and Personality, vol. 41, no. 7, pp. 1153-1163. Copyright © 2013 by Scientific Journal Publishers Limited. Reprinted with permission.

When we evaluated previous studies in which psychosocial aspects of pregnancy were investigated, we saw that there were a limited number of researchers who had targeted the topic of how psychological problems relate to social support (Akbaş, 2006; Altınay, 1999; Büyükkoca, 2001; Okanlı, Tortumluoğlu, & Kırpınar, 2003), and the lack of empirical data on this relationship was the determining factor in planning our study. Our aim was to determine the effect of pregnant women's perception of level of multidimensional social support during the period of pregnancy on their state anxiety level. Therefore, we formulated the following hypothesis:

Hypothesis: Social support of husband, family, and friends will have a positive effect on reducing pregnancy anxiety.

METHOD

We used descriptive research in order to determine the effect of pregnant women's perception of level of multidimensional social support during the period of pregnancy on their state anxiety level.

Place and Characteristics

We undertook this study at the Medical Monitoring Polyclinic for Pregnant Women at Çorum State Hospital. There were four medical monitoring polyclinics for pregnant women at the hospital. Doctors worked in shifts at the polyclinics and one nurse assisted at each polyclinic. Routine follow-ups and screenings of the pregnant women were performed at the polyclinics, and training and counseling were provided by the polyclinic nurses for the pregnant women according to their gestational week.

Sample

The sample population for the research consisted of pregnant women who applied to the Medical Monitoring Polyclinic for Pregnant Women at Çorum State Hospital between March 2011 and June 2011. Using simple random sampling, we selected 160 pregnant women to comprise the research sample.

Women who lived in the city center of Çorum and agreed to participate voluntarily to participate were included in the research. Those women and/or their babies who developed complications during pregnancy (e.g., hemorrhage, infection, intrauterine growth retardation, congenital anomalies) and the women who had chronic diseases (e.g., heart disease, hypertension, diabetes, and renal disease) were excluded from the study because these problems might have affected the results.

Ethical Considerations of the Research

The Ethical Council of the Medicine Faculty of Erciyes University approved the ethical suitability of the research. The necessary official permission from the hospital management was obtained for both the pretest phase and implementation phase of the research which were performed at the Çorum State Hospital. All women were informed of the purpose of the study with written documents and were told that the information would not be disclosed. The women's oral consents were obtained and only those who volunteered for the research were included in the study.

Data Collection Tools

The data were collected using the Descriptive Data Collection Form (DDCF) for the Characteristics of the Pregnant Women (Akbaş, 2006; Büyükkoca 2001; Chou et al., 2008), the Multidimensional Scale of Perceived Social Support (MSPSS), and the State Anxiety Inventory (SAI).

Descriptive Data Collection Form for the Characteristics of the Pregnant Women

The DDCF comprises seven questions addressing information about pregnant women's sociodemographic characteristics of age, educational status, employment status, family type, income status, and harmony between spouses and obstetric information about number of pregnancies and parity, and whether or not it was a desired pregnancy.

Multidimensional Scale of Perceived Social Support (MSPSS)

The MSPSS was developed by Zimet, Dahlem, Zimet, & Farley (1988). Eker and Aker (1995) validated the factor structure and reliability of the MSPSS in a Turkish cultural context and translated the scale into Turkish. The MSPSS consists of 12 items. There were three subscales of four items and the subscales address the source of the support: family (items 3, 4, 8, and 11), friends (items 6, 7, 9, and 12), and significant others (items 1, 2, 5, and 10). Each item is scored between 1 and 7. Subscale scores were obtained by adding the scores of the four items and the total score of the scale was obtained by adding the scores of the four subscales. The lowest score from the scale was 12, whereas the highest score was 84. High scores indicated high levels of perceived social support and low scores indicated that little support was perceived or that the pregnant woman was deprived of support. Eker and Akar (1995) found that the Cronbach's alpha coefficient of the scale was .89 and Cronbach's alpha coefficients for the subscales were .85 for family, .88 for friends, and .92 for significant others.

State Anxiety Inventory (SAI)

This inventory was developed by Spielberger, Gorsuch, and Lushene (1970) using Spielberger's two-factor anxiety theory. The SAI consists of 20 questions addressing how a person feels in a specific situation and at a certain time. Öner and Le Compte (1985) performed the validity and reliability tests of the inventory in a Turkish cultural context and translated the SAI into Turkish. In the test-retest reliability of the inventory, which was administered twice to five different student groups, invariance coefficient calculated using Pearson's product-moment coefficient was between .71 and .86. Internal consistency and homogeneity coefficients calculated using alpha correlations were between .83 and .87, and internal consistency of the scale was between .34 and .72. The scale was scored according to the frequency of the emotion, thought, or behavior described in each item on a 4-point scale ranging from 1 = *almost never* to 4 = *almost always*. There were reversed and nonreversed items. The reversed items signifying positive emotions were scored with 4 demonstrating low anxiety. In nonreversed items signifying negative emotions, the answers scored with 4 demonstrated high anxiety. The state anxiety score was calculated by adding 50 to the difference between total weighted scores of the reversed and nonreversed scores. Higher scores indicated higher anxiety levels and lower scores indicated lower anxiety levels. Scores ≤ 36 indicated no anxiety, scores 37 to 41 indicated mild anxiety, and scores ≥ 42 indicated high anxiety.

Evaluation of the Data

The data obtained from the research were assessed using the SPSS 17.0 statistical package program. Percentages, arithmetic means, and standard deviations were used in the data analysis. We performed a *t* test for the paired-group comparisons of the parameters that followed normal distribution, and one-way ANOVA test was used for the multigroup comparisons.

TABLE 7.1 Sociodemographic Characteristics and Fertility History of Pregnant Women

Characteristics		n	%
Age	18–25	50	31.2
	26–33	70	43.8
	≥ 34	40	25.0
Educational status	Primary school	63	38.2
	Secondary school	33	20.6
	High school and above	66	41.2
Employment status	Yes	28	17.5
	No	132	82.5
Family type	Nuclear	118	73.8
	Extended	42	26.2
Monthly total income (TL)	700–1000	81	50.6
	1001–1300	33	20.6
	1301–1600	46	28.6
Number of pregnancies	Primigravida	63	39.4
	Multigravida	97	60.6
Parity number	Primipara	71	44.4
	Multipara	89	55.6
Total		160	100

TABLE 7.2 Distribution of Pregnant Women in Terms of MSPSS Scores

MSPSS Subscale	X ± SD	Min-Max
Family social support	23.58 ± 5.8	2–28
Significant other social support	24.71 ± 5.3	4–28
Friend social support	18.76 ± 8.08	4–28
Total social support	67.06 ± 15.1	16–84

TABLE 7.3 Anxiety Status of Pregnant Women According to SAI Scores

SAI Scores	n	%
≤36	46	28.8
37–42 (Mild anxiety)	114	71.2
Total	160	100

RESULTS

Nearly half of the participants were between the ages of 26 and 33 years (43.0%), and their educational level was high school graduate or above (41.2%). Most of the women were housewives (82.5%) from nuclear families (73.8%). Approximately half of the women (50.6%) had a total monthly income between 700TL and 1000TL (US$370–US$528), and almost all of them had health insurance (90.6 %). When we analyzed the fertility histories of the women we found that nearly three in five women (60.6%) were multigravida (a woman who is pregnant and has been pregnant at least twice before) and more than half (55.6%) were multipara (a woman who has had two or more pregnancies resulting in viable fetuses; see Table 7.1). Also, not shown in the table, nearly three in five women (60.6%) had a harmonious relationship with their husband and wanted to be pregnant (66.3%).

When we analyzed the women's mean scores obtained from the MSPSS and the distributions of the MSPSS subscales, we found that the mean score from the MSPSS was 67.06±15.1, which showed high social support. The women received social support mostly from significant others during the pregnancy period, and the least social support came from their friends as shown in Table 7.2. According to the scores obtained from the SAI, most of the women experienced anxiety (see Table 7.3). The mean anxiety score obtained from the SAI was 36.95±6.2 (min. = 30, max. = 42).

TABLE 7.4 Factors Affecting SAI Scores of Pregnant Women

Characteristics		M	SD	Test	P
Age	18–25	36.2	6.0		
	26–33	36.0	5.9	$F = .786$	.567
	≥ 34	35.6	6.7		
Educational status	Primary school	35.2	5.5		
	Secondary school	36.5	6.5	$F = .582$	.852
	High school and above	35.1	6.6		
Employment status	Yes	36.5	6.7	$t = .256$	.942
	No	35.4	5.7		
Family type	Nuclear	35.2	5.5	$t = 2.442$	.250*
	Extended	36.7	6.9		
Monthly total income (TL)	700–1000	35.8	5.8		
	1001–1300	36.0	6.3	$F = .686$	.664
	1301–1600	35.0	6.5		
Number of pregnancies	Primigravida	37.2	7.6	$t = 2.021$	.330*
	Multigravida	34.7	4.8		
Parity number	Primipara	36.0	6.4	$t = .612$	.765
	Multipara	35.9	6.0		
Wanted pregnancy	Yes	31.5	6.8	$t = 3.004$	.108*
	No	4.2	5.6	$t = 2.023$	.220*
Harmony with husband	Yes	34.2	4.4		
	No	37.5	7.8		

Note: * $p < .05$.

The analysis of the factors affecting SAI scores indicated that there was no statistically significant difference between mean anxiety scores and age, educational status, employment status, monthly total income, number of pregnancies, and parity ($p > .05$). However, as is shown in Table 7.4, a statistically significant difference was found between mean anxiety scores and family type, desired pregnancy, and harmony between spouses ($p < .05$).

When we analyzed the anxiety levels of the women according to their mean MSPSS scores, we found that mean family social support scores, mean friend social support scores, mean significant other social support scores, and mean total social support scores of those who were mildly anxious during the pregnancy were lower compared to the scores of those who did not experience anxiety. The analysis demonstrated that there was no statistically significant difference between mean family support scores, mean friend support scores, and

TABLE 7.5 Distribution of Pregnant Women's Anxiety Levels According to Mean MSPSS Scores

MSPSS Subscales		n	M	SD	t	P
Family social support	No anxiety	46	24.3	4.7	.976	.325
	Mild anxiety	114	23.2	6.1		
	Total	160	23.5	5.8		
Friend social support	No anxiety	46	20.0	8.1	1.54	7.215
	Mild anxiety	114	18.2	7.9		
	Total	160	18.7	8.0		
Significant other social support	No anxiety	46	26.3	3.3	6.161	.014*
	Mild anxiety	114	24.1	5.8		
	Total	160	24.7	5.3		
Total social support	No anxiety	46	70.6	12.9	3.659	.038*
	Mild anxiety	114	65.6	15.7		
	Total	160	67.0	15.1		

Note: *$p < 0.05$.

the anxiety levels ($p > .05$), whereas there was a statistically significant difference between mean significant other social support scores, total social support scores, and anxiety levels ($p < .05$). These findings showed that pregnant women with higher significant other social support scores and pregnant women with higher mean total social support scores, suffered less anxiety than did those with lower scores (see Table 7.5).

DISCUSSION

The pregnancy period is an important time during which significant biological changes are experienced and during which adaptation to new and different roles is necessary (Heron et al., 2004). Researchers have reported that pregnancy is at the top of a list of stressful events in a woman's life (Heron et al., 2004; Kelly et al., 2001). In the face of stress during pregnancy, women may demonstrate emotional or psychological reactions such as acceptance, resistance, fear, anxiety,

or depression, depending on their behavioral patterns and personal or mental characteristics. The most important emotional reaction or problem known during pregnancy is anxiety (Heron et al., 2004; Kelly et al., 2001). Similarly, we found that nearly 70% of the pregnant women who took part in our study suffered from anxiety according to the SAI scores. Yet, when we evaluated the findings regarding the anxiety levels of the participant women, we noted that these women had mild levels of anxiety (36.95±6.2). There were no findings in our study showing that the participant women had moderate or high levels of anxiety. Heron et al.'s (2004) study revealed that pregnant women had mild levels of anxiety. This was similar to our results, whereas Bhagwanani, Seagravesjk, Dierker, and Lax (1997) and Kelly et al. (2001) reported that pregnant women had high levels of state anxiety.

Social support is one of the key factors that reduce anxiety and stress during pregnancy. It is thought that supportive relations play an important role in both protecting against and reinforcing the efforts to cope with the effects of stress experienced by pregnant women (Chou, Chen, Kuo, & Tzeng, 2006; Jesse et al., 2005). In our study we found that the participant women belonged to a group who had high social support according to the mean MSPSS scores (67.06±15.1). Therefore, the fact that participant women generally belonged to a group with high social support reduced the mean state anxiety scores. In addition, our results showed that family social support scores, significant other social support scores, and mean total social support scores of women who were anxious during pregnancy were lower compared to the scores of those who were not experiencing anxiety during pregnancy. Similarly, McKee et al. (2001) reported that state anxiety means of pregnant women with high social support were lower than those of women with low social support. Chou et al. (2008) also indicated that the perceived stress of the women decreased as their scores of the perceived level of social support during pregnancy increased.

Social support mechanisms assist in improving adaptation and emotional support. Chou et al. (2008) and McKee et al. (2001) reported that as the perceived social support increased, psychological problems created by stressful experiences were reduced. The husband's attitude and the psychosocial environment directly affected the psychological state of the women who took part in our study. Support from significant people in the social environment positively affected the pregnancy experience (Chou et al., 2006; Jesse et al., 2005). In this sense, the most important support sources for pregnant women are close family members, especially husbands. Good communication with friends, relatives, and their husband positively affects the woman's transition to the motherhood role. In previous research it has been found that women whose motherhood role is supported by

their husbands and who can share problems with their husbands experience fewer problems than do those who do not have this support (Chou et al., 2008; Jesse et al., 2005; McKee et al., 2001).

As in previous studies, we found that there was a negative correlation between anxiety levels and both significant other social support scores and mean total social support scores. In other words, as the scores of significant other social support and mean total social support scores increased, anxiety levels of the women decreased. We also found that there was a negative correlation between both harmony between spouses and desiring the baby, and mean state anxiety scores; women who did not have a harmonious relationship with their husband and for whom the pregnancy was unplanned and the baby was unwanted had higher mean state anxiety scores than did those who had a harmonious relationship with their husband and for whom the pregnancy had been planned and the baby was wanted. Chou et al. (2008) also indicated that those whose pregnancy was unplanned had higher state anxiety levels compared to those whose pregnancy was planned. McKee et al. (2001) reported that those who did not have a harmonious relationship with their husband had higher depression scores. Previous researchers have reported that lack of social support and disharmony between spouses are among the most significant causes of depression and anxiety during pregnancy and the postpartum period (Chou et al., 2006; Jesse et al., 2005). Affonso et al. (1991) found that the most important factor that increased depression risk was disharmony between spouses, poor marital relations, and poor social support from husband.

In addition, we found that there was a positive correlation between family type and mean state anxiety scores, in that women living with extended families had higher mean state anxiety scores compared to the scores of those living in nuclear families. Akbaş (2006) reported similar results. The psychological pressures possibly created by authority figures of the traditional family structure, such as a mother-in-law or a father-in-law, may result in problems in self-expression and communication for the pregnant daughter-in-law. Therefore, because the nuclear family type is more open to intrafamilial communication and spouse relations are warmer in the nuclear family compared to those in the extended family type, we concluded that pregnant women living in nuclear families were likely to experience less anxiety than did those in extended families (Akbaş, 2006).

CONCLUSION

In our study we found that 70% of the pregnant women were experiencing mild anxiety. We also noted that pregnant women with higher significant other social support scores and mean total social support scores had lower mean state anxiety scores. The analysis we conducted demonstrated that there was a statistically significant correlation between anxiety levels and mean scores of significant other social support and mean total social support scores, but the correlation between mean scores of family social support and friend social support and anxiety levels was not statistically significant. Based on these findings, we concluded that social support of significant others and total social support during pregnancy affected anxiety levels more than did family and friend support. Based on the results of the study, we made following recommendations:

- The risk factors that facilitate depression and other anxiety disorders among women attending clinics at health institutions during pregnancy should be explored, and the necessary initiatives for those women at risk should be initiated so that their social support systems can be reinforced.
- Psychosocial support systems such as husbands, friends, and families should be integrated with training and counseling during the prebirth period.
- Counseling about issues such as open communication, empathy, and methods for coping with stress should be provided for the pregnant women and their husbands in order to alleviate communication problems in the family.
- Future researchers should include a control group and a bigger sample in their studies so that the findings in our study may be further confirmed and supported with more data.

REFERENCES

Affonso, D., Lovett, S., Paul, S., Arizmendi, T., Nuusbaum, R., Newman, L., & Johnson, B. (1991). Predictors of depression symptoms during pregnancy and postpartum. *Journal of Psychosomatic Obstetrics & Gynecology, 12*, 255–271. **http://doi.org/cq778b**

Akbaş, E. (2006). *Investigation of the relation between pregnant women's depression and anxiety levels and social support* (Master's thesis). Retrieved from **http:// www.belgeler.com/blg/tp5/gebe-kadinlarda-depresyon-ve-anksiyete-duzeylerinin-sosyal-destek-ile-iliskisininincelenmesi-investigation-of-the-relation-between-pregnant-women-s-depression-andanxiety-levels-and-social-support**

Altınay, S. (1999). *Association between sociodemographic variables with the levels of depression and anxiety in pregnancy* (Master's thesis). Retrieved from **http:// www.noropsikiyatriarsivi.com/tr/makale/2622/389/ Tam-Metin**

Bhagwanani, S. G., Seagravesjk, K., Dierker, L. J., & Lax, M. (1997). Relationship between prenatal anxiety and perinatal outcome in nulliparous women: A prospective study. *Journal of the National Medical Association, 89*, 93–98.

Büyükkoca, M. (2001). *To investigate the association between perceived social support and postpartum depression.* Master's thesis, Dokuz Eylül University, Izmir, Turkey.

Chou, F.-H., Avant, K. C., Kuo, S. H., & Fetzer, S. J. (2008). Relationships between nausea and vomiting, perceived stress, social support: Pregnancy planning and psychosocial adaptation in a sample of mothers: A questionnaire survey. *International Journal of Nursing Studies, 45,* 1185–91. **http://doi.org/dsbfb5**

Chou, F.-H., Chen, C.-H., Kuo, S.-H., & Tzeng, Y.-L. (2006). Experience of Taiwanese women living with nausea and vomiting during pregnancy. *Journal of Midwifery & Women's Health, 51,* 370–375. **http://doi.org/c668vb**

Eker, D., & Akar, H. (1995). Factorial structure, validity, and reliability of revised form of the Multidimensional Scale of Perceived Social Support. *Turkish Journal of Psychiatry, 10,* 45–55.

Heron, J., O'Connor, T. G., Evans, J., Golding, J., & Glover, V. (2004). The course of anxiety and depression through pregnancy and the postpartum in a community sample.

Journal of Affective Disorders, 80, 65–73. **http://doi.org/dntp8n**

Jesse, D. E., Walcott-McQuigg, J., Mariella, A., & Swanson, M. S. (2005). Risks and protective factors associated with symptoms of depression in low-income African American and Caucasian women during pregnancy. *Journal of Midwifery & Women's Health, 50,* 405–410. **http://doi.org/dpkbpb**

Kelly, R. H., Russo, J., & Katon, W. (2001). Somatic complaints among pregnant women cared for in obstetrics: Normal pregnancy or depressive and anxiety symptom amplification revisited? *General Hospital Psychiatry, 23,* 107–13. **http://doi.org/cvds6h**

McKee, M. D., Cunningham, M., Jankowski, K. R., & Zayas, L. (2001). Health-related functional status in pregnancy: Relationship to depression and social support in a multi-ethnic population. *Obstetrics & Gynecology, 97,* 988–993. **http://doi.org/b7wsqk**

Okanlı, A., Tortumluoğlu, G., & Kırpınar, İ. (2003). The relationship between pregnant women's perceived social support from family and problem-solving skills. *Journal of Anatolian Psychiatry, 4,* 98–105.

Öner, N., & Le Compte, A. (1985). *State-Trait Anxiety Inventory handbook*. İstanbul: Boğaziçi University Publications.

Spielberger, C. D., Gorsuch, R. L., & Lushene, R. E. (1970). *Manual for State-Trait Anxiety Inventory*. Palo Alto, CA: Consulting Psychologists Pres.

Swallow, B. L., Lindow, S. W., Masson, E. A., & Hay, D. M. (2004). Psychological health in early pregnancy: Relationship with nausea and vomiting. *Journal of Obstetrics & Gynaecology, 24*, 28–32. **http://doi.org/cb6nhd**

Zimet, G. D., Dahlem, N. W., Zimet, S. G., & Farley, G. K. (1988). The Multidimensional Scale of Perceived Social Support. *Journal of Personality Assessment, 52*, 30–41. **http://doi.org/dt7nqw**

PART II

The Social and Cultural Meanings of Illness

Medical sociologists make a distinction between two terms: disease and illness. Whereas *disease* refers to the biophysiological components of an ailment, *illness* is the social counterpart to the disease. Generally, illness refers to the sick individuals' and/or society's perception of the disease. It helps to see disease and illness as two different sides to the same coin. Disease is more of an objective discussion, whereas illness is more subjective. For example, when we discuss the physical symptoms experienced by a person with diabetes, we are talking about the disease. When we discuss the social stigma that a person with type II diabetes experiences, we are referring to the illness. This is an important distinction to make as medical sociologists are generally more concerned with the social experiences of illness rather than its biological components.

In the first reading, entitled "The Social Construction of Illness: Medicalization and Contested Illness," Barker discusses the social constructionist perspective of illness. Social constructionism is the framework within medical sociology that suggests that meanings of health and disease are rooted in cultural and social values. In other words, illness does not just exist biologically. It is also tainted by social and cultural meanings that we attach to these illnesses. Just as a society and its culture decides what is considered good, bad, deviant, or taboo, societies also decide what or who is considered "ill." In many societies, for example, women do not suffer from premenstrual syndrome (PMS) as they do in the United States. Of course, there is nothing biologically different about women in the United States. Rather, we differ in our definition of PMS as a medical condition. Similarly, menopause is not considered a medical condition in some parts of the world. It is simply a natural process of the body that all women of a certain age experience. Likewise, Baker mentions that *susto* and *koro* are illnesses that exist in some parts of the world, but not in the United States. These examples illustrate the notion that a society decides what is an illness and what is not, which is the fundamental idea of the social constructionist perspective.

Another topic discussed in this reading, medicalization, is also a fundamental concept in medical sociology that contributes to the social constructionist perspective. According to Barker, medicalization is the process by which human experiences come to be treated as medical conditions. Things that used to be considered variations in human traits, such as male-pattern baldness and hyperactivity, are now defined as medical problems that need treatment. Another interesting example is childbirth. Prior to the twentieth century, giving birth in a hospital setting was rare. Childbirth was considered a natural, biological process that was mainly a female domestic experience, with little intervention from a doctor. Today, throughout the developed world, medical intervention for childbirth is routine (although there is considerable evidence that it is beginning to reverse). Medical sociologists are interested in the social mechanisms that contribute to the medicalization process over time. They are also interested in the consequences of medicalization, including functioning as a form of social control.

In the second reading, "The Patient's Experience with Illness," Rier discusses the historical progression in the field of medical sociology of the inclusion of a patient focus. This shift in perspective has taught us so much about the importance of identity, support, family, work, and community in regard to health and illness. We have furthered our understanding about how patients manage the sick role and how they maneuver through the stages of an illness. In the third reading, "The Internet and the Experience of Illness," Conrad and Stults expand on our understanding of the illness experience by incorporating the role of the Internet. The authors reflect on patients experience with learning about their illnesses online, engaging in online support groups, finding health care providers, and even receiving treatment virtually. In less than two decades, the Internet has drastically changed the experience of illness in ways we are still just beginning to understand.

Another important concept in the social constructionist perspective of medical sociology is the notion of stigma. In the fourth reading, "Understanding and Addressing the Stigma of Mental Illness with Ethnic Minority Communities," Knifton studies beliefs, stigma, and the effectiveness of existing national mental health campaigns among immigrant communities in the United Kingdom. Across the world, stigma and discrimination against people with mental illness persists. Consistent sentiments include ideas that people are to blame for their conditions or that they are dangerous and unpredicable.

Knifton's study is especially interesting given his focus on immigrant groups who experience material and social disadvantage that puts them at greater risk for mental illness itself, as well as associating stigma and discrimination.

The final reading in Part II is "Nurturing Longevity: Sociological Constructions of Ageing, Care, and the Body." In this article, Fine reiterates that social assumptions not only shape the way we view health and illness, but also care for those who need it.

The Social Construction of Illness

Medicalization and Contested Illness

Kristin K. Barker

This chapter makes a case for the usefulness of a social constructionist approach to medical sociology, emphasizing the analytic potency of social constructionism for explaining a key cultural and historical trend of our time: medicalization (Clarke et al. 2003; Conrad 2007). It includes a detailed discussion of contested illnesses—illnesses where patients and their advocates struggle to have their medically unexplainable symptoms recognized in orthodox biomedical terms—and suggests that lay practices and knowledge, and the consumer demands they engender, are increasingly crucial in advancing medicalization in the twenty-first century.

SOCIOLOGY OF KNOWLEDGE AND THE SOCIAL CONSTRUCTION OF ILLNESS

Social constructionism is a diverse set of theories of knowledge developed and used by social scientists, historians, and cultural studies scholars. From a constructionist perspective, a social construct is an idea that appears to refer to some obvious, inevitable, or naturally given phenomenon, when in fact the phenomenon has been (in full or part) created by a particular society at a particular time. Pointing to the socially constructed character of an idea challenges its taken-for-granted nature and the social practices premised on it. As a case in point,

feminists claim that gender is a social construction, meaning that our current ideas about gender (i.e., norms and standards concerning femininity and masculinity) are not biologically mandated; therefore, the ideas and the social practices they institutionalize are alterable. Social constructionism has been a centerpiece, theoretically and substantively, of the subfield of medical sociology. Stated in brief, its chief contribution has been to demonstrate just how complex the answers are to the seemingly straightforward questions, What is an illness? What is a disease? But before taking on these questions, it's useful to trace the intellectual origins that inform a sociological approach to social constructionism.

From its inception as a discipline, sociology has approached ideas as reflections of the specific historical and social environments in which they are produced. The founding sociological thinkers—Karl Marx (1818–1883), Max Weber (1864–1920), and Emile Durkheim (1858–1917)—each addressed the relationship between the ideas or beliefs of a society and the social and material conditions of that society. Published in 1936, Karl Manheim's *Ideology and Utopia* represented a significant advance in the sociology of ideas. Manheim urged sociology to study empirically how peoples' historical context and their station in life (i.e., class) condition

Kristin K. Barker, "The Social Construction of Illness: Medicalization and Contested Illness," Handbook of Medical Sociology, pp. 147-162. Copyright © 2010 by Vanderbilt University Press. Reprinted with permission.

their ideas. In the 1960s, Berger and Luckmann (1967) articulated the link between ideas, including taken-forgranted or commonsense knowledge about reality, and everyday social interaction. In more recent decades, feminist and postmodern sociologists have demonstrated the relationship between our ideas and our social locations in race, class, and gender hierarchies of power, and have built on Foucauldian views of knowledge as a type of discourse that arbitrarily gives some groups power over others (Collins 1991; Smith 1987). Finally, sociologists contributing to the interdisciplinary field of science studies claim that scientific knowledge, like other ideas, is the outcome of concrete social practices rather than of individual discoveries of truth that "carve nature at its joints" (Knorr Cetina 1997; Latour 1987; Timmerman 2007). This long and venerable tradition—often called the "sociology of knowledge"—studies ideas not as true or false expressions of the world per se, but as the realized expression of particular social interests within particular social systems and contexts (Merton 1973). In other words, from a sociology of knowledge perspective, our ideas are social constructions (Berger and Luckmann 1967).

Sociologists study the social construction of many different ideas, but of interest to us here are sociologists who study ideas about illness. Although perhaps not immediately obvious, the use of social constructionism in medical sociology can be traced to Talcott Parsons's (1951) concept of the *sick role*. The sick role describes illness as a form of medically sanctioned deviant behavior, and specifies the rights and obligations given a sick person to ensure that an episode of sickness doesn't disrupt social order and stability. Despite Parsons's social conservatism, his theoretical claims were premised on the conceptual distinction between the biophysical nature of disease and the social experience of sickness. Over the last fifty-plus

years, medical sociologists have built on this distinction to make more radical and far-reaching claims concerning the social construction of illness and disease (Brumberg 2009; Conrad and Schneider 1992; Freidson 1971; Lorber and Moore 2002).

Social constructionist scholars emphasize the relationship between ideas about illness and the expression, perception, understanding, and response to illness at the individual, institutional, and societal level. Historical and cross-cultural comparisons are effective ways to illustrate social constructionists' claims. Imagine, for example, two societies: one defines illness principally as the outcome of moral failings or spiritual transgressions (on the part of individuals or communities); the other defines illness principally as the result of organic disturbance within an individual human body. Who (or even what) is identified as "ill" in these two societies will differ dramatically, as will arrangements for how and by whom illness is to be treated. In addition, the subjective experience and meaning of being ill will be markedly dissimilar because the two societies provide very different interpretive frameworks of the illness experience. In one society, "the shamed" stand before a sacred figure who rights the wrong, cleanses the soul, or grants mercy; in the other, the individual victim of disease—"the patient"—seeks the physician's technical skills to restore or fix his or her wounded body.

Social constructionists also examine why some illnesses exist in one place and not another, or appear and then disappear in the same place. In many societies, for example, women do not suffer from premenstrual syndrome (PMS) or anorexia nervosa. Likewise, *susto* and *koro* are illnesses that exist only in certain cultures. A number of illnesses that were present in Western societies in the late nineteenth and early twentieth centuries—including fugue, hysteria, and neurasthenia—have now faded from view (Hacking 1998). These so-called culture-bound and transient illnesses effectively advance the social constructionist claim that illness and disease are something beyond fixed physical realities; they are also phenomena shaped by social experiences, shared cultural traditions, and shifting frameworks of knowledge.

From a social constructionist perspective, the task is not necessarily to determine which of the two societies has the *correct* ideas about illness, or which of the illnesses found only in certain places or certain times are *real*. Instead, the task is to determine how and why particular ideas about illness appear, change, or persist for reasons that are at least partly independent of their empirical adequacy vis-à-vis biomedicine. So, for example, social constructionists pay close attention to how and why particular definitions or ideas about illness became dominant in particular places and times and how they marginalize or silence alternative ideas (Conrad and Schneider 1992; Freidson 1971; Starr 1982; Tesh 1988). Additional questions follow: What factors help explain why one society defines illness in moral terms, whereas another eschews such ideas in favor of observable anatomic abnormality? What are the central consequences—for the society at large and for afflicted individuals—of one set of ideas versus another? What dynamics are at play in the appearance and disappearance of a certain illness or in the existence of an illness in one place but its absence elsewhere?

Although these are some archetypal social constructionist questions, questions about reality and truth inevitably arise: Don't some ideas about illness more accurately reflect the truth than others? Doesn't the scientific disease model better explain and treat illness than folkloric or religious approaches? Isn't death definitive proof that illness isn't simply a social construction? These questions arise because not everyone agrees what calling an illness "socially constructed" implies. This is largely because there is no single social constructionist perspective in general, or in medical sociology in particular (Brown 1995).[1] Instead there are several versions of social constructionism used by many different academic disciplines, each drawing on different intellectual assumptions about the relationship between ideas and the material world. The widespread use of several versions of social constructionism, by scholars from a host of disciplines, applied to an increasing array of phenomena (e.g., race, gender, sexuality, quarks, disability, illness) has led to a confused and mulled state of affairs with respect to what exactly is socially constructed about phenomena said to be social constructions.

In his aptly titled book *The Social Construction of What?* philosopher Ian Hacking asks the following types of questions: What does it mean to say that race, or a quark, or an illness is a social construct? Does it mean that we made these *things* and they would not exist as such if we had not made them, and/or we could have made them in a fundamentally different fashion? Or, does it mean that we made our *ideas* about these things, and we could have come up with very different ideas about these things? Does it mean that both the *things* and our *ideas* about the things are socially constructed? Are all things and all ideas social constructions? Or, if all things and all ideas are not equally socially constructed, what makes some things and some ideas social constructions and not others?

Hacking and other analytic philosophers and philosophers of science raise important questions about social constructionism (Boghossian 2001; Hacking 1999; Searle 1995; Slezak 2000). Among the principal charges they raise are that social constructionism explicitly or implicitly denies the existence of the natural world (or at least denies the possibility that we can know about it with some degree of accuracy); and, relatedly, that the approach stumbles over questions concerning whether or not some ideas are better representations of the world than are others. Hacking also alleges that social constructionism inevitably reproduces a false binary between things that are *real* (and therefore have an entirely biophysical basis) and things that are *socially constructed* (and therefore have no biophysical basis whatsoever). As a result, Hacking contends, social constructionism fails to consider the possibility that something can be *both* real *and* socially constructed (Hacking 1999, 31). However, sociologists of medicine have often supported this view, insofar as they believe that the social forces constructing the definition and treatment of illness are themselves real phenomena that can be empirically studied (Brown 1995; Freidson 1971).

What many sociologists mean when they claim that an illness is socially constructed is that the experience of illness is shaped by social and cultural context. The earlier comments concerning the variability in the experience of illness across time (history) and space (culture) are illustrative. Many sociologists have pursued this line of reasoning and in so doing have given us powerful insights into the cultural fabric of illness. Without question, the experience of cancer, epilepsy, or anxiety differs greatly historically and cross-culturally. Insofar as all illness gains meaning within the context of human society, all illness is socially constructed. Yet, if all illnesses are social constructions, then there is no point in singling out any particular illness as being a social construct. In short, the social constructionist perspective loses its expository or investigatory power when followed to its logical conclusion. Even here, however, a core conceptual contribution of social constructionism to medical sociology remains intact: the distinction between the medical model, which emphasizes biological pathology, and the social model, which emphasizes the oft-neglected social causes and character of illness and impairment.

There still is the matter of the social construction of illnesses as things. A strict constructionist position would implicitly or explicitly hold that no illness—cancer, epilepsy, or anxiety—exists outside our socially and historically bound mental constructions. These things exist at all, or exist as they are, only because we created them. Although not about illness, this position, which effectively denies the existence of the ontological world or the reality of what Searle (1995) calls "brute facts" (i.e., facts about the physical and natural world), was famously mocked in 1996 when the physicist Alan Sokal published a hoax article in *Social Text*, a leading journal representing the postmodern critique of science's alleged objectivity in the so-called science wars. Despite the attention given the Sokal hoax and the vocal attacks against the relativism of social constructionism, it is difficult to find scholars who make these strict types of claims. Even Hacking (1999) admits that most social constructionists avoid this pitfall.

A line of inquiry pursued by medical sociologists that thoughtfully negotiates many of these logical problems emphasizes the social construction of medical knowledge. As described by Brown (1995, 37), the social construction of illness stresses the illness experience, whereas the social construction of medical knowledge "deals with the ways of knowing that are based on the dominant biomedical framework" and is chiefly concerned with professional beliefs and diagnoses. Of course, in our society it is impossible to fully disentangle these spheres given that people primarily make sense of and manage illness within the dominant biomedical framework (ibid.). In fact, it is difficult to overstate biomedicine's influence in shaping the prevailing ideas about illness in advanced capitalist societies. Among other things, biomedicine plays a dominant role in organizing our experiences and complaints into disease categories.

A disease does not exist, so to speak, until the social institution of medicine creates a representative diagnostic category (Brown 1995; Freidson 1971). For a disease to exist, in this limited sense, it must be identified. Disease begins with "social discovery" or the "the ways in which people, organizations, and institutions determine that there is a disease or condition" (Brown 1995, 38). This is not to suggest that there are no biological facts concerning disease, nor is the point merely one of semantics. As noted earlier, we can claim that a disease as defined in a diagnostic category is a social construction without implying that the suffering it represents has no biological basis. After all, social constructionists are primarily interested in the empirical adequacy of their own descriptions of the social forces behind medical ideas, be these forces at odds with or supplementary to the empirical adequacy of the corresponding biomedical ideas. Contrary to Hacking's allegations, medical sociologists and anthropologists clearly recognize the possibility that a condition can be both real and socially constructed (Brown 1995; Freidson 1971). For example, such a both/and stance vis-à-vis the real/social-construction dichotomy has been advanced in the case of post-traumatic stress disorder (Young 1995), mood disorders (Horwitz 2002), and anorexia nervosa (Brumberg 2009), to name but a few. Additionally, the social constructionist approach clearly addresses how diagnoses interact with the individuals who are diagnosed, again acknowledging social constructionism's both/and analytic potential (Brown 1995; Freidson 1971; Horwitz 2002).

But not all diseases, as captured in their diagnostic categories, are fundamentally or primarily social constructions. Sometimes the factors behind the creation of a new disease category and its application are straightforwardly biological. A particular type of human distress is linked to biological pathologies, and the new diagnosis represents progress in medical knowledge. In these instances it might be meaningful to talk about the social practices that resulted in the discovery of the disease and its application, but it would not be particularly meaningful to assert that the disease is a social construction simply because social activity led to its discovery. Here the deft historical accounts of the social processes leading up the discovery of tuberculosis (Tomes 1998), end-stage renal disease (Peitzman 1992), and HIV/AIDS (Epstein 1996) come to mind. Often, however, there is a level of arbitrariness concerning why a particular set of attributes comes to be organized and represented under a biomedical diagnosis. Cases characterized by apparent arbitrariness are of most interest to sociologists (Brown 1995). These cases are interesting not because they have no connection to biological facts, but because they demonstrate that "an entity that is regarded as an illness or disease is not ipso facto a medical problem; rather, it needs to become defined as one" (Conrad 2007, 5–6). Hence, the social construction of medical knowledge goes hand in hand with the process known as medicalization.

BIOMEDICAL KNOWLEDGE AND MEDICALIZATION

Medicalization is the process by which an ever-wider range of human experiences comes to be defined, experienced, and treated as medical conditions.

One large sector includes the medicalization of deviance (Conrad and Schneider 1992). Calling a drunk an alcoholic or a gambler an addict are such examples. Social problems are also medicalized, as seen in the case of obesity and antisocial personality disorder (Lorber and Moore 2002). In some cases, "normal" human variation in such things as height, appearance, or temperament is defined as a medical problem and treated accordingly (Conrad

2007). In other instances, it is appropriate to speak of the medicalization of life itself. Medicine, Illich warned us, "can transform people into patients because they are unborn, newborn, menopausal, or at some other 'age of risk'" (Illich 1976, 78). The medicalization of life, therefore, includes natural physical changes ranging from the profound (e.g., senility) to the trivial (e.g., male-patterned baldness). Biotechnology promises to expand the frontier even further as genetic research medicalizes the state of being "at risk" (Skolbekken 2008). Through medicalization, natural human variation, normal experiences, routine complaints, and hypothetical scenarios become medical conditions.

Drawing on social constructionist tenets, feminist scholars have demonstrated how women's bodies and experiences have been particularly susceptible to medicalization. There are many complex reasons for this tendency, including medicine's conceptualization of male physiology as normative. Borrowing Simone de Beauvoir's (1989) central insight, men and men's bodies represent the biomedical standard and women and women's bodies are the biomedical other. It is but a short step to define normal aspects of women's embodiment as biologically aberrant. For example, women's natural reproductive functions are routinely medicalized (e.g., pregnancy, childbirth, menstruation, menopause) (Ehrenreich and English 1973; Lorber and Moore 2002, 2007; Martin 1987). That being said, women have themselves been proactive in processes of medicalization—perhaps because it represents one of a few avenues afforded them to pursue their needs and gain access to resources in a society characterized by gender inequality (Lorber and Moore 2002, 2007; Riessman 1983; Theriot 1993).

Medicalization is a complex process. Although the general historical trend has been toward ever-greater medicalization, it can be a bidirectional process, as the demedicalization of homosexuality

and masturbation attest (Conrad 2007; Clarke et al. 2003). In the 1970s, at the height of the natural childbirth movement, childbirth became less medicalized (Lorber and Moore 2007). Although there is considerable evidence that this trend has reversed itself, the case of childbirth nevertheless illustrates the potential bidirectionality of medicalization. In a somewhat similar vein, there are individuals and groups who reject a medical classification of their behavior, as seen in the contemporary examples of pro-anorexia and self-injury (e.g., cutting, burning, etc.) groups (Adler and Adler 2007; Pascoe and Boero 2008). The actions of these groups have not led to demedicalization per se—the diagnoses these groups reject remain well established—but they do demonstrate pockets of resistance to the medicalization of deviant behaviors. Specifically, these groups actively produce counterconstructions of disordered eating and self-injury, affirm them as alternative lifestyles, and forge virtual subcultures, all far from the dictates of medical practitioners and the clinical gaze. Likewise, although parents and parent groups opposing childhood immunization don't undermine established medical protocol, they do show some individual and collective opposition to unlimited medicalization (Casiday 2007).

There can also be different levels or degrees of medicalization (Conrad 2007). A condition isn't necessarily medicalized or not medicalized. For instance, although a small number of individuals are treated medically for short stature (Conrad 2007), it would be an overstatement to suggest that the general public perceives shortness as an illness. Similarly, individuals who are dissatisfied with their bodily appearance can seek to have it medically altered, but so far being unattractive isn't considered an illness. In contrast to these cases of medical treatment in the absence of illness or disease, celiac disease is an illness without a medical treatment. In the case of celiac disease, the principal treatment is adherence to a gluten-free diet. Because celiac disease requires no medical intervention, it exists somewhere between a medicalized and nonmedicalized condition (Copeland and Valle 2009). Contested illnesses also illustrate different degrees of medicalization insofar as some of these conditions are further down the road toward accepted medical conditions than are others. Sociologists have referred to emergent or partial medicalization (Dumit 2006), or specified different medicalized classifications and categories (Brown 1995) to denote that certain human experiences hit a snag in the process of becoming institutionally accepted medical phenomena.

It is also clear that the principal forces behind medicalization in the present era differ from those that expanded medicine's jurisdiction up through the first three quarters of the twentieth century (Clarke et al. 2003; Conrad 2005). Dramatic changes in the organization of medicine toward the end of the twentieth century, most notably the rise of corporate managed care and the corresponding decline of physicians' professional power, underlie changing patterns of medicalization. One can briefly summarize the standard twentieth-century story of medicalization as follows: physicians carved out a professional niche for themselves by negating lay knowledge and practices and promoting the medical management of natural human experiences, social ills, and personal problems (Conrad and Schneider 1992; Freidson 1970; Illich 1976). The medicalization of childbirth and pregnancy are exemplars (Barker 1998; Wertz and Wertz 1979).

In contrast, when it comes to the forces promoting the expansion of medicine's jurisdiction in the current era, the role of physicians has declined in significance, while that of biotechnology (e.g., pharmaceuticals and genetics) and other corporate health industries (e.g., managed-care organizations), in tandem with the markets and consumers they create and serve, have increased in salience

(Clarke et al. 2003; Conrad 2005). The popularity of elective cosmetic surgery and fertility treatments attests to consumer demands for medical solutions to personal problems and disappointments (Blum 2003; Conrad 2007). Direct-to-consumer pharmaceutical advertising encourages patients to ask their doctor about particular drugs to treat many previously normal or benign symptoms (e.g., toenail discoloration, heartburn) and to consider them specific medical conditions or diseases (e.g., dermatophytes, acid reflux disease) (Moynihan, Heath, and Henry 2002). The availability of a drug or other biotech treatment for a complaint significantly increases the likelihood that the compliant will be medicalized. This raises serious allegations that biotech corporations are engaging in "disease mongering" (Angell 2004; Conrad 2007; McCrea 1983).

There are important consequences of medicalization. By defining disease as a biological disruption residing with an individual human body, medicalization obscures the social forces that influence our health and well-being. Medicalization is depoliticizing: it calls for medical intervention (medication, surgery, etc.) when the best remedy for certain types of human suffering may be political, economic, or social change. Medicalization can also grant the institution of medicine undue authority over our bodies, minds, and lives, thereby limiting individual autonomy and functioning as a form of social control (Illich 1976; Zola 1972). Rarely, however, is medicalization exclusively the result of the medical profession's imperialistic claims. As patient consumers, we are increasingly active participants in the medicalization of our experiences as we earnestly seek to resolve and legitimate our suffering.

A social constructionist perspective that emphasizes the biological arbitrariness of certain diagnoses provides a powerful analytic framework for making sense of medicalization, or the process by which our complaints, disappointments, and experiences come to be defined and treated as medical conditions. In addition, such a perspective circumvents many of the critiques of social constructionism. A close examination of the social construction of contested illnesses further demonstrates these claims.

CONTESTED ILLNESSES

Contested illnesses are conditions in which sufferers and their advocates struggle to have medically unexplainable symptoms recognized in orthodox biomedical terms, despite resistance from medical researchers, practitioners, and institutions (Barker 2008; Conrad and Stults 2008; Dumit 2006). In the last several decades there has been a notable increase in the number of contested illnesses and contested illness sufferers (Barsky and Borus 1999; Henningsen, Zipfel, and Herzog 2007; Manu 2004; Mayou and Farmer 2002). Tens of millions of Americans are diagnosed with one of several syndromes characterized by a cluster of common, diffuse, and disturbing symptoms, ranging from pain and fatigue to sleep and mood disorders. Some of these illnesses include chronic fatigue syndrome/myalgic encephalomyelitis (ME), fibromyalgia syndrome, irritable bowel syndrome, urologic chronic pelvic pain syndrome, temporomandibular dysfunction (TMJ), tension head ache, multiple chemical sensitivity disorder, Gulf War syndrome, and sick building syndrome (Barsky and Borus 1999; Nimnuan et al. 2001; Wessley 2004) many sufferers and some clinician advocates suggest that these disorders—frequently called "functional somatic syndromes" in the medical literature—are unique disease entities with unique natural histories and specific characteristics. At this time, however, there is tremendous medical uncertainty concerning these conditions (Mayou and Farmer 2002).

At the very core of the uncertainty is a lack of medical consensus concerning the biological nature of these illnesses. Despite fierce claims to the contrary, none of these illnesses are associated with any specific organic abnormality. These conditions are not detectable in x-rays, blood tests, CAT scans, or any other high-tech diagnostic tool. Instead, they are diagnosed based on clinical observations and patients' subjective reports of symptoms. They are also diagnosed by exclusion, that is, after other possible explanations for the symptoms have been ruled out. Consequently, many physicians approach these "wastebasket" diagnoses, and those so diagnosed, with considerable skepticism. What is at issue is whether these syndromes are "real" (have organic biological origins) or not (are psychogenic, behavioral, or iatrogenic). With the exception of Gulf War syndrome, these disorders are highly feminized (Mayou and Farmer 2002). This unavoidable fact introduces ruminations that these diagnoses are modern-day labels for hysteria (Bohr 1995; Hadler 1997a, b; Showalter 1997).

The subjective experiences of these illnesses stand in sharp contrast to the medical uncertainty surrounding them. Individual sufferers provide persuasive accounts of their distress (Asbring and Narvanen 2003; Barker 2005; Hayden and Sacks 1998; Koziol et al. 1993; Kroll-Smith and Floyd 1997). They report significant reductions in functional abilities, health status, and quality of life, and little long-term improvement in well-being over time (Manu 2004; Nimnuan et al. 2001; Wessley, Nimnuan, and Sharpe 1999). Living with a contested illness, therefore, means managing a constellation of chronic and often debilitating symptoms, as well as coping with medical uncertainty, skepticism, and disparagement. Indeed these conditions are called "contested" illnesses precisely because of the clash between medical knowledge and patient experience (Conrad and Stults 2008; Dumit 2006; Moss and Teghtsoonian 2008).

A related line of investigation addresses contested environmental illnesses, or illnesses that involve "scientific disputes and extensive public debates over environmental causes" (Brown 2007, xiv). A growing body of research demonstrates that when individuals claim to have an illness caused by exposure to environmental hazards, they meet with considerable resistance (Brown et al. 2004; Zavestoski et al. 2004a, b). Specifically, "corporate, government, and medical authorities" contest environmental illness claims in an effort to defend their organizational, professional, and economic interests (Cable, Mix, and Shriver 2008, 384). The principal contestation is over claims that a specific condition (e.g., breast cancer, asthma, lung cancer) is caused by exposure to a particular environmental hazard. In some cases, however, there are also disputes about the existence of the illness itself (e.g., Gulf War Syndrome, multiple chemical sensitivity disorder) said to be caused by environmental toxins (Kroll-Smith et al. 2000). These latter cases are examples of contested illness as defined in this chapter, but all contested environmental illnesses showcase conflicts between biomedical and lay ways of knowing, and hinge on the inability of medical experts to legitimate lay peoples' symptoms and suffering (ibid., 4).

According to Joseph Dumit (2006, 578), contested illnesses "are researched, discussed, and reported on, but no aspect of them is settled medically, legally, or popularly." Pamela Moss and Katherine Teghtsoonian (2008, 7) describe contested illnesses as "dismissed as illegitimate—framed as 'difficult,' psychosomatic, or even nonexistent—by researchers, health practitioners, and policy makers operating within conventional paradigms of knowledge." More than a decade ago, Brown (1995) identified two types of conflictual or contested diagnoses: conditions that are generally accepted but to which a medical definition is not routinely applied (e.g., environmental diseases);

and conditions that are not generally accepted but to which a medical definition is nevertheless often applied (e.g., chronic fatigue syndrome). In both cases, for different reasons, sufferers have to convince the institution of bio-medicine that their condition is medical in character. Thus, the term "contested" denotes that these illnesses exist somewhere between entirely discredited and fully legitimate diseases.

The particulars concerning the knowledge and experience of individual contested illnesses differ. For example, each condition is coupled with a body of medical research and a case definition or diagnostic criteria (Dumit 2006; Wessley, Nimnuan, and Sharpe 1999). Having been the beneficiaries of more sympathy from mainstream medical professionals, some of these classifications are more widely applied (e.g., fibromyalgia syndrome, irritable bowel syndrome) than others (e.g., sick building syndrome, multiple chemical sensitivity disorder). These illnesses can also be differentiated on the basis of subjective features and accounts: the experience and meaning of living with fibromyalgia is distinct from that of multiple chemical sensitive disorder; and individuals and groups coalesce around specific diagnoses. Nevertheless, these illnesses share a number of key similarities that account for their contested status.

Given that sufferers and their advocates want medically unexplainable symptoms to be medically recognized and legitimated, contested illnesses are examples of conditions for which individual patients and patient groups demand medicalization.[2] That is, they are evidence of a shift in the engines of medicalization: the demands of patient-consumers, rather than the professional agendas of physicians, increasingly underlie medicine's jurisdictional expansion (Conrad 2005). In addition, contested illness and medicalization are tied together conceptually via social constructionism: "Both medicalization and contested illness highlight that illness categories (usually, but not always, diagnoses) are socially constructed and not automatically ascertained from scientific and/or medical discoveries" (Conrad and Stults 2008, 332). What follows is a descriptive account of the social construction of contested illnesses.

Of specific interest to us are the shared factors and influences in the social processes by which contested illnesses were created and propagated. These include public intolerance of or anxiety about medically unexplainable but highly common symptoms; the dynamics of doctor-patient encounters and the corresponding diagnostic imperative; lay knowledge production and the emergence of illness identities and communities; and bureaucratic and institutional demands and practices (Aronowitz 1997; Barsky and Borus 1995; Brown 1995; Freidson 1971; Showalter 1997). I address each in turn.

When delineating the factors contributing to the social construction of contested illnesses, ground zero, so to speak, is the ubiquity of the symptoms they represent. Contested-illness symptoms are widespread in the general public and are particularly common among women (Fillingim 2000; Lorber and Moore 2002; Mayou and Farmer 2002). For example, pain and fatigue are the most common physical aliments reported by the general public (Barsky and Borus 1999). Fatigue is so commonly reported that the acronym TATT (tired all the time) now appears regularly in medical and popular media. The additional symptoms that make up these disorders, including mood, sleep, and bowel disturbances, are also widely prevalent (Mayou and Farmer 2002). This is not to suggest that these disorders are much ado about nothing. Whether these symptoms are common or not, their cumulative effect can be overwhelming. Aggravating this tendency is our cultural impatience with discomfort (Barsky and Borus 1995; Kleinman 1988; Kleinman and Ware 1992).

Accordingly, individuals turn to the institution of medicine for an explanation and remedy. However, even with extensive and very expensive clinical workups, many common symptoms simply can't be explained in biomedical terms (Barsky and Borus 1995; Mayou and Farmer 2002). So it is that sufferers describe a protracted and troubling road into medical uncertainty. "Nothing is wrong," they are told by one doctor after another. And yet they feel very ill indeed. In turn, sufferers must reconcile a subjective certainty of their symptoms with a lack of objective medical evidence regarding the existence of their symptoms (Asbring and Narvanen 2001). Along the way, individuals experience real or perceived accusations that they are faking their symptoms, malingering, or "just plain crazy" (Dumit 2006, 578). Their credibility is called into question. Given the gulf between their distress and the growing mound of negative medical tests, even sufferers sometimes begin to doubt their own grip on reality (Asbring and Narvanen 2003; Banks and Prior 2001). Not surprisingly, many individuals doggedly continue their search for a biological explanation in an effort to prove to medical professionals, their families, and themselves that they really are ill (Dumit 2006). In her research on chronic fatigue syndrome, Pia Bülow (2008) aptly calls this arduous search the "pilgrimage."

The dynamics of countless medical encounters that make up many such pilgrimages stand behind the creation and application of these diagnoses. There are many reasons that doctor-patient encounters favor diagnosing. For the physician, a diagnosis represents codified knowledge about a patient's experience and indicates a treatment protocol. For the patient, a diagnosis gives meaning and legitimacy to worrying symptoms and provides a framework for what he or she is facing (Balint 1957). Thus, when a doctor encounters a patient with distressing symptoms, both parties benefit from a diagnosis: it effectively legitimizes both parties and the doctor-patient relationship itself. Before contested-illness diagnoses could serve this legitimating purpose, however, they had to be created.

The creation of these diagnoses, in terms of both the specific case definitions and the actors advancing those definitions, differ in their particulars (Barsky and Borus 1999; Wessley, Nimnuan, and Sharpe 1999), but two general points can be made. First, each of these diagnoses is a descriptive category or analytic abstraction that stands for otherwise medically unexplainable symptoms (Mayou and Farmer 2002). It has been argued that many medical specialties and subspecialties have at least one functional diagnosis at their disposal to manage a large population of patients whose symptoms lack an understood biological cause; hence the creation of several different, overlapping syndromes (e.g., rheumatology has fibromyalgia, neurologists have tension head ache, gastroenterologists have irritable bowel syndrome, gynecologists have chronic pelvic pain) (Barsky and Borus 1999; Nimnuan et al. 2001). Second, although none of these diagnoses would have come about without the efforts of key players who pushed for their creation—"claims-makers," as Conrad and Schneider (1992) call them—those that were advanced primarily by specialists in the medical mainstream have moved further along in the medicalization process than have those that relied more heavily on lay advocacy or were associated with marginal medical professionals. Examples of the former include fibromyalgia and irritable bowel syndrome. Examples of the latter include multiple chemical sensitivity and chronic fatigue syndrome.[3]

Although some support from sympathetic medical professionals is a necessary part in disease discovery, medical professionals also resist discovery (Brown 1995). Again, this resistance is what defines contested illnesses. Reflecting the most contested end of the continuum, an article published in the prestigious *Annals of Internal Medicine* referred to multiple chemical sensitivity as a "cult" (quoted in Kroll-Smith and Floyd 1997, 29). But even the least contested of the contested illnesses, fibromyalgia, has been resolutely attacked. The essence of the charge, captured in the following quote from a leading rheumatology journal, points to the social construction of the diagnosis: "No one can have fibromyalgia. Fibromyalgia is just a word we use to represent the situation of someone complaining about widespread chronic pain, fatigue, and sleep disturbances. ... It is not a disease, it's a description" (da Silva 2004, 828). The creation of contested illness diagnostic categories represents a decisive move toward the medicalization of common physical and mental distress, but none of these conditions is yet fully medicalized. In the absence of biomedical markers or efficacious treatments, medical professionals will continue to be skeptical of further medicalization.

Where diagnoses have been created—by whatever path and against whatever crystallized medical opposition—a number of factors have ensured their widespread application. First among these is a tendency within medicine to favor assigning illness over health. This is called the "decision rule" (Freidson 1971), but it might also be called the "diagnostic imperative." Concerned about their patients and trained to be proactive, physicians prefer to diagnose illness rather than health. Consequently, the existence of these diagnoses gives medical practitioners a new tool for managing the steady influx of patients with otherwise unexplainable symptoms. Under the weight of the decision rule, even physicians who are skeptical about contested illnesses are inclined to diagnose them.

The diagnosing behavior of physicians is only one side of the story. Once contested illnesses exist, again in the narrow sense of the creation of a diagnostic classification, individuals in distress encounter them. This makes possible perhaps the most crucial moment in the patient's pilgrimage (Bülow 2008)—the moment when her suffering is at last given a name. A diagnosis brings a coherence and order to a collection of symptoms that have heretofore been incoherent and unruly. Perhaps even more important, the diagnosis validates the sufferer and her suffering after a protracted period of disparagement (Asbring and Narvanen 2003; Barker 2005; Dumit 2006). In practical terms, a diagnosis is required to receive health care, disability compensation, and other social reparations. For all these reasons, individuals often strongly identify with their diagnosis. These are also all key factors that motivate sufferers to demand greater medicalization of their condition.

The means by which individuals encounter their diagnosis is also of interest. In some instances, the patient learns about her diagnosis only when a sympathetic (or agnostic) medical provider diagnoses her. Increasingly, however, individuals discover their diagnosis without the aid of their health-care provider. Some happen upon their diagnosis by way of a family member or friend battling the same symptoms. Others come to their diagnosis after reading a magazine or newspaper article that describes a condition that fits their symptoms to a tee. As the Internet becomes a primary source of health-related information (Fox and Fallows 2003), an ever-greater number of individuals find their diagnosis by typing their symptoms into an online search engine. In turn they connect to an extensive network of commercial and nonprofit websites that describe their symptomatic experience as evidence of a diagnosable disease about which they were previously unaware (Barker 2008; and see Conrad and Stults, this volume). Now that the FDA has approved the first drug for the treatment of fibromyalgia, some individuals find out they have this disease courtesy of a direct-to-consumer pharmaceutical advertisement.

Although commonplace, self-diagnosis is insufficient; individuals need medical corroboration. Sometimes doctors are amenable, especially given the inertia of the decision rule. But many clinicians are hesitant to diagnose patients with a contested illness. Some patients go from doctor to doctor in search of a willing diagnostician. For this reason, Dumit (2006, 577) calls these "illnesses you have to fight to get." Again, issues surrounding self-validation and health/disability compensation make the fight for a diagnosis particularly salient.

Illness support communities also play an important role in the social construction of contested illnesses. Although patient advocacy, education, and mutual support are increasingly common in relation to many illnesses, contested-illness sufferers are particularly eager to affiliate with those who share their experiences. To use Bülow's (2008) metaphor again, these communities provide a welcomed shelter for the weary pilgrim. Through a variety of sources (e.g., best-selling self-help books, real and virtual support groups, and a host of advocacy organizational websites), individuals learn the biological facts—those denied by the uninformed in the medical mainstream—about their "real" disease. They also learn how to manage symptoms, deflect medical derision, and find a friendly provider who will diagnosis and treat their disease. Illness support communities produce and disseminate knowledge of sufferers' shared embodied experiences in an effort to support fellow sufferers, produce logical accounts of their distress, and challenge medical critics (Barker 2008; Dumit 2006; Kroll-Smith and Floyd 1997). At the level of experience, therefore, affiliation with a contested-illness community validates an individual's diagnosis and the diagnostic category. It would be difficult to overstate the degree to which the Internet has increased the reach and influence of these communities

(Barker 2008; and see Conrad and Stults, this volume).

In this way, contested illnesses are examples of what Hacking (1999) calls "interactive kinds of things." Herein lies another important factor fueling the development of contested illnesses. In the case of interactive kinds of things, individuals react to being classified in particular ways. Unlike calling a quark a quark, which Hacking notes makes no difference to the quark, an individual reacts to being diagnosed with fibromyalgia or chronic fatigue syndrome or irritable bowel syndrome. Individuals come to see themselves as having a particular disease and reorient their symptoms and sense of self in relationship to that disease designation. This is starkly seen with respect to the self-validation that being diagnosed represents. The diagnosis launches a particular illness career, contributes to the creation of an illness identity, and makes possible affiliation with an illness community. Additionally, the creation and application of these diagnoses result in their reification: although these diagnoses are conceptual abstractions, they have come to garner status as "things." Because contested illnesses include many common symptoms and provide no exclusionary criteria, sufferers can readily see the parallels between their own illness experience and the illness experience of fellow sufferers. Not only are contested illnesses interactive kinds of things in terms of how the designation interacts with the individual so designated, but their interactive quality also creates a cultural milieu wherein even more individuals, through their brief or extensive encounters with illness support communities, come to locate themselves within these designations.

Finally, organizational imperatives and dynamics also critically influence "the type and amount of conditions discovered" (Brown 1995, 45). Patients with unexplainable symptoms can be very costly. Although managed-care organizations erect barriers to limit health-care utilization, these barriers force patients to "express their 'disease' in more urgent and exaggerated terms in order to gain access to the physician" (Barsky and Borus 1995, 1931) Additionally, health-care providers use these diagnoses to help patients gain access to health-care resources within the constraints of managed care. Curiously, a case can also be made that these diagnoses might, in the end, work to the financial advantage of managed-care organizations. When patients with medically unexplainable symptoms are diagnosed with a contested illness in its early stages, health-care costs are reduced by limiting the number of expensive diagnostic tests, referrals to specialists, and surgical procedures that otherwise characterize the contested-illness experience. Because the standard treatment protocol is often relatively inexpensive (e.g., pain, sleep, and anti-depressant medications, as well as behavioral and exercise therapies), managed-care organizations may use contested-illness diagnoses as part of their agenda for cost containment.

In sum, contested illnesses reveal the conceptual union between social constructionism and medicalization. Specifically, contested illnesses are social constructions that give biomedical meaning to a broad range of distress and suffering that characterize the lives of many individuals, especially women. The contested status of these diagnoses, however, signifies only partial medicalization. Whereas advocates for contested illnesses demand greater medicalization as a route to legitimate the sufferer and secure necessary health and welfare reparations, critics hope to stem the medicalization tide to which these diagnoses contribute (Conrad and Stults 2008). There are two obvious paths toward increasing the degree to which contested illnesses are medicalized. The first includes identifying biological markers upon which the "social legitimacy and intellectual plausibility of contemporary disease categorizations often hinge" (Shostak, Conrad, and Horwitz 2008, 310). For example, recent reports of potential genetic variations associated with restless leg syndrome bode well for this condition's further medicalization (Shostak, Conrad, and Horwitz 2008). The second path includes a specific treatment option. Based on my current research, for example, sufferers and their clinician-advocates have enthusiastically embraced the recent FDA approval of the first drug specifically for the treatment of fibromyalgia syndrome, more for the drug's disease-legitimating potential than for its therapeutic efficacy.

It is worth restating what it means to call contested illnesses socially constructed. As they currently exist, these diagnoses are best understood as intellectual categories whose social etiological is more clearly understood than is their biomedical etiology. The diagnostic criteria for these illnesses are descriptive, subjectively determined, and inexactly and inconsistently applied. The creation of these diagnostic categories has more to do with the social dictates of clinical encounters, the influence of illness communities, and institutional demands than with scientific or medical discoveries. Contested illnesses are very large conceptual tents under which many dissimilar types of symptoms and distress can be located. What is more, these types of symptoms and distress are widespread in general, and particularly common among women.

Calling these syndromes socially constructed, however, does not deny the reality of their symptoms. It is clear that the suffering of those so diagnosed is real: their quality of life is significantly eroded and they would do almost anything to be well (Asbring and Narvanen 2001; Bülow 2008; Kroll-Smith and Floyd 1997). Although the diagnostic labels are social constructions, they might, in fact, represent a number of things that have biomedical correlates that are currently unknown.

The socially constructed meanings that mediate our experience of a disorder or condition can be overly simplistic, imperfect, or vague, but that does not mean that the symptoms that comprise the disorder have no biological basis or that they would cease to exist in the absence of a specific diagnosis. Instead, as Hacking has claimed, things can be *both* socially constructed *and* real; this may, in fact, prove to be the case with one or more contested illnesses.

CONCLUSION

All illnesses, not just those that are contested, are in some general sense socially constructed. Without exception, the meaning and experience of all illness is innately social. In this regard we can speak of the social construction of epilepsy. To be sure, the seizures are real. At the same time, however, the meaning of the seizures (possession vs. disease) and their experience (stigmatized vs. medicalized) is socially contingent. This chapter has emphasized the social construction of illness in a more limited or restricted sense, focusing on the social creation of new biomedical diagnostic categories for human experiences that do not lend themselves to such categorization, with contested illnesses as a case in point. A restricted definition of the social construction of illness gives medical sociologists a powerful expository tool for charting the concrete social forces that promote medicalization. Insofar as lay people, not the medical profession, demand the medicalization of contested illnesses, the creation of contested-illness categories is paradigmatic of the shifting engines of medicalization (Conrad 2005).

It is important to put the social construction of contested illnesses into larger perspective. Many widely accepted disorders are also characterized by uncertainties. Many uncontested conditions lack diagnostic precision or are difficult to diagnose (e.g., asthma, osteoarthritis, rheumatoid arthritis); the causal mechanisms of some illnesses are poorly understood or unknown (e.g., lupus, multiple sclerosis, scoliosis, allergies); and many conditions respond poorly or only marginally to medical therapeutics (e.g., Alzheimer's disease, pancreatic cancer). None of these disorders are discredited as biologically unreal on such grounds. Some of these conditions can hardly be in doubt, given that they dramatically and unambiguously manifest themselves in bodily disfigurement or death. But others are neither disfiguring nor deadly. In short, imperfect medical knowledge is ubiquitous to contemporary biomedicine.

One might argue that contested illnesses are but exaggerated or extreme cases of contemporary medicine's inevitable encounter with uncertainty. To a large degree, this can be attributed to the intrinsic difficulties many chronic conditions pose to conventional biomedicine, which proved far more effective in slaying our earlier infectious enemies. But biomedical uncertainty alone is an insufficient explanation. Biomedicine's lack of certitude about contemporary illnesses is also the result of its dealings with an ever-expanding range of complex human distresses. Uncertainty grows as patients and clinicians alike seek to frame multifaceted forms of human suffering within the confines of the conventional biomedical model. That is, uncertainty grows as we push for greater medicalization. Most of us live or will live with a number of long-term afflictions that are medically diffuse and elusive but that nevertheless, negatively and very tangibly, impact the quality of our lives. The creation of contested-illness diagnoses puts into sharp relief our sociocultural response to this larger dilemma, suggesting that we either come to acknowledge and address the normalization of suffering, or expect to see the creation of many new contested-illness diagnoses in the future.

NOTES

Some of the material in this chapter appears in Barker 2002, 2005, and 2008.

1 Brown (1995, 34–35) suggests that there are three versions of social constructionism in medical sociology. The first emerges from social problems scholarship that addresses the contingent processes by which specific phenomena come to be identified as social problems. The second version draws on the Focauldian tradition and emphasizes how medical knowledge and discourse give meaning to illness. The third version, aligned with the interdisciplinary field of science studies, argues that the production of scientific facts emerges from everyday social actions and interactions in clinical settings.

2 Given the definition of contested illness, it is possible to consider post-traumatic stress disorder (PTSD) and attention deficit hyperactivity disorder (ADHD) under the rubric of contested illnesses. More generally, many mental illnesses are contested, since sufferers and advocates claim the existence of a biophysical basis for these conditions that is not currently acknowledged by medical experts. In this chapter, contested illnesses are limited to the overlapping conditions referred to as "functional" in the medical literature.

3 The campaign behind chronic fatigue syndrome originated with the claims of two physicians in Lake Tahoe concerning a link between mysterious symptoms and the Epstein-Barr virus. The subsequent path to medicalize CFS, however, was heavily lay forged (Aronowitz 1997; Showalter 1997). Along with other contested environmental illnesses, the emergence of multiple chemical sensitivity disorder also relied overwhelmingly on lay advocacy. The legitimacy of contested environmental illnesses has been further hindered (or at least not advanced) by their association with health professionals practicing in specialties that the American Medical Association does not recognize (e.g., clinical ecology and environmental medicine).

REFERENCES

Adler, Patricia A., and Peter Adler. 2007. "The Demedicalization of Self-Injury: From Psychopathology to Sociological Deviance." *Journal of Contemporary Ethnography* 36:537–70.

Angell, Marcia. 2004. *The Truth about the Drug Companies.* New York: Random House.

Aronowitz, Robert. 1997. "From Myalgic Encephalitis to Yuppie Flu: A History of Chronic Fatigue Syndrome." In *Framing Disease,* ed. Charles Rosenberg and Janet Golden, 155–81. New Brunswick, N.J.: Rutgers University Press.

Asbring, Pia, and Anna-Liisa Narvanen. 2001. "Chronic Illness—A Disruption in Life: Identity-Transformation among Women with Chronic Fatigue Syndrome and Fibromyalgia." *Journal of Advanced Nursing* 34:312–19.

———. 2003. "Ideal versus Reality: Physicians' Perspectives on Patients with Chronic Fatigue Syndrome (CFS) and Fibromyalgia." *Social Science and Medicine* 57:711–20.

Balint, Michael. 1957. *The Doctor, His Patient and the Illness.* New York: International Universities Press.

Banks, Jonathan, and Lindsay Prior. 2001. "Doing Things with Illness: The Micro Politics of the CFS Clinic." *Social Science and Medicine* 52:11–23.

Barker, Kristin. 1998. "A Ship upon a Stormy Sea: The Medicalization of Pregnancy." *Social Science and Medicine* 47:1067–76.

———. 2002. "Self-Help Literature and the Making of an Illness Identity: The Case of Fibromyalgia Syndrome." *Social Problems* 49:279–300.

———. 2005. *The Fibromyalgia Story: Medical Authority and Women's Worlds of Pain.* Philadelphia: Temple University Press.

———. 2008. "Electronic Support Groups, Patient-Consumers, and Medicalization: The Case of Contested Illness." *Journal of Health and Social Behavior* 49:20–36.

Barsky, Arthur, and Jonathan Borus. 1995. "Somatization and Medicalization in the Era of Managed Care." *Journal of the American Medical Association* 274:1931–34.

———. 1999. "Functional Somatic Syndromes." *Annals of Internal Medicine* 130:910–21.

Berger, Peter, and Thomas Luckmann. 1967. *The Social Construction of Reality: A Treatise in the Sociology of Knowledge.* New York: Anchor.

Blum, Virginia. 2003. *Flesh Wounds: The Culture of Cosmetic Surgery.* Berkeley: University of California Press.

Boghossian, Paul. 2001. "What Is Social Construction?" *Times Literary Supplement,* February.

———. 2006. *Fear of Knowledge: Against Relativism and Constuctivism.* New York: Oxford University Press.

Bohr, T. W. 1995. "Fibromyalgia Syndrome and Myofascial Pain Syndrome: Do They Exist?" *Neurologic Clinics* 13:365–84.

Brown, Phil. 1995. "Naming and Framing: The Social Construction of Diagnosis and Illness." *Journal of Health and Social Behavior,* extra issue: 34–52.

———. 2007. *Toxic Exposures: Contested Illnesses and the Environmental Health Movement.* New York: Columbia University Press.

Brown, Phil, Stephen Zavestoski, Sabrina McCormick, Brian Mayer, Rachel Morello-Frosch, and Rebecca Gesior Altman. 2004. "Embodied Health Movements: New Approaches to Social Movements in Health." *Sociology of Health and Illness* 26:50–80.

Brumberg, Joan Jacobs. 2009. "Anorexia Nervosa in Context." In *The Sociology of Health and Illness: Critical Perspectives,* 8th ed., ed. Peter Conrad, 107–20. New York: Worth.

Bülow, Pia H. 2008. "Tracing Contours of Contestation in Narratives about Chronic Fatigue Syndrome." In *Contesting Illness: Processes and Practices,* ed. Pamela Moss and Katherine Teghtsoonian, 123–41. Toronto: University of Toronto Press.

Cable, Sherry, Tamara L. Mix, and Thomas E. Shriver. 2008. "Risk Society and Contested Illness: The Case of Nuclear Weapons Workers." *American Sociological Review* 73:380–401.

Casiday, Rachel Elizabeth. 2007. "Children's Health and the Social Theory of Risk: Insights from the British Measles, Mumps and Rubella (MMR) Controversy." *Social Science and Medicine* 65:1059–70.

Clarke, Adele, Laura Mamo, Jennifer R. Fishman, Janet K. Shim, and Jennifer Ruth Fosket. 2003. "Biomedicalization: Technoscientific Transformations of Health, Illness, and U.S. Biomedicine." *American Sociological Review* 68:161–94.

Collins, Patricia Hill. 1991. *Black Feminist Thought: Knowledge, Consciousness, and the Politics of Empowerment.* New York: Routledge.

Copeland, D. A. and Valle, G. 2009. "You Don't Need a Prescription to Go Gluten-Free": The Scientific Self-Diagnosis of Celiac Disease. *Social Science and Medicine* 69:623–31.

Conrad, Peter. 2007. *The Medicalization of Society: On the Transformation of Human Conditions into Treatable Disorders*. Baltimore: Johns Hopkins University Press.

———. 2005. "The Shifting Engines of Medicalization." *Journal of Health and Social Behavior* 46:3–14.

Conrad, Peter, and Joseph W. Schneider. 1992. *Deviance and Medicalization: From Badness to Sickness*. Philadelphia: Temple University Press.

Conrad, Peter, and Cheryl Stults. 2008. "Contestation and Medicalization." In *Contesting Illness: Processes and Practices*, ed. Pamela Moss and Katherine Teghtsoonian, 323–35. Toronto: University of Toronto Press.

da Silva, Luiz Claudio. 2004. "Fibromyalgia: Reflections about Empirical Science and Faith." *Journal of Rheumatology* 31:827–28.

de Beauvoir, Simone. 1989 [1953]. *The Second Sex*. Translated by H. M. Parshley. New York: Knopf.

Dumit, Joseph. 2006. "Illnesses You Have to Fight to Get: Facts and Forces in Uncertain, Emergent Illnesses." *Social Science and Medicine* 62:577–90.

Ehrenreich, Barbara, and Deirdre English. 1973. *Complaints and Disorders: The Sexual Politics of Sickness*. New York: Feminist Press.

Epstein, Steven. 1996. *Impure Science: AIDS, Activism, and the Politics of Knowledge*. Berkeley: University of California Press.

Fillingim, Roger. 2000. *Sex, Gender, and Pain*. Seattle, Wash.: IASP Press.

Fox, Susannah, and Deborah Fallows. 2003. Internet Health Resources. Pew Internet and American Life Project. www.pewinternet.org. Accessed November 26, 2005.

Freidson, Eliot. 1970. *Profession of Medicine: A Study of the Sociology of Applied Knowledge*. New York: Harper and Row.

Hacking, Ian. 1998. *Mad Travelers: Reflections on the Reality of Transient Mental Illnesses*. Charlottesville: University of Virginia Press.

———. 1999. *The Social Construction of What?* Cambridge, Mass.: Harvard University Press.

Hadler, N. M. 1997a. "Fibromyalgia, Chronic Fatigue, and Other Iatrogenic Diagnostic Algorithms. Do Some Labels Escalate Illness in Vulnerable Patients?" *Postgraduate Medicine* 102:262–77.

———. 1997b. "La Maladie Est Morte, Vive le Malade." *Journal of Rheumatology* 24:1250–51.

Hayden, Lars-Christer, and Lisbeth Sacks. 1998. "Suffering, Hope and Diagnosis: On Negotiation of Chronic Fatigue Syndrome." *Health* 2:175–93.

Henningsen, P., S. Zipfel, and W. Herzog. 2007. "Management of Functional Somatic Syndromes." *Lancet* 369:946–55.

Horwitz, Allan V. 2002. *Creating Mental Illness*. Chicago: University of Chicago Press.

Illich, Ivan. 1976. *Medical Nemesis: The Expropriation of Health*. New York: Pantheon.

Kleinman, Arthur. 1988. *The Illness Narratives: Suffering, Healing and the Human Condition*. New York: Basic Books.

Kleinman, Arthur, and Norma C. Ware. 1992. "Culture and Somatic Experience: The Social Course of Illness in Neurasthenia and Chronic Fatigue Syndrome." *Psychosomatic Medicine* 54:546–60.

Knorr Cetina, Karin. 1997. "Sociality with Objects: Social Relations in Postsocial Knowledge Societies." *Theory, Culture and Society* 14:1–30.

Koziol, J. A., D. C. Clark, R. F. Gittes, and E. M. Tan. 1993. "The Natural History of Interstitial Cystitis: A Survey of 374 Patients." *Journal of Urology* 149(3): 465–69.

Kroll-Smith, Steve, Phil Brown, and Valerie J. Gunter. 2000. *Illness and the Environment: A Reader in Contested Medicine*. New York: New York University Press.

Kroll-Smith, Steve, and H. Hugh Floyd. 1997. *Bodies in Protest: Environmental Illness and the Struggle over Medical Knowledge*. New York: New York University Press.

Latour, Bruno. 1987. *Science in Action: How to Follow Scientists and Engineers through Society*. Cambridge, Mass.: Harvard University Press.

Lorber, Judith, and Lisa Jean Moore. 2002. *Gender and the Social Construction of Illness*. 2nd ed. Lanham, Md.: Rowman Altamira.

———. 2007. *Gendered Bodies: Feminist Perspectives*. Los Angeles: Roxbury Publishing.

Mannheim, Karl. 1936. *Ideology and Utopia*. New York: Harcourt, Brace.

Manu, Peter. 2004. *The Psychopathology of Functional Somatic Syndromes*. New York: Haworth Medical Press.

Martin, Emily. 1987. *The Woman in the Body: A Cultural Analysis of Reproduction*. Boston: Beacon Press.

Mayou, Richard, and Andrew Farmer. 2002. "Functional Somatic Symptoms and Syndromes." *British Medical Journal* 325:265–68.

McCrea, Frances. 1983. "The Politics of Menopause: The 'Discovery' of a Deficiency Disease." *Social Problems* 31:111–23.

Merton, Robert. 1973. *The Sociology of Science: Theory and Empirical Investigations.* Chicago: Chicago University Press.

Moss, Pamela, and Katherine Teghtsoonian. 2008. "Power and Illness: Authority, Bodies, and Context." In *Contesting Illness,* ed. Pamela Moss and Katherine Teghtsoonian, 3–27. Toronto: University of Toronto Press.

Moynihan, R., I. Heath, and D. Henry. 2002. "Selling Sickness: The Pharmaceutical Industry and Disease Mongering." *British Medical Journal* 324:886–91.

Nimnuan, Chaichana, Sophia Rabe-Hesketh, Simon Wessley, and Matthew Hotopf. 2001. "How Many Functional Somatic Syndromes." *Journal of Psychosomatic Research* 51:549–57.

Parsons, Talcott. 1951. *The Social System.* Glencoe, Ill.: Free Press.

Pascoe, C. J., and Natalie Boero. 2008. *No Wannarexics Allowed: An Analysis of Pro-Eating Disorder Online Communities.* Typescript.

Peitzman, Steven J. 1992. "From Bright's Disease to End-Stage Renal Disease." In *Framing Disease: Studies in Cultural History,* ed. Charles Rosenberg and Janet Golden, 3–19. New Brunswick, N.J.: Rutgers University Press.

Riessman, Catherine. 1983. "Women and Medicalization: A New Perspective." *Social Policy* 14:3–18.

Searle, John R. 1995. *The Construction of Social Reality.* New York: Free Press.

Shostak, Sara, Peter Conrad, and Allan Horwitz. 2008. "Sequencing and Its Consequences: Path Dependency and the Relationships between Genetics and Medicalization." *American Journal of Sociology* 114:287–316.

Showalter, Elaine. 1997. *Hystories: Hysterical Epidemics and Modern Media.* New York: Columbia University Press.

Skolbekken, John-Arne. 2008. "Unlimited Medicalization? Risk and the Pathologization of Normality." In *Health Risk and Vulnerability,* ed. Ian Wilkinson, 16–29. New York: Routledge.

Slezak, Peter. 2000. "A Critique of Radical Social Constructionism." In *Constructivism in Education: Opinions and Second Opinions on Controversial Issues,* ed. D. C. Philips, 91–126. Chicago: University of Chicago Press.

Smith, Dorothy. 1987. *The Everyday World as Problematic: A Feminist Sociology.* Boston: Northeastern University Press.

Sokal, Alan. 1996. "Transgressing the Boundaries: Towards a Transformative Hermeneutics of Quantum Gravity." *Social Text* 46/47:217–52.

Starr, Paul. 1982. *The Social Transformation of American Medicine.* New York: Basic Books.

Tesh, Sylvia Noble. 1988. *Hidden Arguments: Political Ideology and Disease Prevention Policy.* New Brunswick, N.J.: Rutgers University Press.

Theriot, Nancy. 1993. "Women's Voices in Nineteenth-Century Medical Discourse: A Step toward Deconstructing Science." *Signs* 19:1–31.

Timmerman, Stefan. 2007. *Postmortem: How Medical Examiners Explain Suspicious Deaths (Fieldwork and Discoveries).* Chicago: University of Chicago Press.

Tomes, Nancy. 1998. *The Gospel of Germs: Men, Women, and the Microbe in American Life.* Cambridge, Mass.: Harvard University Press.

Wertz, Richard, and Dorothy Wertz. 1979. *Lying-In: A History of Childbirth in America.* New York: Schocken.

Wessley, S. 2004. "There Is Only One Functional Somatic Syndrome: For." *British Journal of Psychiatry* 185:95–96.

Wessley, S., C. Nimnuan, and M. Sharpe. 1999. "Functional Somatic Syndromes: One or Many?" *Lancet* 354:936–39.

Young, Allan. 1995. *The Harmony of Illusions: Inventing Post-Traumatic Stress Disorder.* Princeton, N.J.: Princeton University Press.

Zavestoski, Stephen, Phil Brown, Sabrina McCormick, Brian Mayer, Maryhelen D'Ottavi, and Jamie C. Lucove. 2004a. "Embodied Health Movements and Challenges to the Dominant Epidemiological Paradigm." *Research in Social Movements, Conflicts and Change* 25:253–78.

———. 2004b. "Patient Activism and the Struggle for Diagnosis: Gulf War Illnesses and Other Medically Unexplained Physical Symptoms in the U.S." *Social Science and Medicine* 58:161–75.

Zola, Irving Kenneth. 1972. "Medicine as an Institution of Social Control." *Sociological Review* 20:487–504.

The Patient's Experience of Illness

David A. Rier

What happens when someone gets sick? What is it like to *be* sick? This review considers the patient's experience of illness, broadly defined. Rather than a comprehensive survey, it is a selective look at some of the main contributions of research on the illness experience over the years and, more briefly, certain newer research areas, some suggestions for future research, and an assessment of the field's contributions. Insofar as possible, it emphasizes topics less widely covered in earlier reviews or by other chapters in this volume.[1] Also, given the enormity of the literature, it deals mainly with qualitative research. The topic encompasses illness narratives, but this chapter deals more with content than with format and epistemology, which Bell's (2000) piece in the previous edition of this handbook addressed well.

One way to appreciate how medical sociology has changed in how it understands the experience of illness is to begin with Parsons's (1951) statement of the sick role, which will provide both framework and foil for parts of our discussion. This model involved a pair of duties and a pair of privileges. Specifically, the sick person must recognize that it's bad to be sick and must also seek competent help (i.e., consult a physician) and comply with treatment. The sick are excused from their normal obligations (to family, community, job, etc.), and are also excused from blame for becoming ill. This model helped set the terms of discussion for over a

generation but has also sustained varied criticism from subsequent writers, fueling decades of debate (Parsons 1975; Levine and Kozloff 1978; Gallagher 1979; Gerhardt 1989; Turner 1990; Williams 2005). Relevant to this chapter are criticisms of the model for ignoring self-management, for its paternalism, and for its simplistic conceptualization of time. Most relevant for our purposes is what now seems the glaring absence of the patient's perspective from the model.

This absence of patient perspectives also characterized the first edition of the *Handbook of Medical Sociology* (Freeman, Levine, and Reeder 1963), and subsequent generations of medical sociology textbooks and anthologies, which placed hospitals and physicians squarely at the center. There was little focus on patients beyond their interactions with the medical system, involving such issues as debates over Parsons's sick role, the sick "career," help-seeking behavior, and provider-patient relationships (Twaddle and Hessler 1977; Mechanic 1978; Jaco 1979; Wolinsky 1980; Maykovich 1980). Even in the fourth edition of this handbook (Freeman and Levine 1989), the section headings tell the story: after an introductory section composed of two pieces—"The Present State of Medical Sociology" and "Trends in Death and Disease and the Contribution of Medical Measures"—subsequent pieces were grouped under "Sociological Perspectives in

David A Rier, "The Patient's Experience of Illness," Handbook of Medical Sociology, pp. 163-178. Copyright © 2010 by Vanderbilt University Press. Reprinted with permission.

Disease Causation," "The Organization of Health Services," "Use of Health Services," and "Health Care Providers."[2] All this reflects an era in which patients were not directly at the heart of medical sociology, and in which, even when their views were solicited, this was accomplished often through questionnaires designed around topics salient to researchers.

In medicine, too, the patient's perspective has not always received significant attention. Asymmetries in knowledge, status, and authority have traditionally helped doctors control communication with patients and compel patients to function according to the physician's definition of the situation (Anderson and Helm 1979). The physician's definition may differ substantially from that of the patient. According to Kleinman's (1988) distinction between disease and illness, disease is a physiological, clinical entity, which physicians are taught to approach in objective, empirical fashion. Illness, by contrast, is the subjective, lived experience of patients (and their families and perhaps social networks), within the context of their wider existence. It is comprised of elements such as fear, suffering, hope, stigma, support, and shame. Patients often frame their health problems as they subjectively experience them, as part of their lifeworlds. Yet Mishler's fine-grained analyses of patient-doctor communication demonstrated that, when seeing patients, doctors use various techniques, including interruptions, to guide patients into presenting their stories within the "disease" framework of biomedicine. This accords with biomedicine's goal of isolating and quantifying certain discrete, technical parameters for determining diagnosis and treatment. Mishler provides a powerful example of what this can mean in practice. In answer to a doctor's question about how long the patient had been drinking heavily, the patient answered, "Since I've been married." Rather than pursuing this comment as a clue to the patient's drinking

problems, the doctor treated it as something of a non sequitur, asking, "How long is that?" (Mishler 1984, 114). As Anderson and Helm and Mishler suggest, doctor-patient communication partly represents a struggle between the voices of the lifeworld and biomedicine.

Mirroring in part a gradual recognition of the value of eliciting patients' perspectives in medicine (Armstrong 1984) and a wider interest in narrative among social scientists (Hydén 1997), contemporary medical sociology has helped reverse the inattention to patients and their perspectives by highlighting the voice and experience of the lifeworld (Rosenfeld 2006, 65). This reflects and contributes to a redirection of interest away from the medical profession to the patient as a focus of inquiry in medical sociology.

SOME HIGHLIGHTS OF RESEARCH ON THE EXPERIENCE OF ILLNESS

Managing Chronic Illness

The overwhelming majority of research on the illness experience has involved chronic illness. Coping emerged early as a major concern. Strauss (1975), relying largely on sets of ethnographic studies, delineated key aspects of managing chronic illness. For example, he pointed out how coping with the daily regimens (of medication, exercise, therapy, etc.) necessary to preserve function and prevent further declines can take a major portion of one's time and energy and, in some cases, may even become the focal point of life. He described individuals' efforts to "normalize" their lives insofar as the disease allowed. Significantly, he also located problems of chronic illness in their wider policy context, such as when discussing the failure of U.S. communities to design facilities accessible to the chronically ill. Charmaz (1991), with greater use of direct interview data on the personal experience of illness, contributed additional insights. For example, she described trade-offs, compromises necessary in confronting the demands and limitations of the disease while preserving as much as possible of one's pre-illness life. A particularly valuable contribution has been her work on disclosure—the various calculations necessary to decide whether, when, how, and to whom one reveals one's physical condition (Strauss had discussed disclosure and concealment, but more briefly). Such maneuvering can leave the chronically ill maintaining complex webs of truth and lies. Crucially, Charmaz's analysis was also explicitly located within the dimension of time (to which we will return).

Definitions of Illness

Since Parsons (1951) published his original model of the sick role, numerous challenges have arisen. For example, determination of illness and assignment of the sick role are far from simple. Patients may struggle for years in their quest for the validation of an official diagnosis (Stewart and Sullivan 1982).

More recent work has highlighted other facets of the assignment of the sick role. First, there is the phenomenon of contested diseases and symptoms, in which providers and others reject patients' claims to be genuinely ill. Examples include chronic fatigue syndrome and myalgic encephalomyelitis, as well as unexplained constellations of symptoms (Cooper 1997; Nettleton et al. 2004; Sim and Madden 2008). Apart from the pain, loss of function, and other experiences common to various types of illnesses, in these cases patients' difficulty in securing a definitive diagnosis undermines their credibility with health providers and friends and family as well. Even patients themselves may question whether their ailments have psychological, rather than strictly somatic, origins. Back pain is among the most common forms of contested illness; absence of clinically observable signs means patients worry that others regard them as malingerers (Glenton 2005). Though Glenton regards Parsons's model of the sick role as inappropriate to the case of back pain, she observes that patients themselves *do* embrace its expectations, as they seek the legitimation and validation of a medical diagnosis (thus according the medical profession additional power). Indeed, she notes that, unlike most sufferers, for whom a medical diagnosis is generally unpleasant news, those living with back pain often welcome it as conferring a form of "absolution" (2249–50). But living with a contested disease may also politicize patients, causing them to resist (and lose faith in) their physicians. Discussing Gulf War syndrome, Brown and colleagues (2001) demonstrated how issues of contestation can play out against a wider social context of relations between laypersons, scientific expertise, and social activism. In this case, veterans pursued various strategies to legitimate their claims (disputed by government officials) to be suffering from service-related, somatic illnesses "worthy" of compensation. They met with only mixed success. Difficulties included incommensurable paradigms regarding disease criteria and standards of scientific evidence, bureaucratic inertia, and the fact that their claimed maladies were not readily traceable to specific exposures. A special case of contested disease is the phenomenon of the "worried well," particularly as regards HIV/AIDS. This refers mainly to individuals who, despite not having been diagnosed as HIV+, are convinced that they have been infected with the virus (Lombardo 2004).

Contestation cuts both ways, however. Individuals may resist efforts of professionals and society to label them ill. By 1979, Lorde (1997) was already resisting social pressure to label her, following mastectomy, as disfigured and requiring concealment via prosthetics. Still, she certainly viewed breast cancer as an actual disease. Yet some deaf activists resist the view of deafness as disability, seeing it instead as membership in an alternative "linguistic minority" (Lane 2006). A striking example of resistance is the "pro-ana" movement (especially online), in which those living with anorexia attempt to dissuade others from pursuing recovery (Fox, Ward, and O'Rourke 2005b; Gavin, Rodham, and Poyer 2008).

Second, there is the rich body of work on medicalization (e.g., Conrad and Schneider 1992). Conditions such as hyperactivity, homosexuality, and alcoholism have undergone sociocultural shifts, leading them to be considered, at various times and places, as sins, crimes, diseases, normal, and alternative lifestyle choices. Indeed, medicalization is one segment of a spectrum that can include de- and remedicalization, with given conditions moving in and out of medical frameworks and jurisdictions at different times and places. More recently, Conrad (2007) and others have highlighted how enhancement and augmentation to correct or supplement "normal" attributes have become more popular. Here, too, contemporary research has taken us far beyond Parsons's original formulation, which did not treat the actual determination of disease or illness (hence, patient) status as especially problematic.

The Politics of Patienthood

Parsons defined the patient nearly completely in terms of his or her relationship with physicians. Yet it is now clear that this is far too narrow a model. First, at least for chronic illness, those dealing with illness spend only limited time in direct contact, *as patients*, with the medical system (particularly since hospitalizations have shortened over the past several decades.) Today, much of the illness experience takes place well beyond the doctor-patient relationship. In particular, the community—rather than the hospital or doctor's office—has become

the locus of much management, with self-management an important element.

Second, patients themselves have demonstrated a far broader definition of their role. Not relying only on physicians, they rely on themselves, their families, and, via activist networks or online and offline support groups, on each other as well. Nowhere was this made more explicit than with the response to AIDS, where those living with HIV/AIDS engaged in informed critiques of the biomedical establishment's handling of research and policy; they even engaged in the production and dissemination of their own scientific data (Epstein 1996; Indyk and Rier 1993). One aspect of their activism was explicit resistance to the dominant model, which defined them, always, as patients. Consider AIDS activists' 1983 "Denver Principles" manifesto, which included the important statement: "we are only occasionally 'patients,' a term which implies passivity, helplessness, and dependence upon the care of others" (Advisory Committee of People with AIDS, quoted in Callen 1988, 294). By redefining patienthood and renegotiating definitions of expertise, AIDS activists have influenced activists for other diseases, from breast cancer to disability (Epstein 1996; Indyk and Rier 1993). As Prior (2003) shows, however, contemporary medical sociology may exaggerate such trends, sometimes conflating lay experiences with actual biomedical knowledge and expertise.

Internet

One realm in which individuals enact the post-Parsonian patient role, with its scope for much wider patient initiative and involvement, is on the Internet. The Internet arguably constitutes the single greatest change in the experience of illness over the last two decades. First, it is an extremely powerful tool for gaining information about symptoms, diagnosis, and treatment. There are now countless sites maintained by health authorities, universities, and various private and activist entities. There are also numerous sites operated by patients themselves. Often these take the form of support groups, in which those confronting various diseases post questions and comments and view the responses. Unlike traditional face-to-face support groups, participation is not limited to those who can fit in the same room at the same time; instead, membership can be truly global. To an extent Parsons could scarcely have envisioned in 1951, this helps individuals bypass their physicians and affords them wide access to those facing similar issues with whom to trade information and tips. Although it does not guarantee a revolution in doctor-patient relations (Broom 2005), such information empowers participants to question their doctor and form their own opinions about managing their illness (Hardey 1999; Ziebland 2004). Personal home pages become a means for private citizens to produce and disseminate their own information about illness (Hardey 2002).

Electronic groups also provide social and emotional support (Sharf 1997; Bar-Lev 2008). The anonymity they offer helps create an aura of a "safe space" where intimate issues can be discussed without fear of censure or stigma. Members may engage in intricate interactional practices to preserve this environment (Walstrom 2000). Online support groups may also serve as devices for communally debating, crystallizing, and attempting to enforce moral codes (Rier 2007a, b).

As suggested earlier, we may view the medical interview as partly a struggle between the voices of the lifeworld and of biomedicine. Online discussion and support groups, by contrast, are largely free of direct interference from professional and expert authorities (see Connery 1997). We might thus expect these channels to help liberate the traditionally subjugated voice of the lifeworld and create new, alternative types of illness discourses. However, such changes do not necessarily occur.

Pitts (2004) has criticized the personal webpages of breast cancer patients for reproducing both biomedical linguistic framing and the wider societal discourse of personal responsibility. Fox, Ward, and O'Rourke (2005a) found, in their study of an online support group for users of a weight-loss drug, that the group helped develop informed patients, but that online discussions replicated biomedical and societal discourses regarding obesity and weight loss. A study of how online HIV/AIDS support groups discussed seropositivity disclosure found that most posts replicated traditional, offline views of moral responsibility (Rier 2007b). Studies of online HIV/AIDS (Bar-Lev 2008) and breast cancer (Sandaunet 2008) support groups found that, while these groups did offer alternative spaces for airing personal concerns and exchanging support, they did not encourage certain "negative," socially undesirable comments.

Apart from what it means for patients, the Internet can influence how researchers study the experience of illness. In her study of agency and empowerment, Pitts (2004) examined webpages of women who confronted breast cancer. The online DIPEx video archive (recently redesigned as healthtalkonline.org) affords researchers the opportunity to conduct secondary analysis of interviews with those (or actors playing them, speaking their words) living with a range of diseases (Ziebland and Herxheimer 2008). The transparency of many online support groups turns them into a fascinating opportunity for researchers to treat them as subject-initiated, floating focus groups in which crystallization of community norms—and their enforcement—can be tracked in real time (Rier 2007a, 244).

Time

Parsons's original model was based on a patient who is healthy, gets sick, seeks medical help, and then gets better. Yet much of the work on the experience of illness points to far more complicated temporal patterns. In fact, the dimension of time pervades research on the experience of illness.

Trajectories

At least since Roth's (1963) early work on the illness trajectory of hospital patients, and Davis's ([1963] 1991) study of the various stages through which families pass when a child contracts polio, the time dimension has been a part of social science work on the illness experience. Strauss (1975, 47) noted, regarding chronic illness, that trajectories "may plunge straight down; move slowly but steadily downward; vacillate slowly, moving slightly up and down before diving downward radically; move slowly down at first, then hit a long plateau, then plunge abruptly, even to death." Charmaz (1991) devoted considerable attention to the dimension of time. She described how patients may subjectively experience illness: as interruption, intrusion, or immersion. Soon after onset, patients often viewed the illness as an interruption in the normal flow of their lives. They expect recovery and, as in Parsons's sick role, resumption of prior roles and identities. Often, however, patients came to experience their illness as a chronic, demanding intrusion requiring significant attention and trade-offs to manage their regimens, debilities, and other disruptions, while also trying to preserve as much day-to-day life as possible. More advanced, serious illness might lead to immersion, as the disease consumes more and more of one's daily life.

Yoshida (1993) contributed substantially to our grasp of the types of identity threat and reconstruction that can occur after disabling injury and how these unfold over time. Yoshida's mostly young respondents had experienced traumatic spinal cord injury. Though discussions of the illness trajectory had invariably portrayed it in linear fashion, Yoshida found that it described a pendular pattern. Specifically, these individuals oscillated between their "baseline" (preaccident) healthy, "whole" identity and the physically diminished, highly dependent self of their postaccident lives. Over time, the swings between these poles diminished, as the individuals settled into a middle ground in which they refashioned their identity to accommodate their disability without surrendering to it.

Illness States

Questions of time also bear directly upon the definitions of illness states. For example, there is the increasing significance of the "preemptive" or "preliminary" sick role. For Parsons, the sick role effectively commenced with manifestation of physical restrictions on fulfilling normal roles. Yet this is no longer true. By the 1980s, many confused testing seropositive for the HIV virus with being sick, triggering such risks as fear and stigma (Sontag 1990a, 120–21)—despite the fact that HIV+ individuals might not develop AIDS for years, if ever. The burdens of genetic testing provide another example. Cox and McKellin (1999) showed how healthy people known to be at risk for Huntington's disease apply a variety of subjective mental devices to decide whether to seek testing. Women with family risk of breast and ovarian cancer, even before the appearance of clinical signs of disease or definitive results of genetic testing, may regard themselves as bearing special responsibilities, particularly to their families. This can lead to phenomena such as high-risk women, with no evidence of actually having cancer, choosing elective, prophylactic mastectomy. Often, this choice involves complex feelings about their duties to their families, including questions of disclosure, such as to unmarried daughters (Hallowell 1999). The case of Machado-Joseph disease shows there may be feelings of guilt and responsibility among family members even when no genetic test exists (Boutte 1990). However, as genetic tests become increasingly available, these experiences will grow more common. Knowing one's genetic fate may be a mixed blessing, particularly in the absence of effective prevention or therapy (Kenen 1996). More recently, Arribas-Ayllon, Sarangi, and Clarke (2008) have detailed the dilemmas parents face regarding assuming or attributing responsibility for disclosing their children's genetic test results. A corollary category, resembling somewhat the experience of living with genetic risk, involves those receiving early detection of slow-moving cancers, such as prostate cancer (Oliffe et al. 2009). Such individuals confront not only existential uncertainty about their future, but also substantial clinical uncertainty about whether active management or "watchful waiting" is appropriate.

Time is also bound up with definitions of illness at the other end of the illness trajectory: the issue of resolution. Although in Parsons's model the patient simply seeks treatment, complies, and is cured, achieving such closure in practice is far from simple. With cancer, for example, even after passing the technical five-year survival milestone, former patients still face the possibility that their apparent cure is merely a remission, subject to recurrence. Physicians often have great difficulty in answering such questions as, "What are my odds, Doc?" or "How much time have I got?" (Christakis 1999). Describing his status after treatment (including bone marrow transplantation) for his rare blood disorder, patient/physician Biro spoke for many: "My story is far from over. Questions remain. … Will my disease return … ? No answers. … Cure? Depends on what you mean, who you ask. In my book, no. I will always remain a patient" (Biro 2000, 286).

Remission, Liminality, Survival

Indeed, Frank ([1991] 2002, 138–39) has written famously of a "remission society." Thanks to medical advances, it is inhabited by a growing number of people whose experiences of serious illness place them in a "chronically critical," indeterminate state between health and illness. Building partly on van Gennep's work on rites of passage, Miles Little and his colleagues (1998) formulated the concept of liminality as crucial for understanding this aspect of the illness experience. It highlights how disease removes individuals from their prior life but often, *contra* Parsons, the complete return to that life is far from seamless, or even impossible. Anthropologist Robert Murphy (1990, 131) claimed that the disabled spend their entire lives in the liminal stage. Experiencing chronic illness, or surviving a severe illness, places someone forever on a spectrum between, in Sontag's (1990b, 3) classic terms, the kingdom of the sick and the kingdom of the well. Following Bellaby (1995), we might regard the case of severe head trauma as involving double liminality: many such patients are young males who were already "liminal," located between adolescence and adulthood; then the accident removed them from their prior status while leaving uncertain their future status.

Beyond remission and liminality, there remains much to learn about what happens "after" illness. Thomas (2004, 13) observed that medical sociology has devoted scant attention to recovery and reengagement with pre-illness roles and identities. Since then, Ville (2005) has explored how those surviving severe spinal cord damage gradually confront the possibility of returning to work. Janet Parsons and her colleagues showed that, for young cancer patients, reentry to their normal social roles of completing their education and establishing their careers is complicated by the need to attend also to their disease and to the reconstruction and repair of their identities (Parsons et al. 2008).

HIV/AIDS disease in the current era of effective antiretroviral therapy is a particularly interesting site for examining reentry. By the late 1990s, the "Lazarus Syndrome" (Trainor and Ezer 2000) had been noted, in which those literally near the brink of death experienced seemingly miraculous recoveries. Their being, in Dickens's phrase, "recalled to life" challenged them to rebuild and reconstitute relationships, jobs, and other elements of their lives to which they had already bade farewell. Later, awareness of toxicity and other problems with the AIDS cocktails demonstrated that even patients who have entered what is sometimes considered a type of remission might face severe medical problems. As one informant remarked about the difficulties others had in grasping his fluid health status: "They wouldn't dream that I have AIDS and that I'm attached to an IV pole once a week … and yet it's true, and both realities are true: The Thursday afternoons at the gym is true, and the Wednesday afternoons at the clinic is true" (ibid., 652). Significantly, each of the seven respondents in Trainor and Ezer's study reported that adjusting to their new situation was more difficult than when they had been dying; in the latter instance, they at least had a clearly defined social role to play.

Frank (1995) has examined survival as project, in explicitly moral terms, such as the obligation to bear witness. He has likened survival to craft work, documenting two very different socially constructed templates through which survivors might define what their illness experience implies for their subsequent lives (Frank 2003). According to the narrative of extensive responsibility, survivors see their experience as imposing some duty, essentially a calling, on them. This might involve engaging in activism, providing support, or simply bearing witness. By contrast, the narrative of limited liability regards the illness as an obstacle to be surmounted and then left behind.

Looking at cancer survivors, Kaiser (2008) used interviews with women who had completed breast cancer treatment to show how the "breast cancer culture" influenced cultural scripts and expectations, and how women sometimes resisted these expectations and even the survivor identity itself. Some defined themselves as survivors not because they thought they actually had beaten cancer, which they believed could always recur, but because they had fought the disease as best they could. Also, even Kaiser's "relatively homogenous" sample of women interviewed at similar stages of breast cancer survival varied substantially among themselves in how they understood survival (86).

This work suggests that the post-illness phase merits closer attention. Future studies could compare what survival and recovery mean across disease, age, sex, ethnic, class, and cultural categories, and how these definitions change over time. Reminding us that some patients actually do get better, just as Parsons's model assumed, Thomas (2004) has proposed a sociology of recovery which, on the microsociological level, would explore such areas as physical and psychological restoration and exiting the patient role.

Some Methodological Implications

Another significant point about time is methodological. Pierret (2001, 2007) and Trainor and Ezer (2000) have demonstrated the value of returning to the field at various time intervals. Such long-range perspectives are particularly important for understanding the experiences of illnesses that are rapidly moving targets, such as HIV/AIDS. Indeed, Baumgartner (2007) has recently shown how identity shifted across three time points over a period of almost five years. Though this range was not particularly large, it coincided with the introduction of antiretroviral treatment that helped redefine AIDS from terminal to chronic illness. However, there has not been enough of such work, presumably because of logistic difficulties such as deadline pressure and limited budgets.

Not only is it valuable to collect data at different points over a patient's illness experience, it can be most fruitful to *analyze* data at different points in a researcher's career. Riessman (1990) detailed the rhetorical strategies of impression management employed by a man suffering from multiple sclerosis to present himself either as successful or as mostly blameless for a life that was (by most objective measures) in profound disarray. Over a decade later, Riessman (2003) published a follow-up piece in which she returned to this man's story, pointing out several ways in which her initial "reading" had evolved since she had originally analyzed it, several years before publishing the first article. In this newer reading, she located his story within the wider context of contemporary disability politics and a critique of market capitalism. These perspectives helped her understand his social isolation as an unemployed disabled man. Surely, many studies would yield new insights if investigators returned to their data at various points in their intellectual development, political awareness, and ideological orientations. This point mirrors an insight about patients' narrative recounting over time encapsulated in Gareth Williams's (1984, 179) citation of R. G. Collingwood's observation that " every present has a past of its own."

NEWER TOPICS OF INTEREST

The previous section presented highlights of research on the patient's experience of illness. This section focuses specifically on two types of diseases to which this literature has only recently begun to attend.

Alzheimer's

The perspectives of Alzheimer's patients were long ignored in the literature (MacRae 2008, 397; Beard and Fox 2008, 1510). Traditionally, senile dementia has been regarded as a form of social death, as Sweeting and Gilhooly's (1997) research on family caretakers of such individuals illustrated.

Yet the Alzheimer's patients Snyder (1999) interviewed were often able to articulate the accretion of losses—of memory, of independence, of identity, of social ties—that their condition brought in its wake. One declared, "I want to cry and whine and kick!" (71). In describing her situation, another offered one of the most arresting remarks in the entire literature on the illness experience: "You aren't you anymore" (62). As Charmaz had noted about the chronically ill, persons living with Alzheimer's often must fight to preserve as much of their original routines as possible. For—though the popular image is dominated by latter stages of the disease, in which people may not recognize even close family—Snyder's informants remind us that declines can be gradual. Such Alzheimer's patients occupy a liminal stage in which they remain aware enough to recognize and describe what is happening, and integrated enough into their predisease roles, networks, and identities to be able to mourn their losses.

Subsequent work has confirmed the ability of Alzheimer's patients movingly to describe their inner and social worlds (Clare 2003), even when already confined to institutions (Clare et al. 2008). MacRae (2008) demonstrated how such early-stage Alzheimer's patients—much like the disabled discussed in Lutz and Bowers (2005)—resist stereotypical constructions of their situation as devastated victims, and employ numerous coping mechanisms to preserve their identities and manage others' perceptions of them. These include such techniques as positive thinking, humor, cultivating hope, preemptive disclosure, and normalization (in which patients attempt to integrate their disease into their daily lives). Beard and Fox (2008) showed how, beyond resisting dominant constructions, Alzheimer's patients can manipulate their diagnosis, using it as a resource for managing their condition. Beard and Fox also examined how support groups shape the illness experience, in this case by discussing how these groups influenced constructions of illness identities. Medical advances in earlier detection present the possibility of additional research into the subjective experience of dementia, since the illness trajectory has effectively been extended backward in time to a period in which those affected remain articulate and reflective.

Mental Illness

Another example of interesting new work in previously neglected areas is research into the experience of mental illness (Kangas 2001). Karp (1996, 11) has observed that when he first began writing on depression, the existing literature contained the voices of countless experts but never those of the depressed themselves. Based on interviews with a diverse sample of individuals with depression, Karp's sociologically grounded analysis explored topics such as the threat to one's identity, the web of family and friends who may attempt to lend emotional support and instrumental assistance, and the range of coping strategies employed to negotiate daily life. Karp attempted to link the growing prevalence of depression in the United States to wider structural and sociocultural trends. These included: a "therapeutic," self-help culture, postmodern social alienation, postindustrial economic dislocation and loss of valued identities, and consumerism that converts happiness (and other emotions) into marketable commodities.

Kangas (2001) examined lay sense making and attribution among the depressed. Emslie and her colleagues (2006) discussed how depressed men attempted to preserve or reconstruct their masculine identities as part of recovery. Pollock (2007) detailed how, during doctor visits, her sample of depressed individuals engaged in face-saving strategies that could undermine their treatment by leading them to deny the extent of their illness, including in response to their doctors' queries. Often, patients feared to drop their "masks" of normalcy and admit to their illness. Sometimes, however, they were attempting to protect the doctor from the time and bother of confronting a difficult problem, and so concealed it. More generally, according to Pollock, these patients attempted to make the visit proceed smoothly, as a social encounter; they felt that admitting the extent of their depression would spoil this interaction. Such practices, Pollock concluded, impeded treatment.

Despite the existence of research on depression, the sociological literature includes less material on other forms of mental illness. Among the limited body of work not specifically dealing with depression, Crossley and Crossley (2001) cleverly documented changes over time in how persons diagnosed as mentally ill constructed their identity. They compared narratives published in two anthologies, *The Plea for the Silent* (published in 1957) and *Speaking Our Minds* (published in 1996). These titles alone eloquently attest to significant changes. Similarly, Cresswell (2005) has described how those suffering from "self-harm" came to define themselves as "survivors"—not of mental illness, but of psychiatric *treatment*—and began to practice a form of self-advocacy that asserted their right to voice their views. They resisted or rejected certain professional and societal labels, and offered alternative "truth-claims" grounded in their personal experiences, which Cresswell defined as "testimony." Lester and Tritter (2005) conducted focus groups with those experiencing schizophrenia, depression, and other significant mental problems. Participants described such difficulties as service access, unemployment, medication side effects, and social isolation. Many wished to volunteer to help others navigate services. Most recently, Moses (2009) used a mixed-method approach, including semi-structured interviews, to explore how adolescents receiving mental health services related to mental illness labels. Most were either unsure whether, or denied that, they were mentally ill; some moved in and out of accepting this identity. Only one-fifth clearly accepted this label.

Despite such studies, we still know comparatively little about the experience even of such common conditions as schizophrenia and phobia. Additional research is needed to examine more fully such questions as: How does society label and stigmatize the mentally ill? How do they manage their disease across its particular trajectory? Do they attempt to resist their diagnosis and its attendant stigma? If so, how successfully? How do these patterns vary by gender, class, and ethnicity?

UNCHARTED TERRITORY: CRITICAL ILLNESS

The existing sociological literature on the illness experience has focused on chronic (Bell 2000) rather than on acute (Faircloth et al. 2004; Rosenfeld 2006) and critical (Rier 2000) illness. Sociological (Zussman 1992) and anthropological (Cassell 2005; Kaufman 2005) ethnographies have explored the intensive care unit (ICU). But Zussman and Cassel related to patients only as passive objects, while Kaufman emphasized end-of-life decisions rather than patients' experiences.

First-person, nonacademic accounts (Simpson 1982; Baier and Schomaker [1986] 1995; Bauby 1997) have shed some light on patients' experiences of critical illness. The latter two works deserve special mention for opening up new worlds in our understanding. The authors were both paralyzed and ventilator dependent; they communicated and dictated their thoughts by blinking their eyes. Perhaps their single greatest contribution lies in their having revealed what even many ICU staff may not recognize: that such patients, despite their dire physical condition, retained awareness, hopes, dreams—in short, an inner life. Simpson wrote wisely about the cultivation of hope, and how this

might require lying to critically ill patients (32, 108, 116).

Yet, with such limited exceptions as first-hand accounts (Robillard 1994; Richman 2000; Rier 2000), the sociology literature says little about the experiences of the critically ill (Rier 2000, 2008). Therefore, debates over such questions as autonomy, paternalism, empowerment, and disclosure of information to patients take place with little input from patients themselves (Rier 2000, 2008). In particular, critical illness still awaits its Strauss (1975) and Charmaz (1991), who bequeathed to students of chronic illness a magnificent set of conceptual tools for their work. One major difference between most chronic illness and critical illness is that, whereas the former typically involves the struggle to integrate illness into the routines of one's daily life, critical illness is likelier to *replace* one's existing life (Rier 2000, 72) in a more advanced form of the "immersion" (Charmaz 1991) described earlier.

A major reason for the lack of focus on the ICU patient experience is the significant methodological difficulty in studying these patients. ICUs have high mortality rates, many survivors are too weak to be interviewed, and many remember very little of their experiences, particularly given the heavy sedation they often received. One attempt to address such limitations comes from the nursing/critical care literatures, where researchers have interviewed ICU patients about their experiences (e.g., Granberg, Engberg, and Lundberg 1998; Johnson 2004; Magarey and McCutcheon 2005; Karlsson and Forsberg 2008). This work has yielded important insights into elements of the experience, such as dreams, fears, and feelings of helplessness. However, such studies have typically been based on small samples.

Some studies (e.g., Bergbom et al. 1999; Bäckman and Walther 2001; Combe 2005; Egerod and Christensen 2009; Egerod et al. 2007; Roulin,

Hurst, and Spirig 2007) have used ICU "diaries," summaries of daily events in the ICU written by nurses and family on behalf of and for the patient, not by the patient. Such texts clearly help former patients make sense of their time in the ICU. Yet, authored by others, these top-down diaries cannot necessarily help patients recapture their inner world or restore their voice; neither can they really help us understand what such patients experience. Therefore, Rier (2000) has proposed a method of offering nonvocal patients the chance to write as a means of communication while in the ICU, then using this writing as a memory aid for postdischarge interviews.[3]

That so few studies of the ICU patient experience engage with the rich medical sociology literature leaves much work for sociologists. For example, the contemporary, post-Parsonian discourse of patient empowerment may not be relevant to the high dependency of the ICU (Rier 2000). Among other areas for research are gender (which existing studies of the critical illness experience rarely address) and the timing and extent of disclosure of information to ICU patients. Another area arises from the fact that, partly as a means of controlling infection, newer ICUs often have individual patient rooms. Little is known about how such ecological changes in the ICU affect patients.

CONCLUSION

Over the past generation or so, the patient has emerged as a focus of medical sociology research, joining providers, hospitals, and health systems. Studying patients' experiences has taught us much about how body, self, and society interact. This includes such specific topics as: identity; support; how patients integrate their illness into daily routines and family, community, and work lives; how patients resist or negotiate professional authority, societal labels, and sociocultural expectations; moral dilemmas; and how the illness experience develops over time. It is interesting to speculate, How might Parsons's sick-role model have looked, had his generation already produced a substantial body of research on patient experiences?

Research on patient experiences also allows physicians to transcend blood gases and x-rays, teaching them about pain, loneliness, dread—but also hope, dreams, courage. It underscores the humanity and agency of disabled, demented, and mentally, critically, and terminally ill persons. Clinicians are learning to apply illness narratives to improve how they communicate with, support, and treat their patients (Charon 2006; Overcash 2003). Such research is also a tool for medical education (Childress 2002) and bioethics (Charon and Montello 2002). Without understanding the meanings patients give to central elements of their experiences such as pain, fear of death, guilt, and quality of life, clinicians and bioethicists may be reduced to guessing patients' needs. Clinicians are currently developing illness narratives as a form of evidence-based medicine (Charon and Wyer 2008), treating them as one source of data, alongside more traditional sources such as randomized clinical trials, for improving clinical decision making.

Yet so much remains undone. Recovery (i.e., actually getting better) has received insufficient attention. Immense work remains in understanding different forms of mental illness. Sociological research on the patient's critical illness experience has barely begun. Also, if physicians must look beyond their biomedical measures to the wider psychosocial context, social scientists must look beyond the psychosocial context to attend to the body and its pathology as direct influences on the illness experience (Timmermans and Haas 2008). Research on illness trajectories does typically correlate experience with disease stage. Yet sociological writing too often brackets off the actual physical disease, ignoring the proverbial elephant in the room in an attempt to highlight purely social aspects of illness. Taking the body seriously, for example, would provide a useful counterweight to radical critiques of disability as a purely social construct (Bury 2000). Methodologically, moreover, it is sloppy to interview, say, dozens of cancer patients without careful attention to, not just age or sex, but also disease stage, symptoms, and side effects. Despite various obstacles to gaining access to clinical charts, correlating biomedical status with lifeworld experience can yield rich benefits. In fact, perhaps the disease/illness distinction has by now been overstated.

Still, research on the illness experience is flourishing. It is a large, lively, diverse field. Thus, there is ample reason to expect that it will continue to illuminate new areas of the illness experience, generating insights for social science, health practice and policy, and beyond.

NOTES

The author gratefully acknowledges his conversations with Miles Little and Hilary Thomas, and the editorial advice of Stefan Timmermans.

1   There exist numerous social science reviews of the large body of literature on the illness experience. Bury (1991) and Charmaz (2000) focused on chronic illness. Frank (1995), Hydén (1997), and Bell (2000) reviewed the narrative recounting of such experiences. Anthropologists Kleinman and Seeman (2000) located the illness experience within a socially and politically critical framework. Lawton (2003) and Pierret (2003) focused specifically on material published in the first quarter-century of the journal *Sociology of Health and Illness.*

2   However, the fifth edition of this handbook (Bird, Conrad, and Fremont 2000) included Bell's chapter on illness narratives plus Bury's theoretical chapter on chronic illness and disability. Also, the third edition of Graham Scambler's (1991) medical sociology text already included Locker's chapter on living with chronic illness.

3   Development of this technique parallels use of a set of techniques described in recent studies employing photography as a means through which the sick can capture and reconstruct their experiences and narrate their own stories (Bell 2002; Radley and Taylor 2003a, b; Oliffe and Bottorff 2007; Frith and Harcourt 2007).

REFERENCES

Anderson, W. Timothy, and David T. Helm. 1979. "The Physician-Patient Encounter: A Process of Reality Negotiation." In *Patients, Physicians, and Illness*, 3rd ed., ed. E. Gartly Jaco, 259–71. New York: Free Press.

Armstrong, David. 1984. "The Patient's View." *Social Science and Medicine* 18(9): 737–44.

Arribas-Ayllon, Michael, Srikant Sarangi, and Angus Clarke. 2008. "Managing Self-Responsibility through Other-Oriented Blame: Family Accounts of Genetic Testing." *Social Science and Medicine* 66(7): 1521–32.

Bäckman, C. G., and S. M. Walther. 2001. "Use of a Personal Diary Written on the ICU during Critical Illness." *Intensive Care Medicine* 27(2): 426–29.

Baier, Sue, and Mary Z. Schomaker. [1986] 1995. *Bed Number Ten*. Reprint. Boca Raton, Fla.: CRC Press.

Bar-Lev, Shirly. 2008. "'We Are Here to Give You Emotional Support': Performing Emotions in an Online HIV/AIDS Support Group." *Qualitative Health Research* 18(4): 509–21.

Bauby, Jean-Dominique. 1997. *The Diving-Bell and the Butterfly*. Translated by Jeremy Leggatt. New York: Vintage.

Baumgartner, Lisa M. 2007. "The Incorporation of the HIV/AIDS Identity into the Self over Time." *Qualitative Health Research* 17(7): 919–31.

Beard, Renee L., and Patrick J. Fox. 2008. "Resisting Social Disenfranchisement: Negotiating Collective Identities and Everyday Life with Memory Loss." *Social Science and Medicine* 66(7): 1509–20.

Bell, Susan, 2000. "Experiencing Illness in/and Narrative." In *Handbook of Medical Sociology*, 5th ed., ed. Chloe E. Bird, Peter Conrad, and Allen M. Fremont, 184–99. Upper Saddle River, N.J.: Prentice Hall.

———. 2002. "Photo Images: Jo Spence's Narratives of Living with Illness." *Health* 6(1): 5–30.

Bellaby, Paul. 1995. "The World of Illness of the Closed Head Injured." In *Worlds of Illness: Biographical and Cultural Perspectives on Health and Disease*, ed. Alan Radley, 161–78. London: Routledge.

Bergbom, Ingegerd, Carina Svensson, Elisabeth Berggren, and Marie Kamsula. 1999. "Patients' and Relatives' Opinions and Feelings about Diaries Kept by Nurses in an Intensive Care Unit: Pilot Study." *Intensive and Critical Care Nursing* 15(4): 185–91.

Bird, Chloe E., Peter Conrad, and Allen M. Fremont, eds. 2000. *Handbook of Medical Sociology*. 5th ed. Upper Saddle River, N.J.: Prentice Hall.

Biro, David. 2000. *One Hundred Days: My Unexpected Journey from Doctor to Patient*. New York: Pantheon.

Boutte, Marie I. 1990. "Waiting for the Family Legacy: The Experience of Being at Risk for Machado-Joseph Disease." *Social Science and Medicine* 30(8): 839–47.

Broom, Alex. 2005. "Virtually He@lthy: Impact of Internet Use on Disease Experience and the Doctor-Patient Experience." *Qualitative Health Research* 15(3): 324–45.

Brown, Phil, Stephen Zavetoski, Sabrina McCormick, Meadow Linder, Joshua Mandelbaum, and Theo Luebke. 2001. "A Gulf of Difference: Disputes over Gulf War–Related Illnesses." *Journal of Health and Social Behavior* 42(3): 235–257.

Bury, Mike. 1991. "The Sociology of Chronic Illness: A Review of Research and Prospects." *Sociology of Health and Illness* 13(4): 451–68.

———. 2000. "On Chronic Illness and Disability." In *Handbook of Medical Sociology*, 5th ed., ed. Chloe E. Bird, Peter Conrad, and Allen M. Fremont, 173–83. Upper Saddle River, N.J.: Prentice Hall.

Callen, Michael, ed. 1988. *Collected Wisdom*. Vol. 2 of *Surviving and Thriving with AIDS*. New York: People with AIDS Coalition.

Cassell, Joan. 2005. *Life and Death in Intensive Care*. Philadelphia: Temple University Press.

Charmaz, Kathy. 1991. *Good Days, Bad Days: The Self in Chronic Illness and Time*. New Brunswick, N.J.: Rutgers University Press.

———. 2000. "Experiencing Chronic Illness." In *The Handbook of Social Studies in Health and Medicine*, ed. Gary L. Albrecht, Roy Fitzpatrick, and Susan C. Scrimshaw, 277–92. London: Sage.

Charon, Rita. 2006. *Narrative Medicine: Honoring the Stories of Illness*. Oxford: Oxford University Press.

Charon, Rita, and Martha Montello, eds. 2002. *Stories Matter: The Role of Narrative in Medical Ethics*. London: Routledge.

Charon, Rita, and Peter Wyer [for the NEBM Working Group]. 2008. "Narrative Evidence Based Medicine." *Lancet* 371(9609): 296–97.

Childress, Marcia D. 2002. "Of Symbols and Silence: Using Narrative and Its Interpretation to Foster Physician Understanding." In *Stories Matter: The Role of Narrative in Medical Ethics*, ed. Rita Charon and Martha Montello, 119–25. London: Routledge.

Christakis, Nicholas A. 1999. *Death Foretold: Prophecy and Prognosis in Medical Care*. Chicago: University of Chicago Press.

Clare, Linda. 2003. "Managing Threats to Self: Awareness in Early-Stage Alzheimer's Disease." *Social Science and Medicine* 57(6): 1017–29.

Clare, Linda, Julia Rowlands, Errollyn Bruce, Claire Surr, and Murna Downs. 2008. "'I Don't Do Like I Used to Do': A Grounded Theory Approach to Conceptualising Awareness in People with Moderate to Severe Dementia Living in Long-Term Care." *Social Science and Medicine* 66(11): 2366–77.

Combe, Denise. 2005. "The Use of Patient Diaries in an Intensive Care Unit." *Nursing in Critical Care* 10(1): 31–34.

Connery, Brian A. 1997. "IMHO: Authority and Egalitarian Rhetoric in the Virtual Coffeehouse." In *Internet Culture*, ed. David Porter, 161–79. New York: Routledge.

Conrad, Peter. 2007. *The Medicalization of Society: On the Transformation of Human Conditions into Treatable Disorders*. Baltimore: Johns Hopkins University Press.

Conrad, Peter, and Joseph W. Schneider. 1992. *Deviance and Medicalization: From Badness to Sickness*. 2nd ed. Philadelphia: Temple University Press.

Cooper, Lesley. 1997. "Myalgic Encephalomyelitis and the Medical Encounter." *Sociology of Health and Illness* 19(2): 186–207.

Cox, Susan M., and William McKellin. 1999. "'There's This Thing in Our Family': Predictive Testing and the Construction of Risk for Huntington Disease." *Sociology of Health and Illness* 21(5): 622–46.

Cresswell, Mark. 2005. "Psychiatric 'Survivors' and Testimonies of Self-Harm." *Social Science and Medicine* 61(8): 1668–77.

Crossley, Michelle L., and Nick Crossley. 2001. "'Patient' Voices, Social Movements and the Habitus: How Psychiatric Survivors 'Speak Out.'" *Social Science and Medicine* 52(2): 1477–89.

Davis, Fred. [1963] 1991. *Passage through Crisis: Polio Victims and their Families.* Reprint. New Brunswick, N.J.: Transaction.

Egerod, Ingrid, and Doris Christensen. 2009. "Analysis of Patient Diaries in Danish ICUs: A Narrative Approach." *Intensive and Critical Care Nursing* 25(5): 268–77.

Egerod, Ingrid, Kathrine H. Schwartz-Nielsen, Glennie M. Hansen, and Eva Laerkner. 2007. "The Extent and Application of Patient Diaries in Danish ICUs in 2006." *Nursing in Critical Care* 12(3): 159–67.

Emslie, Carol, Damien Ridge, Sue Ziebland, and Kate Hunt. 2006. "Men's Accounts of Depression: Reconstructing or Resisting Hegemonic Masculinity?" *Social Science and Medicine* 62(9): 2246–57.

Epstein, Steven. 1996. *Impure Science: AIDS, Activism, and the Politics of Knowledge.* Berkeley: University of California Press.

Faircloth, Chris A., Craig Boylstein, Maude Rittman, Mary E. Young, and Jaber Gubrium. 2004. "Sudden Illness and Biographical Flow in Narratives of Stroke Recovery." *Sociology of Health and Illness* 26(2): 242–61.

Fox, Nick, Katie Ward, and Alan O'Rourke. 2005a. "The 'Expert Patient': Empowerment or Medical Dominance? The Case of Weight Loss, Pharmaceutical Drugs and the Internet." *Social Science and Medicine* 60(6): 1299–1309.

———. 2005b. "Pro-anorexia, Weight-Loss Drugs and the Internet: An 'Anti-Recovery' Explanatory Model of Anorexia." *Sociology of Health and Illness* 27(7): 944–71.

Frank, Arthur W. 1995. *The Wounded Storyteller: Body, Illness, and Ethics.* Chicago: University of Chicago Press.

———. [1991] 2002. *At the Will of the Body: Reflections on Illness.* Reprint. Boston: Houghton Mifflin.

———. 2003. "Survivorship as Craft and Conviction: Reflections on Research in Progress." *Qualitative Health Research* 13(2): 247–55.

Freeman, Howard E., and Sol Levine. 1989. *Handbook of Medical Sociology.* 4th ed. Englewood Cliffs, N.J.: Prentice Hall.

Freeman, Howard E., Sol Levine, and Leo G. Reeder. 1963. *Handbook of Medical Sociology.* Englewood Cliffs, N.J.: Prentice Hall.

Frith, Hannah, and Diana Harcourt. 2007. "Using Photographs to Capture Women's Experiences of Chemotherapy: Reflecting on the Method." *Qualitative Health Research* 17(10): 1340–50.

Gallagher, Eugene B. 1979. "Lines of Reconstruction and Extension in the Parsonian Sociology of Illness." In *Patients, Physicians, and Illness*, 3rd ed., ed. E. Gartly Jaco, 162–83. New York: Free Press.

Gavin, Jeff, Karen Rodham, and Helen Poyer. 2008. "The Presentation of 'Pro-Anorexia' in Online Group Interactions." *Qualitative Health Research* 18(3): 325–33.

Gerhardt, Uta. 1989. *Ideas about Illness: An Intellectual and Political History of Medical Sociology.* New York: New York University Press.

Glenton, Claire. 2005. "Chronic Back Pain Sufferers: Striving for the Sick Role." *Social Science and Medicine* 57(11): 2243–52.

Granberg, Anetth, Ingegerd Bergbom Engberg, and Dag Lundberg. 1998. "Patients' Experience of Being Critically Ill or Severely Injured and Cared for in an Intensive Care Unit in Relation to the ICU Syndrome. Part 1." *Intensive and Critical Care Nursing* 14(6): 294–307.

Hallowell, Nina. 1999. "Doing the Right Thing: Genetic Risk and Responsibility." *Sociology of Health and Illness* 21(5): 597–621.

Hardey, Michael. 1999. "Doctor in the House: The Internet as a Source of Lay Health Knowledge and the Challenge to Expertise." *Sociology of Health and Illness* 21(6): 820–35.

———. 2002. "'The Story of My Illness': Personal Accounts of Illness on the Internet." *Health* 6(1): 31–46.

Hydén, Lars-Christer. 1997. "Illness and Narrative." *Sociology of Health and Illness* 19(1): 48–69.

Indyk, Debbie, and David A. Rier. 1993. "Grassroots AIDS Knowledge: Implications for the Boundaries of Science and Collective Action." *Knowledge: Creation, Diffusion, Utilization* 15(1): 3–43.

Jaco, E. Gartly, ed. 1979. *Patients, Physicians, and Illness.* 3rd ed. New York: Free Press.

Johnson, Patricia. 2004. "Reclaiming the Everyday World: How Long-Term Ventilated Patients in Critical Care Seek to Gain Aspects of Power and Control over Their

Environment." *Intensive and Critical Care Nursing* 20(4): 190–99.

Kaiser, Karen. 2008. "The Meaning of the Survivor Identity for Women with Breast Cancer." *Social Science and Medicine* 67(1): 79–87.

Kangas, Ilka. 2001. "Making Sense of Depression: Perceptions of Melancholia in Lay Narratives." *Health* 5(1): 76–92.

Karlsson, Veronika, and Anna Forsberg. 2008. "Health Is Yearning: Experiences of Being Conscious during Ventilator Treatment in a Critical Care Unit." *Intensive and Critical Care Nursing* 24(1): 41–50.

Karp, David A. 1996. *Speaking of Sadness.* Oxford: Oxford University Press.

Kaufman, Sharon R. 2005. *… And a Time to Die: How Hospitals Shape the End of Life.* Chicago: University of Chicago Press.

Kenen, Regina H. 1996. "The At-Risk Health Status and Technology: A Diagnostic Invitation and the 'Gift' of Knowing." *Social Science and Medicine* 42(11): 1545–53.

Kleinman, Arthur. 1988. *The Illness Narratives.* New York: Basic Books.

Kleinman, Arthur, and Don Seeman. 2000. "Personal Experience of Illness." In *The Handbook of Social Studies in Health and Medicine*, ed. Gary Albrecht, Roy Fitzpatrick, and Susan C. Scrimshaw, 230–42. London: Sage.

Lane, Harlan. 2006. "Construction of Deafness." In *The Disability Studies Reader*, 2nd ed., ed. Lennard Davis, 79–92. New York: Routledge.

Lawton, Julia. 2003. "Lay Experiences of Health and Illness: Past Research and Future Agendas." *Sociology of Health and Illness* 25(3): 23–40.

Lester, Helen, and Jonathan Q. Tritter. 2005. "'Listen to My Madness': Understanding the Experiences of People with Serious Mental Illness." *Sociology of Health and Illness* 27(5): 649–69.

Levine, Sol, and Martin A. Kozloff. 1978. "The Sick Role: Assessment and Overview." *Annual Review of Sociology* 4:317–43.

Little, Miles, Christopher F. C. Jordens, Kim Paul, Kathleen Montgomery, and Bertil Philipson. 1998. "Liminality: A Major Category of the Experience of Cancer Illness." *Social Science and Medicine* 47(10): 1485–94.

Locker, David. 1991. "Living with Chronic Illness." In *Sociology as Applied to Medicine*, ed. Graham Scambler, 81–92. London: Bailliere Tindall.

Lombardo, Anthony P. 2004. "Anatomy of Fear: Mead's Theory of the Past and the Experience of the HIV/

AIDS 'Worried Well.'" *Symbolic Interaction* 27(4): 531–48.

Lorde, Audre. 1997. *The Cancer Journals.* Special ed. San Francisco: Aunt Lute.

Lutz, Barbara J., and Barbara J. Bowers. 2005. "Disability in Everyday Life." *Qualitative Health Research* 15(8): 1037–54.

MacRae, Hazel. 2008. "'Making the Best You Can of It': Living with Early-Stage Alzheimer's Disease." *Sociology of Health and Illness* 30(3): 396–412.

Magarey, Judith M., and Helen H. McCutcheon. 2005. "'Fishing with the Dead': Recall of Memories from the ICU." *Intensive and Critical Care Nursing* 21(6): 344–54.

Maykovich, Minako K. 1980. *Medical Sociology.* Sherman Oaks, Calif.: Alfred Publishing.

Mechanic, David. 1978. *Medical Sociology.* 2nd ed. New York: Free Press.

Mishler, Elliot G. 1984. *The Discourse of Medicine: Dialectics of Medical Interviews.* Norwood, N.J.: Ablex.

Moses, Tally. 2009. "Self-Labeling and Its Effects among Adolescents Diagnosed with Mental Disorders." *Social Science and Medicine* 68(3): 570–78.

Murphy, Robert F. 1990. *The Body Silent.* New York: W. W. Norton.

Nettleton, Sarah, Lisa O'Malley, Ian Watt, and Philip Duffey. 2004. "Enigmatic Illness: Narratives of Patients Who Live with Medically Unexplained Symptoms." *Social Theory and Health* 2(1): 47–66.

Oliffe, John L., and Joan L. Bottorff. 2007. "Further Than the Eye Can See? Photo Elicitation and Research with Men." *Qualitative Health Research* 17(6): 850–58.

Oliffe, John L., B. Joyce Davison, Tom Pickles, and Lawrence Mróz. 2009. "The Self-Management of Uncertainty among Men Undertaking Active Surveillance for Low-Risk Prostate Cancer." *Qualitative Health Research* 19(4): 432–43.

Overcash, Janine A. 2003. "Narrative Research: A Review of Methodology and Relevance to Clinical Practice." *Critical Reviews in Oncology/Hematology* 48(2): 179–84.

Parsons, Janet A., Joan M. Eakin, Robert S. Bell, Renée-Louise Franche, and Aileen M. Davis. 2008. "'So, Are You Back to Work Yet?' Re-conceptualizing 'Work' and 'Return to Work' in the Context of Primary Bone Cancer." *Social Science and Medicine* 67(11): 1826–36.

Parsons, Talcott. 1951. *The Social System.* Glencoe, Ill.: Free Press.

———. 1975. "The Sick Role and Role of the Physician Reconsidered." *Milbank Memorial Fund Quarterly* 53(3): 257–78.

Pierret, Janine. 2001. "Interviews and Biographical Time: The Case of Long-Term HIV Nonprogressors." *Sociology of Health and Illness* 23(2): 159–79.

———. 2003. "The Illness Experience: State of Knowledge and Perspectives for Research." 25(3): 4–22.

———. 2007. "An Analysis over Time (1990–2000) of the Experiences of Living with HIV." *Social Science and Medicine* 65(8): 1595–1605.

Pitts, Victoria. 2004. "Illness and Internet Empowerment: Writing and Reading Breast Cancer in Cyberspace." *Health* 8(1): 33–59.

Pollock, Kristian. 2007. "Maintaining Face in the Presentation of Depression: Constraining the Therapeutic Potential of the Consultation." *Health* 11(2): 163–80.

Prior, Lindsay. 2003. "Belief, Knowledge and Expertise: The Emergence of the Lay Expert in Medical Sociology." *Sociology of Health and Illness* 25(3): 41–57.

Radley, Alan, and Diane Taylor. 2003a. "Images of Recovery: A Photo-Elicitation Study on the Hospital Ward." *Qualitative Health Research* 13(1): 77–99.

———. 2003b. "Remembering One's Stay in Hospital: A Study in Photography, Recovery and Forgetting." *Health* 7(2): 129–59.

Richman, Joel. 2000. "Coming out of Intensive Care Crazy: Dreams of Affliction." *Qualitative Health Research* 10(1): 84–102.

Rier, David A. 2000. "The Missing Voice of the Critically Ill: A Medical Sociologist's First-Person Account." *Sociology of Health and Illness* 22(1): 68–93.

———. 2007a. "The Impact of Moral Suasion on Internet HIV/AIDS Support Groups: Evidence from a Discussion of Seropositivity Disclosure Ethics." *Health Sociology Review* 16(3–4): 237–47.

———. 2007b. "Internet Support Groups as Moral Agents: The Ethical Dynamics of HIV+ Status Disclosure." *Sociology of Health and Illness* 29(7): 1043–58.

———. 2008. "'The Missing Voice of Critical Illness,' Ten Years Later: In Sociology, Still Missing." Presented to the American Sociological Association 103rd Annual Meeting, Boston, August 1–4.

Riessman, Catherine K. 1990. "Strategic Uses of Narrative in the Presentation of Self and Illness: A Research Note." *Social Science and Medicine* 30(11): 1195–1200.

———. 2003. "Performing Identities in Illness Narrative: Masculinity and Multiple Sclerosis." *Qualitative Research* 3(1): 5–33.

Robillard, Albert B. 1994. "Communication Problems in the Intensive Care Unit." *Qualitative Sociology* 17(4): 383–95.

Rosenfeld, Dana. 2006. "Similarities and Differences between Acute Illness and Injury Narratives and Their Implications for Medical Sociology." *Social Theory and Health* 4(1): 64–84.

Roth, Julius. 1963. *Timetables: Structuring the Passage of Time in Hospital Treatment and Other Careers*. Indianapolis: Bobbs-Merrill.

Roulin, Marie-José, Samia Hurst, and Rebecca Spirig. 2007. "Diaries Written for ICU Patients." *Qualitative Health Research* 17(7): 893–901.

Sandaunet, Anne-Grete. 2008. "A Space for Suffering? Communicating Breast Cancer in an Online Self-Help Context." *Qualitative Health Research* 18(12): 1631–41.

Scambler, Graham, ed. 1991. *Sociology as Applied to Medicine*. London: Bailliere Tindall.

Sharf, Barbara F. 1997. "Communicating Breast Cancer On Line: Support and Empowerment on the Internet." *Women and Health* 26(1): 65–84.

Sim, Julius, and Sue Madden. 2008. "Illness Experience in Fibromyalgia Syndrome: A Metasynthesis of Qualitative Studies." *Social Science and Medicine* 67(1): 57–67.

Simpson, Elizabeth L. 1982. *Notes on an Emergency: A Journal of Recovery*. London: W. W. Norton.

Snyder, Lisa. 1999. *Speaking Our Minds: Personal Reflections from Individuals with Alzheimer's*. New York: W. H. Freeman.

Sontag, Susan. 1990a. "AIDS and Its Metaphors." In *Illness as Metaphor and AIDS and Its Metaphors*, 93–183. New York: Anchor Books/Doubleday.

———. 1990b. "Illness as Metaphor." In *Illness as Metaphor and AIDS and Its Metaphors*, 3–87. New York: Anchor Books/Doubleday.

Stewart, David C., and Thomas J. Sullivan. 1982. "Illness Behaviors and the Sick Role in Chronic Disease: The Case of Multiple Sclerosis." *Social Science and Medicine* 16(15): 1397–404.

Strauss, Anselm L. 1975. *Chronic Illness and the Quality of Life*. St. Louis: C. V. Mosby.

Sweeting, Helen, and Mary Gilhooly. 1997. "Dementia and the Phenomenon of Social Death." *Sociology of Health and Illness* 19(1): 93–117.

Thomas, Hilary. 2004. "From Patient to Person: Identifying a Sociology of Recovery." Paper presented at the American Sociological Association 99th Annual Meeting, San Francisco, August 14–17.

Timmermans, Stefan, and Steven Haas. 2008. "Towards a Sociology of Disease." *Sociology of Health and Illness* 30(5): 659–76.

Trainor, Andrea, and Hélène Ezer. 2000. "Rebuilding Life: The Experience of Living with AIDS after Facing Imminent Death." *Qualitative Health Research* 10(5): 646–60.

Turner, Bryan S. 1990. *Medical Power and Social Knowledge.* London: Sage.

Twaddle, Andrew C., and Richard M. Hessler. 1977. *A Sociology of Health.* St. Louis: C. V. Mosby.

Ville, Isabelle. 2005. "Biographical Work and Returning to Employment Following a Spinal Cord Injury." *Sociology of Health and Illness* 27(3): 324–50.

Walstrom, Mary K. 2000. "'You Know, Who's the Thinnest?': Combating Surveillance and Creating Safety in Coping with Eating Disorders Online." *CyberPsychology and Behavior* 3(5): 761–83.

Williams, Gareth. 1984. "The Genesis of Chronic Illness: Narrative Re-construction." *Sociology of Health and Illness* 6(2): 175–200.

Williams, Simon J. 2005. "Parsons Revisited: From the Sick Role to … ?" *Health* 9(2): 123–44.

Wolinsky, Frederick D. 1980. *The Sociology of Health: Principles, Professions, and Issues.* Boston: Little, Brown.

Yoshida, Karen K. 1993. "Reshaping of Self: A Pendular Reconstruction of Self and Identity among Adults with Traumatic Spinal Cord Injury." *Sociology of Health and Illness* 15(2): 217–43.

Ziebland, Sue. 2004. "The Importance of Being Expert: The Quest for Cancer Information on the Internet." *Social Science and Medicine* 59(9): 1783–93.

Ziebland, Sue, and Andrew Herxheimer. 2008. "How Patients' Experiences Contribute to Decision Making: Illustrations from DIPEx (Personal Experiences of Health and Illness)." *Journal of Nursing Management* 16(4): 433–39.

Zussman, Robert. 1992. *Intensive Care: Medical Ethics and the Medical Profession.* Chicago: University of Chicago.

The Internet and the Experience of Illness

Peter Conrad and Cheryl Stults

Sociologists have studied the experience of illness for at least the past four decades (Conrad 1987). The earliest studies focused on how patients managed the sick role (Parsons 1951) or how they maneuvered through the stages of an illness career (Suchman 1965). Beginning with the work of Anselm Strauss and his colleagues (Glaser and Strauss 1965; Strauss and Glaser 1975), sociological researchers started investigating the experience of illness by examining the illness experience from the patient's viewpoint. This has led to several lines of work that focused on how people live with and in spite of their illness, the subjective experience of illness, and strategies sufferers develop to manage their illnesses and lives (e.g., Charmaz 1999; Bury 1982; Bell 2000). Researchers have typically used qualitative research methods, especially interviews, to examine the experience of illness (Conrad 1987; Charmaz 1999) and have studied stigmatized illnesses like epilepsy (Schneider and Conrad 1983) and HIV/AIDS (Weitz 1991; Klitzman and Bayer 2003), contested illnesses like fibromyalgia (Barker 2005), psychiatric disorders like major depression (Karp 1997), and medical conditions such as infertility (Greil 1991) and genetic disorders (Cox and McKellin 1999). Numerous studies have focused on how sufferers manage their identity (Charmaz 1991),

stigma (Weitz 1991), biographical disruption (Bury 1982), or narrative reconstruction (Williams 1984).

Two consistent findings from experience-of-illness studies through roughly the year 2000 are that with few exceptions there were no illness subcultures and that illness was a profoundly privatizing experience. In an early statement, Parsons and Fox (1952, 137) observed that "illness usually prevents the individual from attaching himself to a solidary subculture of similarly oriented deviants." Sociologists who studied the experience of illness studied individuals through interviews and, in contrast to a field like deviance, could not render ethnographies of illness subcultures, for they essentially did not exist. There were a few cases where sociologists could study patient subcultures in hospitals, the most famous of which are the classic studies of TB hospitals (Roth 1963) and mental institutions (Goffman 1961), but these were studies of the experience of patienthood more than of the experience of illness. Other than hospitals, there were few settings where people with the same illness interacted with one another. There have been a few studies of self-help groups for people with illness, especially post-illness, but studies of these were more about self-help than about the experience of illness (Borkman 1999). In a few rare

Peter Conrad and Cheryl Stults, "The Internet and the Experience of Illness," Handbook of Medical Sociology, pp. 179-191. Copyright © 2010 by Vanderbilt University Press. Reprinted with permission.

instances, such as the early days of end-stage renal disease (ESRD), there was sufficient interaction to begin to create some kind of illness subculture (e.g., Kutner 1987), but for the most part patients were treated separately and rarely interacted in meaningful ways with others who had the same illness. One can say with reasonable certainty that there were very few illness subcultures (had there been more, sociologists and others would certainly have studied them.)

Until recently, illness in general was a privatizing experience discussed only with one's doctor, family, and perhaps a few good friends. It was not unusual for individual sufferers of an illness never to have spoken to another person with the same illness or to have known someone who shared the same illness. In a 1983 study of the experience of epilepsy, when Schneider and Conrad interviewed eighty people with epilepsy, no more than five had ever spoken to another person with epilepsy about their illness experience. It may be in part the stigma that discouraged revealing one's illness and communication, but for the overwhelming majority of those interviewed illness remained a private experience. With specific illnesses such as HIV/AIDS, where a large and active gay subculture organized around the illness, there was surely more interaction among those with the illness. But this was an unusual situation; typically illnesses were privatized, and most sufferers had little or no communication with people suffering the same disorder.

In the past two decades the Internet has changed all that. There are now hundreds, probably thousands, of illness subcultures on the Internet, and illness is now a public as well as a private experience. In short, for many people, the Internet has changed the experience of illness.

COMING OF THE INTERNET

What we now term "the Internet" began in 1969 when four computers in the United States were linked together to pass military information to one another. Until the late 1980s, most communication over the Internet was text-based e-mails (Hardey 1999). The initial Web browser, the World Wide Web (WWW), was created to allow users to search for information rather than rely on authors to distribute it. The WWW "through a browser enables users to point and click their way across the Internet," placing information at only a mouse click away (Hardey 1999, 825). The first browser for the masses, Mosaic, appeared in 1993; Google as an Internet search engine appeared in 1998. This access to online information and interconnectivity has impacted many aspects of communication, including business and commerce, government, education, news, personal communication, and information acquisition.

The Internet has grown enormously in the past fifteen years, as has the number of users, with roughly 360 million users in 2000 and an estimated 1.5 billion in 2007 (Internet World Stats 2008). The greatest penetration of usage is of course in the developed world, but China has pulled ahead of the United States with the largest number of Internet users (Barboza 2008); according to recent statistics, North America has roughly 250 million Internet users. It has become increasingly easier to access the Internet with computers in all schools, most businesses, public libraries, Internet cafés, and millions of homes. And the Internet is available 24/7; it never shuts down. Sophisticated search engines like Google make accessing relevant information quick and simple. It is not an exaggeration to observe that despite the existence of a real but shrinking Internet divide (Marriott 2006), there has been a digital revolution in the past two decades. Virtually everything about the Internet is growing or increasing. The Internet revolution has affected health information and communication as well.

Estimates of Internet use vary and change by the month. In the United States, nearly 100 million people regularly access the Internet for health information, and most (66 percent) are searching for information about specific diseases (Fox 2005; Blumenthal 2002). Other sources suggest that 80 percent (113 million) of adults who use the Internet have searched for health information online, a 250 percent increase since 1998 (Miah and Rich 2008; Ayers and Kronenfeld 2007). Health-related websites and discussion lists are some of the most popular resources on the Web (Miah and Rich 2008). On any given day more people in the United States go online for health information than consult a health professional (Ayers and Kronenfeld 2007; Nettleton, Burrows, and O'Malley 2005). However, while on some level the Internet is the great equalizer, allowing individuals the same access to information as the experts, a digital divide has emerged. People with lower incomes access or utilize the Internet less often for health information than do people with higher incomes (Ayers and Kronenfeld 2007). Somewhat more whites than African Americans utilize the Internet for health information (Fox and Fallows 2003, 5; cf. Lieberman et al. 2005). Women utilize the Internet more for health information than men do (54 percent to 46 percent) and report significantly more interest in information about specific diseases (69 percent to 58 percent) and certain treatments than do men (54 percent to 47 percent) (Fox 2006). In addition to women, individuals with more education, health insurance, and younger persons are those more likely to use the Internet to search for health information (Ayers and Kronenfeld 2007). The digital gap among minority groups is decreasing, with 43 percent of African Americans and 59 percent of Hispanics reporting access to the Internet (Lieberman et al. 2005).

Individuals who access the Internet are able to locate vast amounts of information about any health condition from sites sponsored by governments, hospitals, national organizations, medical information collections, and even individuals. Beyond these institutional sites (including mega-sites like WebMD.com), one finds personal webpages, weblogs (blogs), online chat rooms, bulletin boards, and discussion sites where individuals can participate and share their knowledge and experience. Many sites allow participation or interaction by posting, or individuals can choose to be "lurkers," who read the messages but do not post or add to the conversations. The number of lurkers on a site can greatly exceed the number of active members—one study found twenty lurkers for each participant (Loader et al. 2002). Thus Internet participation can occur in both interactional and observational ways. The net accumulation is a tremendous amount of health information available on the Internet, some scientific, some personal or experiential, and some commercial. While virtually any illness now has its own site or numerous electronic support groups (ESGs) or informational sites, the actual information must be evaluated with a careful eye. The quality of information may be improving, however; in a recent study analyzing 343 websites about breast cancer, the authors found that only 5.2 percent of the sites contained inaccurate information (Bernstam et al. 2008).

While the Internet has helped patients become more active consumers by providing them a means for finding information and occasionally purchasing treatments, it has also transformed individuals into producers of knowledge. In this Web 2.0 (more interactive) era, individuals can construct their own websites or home pages or develop blogs about their health issues, transforming them from "consumers of health information and care to producers of health information and care" (Hardey 2002, 31). In his study, Hardey (2002) chose

132 webpages through search engines (Yahoo, Alta Vista, Dogpile), newsgroups, and ICQ ("I seek you") chat rooms; 74 webpage constructors returned an e-mail questionnaire that investigated information not included on the websites. Based on these two sources (home pages and questionnaires), Hardey generated four categories of motives for constructing these pages: (1) explain illness; (2) give "expert advice" to others: (3) promote an approach to the illness; and (4) indirect or direct selling of products. "Explaining myself" was one of the main reasons indicated by 43 percent of respondents for placing information on their webpage. Many, in the midst of their narrative, included a hypertext link to a particular aspect of their account (e.g., treatment regimen). Hardey found that while many were skeptical about the efficacy of traditional medicine, they were just as skeptical about alternative treatments. These webpage producers presented information as if they were the "experts" because they had experienced the illness. At times, they felt that this experience was more valid than medical training. Finally, in several cases, the websites not only provided experience-based advice but also a "sales pitch" for a particular treatment.

Internet sources such as personal websites, bulletin boards, and electronic support groups produce a significant amount of lay knowledge based on embodied expertise that can be shared and that sometimes is used to challenge physician or dominant medical perspectives (Barker 2008). While experiential knowledge was embedded in sources like the feminist book *Our Bodies, Ourselves*, published in 1970, the Internet, due to its vast nature and accessibility, amplifies such knowledge and in its sheer ubiquity helps legitimize it as well. This blurs some distinctions between patient and expert, developing what Collins and Evans (2002, 238) call "experience-based experts," who have "special technical expertise by virtue of experience that is not recognized by degrees or other certificates."

The Internet can also empower patients with knowledge and options by offering information previously limited to medical experts (or available only through extensive library research) and the potential to increase control over their health. Pitts (2004) examined fifty personal webpages of women with breast cancer to see if their information and stories portrayed evidence of empowerment. She found the women often referred to the Internet as a "virtual library" where they could "arm themselves" with information that they could take to medical appointments to challenge or question doctors about the care and treatments they felt they should be receiving. The process of writing out their experiences helped them better understand medical language. Several women portrayed the Internet as a "beacon of hope," since it can potentially provide life-saving information. However, this may become a double-edged sword if women blame themselves if the treatment or course of illness goes awry, despite the illness trajectory being beyond their control. As Pitts notes: "The idea that breast cancer kills only the unaware is blatantly wrong—it also kills the aware, the 'tested'—and implies that women who do get sick or die could have prevented this fate" (48). Thus, women feel a responsibility to save themselves in what Pitts calls the "individual responsibility ethic." Pitts shows that while the Internet can be empowering and creates something of a cyberspace breast cancer community, it also reinforces dominant cultural norms like femininity, consumerism, and individualism. It enables women to feel that they "were not alone" and that it was their "ethical imperative" and responsibility to share their experience so that it might benefit others. This empowerment provides a venue for activism in order to possibly "ameliorate the alienating aspects of medicine" (ibid.) and, perhaps unwittingly, transform breast cancer from a personal to a public issue.

SUPPORT GROUPS

In-person self-help groups have a long and winding history with health and illness but are actually quite limited in their population penetration (Borkman 1999). In a way, the Internet is just an extension of the self-help tradition, but it also revolutionizes it. The Internet has most directly and dramatically altered the experience of illness through online electronic support groups (ESGs). For most people, as noted earlier, illness was a private affair before the advent of the Internet, often isolating individuals; most people didn't communicate with others who suffered from the same illness. Through interconnectivity on the Internet, we have seen the emergence of illness subcultures and, for many people, illness is now a more shared and public experience. As Barker (2008, 21) notes: "The process of understanding one's embodied distress has been transformed from an essentially private affair between doctor and patient to an increasingly public accomplishment among sufferers in cyberspace." Increasingly, individuals are also communicating with others who have the same illness, thereby creating thousands of virtual self-help groups incorporating nearly all illnesses, many with a range of groups from different sources and angles. Many "connectors" have been around for years, as the first newsgroups appeared on the Internet in 1981 (Richardson 2005). What began with illness-oriented newsgroups and bulletin boards has expanded to a large variety of interactive virtual realms, facilitated by expanding Web access and the speed of broadband cable Internet.

An estimated 9 percent of Internet users have visited online support groups (Lieberman et al. 2005). Tens of thousands of ESGs are "accessed as bulletin boards, newsgroups, listserves, and chat rooms" in postings of individuals (Barker 2008, 20). In another vein, computer-mediated social support (CMSS) occurs when medical consultations, prescriptions, and advice from health-care providers can be accessed by the patient, that is, the patient can receive information about diagnosis and treatment. But beyond accessing knowledge, patients can connect with other individuals who are having similar experiences. As just one example, in 2002 Usenet was estimated to have 15,000+ newsgroups and 20,000 people posting 300,000 messages daily (Loader et al. 2002). No doubt with today's greater variety of venues, these numbers are much larger.

The disorders represented on the Internet differ from traditional self-help groups. Davison Pennebaker, and Dickerson (2000) investigated community-based (in-person) and Internet-based self-help groups (5,440 Internet posts to newsgroups and bulletin boards over a two-week period) for twenty illnesses in four metropolitan areas. The most common community-based self-help group was Alcoholics Anonymous (AA), while chronic fatigue syndrome in-person self-help groups were uncommon. In contrast, chronic fatigue syndrome had the most self-help groups on the Internet, while AA was not among the top three. This suggests that Internet-based self-help groups may be especially attractive to individuals who experience chronic illnesses or illnesses that have contested viewpoints. As the authors note: "The on-line domain may be particularly useful in bringing together those who suffer from rare and debilitating conditions, in which getting together physically would present a number of practical barriers" (8). In addition, Internet technology may allow individuals who experience contested illnesses like fibromyalgia and chronic fatigue syndrome or socially stigmatizing illnesses such as epilepsy and sexually transmitted diseases (STDs) to communicate with others who have the same condition in relative privacy and without fear of discrimination. The anonymity of the Internet, buffered by the ability to create screen names and extended by the possibility of simply lurking to view others' experience, creates a relatively safe and private environment for communication and observing others' illness experience.

The "compensation model of Internet use" posits that those who are the most socially awkward will utilize and derive more "benefit" from the Internet (Guo, Bricout, and Huang 2005). The experience of those suffering from stigmatized illnesses, physical disabilities, and multiple chronic illnesses could potentially be the most affected by Internet interaction. In a national survey, Berger, Wagner, and Baker (2005) studied how U.S. adults utilize the Internet for health conditions. Comparing nonstigmatized and stigmatized illnesses, they found that those with stigmatized illness were statistically significantly more likely to use the Internet to obtain health information, communicate with health-care practitioners about their condition, and apply the information they had found to increase their utilization of health care. However, no statistically significant relationship occurred between length of time spent online, frequency of Internet usage, satisfaction with discovered health information, and discussing findings with health care providers. They then separated the group "stigmatized illnesses" into four specific conditions: anxiety, depression, herpes, and urinary incontinence. Upon comparison, the psychiatric stigmatized illnesses (anxiety and depression) were more likely to go online to find health information and to converse with a health provider. These results suggest that overall, individuals with stigmatized illnesses utilize the Internet more than do those with nonstigmatized conditions; however, differences emerge among types of stigmatized illnesses, with higher use by those with psychiatric illnesses (Berger, Wagner, and Baker 2005). Internet communication is particularly attractive to people suffering from physical disabilities and mobility impairments. Individuals with disabilities can access information from their homes.

Guo, Bricout, and Huang (2005) surveyed Internet users in China with a disability about their online interactions. One benefit of online communication was that it allowed disabled individuals to choose whether or not to disclose their disability to other users. Fifty-four percent of respondents felt that the Internet reduced the amount of social discrimination they experience, while 77 percent expressed that online use provided them increased social integration and reduced isolation. Only 32 percent responded that online interactions increased societal concern for disabilities. While their individual isolation was lessened, the Internet appears to have a limited impact on real-world change. Thus, "the Internet cannot by itself remedy the social exclusion faced by persons with disabilities, but must instead be part of a larger programme fueled by social development" (65).

Uncertainty about illness seems to be a factor driving Internet usage. According to a recent study, individuals with multiple chronic illnesses utilized the Internet more than did other respondents (regardless of conditions) due to an increased amount of uncertainty with their situations (Ayers and Kronenfeld 2007). These users seek information to attempt to decrease both social and medical uncertainty. But not all users envisage Internet use in the same way. One study that compared prostate and breast cancer online message boards found different emphases for men and women. Consistent with other studies, both men and women could mention topics that they might not feel comfortable discussing in person. Women allowed more direct emotional expressions of support and criticized the health information found on Internet; men were more likely to search for information about treatments/diseases (Seale, Ziebland, and Charteris-Black 2006).

We know little about what differentiates individuals who do not participate in ESGs from those who do. One study of Norwegian breast cancer patients provides us a little insight. Breast cancer patients are among the illness groups that have the highest participation in both online and offline support groups, according to Sandaunet (2008), who examined why individuals do not join ESGs or become members and then leave them. She found that among her sample, those who did not participate (or left) online breast cancer support groups did so because they did not like to hear stories about death, given their own mortal situations. Other nonparticipators felt that they were not "ill enough" or that they did not have anything to contribute to the discussion. Some women felt that if they participated in the online group, their posts would contain "too much complaining." Sandaunet's results align with previous findings that Western illness narratives are often mediated by a moral imperative to be "successfully ill" and to "rise to the occasion" when sick (Miah and Rich 2008, 62).

Moral or value issues are common among ESGs. Rier researched HIV message boards and found that besides giving emotional support, moral dilemmas about living with HIV were debated online, bringing out sharp moral judgments. This research demonstrates that this new medium, the Internet, does not necessarily mean a new message is being conveyed: "If these boards are seldom generators of genuinely new moral discourse, they do seem clearinghouses for and *transmitters* of existing alternative discourses. Debates over disclosure ethics were witnessed not only by active posters, but also those merely lurking on the boards" (Rier 2007, 1054).

The emergence and popularity of ESGs for virtually any illness may be the most unique and consequential effect of the Internet on illness experience. Not only are these active illness subcultures, but also they move the illness experience from the private to the public sphere and in some cases, allow a kind of collective activism in the name of whatever illness the group represents.

INTERNET ILLNESS SOCIAL MOVEMENTS

Another manifestation of illness on the Internet has been the rise of what might be termed "online social movements." In general these are not extensions of extant social movements but phenomena spawned on the Internet and largely a function of Internet interaction. In this instance, groups move beyond experiential exchange and support to advocate for an alternative interpretation of an illness or the recognition of a previously unknown condition as an illness.

The most developed examples of such social movements are the so-called pro-anorexia (pro-ana) websites. The pro-ana sites have their origin as support groups but have become online communities for people with eating disorders that challenge the dominant medical treatment model of anorexia (see Miah and Rich 2008, 91–106). Pro-ana groups present a very different viewpoint: they attempt to help members and visitors become "better" anorexics, with information as to how to eat fewer calories and survive, hide their anorexia from friends and family, share "anorexic tricks," and avoid medical treatment. They extol the joys and benefits of extreme thinness and develop a counternarrative to the medical view, such as "anorexia is a lifestyle, not an illness." They often consider themselves an "Anorexic Nation." Part of many pro-ana sites is "thinspiration," photos ranging from ultrathin models to skin-and-bones anorexic women who look to most people emaciated and sickly. Beyond message boards, thinspiration videos have begun to emerge on the Internet. Most videos have no dialogue but show faceless, still photos of ultra-thin bodies (Heffernan 2008). One video placed a line of text underneath the photos: "Time spent wasting is not wasted time" (ibid.).

Among the few studies of pro-ana websites is a study of an online support group, Anagrl, in which Fox, Ward, and O'Rourke (2005b) found that the participants viewed the site as a "refuge" for anorexics. Many of the participants did not want the site to become a place to "teach" individuals about how to become an anorexic; rather, the goal of this pro-ana site is to "sustain life in the healthiest way possible for an anorexic" and not force individuals into treatment and eradicate their lifestyle choice (959). The authors termed this view the "anti-recovery stance," meaning that "the movement is there to support its members through life problems, helping them manage anorexia safely, without removing the crutch that it provides them" (963). The response of one Anagrl member described the difference of this site as being "proanorectics," not "proanorexia" (ibid.).

One of the main arguments supporting the pro-anorexia "community" is that the Internet creates "the first truly equal communications platform" by providing a medium where people are not judged upon their appearance—race/ethnicity, gender, or social class—but where all are "neutral and unmarked" (Ferreday 2003, 279). But Ferreday argues that bodies still matter, since they are what house the virtual subject. She suggests there is a powerful resistance to the pro-ana sites because they are uniting individuals based upon how their body looks. These sites post images on their thinspiration pages of anorexic torsos and links to potentially anorexic models to entice others to investigate this whole process. This imagery demonstrates "the hypocrisy of a society that positions anorexics as sick, while continually celebrating and displaying extremely thin bodies" (286).

Pro-ana groups have become very controversial. Nonanorexic viewers often comment that anorexics don't know how "disgusting their bodies are" (Ferreday 2003, 288), although many lurkers visit the sites. Critics have accused the pro-ana sites of recruiting young women to extreme dieting and thinness, teaching them how to become anorexics, or at least glorifying what can be a deadly disorder. Many Internet service providers have removed or blocked their sites in the name of public health, but the sites keep reappearing. In April 2008, the lower house of France's parliament proposed banning any "online incitement" to anorexia, which includes thinspiration videos and more than four hundred websites (Heffernan 2008).

The Internet has also become a forum for conditions or desires once considered anomalies or oddities to develop a collective voice. There have probably always been rare individuals who admired amputees, for example, and a few who desired to become one. These individuals, if they expressed or acted out on their desires, were likely considered disturbed or even mentally ill. The idea of a perfectly healthy individual who has an intense desire to have an amputation of one (or multiple) limbs, or someone who has actually performed a self-amputation of an extremity, is a rare condition (First 2004). The technical term for the attraction to becoming an amputee is "apotemnophilia," coined in 1977 by Johns Hopkins psychologist John Money (Elliott 2000). On the Internet there are now websites created by and catering to "wannabes," which is how these individuals refer to themselves (for "wannabe" an amputee). They write about how this leg shouldn't be there, it's not meant to be their leg, and they need to have it removed to become their ideal self. They have found support and solace in the hundreds of other wannabes worldwide who post on the sites and exchange information about seeking (with little success) surgeons to remove their "unnecessary" limb or other ways that individuals could reach an amputee state. While the medical world in general opposes the amputation of healthy limbs, wannabes are working to get their disorder legitimated in the next edition of the DSM, perhaps as "amputee identity disorder" or "body integrity identity disorder" (BIID), with the hope that this would enable them to find physicians to "treat" their disorder with surgery (Elliott 2000). The wannabes use a claim similar to that of transsexuals—they are "trapped in the wrong body," and medical treatment could fix this.

In another frame, these two examples illustrate that the Internet can be a conduit for issues around medicalization (Conrad 2007). Pro-ana groups are a movement seeking the demedicalization of anorexia, while the wannabes are seeking medicalization as BIID in their quest to become amputees. Both are using the Internet to legitimize their views of what others might well see as illnesses. Recently there has been an upsurge of interest in a new contested illness called Morgellons syndrome, an alleged skin disorder with protruding florescent fibers that is eschewed by dermatologists but that the Centers for Disease Control has actually begun to investigate (Fair 2010). The Internet can operate as an organizing vehicle for or against medicalization of a particular problem and as a medium for the wider dissemination of medicalized claims and counterclaims.

Other illness-oriented groups that have used the Internet as a basis for social movements include mental illness web activists who are trying to reclaim "mad" as a positive term, similar to the way gay activists reclaimed the term "queer." One site has expanded offline to face-to-face support groups in some areas. From its five thousand unique monthly visitors, a New York–based online support group, the Icarus Project, has formed local chapters

in Oregon, Missouri, and Virginia (Glaser 2008). HIV-AIDS activism is also visible on the Internet. Gillet (2003) found numerous activist orientations on AIDS websites, going far beyond the interests of AIDS ESGs. These websites both reflect and reinforce other media activism, but what makes them different is they are explicitly located in the illness experience of individuals. It seems clear that many illness experiences can lead to some kind of activism and social movement activity; the pro-ana and wannabe cases are unique in that they would not exist without the Internet. As Epstein (2008, 514) notes: "In a globally wired world, location doesn't *always* matter—at least not always to the same degree—and the birth and development of the Internet is … why patient and health movements have taken particular forms in recent years."

CHALLENGING PHYSICIAN AUTHORITY?

If the Internet provides patients with independent health information, and if ESGs provide external support and empowerment, is the Internet a medium for challenging physician authority? Blumenthal suggests patients' online interactions will lead to diminished physician authority since the medical information available on the Internet reduces the patients' dependence upon the physician as the "expert" but may also lead to a new role for physicians as consultants. Such a consultant plays two roles: "decision analyst" and "health care informatician." A decision analyst is able to make rational decisions in the presence of uncertainty that also incorporate the patient's preferences. A health-care informatician is an expert in all information technologies, having a vast knowledge of what is available. The acquisition of these skills is a double-edged sword: if the doctor consults a computer in front of some patients, it may undermine the patient's confidence in the physician; but if doctors are unacquainted with technologically advanced sources, many patient-consumers may lose confidence in them as well. Overall, Blumenthal (2002) concludes that while information technologies will cause a decline in physician authority, they will change but not remove the importance and functions of an expert physician. Some have suggested that the Internet and the wide access to medical information give the appearance of informational empowerment for patients but "may be *extending* the reach and power of medicine by creating a kind of 'indirect management of the population'" (Pitts 2004, 53).

The new information available on the Internet is not just replacing previous knowledge but is merging with a mix of sources. All this knowledge has escaped from the sole control of medical experts, potentially reducing their authority. One important area that needs to be studied is how medical professionals are regulating, using, and responding to this knowledge that is widely available to the public. This "e-scaped medicine" is a shift away from the expert provider toward the individuals who are learning and gathering information about their health concerns (Nettleton and Burrows 2003). Overall, it is likely that Internet-based medical information will become an additional resource for patients to manage their experience of illness. Some researchers have shown that the Internet is not used in place of physicians but rather as a supplement. According to one study, 61 percent of Internet health searchers sought health information online in conjunction with their physician visit, to supplement and "get more" from their visit (Ayers and Kronenfeld 2007).

Based on interviews with physicians in Australia, Broom found that doctors responded to the Internet-informed patient in a strategic way to avoid a breakdown of their authority. Several Australian practitioners encouraged their patients to seek information on the Internet, believing that an informed patient could improve the

doctor-patient relationship by taking an active role with aspects of their health: "What emerged from these interviews was a view of the 'active' patient or 'informed' patient as safer than the so-called 'obedient' or 'passive' patient" (Broom 2005, 326). However, not all physicians' views of informed patients were so positive and cooperative. Many doctors liked having informed patients because they were more "compliant" with the treatment options prescribed to them (ibid.). These examples suggest that the Internet may alter ways in which physicians interact with their patients but has not eliminated the need for them. Some might argue that with so much information out there, patients are in greater need of physicians to clarify it.

In sum, our understanding of the impact of the Internet on physician authority is limited. There is considerable evidence that physician authority is decreasing (Mechanic 1996; McKinlay and Marceau 2002), so it would not be surprising if the Internet reinforced this decline. Our best guess now is that the Internet empowers patients, supplements and sometimes challenges physicians' expertise, and provides broader perspectives on illness experience. This probably does erode physician authority to some degree, but to what extent and with what consequences are not yet understood.

EVALUATION OF INFORMATION ON THE INTERNET

Sociological research on the Internet and health has focused upon the interaction of patients and consumers with the vast amount of information found on the Internet. Some articles frame their research in terms of a "reliability discourse" about the quality of health information on the Web and the ability of patients to evaluate it. Various organizations including "the Federal Trade Commission and the U.S. science panel on interactive health communication have warned that much of the information available online may be misleading and potentially harmful" (Miah and Rich 2008, 44). Some critics suggest a paradox, when "such highly rational productions result in the incredible irrationality of information overloads, misinformation, disinformation, and out-of-control information. At stake is a disinformed society. … Thus, while we may appear to be 'smarting up,' the sheer proliferation of decontextualized information means that we are, in fact, experiencing a 'dumbing down'" (Nettleton and Burrows 2003, 174). While this is clearly an overstatement, there is some truth to the contention that there is much bad, wrong, and misleading information on the Internet and that consumers need to be able to evaluate online sources. In a study of the accuracy of information, Loader and colleagues (2002) asked four consultant diabetologists to evaluate sixty-one threads on an Internet newsgroup to determine if there was a gap between lay information and a more traditional medical view. Of the sixty-one, forty were graded B ("less good, some details") or C ("poor, little detail"), with 137 of 242 replies being personal opinion/anecdote. Only 5 of the 242 replies were "possibly dangerous," such as recommending more insulin for exercise.

One common criticism is that Internet information may be "problematic or even harmful" due to its potential to sway individuals away from biomedical treatments with inaccurate information or "unproven" complementary or alternative medical (CAM) treatments. To test this allegation, Broom and Tovey (2008) interviewed cancer patients from around the United Kingdom. Patients who used the Internet for CAM sought validation of the presented claims of others like family members, friends, or physicians. Several patients were skeptical not only of CAM but also of biomedicine information on the Internet and trusted only a few institutional sites. Overall, the Internet reenforced medical views: "Particularly for cancer patients

who are CAM users, the Internet can be a form of virtual re-biomedicalization, imposing the biomedical diagnosis and prognostic knowledge in a context where they are attempting to pursue alternative models of healing" (150). So Internet information, even about CAM, did not necessarily undermine strong biomedical perspectives.

Finally, a word about ESGs, because of their interconnectivity and because they are perhaps the most unique aspect of the Internet. It seems clear that participants in Internet online illness groups are self-selected. While many individuals may access ESGs, only a small proportion seems to actually participate or post messages (Barker 2008; Stults 2007). There may be some evidence that individuals who have more difficulties with their illness, its treatment, or their medical care are more likely to post or seek information or affirmation (Ayers and Kronenfeld 2007). This could possibly self-select for the more severe forms of the illness, or individuals who are more apt to be dissatisfied or frustrated with their experience. Our assumption is that individuals with few problems with their illness might be less likely to participate or post in online groups. One outcome of this might be that ESGs can present an unbalanced picture of the experience of illness.

EMERGING DIRECTIONS OF ILLNESS ON THE INTERNET

While online electronic support groups have been one of the most transformational aspects of the experience of illness, other forms of interactive sites are starting to emerge. A major Internet development of the 2000s has been the emergence of social networking sites such as Facebook or My Space. These sites allow Internet users to join groups connected with their university, hometown, occupation, or hobby. Illness groups too have formed on Facebook, creating new links among people around the world. These connections are similar to Internet support groups, creating online links and community, yet they differ in that the individuals are linked to individual profile pages. These social network groups seem to be replacing the older bulletin board or chat room groups; illness becomes just another way of having some interest in common with other people.

A different kind of online networking illness site has emerged that may be a harbinger of future sites. An exemplar is Patients Like Me, an innovative and expanding site where individuals not only connect and report their symptoms, pains, experiences, or treatment regimens, but also quantify these aspects of their illness: "They note what hurts, where and for how long. They list their drugs and dosages and score how well they alleviate their symptoms. All this gets compiled over time, aggregated and crunched into tidy bar graphs and progress curves by the software behind the site" (Goetz 2008). All this information is available for other group members to examine and evaluate against their own graphs. With so much information available, "the members of Patients LikeMe are creating a rich database of disease treatment and patient experience" (Goetz 2008). The site began in 2004 with a group of individuals with amyotrophic lateral sclerosis (ALS), or Lou Gehrig's disease. As of July 2008, Patients Like Me had organized communities for anxiety, bipolar, depression, HIV/AIDS, multiple sclerosis, obsessive-compulsive disorder, Parkinson's disease, progressive muscular atrophy, primary lateral sclerosis, and post-traumatic stress disorder. The website creators note that they began this site to help empower patients: "We're here to give patients the power to control their disease and to share what they learn with others." The funding for the site comes from health-care providers, pharmaceutical and medical device companies, research institutions, and nonprofit organizations, who pay

to utilize the anonymous data from the members to "drive treatment research and improve medical care" (PatientsLikeMe 2008). Pharmaceutical companies and other research groups conducting clinical trials can advertise on the site for member participation. While such sites provide illness sufferers with comparative information they never had before, there is of course a real danger of this experiential information being appropriated by corporate interests for commercial purposes.

There is always the risk that the Internet may be creating "cyberchondria," a condition in which individuals read too much into the information they unearth about diagnoses and think they are suffering from six or seven "problems" (Gray et al. 2005, 1473). Beyond the problem of excessive self-diagnosis, the Internet allows easy and accessible purchasing of many "prescription" drugs without a prescription. Some sites supply prescription drugs according to an online questionnaire the consumer completes (Fox et al. 2005a). Other suppliers in foreign countries like Canada or Mexico do not require prescriptions for most of their pharmaceuticals; patients may have these medications—some of which have not been officially approved by the U.S. Food and Drug Administration—shipped to them in the United States. Clearly this goes beyond the experience of illness, but such increased access to pharmaceuticals can affect how individuals manage their symptoms and illness. One of the most recent proposals has been to place patients' complete medical records online through providers like Google and Microsoft. These consumer-driven online electronic health records in theory should be able to link up with the records from doctors and hospitals, which could greatly ease the communication among physicians and providers to better coordinate care and reduce medical errors and records available in potentially lifesaving situations. The issues of privacy and confidentiality of these records remain an issue, with concern about the potential of inappropriate disclosure of patient information to unauthorized providers (Lohr 2008). But it seems likely that the Internet will become more of a repository of medical and experiential information about one's illness, and at least some of that will be available to others.

The extant sociological knowledge about the impact of the Internet on illness is still preliminary. At the moment we have growing evidence of the impact of the Internet on illness experience. But as yet, we have no publicly available data that have measured whether utilizing the Internet for illness has any effect on the morbidity or trajectory of the condition itself. A different kind of research will be necessary to ascertain whether Internet usage has any impact on health outcomes, and if it does,

the type, extent, and context of such use. But it is clear that it can have a transformative effect on subjective aspects of illness.

In conclusion, the Internet has revolutionized aspects of illness experience in less than two decades. We now see established online illness subcultures, growing venues of social support for specific illnesses, important sources of information and information exchange, and increased accessibility to and perhaps value of experiential illness information. Advancing technology, innovative communication media, and increased global accessibility suggest that we may be only beginning to recognize the impacts of the Internet on the experience of illness.

NOTE

Our thanks to Kristin Barker and Stefan Timmermans for comments on an earlier draft of this chapter.

REFERENCES

Ayers, Stephanie L., and Jennie Jacobs Kronenfeld. 2007. "Chronic Illness and Health Seeking Information on the Internet." *Health: An Interdisciplinary Journal for the Social Study of Health, Illness and Medicine* 11(3): 327–47.

Barboza, David. 2008. "China Passes U.S. in Number of Internet Users." *New York Times*, July 26.

Barker, Kristin K. 2005. *The Fibromyalgia Story*. Philadelphia: Temple University Press.

———. 2008. "Electronic Support Groups, Patient-Consumers, and Medicalization: The Case of Contested Illness." *Journal of Health and Social Behavior* 49:20–36.

Bell, Susan. 2000. "Narratives." In *Handbook of Medical Sociology*, 5th ed., ed. Chloe Bird, Peter Conrad, and Allen Fremont, 184–99. New York: Prentice Hall.

Berger, Magdalena, Todd H. Wagner, and Lawrence C. Baker. 2005. "Internet Use and Stigmatized Illness." *Social Science and Medicine* 61:1821–27.

Bernstam, Elmer V., Muhammed F. Walji, Smitha Sagaram, Deepak Sagaram, Craig W. Johnson, and Funda Meric-Bernstam. 2008. "Commonly Cited Website Quality Criteria Are Not Effective at Identifying Inaccurate Online Information about Breast Cancer." *Cancer* 112(6): 1206–13.

Blumenthal, David. 2002. "Doctors in a Wired World: Can Professionalism Survive Connectivity?" *Milbank Quarterly* 80(3): 525–46.

Borkman, Thomasina. 1999. *Understanding Self-Help/Mutual Aid: Experiential Learning in the Commons*. New Brunswick, N.J.: Rutgers University Press.

Broom, Alex. 2005. "Medical Specialists' Accounts of the Impact of the Internet on the Doctor/Patient Relationship." *Health: An Interdisciplinary Journal for the Social Study of Health, Illness and Medicine* 9(3): 319–38.

Broom, Alex, and Philip Tovey. 2008. "The Role of the Internet in Cancer Patients' Engagement with Complementary and Alternative Treatments." *Health: An*

Interdisciplinary Journal for the Social Study of Health, Illness and Medicine 12(2): 139–55.

Bury, Michael. 1982. "Chronic Illness as Biographical Disruption." *Sociology of Health and Illness* 4:167–82.

Charmaz, Kathy. 1991. *Good Days, Bad Days.* New Brunswick, N.J.: Rutgers University Press.

———. 1999. "Experiencing Chronic Illness." In *Handbook of Social Studies in Health and Medicine*, ed. Gary L. Albrecht, Ray Fitzpatrick, and Susan Scrimshaw, 277–92. Thousand Oaks, Calif.: Sage.

Collins, H. M., and Robert Evans. 2002. "The Third Wave of Science Studies: Studies of Expertise and Experience." *Social Studies of Science* 32(2): 235–96.

Conrad, Peter. 1987. "The Experience of Illness: Recent and New Directions." In *The Experience and Management of Chronic Illness*, ed. Peter Conrad and Julius A. Roth, 1–32. Vol. 6 of *Research in the Sociology of Health Care.* Greenwich, Conn.: JAI Press.

———. 2007. *The Medicalization of Society: On the Transformation of Human Conditions into Treatable Disorders.* Baltimore: Johns Hopkins University Press.

Cox, Susan, and William McKellin. 1999. "'There's This Thing in our Family': Predictive Testing and the Construction of Risk for Huntington Disease." In *Sociology Perspectives in the New Genetics*, ed. Peter Conrad and Jonathan Gabe, 121–47. Oxford: Blackwell.

Davison, Kathryn P., James W. Pennebaker, and Sally S. Dickerson. 2000. "Who Talks? The Social Psychology of Illness Support Groups." *American Psychologist* 55:205–17.

Elliott, Carl. 2000. "A New Way to Be Mad." *Atlantic Monthly* 286:72–84.

Epstein, Steven. 2008. "Patient Groups and Health Movements." In *The Handbook of Science and Technology Studies*, 3rd ed., ed. Edward J. Hackett, Olga Amsterdamska, Michael Lynch, and Judy Wacjman, 499–539. Cambridge, Mass.: MIT Press.

Fair, Brian. 2010. "Morgellons: Contested Illness, Diagnostic Compromise, and Medicalisation." *Sociology of Health and Illness* 32(4):597–612.

Ferreday, Debra. 2003. "Unspeakable Bodies: Erasure, Embodiment and the Pro-Ana Community." *International Journal of Cultural Studies* 6(3): 277–95.

First, Michael B. 2004. "Desire for Amputation of a Limb: Paraphilia, Psychosis, or New Type of Identity Disorder." *Psychological Medicine* 34:1–10.

Fox, N. J., K. J. Ward, and A. J. O'Rourke. 2005a. "The 'Expert Patient': Empowerment or Medical Dominance? The Case of Weight Loss, Pharmaceutical Drugs, and the Internet." *Social Science and Medicine* 60:1299–1309.

———. 2005b. "Pro-anorexia, Weight-Loss Drugs, and the Internet: An 'Anti-Recovery' Explanatory Model of Anorexia." *Sociology of Health and Illness* 60:944–71.

Fox, Susannah. 2005. "Health Information Online." Pew Internet and American Life Project. pewinternet. org/~/media//Files/Reports/2005/PIP_Healthtopics_May05.pdf.pdf.

———. 2006. "Online Health Search 2006." Pew Internet and American Life Project. pewinternet. org/~/media//Files/Reports/2006/PIP_Online_Health_2006.pdf.pdf.

———. 2008. "The Engaged E-patient Population." Pew Internet and American Life Project. pewinternet.org/~/media//Files/Reports/2008/PIP_Health_Aug08.pdf.pdf.

Fox, Susannah, and Deborah Fallows. 2003. "Internet Health Resources." Pew Internet and American Life Project. pewinternet.org/~/media//Files/Reports/2003/PIP_Health_Report_July_2003.pdf.pdf.

Gillet, James. 2003. "Media Activism and Internet Use by People with HIV/AIDS." *Sociology of Health and Illness* 25(6): 608–42.

Glaser, Barney G., and Anselm L. Strauss. 1965. *Awareness of Dying.* Chicago: Aldine.

Glaser, Gabrielle. 2008. "'Mad Pride' Fights a Stigma." *New York Times*, May 11.

Goetz, Thomas. 2008. "Practicing Patients." *New York Times Magazine*, March 23.

Goffman, Erving. 1961. *Asylums.* New York: Doubleday.

Gray, Nicola J., Jonathan D. Klein, Peter R. Noyce, Tracy S. Sesselberg, and Judith A. Cantrill. 2005. "Health-Information Seeking Behavior in Adolescents: The Place of the Internet." *Social Science and Medicine* 60:1467–78.

Greil, Arthur L. 1991. *Not Yet Pregnant: Infertile Couples in Contemporary America.* Philadelphia: Temple University Press.

Guo, Baorong, John C. Bricout, and Jin Huang. 2005. "A Common Open Space or a Digital Divide? A Social Mobility Perspective on the Online Disability Community in China." *Disability and Society* 20(1): 49–66.

Hardey, Michael. 1999. "Doctor in the House: The Internet as a Source of Lay Health Knowledge and the Challenge to Expertise." *Sociology of Health and Illness* 21(6): 820–35.

———. 2002. "'The Story of My Illness': Personal Accounts of Illness on the Internet." *Health: An Interdisciplinary Journal for the Social Study of Health, Illness, and Medicine* 6(1): 31–46.

Heffernan, Virginia. 2008. "The Medium: Narrow Minded." *New York Times*, May 25.

Internet World Stats. 2008. "Usage and Population Statistics." internetworldstats.com/stats.htm.

Karp, David. 1997. *Speaking of Sadness.* Oxford: Oxford University Press.

Klitzman, Robert, and Ronald Bayer. 2003. *Mortal Secrets: Truth and Lies in the Age of AIDS.* Baltimore: Johns Hopkins University Press.

Kutner, Nancy. 1987. "Social Worlds and Identity in End Stage Renal Disease." In *The Experience and Management of Chronic Illness*, ed. Peter Conrad and Julius A. Roth, 33–72. Vol. 6 in *Research in the Sociology of Health Care*. Greenwich, Conn.: JAI Press.

Lieberman, Morton A., Andre Winzelberg, Mitch Golant, Mari Wakihiro, Mariann DiMinno, Michael Aminoff, and Chadwick Christine. 2005. "Online Support Groups for Parkinson's Patients: A Pilot Study of Effectiveness." *Social Work in Health Care* 42(2): 23–38.

Loader, Brian D., Steve Muncer, Roger Burrows, Nicholas Pleace, and Sara Nettleton. 2002. "Medicine on the Line? Computer-Mediated Social Support and Advice for People with Diabetes." *International Journal of Social Welfare* 11:53–65.

Lohr, Steve. 2008. "Most Doctors Aren't Using Electronic Health Records." *New York Times*, June 19.

Marriott, Michel. 2006. "Digital Divide Closing as Blacks Turn to Internet." *New York Times*, March 31.

McKinlay, John B., and Lisa D. Marceau. 2002. "The End of the Golden Age of Doctoring." *International Journal of Health Services* 32:379–416.

Mechanic, David. 1996. "Changing Medical Organization and Erosion of Trust." *Milbank Quarterly* 74: 171–89.

Miah, Andy, and Emma Rich. 2008. *The Medicalization of Cyberspace.* New York: Routledge.

Nettleton, Sarah, and Roger Burrows. 2003. "E-scaped medicine? Information, Reflexivity, and Health." *Critical Social Policy* 23(2): 165–85.

Nettleton, Sarah, Roger Burrows, and Lisa O'Malley. 2005. "The Mundane Realities of the Everyday Lay Use of the Internet for Health, and Their Consequences for Media Convergence." *Sociology of Health and Illness* 27(7): 972–92.

Parsons, Talcott. 1951. *The Social System.* New York: Free Press.

Parsons, Talcott, and Renée Fox. 1952. "Illness, Therapy and the Modern American Family." *Journal of Social Issues* 8:31–44.

PatientsLikeMe. 2008. patientslikeme.com/. Pitts, Victoria. 2004. "Illness and Internet Empowerment: Writing and Reading Breast Cancer in Cyberspace." *Health: An Interdisciplinary Journal for the Social Study of Health, Illness, and Medicine* 8(1): 33–59.

Richardson, Jane C. 2005. "Establishing the (Extra) ordinary in Chronic Widespread Pain." *Health: An Interdisciplinary Journal for the Social Study of Health, Illness, and Medicine* 9(1): 31–48.

Rier, David. 2007. "Internet Social Support Groups as Moral Agents: The Ethical Dynamics of HIV+ Status Disclosure." *Sociology of Health and Illness* 29(7): 1043–58.

Roth, Julius A. 1963. *Timetables.* Indianapolis: Bobbs-Merrill.

Sandaunet, Anne-Grete. 2008. "The Challenge of Fitting In: Non-Participation and Withdrawal from an Online Self-Help Group for Breast Cancer Patients." *Sociology of Health and Illness* 30(1): 131–44.

Seale, Clive, Sue Ziebland, and Jonathan Charteris-Black. 2006. "Gender, Cancer Experience, and Internet Use: A Comparative Keyword Analysis of Interviews and Online Cancer Support Groups." *Social Science and Medicine* 62:2577–90.

Schneider, Joseph W., and Peter Conrad. 1983. *Having Epilepsy: The Experience and Control of Illness.* Philadelphia: Temple University Press.

Strauss, Anselm, and Barney G. Glaser. 1975. *Chronic Illness and the Quality of Life.* St. Louis: Mosby.

Stults, Cheryl. 2007. "Chronic Pain on the Internet: The Case of Arthritis and Fibromyalgia." Presented at the annual meeting of the Society for the Study of Social Problems, New York, August.

Suchman, Edward A. 1965. "Social Patterns of Illness and Medical Care." *Journal of Health and Human Behavior* 6:114–28.

Weitz, Rose. 1991. *Life with AIDS.* New Brunswick, N.J.: Rutgers University Press.

Williams, Gareth. 1984. "The Genesis of Chronic Illness: Narrative Reconstruction." *Sociology of Health and Illness* 6:175–200.

Understanding and Addressing the Stigma of Mental Illness with Ethnic Minority Communities

Lee Knifton

ABSTRACT

Higher income societies have moved from institutional to community-based care for people experiencing mental illness. However, stigma and discrimination persists and undermines help-seeking, recovery and life chances. Mental illness prevalence is higher amongst communities that face multiple prejudices and disadvantages within society, including Black and minority ethnic communities who may experience migration trauma, racism, acculturation and adverse social circumstances. This study examines beliefs, stigma and the effectiveness of existing national mental health campaigns with Pakistani, Indian and Chinese heritage communities in Scotland, UK, using community based participatory research. Community organisers were trained and supported to co-facilitate focus groups with 87 people using a range of languages. Whilst diversity within and between communities was apparent, important trends emerged. People with mental illness experience high levels of stigma from communities. Families experience significant associated stigma. This shame combines with culturally inappropriate services to reduce help-seeking from mental health services, friends and families. Existing anti-stigma campaigns have failed to reach or engage with communities due to a combination of practical issues such as the use of inappropriate language, imagery and media, but also due to assuming western medical concepts of illness. Participants suggested a new model for national campaigns placing greater emphasis upon community development, cultural events, positive contact and dialogue with families, faith leaders and youth groups. National anti-stigma programmes must develop more effective partnerships with communities or risk magnifying existing inequalities. Despite a range of national programmes to address stigma towards people with mental illness, it remains as the major barrier to social inclusion for people with mental illness living in communities. Stigma is particularly severe if people have a mental illness and are also economically disadvantaged or face multiple stigmas. By adopting community based participatory research (CBPR) approaches with three Black and ethnic minority

Lee Knifton, "Understanding and Addressing the Stigma of Mental Illness with Ethnic Minority Communities," Health Sociology Review, vol. 21, no. 3, pp. 287-298. Copyright © 2012 by Taylor & Francis Group. Reprinted with permission. Provided by ProQuest LLC. All rights reserved.

communities in Scotland, this study makes the case that stigma can only be understood and effectively addressed with reference to its socio-cultural context.

KEYWORDS

mental illness, sociology, ethnic minority, stigma, discrimination, culture

The way in which we support people with enduring mental health problems in affluent countries is changing. Deinstitutionalisation and recovery-focused models of care are frequently accompanied by rights-based legislation in relation to health-care treatment, employment and education. Yet in contemporary societies, the intense stigma and discrimination that people with mental health problems continue to face results in a series of 'social injuries' that are profoundly damaging (Rogers & Pilgrim, 2003).

Sociologists Link and Phelan (2001) provide a strong model for understanding mental health stigma. They acknowledge that stigma includes a combination of inaccurate or distorted beliefs, negative attitudes and discriminatory behaviour. They describe stigma as the co-occurrence of labelling of difference, stereotyping, separation of 'us' and 'them', followed by discrimination and status loss. This model acknowledges that it is easier to discriminate against groups who have less power, and that stigma can exist at a number of levels in society: internalised stigma (or anticipated discrimination) for the person affected; social stigma experienced in everyday interactions with friends, family and the wider community; and structural stigma (or institutional discrimination) whereby prejudice is embedded into legal systems, the media, cultural and businesses institutions. Family and friends can also be stigmatised by association with the labelled person or group although this dimension has received less attention (Goffman, 1963).

The impact of stigma is profound. People with mental health problems frequently delay help-seeking for fear of the social consequences (Schomerus & Angermeyer, 2008). Life chances and opportunities are consistently restricted (Rosenfield, 1997). Harassment in the community remains a common phenomenon (Berzins, Petch, & Atkinson, 2003). Employment rates remain at under 20% across Europe compared to over 40% of all people with a disability (Williams, Copestake, Eversley, & Stafford, 2008) and stigma from employers and colleagues is a major cause (Arthur, Knifton, Park, & Doherty, 2008; Faulkner & Layzell, 2000). The cumulative effects of this income and status loss, combined with fear of rejection from friends, families and partners, frequently results in lowered self-esteem (Wright, Gronfein, & Owens, 2000). Enduring stigma can lead to people living in states of constant stress, worsening the initial mental health problem (Link & Phelan, 2006). Under-investment in health services from governmental institutions contributes towards a gap between mental health need, services and support, especially amongst disadvantaged social groups (Patel et al., 2010).

In Scotland, the location of this study, stigma and discrimination against people with mental illness continues to be a major issue. Dangerousness remains a commonly reported belief in public surveys and in the media, along with notions that people are to blame for their condition, are unwilling or unable to work, make little social contribution and are unsuitable as partners (Knifton

& Quinn, 2008). Beliefs about danger increased as we moved from institutions to community care, with a shift from 'becoming mad' to 'fear of the other' (Maclean, 1969). Danger and unpredictability remain highly associated with people with severe and enduring mental illnesses including psychoses and schizophrenia. Other conditions, such as depression, attract more subtle forms of stigma related to ability to work and being difficult to talk to (Crisp, Gelder, Rix, Meltzer, & Rowlands, 2000).

This study engages with communities that experience multiple forms of disadvantage and disempowerment, and the case for understanding and addressing mental health stigma in the context of inequalities is compelling. Globally the prevalence of mental health problems is high and increasing (World Health Organization, 2001) and the burden does not fall equally within societies. Those experiencing material and social disadvantage have much higher rates of mental illness (Pickett, James, & Wilkinson, 2006). In particular mental illness and distress is caused and perpetuated by relative inequality, meaning that it is not the absolute levels of poverty or disadvantage that matter as much as the differences within a society between those who have most and those who have least. The greater the disparity, the greater the levels of mental illness and distress (Friedli, 2009). This social gradient in health was outlined in the UK by Marmot (2010) in his recent review and he recommended proportionate universalism as a response from health and public agencies to reduce health inequalities. This means that universal health and social programmes should invest more resources and effort into areas and communities according to the level of need.

In relation to mental health stigma specifically, greater prevalence is reported from members of communities in disadvantaged areas (Braunholtz, Davidson, Myant, & O'Connor, 2006). So not only

is someone more likely to experience mental illness in an area of deprivation, they may have less access to support, have fewer opportunities for employment, and will likely face a more stigmatising community response.

When people face multiple disadvantages, mental health stigma needs to be considered in this wider context. This study explores mental health stigma with the three largest Black and minority ethnic (BME) communities in Scotland, comprising citizens with Pakistani, Chinese and Indian heritage who encompass a variety of cultures and religious beliefs. Mental health services and campaigns rarely target BME communities consistently. Yet BME communities frequently experience high rates of mental health problems linked to social circumstances such as unemployment, stress and living conditions (Williams & Hunt, 1997) and life events such as family absence, acculturation and migration trauma (Myers, McCollam, & Woodhouse, 2005).

These problems are consistently exacerbated by racism from communities and services (Chakraborty, McKenzie, Hajat, & Stansfeld, 2010). In the UK, BME communities frequently receive inadequate mental health service provision. In some cases, particularly amongst Asian minorities, services fail to reach or engage with communities where there is need. In other cases there can be an excess of compulsory admissions and restrictive treatments (Fernando, 2003). This can be attributed to racial prejudice and fear amongst practitioners. It is also seen as a consequence of prejudice embedded within psychiatry and the diagnostic process itself, which takes little account of cultural differences. So if mental health services are seen as part of a system that diminishes your cultural beliefs, or exerts restrictive power over you, then mental illness itself can become something to fear, avoid or reject. When that same system dominates campaigns to reduce stigma both the messages and their source may lack credibility. In Scotland this dual stigma shows little improvement despite various equalities initiatives (Grant & Jackson, 2005). High levels of social isolation and significant racism are reported by all three major BME communities and dissatisfaction with services is highest amongst Chinese minorities (Heim & MacAskil, 2006).

Layered onto these social issues, it is important to consider cultural beliefs as a potentially important factor influencing social stigma towards people with mental illness. In international cross-cultural studies the emerging trends are that the impact of stigma and discrimination affects similar domains of individual's lives, for example employment, community harassment or marriage. However the intensity of impact varies and the forms and nature of stigmatising beliefs that people and communities hold also varies widely according to cultural beliefs (Van Brakel, 2006).

There is a significant amount of literature on cross-cultural dimensions of mental illness and social stigma. Fabrega (1991) reviewed the literature on psychiatric stigma in India, China and in Islamic countries including Pakistan, the countries of origin of the minority communities in this study, and found consistently high levels of stigma. More recent reviews across several Asian countries by Ng (1997) and Lauber and Rossler (2007) highlight variations within and across countries and cultures in the intensity of stigma. However overall stigma and discrimination are prevalent and common patterns emerge. Dangerousness is a common belief and often leads to social distance and isolation. Families can both stigmatise the person with mental illness and in turn, themselves be stigmatised through association by the community. A consequence is that relatives are devalued as potential marriage partners.

It is also important to acknowledge that psychiatric illness categories are western cultural constructs. Other cultures may not conceptualise distress as illness (Kleinman, 1987). Many Asian cultures use supernatural and religious explanations for what psychiatry sees as severe mental illnesses and common mental health problems are frequently expressed as physical health problems, which can be less socially disadvantageous (Fabrega, 1992; Lauber & Rossler, 2007). Knowing who is labelled as having a mental illness in a community is fundamental to knowing how to approach tackling stigma.

We are not certain how beliefs and stigmas that are common in people's countries of origin change amongst first, second and third generation minorities. There is a lack of research concerning the nature and impact of mental health stigma amongst BME communities in the UK or Scotland specifically. National mental health surveys in Scotland on awareness and attitudes did not focus upon BME communities. Of the UK studies available, family reputation and marriage concerns do feature heavily amongst South Asian minority communities. There is evidence that some cultural and religious beliefs about causation can lead to shame and blame (Hatfield, Mohammad, Ahim, & Tanweer, 1996; Tabassum, Macaskill, & Ahmad, 2000). Shame, guilt and losing 'face' also emerged in studies with Chinese ethnic minority communities. Perceptions of dangerousness are reported along with hiding the condition from friends, family and health services (Blackwell, 1997; Li, Logan, Yee, & Ng, 1999; Wong & Richman, 2004; Yeung, 2004).

Wider international studies with BME communities in affluent countries indicate that culture does play a significant role in shaping mental health stigma. For example in the US, Gary (2005) explores the mental health stigma experienced by four ethnic minority communities. She notes how the prejudice experienced by ethnic group affiliation leads to dual stigma, and results in reduced help-seeking and a widening of mental health disparities.

Scotland has had a national programme to improve the public's mental health since 2003. This has developed as a public health approach and aims to promote positive mental health for all, prevent common disorders, and enhance the quality of life of people with mental illness. This includes a national campaign to reduce the stigma associated with mental illness, now in its eighth year. The campaign is well funded in international terms and to date activities of the campaign have been aimed at the general population or specific setting such as workplaces or schools. The main methods that it uses to tackle stigma include national advertising campaigns with key messages about stigma, media lobbying to protest against negative reporting, supporting local mental health groups to develop anti-stigma events and persuading major organisations to pledge to reduce stigma associated with mental illness. There is a focus upon producing resources such as posters and flyers for general distribution by mental health groups, health providers and government agencies. It describes itself as adopting a social marketing approach. Yet there is compelling evidence that mental illness stigma must be understood, and perhaps addressed, in relation to its social and cultural context. Little research has been undertaken with BME communities in Scotland to understand if there are important differences in beliefs about mental illness or patterns of stigma, or the extent to which the national programme has reached and influenced these communities.

This study undertakes research with members of the three largest BME communities in Scotland that have migrated from China, Pakistan and India. We explored commonly held beliefs about mental illness, patterns of stigma and discrimination and perceptions about the current national anti-stigma campaign in order to inform future action.

METHODS

A broad based community coalition was established over the 2-year duration of the study, involving 12 partner organisations including universities, mental health agencies, the national anti-stigma campaign team and community groups representing the three largest BME communities in Scotland. This was an example of a community of learning and practice (Wenger, 1998). This coalition supported the study through a series of meetings with researchers helping to identify community projects and advising on methods of engagement. By developing a research partnership of stakeholders who both affect and are affected by mental illness and stigma the research was intended to be more equitable and collaborative (Cargo & Mercer, 2008). Drawing upon different strengths and insights can lead to changes that improve health (Israel, Schulz, Parker, & Becker, 1998). This coalition also has the potential to move from learning to action and use the research findings to help to develop improved methods of tackling stigma with BME communities (Israel et al., 1998).

In previous health research the coalition indicated that many people in BME communities felt like research subjects rather than partners. Staff in the community projects were keen to develop capacity in research skills, but also sought assurances that they would be involved in any future projects to improve mental health. This study, therefore, adopted a CBPR approach. This approach is based upon the belief that research is strengthened when formal researchers from outside the community partner with community representatives and organisers who have direct inside knowledge, experience and access to the communities (Minkler, 2004). Community organisers were drawn from the Chinese, Pakistani and Indian ethnic minority communities and shared their inside knowledge of community structures and responses to mental health issues in order to shape the design and focus of the study. In return the researchers helped to develop the formal research capacities of the community partners through training sessions and mentoring. They jointly developed the research method and materials, identified participants and collected data. CBPR was seen as particularly relevant in this context as it builds upon community strengths, can create more trust about a health topic that is heavily stigmatised, and sees people in the context of their social and cultural environments (Minkler & Wallerstein, 2003).

The study aimed to gain an in-depth understanding of mental illness and stigma in its social and cultural context and its meanings to participants. Qualitative research was adopted to enable us to capture subjective experiences and complexity. Focus groups were identified as the most culturally appropriate method across the communities involved. They also provided for a safe and supportive setting. Focus groups allow participants to share their collective knowledge more fully, and importantly why these views are held (Bryman, 2004). They enable participants to raise issues and explore and contextualise them, and the researchers to reflect back to participants to ensure shared understandings. The focus group schedule was developed in conjunction with community agencies and covered: beliefs about mental illness and its causes; stigma and discrimination in communities; and opinions about the national anti-stigma campaign. Groups lasted between 90 minutes and 2 hours. Questions about mental health, stigma and discrimination were asked in the third person 'in your community' rather than about the person or people themselves. It was felt that this would elicit more honest findings and minimise social desirability bias.

The community projects were responsible for recruiting to and hosting the focus groups. Ten focus groups were conducted involving 87 participants. The sampling was designed to include a mix of participants according to age, gender and faith. Within this outline framework, participants were recruited through community organisations using purposive sampling, and through local advertising by projects. This means that it was not important to be 'representative' but rather typical. Urdu, Punjabi, Hindi and Cantonese translators were provided in the relevant focus groups to ensure that we could reach and engage with participants who did not have good English language skills.

The focus groups were co-facilitated by experienced formal researchers alongside community workers from participating BME community projects who were trained in research methods. To ensure that complex and subtle points were not missed or misinterpreted, facilitators regularly checked emerging points and themes with the group throughout the session. The facilitators and translators also jointly reviewed the focus group after the session to clarify any points that were specific to certain cultures or faiths, or which were difficult to translate. The focus group data were analysed systematically to allow key themes and issues to be identified. Data were analysed using our initial 'focusing factors' (Silverman, 2004) of 'beliefs about mental illness', 'stigma' and 'a national anti-stigma campaign'. A grounded theory technique was used to analyse the data for emerging themes and topics. Comments were analysed, described and labelled and then grouped into broad categories. Relationships between categories were examined within and between the groups and key themes identified. Whilst the analysis followed the principles of Glaser and Strauss' (1967) grounded theory, in practice CBPR involves researchers sharing concepts, perspectives and theoretical positions in designing the study and analysing the data. Therefore the process inevitably involved 'subtle interplay between theory, concepts and data' (Silverman, 2004) and could not be entirely inductive (see Corbin & Strauss, 2008).

FINDINGS

The findings across the groups were both rich and complex. There was general agreement that mental health stigma and its consequences were profound and deeply embedded across and within the three communities. There was considerable variation within and between communities about perceived causes and meanings associated with mental illness and stigma. Older and lower income participants and first generation citizens held more traditional beliefs. Interestingly older and younger generations were well aware of the beliefs of each other. For the purposes of this paper, we focus upon beliefs and stigma and then the more specific data that relates the provision of mental health services and anti-stigma campaigns. The main themes are outlined in four sections: beliefs and stigma; mental health treatment and services; the existing national anti-stigma campaign; and alternative models and approaches to engaging with BME communities.

Beliefs and Stigma Associated with Mental Health Problems

Across the ethnic minority groups, high levels of mental health problems were attributed to a combination of stressful social circumstances faced by many people including economic deprivation, greater social isolation and pressures of family responsibilities. Amongst Chinese minority communities this was consistently reported as pressures of life. Newer migrants highlighted how processes of migration lead to particular stresses including often living in poor accommodation, language

barriers and consistently experiencing high levels of racism from the wider community. South Asian participants reported poor living conditions, prejudice and violence more directly as contributing to mental health problems.

Mental health problems were seen to be prevalent across the communities, however respondents mainly referred to more severe and enduring mental health problems rather than more common conditions such as anxiety and depression. Most participants resisted the idea that the latter are medical conditions as they are more commonly seen as responses to social problems, crises of faith or just 'part of life'. Amongst the more 'severe conditions' many people in communities frequently do not differentiate conditions such as schizophrenia or bipolar illness and more commonly view them as 'just madness'.

In addition to mental health problems being a major issue, all groups reported that people with mental health problems are frequently and heavily stigmatised within communities. This stigma takes several forms and often relates to underlying cultural and religious beliefs about causes. One set of explanations framed mental health problems in the context of blame for example as a punishment from God for a sin in a person's current or past life, or caused by spirits or *jinn*. Each of the Chinese and Hindu groups discussed linked *karma* to blame. A further theme was communities viewing mental illness as inherited through families. This frequently taints not just the person affected but the whole family within the community. This was reported across communities but the strongest examples emerged amongst Hindu, Sikh and Muslim communities. Here, respondents described examples of how extended family structures and a focus upon marriage magnifies the impact of stigma upon the person and the whole family. Maintaining family reputation could lead to hiding the problem and isolation for people affected.

Amongst a wide range of responses, a number of consistent beliefs were reported both across and within groups. These include people with mental health problems being dangerous and unpredictable, less intelligent, unable to work effectively, and unsuitable as a marriage partner. These are fundamental aspects of affected people's social identity that are diminished. They are compounded by commonly reported beliefs that severe mental illness is incurable, with little possibility for recovery. It is therefore unsurprising that across all community groups 'shame' emerged as the most common response to mental health problems. This was expressed in different ways such as 'face' amongst Chinese communities, but with similar consequences.

Many of these findings about beliefs and stigma have been identified in previous international cross-cultural studies outlined in the introduction. Kleinman (1987), Fabrega (1992) and Lauber and Rossler (2007) consistently demonstrate that concepts of mental health may not be culturally constructed as illness, that stigma can affect families and not just individuals, and that beliefs about danger and unsuitability for marriage can lead to shame or social isolation for the person affected. Our findings highlight how these beliefs persist amongst migrant communities in Scotland. They reinforce some of the English studies with first and second generation Asian ethnic minority communities, which found that religious and cultural beliefs still lead to shame and blame (Hatfield et al., 1996; Tabassum et al., 2000). The study does not enable us to make detailed comparisons within and between communities. However, it was reported that more traditional beliefs were held less strongly by younger generations, professionals and those with higher economic status.

Perceptions of Mental Health Treatment and Services

Groups explored both the experience of mental health services and reasons for or against seeking treatment. Common themes about treatment emerged from each of the BME community discussions.

Stigma and recovery pessimism reduce help-seeking. One reason for avoiding help-seeking from health services stated by all generations was the shame associated with mental illness amongst communities, tying in with international research (Fabrega, 1991). This shame was also experienced by families within communities, which reduced support and motivation for individuals to seek medical help. Amongst older and first generations recovery-pessimism was common. A consistent reason for not seeking help from mental health services was a belief that it would not be effective in improving the mental health condition, that 'it will not work' or 'there is no cure'.

Many participants from Muslim, Hindu and Sikh heritage talked about a community belief that mental health problems are not an illness—but are caused by factors such as the will of God, inheritance, 'black magic' or 'spirits'; consequently medication is not seen to help. Many community members were reported as holding a number of beliefs about causation in parallel; including social, religious and medical explanations which, again, supports wider international findings on cultural beliefs and stigma (Lauber & Rossler, 2007). For a high proportion of respondents, religious leaders were seen as the first and foremost point of contact and support, particularly for those with Muslim, Hindu and Sikh heritage. Traditional treatments were reported as a common alternative to medical help seeking amongst those who have migrated from mainland China and Hong Kong. Social responses to treating mental illness permeated group discussions across communities, for example the belief that with family support people 'will get over it' or that 'lots of love will solve it'.

Confidence with language was an important factor in using mental health services. Newer and first generation migrants, and those with lower confidence in English language ability will frequently seek help from religious leaders, as respected members of their community with whom they can communicate easily, rather than seeking help outside the community. Although interpreters are used across the three communities in other areas of life, there were perceived issues of confidentiality and a sense that it is difficult to convey feelings and emotions accurately through an interpreter.

The groups did not cite overt prejudice from health services as a reason for avoiding mental health services. However, respondents explained that there was a level of general distrust of social workers and doctors in some sections of the communities. Participants expressed more direct fear of being asked 'too many questions' either by the doctor or by others in the waiting room. They also expressed a lack of trust in personal information remaining confidential. A smaller proportion of respondents expressed fears of extreme measures. These concerns were expressed most strongly amongst respondents from Muslim communities, several of whom expressed concerns about 'ending up in an asylum'. Few people felt that provision of mental health services within and by members of the communities would significantly increase uptake, instead people generally restated concerns about confidentiality within relatively small communities.

Across the three BME communities, there was unanimity that members of the communities that were second and third generations, and those with high levels of education and language confidence were more likely to engage earlier and more readily with mental health services if needed. However,

personal and family stigma was consistent across generations, acting as a barrier.

Effectiveness of an Existing National Anti-Stigma Campaign

Scotland has had a national anti-stigma campaign since 2003. Although there has been a sustained national campaign for several years, the groups expressed profound concerns about its reach, materials and overall approach in terms of engaging the BME communities. The findings were consistent across groups about its weaknesses, highlighting practical and conceptual issues.

A set of problems relate to language. The printed and advertising materials were all in English language and unavailable as translated resources. This excludes a significant number of people within the BME communities who have less confidence with English language from the campaign. This very likely includes those in most need. The language that is used is also quite subtle, cryptic and indirect and seen to require a good degree of proficiency to have a full effect. This criticism of language even applied to the term 'see me' which several of the groups felt was a particularly individualistic term and might have greater impact if it was a term that stressed people in the context of community and family.

Imagery was also raised. One concern across groups was the lack of multi-racial images. Images on materials were of white people. The groups felt that this should be more balanced, but not have such a high proportion of people from BME communities that it could imply these communities were 'mad' and risk reinforcing racism. Several of the groups also noted that they had not seen anyone from an ethnic minority community present in any of the television and media adverts, nor as volunteer speakers in the media. In addition to people, there were comments that the 'cultural activities' shown such as football were less likely to engage these three communities.

Members of all groups felt that national campaign materials had not reached their communities. They were distributed primarily through health services and local councils, but also through mental health consumer groups. Few of the campaign materials had been seen in religious, cultural or community centres. Existing press, radio and television communications were seen to be partially useful but it was noted that little attention was given to press, radio and television stations that are accessed by many in BME communities.

Respondents felt that little consideration appeared to be given to race or culture when the campaign was designed. Groups identified a number of steps (in addition to addressing the problems identified in this section) that could be taken to make the campaign more relevant and effective. One example was to use simpler but more positive messages that involve key opinion formers including faith leaders and health professionals. They also suggested targeting community newspapers (especially free newspapers), community radio channels and key satellite television channels that use a range of languages. Perhaps most importantly it was argued that the use of the word 'me' in 'see me' should be changed to something less individualistic, and that the slogan 'one in four' was inappropriate. New media was seen to be entirely appropriate by younger generations.

Overall, discussions centred on the value of community involvement from the outset in order to have relevant campaigns that reach those who need it most. Within communities, generations have very different views and a series of mini campaigns were suggested in addition to modifications to the existing national approach. However, respondents were generally pessimistic about the likelihood of an information-giving campaign being successful in addressing deeply held prejudices.

New Approaches

When asked more freely about what approaches would work to address mental health stigma within their communities, a very different set of priorities and actions emerged challenging classic social marketing and public education models. A set of linked solutions and activities were suggested which are characterised by some core processes; community development, personal contact, dialogue and respecting different beliefs. These approaches were felt to be more likely to address some of the fundamental stigma that people with mental illness faced, specifically being seen as 'dangerous', to 'blame', and 'unsuitable for marriage'. Three approaches were favoured.

Participants stressed the embedded nature of stigma within communities, and the different beliefs that people held about what mental illness is, what causes it, and its impact. It was consistently stated that conversation and dialogue would be much more effective than just receiving information in writing or advertisements. Across the groups it was felt that this form of community dialogue or workshops would be culturally appropriate, and more effective if delivered by people from within the community. This finding is not new and has been found in many other studies across communities who are disempowered for a range of health issues. Wallerstein and Bernstein (1988) critiqued how health promotion has persistently used community-wide programmes that have targeted individual behaviours and have failed to reach poor and minority sections of communities. Countering this model with ideas from Freire they argued knowledge does not come from 'experts inculcating their information and imposing their cultural values, but collective knowledge should emerge from group-sharing experiences, where people can engage in mutual reflection and authentic dialogue'. This model, advocated by communities, would allow people to explore their views and understand the impact of stigma on others. Schools, community centres, religious settings and some workplaces were seen as realistic locations from which to access a wide range of people. This approach seemed to be more popular amongst female participants in the study.

An approach that emerged very strongly amongst groups with Pakistani and Indian heritage was the potential of cultural engagement; using events and different art forms to explore mental illness and stigma. Participants highlighted how stories are often used within families and communities. They also pointed out the potential of populist cultural forms, such as Hindi cinema and drama, to engage people. Ideas ranged from developing arts programmes to influence communities, through to using pre-existing, large-scale cultural events and festivals as a setting in which to engage people in a positive way.

Finally, opinion formers were viewed as very important in shaping community perceptions and responses towards people with mental illness and their families. Some, such as faith leaders, were also identified as gatekeepers to accessing services. The most significant and frequently mentioned opinion formers were religious leaders, particularly amongst those from Pakistani and Indian heritage, and most strongly from Muslim participants. Employers were also seen as key opinion formers. This was particularly so for groups of people that work long hours, and the Chinese heritage groups consistently identified the restaurant trade as an example. It is important to note opposing views that were less common but strongly felt. For example several of the female participants felt that women's groups and community development workers were more important people to engage with.

IMPLICATIONS

The findings presented here raise a number of issues that have implications for mental health policy, practice and research both locally and internationally. Overall the study confirms that stigma towards people with mental illness amongst the three BME communities was significant and deeply held, and is a significant factor in the treatment gap we outlined in the review (Patel et al., 2010). It supports aspects of the critiques of community care by authors such as Chesters (2005) who argue that merely being in community settings does not promote humane or effective care. The social support of families and communities is required in order for people with mental illness to live fulfilling lives and stigma remains a barrier to this.

This local study illustrated the importance of understanding and addressing stigma in its socio-cultural context. Community beliefs showed significant diversity but were frequently connected to underlying social and cultural beliefs about causation. What is clear is that we cannot assume that all sections of our communities share a medical, psychiatric view of mental illness. Mental illness is an essentially contested concept (Foucault, 1988). This is reflected in the range of services and treatments that people accessed. Stakeholders should engage communities in order to understand and respond to these social and cultural influences.

In this study stigma is viewed as a more collective experience. Families are often stigmatised as a group, and this can be due to beliefs about contagion and inheritability and blame for previous sin. It acts to reinforce the sense of shame for the individual and hiding of the problems from the wider community and health services. It suggests that in engaging with cultures that have strong community and family connectedness, we should reconsider the importance of associated stigma for families, spouses and friends. Almost half a century ago Goffman (1963) highlighted the stigma that people can face if they are closely associated with someone who is labelled as having a mental illness, particularly families. Current campaigns and mental health services primarily focus upon the individual, reflecting wider political trends in affluent western societies. However, the findings suggest we should give greater attention to this dimension of stigma and challenge individualism as the only basis of health actions and campaigns.

Responses to the national campaign force us to reconsider the value of general approaches in mental health awareness campaigns and service provision. The national anti-stigma campaign, in aiming to make best use if its resources, favoured a single approach. This arguably aimed to provide the greatest health gain at a population level within its resources. The risk though is that it fails to reach those who experience multiple disadvantage, thus widening mental health inequalities, and worsening the experiences of stigma by those at most risk. This consequence appears to be borne out across the three communities. The implication is that we need to rebalance campaigns and develop them with communities, recognising the diversity between and within them. The CBPR model adopted in this study means that key organisations can use these findings to collectively address stigma.

Whilst these findings relate to three BME communities in Scotland specifically, they do raise questions for policy makers more generally about the value of persisting with public education approaches as a route to tackling stigma at all. Anti-stigma campaigns are rooted in positivistic notions of self and society. Campaigns are frequently dominated by medical models and health education messages. This frames the problem as ignorance of 'facts' and sees the challenge as providing the 'right' information to those who are less well informed in the 'right way'. The public will then rationally modify the way that they interact with people with mental illness. Seen in this context, its sociological naivety is clear. Just as it failed to engage at all with communities holding diverse beliefs, it ignores the barriers to change such as prejudice, and power relationships. There are interesting links between the community-generated preferences for tackling stigma in this study and wider evidence about 'what works'. There is evidence that positive contact, narratives and the arts can be effective in reducing stigma (Corrigan, River, Lundin, & Penn, 2001; Knifton et al., 2010). So an over-reliance on education campaigns perhaps partially explains the persistence of stigma more widely.

This study provides important insights into some of the social and cultural issues in three BME communities which affect how they respond to mental illness and mental health services. It provides insights into why stigma persists and why existing approaches to tackling stigma are ineffective. Our respondents were typical rather then representative meaning themes that emerged are tentative and hypothesis generating. However, an emerging potential model for national campaigns must place greater emphasis upon community development, positive contact, community dialogue and engaging with diverse beliefs. Such approaches need to understand and respond to the socio-cultural needs of communities. To succeed, mental health campaigns must develop more effective partnership with community agencies, or risk magnifying existing inequalities.

ACKNOWLEDGEMENTS

I would like to acknowledge the individuals, groups and organisations in involved in the Mosaics of Meaning project.

REFERENCES

Arthur, B., Knifton, L., Park, M., & Doherty, E. (2008). Cutting the dash: Experiences of mental health and employment. *Journal of Public Mental Health, 7*(4), 51–59.

Berzins, K. M., Petch, A., & Atkinson, J. M. (2003). Prevalence and experience of harassment of people with mental health problems living in the community. *British Journal of Psychiatry, 183*(12), 526–533.

Blackwell, M. J. (1997). *Chinese mental health issues in Britain.* London, England: Chinese Mental Health Association/Mental Health Foundation.

Braunholtz, S., Davidson, S., Myant, K., & O'Connor, R. (2006). *Well? What do you think? The third National Scottish Survey of public attitudes to mental health, mental wellbeing and mental health problems.* Edinburgh, Scotland: Scottish Government.

Bryman, A. (2004). *Social research methods.* Oxford, England: Oxford University Press.

Cargo, M., & Mercer, S. L. (2008). The value and challenges of participatory research: Strengthening its practice. *Annual Review of Public Health, 29*, 325–350.

Chakraborty, A. T., McKenzie, K. J., Hajat, S., & Stansfeld, S. A. (2010). Racism, mental illness and social support in the UK. *Social Psychiatry and Psychiatric Epidemiology, 45*(12), 1115–1124.

Chesters, J. (2005). Deinstitutionalisation: An unrealised desire. *Health Sociology Review, 14*(3), 272–282.

Corbin, J., & Strauss, A. (2008). *Basics of qualitative research: Techniques and procedures for developing grounded theory.* Thousand Oaks, CA: Sage.

Corrigan, P. W., River, L. P., Lundin, R. K., & Penn, D. L. (2001). Three strategies for changing attributions about severe mental illness. *Schizophrenia Bulletin, 27*(2), 187–195.

Crisp, A., Gelder, M., Rix, S., Meltzer, H., & Rowlands, O. (2000). Stigmatisation of people with mental illnesses. *British Journal of Psychiatry, 177*, 4–7.

Fabrega, H. (1991). Psychiatric stigma in non-Western societies. *Comprehensive Psychiatry, 32*(6), 534–551.

Fabrega, H. (1992). The role of culture in a theory of psychiatric illness. *Social Science & Medicine, 35*(1), 91–103.

Faulkner, A., & Layzell, S. (2000). *Strategies for living.* London, England: Mental Health Foundation.

Fernando, S. (2003). *Cultural diversity, mental health and psychiatry. The struggle against racism.* Hove, England: Brunner-Routledge.

Foucault, M. (1988). An aesthetics of existence. Sheridan, A., trans. In L. D. Kritzman (ed.), *Politics philosophy culture. Interviews and other writings 1977–1984.* London, England: Routledge.

Friedli, L. (2009). *Mental health, resilience and inequalities.* Copenhagen, Denmark: World Health Organization and Mental Health Foundation.

Gary, F. (2005). Stigma: Barrier to mental health care amongst ethnic minorities. *Issues in Mental Health Nursing, 26*(10), 979–999.

Glaser, B., & Strauss, A. (1967). *The discovery of grounded theory: Strategies for qualitative research.* Chicago, IL: Aldine.

Goffman, E. (1963). *Stigma: Notes on management of spoiled identity.* Upper Saddle River, NJ: Prentice Hall.

Grant, S., & Jackson, J. (2005). *Equal services.* Edinburgh, Scotland: National Resource Centre for Ethnic Minority Health.

Hatfield, B., Mohammad, H., Ahim, Z., & Tanweer, H. (1996). Mental health and the Asian communities: A local survey. *British Journal of Social Work, 26*(3), 315–336.

Heim, D., & MacAskill, S. (2006). *Black and minority ethnic health in greater Glasgow.* Glasgow, Scotland: Greater Glasgow NHS.

Israel, B. A., Schulz, A. J., Parker, E. A., & Becker, A. B. (1998). Review of community-based research: Assessing partnership approaches to improve public health. *Annual Review of Public Health, 19*, 173–202.

Kleinman, A. (1987). Anthropology and psychiatry: The role of culture in cross-cultural research on illness. *British Journal of Psychiatry, 151*(4), 447–454.

Knifton, L., & Quinn, N. (2008). Media, mental health and discrimination: A frame of reference for understanding reporting trends. *International Journal of Mental Health Promotion, 10*(1), 23–31.

Knifton, L., Gervais, M., Newbigging, K., Mirza, N., Quinn, N., Wilson, N., & Hunkins-Hutchison, E. (2010). Community conversation: Addressing mental health stigma with ethnic minority communities. *Social Psychiatry and Psychiatric Epidemiology, 45*(4), 497–504.

Lauber, C., & Rossler, W. (2007). Stigma towards people with mental illness in developing countries in Asia. *International Review of Psychiatry, 19*(2), 157–178.

Li, P. L., Logan, S., Yee, L., & Ng, S. (1999). Barriers to meeting the mental health needs of the Chinese community. *Journal Public Health Medicine, 21*(1), 74–80.

Link, B. G., & Phelan, J. C. (2001). Conceptualising stigma. *Annual Review of Sociology, 27*(1), 363–385.

Link, B. G., & Phelan, J. C. (2006). Stigma and its public health implications. *The Lancet, 367*(9509), 528–529.

Maclean, U. (1969). Community attitudes to mental illness in Edinburgh. *British Journal of Preventative and Social Medicine, 23*(1), 45–52.

Marmot, P. (2010). *Marmot review—Fair society, healthy lives: Strategic review of health inequalities in England post-2010.* London, England: Marmot Review.

Minkler, M., & Wallerstein, N. (2003). Introduction to community-based participatory research. In M. Minkler & N. Wallerstein (Eds.), *Community-based participatory research for health.* San Francisco, CA: Jossey-Bass.

Minkler, M. (2004). Ethical challenges for the 'outside' researcher in community based participatory research. *Health Education and Behaviour, 31*(6), 684–697.

Myers, F., McCollam, A., & Woodhouse, A. (2005). *Equal minds: Addressing mental health inequalities in Scotland.* Edinburgh, Scotland: Scottish Executive.

Ng, C. H. (1997). The stigma of mental illness in Asian cultures. *Australian and New Zealand Journal of Psychiatry, 31*(3), 382–390.

Patel, V., Maj, M., Flisher, A. J., De Silva, M. J., Koschorke, M., Prince, M., & WPA Zonal and Member Society Representatives. (2010). Reducing the treatment gap for mental disorders: A WPA survey. *World Psychiatry, 9*(3), 169–176.

Pickett, K. E., James, O. W., & Wilkinson, R. G. (2006). Income inequality and the prevalence of mental illness: A preliminary international analysis. *Journal of Epidemiology and Community Health, 60*(7), 646–647.

Rogers, A., & Pilgrim, D. (2003). *Inequalities and mental health.* London, England: Palgrave Macmillan.

Rosenfield, S. (1997). Labelling mental illness: The effects of received services and perceived stigma on life satisfaction. *American Journal of Sociology, 62*(4), 660–672.

Schomerus, G., & Angermeyer, M. C. (2008). Stigma and its impact on help-seeking for mental disorders: What do we know? *Epidemiologica Psichiatria Sociale, 17*(1), 31–37.

Silverman, D. (2004). *Doing qualitative research* (2nd ed.). London, England: Sage.

Tabassum, R., Macaskill, A., & Ahmad, I. (2000). Attitudes towards mental health in an urban Pakistani community in the United Kingdom. *International Journal of Social Psychiatry, 46*(3), 170–181.

Van Brakel, W. (2006). Measuring health-related stigma: A literature review. *Psychology, Health and Medicine, 11*(3), 307–334.

Wallerstein, N., & Bernstein, E. (1988). Empowerment education: Freire's ideas adapted to health education. *Health Education and Behaviour, 15*(4), 379–396.

Wenger, E. (1998). *Communities of practice: Learning, meaning and identity.* New York, NY: Cambridge University Press.

Williams, R., & Hunt, K. (1997). Psychological distress among British South Asians: The contribution of stressful situations and sub-cultural differences in the West of Scotland Twenty-07 study. *Psychological Medicine, 27*(5), 1173–1181.

Williams, B., Copestake, P., Eversley, J., & Stafford, B. (2008). *Experiences and expectations of disabled people.* London, England: Office for Disability Issues.

Wong, L., & Richman, J. (2004). Chinese understanding of *diankuang* in a metropolitan city in the United Kingdom. *International Journal of Mental Health, 32*(3), 5–30.

World Health Organization. (2001). *The world health report 2001—Mental health: New understanding, new hope.* Geneva, Switzerland: Author.

Wright, E. R., Gronfein, W. P., & Owens, T. J. (2000). Deinstitutionalization, social rejection, and the self-esteem of former mental patients. *Journal of Health and Social Behaviour, 41*(1), 68–90.

Yeung, E. (2004). *Improving accessibility to mental health services for Chinese people.* Liverpool, England: Merseyside Health Action Zone.

READING 12

Nurturing Longevity

Sociological Constructions of Ageing, Care, and the Body

Michael Fine

ABSTRACT

This paper examines assumptions that surround the way that aged care and assistance is conceptualised and discussed. Problems with the concept of care became apparent with the critique of care theory by the disability movement in the 1980s and continue to this day. Debates arose initially between those who sought to identify care as a gender-based duty that serves to burden those who take responsibility for it, and those who reject the concept as a form of socially constructed dependency. The paper considers the problematic sociological foundations of this critique—the failure to incorporate an understanding of the body into much sociological theory and the significance that the conceptualisation has for understanding the need for personal assistance in advanced old age. While the disability critique of care is firmly grounded in a sociological analysis, it overemphasises the social construction of social relations and ignores the visceral reality of the body. Longevity care, in contrast, needs to explicitly acknowledge that ageing is an embodied and physical process that generates a need for care. The conclusions are tested against recent Australian data and research on care needs and preferences amongst older people.

KEYWORDS

ageing, care, gender, sociology of the body, disability theory, aged care, social policy

Longevity comes with many costs and challenges, none more important than that of ensuring the availability of care in the final years of life. Increasing numbers of those who need care or who will require it in the near future, as a result of profound disability or chronic disease associated with advanced age, challenge individuals, families, governments and communal social institutions in the twenty-first century (Organisation for Economic Co-operation and Development [OECD], 2000). The restructuring and reorganisation of care systems is justified as both preparation and response to this demographic transformation. At the same time, a plethora of official reports and

Michael Fine, "Nurturing Longevity: Sociological Constructions of Ageing, Care and the Body," Health Sociology Review, vol. 23, no. 1, pp. 33-42. Copyright © 2014 by Taylor & Francis Group. Reprinted with permission. Provided by ProQuest LLC. All rights reserved.

plans demonstrate ongoing concern about the costs and availability of health and medical care for an ageing population, as well as the needs for, costs of and availability of, more specialised forms of paid formal aged care and informal care (both paid and unpaid care provided by family or intimate friends) (Murphy, 2011).

Population ageing is itself a significant force for change (Hugo, 2007), but is not the only development forcing the reorganisation of the way that care is provided. Changes in women's lives associated with the emancipatory social movement of feminism, and the shift to employment outside the home that has accompanied this, have fundamentally altered the availability of unpaid female domestic labour that, until recently, underpinned the way that care was understood (Fine, 2007a). Similarly, the lives and expectations of people with disabilities have been reshaped by the human rights perspectives movements and changes in policy that have come about as a result of the rise of disabled persons' movements and by developments in medical technology. These and other related social changes have profoundly affected both the need for care and the way it is understood and provided.

In the context of population ageing, policy debates about aged care tend to focus on questions concerned with ensuring the viability of formal systems of support. Issues of resource adequacy, in particular the financing of aged care, including different mechanisms for maintaining cost control; the challenges of the aged care workforce; and ways of increasing the efficiency of service provision, through reform, restructuring, privatisation, and increased substitution of low cost for high cost interventions, dominate the public discussion (Kendig & Duckett, 2001; OECD, 1998, 2011; Productivity Commission, 2011). Yet, many of the most fundamental questions remain beyond the horizon of his debate (Lymbery, 2010). In this paper I seek to address one of the most fundamental of these—assumptions that surround the way that care and assistance are conceptualised and discussed. I argue that, despite the general acknowledgement of the importance of informal care and of the work of unpaid carers, attention continues to be focussed mainly on formal care provisions, with little analysis given to the questions of informal care.

The significance of the concept of care became apparent with the critique of care theories by the disability movement in the 1980s and continues to this day. The following two sections of this paper, therefore, return to the debates from this time. The debates arose initially between those who sought to identify care as a gender-based duty that serves to burden those who take responsibility for it, and those who reject the concept as a form of socially constructed dependency. The paper then moves to consider the problematic sociological foundations of this critique—the failure to incorporate an understanding of the body into much sociological theory and the significance that the conceptualisation has for understanding the need for personal assistance in advanced old age. While the disability critique of care is firmly grounded in a sociological analysis, I argue that it overemphasises the social construction of social relations and ignores the visceral reality of the body. Longevity care, in contrast, needs to explicitly acknowledge that ageing is an embodied and physical process that generates a need for care. Testing these conclusions against recent Australian data and research on care needs and preferences amongst older people, it is argued that developing new sociological understandings of care remains an important challenge for sociologists concerned with ensuring sustainable and just support arrangements in the context of population ageing over the coming decades of the twenty-first century.

CARE AND THE DISABILITY CRITIQUE

Care research and theory, in its contemporary form, arose in the wake of feminism in the mid to late 1970s (Rummery & Fine, 2012; Thomas, 1993). Interest arose initially as a concern with the unpaid work carried out by women within the family as women went public and interest moved from the domestic sphere, as I have argued elsewhere (Fine, 2007a). Care came to be seen as a burden as the unpaid domestic responsibilities of women, holding them back from achievements in other areas of life (Land, 1978; Oakley, 1974). Moreover, care has been equated with the household duties of married women, which focussed on 'caring for their children, their elderly or sick relatives and, of course, their husbands' (Land, 1978, p. 360). This approach was soon applied to other forms of care, in particular to care of the elderly and of children with disabilities (Finch & Groves, 1983). Care was understood as the 'labour of love' (Graham, 1983) provided in the home by unpaid and unrecognised female relatives of the recipients.

Care theory was not simply about feminism. It articulated concerns from what might be thought of as a labour perspective, identifying the hidden, even suppressed interests of the workers responsible for providing care. Recognising that feminism sought to lift the cloak of 'invisibility' from women carers, feminist and other disability activists from the UK (including Jenny Morris and Lois Keith) wanted recognition of the recipients of care (Keith, 1992; Keith & Morris, 1996; Morris, 1994, 1997). Drawing on principles that formed part of the 'social model of disability' (Oliver, 1990; Oliver & Barnes, 1998) as well as those of feminism, Morris (1993b, p. 49) argued that the problems with the feminist conceptions of care could be traced to a failure to examine the factors which underlie the need for assistance in the first place:

By taking the need for care for granted and by assuming the dependency of older and disabled people, feminist research and carers as a pressure group have not only failed to address the interests of older and disabled people but they have, unwittingly, colluded with both the creation of dependency and the state's reluctance to tackle the social and economic factors which disable people.

Morris went further, calling for the complexity involved in interpersonal support to be recognised. Pointing out that as a mother she was not just a dependent recipient but was responsible for the care of her own children, she personally sought recognition of the fact that 'disabled women' are care-givers in their own right. In the process, she chastised feminists such as Clare Ungerson, whom she accused of portraying care recipients as a burden.

This separating out of disabled and older women from the category 'women' comes about because these feminist researchers fail to identify with the subjective experience of 'such people'. The principle of 'the personal is political' is applied to carers but not to the cared for. (Morris, 1993a, p. 157)

Other writers from a disability perspective have been even harsher in their criticisms:

The discovery of the 'carer' in the late capitalist welfare state has sharpened the contradictions imposed by the approach to families of welfare state policies. Constructing the category carer and developing policies in respect of this group has neither enabled disabled people to become independent nor freed other family members from their 'caring' duties. In fact, apart from inventing a new word and giving employment to yet more welfare professionals and opportunistic voluntary organizations, nothing much has changed and the contradictions of family life remain. (Oliver & Barnes, 1998, p. 8)

In advancing this radical rejection of care theory, disability advocates adopted what might be considered a consumer stance, speaking for the interests of the recipients of care, not the workers charged with undertaking the work. The feminist theorists who had helped promote the concept of carers to illuminate and name the hidden oppression that assuming responsibility for unpaid domestic duties involved, found that instead of solidarity between the two oppressed groups—the care-givers and those who relied on their unpaid efforts—there was an active accusation that they were being identified as self-interested oppressors themselves.

The overtly political character of this rhetoric is clear, although the consequences are perhaps much murkier than might have been imagined. The result was not common cause but division and suspicion. The disability movement's critique of the concept of care as burden in this way served as an important driver of revision. It reminded us that care involves transactions between two or more people and cannot be understood simply from the perspective of the giver of care alone.

Disability activists such as Morris, Oliver and Barnes, drew attention to what they saw as the social causes underlying the need for care. In doing so, they have typically advocated for the implementation of policies and approaches that would invert the relations of power—the disabled consumer would cease to be dependent but would instead become the employer. It is here that we find the origins of schemes such as consumer-directed care (CDC) (Batavia, DeJung, & McKnew, 1990; Eustis, 2000) that are today held up as models

for aged care policy in Australia and elsewhere (Department of Health and Ageing, 2012; Productivity Commission, 2011; Ungerson, 2004). This approach, based on the ideals of consumer sovereignty, has found favour among policy-makers who have used it to help promote the marketisation of care services, as cash for care or CDC.

Despite these critiques of the way that care has been conceived and constructed, recognising the validity of the disability critique does not require abolishing the concept of care (Fine & Glendinning, 2005). However, it is clear that if care is conceptualised primarily in a way that is designed solely to draw attention to the oppression of women, it cannot provide a model for future social solidarity or for a wider form of social emancipation (Parker & Clarke, 2002).

The social model of disability, as Corker and Shakespeare (2002) point out, has its roots in historical materialism. Despite its embrace of consumer theory, it incorporates many elements of a modern socialist critique of capitalist society. The model makes a conceptual distinction between impairment (a bodily deficit) and disability (a socially constructed limitation) in a manner similar to the feminist distinction between sex and gender. Disability is seen as socially constructed on the basis of impairment, placing 'the explanation of its changing character in the social and economic structure and culture of the society in which it is found' (Corker & Shakespeare, 2002, p. 3). Clearly, this suggests that the need for care can be reduced—indeed care may not even be necessary. What is needed, instead, is something much less emotive—cold, hard, support. If the need for care is socially constructed, so can it be ignored and reduced. More recently, however, a number of writers from the disability movement have called for recognition of the lived reality of the body and of embodied determinants of physical or mental incapacity (Crow, 1996; Morris, 2001; Price & Shildrick, 2002; Thomas & Corker, 2002).

THE BODY IN SOCIOLOGY, CARE AND DISABILITY THEORY

The social relations of disability approach is built on solid sociological foundations which, since the 1960s, has stressed the 'social construction' of social life (Berger & Luckmann, 1967). Recently Bryan Turner, amongst others, has chosen to speak out against the logical extension of this proposition (Turner & Rojek, 2001). The body, Turner demonstrates, has come to be portrayed in much contemporary social research as no more than a cultural text.

Life events, including birth, death and disability are, of course, shaped by social expectations, enacted as rituals and given symbolic meanings, and these are often inscribed on the body in various forms, some relatively temporary in nature, such as hair styles or body painting, while others, such as tattoos and circumcisions, are more enduring. But the body cannot be simply reduced to a social construction. It has a materiality, a visceral, biologically based physical presence absent in purely symbolic social phenomena. Importantly, the body is part of a living, conscious being that, in the nature of its existence, participates in but is distinct from the social relationships and cultural forms that shape social life (Twigg, 2002, 2006). Just as Wrong (1961) in the early 1960s argued against an overly deterministic form of social explanation that emphasised the importance of social structure but seemingly denied a place for agency, so too is it important today for sociologists to draw attention to the importance of the physical reality of the body as a corrective to what might be called the over-constructed life. Recognising the body in this way as a foundation for life and society reminds us of the limits of the social construction approach

that lies at the centre of the theoretical rejection of care by those associated with the social relations of disability approach.

This is not to suggest that social conditions are not significant at each point in an individual's life. The food we eat is necessarily biological in its origin, but the way it is produced and prepared for the table and the way it is consumed are clearly shaped by culture and social conditions. Similarly, there is a biological imperative underlying our personal conduct towards our bodies in meeting the physical needs for such life necessities as food, shelter, and self maintenance. These aspects of our existence are evidence of the cultural shaping of our responses to biological urges. They cannot be understood purely as social constructs in the way of, for instance, a uniform or a national flag.

Ageing is a lifelong process that occurs at both the cellular level as well as in the social domain. There are important socially constructed markers, such as the age of eligibility for retirement, but ageing cannot be reduced to these markers or understood without an understanding of the body as a biological entity. So it is that the ageing body reflects social conditions of existence such as social class, gender and access to medical care, but this does not mean that ageing is simply a construct of society. Instead, it needs to be acknowledged as an organic process that is central to biological life of all kinds, including human life. Cultural practices and social determinants in this way shape the way that our physical existence is played out, but our physical existence cannot be reduced to a social or cultural text. Like ageing, care and the ritualised forms of behaviour associated with the social management of death need to be understood, I argue, as a social response to the needs for personal support arising from the vulnerabilities and inadequacies of the body.

CARE AND THE AGEING BODY

Providing what in nursing is referred to as 'personal care' inevitably involves physical contact between a care-giver while she or he attends to the support of the bodily functions of another (Twigg, 2000). Indeed, it can be argued that at the final point of delivery, care is necessarily concerned with practices that require tending the body of another. Care, at this level, is an active social relationship in which sustaining a person's bodily existence is the most basic priority. It is a bodily engagement in two senses. First, personal care involves attending to the body and bodily needs of the recipient. Second, the act of providing care, too, involves direct physical engagement and bodily exertion from care-givers. The body of the care-giver as much as that of the care recipient is central to developing an understanding of care.

Stripped of the sentimentality that often attends discussions of care-giving, much of the physical and typically repetitive work involved can be seen as analogous to, although not reducible to, manual labour. The physical demands on carers are extensive, their hours of work often extreme (Schofield et al., 1998) and, like other manual workers, their level of recognition is low. Yet, unlike most other physical work, what Hochschild has termed 'emotional labour' is also central to the work of care (Himmelweit, 1999; Hochschild, 1983; Wharton, 2009). Emotional labour is a crucial, defining component of the physically and emotionally draining character of many acts of care-giving, and is closely linked to the physical aspects through direct bodily contact. Interpersonal physical contact is essential for attending to the needs of frail older people, disabled people, the sick, where it is necessary for providing support to assist the other directly in tasks that s/he is physically unable to complete without assistance. Providing care, tending to the wellbeing of others involves not just muscle power. As Twigg (2004)

has shown, touch is a fundamental, not just incidental, feature of providing care.

Some of the potential of recognising the links between the body and the social response of care is captured in the following brief extract from Julie Godyer's moving account of caring for patients with Alzheimer's disease in the days before any pharmacological intervention was found to be effective:

I had never been so conscious of people's bodies as when I began working in nursing homes. Patients, especially those with dementias like Alzheimer's disease, were often handled without any awareness or consideration of their 'selfness', handled as if they were only bodies and nothing else. Often they were wrenched from slumber in the very early hours, pulled forcibly out of bed, placed firmly on commode chairs and wheeled to the shower. Here they were stripped, washed, dried and dressed again—often without a word of explanation, because of a belief that they didn't understand what was going on anyway. The daily routines pivoted around getting food into the patients and ensuring the subsequent and required daily bowel motion.

…The intimacy of physical contact necessary for these routines between nurse and patient was something over which patients had no control. They were touched, handled, repositioned, toileted and so on constantly throughout the day and had no choice over when or where they were touched. Many became limp, immobilized, refusing to move themselves or help in any way even if they could. Refusing also to speak, these patients began to seem like heavy lumps of flesh, nothing else—all body. This treatment of people with Alzheimer's Disease

TABLE 12.1 Disability Rates by Age Group, All Persons, Australia 2009

Age Group (Years)	Profound Core Activity Limitation[a] Pct	Severe Core Activity Limitation[a] Pct	Moderate Core Activity Limitation[a] Pct	Mild Core Activity Limitation[a] Pct	Total Population '000
0–4	1.3	0.9	0.1	–	1411.3
5–14	2.6	2.2	0.3	1.4	2734.0
15–24	1.0	0.8	0.4	1.8	3081.7
25–34	0.7	1.3	1.0	2.2	3083.2
35–44	0.9	1.9	1.9	3.5	3119.0
45–54	1.2	3.0	3.5	5.2	2989.8
55–59	2.1	4.7	6.1	8.4	1297.4
60–64	2.8	5.7	8.2	11.7	1163.7
65–69	3.8	5.0	8.8	14.8	863.7
70–74	7.0	7.0	9.9	17.9	683.2
75–79	11.2	6.5	9.4	22.0	547.6
80–84	17.6	10.4	10.7	23.4	438.0
85–89	33.5	13.4	8.9	20.3	265.2
90+	59.9	10.4	3.8	13.8	105.5
Total	2.9	2.9	3.0	5.6	21,783.2

Source: Table 1, ABS (2011). *Disability and long-term health conditions,* Australia, 2009, Report 4433.0 (Released 9 December 2011).

[a]Core activities comprise communication, mobility and self care. For further details of disability classification see Appendix 2 in ABS (2009).

was not (in my nursing experience) seen to be either unfair or unusual in an institution where the control of bodies is sanctioned by a medical discourse, and, subsequently, a society, which has already abjected those with dementias such as Alzheimer's Disease. This was simply called 'care'. (Goyder, 2001, pp. 123–124)

It would be easy to mistake Alzheimer's disease and other forms of dementia as psychological, rather than as bodily conditions. However, this would be to ignore the medical research on the physical aetiology and effects of these conditions over time that, in the case of Alzheimer's disease in particular, result in progressive physical paralysis and are ultimately terminal (Dash & Villemarette-Pittman, 2005; Huang & Mucke, 2012). It is also to misunderstand Godyer's point about the care of dementia sufferers as bodies. Godyer signals her disillusion with the character and nature of the support provided to those no longer able to act as conscious, intelligent people, by placing the term 'care' in inverted commas, asking in this way if looking after these people's bodies is meaningful.

Her descriptions of this work help open questions about the cultural and social forms that this care has taken. Is tending to a person's living body when their mind, their consciousness, their sense of identity and purpose is no longer present anything more than a ritualised, socially and medically sanctioned form of sequestration? Where quality of life no longer exists and where conditions for eligibility for alternative solutions, such as euthanasia, are not capable of being met or are simply not legal, care is often no more than a polite word used to describe management of the problem. While the form that care takes is socially shaped, it would be wrong to ignore either the physical aspects of incapacity or bodily dependency that underlie either the need for assistance or the physical, embodied form that its provision entails. Rather than seeing care as responsibility solely for the care-giver, recognition of the body of both the care recipient and the care-giver reinforces the view that caring needs to be understood as a 'widespread activity in which we are all implicated,' with a need to 'balance the rights of both people in the caring relationship' (Lloyd, 2000, p. 148). Henderson and Forbat (2002) similarly seek not just to incorporate the views of care recipients and service users in care policy, and call for an understanding of care as a 'relationship-based' activity.

AGEING AND INFORMAL CARE

The theoretical significance of understanding care as a relationship-based activity undertaken in response to bodily needs can be tested against research data. It is not possible here to do

TABLE 12.2 Persons Aged 65 and Over, Disability, Living Arrangements and Sex, Australia 2009

ABS Estimates	All with a Disability[a] Pct	All Persons Pct
Males		
In private dwellings		
With partner	67.3	71.8
With relatives	4.2	3.6
With non-relatives	1.2	1.3
Lives alone	17.9	16.9
Total in private dwellings	90.6	93.5
In non-private dwellings		
Cared accommodation[b]	6.0	3.3
Other dwellings[c]	3.4	3.2
Total	9.4	6.5
Total Pct	100.0	100.0
Number	707,400	1,322,100
Females		
In private dwellings		
With partner	35.3	44.5
With relatives	12.6	11.5
With non-relatives	0.7	0.6
Lives alone	34.2	32.1
Total in private dwellings	82.8	88.8
In non-private dwellings		
Cared accommodation[b]	12.0	6.6
Other dwellings[c]	5.2	4.6
Total	17.2	11.2
Total Pct	100.0	100.0
Number	844,400	1,581,100
Persons		
In private dwellings		
With partner	49.9	56.9
With relatives	8.8	7.9
With non-relatives	0.9	0.9
Lives alone	26.8	25.2
Total in private dwellings	86.3	90.9
In non-private dwellings		
Cared accommodation[b]	9.2	5.1
Other dwellings[c]	4.4	4.0
Total	13.6	9.1
Total Pct	100.0	100.0
Number	1,551,800	2,903,100

[a]Total may be less than the sum of the components as persons may be counted in more than one disability group. [b]Includes hospitals, homes for the aged, other home or accommodation for the aged/retired. [c]Includes self care special dwellings and other special dwellings.

Source: Table 7, ABS (2011). *Disability and long term health conditions.* Publication no. 4433.0, 2009 (Released 9 December 2011).

so exhaustively, but drawing on research over a number of decades it is possible to go well beyond conjecture and hypothesis.

The most recent official figures for Australia from the national survey of *Disability, Ageing and Caring*, undertaken by the (Australian Bureau of Statistics [ABS], 2009), show that disability rates increase markedly with age (see Table 12.1). Importantly, the rates of profound disability, requiring ongoing support with personal care, are highest for those in the oldest age groups, with almost 60% of those aged 90 or over requiring ongoing assistance as a result of what the ABS classifies as a 'profound activity restriction' (disability). In a pattern consistent with epidemiological evidence in other comparable countries (Freedman et al., 2004; Mathers, 2002), a significant level of profound disability is evident amongst children, but this falls slightly in early adulthood—reflecting both the impact of successful early interventions, and the impact of mortality in the early age groups. After a slight fall in the early twenties, levels of need for assistance gradually increase with age from the early twenties. The rate of increase is markedly higher from the age of 75 onwards, so that the rates of profound disability begin to exceed the rates of severe and moderate levels of disability. Nonetheless, disability is not confined to older age groups as the need for support resulting from physical and cognitive limitations to activity affects significant numbers of people at all age groups. The impact that this has on the need and type of support required, as well as the likely source of this support, varies significantly at different points in the life course.

Amongst those over 65 who need assistance as a result of disability, over 90% report receiving that help in their own home, far exceeding the proportion admitted to a specialised residential care facility. While approximately half of all those who need care live at home with their partner, from

whom they are most likely to receive the help they need, there are significant differences between men and women, as the data in Table 12.2 shows. Men aged 65 and over are more likely to be living with their partner and to receive help from this source than women of the same age. Approximately two of every three men who need assistance live at home with their partners. In contrast, only one in three women above 65 who need help, however, live with their partner. The most likely explanation for this is the age difference between married men and women and the different life expectancies of men and women (de Vaus, 2004, pp. 100–109). Although women aged over 65 today tended to marry men who were on average 5 years older than themselves when they were first married, men have a shorter life expectancy than women and, as a result, women are more likely to have a prolonged period of widowhood at precisely the ages they are most likely to need care as a result of age related disability.

Importantly, other research evidence shows most older people are willing to accept care from people other than partners. In addition to care from children and other family members, it is clear that considerable assistance is received at home from community care services that supplement and extend that provided by family members (Fine, 2007a, 2007b). Services at home are generally preferred over residential care services—although accommodation options that offer security, independence and a guarantee of care should it be needed, are amongst the options that find favour among older single women and some men who seek out secure retirement accommodation with care.

Analysis of empirical evidence from the British 1980 General Household Survey (GHS) was the first to show that while women are overwhelmingly responsible for the majority of informal care in the home, around a third of co-resident carers of older people (those likely to be most intensively involved) were men (Arber & Gilbert, 1989; Arber & Ginn, 1990). Further research from the UK and elsewhere has consistently confirmed a similar pattern in which men, particularly the husbands and partners of older women, are more likely to take responsibility for personal care than a purely gendered model might predict (Fine & Glendinning, 2005; Hirst, 2001). As for other English speaking countries there is evidence of a hierarchy of preferences concerning care amongst older Australians to date. This set of preferences is one that is both shared and negotiated between care recipients and family members.

The 'hierarchical compensation model' is the term first introduced by Marjorie Cantor to explain the pattern of care preferences. Using her experience in New York, Cantor argued that when care is required, older people usually tried to remain independent but, if pressed, would chose help from close family members or others with whom they had intimate and longer-term relationships to supplement formal services (Cantor, 1989; Cantor & Little, 1985). Assistance from marital partners was the first preference but if not available, care provided by daughters was a close second. Care from sons and other family members followed, in that order of preference, over help from state supported, non-profit or commercial organisations. The approach suggests that help would likely be sought from formal services only when these informal care-givers were inadequate or needed supplementation. Research in the UK (Qureshi & Walker, 1989) and Australia (Fine & Thomson, 1997) provides some support for this approach.

Following extensive ethnographic research in England concerning the obligations of adult children to care for their parents, Finch and Mason (1993) have shown that preferences for care by female family members derive from, and demonstrate the existence of, a 'public normative consensus,' with family members and service providers alike sharing a consensus that care for aged parents is an essentially female duty. It is not simply the national culture or the unique choices of each individual, but the broader system of social policy, market and political economy that enables and limits access to resources outside the family, as Qureshi (1990) has shown.

CARING TO THE END

The Canadian sociologist Chappell (1992) has long argued that care can be best understood as the extension, indeed the most intense expression, of social support. Understanding care in this way serves to remind us why informal care continues to be so significant a force shaping our lives. In aged care it shapes not just the lives of the older recipients of care but those of the people who provide the care as well.

Ageing and care are each at once social phenomena and expressions of our embodied and physically vulnerable existence. As demographic ageing continues over the next three to four decades of the twenty-first century, the numbers of frail older people will continue to rise. Rather than rejecting the concepts of care, as the disability critique first sought to achieve, what is needed is for care to be continually rethought so that it may be reconstructed in sustainable and productive ways. It is not desirable for the availability of care to continue to be premised on the denial of the rights of unpaid women carers, or to be based on the exploitation of low paid staff. Nor is it satisfactory to require the neglect of those who need assistance. For reasons of economic sustainability as well as for ethical reasons concerning recognition and social justice, care must be understood in a more complex way—as involving disposition, activity (work and competence) and as a relationship-based process.

Current data, some of which were presented in this paper, shows that a significant proportion of the work of care is already undertaken by those who are themselves aged. Developing systems of care that will build on this, by ensuring adequate formal provisions alongside support for informal care-givers, must be a central part of the approach to the way care is made sustainable and equitable. How this more inclusive approach might be shaped and practiced is evident in recent writings that seek to incorporate the perspectives of those reliant on care. The disability critique outlined earlier needs to be taken seriously—not at the level of an essentialist attack on care, but as a valuable reminder that care, based on bodily vulnerabilities, is both essential and universal. The use of sociological research and analysis needs to continue to facilitate social ideals, not deny them.

REFERENCES

Arber, S., & Gilbert, N. (1989). Men: The forgotten carers. *Sociology, 23*(1), 111–118.

Arber, S., & Ginn, J. (1990). The meaning of informal care: Gender and the contribution of elderly people. *Ageing and Society, 10*(4), 429–454.

Australian Bureau of Statistics. (2009). *Disability, ageing and carers: Summary of findings*. Canberra, ACT: Author. [Cat No. 4430.0].

Batavia, A. I., DeJung, G., & McKnew, L. B. (1990). Toward a national personal assistance program: The independent living model of long-term care for persons with disabilities. *Journal of Health Politics, Policy and Law, 16*(3), 523–545.

Berger, P., & Luckmann, T. (1967). *The social construction of reality*. Garden City, NY: Doubleday.

Cantor, M., & Little, V. (1985). Aging and social care. In R. H. Binstock & E. Shanas (Eds.), *Handbook of aging and the social sciences* (pp. 745–781). New York, NY: Van Nostrand Reinhold.

Cantor, M. H. (1989). Social care: Family and community support systems. *The Annals of the American Academy of Political and Social Science, 503*, 99–112.

Chappell, N. L. (1992). *Social support and aging*. Toronto, ON: Butterworths.

Corker, M., & Shakespeare, T. (2002). Mapping the terrain. In M. Corker & T. Shakespeare (Eds.), *Disability/postmodernity. Embodying disability theory* (pp. 1–17). London, England: Continuum.

Crow, L. (1996). Including all our lives: Renewing the social model of disability. In J. Morris (Ed.), *Encounters with strangers: Feminism and disability* (pp. 206–226). London, England: Women's Press.

Dash, P., & Villemarette-Pittman, N. (2005). *Alzheimer's disease*. New York, NY: American Academy of Neurology.

de Vaus, D. (2004). *Diversity and change in Australian families: Statistical profiles*. Melbourne, VIC: Australian Institute of Family Studies.

Department of Health and Ageing. (2012). *Living longer, living better. Aged care reform package 2012*. Canberra, ACT: Author.

Eustis, N. N. (2000). Consumer-directed long-term-care services: Evolving perspectives and alliances. *Generations, 24*(111), 10–15.

Finch, J., & Groves, D. (Eds.). (1983). *A labour of love: Women, work, and caring*. London, England: Routledge & Kegan Paul.

Finch, J., & Mason, J. (1993). *Negotiating family responsibilities*. London, England: Routledge.

Fine, M. (2007a). *A caring society? Care and the dilemmas of human service in the 21st century*. Houndmills, England: Palgrave Macmillan.

Fine, M. (2007b). Uncertain prospects: Aged care for a long-lived society. In A. Borowski, S. Encel, & E. Ozanne (Eds.), *Longevity and social change in Australia* (pp. 265–295). Sydney, NSW: UNSW Press.

Fine, M., & Glendinning, C. (2005). Dependence, independence or inter-dependence? Revisiting the concepts of 'care' and 'dependency'. *Ageing and Society, 25*(4), 601–621.

Fine, M., & Thomson, C. (1997). Beyond caring: Informal care and the use of community support services by home and community care clients. In V. Minichiello, N. Chappell, H. Kendig, & A. Walker (Eds.), *Sociology of aging: International perspectives* (pp. 207–225). London, England: International Sociological Association.

Freedman, V. A., Crimmins, E., Schoeni, R. F., Spillman, B. C., Aykan, H., Kramarow, E., Waidmann, T. (2004). Resolving inconsistencies in trends in old-age disability: Report from a technical working group. *Demography, 41*(3), 417–441.

Goyder, J. (2001). *We'll be married in Fremantle*. Fremantle, WA: Fremantle Arts Centre Press.

Graham, H. (1983). Caring: A labour of love. In J. Finch & D. Groves (Eds.), *A labour of love: Women, work and caring* (pp. 13–30). London, England: Routledge & Keegan Paul.

Henderson, J., & Forbat, L. (2002). Relationship-based social policy: Personal and policy constructions of care. *Critical Social Policy, 22*(4), 669–687.

Himmelweit, S. (1999). Caring labor. *The Annals of the American Academy of Political and Social Science, 561*(1), 27–38.

Hirst, M. (2001). Trends in informal care in Britain. *Health and Social Care in the Community, 9*(6), 348–357.

Hochschild, A. R. (1983). *The managed heart: Commercialization of human feeling*. Berkeley, CA: University of California Press.

Huang, Y., & Mucke, L. (2012). Alzheimer mechanisms and therapeutic strategies. *Cell, 148*(6), 1204–1222.

Hugo, G. (2007). Contextualising the 'crisis in aged care': A demographic perspective. *The Australian Journal of Social Issues, 42*(2), 169–182.

Keith, L. (1992). Who cares wins? Women, caring and disability. *Disability and Society, 7*(2), 167–175.

Keith, L., & Morris, J. (1996). Easy targets: A disability rights perspective on the 'children as carers' debate. In J. Morris (Ed.), *Encounters with strangers: Feminism and disability* (pp. 89–116). London, England: Women's Press.

Kendig, H. L., & Duckett, S. (2001). *Australian directions in aged care: The generation of policies for generations of older people*. Australian Health Policies Institute, Commissioned Paper Series 2001/05, Sydney. Sydney, NSW: University of Sydney.

Land, H. (1978). Who cares for the family? *Journal of Social Policy, 3*(7), 357–384.

Lloyd, L. (2000). Caring about carers: Only half the picture? *Critical Social Policy, 20*(1), 136–150.

Lymbery, M. (2010). A new vision for adult social care? Continuities and change in the care of older people. *Critical Social Policy, 30*(1), 5–26.

Mathers, C. (2002). *The burden of disease and injury in Australia*. Canberra, ACT: Australian Institute of Health & Welfare.

Morris, J. (1993a). 'Us' and 'Them'? Feminist research and community care. In J. Bornat, C. Pereira, D. Pilgrim, & F. Williams (Eds.), *Community care: A reader* (pp. 156–166). Houndmills, England: Macmillan.

Morris, J. (1993b). *Independent lives? Community care and disabled people*. London, England: Macmillan.

Morris, J. (1994). Community care or independent living? *Critical Social Policy, 40*(1), 24–45.

Morris, J. (1997). Care or empowerment: A disability rights perspective. *Social Policy & Administration, 31*(1), 54–60.

Morris, J. (2001). Impairment and disability: Constructing an ethics of care that promotes human rights. *Hypatia, 16*(4), 1–16.

Murphy, M. (2011). Long-term effects of the demographic transition on family and kinship networks in Britain. *Population and Development Review, 37*(Suppl.), 55–80.

Oakley, A. (1974). *The sociology of housework*. Oxford, England: Martin Robertson.

OECD. (1998). *Ageing and care for frail elderly persons: An overview of international perspectives*. Paris, France: Author.

OECD. (2000). *Reforms for an ageing society*. Paris, France: Author.

OECD. (2011). *Paying for the past, providing for the future: Intergenerational solidarity*. Paris, Retrieved from http://www.oecd.org/dataoecd/8/42/47712019.pdf

Oliver, M. (1990). *The politics of disablement*. Basingstoke, England: Macmillan.

Oliver, M., & Barnes, C. (1998). *Disabled people and social policy: From exclusion to inclusion*. London, England: Longman.

Parker, G., & Clarke, H. (2002). Making the ends meet: Do carers and disabled people have a common agenda? *Policy & Politics, 30*(3), 347–359.

Price, J., & Shildrick, M. (2002). Bodies together: Touch, ethics and disability. In M. Corker & T. Shakespeare (Eds.), *Disability/postmodernity: Embodying disability theory* (pp. 62–75). London, England: Continuum.

Productivity Commission. (2011). *Caring for older Australians*. Report No. 53, Final inquiry report. Canberra, ACT: Author.

Qureshi, H. (1990). Boundaries between formal and informal care-giving work. In C. Ungerson (Ed.), *Gender and caring: Work and welfare in Britain and Scandinavia* (pp. 59–79). Hemel Hemstead, England: Harvester.

Qureshi, H., & Walker, A. (1989). *The caring relationship: Elderly people and their families*. Houndmills, England: MacMillan.

Rummery, K., & Fine, M. (2012). Care: A critical review of theory, policy and practice. *Social Policy & Administration, 46*(3), 321–343.

Schofield, H., Bloch, S., Herman, H., Murphy, B., Nankervis, J., & Singh, B. (1998). *Family care-givers: Disability, illness and ageing*. Sydney, NSW: Allen & Unwin.

Thomas, C. (1993). De-constructing concepts of care. *Sociology, 27*(4), 649–670.

Thomas, C., & Corker, M. (2002). A journey around the social model. In M. Corker & T. Shakespeare (Eds.), *Disability/postmodernity: Embodying disability theory* (pp. 18–31). London, England: Continuum.

Turner, B., & Rojek, C. (2001). *Society and culture: Principles of scarcity and solidarity.* London, England: Sage.

Twigg, J. (2000). *Bathing—The body and community care.* London, England: Routledge.

Twigg, J. (2002). The body in social policy: Mapping a territory. *Journal of Social Policy, 31*(3), 421–439.

Twigg, J. (2004). The body, gender, and age: Feminist insights in social gerontology. *Journal of Aging Studies, 18*(1), 59–73.

Twigg, J. (2006). *The body in health and social care.* Houndmills, England: Palgrave Macmillan.

Ungerson, C. (2004). Whose empowerment and independence? A cross-national perspective on 'cash for care' schemes. *Ageing & Society, 24*(2), 189–212.

Wharton, A. S. (2009). The sociology of emotional labor. *Annual Review of Sociology, 35*, 147–165.

Wrong, D. (1961). The oversocialized conception of man in modern sociology. *American Sociological Review, 26*(2), 183–193.

COPYRIGHTED MATERIAL — DO NOT DUPLICATE, DISTRIBUTE, OR POST

PART III

Health Care Systems/Delivery

In sociology, the study of power is a common theme, derived largely from the work of Karl Marx. He discussed the conflict in power between the ruling class (known as the bourgeoisie) and the working class (known as the proletariat). In medical sociology, this power struggle is demonstrated not as ruling class versus the working class, but as patient versus health care provider. In this part, we look at the evolving relationship between health care providers and patients. We ask the question: How much power does a health care provider have over the patient? With the rise in technology allowing patients better access to health information it is no longer an asymmetrical relationship, but evolving into a partnership. From the power of diagnosing to technological advances, this part takes an investigative look at the power play between health care providers and patients.

In the article, "Who's the Boss?" Jenkins discusses the power that society gives health care providers (doctors) willingly. We have all heard the saying, "Doctor knows best." Why do they know best though? Health care providers have the medical authority to diagnosis. Jenkins states that because of a combination of evidence-based medicine and the process of elimination, health care providers are able to diagnose patients with accuracy. As part of American sociologist Talcott Parsons notion of "the sick role," patients need their health care providers to legitimatize that they are sick, giving health care providers more power over the patients. Jenkins also looks at technology as a double-edged sword. Patients are dependent on health care providers for access to certain technology such as a magnetic resonance imaging (MRI). Yet, at the same time technology can cause mistrust and doubt in patients.

When technology gives patients access to thousands of "doctors," who can they trust? Do they trust their face-to-face health care provider or the Internet? In the article, "My (Smartphone) Doctor," Topol, sheds light onto the increased use of telemedicine (technology) to help reach patients. Topol estimated the current average wait time to see a health care provider is about 2.5 weeks. With the increased use of smartphones, patients are now able to self-diagnose and improve self-care, creating a new era of patient engagement (with hopes of lowering this wait time). Medical sociologists ask questions such as: Are patients able to make appropriate health care decisions? Health insurance companies do not believe patients are, so instead they are embracing telemedicine/smartphone usage by having more health care providers available through patients' mobile device, known as virtual visits. However, many health care providers are feeling marginalized because they are not being able to give thorough examinations to patients. Do you think the increase in technology provides a positive or negative impact for the providers and the patients?

The last article in this part suggests that technology is an attack on the health care providers. In "The Urgent Need to Preserve and Enhance Physician Careers," authors Cochran and Kenny state the elephant in the room is liability. It is a paradoxical situation; health care providers must use technology to treat patients, and yet technology is used against providers increasing the fear of liability which results in some to overtreat and question their training. The authors suggest that health care providers need to be trained on how to disclose errors to patients. There needs to be a culture shift away from a fee-for-service model to payment for population health. It is time for health care providers to lead the way in change and embrace all aspects of technology to remain effective. Cochran and Kenny hope to see "the best work anywhere should be the standard everywhere" in the coming years, or in other words, a unified effort by all providers to improve the delivery of health care across our country.

The health care system in the United States is constantly evolving, which requires the need for change in the way health care is delivered. While you are reading the articles in this part, take a moment to think about how the relationship of health care provider and patient has changed and what do you think will happen in the future? Does technology improve this relationship or harm it? Who ultimately has the power? If it is the patient who is in charge, then is Parson's "sick role" still relevant? If it is the doctor who has all the power, does society still think the "doctor knows best"?

READING 13

Who's the Boss?

Diagnosis and Medical Authority

Tania M. Jenkins

STARTING POINTS

- Society often believes that "doctor knows best," but where did that belief come from?
- Doctors control access to the sick role by making diagnoses.
- Physicians rely on tools, such as technology, to make diagnoses.

The onset was sudden. Laura Hillenbrand, author of the famed book that later became a major motion picture, *Seabiscuit,* was a healthy college student who within weeks became so sick she had to drop out of school. Her symptoms were all over the map: nausea, fever, chills, joint pain, stiffness, sore throat, confusion, disorientation, aphasia, weight loss. Her internist ran test after test but could find nothing wrong with her: "My problem, he said gravely, was not in my body but in my mind; the test results *proved* it. He told me to see a psychiatrist" (Hillenbrand 2003; emphasis added). When she went to see a psychiatrist, he sent her back to her internist. According to him, "I was mentally healthy but suffering from a serious physical illness." Over the course of the next few months, Hillenbrand's condition worsened but she was no closer to a diagnosis. Her peers began to lose patience: "Without my physicians' support, it was almost impossible to find

support from others. People told me I was lazy and selfish" (Hillenbrand 2003).

Hillenbrand's experience highlights the power that a diagnosis can carry in legitimizing a **patient**'s suffering, revealing that the process of diagnosis is an act of power, one where the physician traditionally exercises authority over a set of social actors—usually the patient, but also friends, family, and the public at large. This chapter describes how physician authority both manifests in—and gets reinforced by—medical diagnosis. It also examines how recent social changes have affected medical authority, challenging both the legitimacy of and our dependency on the medical profession, with diagnosis at the center of these shifts.

MEDICAL AUTHORITY = LEGITIMACY + DEPENDENCE

To understand how diagnosis and authority interact, we must first establish what we mean by medical authority. In his seminal treatise on the rise (and fall) of the American physician, Paul Starr (2004) writes that medical authority, "in its classical sense, signifies the possession of some status, quality, or claim that compels trust or obedience" (580). Perhaps this quality is the scientific ability to heal—after all, we do turn to physicians for tried and tested solutions to our medical problems. It is not enough for Starr, however, that physicians lay claim to science for healing purposes, and he points to instances where allopathic (or mainstream) physicians, such as those in Soviet Russia, still used scientific methods but did not rise to the same level of authority as in the West. He goes on to designate two particular dimensions that distinguish Western physicians from other healers; on the one hand, they have legitimacy as a group of professionals, and on the other, there is social dependence on their services. Let us unpack these concepts by seeing how they apply to diagnosis.

A MONOPOLY OVER DEFINING DISEASE

As mentioned above, physicians' monopoly over healing historically came from more than just the improvement in scientific approaches to disease. In fact, the regulation of the medical profession in many countries occurred well before experimentation and the use of statistical tests in assessing clinical effectiveness gained a foothold in medical research (see Hacking 1990; Porter 1995). In the late nineteenth and early twentieth centuries, physicians managed to convince governments that their knowledge was so esoteric (understood by such a small group) that only other physicians could regulate the profession. This control gave doctors government-sanctioned oversight of training, licensing, and ultimately the authority to diagnose (Freidson 1970; Starr 2004). The combination of government support and dominance over other health practitioners gave the medical profession the ultimate authority to name disease, although this power was never an absolute, as "alternative" health practitioners and even laypeople (see chap. 12) have named disease. Nevertheless, medical diagnosis wields power in courts, death certificates, and compensation and insurance claims; allows access to a range of health resources and services; and gives permission to miss work,

have special conditions for taking examinations, obtain parking permits, and other special considerations. As a result, diagnosis (or the naming of disease) is inherently a function of the "legitimacy" dimension of physicians' authority.

But Starr and Freidson remind us that having the legitimate right to practice medicine is meaningless without patients' trust in medical professionals. As patients, we trust in and depend on medicine's ability to make use of esoteric knowledge to evaluate and fulfill our health needs (Starr 2004). For medical authority to exist, it must be characterized by both legitimacy and dependence.

The **sick role**, as defined by the well-known American sociologist Talcott Parsons (1951), is a great example of how the two concepts of legitimacy and dependence work together. When a patient receives a diagnosis, she also receives access to the sick role, which is associated with specific rights and obligations. The patient is exempt from the normal duties of everyday life (such as chores and work obligations), and exempt from blame for her inability to fulfill those everyday duties. In exchange for these exemptions (granted by a physician), the patient is required to attempt to get better. That obligation is both defined and facilitated by competent, expert medical help.

The physician in turn has the corresponding obligation to serve the patient's best interests and to do so with professional competence, expertise, altruism, and affective neutrality, the latter being a requirement that all patients should be treated in the same way and that health professionals should not respond in relation to whether they like or dislike a patient (Gehardt 1987). In this way, the sick role is both contingent on physician authority, as it requires the legitimacy of a medical license and expert knowledge, and contributive to that authority, because it establishes that physicians should act in the best interest of their patients, which inspires both trust in—and dependence on—the medical profession. Diagnosis is pivotal for a patient to be a patient, with all of the accompanying social exemptions such as taking time off work, getting light duty, and receiving other special considerations. In this way, physicians have the authority to transform social roles through their allocation of the sick role. And while the doctor-patient relationship may no longer conform exactly to the traditional sick role (Parsons 1975; Rier 2010), it remains that the diagnostic encounter, where the sick role is bestowed, is both a manifestation and reinforcement of physician authority.

DIFFERENTIAL DIAGNOSIS

Consider a more concrete example of how diagnosis can be both a cause and consequence of medical authority by looking at the history of psychiatry as a sub-discipline of medicine. Today, physicians pride themselves on espousing rigorous scientific principles, such as those contained in **evidence-based medicine** (the **gold standard** of "scientific" medicine), and differential diagnosis, the systematic method of arriving at a diagnosis through a process of elimination. This process of elimination requires adherence to and knowledge of a diagnostic nosology that catalogues various alternative diagnoses for a given symptomatology (see chap. 1, on classification, and chap. 2, on the diagnostic process). This practice of differential diagnosis lends scientific credibility to the diagnostic process and to the profession as a whole. In some ways, differential diagnosis can be considered a defining characteristic of modern medical practice, distinguishing it from other forms of healing. Without differential diagnosis, the practice of medicine would be considered merely speculative.

The attending interrupts—"What's the differential diagnosis before we see the CT?" Suggestions get tossed about the room: Could be osteonecrosis? An abscess? Lipoma?

"Femoral hernia?," asks one resident. The attending interjects, "Ah, but you'd feel it." They decide to look at the CT scan results together. Finally, they stop at a large white spot in the leg and, almost in unison, the doctors nod their heads, murmuring "abscess." The patient will be sent to interventional radiology for treatment. (Author's field notes from ethnographic research at a community hospital)

An example of differential diagnosis.

Making diagnoses on the basis of evidence was not always standard practice for all branches of medicine, however. Until the middle to late twentieth century, psychiatry did not employ differential diagnostic methods, relying instead on psychoanalytic and idiopathic approaches. These approaches viewed each patient as unique and did not attempt to find trends or patterns among symptoms and diseases, thereby making it difficult for psychiatrists to even speak of diagnosis per se, as they did not have the tools to describe commonalities between patients.

This meant that psychiatry also did not have a nosology, or a systematic and hierarchical means of classifying mental disorders. Psychiatry was therefore not as well respected as a subspecialty, and numerous other **professions** in the counseling field encroached upon its authority, a situation that the discipline attempted to remedy with the diagnostic process. Early attempts at a nosology, resulting in the first (1952) and second (1968) editions of the *Diagnostic and Statistical Manual of Mental Disorders* (DSM), were not well organized and thus rarely used. In preparing the third edition, however, psychiatrists wanted to improve their position within the broader profession of medicine and to increase the legitimacy of their work (Young 1997). As a result, they worked within a neo-Kraepelinian framework based on the work of German psychiatrist Emil Kraepelin, who was thought to have come up with the idea of differential diagnosis in mental disorders.

The new framework abandoned the idiopathic approach and advocated careful record keeping in order to uncover the etiologies of mental disorders. The DSMIII, containing 265 disorders, was released in 1980 (up from 106 in DSM-I and 182 in DSM-II) and was considered a major step forward in granting authority to the fledgling discipline. By adopting a nosology with standardized diagnostic criteria, giving psychiatrists the ability to conduct differential diagnosis, psychiatry obtained a monopoly over medically defining mental illness, thereby making it less subjective and more legitimate than other professions, such as psychoanalysis. By improving their legitimacy, psychiatrists also increased patients' dependence on them as the sole arbiters of sanity. In this way, the process of differential diagnosis, made possible by the creation of the DSM-III, both delegated psychiatry authority over mental health vis-à-vis other practitioners and reaffirmed that authority by making patients dependent on psychiatrists for their mental health care.

MEDICALIZATION AND AUTHORITY

Through the creation of new diagnoses, medical subspecialties can enhance their standing within the profession while also extending their authority to new social realms. Stephen Pfohl (1977) has written about pediatric radiologists' "discovery" of "battered child syndrome" (or child abuse) as a diagnostic category in the early 1960s, and about the various circumstances that led to the creation of that diagnosis.

Pfohl describes an American historical tradition that until the first half of the twentieth century legitimized violence toward children, such that parents would only be criminally liable for physically disciplining their children if their actions resulted in permanent injury. In more serious cases, when children were brought to the emergency room after having sustained injuries from their parents, emergency physicians were reluctant to make a diagnosis of abuse because of (1) concerns about doctor-patient confidentiality and fears of litigation; (2) not wanting to get involved in family affairs; (3) disbelief that parents could harm their children in this way; and (4) ignorance that a diagnosis of abuse was even an option, as this diagnosis did not yet exist.

Pediatric radiologists, however, increasingly found that the radiographic evidence did not support the claims that particular injuries were caused by childhood accidents. In 1962, they created the diagnosis of battered child syndrome to rectify this discrepancy. Pfohl (1977) attributes this discovery to three major characteristics that pertain to pediatric radiology: (1) radiologists enjoyed a certain social distance from patients and their parents, such that X-rays "carry little of the horror of bloody assault" (317); (2) at the time, radiologists did not share emergentologists' concerns about violating confidentiality, once again because of this social distance; and, perhaps most relevant to our purposes, (3) the field of pediatric radiology was looking for an opportunity for an intraprofessional advance in prestige and the chance to name and label a disease of its own. Pediatric radiology at the time was marginalized within the profession for not performing risky procedures, not dealing with blood and guts, and having little life-or-death decision-making authority. Of course, professional advancement was not the only motivator for creating the diagnosis of battered child syndrome, but, combined with the undeniable "objective" radiographic evidence before them, the desire to advance the field gave pediatric radiologists the impetus needed to establish a new disease category.

Creating this diagnosis provided pediatric radiologists an opportunity to improve their status within the broader medical profession as they made their entrée into the diagnostic arena:

"By linking themselves to the problem of abuse, radiologists became indirectly tied into the crucial clinical task of patient diagnosis" (Pfohl 1977, 318). At the same time, the medical profession as a whole extended its authority into moral and family matters—an area in which government wanted to avoid getting involved. The diagnosis eventually led to the criminalization of child abuse. By capturing this particular action in medical definitional terms (see chap. 8, on **medicalization**), medicine positions itself to make moral judgments, as if it were a "repository of truth, the place where absolute and often final judgments are made by supposedly morally neutral and objective experts" (Zola 2009, 470). The diagnosis of battered child syndrome is a positive intervention, but it also illustrates how medical specialties use diagnosis as a means for overcoming marginalization, and how the profession as a whole works to improve its overall authority within society.

In sum, medical authority is both enshrined in diagnosis and continually reinforced through patients' dependency on physicians for access to resources, achieved through conferring the status of the sick role to patients as well as through the expansion of medicine into new domains. Physicians' authority is not static, however; while there may be several factors that enhance it, as described above, recent changes in the medical system have also challenged physicians' sovereignty. These changes include encroachment by other health practitioners, shifting patient roles, and the divergent effect of technology, which both enhance and undermine physician authority. And yet, despite all of these changes, physicians continue to maintain their authority.

CHALLENGES TO MEDICAL AUTHORITY

The Growing Nonexclusivity of Diagnosis

A number of broad trends during the 1970s and 80s weakened physicians' legitimacy and led to the undoing of medical sovereignty over diagnosis. Poor-quality outcomes, an increasingly specialized yet fractured profession, and, the emergence of antitrust laws prohibiting physicians in the United States from having a monopoly over patient care facilitated the existence of competition (Light 2010; Mendel and Scott 2010; Ritzer and Walczak 1988; Scott 2003). The result is that physicians no longer bear the exclusive right to make diagnoses that allow access to health resources and services; increasingly, other health professionals are permitted to make diagnoses (such as nurse practitioners, optometrists, and even physical therapists), all of which has diluted the exclusivity that physicians traditionally enjoyed.

Nurses who prescribe medicine threaten this exclusivity. In many countries, clinical nurse specialists are joining nurse practitioners to prescribe quasi-independently an ever-growing list of medications. Nurse prescription has selectively shifted responsibility for certain clinical activities from one professional group to another, freeing up physicians to focus their time on more complex medical issues in a system that is already overtaxed (Kemp 2007). By the same token, however, the policy has also shifted part of the authority to diagnose to nurses and away from physicians in a move that can be described as professional encroachment. Similarly, alternative health practitioners are also challenging doctors as diagnosticians by increasingly becoming professionalized and scientized (Goldner 2004; Hirschkorn 2006).

By having lost their monopoly over diagnosis through the encroachment of other health practitioners, physicians have experienced a corresponding decline in authority, which is only exacerbated by the dissemination of medical information to other practitioners and the general public (see below) through channels like the Internet. Yet physicians remain society's primary diagnosticians, and while their authority might be in flux, it is still firmly entrenched. In some jurisdictions, for example, health professionals who can diagnose (such as nurse practitioners and midwives) must still work under the supervision of a physician, suggesting that while there may be a wider variety of diagnosticians in society, physicians still maintain tight control over the process.

[It] is a very specific prescription that actually has my signature, my name, my license number; that's my very own prescription. (Primary care nurse with six years of experience)
Registered nurses in Quebec, Canada, now have the ability to prescribe certain medications after legislation was passed that expanded their clinical responsibilities.

The Empowered Patient

[...] On the diagnostic relationship, patients are becoming increasingly informed and mobilized as a result of easier access to medical knowledge. Health information has become "e-scaped" through the explosion of web-based resources (Nettleton 2004), providing a leveling effect on the traditionally paternalistic doctor-patient relationship (Bury 2004). Increases in lay knowledge have meant that patients often come to a clinical encounter with a diagnosis in mind, which they put forward and negotiate. Rather than approaching physicians as experts who have unique knowledge (i.e., in a traditional dependence framework set out by the sick role), patients increasingly are consulting doctors for support in making choices—including diagnostic decisions—about their health (in a phenomenon known as "physician compliance"; see Barker 2008). This has meant that physician authority has been countered by rising patient empowerment in the form of medical knowledge and social support, as we are less dependent on physicians than before. About 95% of Americans today (referred to as the "informed-by-Google generation") look for health information on the Internet, where it is available twenty-four hours a day, seven days a week, free of charge (Sanders 2009). Patients are also increasingly turning to the Internet as a source of social support when physicians do not grant them the sick role for medically unexplained symptoms (Barker 2008; Dumit 2006). Disillusioned by physicians' unbridled autonomy, which led to mistakes and quality issues (Light 2010), patients have begun to question medicine's legitimacy and to take matters into their own hands, reducing their dependence on the profession, a position that was less likely only a few decades ago, when information was less accessible.

Despite this growing empowerment, patients' dependence on physicians persists. Recent developments in **health social movements** and health legislation may have improved patients' standing vis-à-vis physicians, but they remain reliant on doctors' social legitimacy (composed, among other things, of specialized knowledge and altruism) in order to access certain resources. Patients might feel like they have more of a say in their health (care) these days, but these choices largely remain within a biomedical framework, where physicians remain at the helm. While patients may have more choices to look elsewhere, those alternatives are largely other medical authorities.

They come to see me, they ask my advice, and then they go tootling off to the Internet to find some website which tells them not to do what I just recommended, and they come back three months later, much worse, and still not willing to follow my advice. What can I do?!

Medical authority is no longer immutable. Access to other forms of information challenges the way doctors practice today.

Social Movements

Patients have become increasingly involved in their health and the health of others, fighting to be heard alongside (or in spite of) dominant medical science. One way they have done this is through health social movements. Brown et al. (2004) have distinguished between three different types of health movements: (1) health access movements that seek to correct inequalities in access to health-care services; (2) constituency-based health movements that seek to redress inequalities in health on the basis of social categories such as race, gender, and sexual preference; and (3) embodied health movements, which are premised on the idea that patients have valuable contributions to debates about disease diagnosis, etiology, and treatment based on their own embodied experience of illness. These movements blur the boundary between experts and laypeople, as individuals driven by their own lived experience of a disease become experts in the science. They therefore also blur the line between what is considered to be "good" and "bad" science, as they often bring to the table more subjective knowledge generated from individual experience, while scientists place priority over so-called rigorous and objective science.

The environmental breast cancer movement is a good example of an embodied social movement, as it centers itself on the body and on the lived experiences of women suffering from the disease. Laypeople draw on their own knowledge production in order to counter common conceptions of etiological processes that lead to disease. Directly challenging the paternalistic model of medicine that reigned during the golden era of the early twentieth century, these movements seek to shift the power dynamic between physicians and laypeople in order to afford individuals a better chance at the diagnostic negotiation table when it comes to determining etiology. They do not, however, seek to overturn physician authority altogether; instead, they often establish citizen-science alliances or "lay-professional collaborations in which citizens and scientists work together on issues identified

by lay people" (Brown 2007, 33). In fact, embodied health movements are defined not only by the fact that they challenge current science, but also that they work in collaboration with experts in order to improve treatment, prevention, research, and funding outcomes. In this way, while patients may be growing more empowered, they are still reliant on physician authority to achieve their goals.

A good example of one such citizen-science alliance occurred in Woburn, Massachusetts, in the 1980s. From 1966 to 1986, twenty-eight cases of childhood leukemia developed among Woburn children, a rate four times higher than expected at a national level (Brown and Mikkelsen 1990; Durant et al. 1995). A later study found that six of the children with leukemia lived within close proximity of one another, a staggering seven and a half times the expected number in that geographic location (Cutler et al. 1986). Other health problems were also more common than normal, including adult-onset leukemia and renal cancer (Brown and Mikkelsen 1990). The families of these sick individuals began to suspect that their health problems were linked to drinking water contaminated by dumped industrial waste in the local water source. In 1979, 184 fifty-five-gallon drums were discovered next to the Aberjona River, and water samples from underground wells near the site were found to contain up to forty times the permissible concentrations of known toxic and carcinogenic chemicals (Brown and Mikkelsen 1990; Lagakos et al. 1986).

The discovery of these pollutants and their link to leukemia was largely based on the efforts of the laypeople in Woburn. Families banded together to form the social movement organization For a Cleaner Environment (FACE) to help address the toxic waste problems of the community. This group almost single-handedly detected a cancer cluster, incited the government to clean up the toxic sites, brought two major national corporations to court, pioneered a health study surrounding the effects of toxic chemicals on cancer, and while doing so drew national attention to the broader issue of environmental health (Brown and Mikkelsen 1990). It started in 1979 when two members of the Woburn community (a mother and her pastor) joined forces with a local physician and mapped all the cases of childhood leukemia in the city. This effort eventually led to an alliance with three Harvard scientists and ultimately the design and implementation of the Woburn Harvard/FACE study. The goal of the study was to provide more systematic data on the cancer cluster and its link to contaminated water, and it is now considered a model for citizen-practitioner alliances. A group of 235 volunteers surveyed 57% of Woburn's population, an impressive size given the study's dearth of research funding ($10,000 for a study that would have ordinarily cost between $500,000 and $750,000; Brown and Mikkelsen 1990; Lagakos et al. 1986). Twenty cases of childhood leukemia diagnosed between 1964 and 1983 were further studied alongside a hydrogeological model for the groundwater (Lagakos et al. 1986). Perhaps unsurprisingly, the study found positive significant associations between the toxic water and childhood leukemia, perinatal deaths and certain types of childhood diseases, including congenital abnormalities (Lagakos et al. 1986). These findings were enough to incite eight families to go to trial.

The Woburn case is important because "the children died. Six-teen children died in Woburn. I think it had to do with the fact that the children died of leukemia and some mothers got very involved. They tell a very unhappy story and I think people relate to that. It is a human tragedy." (Gretchen Latowsky, community organizer, cited in Brown and Mikkelsen 1990, 47, emphasis added)

Why popular epidemiology came about in Woburn, and why it is such an important case study.

The example above powerfully illustrates the ability of laypeople to piggyback on medical authority by creating links between diagnoses and causes. In other instances, this kind of alliance may be harnessed to recognize and even name diseases. Lyme disease is an important case in point. As Robert Aronowitz (1998) has written, some Connecticut mothers (from the area around the town of Lyme) recognized that a number of children were suffering from similar low-grade fevers, headaches, malaise, and joint pain. Bringing this disease cluster to the attention of the U.S. Centers for Disease Control and Prevention (CDC) with the support of their local doctors was the first step in disease recognition. Had the cases been more geo graphically dispersed, the sufferers less articulate, or public health officers less receptive to its description as a unified condition, Lyme disease might never have been named.

The fact that the community members, starting with mothers in both of these cases, were able to effectively create new science that in the first case linked toxic chemicals to leukemia, and in the second gave meaning to general systemic symptoms of infectious disease, is evidence of a significant shift in social relations between physicians, scientists, and laypeople. But their efforts were made possible due to the alliances they made with physicians. The people of Woburn encountered initial resistance from the CDC, which would not seriously entertain their requests for water testing, and only agreed after the citizens of Woburn sought a physician's help. While it remains true that social movements sometimes seek to challenge extant social relations between patients and doctors, they also require the authority of physicians to get their message across.

Legal Challenges to Medical Authority

In some cases, it is not social movements that challenge physician authority, but rather social **institutions**, like the law. Patients have become increasingly empowered through the rise of malpractice lawsuits that seek to redress wrongs performed by physicians, especially as a result of not disclosing full information to patients. In part due to health social movements, full disclosure of medical information has become the legal norm, such that patients are expected to want and to be able to handle full disclosure about their diagnosis, prognosis, and treatment. In the United States, the Patient Self-Determination Act of 1991 says that competent individuals have a right to make decisions about their health care, including end-of-life care (Luce and Alpers 2001). This codification of patient autonomy constitutes a major reversal of previous informal practices, where physicians would paternalistically make life-and-death decisions on patients' behalf (Burns et al. 2003; Klawiter 2004; Veatch 2003). Today, patients have increasing control over technical, medical matters that were formerly thought to be too complicated for laypeople to handle (Veatch 2003). Physicians have thus been legally stripped of their exclusive authority to make life-and-death decisions without first consulting their patients.

The result is that patients are now legally included in decision making about their health, which has shifted the way patients are seen by physicians: "The lay person who consults the health care professional is no longer the submissive and compliant 'patient' but an expert *partner* who brings his or her experience of illness to the differentially specialized medical practitioner" (Jutel 2011, 69).

But including patients in the decision-making process can lead some physicians to willfully abdicate their responsibility (and perhaps their authority) vis-à-vis patients, as the text box suggests. Consider a patient who enters a doctor's office with a presumptive diagnosis and demands antibiotics for what is clearly (to the physician) a viral respiratory infection: the doctor who complies with this request for fear of being sued or to avoid explaining the pharmacology of antibiotic therapy may in fact be harming her patient. In an attempt to decrease **paternalism** within medicine by including the patient as an active partner, we may inadvertently be threatening one of the very

cornerstones of sound medical practice and physician authority—discretion.

When I started residency, I viewed patient autonomy as an absolute good, an ethical imperative that trumped all others … Informed consent was supposed to guard against such abuses. But informed consent is practiced very differently from the way ethicists envisioned it. It was supposed to protect patients from doctors. Instead, it is used to protect doctors from patients, or rather, from the hard decisions that patient care demands. *Doctors nowadays sometimes use informed consent as a crutch to abdicate responsibility. (Jauhar 2008, 231, emphasis added)*

Changing attitudes and practices toward patient autonomy.

Professional Challenges to Clinical Authority

This brings us to the issue of how professions can sometimes constrain their own authority. Professional governing bodies establish the standards by which members of their group are held accountable. In the case of medicine, members of the profession must be able to demonstrate how their actions comply with established standards embodied in guidelines, protocols, and practice policies. These are procedural standards that attempt to specify the processes by which diagnoses are made and how treatment plans are determined and implemented (Timmermans and Berg 2003). Practitioners are also regularly assessed by quality assurance and quality improvement processes. Deviations from such standards must be justified by a warrant for their nonconformity. The individual clinician's authority is thus challenged in relation to professional standards, which attempt to standardize medicine and in so doing define medical practice as the logical and sequential application of science.

Standardization is a way of dealing with huge variations in medical practice with widely varying outcomes, but one of its consequences is limiting clinical autonomy and patient choice. It cannot be assumed that attempts to standardize medical practices through such means as requiring the use of protocols will have the intended outcome. As demonstrated by detailed analysis of interactions between patients and clinicians, there are many means by which clinicians can ignore, undermine, or utilize protocols and standardized procedures (Dew et al. 2005; 2010)

As Freidson (1970) writes, "In order to provide a truly human service, practitioners must have a significant degree of autonomy within reasonable limits dictated by patients' rights, official standards, and accountability" lest we "reduc[e] practitioners to passive cogs in a rationalized system" (391). Despite these warnings, however, it appears that enshrining patient autonomy in the law and clinical accountability in protocols has not gone so far as to completely eradicate physician authority in the context of medical decision making. Patient autonomy laws and attempts to standardize clinical practice might challenge this authority, but it is a long way from being undermined altogether.

Technology as a Double-Edged Sword

[…] On diagnostic technology, while most doctors can interpret some diagnostic tests (complete blood count, for example), specialist medical interpretation may be required for others, such as magnetic resonance imaging (MRI) and other technical imaging procedures. The need for specialization adds to the dependence dimension of their authority; we are dependent on physicians for access to certain resources, including technology. But this monopoly can also (paradoxically perhaps) threaten clinical legitimacy. Having control over diagnostic technologies may enhance physicians' ability to diagnose, but overreliance on technology can also lead to mistrust and devaluation of clinical acumen: "the development of newer and better technologies— the mammogram, ultrasound and most recently the MRI—has caused doctors to doubt the value of what their hands can tell them" (Sanders 2009, 52). Some fear that advances in technology are

leading to the demise of the physical exam, which used to be at the center of diagnosis but is now only performed perfunctorily. Some physicians view it as a waste of time, and while most agree that the physical exam is important, it is often subtly dismissed as unreliable compared to the results of diagnostic technology.

Seeing the physical exam as being potentially unreliable can have important implications for physician authority as it affects the sick role; according to Parsons (1951), physicians ought to have unimpeded access to the body in order to reach a diagnosis. As physician Lisa Sanders (2009) writes, "the act of placing your hand upon another's body is, in many ways, the hallmark of the physician" (47). Given that the increasing use of technology detracts from the importance of the "laying of hands" upon patients' bodies and that these technologies can make physicians doubt their own clinical acumen, does this start to undermine patient dependence on the physician? The fine line between the authority of having control over access to diagnostic technologies and the reduced importance of the actual clinical skills of the physician will become increasingly tricky to navigate in the future, as diagnostic technologies proliferate even further.

DIAGNOSIS: A PRODUCT AND ENGINE OF MEDICAL AUTHORITY

Diagnosis is both a manifestation and reinforcement of physician authority. But that authority is also contingent upon broader social changes, such as the rising professionalization of other health practitioners and shifts in power between doctors and patients. As a clinician, it is important to be aware of how diagnosis is embedded not only in scientific knowledge but myriad social relations that variously affect our dependency on the medical profession and its legitimacy.

This brings us full circle to Laura Hillenbrand's ordeal. Nearly a year after the initial onset of her symptoms, Hillenbrand was diagnosed with chronic fatigue syndrome, a poorly understood, incapacitating illness. By getting that label from a physician, she was able to receive the support and recognition she needed from her peers. She—just like all of us—was dependent on the authority vested in her physician to pronounce a diagnosis, which granted her access to the resources necessary to get help. In this way, her diagnosis was both a product and an engine of medical authority.

TAKEAWAY POINTS

- Diagnosis is an act of power.
- Medical authority is manifested and reinforced by diagnosis.
- Diagnosis can also challenge medical authority, especially when other actors (including patients and other professionals) compete for access to the diagnostic process.
- Diagnosis is embedded in scientific knowledge as well as the social relations that variously affect our dependency on the medical profession.

DISCUSSION QUESTIONS

1. Reflect on a recent diagnostic encounter where you were either patient or clinician. In what ways was authority present in this encounter? Are there ways in which your clinician (if you were the patient) or you (if you were the clinician) can become more aware it?

2. How do you feel about challenges to physicians' authority? Do you think there ought to be more checks and balances to keep physicians from having too much power, or should they be given even more authority to exercise full clinical discretion?

3. Can you think of any diagnoses in your field that may have been linked to a power struggle by the profession?

REFERENCES

Aronowitz, R. 1998. *Making Sense of Illness: Science, Society and Disease.* Cambridge: Cambridge University Press.

Barker, K. 2008. "Electronic Support Groups, Patient-Consumers, and Medicalization: The Case of Contested Illness." *Journal of Health and Social Behavior* 49(1): 20–36.

Brown, Phil. 2007. *Toxic Exposures: Contested Illnesses and the Environmental Health Movement.* New York: Columbia University Press.

Brown, Phil, and Edwin J. Mikkelsen. 1990. *No Safe Place: Toxic Waste, Leukemia and Community Action.* Berkeley: University of California Press.

Brown, Phil, Stephen Zavestoski, Sabrina McCormick, Brian Mayer, Rachel Morello-Frosch, and Rebecca Gasior Altman. 2004. "Embodied Health Movements: New Approaches to Social Movements in Health." *Sociology of Health and Illness* 26(1): 50–80.

Burns, J. P., J. Edwards, J. Johnson, N. H. Cassem, and R. D. Truog. 2003. "Do-Not-Resuscitate Order after 25 Years." *Critical Care Medicine* 31(5): 1543–50.

Bury, M. 2004. "Researching Patient-Professional Interactions," supplement, *Journal of Health Services Research and Policy* 9(1): 48–54.

Cutler, J. J., G. S. Parker, S. Rosen, B. Prenney, R. Healey, and G. G. Caldwell. 1986. "Childhood Leukemia in Woburn, Massachusetts." *Public Health Reports* 101(2): 201–5.

Dew, K., J. Cumming, D. McLeod, S. Morgan, E. McKinlay, A. Dowell, and T. Love. 2005. "Explicit Rationing of Elective Services: Implementing the New Zealand Reforms." *Health Policy* 74(1): 1–12.

Dew, K., Maria Stubbe, Lindsay Macdonald, Anthony Dowell, and Elizabeth Plumridge. 2010. "The (Non) Use of Prioritisation Protocols by Surgeons." *Sociology of Health and Illness* 32(4): 545–62.

Dumit, J. 2006. "Illnesses You Have to Fight to Get: Facts as Forces in Uncertain, Emergent Illnesses." *Social Science and Medicine* 62(3): 577–90.

Durant, J. L., J. Chen, H. F. Hemond, and W. G. Thilly. 1995. "Elevated Incidence of Childhood Leukemia in Woburn, Massachusetts: Niehs Superfund Basic Research-Program Searches for Causes," supplement, *Environmental Health Perspectives* 103(6): 93–98.

Freidson, Eliot. 1970. *Profession of Medicine: A Study of the Sociology of Applied Knowledge*. Chicago: Chicago University Press.

Gerhardt, U. 1987. "Parsons, Role Theory, and Health Interaction." In *Sociological Theory and Medical Sociology*, edited by G. Scambler, 110–33. London: Tavistock.

Goldner, M. 2004. "The Dynamic Interplay between Western Medicine and the Complementary and Alternative Medicine Movement: How Activists Perceive a Range of Responses from Physicians and Hospitals." *Sociology of Health and Illness* 26(6): 710–36.

Hacking, Ian. 1990. *The Taming of Chance*. Cambridge: Cambridge University Press.

Hillenbrand, Laura. 2003. "A Sudden Illness." *New Yorker*, July 7, 56–65.

Hirschkorn, K. A. 2006. "Exclusive versus Everyday Forms of Professional Knowledge: Legitimacy Claims in Conventional and Alternative Medicine." *Sociology of Health and Illness* 28(5): 533–57.

Jauhar, Sandeep. 2008. *Intern: A Doctor's Initiation*. New York: Farrar, Strauss and Giroux.

Jutel, Annemarie Goldstein. 2011. *Putting a Name to It: Diagnosis in Contemporary Society*. Baltimore: Johns Hopkins University Press.

Kemp, K. A. 2007. "The Use of Interdisciplinary Medical Teams to Improve Quality and Access to Care." *Journal of Interprofessional Care* 21(5): 557–59.

Klawiter, M. 2004. "Breast Cancer in Two Regimes: The Impact of Social Movements on Illness Experience." *Sociology of Health and Illness* 26(6): 845–74.

Lagakos, S. W., B. J. Wessen, and M. Zelen. 1986. "An Analysis of Contaminated Well Water and Health Effects in Woburn, Massachusetts." *Journal of the American Statistical Association* 81(395): 583–96.

Light, Donald W. 2010. "Health-Care Professions, Markets, and Countervailing Powers." In *Handbook of Medical Sociology*, edited by Chloe E. Bird, Peter Conrad, Allen M. Fremont, and Stefan Timmermans, 270–89. Nashville, TN: Vanderbilt University Press.

Luce, J. M., and A. Alpers. 2001. "End-of-Life Care: What Do the American Courts Say?" *Critical Care Medicine* 29(2): N40–N45.

Mendel, Peter, and W. Richard Scott. 2010. "Institutional Change and the Organization of Health Care: The Dynamics of 'Muddling Through.'" In *Handbook of Medical Sociology*, edited by Chloe E. Bird, Peter Conrad, Allen M. Fremont, and Stefan Timmermans, 249–69. Nashville, TN: Vanderbilt University Press.

Nettleton, Sarah. 2004. "The Emergence of E-Scaped Medicine." *Sociology* 38(4): 661–79.

Parsons, Talcott. 1951. "Social Structure and Dynamic Process: The Case of Modern Medical Practice." In *The Social System*, 436–39. New York: Free Press.

———. 1975. "The Sick Role and the Role of the Physician Reconsidered." *Milbank Memorial Fund Quarterly: Health and Society* 53(3): 257–78.

Pfohl, Stephen J. 1977. "The 'Discovery' of Child Abuse." *Social Problems* 24(3): 310–23.

Porter, Theodore. 1995. *Trust in Numbers: The Pursuit of Objectivity in Science and Public Life*. Prince ton, NJ: Prince ton University Press.

Rier, David A. 2010. "The Patient's Experience of Illness." In *Handbook of Medical Sociology*, edited by Chloe E. Bird, Peter Conrad, Allen M. Fremont, and Stefan Timmermans, 163–78. Nashville, TN: Vanderbilt University Press.

Ritzer, G., and D. Walczak. 1988. "Rationalization and the Deprofessionalization of Physicians." *Social Forces* 67(1): 1–22.

Sanders, Lisa. 2009. *Every Patient Tells a Story*. New York: Broadway.

Scott, W. Richard. 2003. "The Old Order Changeth: The Evolving World of Health Care Organizations." In *Advances in Health Care Organization Theory*, edited by Stephen S. Mick and Mindy E. Wyttenbach, 23–43. San Francisco: Jossey-Bass.

Starr, Paul. 2004. "Précis of Paul Starr's the Social Transformation of American Medicine." *Journal of Health Politics, Policy and Law* 29(45): 575–620.

Timmermans, Stefan, and Marc Berg. 2003. *The Gold Standard: The Challenge of Evidence-Based Medicine and Standardization in Health Care*. Philadelphia: Temple University Press.

Veatch, R. M. 2003. "Do Not Resuscitate: Ordering Nonassault and Charting Patients' Decisions to Forgo Cardiopulmonary Resuscitation." *Critical Care Medicine* 31(5): 1593–95.

Young, Allan. 1997. *The Harmony of Illusions: Inventing Post-Traumatic Stress Disorder*. Prince ton, NJ: Prince ton University Press.

Zola, Irving Kenneth. 2009. "Medicine as an Institution of Social Control." In *Sociology of Health and Illness*, 9th ed., edited by Peter Conrad, 470–80. New York: Worth.

My (Smartphone) Doctor

Eric Topol

"I am more certain than ever that iDoc is the future of medicine in the digitalized world. Doctors had their chance to lead medicine, but they didn't take it."

—FROM ROBIN COOK'S *CELL*[1]

"mHealth is about fundamentally changing the social contract between patients and doctors. Physicians are likely to resist the loss of power implicit in greater patient control."

—ERIC DISHMAN, INTEL[2]

"Today the ASK WATSON button provides a second opinion for oncologists. But as it grows more reliable, might it replace some of them entirely?"

—JESSI HEMPEL, *FORTUNE*[3]

How can we expect radical changes that are occurring everywhere besides medicine to leave the health care landscape untouched?[4] W. Brian Arthur, a researcher at the Xerox Palo Alto Research Center, rightly says "It will change every profession in ways we have barely seen yet."[5] You can just take lessons from history to see how technology radically affects what people do. For example, in 1900 41 percent of Americans worked in agriculture; this has been profoundly reduced to 2 percent a century later. Or Americans employed in manufacturing, which has declined from 30 percent in the 1950s to less than 10 percent today, due to automation. There is indeed now a "race against machines" that is pervasive, and it would be naïve to think that medicine is immune from the impact.[6]

The medical thriller novelist and physician Robin Cook wrote *Cell*, his thirty-third book, about iDoc—"a smartphone functioning as a twenty-first-century primary-care physician,"[7] an avatar doctor equipped with algorithms to "create a true ersatz physician on duty twenty-four-seven for a particular individual, truly personalized medicine."[7] Each individual signing up selects an avatar doctor, choosing their gender, attitude, whether they are paternal or maternal in tone, and how they want to be notified.

The system involves a remote command center staffed with hundreds of physicians who work four-hour shifts to keep them mentally crisp, and a supercomputer that, in real time, continuously monitors extensive physiological data on all iDoc users. Here is an excerpted dialogue from *Cell* between two doctors:

> "It's simple. iDoc is able to titrate life-saving medication according to real-time physiological values rather than trying to treat symptoms, which is the old 'sick' care medical paradigm. iDoc is the perfect primary-care doctor since it is based on an algorithm that is capable of learning and will be continually upgraded as new medical information is incorporated."
>
> "I'm concerned it can't handle what's on its plate now."

"You know what a Luddite doctor is, George? I run across them all the time. MDs who have been dragging their feet in the acceptance of digitalized medicine, even something as intuitive as electronic records. Come on! This is a no-brainer!"[8]

Unfortunately, an insurance company (called Amalgamated Healthcare) acquires the technology and hijacks it, killing off individuals who have been newly diagnosed with a fatal illness in order to cut costs.

A nonmedical version of this narrative, with some common threads, is the sci-fi romantic comedy movie *Her* in which Joaquin Phoenix falls in love with his computer and smartphone avatar, whose advanced operating system (iOS 10) voice is played by Scarlett Johansson. Here the monitoring capability coupled with machine learning sets up a progressively stronger, intimate relationship culminating in love (and later tragedy).

The book *Cell* and movie *Her* are not at all far-fetched. All of the technology to do this exists today. Robin Cook just went a bit fast-forward to portray the command centers equipped with massive computing capability and hundreds of doctors. Although it may not be the precise configuration for a future health system, it certainly represents a likely scenario. Unfortunately the risks are real, too, even if they probably won't involve murderous insurance companies. While Robin is as enthusiastic as I am for digital medicine to be transformative,[9] the potential for misuse and exploitation must always be kept in mind. As he explained to me, his winning formula for a medical thriller obligates there being a big-time villain. In this case the health insurance company, an easy target, since many have long viewed these companies as villains. The security and privacy of digital medical data, and its potential for misappropriation, are not to be underemphasized, and we will

review these issues later. For now, I want to set the stage for the future smartphone doctor era of medicine. You may have noticed that I have put *smartphone* in parentheses in the title of this chapter. That's because smartphone-mediated medicine offers two possible smartphone doctors. Users may be engaging with a real doctor, but they may just as likely be calling an avatar or algorithm with a connection to the cloud or supercomputer.

THE WARM-UP

For a variety of reasons, between 2009–2011 in the United States, the number of physician visits fell 17 percent among privately insured patients.[10] And that decline is continuing despite the aging of the population and their high density of comorbidities. One of the reasons may be cost, but surely a contributing factor is that there are many emerging alternatives, from retail clinics with nurses to do-it-yourself (DIY) care. Precivil Carrera, a physician in the Netherlands, defined modern DIY medicine as "a form of self-care involving the use of consumer-directed health informatics technologies and applications that allow consumers to track and manage their health by themselves or together with professionals, and that guide consumers' use of health care."[11]

There is considerable evidence that deeper engagement of consumers in their health care yields superior results. For blood pressure, a review of fifty-two prospective, randomized studies showed that people who took self-measurements had better blood pressure management versus those whose only monitoring came through usual care (e.g., at the doctor's office).[12] Beyond self-care, those who interacted with a pharmacist via telemonitoring also showed superior blood pressure control in a randomized trial, with 72 percent of patients achieving controlled blood pressure as compared to only 57 percent with usual care (the national norm is 50 percent).[13] Furthermore, the blood pressure control advantage in the pharmacist arm was quite durable, extending many months after the random assignment of the intervention. Blood pressure is not the only condition successfully treated this way. Using mobile phones to engage adults with diabetes in a randomized trial, researchers at the University of Chicago showed superior glycemic control compared with usual care, at lower costs and higher satisfaction.[14]

Better outcomes have been demonstrated for engaged, activated patients as compared with usual care for a wide variety of conditions, including hypertension, diabetes, obesity, multiple sclerosis, hyperlipidemia, and many types of mental health disorders. Based on this sort positive data, Leonard Kish, a health information technologist, has rightfully called the engaged patient the "blockbuster drug of the century."[15] These successes subsequently led the journal *Health Affairs* to have a dedicated issue on "the new era of patient engagement."[16–18] Engagement can be conceived as patient activation—"understanding one's own role in the care process and having the knowledge, skills, and confidence to take on that role."[16]

Besides self-care, there is the link to nurses. There are approximately one hundred million outpatient visits in the United States per year, with over six million in retail clinics that typically employ nurse practitioners.[19–22] Clinics in pharmacies, like the Minute Clinics at CVS, or in chain stores like Walmart, Kroger, and Target, cropped up about a decade ago and have cumulatively accrued twenty million patient visits in now over sixteen hundred sites. CVS has plans to double their Minute Clinics to be at fifteen hundred by 2017; Walgreens is adding one hundred more clinics this year to get to five hundred total. Both the difficulty involved in getting conventional physician appointments and the convenience for

patients that retail clinics afford have been well documented.[23]

Nonetheless, there are regulatory limits on the practice of nurses in many states, and there is reduced insurance reimbursement for nurses as compared with doctors. Moreover, there is considerable tension between physicians and nurses about delivery of care. For example, after Walgreens announced the expansion of its 330 Take Care clinics, which are staffed by nurse practitioners, the American Academy of Family Physicians claimed the development would ultimately "lower quality, increase costs and pose a risk to patients' long-term health outcomes."[24] In 2014, the American Academy of Pediatrics was up in arms about retail-based clinics and issued a statement that they "are an inappropriate source of primary care for pediatric patients, as they are detrimental to the medical home concept of longitudinal and coordinated care."[23,25] Indeed, the American Medical Association and many other physician groups have issued restrictive policies and regulations about the "scope of practice" available to nurses, dictating what a health care provider can do based on experience, education, and training.[24]

This is not a problem confined to outpatient clinics; the tension extends to hospital services. Even though there have been studies that have shown no differences in outcomes for patients having their anesthesia administered by an anesthesiologist or a nurse anesthetist, the American Society of Anesthesiologists (representing over fifty thousand doctors) has issued warnings that quality of care may be diminished by care provided by nurse anesthetists.[26]

Independent assessments make such criticism look more like turf protection than patient protection. For example, a group of experts from the Institute of Medicine studied the problem and issued a report that provided backing for nurses to practice "to the full extent of their education and training" and called for eliminating regulations that suppress their role.[27] The National Governors Association and the Federal Trade Commission reinforced these recommendations, but the turf battle between physicians and nurses remains unsettled.[26,28–30]

There is only 1 licensed doctor for every 370 people in the United States. In most of the one-quarter of the United States that is considered rural, there is less than one doctor per thirty-five hundred people.[31] The average wait time to see a primary care doctor across the country is about 2.5 weeks, and as high as 66 days in Boston (Figure 14.1).[32,33] That's now, but by 2023, with the baby boomers coming to age, there is a projected 40 percent increase in heart disease and 50 percent increase in cancer and diabetes, which should make competition for appointments even fiercer. And these statistics don't even take into account increased access for forty million citizens who were previously uninsured. Although self-care and physician extenders, including nurses and physician assistants, can help, surely they won't be the whole solution. New tools must be brought to bear. While the medical community is slow to embrace digital and network solutions, these solutions are nonetheless erupting. Take the online health communities like PatientsLikeMe, CureTogether, Insight, and countless others, which provide peer-to-peer connectivity for patients with similar conditions. Many participants say they put more trust in their peers of these communities than in their doctors. In just a span of five years, these eHealth networking sites have attracted millions of consumers and are continuing to grow as a prominent medical information resource. Remarkably, this is certainly one key component of the movement toward the democratization of medicine.

Another emerging digital solution is the advanced Siri for medical guidance—the

FIGURE 14.1 The average wait time for a new patient to see a doctor for family practice (nonemergency issues) by city.

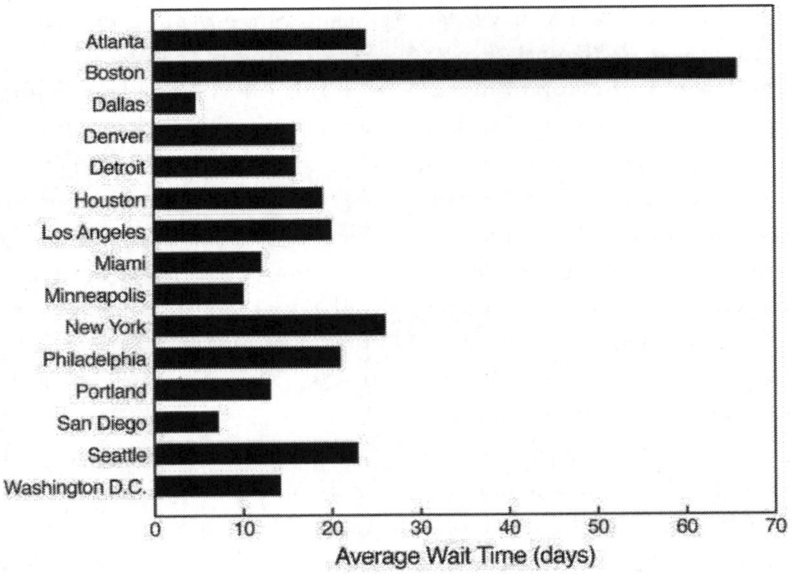

Source: Adapted from "How Long Will You Wait to See a Doctor?" CNN Money, accessed August 14, 2014, http://money.cnn.com/interactive/economy/average-doctor-wait-times/.

emergence of virtual health assistants (VHAs).[34,35] AskMD is one of the first Siri-like entries for this concept. A free smartphone app is downloaded, allowing the consumer to enter symptoms, either by typing them in or by voice recognition–embedded software, and tap into its pattern recognition database for feedback. When I visited the *Colbert Report,* Stephen Colbert had already caught on. He said, "I have a smart-phone. Am I a doctor? How can my smartphone tell me about me? Is Siri a doctor?" Then he held his smartphone to his chest and asked "Siri, am I dying?" And Siri responded, "I really can't say."

While that got plenty of laughs, virtual health assistants should be taken seriously. Given a device with access to a large database as well as machine learning capabilities, surely we can see an effective, intelligent VHA developed that integrates the individual's medical record, medications, and relevant data monitoring. It would not take much to see a device help guide medication adherence, coach a healthy lifestyle, and respond to questions customized to the individual patient's circumstances and needs.

THE OUTPATIENT VISIT OF THE FUTURE

It seems like every week there is a new headline for an article related to who will see you (the smartphone, robot, avatar, algorithm, or Dr. Siri) for medical care or how you will be seen (cellphone, smartphone, Skype) (Figure 14.2).[23,36–49] *Fast Company* had an article titled "Could ePatient Networks Become the Superdoctors of the Future?" and asserted "the idea of going down to your doctor's office is going to feel as foreign as going to the video store."[50] That may seem bold, but they got that one right. Physical office visits are on their way out. Cisco surveyed over fifteen hundred Americans and found that 70 percent prefer virtual rather than physical visits with their doctors.[51] That's not too surprising, given that the average return visit in the United States lasts seven minutes and new consultation twelve minutes, and that only after an average wait of sixty-two minutes to get into the exam room and be seen. Or not being seen because the doctor is predominantly looking at the keyboard to type into the electronic medical record.

FIGURE 14.2 Headlines of various articles in the past two years related to smart-phone office visits.

The Smartphone Will See You Now
The Avatar Will See You Now
The Robot Will See You Now
The Doctor Will Skype You Now
How Smartphones Are Trying to Replace Your Doctor
The Doctor Will See You Now—On Your Cellphone
When Your MD Is an Algorithm
Dr. Smartphone: 5 Ways Your Doctor Can Diagnose You
Paging Dr. Siri: How Your iPhone Can Diagnose Disease
Can a Smartphone Replace Your Doctor?

From *Macleans, MIT Technology Review, The Atlantic, TIME, Gizmodo, Mashable, Wall Street Journal, Popular Mechanics, The Telegraph, Euronews,* respectively

Insurers are taking the lead in expanding these services.[37,52–54] Health Partners, a health insurer based in Minnesota, conducted a study of virtual visits using their web-based Virtuwell platform. They showed that virtual visits not only were substantially preferred, but they also reduced the average cost by $88 compared with physical visits, likely related to increased efficiency and reduced ancillary testing.[37] The University of Pittsburgh compared more than eight thousand e-visits ("Anywhere Care") and office visits and also found virtual connects cheaper, without compromising of quality according to key measures such as misdiagnosis, and considerably more popular among its patients. United Healthcare, one of the largest private insurers, started the NowClinic to give individuals immediate access to physicians for ten-minute secured live chat by phone or webcam. Wellpoint operates LiveHealthOnline, which charges $49 for a videoconference with physicians. Kaiser Permanente has been using virtual visits for several years, predominantly by secure e-mails and telephone calls and a minority of video encounters.[55] For the eight thousand doctors and 3.4 million members of Kaiser Permanente Northern California, virtual visits grew from 4.1 million in 2008 to 10.5 million in 2013 and are projected to exceed physical visits by 2016, according to Kaiser.[55,56] Nevertheless, while it appears that there has not been a decrease for in-person visits, more recent data that accounts for membership growth shows an inflection to be the case. Members strongly preferred virtual visits, while the "physicians have been slow to integrate new technologies into their practices, and most are leery of moving in this direction."[55]

There are many new players that are offering immediate virtual visits,[57] including Doctor on Demand, MD Live, American Well, Ringadoc, Teladoc, Health Magic, MedLion, InteractiveMD, and First Opinion.[58–75] You can hardly miss the pitches: "For $69 and your smartphone in hand, a board certified dermatologist will look at your rash" (from Dermatologist On Call) or "For $49, a doctor will see you now—online" (from American Well). Some of these connect for only telephone or text consults; a few of these companies offer secure video encounters. First Opinion is a text-only service that keeps the user's identity anonymous, circumventing the need for HIPAA approval.[68] There is a subscription fee of $9 per month after the first consult, and assurance that the same doctor will be linked for all subsequent consults. Google Helpouts, which are secure video meetings that are fully HIPAA compliant, have been adopted by One Medical Group, a very progressive, boutique medical practice based in San Francisco that received $40 million of investment from Google.[76–78] There are other very interesting entries to virtual video medical visits, including Verizon and the Mayo Clinic.[79–83] The latter is through a mobile health startup company called Better, which links the user to a Mayo Clinic nurse and charges a $50 monthly fee per household for unlimited access.[79–83] Its website bills it as "Your Personal Health Assistant" and having a nurse in your pocket.

One of the largest outpatient telehealth providers, Teladoc, published in 2014 on its 120,000 consults. It charges $38 per visit, operates 24/7, and the top three reasons for visits were acute respiratory illness, urinary tract symptoms, and skin problems. Overall, the cost for a video visit for most of these services is about $40, lasting from fifteen to twenty minutes. That is noteworthy, since a co-payment to see a doctor physically costs about the same. But there is 24/7 availability, wait time is zero, and it's as simple as tapping your smartphone to get connected with a physician.[51,84a] In some ways it can be likened to Uber as we get used to on-demand service via our smartphones.

Indeed, two companies have now launched the real equivalent to Uber for medical house calls. In select cities, Medicast and Pager offer doctors on demand on a 24/7 basis. It's just like summoning a car via Uber or Lyft, but instead of seeing information about the driver and car on your smartphone screen, you see the doctor's picture, his or her profile, and the length of time it will take him or her to be at your house. It's no surprise that these companies are so similar to Uber—Pager was started by one of Uber's co-founders.[84b]

There has also been the emergence of health visit kiosks. One, called Healthspot, looks like a hybrid of a sleek, futuristic phone booth and automated teller machine (ATM). In these kiosks, which are appearing in department stores like Target, a medical assistant escorts the consumer into the private booth for a secure video visit with a physician. The kiosk is equipped with some of the tools to obtain metrics such as blood pressure. Lee Schwamm, a physician proponent of telehealth, has pointed out that its implementation is much like ATMs for banks. The latter had a shaky start in the 1970s when they were expensive to manufacture, a loss leader for the banks, and quite clunky with limited capabilities.[85] Over time, however, they became fully integrated with global banking and financial services and remarkably consumer-centric. It has become unimaginable to have a bank without full ATM services for 24/7 access anywhere in the world. Dr. Peter Antall, a medical director for American Well compared the new phenomenon of telehealth to that of online banking: "Patients do have to get comfortable with this, but I remember a time where we were worried about electronic banking, and we got over that."[61] Now, of course, most of us do some banking online. Similarly, Randy Parker, the CEO of MDLive said, "Within the next few years, no consumer will even remember not being able to be connected to their providers through telehealth."[86a] The projections from the Deloitte consulting firm support Parker's assertion that telemedicine is growing rapidly. By the end of 2014, nearly 1 in 6 doctor visits in the United States will be virtual, and it is expected that the increase in over one hundred million virtual visits will potentially save $5 billion compared with traditional physical office visits.[86b,86c]

An unexpected example of the efficacy of teleconsults was demonstrated with genetic counselors. A randomized trial was undertaken of 669 women receiving new data on their BRCA gene mutations who were assigned to either an in-person or telephone consult. Extensive evaluation after the information was reviewed showed the telephone consults were just as effective.[87,88] With less than three thousand genetic counselors for a population in the United States of 330 million, surely this is good news for fixing the incongruous mismatch between the supply of this expertise and its increasing demand.

Nonetheless, there are significant obstacles for the widespread adoption of telemedicine. For one, there are archaic state laws for the practice of medicine that restrict a physician's practice to be limited to the state where he or she is licensed. They are a throwback to the late nineteenth century in response to unrestrained entry of medical practice during the Civil War! As a result such laws reflect none of the changes that medical training has undergone. For example, all MD physicians have to take the US Medical Licensure Examination (USMLE), and all medical education and training is set by national standards, which means state-by-state licensing is pointless.[89,90] Another obstacle results from state laws mandating that a patient has to have a physical visit with the doctor before a virtual visit is allowed. So in order for these companies to operate, it has been necessary to enlist doctors in all fifty states, or restrict their practice to particular states that are covered by licensed physicians. It remains unclear when these antiquated state laws will be overridden. But at least in 2014 former Senator Tom Daschle formed a group known as the Alliance for Connected Care to address the need for a federal telemedicine law.[91] Building on that, the Federation of the Medical Boards have recently drafted into legislation to "create a new pathway to speed the licensing of doctors practicing medicine in multiple states."[92a] Known as the Interstate Medical Licensure Compact, the legislation is expected to be approved by many states in 2015 and "herald a major reform in medical licensing."[92b]

Telehealth will certainly not solve every problem facing medicine. Many of the models for these telehealth providers are fee-for-service, representing an extension of the pervasive and perverse way that American medicine is practiced. While they provide the foundation for a technology to reach remote areas that are medically underserved, the problems accompanying reimbursement and the medicine-by-the-yard model mean that telehealth won't necessarily help move us toward a health system motivated to preserve health, provide broad access to quality care, and avoid fees for episodic evaluation or treatment. Large employers in the United States have been embracing telehealth. Many reimburse the cost of such consultations, and the number offering access to them grew from 12 percent of companies in 2012 to 17 percent in 2013. An upbeat perspective on these developments comes from Dr. Zachary Landman, chief medical officer of DoctorBase. Landman tells the story of when his grandfather had a heart attack in 1950; the doctor tended to him at his home and charged $3.50.[93] He wrote about mobile health now letting doctors practice like it's 1950: "the mHealth movement has democratized mobile-based secure healthcare communication allowing every electing doctor to work in teams, message, share photos, and exchange files on HIPAA-secure mobile platforms."[93]

That indeed may be true one day, but we've already seen how doctors are reluctant to adapt the technology. Half of American physicians are over age fifty-five, far removed from digital native status (under age 30) and any propensity for adopting little wireless devices for their practice of medicine. Nevertheless, innovations abound, and a virtual physical may not be close to common but it is very close to possible. We've already covered a range of apps and hardware extensions—call them add-appters—that enable checking everything from pulse to breathing to eardrums with smartphones, and new devices, such as one from the Israeli company Tyto, which have tiny cameras and microphones that "can perform almost a complete checkup of the body."[94,95a] Besides the virtual physical during a one-off visit, there's remote monitoring of all vital signs and a range of important physiologic metrics, as we've already reviewed.

This is really transformative, multidimensional information—in time, space, and person. First, there's a much higher frequency of data that is gathered in the individual's "wild" rather than in a strained medical setting. That could be either continuous or intermittent, but often data that are being captured were not previously attainable. Examples would be blood pressure or blood oxygen saturation during sleep, or quantitative physiologic metrics (like HRV, GSR) during a traffic jam or an argument with one's spouse. Soon most and someday all the blood tests that would normally be done in a hospital or clinic laboratory will also be obtainable by smartphone add-appters. Second, the individual is looking at all this data on a frequent basis, in contrast to not even having access to it previously. This provides precious contextual insight. For example, some patients of mine tell me their blood pressure is invariably in the normal range except for Monday morning when they go back to work, or that the new medication that was added is not having any effect, or that "long acting" medicines taken in the morning seem to be wearing off by the evening. Patients with a history of heart rhythm abnormalities can see their ECG on the phone screen along with its computer reading. From that they can begin to learn what symptoms are the real deals, significant arrhythmias, as compared to innocent extra beat clustering. Individuals who are at risk for diabetes learn, for the first time, what particular foods or activities lead to better or worse glucose regulation. There could be a much longer list here but hopefully this conveys the power of critical data, simply and graphically displayed on the smartphone screen, to be uniquely and highly informative to the individual.

Third, there's the doctor's enhanced window to the patient's information, much of which wasn't available before, now contextualized by real world experience. Add to that the enhanced engagement of the patient and we begin to see how powerful an enabled patient can be. Let's consider a patient with depression, a condition for which mobile apps are already starting to make a difference.[95b] A medication has been prescribed and there is a question as to whether it is working. The patient reports feeling subjectively better, but all of the objective indices—tone and inflection of voice, frequency of communication, activity and movement, breathing pattern, facial expression, vital signs, HRV and GSR—show no sign of improvement whatsoever. Does this diagnose a placebo effect of the medication? The patient looks at the integrated data and notes a dissociation of symptoms and the metrics. A whole new discussion can ensue as to whether a medication is necessary, whether it's really working, and the potential to explore other alternative nonmedical treatments. Or another patient with a history of frequent asthma attacks is now using the lung smartphone add-appter, which gathers environmental exposures that include pollen count and air quality, ambient temperature and humidity, along with activity, vital signs, lung function (forced expiratory volume in one second via the microphone), chest movement, and breathing

pattern. The integrated asthma dashboard shows that the combination of cold air and exercise, on days with poor air quality, explains nearly all of the exacerbations of asthma. Now the patient and doctor can come up with a new plan of anti-attack—with emphasis of preventive inhaler use (and specific types of inhalers) timed to this individual's exposure triggers. That also allows for reduction of medications for the rest of the time, reducing the chances for side effects and expense.

So the real office visit has a whole different look, highly enriched by data that was patient-generated, but also visualized and, at least to some extent, processed by the patient. This sets up an opportunity to strengthen the bond between the patient and doctor. The activated patient has now assumed the role of "data-gatherer" who sends this trove of information for additional guidance and input to the physician. The data can be sent ahead anytime, either during or before a virtual or real office visit. Indeed, the data might even preempt the need for a "visit," and when they do prove necessary, they will no longer be visits or appointments but informative, data-driven discussions. There you have my sense of why recommending medical apps and add-appters makes for such an exciting and intimate way to practice medicine. Perhaps that's why even back in 2012 England's National Health Service (not known as the most progressive health system in the world) requested general practitioners to recommend apps to their patients for managing conditions ranging from diabetes to depression "in an attempt to give patients more power and reduce visits to doctors."[96,97] For this initiative, the health secretary, Andrew Lansley, said: "I want to make using apps to track blood pressure, to find the nearest source of support when you need it and to get practical help in staying healthy the norm. With more information at their fingertips, patients can truly be in the driving seat."[96]

[…] We will get away from keyboards in the office, also known as "death by a thousand clicks," and replace them with computer processing of natural language into notes.[98–100] This sort of data, combined with a machine-learning powered app to turn spoken words into notes, will truly revolutionize the doctor's visit of the future—assuming, of course, that we need the routine visits at all.

DOCTORS DISINTERMEDIATED?

We've already seen some examples of how physicians react to the threat of being marginalized, along with their general reluctance to adapt to new technology. Now we get into the "Second Machine Age"[101] question as to whether the new digital landscape will reboot the need for doctors and health professionals. Kevin Kelly, a cofounder of *Wired*, has asserted: "The role tasks of any information-intensive job can be automated. It doesn't matter if you are a doctor, lawyer, architect, reporter, or even programmer: The robot takeover will be epic."[102] An emergency medicine physician likened the current practice of medicine to a Radio Shack store in his piece "Doctor Dinosaur: Physicians may not be exempt from extinction."[103] In late 2013, Korean doctors threatened to go on an all-out strike if the government went ahead with new telemedicine laws that would support clinical diagnoses to be made remotely. Their fear of losing fifty thousand jobs was articulated by one of the medical group leaders: "The government's plans will only bring the collapse of the country's healthcare system and polarization between large hospitals and small clinics."[104] When Johnson & Johnson introduced a computerized conscious sedation machine called Sedasys, the company proclaimed: "This is truly a first-in-kind medical technology that has the potential to redefine the way sedation is administered" and "is a great way to improve care

and reduce costs."[105] In contrast, a physician leader of the American Society of Anesthesiologists responded, "Everyone is so hot on technology, but you have to balance the fiduciary duties of the company with the physicians' interest in ensuring the highest quality and safest care for the patient."[105] The founders of PatientsLikeMe, the largest online health community, have asked, "Who will be the best to interpret your MRI? A radiologist? Or a computer?"[106a] It's just a question of time. You can only imagine how radiologists react to robotic replacement affirmations. Or oncologists after reading a *Fortune* magazine feature article on IBM Watson that has been deployed in several cancer centers asking whether cancer doctors will be replaced by a supercomputer.[3] Add to that psychiatrists who read an article in *The Economist* that a virtual shrink may be better than a real one, reviewing a study that showed that patients are more apt to confide and be open and honest with a computer avatar than with a counselor.[106b,106c]

FIGURE 14.3 Projection by American Association of Medical Colleges of physician shortage in the United States.

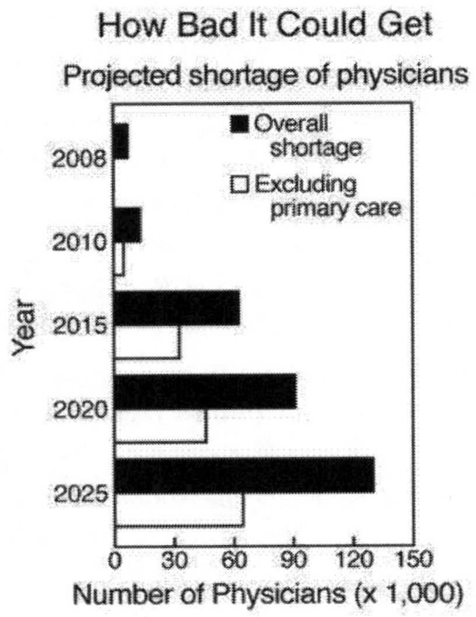

Source: Adapted from "Physician Shortages to Worsen Without Increases in Residency Training," American Association of Medical Colleges, 2014, https://www.aamc.org/download/153160/data/physician_shortages_to_worsen_without_increases_in_residency_tr.pdf.

The need for doctors will be reduced, so there certainly is reason to question the projection of a profound shortage of doctors that looms ahead. Already in 2015 it is estimated by the American Association of Medical Colleges that there are almost 63,000 less doctors than needed in the United States. This figure jumps to over 130,000 short in a decade (Figure 14.3).[106d] The shortage is not confined to the United States—the World Health Organization claims there is already an alarming worldwide shortage of 4.3 million doctors and nurses of the 27.3 million combined global workforce.

In 2014, the Institute of Medicine issued a report on medical education, assessing the physician workforce with a key conclusion about the looming shortage: "does not find any credible evidence to support such claims."[106e] Echoing this conclusion, a most unlikely bipartisan combination of authors—Scott Gottlieb and Ezekiel Emanuel—representing extreme views of the Republican and Democratic parties, respectively, wrote a pointed piece, "No, There Won't Be a Doctor Shortage."[107] While acknowledging the aging of the population and the increased demand related to thirty million newly insured Americans via the Affordable Care Act, they declared: "The road to Obamacare has seen its share of speed bumps, as well as big potholes. But a physician shortage is unlikely to be one of its roadblocks."[107] Beyond echoing the use of nurses, pharmacists, dieticians, health aides, and other non-physicians, and the profound waste in American health care […], they aptly point out: "Innovations, such as sensors that enable remote monitoring of disease and more timely interventions, can help preempt the need for inpatient treatment."[107] And that is just the beginning of how innovative technology and unplugged medicine can markedly improve the efficiency of physicians.

SMARTPHONE MEDICINE TO THE RESCUE?

Unfortunately, most physicians don't get it yet and are somewhat vulnerable to being marginalized or disintermediated. They haven't gone digital. Jay Parkinson, who originated and runs a progressive primary care physician practice, wrote in the *New Yorker*, "I've hired two generations of doctors—one from my parents' generation and one from my own. The differences are striking. One feels right at home, empowered and enabled, and the other thinks she's going to break something. The older physician still loves what she does, and enjoys learning out of curiosity, but computers just aren't hardwired into her brain like the younger one."[108]

Earlier in the chapter I mentioned that about half of the physicians in the United States are over age fifty-five. Two out of three won't e-mail with their patients, which has been proven in multiple studies to markedly improve efficiency of practice.[109] To this end, *Consumer Reports* in December 2013 had a digital doctor's office feature, "The Doctor Will e-mail You Now" with a key projection: "You may find your doctor actively encouraging you to send her an e-mail."[110] That does seem quite logical. But a Price Waterhouse Coopers report on mHealth suggested otherwise, headlined "42% of Docs Fear mHealth Will Lessen Their Power Over Patients."[111] (That's engrained paternalism, […].) There's also the fear of malpractice, which was picked up on by *The Economist*: "The irony is that a doctor is more comfortable with the liability in a system that does not have rich data than in a system that does have rich data."[112]

Sometimes it takes a fresh, outside view to provide insight and impetus to change. At a meeting of the Semiconductors Industry Association of America in late 2013, I had the opportunity to meet Mike Splinter, the chairman of Applied Material, one of the largest chip manufacturers in the world. He asked me, "Why are doctors still using the stethoscope and manila folder?" I said he was asking the wrong guy but turned it back to him to write it out, which he did, here excerpted:

And while the tubes have transformed from wood to rubber, and sensing plates are now metal, not much else has changed in this pre–Civil War medical instrument. As my granddaughter would say, "Are you kidding me?" Even though we call the stethoscope a scope, it does not scope anything. It simply is a little amplifier analogous to the Edison phonograph or a Victrola—like the ones you see with big horns in the old-time movies. Sadly, I am not joking. This is a truly archaic device, and yet we trust our lives and health to it in a way that is out of touch with the world we live in today. The stethoscope has no ability to record information; it has no ability to analyze information. Its successful usage depends totally on the practitioner at the moment.[113]

But age and the medical community's resistance to change are certainly interdependent, major factors. New technology just doesn't go over well. I took a hit on this topic with a "white coat lecture" by Donald M. Knowlan, MD, at the Georgetown University School of Medicine in 2013.[114] A white coat lecture is a tradition at medical schools on or around the first day, when a faculty member gives an inspirational talk. For anchoring, please remember that Georgetown was the home of Dr. Proctor Harvey, one of the most well-regarded bedside cardiologists. Here is what Dr. Knowlan, age eighty-six, included in his address to the incoming students:

But what can you, the class of 2017, expect? In a recent thought-provoking book, *The Creative Destruction of Medicine* ... [Topol] anticipate[d] future changes in the health care delivery system. He commented on changes such as use of smartphones for complex diagnostic challenges and personalized medicine with use of genetic information. He even suggested that the stethoscope, so revered here at Georgetown, will be replaced by a handheld ultrasound device. He admitted to not using his own stethoscope for over 2 years, which suggests to me he never learned to use it properly and appreciate its value. Despite all these future advances, he probably hardly scratches the surface.[114]

I've never met Dr. Knowlan, and he has no awareness that one of my favorite things in medicine for decades was to teach the bedside cardiovascular physical exam to medical students, residents, and advanced trainees. Indeed my idol in cardiology is Kanu Chatterjee, a master clinician like Proctor Harvey who emphasized the intricacies of the bedside exam as he taught my fellow students and me at UCSF. Most of that centered on the stethoscope, learning how to hear and interpret the whole gamut of subtle heart sounds—well beyond lub dub. But unfortunately that is old history now.[115–119] That physicians like Dr. Knowlan still emphasize the old ways is no doubt a result of having trained before ultrasound was standard. But for many, such resistance can be, as Drs. Nelson and Narula put it, a part of a "philosophical and practical gap between comprehensive imaging by a consultant and bedside physical examination."[118]

Another eminent, elder statesman, Dr. Arnold "Bud" Relman, former editor of the *New England Journal of Medicine*, who recently died at age ninety-one, also expressed his concerns about the future of medical care highly influenced by digital devices.[120] He believed my view was "much too sanguine" and "not sufficiently concerned about its

FIGURE 14.4 Doctors are getting squeezed like never before.

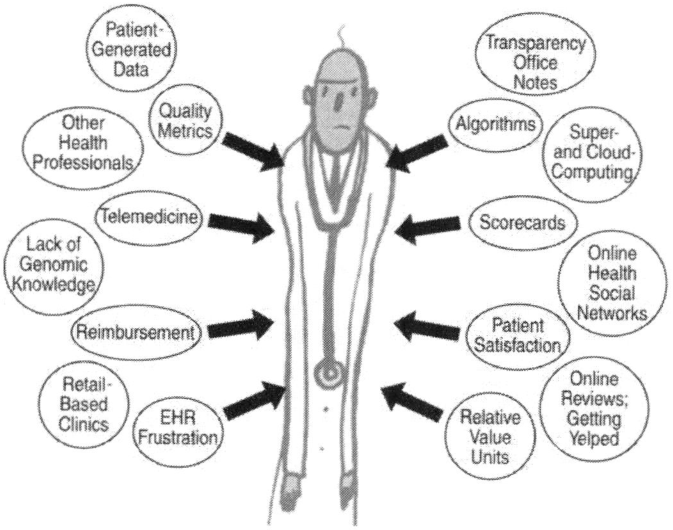

limitations." These views that challenge the active role of consumers, social networks, and technology that would dare to replace the treasured medical icon are to be expected. While they come from physicians of advanced age, they are indeed representative of the majority of doctors today.

But doctors are facing unprecedented pressures coming from all directions, many of which we have already reviewed (Figure 14.4).[111,121–133] This has understandably led to marked disillusionment, which has been amply documented. When I talk with many of my colleagues about this oppressive squeeze, diminishing reimbursement for their work often crops up in the discussion. But there's something about what motivates physicians that is more compelling than financial incentives.[134–136] Jonathan Kolstad, a Wharton health economist, received the prestigious Arrow Award for a study that showed what really drives physicians is their performance compared with their peers—that was four times more powerful than financial incentives. He used the report-card system for cardiac surgeons in

Pennsylvania as the basis of understanding physician behavior.[134–136]

That's an important finding that certainly resonates with me and can be the basis for adaptation to the way medicine will move forward. Physicians generally want to be the best performer among their peers; they are inherently competitive and data-driven. There isn't any question that, with rare exceptions, they're deeply committed to their patients. So how do we use this lever?

Online evaluations of physicians, like Yelp!, Vitals.com, Healthgrades, RateMDs, and Angie's List really don't achieve this goal.[137–141] While they can provide some objective assessment for metrics like waiting time and parking conditions, much is subjective, such as how friendly and courteous the office staff is, or the communicative skills of the doctor. This information is certainly very useful for consumers but doesn't get to the quality of medical care,[142–144] even though many physicians are responsive and do whatever they can to ameliorate their ratings.[145] Similarly, patient satisfaction surveys, which are widely used for rating physicians and hospitals and are embraced by the US government, have major flaws.[146] It turns out scoring is highly influenced by the patient getting a prescription, such as an antibiotic or narcotic pain medication, or a scan—even though this is all too often contraindicated.

But what if physicians incorporated the powerful microcomputer to decompress their dispensable duties, transferring responsibility for generating data, surveillance, and much of disease management to patients?[147,148] The term *letting go* in medicine usually refers to end-of-life care, and willingness to stop resuscitation or heroic efforts. But here I am invoking *letting go* to denote readiness of physicians and the medical community for patients to take charge. The opportunity now is for physicians to compete for performance—adapting to a democratized form of medicine—fostering e-mail communication with patients, supporting use of mobile device add-appters patient-generated data, and online social health networks, sharing and co-editing office notes, and all aspects of consumer-driven health care. Off-loading data and information is liberating for the physician, just as it is empowering to the patient. This is not about letting go of the importance of human touch and compassion, which can never be trumped by technology.[132,149–151] When I gave a medical school commencement address in 2014, I spoke about artificial intelligence [...] and real, digital intelligence in medicine, as measured by the "DQ"—digital quotient. Here were my five questions for the DQ of the new physician graduates:

1. Can you see every patient as an individual—learn everything possible about what makes them tick with our new digital tools of sequencing, sensors, imaging?

2. Are you going to advocate patient-generated data so each of your patients is using his or her smartphone or tablet to capture essential data, relevant to his or her medical condition?

3. Will you be fully supportive of activating your patients, getting them maximally engaged in the new form of consumer-driven health care that is just starting to take hold?

4. Will you share all your notes with your patients, and treat them with the utmost respect as a partner for whom you will be giving advice, counsel, and most importantly providing exquisite communication, empathy, and compassion?

5. Will you keep up with all the new information, such as following trusted medical sources on Twitter? And challenge existing dogma and guidelines when it comes down to the unique patient in front of you?[152]

The smartphone is just a pipe, a conduit of flowing data. On either end of it are intelligent human beings who are ready to assume quite different roles from what the history of medicine has established. Patients will always crave and need the human touch from a doctor, but that can be had on a more selective basis with the tools at hand. Instead of doctors being squeezed, resorting to computer automation can actually markedly expand their roles. As Kevin Kelly wrote, "the rote tasks of any information-intensive job can be automated. It doesn't matter if you are a doctor, lawyer, architect, reporter, or even programmer."[102] *The Economist* weighed in on this too: "The machines are not just cleverer, but they also have access to far more data. The combination of big data and smart machines will take over some occupations wholesale."[153] But smart doctors need not feel threatened, for their occupation is secure. Letting go and competing on embracing digital medicine may turn out to be the best way to prevent disintermediation and disillusionment in the long run.

NOTES

1. R. Cook, *Cell* (New York, NY: Penguin, 2014), 216.

2. M. Miliard, "Q&A: Eric Dishman on Patient Engagement," *Healthcare IT News*, April 10, 2012, http://www.healthcareitnews.com/eric-dishman-interview.

3. J. Hempel, "IBM's Massive Bet on Watson," *Fortune*, September 19, 2013, http://fortune.com/2013/09/19/ibms-massive-bet-on-watson/.

4. D. Rotman, "How Technology Is Destroying Jobs," *MIT Technology Review*, June 12, 2013, http://www.technologyreview.com/featuredstory/515926/how-technology-is-destroying-jobs/.

5. W. B. Arthur, *The Nature of Technology* (New York, NY: Penguin, 2009).

6. E. Brynjolfsson and A. McAfee, *Race Against the Machine* (Lexington, MA: Digital Frontier Press, 2011).

7. Cook, *Cell*, 30.

8. Ibid., 216–217.

9. R. Cook and E. Topol, "Cook and Topol: How Digital Medicine Will Soon Save Your Life," *Wall Street Journal*, February 21, 2014, http://online.wsj.com/news/articles/SB100014240527023039737045793510800028045594.

10. "A Survey of America's Physicians: Practice Patterns and Perspectives," The Physicians Foundation, September 21, 2012, http://www.physiciansfoundation.org/healthcare-research/a-survey-of-americas-physicians-practice-patterns-and-perspectives.

11. P. Carrera, "Do-It-Yourself Health Care," *Health Affairs* 32, no. 6 (2013): 1173.

12. K. Uhlig et al., "Self-Measured Blood Pressure Monitoring in the Management of Hypertension: A Systematic Review and Meta-Analysis," *Annals of Internal Medicine* 159, no. 3 (2013): 185–194.

13. K. L. Margolis et al., "Effect of Home Blood Pressure Telemonitoring and Pharmacist Management on Blood Pressure Control: A Cluster Randomized Clinical Trial," *Journal of the American Medical Association* 310, no. 1 (2013): 46–56.

14. S. Nundy et al., "Mobile Phone Diabetes Project Led to Improved Glycemic Control and Net Savings for Chicago Plan Participants," *Health Affairs* 33, no. 2 (2014): 265–272.

15. L. Kish, "The Blockbuster Drug of the Century: An Engaged Patient," *HL7 Standards*, August 28, 2012, http://www.hl7standards.com/blog/2012/08/28/drug-of-the-century/.

16. S. Dentzer, "Rx for the 'Blockbuster Drug' of Patient Engagement," *Health Affairs* 32, no. 2 (2013): 202.

17. L. Ricciardi et al., "A National Action Plan to Support Consumer Engagement via E-Health," *Health Affairs* 32, no. 2 (2013): 376–384.

18. J. H. Hibbard and J. Greene, "What the Evidence Shows About Patient Activation: Better Health Outcomes and Care Experiences; Fewer Data on Costs," *Health Affairs* 32, no. 2 (2013): 207–214.

19. S. Bouchard, "Harnessing the Power of Retail Clinics," *Healthcare Finance News*, April 25, 2014, http://www.healthcarefinancenews.com/news/harnessing-power-retail-clinics.

20. M. Hamilton, "Why Walk-in Health Care Is a Fast-Growing Profit Center for Retail Chains," *Washington Post*, April 4, 2014, http://www.washingtonpost.com/business/why-walk-in-health-care-is-a-fast-growing-profit-center-for-retail-chains/2014/04/04/a05f7cf4-b9c2-11e3-96ae-f2c36d2b1245_story.html.

21. S. Reddy, "Drugstores Play Doctor: Physicals, Flu Diagnosis, and More," *Wall Street Journal*, April 7, 2014, http://online.wsj.com/news/articles/SB10001424052702304819004579487412385359986.

22. K. Koplovitz, "Healthcare IT—An Investment Choice for the Future," *Forbes*, February 2, 2014, http://www.forbes.com/sites/kaykoplovitz/2014/02/04/healthcare-it-an-investment-choice-for-the-future/.

23. M. Beck and T. W. Martin, "Pediatrics Group Balks at Rise of Retail Health Clinics," *Wall Street Journal*, February 24, 2014, http://online.wsj.com/news/article_email/SB1000142405270230483470457940096232839387 6-lMyQjAxMTA0MDIwNDEyNDQyWj-printMode.

24. B. Japsen, "As Walgreen Plays Doctor, Family Physicians Bristle," *Forbes*, April 6, 2013, http://www.forbes.com/sites/brucejapsen/2013/04/06/as-

walgreen-plays-doctor-family-physicians-bristle/print/.

25 M. Healy, "Docs Oppose Retail-Based Clinics for Kids' Care," *USA Today*, February 24, 2014, http://www.usatoday.com/story/news/nation/2014/02/24/pediatrician-retail-health-clinics/5688603/.

26 M. Beck, "At VHA, Doctors, Nurses Clash on Oversight," *Wall Street Journal*, January 26, 2014, http://online.wsj.com/news/articles/SB10001424052702304856504579340603947983912.

27 "The Future of Nursing: Leading Change, Advancing Health Report Recommendations," Institute of Medicine, November 17, 2010, http://www.iom.edu/Reports/2010/The-Future-of-Nursing-Leading-Change-Advancing-Health/Recommendations.aspx.

28 C. Gounder, "The Case for Changing How Doctors Work," *New Yorker*, October 1, 2013, http://www.newyorker.com/online/blogs/currency/2013/10/changing-how-doctors-work.html?printable=true&currentPage=all.

29 S. Jauhar, "Nurses Are Not Doctors," *New York Times*, April 30, 2014, http://www.nytimes.com/2014/04/30/opinion/nurses-are-not-doctors.html.

30 O. Khazan, "The Case for Seeing a Nurse Instead of a Doctor," *The Atlantic*, April 2014, http://www.theatlantic.com/health/print/2014/04/the-case-for-seeing-a-nurse-instead-of-a-doctor/361111/.

31 L. Uscher-Pines and A. Mehrotra, "Analysis of Teladoc Use Seems to Indicate Expanded Access to Care for Patients Without Prior Connection to a Provider," *Health Affairs* 33, no. 2 (2014): 258–264.

32 "How Long Will You Wait to See a Doctor?," *CNN Money*, accessed August 19, 2014, http://money.cnn.com/interactive/economy/average-doctor-wait-times/.

33 E. Rosenthal, "The Health Care Waiting Game," *New York Times*, July 6, 2014, http://www.nytimes.com/2014/07/06/sunday-review/long-waits-for-doctors-appointments-have-become-the-norm.html.

34 T. Morrow, "How Virtual Health Assistants Can Reshape Healthcare," *Forbes*, March 13, 2013, http://www.forbes.com/sites/ciocentral/2013/03/13/how-virtual-health-assistants-can-reshape-healthcare/print/.

35 T. Morrow, "Virtual Health Assistants: A Prescription for Retail Pharmacies," *Drug Store News*, July 18, 2013, http://www.drugstorenews.com/article/virtual-health-assistants-prescription-retail-pharmacies.

36 T. McMahon, "The Smartphone Will See You Now," *MacLean's Magazine*, March 4, 2013, 46–49.

37 A. Carrns, "Visiting the Doctor, Virtually," *New York Times*, February 13, 2013, http://bucks.blogs.nytimes.com/2013/02/13/visiting-the-doctor-virtually/.

38 T. Wasserman, "The Doctor Will See You Now—On Your Cellphone," *Mashable*, December 10, 2013, http://mashable.com/2013/12/10/doctor-on-demand-app/.

39 R. Xu, "The Doctor Will See You Onscreen," *New Yorker*, March 10, 2014, http://www.newyorker.com/online/blogs/currency/2014/03/the-doctor-will-see-you-on-screen.html?printable=true&currentPage=all.

40 A. Sifferlin, "The Doctor Will Skype You Now," *TIME*, January 13, 2014, http://content.time.com/time/subscriber/printout/0,8816,2161682,00.html.

41 K. Bourzac, "The Computer Will See You Now," *Nature* 502 (2013): 592–594.

42 "The Robots Are Coming. How Many of Us Will Prosper from the Second Machine Age?," *Raw Story*, January 4, 2014, http://www.rawstory.com/rs/2014/01/04/the-robots-are-coming-how-many-of-us-will-prosper-from-the-second-machine-age/.

43 J. Marte, "The Doctor Visit of the Future May Be a Phone Call," *Market Watch*, March 3, 2014, http://www.marketwatch.com/story/the-doctor-will-facetime-you-now-2014-03-03/print?guid=D2E3D006-A2D6-11E3-BC16-00212803FAD6.

44 L. Landro, "A Better Online Diagnosis Before the Doctor Visit," *Wall Street Journal*, July 22, 2013, http://online.wsj.com/article/SB10001424127887324328904578621743278445114.html.

45 S. Koven, "Doctors, Patients, and Computer Screens," *Boston Globe*, February 24, 2014, http://www.bostonglobe.com/lifestyle/health-wellness/2014/02/24/practice-doctors-patients-and-computer-screens/JMMYaCDtf3mnuQZGfkMVyL/story.html.

46 L. Landro, "The Doctor's Team Will See You Now," *Wall Street Journal*, February 17, 2014, http://online.wsj.com/news/articles/SB10001424052702304899704579389203539061082.

47 T. W. Martin, "When Your M.D. Is an Algorithm," *Wall Street Journal*, April 11, 2013, http://online.wsj.com/article/SB10001424127887324010704578414992125798464.html.

48 A. Vaterlaus-Staby, "Is Data the Doctor of the Future?," *PSFK*, March 11, 2014: http://www.psfk.com/2014/03/data-doctor-future-future-health.html#!bGg2V0.

49 S. Bader, "The Doctor's Office of the Future: Coffeeshop, Apple Store, and Fitness Center," *Fast Company*, December 11, 2013, http://www.fastcoexist.com/3023255/futurist-forum/the-doctors-office-of-the-future-coffeeshop-apple-store-and-fitness-center.

50 A. Hamilton, "Could ePatient Networks Become the Superdoctors of the Future?," *Fast Company*, September 28, 2014, http://www.fastcoexist.com/1680617/could-epatient-networks-become-the-superdoctors-of-the-future.

51 S. D. Hall, "The Idea of Virtual Doctor Visits Is Growing on Us," *Fierce Health IT*, March 7, 2013, http://www.fiercehealthit.com/node/19095/print.

52 S. Mace, "Developing Telemedicine Options," *Health Leaders Media*, April 11, 2014, http://www.healthleadersmedia.com/print/MAG-303102/Developing-Telemedicine-Options.

53 K. Lee, "'Telehealth' Evolving Doctor-Patient Services with Online Interactions," *NECN*, January 21, 2014, http://www.necn.com/01/21/14/Telehealth-evolving-doctor-patient-servi/landing.html?blockID=861 974.

54 C. Lowe, "The Future of Doctors," TeleCare Aware, January 23, 2014, http://telecareaware.com/the-future-of-doctors/.

55 R. Pearl, "Kaiser Permanente Northern California: Current Experiences with Internet, Mobile, and Video Technologies," *Health Affairs* 33, no. 2 (2014): 251–257.

56 D. Raths, "Kaiser N. Calif. Topped 10 Million Virtual Visits in 2013," *Healthcare Informatics*, February 11, 2013, http://www.healthcare-informatics.com/print/blogs/david-raths/kaiser-n-calif-topped-10-million-virtual-visits-2013.

57 "Why Telemedicine Is the Future of the Health Care Industry," *The Week*, April 23, 2014, http://theweek.com/article/index/260330/why-telemedicine-is-the-future-of-the-health-care-industry.

58 D. Liu, "Vinod Khosla: Technology Will Replace 80 Percent of Docs," *Health Care Blog*, August 31, 2014, http://thehealthcareblog.com/blog/2012/08/31/vinod-khosla-technology-will-replace-80-percent-of-docs/.

59 L. Gannes, "Doctor on Demand App Gives $40 Medical Consultations from the Comfort of Your Smartphone," *All Things D*, December 10, 2013, http://allthingsd.com/?p=377886&ak_action=printable.

60 "MedLion Direct Primary Care Partners with Helpouts by Google to Give Patients Live Video Appointments," *PRWeb*, April 2, 2014, http://www.prweb.com/releases/2014MedLionGoogleHelpouts/04/prweb11730367.htm.

61 E. A. Moore, "For $49, a Doctor Will See You Now—Online," *CNET*, October 9, 2013, http://news.cnet.com/8301-17938_105-57606794-1/for-$49-a-doctor-will-see-you-now-online/.

62 A. Nixon, "Virtual Doctor's Office Visits via Telemedicine to be Norm," *TribLive*, October 31, 2013, http://triblive.com/business/headlines/4976316-74/doctor-patients-telemedicine?printerfriendly=true.

63 J. Bellamy, "Telemedicine: Click and the Doctor Will See You Now," *Science Based Medicine*, May 1, 2014, http://www.sciencebasedmedicine.org/telemedicine-click-and-the-doctor-will-see-you-now/.

64 W. H. Frist, "Connected Health and the Rise of the Patient-Consumer," *Health Affairs* 33, no. 2 (2014): 191–193.

65 L. Freeman, "Patients Skipping Waiting Room in Favor of Visiting Doctor Online," *23 ABC*, August 9, 2013, http://www.turnto23.com/web/kero/lifestyle/health/patients-skipping-waiting-room-in-favor-of-visiting-doctor-online-1.

66 R. Flinn, "Video Dial-a-Doctor Seen Easing Shortage in Rural U.S.," *Bloomberg Businessweek*, September 5, 2012, http://www.businessweek.com/printer/articles/319338?type=bloomberg.

67 C. Farr, "Former Apple CEO Backs Virtual Doctor's Office to Create the 'Consumer Era' of Medicine," *Venture Beat*, January 22, 2014, http://venturebeat.com/2014/01/22/former-apple-ceo-backs-virtual-doctors-office-to-create-the-consumer-era-of-medicine/.

68 R. Empson, "With $1.2M from Greylock, Yuri Milner and 500 Startups, First Opinion Lets You Text a Doctor Anytime," *TechCrunch*, January 14, 2014, http://techcrunch.com/2014/01/14/with-1-2m-from-greylock-yuri-milner-and-500-startups-first-opinion-lets-you-text-a-doctor-anytime/.

69 O. Kharif, "Telemedicine: Doctor Visits via Video Calls," *Bloomberg Businessweek*, February 27, 2014, http://www.businessweek.com/articles/2014-02-27/health-insurers-add-telemedicine-services-to-cut-costs.

70 W. Khawar, "For $69 and Your Smart Phone in Hand, a Board Certified Dermatologist Will Look at Your Rash," *iMedical Apps*, August 19, 2013, http://www.imedicalapps.com/2013/08/smartphone-dermatologist-rash/.

71 L. Dignan, "Expanding Amazon's Mayday Button: Five New Uses to Ponder," *ZDNet*, January 3, 2014,

http://www.zdnet.com/expanding-amazons-mayday-button-five-new-uses-to-ponder-7000024741/.

72 D. Pogoreic, "MDs, AT&T Alum Look to Test the Market for Virtual Concierge Care in California via Crowdfunding," *MedCity News*, March 4, 2014, http://medcitynews.com/2014/03/crowdfunding-lean-mhealth-startup-att-mhealth-alum-test-market-virtual-concierge-care/.

73 "How Digital Checkups Provide Better Patient Care [Future of Health]," *PSFK*, March 6, 2014, http://www.psfk.com/2014/03/remote-health.html.

74 L. H. Schwamm, "Telehealth: Seven Strategies to Successfully Implement Disruptive Technology and Transform Health Care," *Health Affairs* 33, no. 2 (2014): 200–206.

75 C. Brown, "Bringing Home the Value of Telehealth," *Business Innovation*, February 18, 2014, http://www.business2community.com/business-innovation/bringing-home-value-telehealth-0783860#!bGhsGA.

76 C. Farr, "Google Jumps into the Healthcare Field with Video Service Helpouts," *MedCity News*, November 20, 2013, http://medcitynews.com/2013/11/google-jumps-healthcare-field-video-service-helpouts/.

77 J. Roettgers, "Google's Helpouts Could Be the Company's Secret Weapon to Take on Healthcare," *Tech News and Analysis*, November 4, 2013, http://gigaom.com/2013/11/04/googles-helpouts-could-be-the-companys-secret-weapon-to-take-on-healthcare/.

78 D. Tahir, "Verizon Introduces Virtual Visits, New Telehealth Offering," *Modern Healthcare*, June 25, 2014, http://www.modernhealthcare.com/article/20140625/NEWS/306259948.

79 "For $50 a Month, These Health Advisors Will Answer All Your Paranoid Medical Questions," *Fast Company*, April 17, 2014, http://www.fastcoexist.com/3029237/for-50-a-month-these-health-advisors-will-answer-all-your-paranoid-medical-questions.

80 G. Clapp, "Meet Better—Your Personal Health Assistant," Better, April 15, 2014, http://www.getbetter.com/blog/2014/4/15/meet-better-your-personal-health-assistant.

81 N. Ungerleider, "The Mayo Clinic's New Doctor-in-an-iPhone," *Fast Company*, April 18, 2014, http://www.fastcompany.com/3029304/the-mayo-clinics-new-doctor-in-an-iphone.

82 L. Rao, "Better Raises $5M from Chamath Palihapitiya and Mayo Clinic to Be Your Personal Health Advocate," *TechCrunch*, April 16, 2014, http://techcrunch.com/2014/04/16/

better-raises-5m-from-chamath-palihapitiya-and-mayo-clinic-to-be-your-personal-health-advocate/.

83 B. Dolan, "Mayo Clinic–Backed Better Launches Personal Health Assistant Service," *Mobi-HealthNews*, April 16, 2014, http://mobihealthnews.com/32130/mayo-clinic-backed-better-launches-personal-health-assistant-service/.

84a G. Pittman, "Virtual Visits to Doctor May Be Cheaper Than and as Effective as In-Person Visits," *Washington Post*, January 18, 2013, http://www.washingtonpost.com/national/health-science/virtual-visits%C9n-visits/2013/01/18/8237c028-601e-11e2-a389-ee565c81c565_print.html.

84b C. Schmidt, "Uber-Inspired Apps Bring a Doctor Right to Your Door," *CNN*, July 31, 2014, http://www.cnn.com/2014/07/31/health/doctor-house-call-app/.

85 L. H. Schwamm, "Telehealth: Seven Strategies to Successfully Implement Disruptive Technology and Transform Healthcare," *Health Affairs* 33, no. 2 (2014): 200–206.

86a H. Gregg, "WellPoint's Telemedicine Service Saves Patients $71 per Visit," *Beckers Hospital Review*, March 6, 2014, http://www.beckershospitalreview.com/healthcare-information-technology/wellpoint-s-telemedicine-service-saves-patients-71-per-visit/print.html.

86b "Technology, Media & Telecommunications Predictions," Deloitte Global Report, 2014, http://www2.deloitte.com/global/en/pages/technology-media-and-telecommunications/articles/tmt-predictions-2014.html.

86c L. Mearian, "Almost One in Six Doctor Visits Will Be Virtual This Year," *Computer World*, August 9, 2014, http://www.computerworld.com.au/article/552031/almost_one_six_doctor_visits_will_virtual_year/.

87 D. F. Maron, "Virtual Doctor Visits Gaining Steam in 'Geneticist Deserts,'" *Scientific American*, April 21, 2014, http://www.scientificamerican.com/article/virtual-doctor-visits-gaining-steam/?print=true.

88 "Genetic Counseling via Telephone as Effective as In-person Counseling," Lombardi News Release Archive, January 22, 2014, http://explore.georgetown.edu/documents/74419/?PageTemplateID=141.

89 J. Adler-Milstein, J. Kvedar, and D. W. Bates, "Telehealth Among US Hospitals: Several Factors, Including State Reimbursement and Licensure Policies, Influence Adoption," *Health Affairs* 33, no. 2 (2014): 207–215.

90 R. Kocher, "Doctors Without State Borders: Practicing Across State Lines," *Health Affairs*, February 18, 2014, http://healthaffairs.org/blog/2014/02/18/doctors-without-state-borders-practicing-across-state-lines/.

91 M. Ravindranath, "Daschle, Former Senators Form Alliance to Lobby for New Telehealth Rules," *Washington Post*, March 1, 2014, http://www.washingtonpost.com/business/on-it/daschle-former-senato%C9h-rules/2014/03/01/194bc356-98ef-11e3-80ac-63a8ba7f7942_story.html.

92a R. Pear, "Medical Boards Draft Plan to Ease Path to Out-of-State and Online Treatment," *New York Times*, June 30, 2014, http://www.nytimes.com/2014/06/30/us/medical-boards-draft-plan-to-ease-path-to-out-of-state-and-online-treatment.html.

92b R. Steinbrook, "Interstate Medical Licensure: Major Reform of Licensing to Encourage Medical Practice in Multiple States," *Journal of the American Medical Association* 312, no. 7 (2014): 695–696.

93 Z. Landman, "Mobile Health Lets Doctors Practice Like It's 1950," *Huffington Post*, November 12, 2013, http://www.huffingtonpost.com/zachary-landman/mobile-health-lets-doctor_b_426 229 9.html.

94 I. Gal, "Israeli Invention May Spare Visit to Doctor," *YNet News*, November 4, 2013, http://www.ynetnews.com/articles/0,7340,L-444 364 8,00.html.

95a "New Medical Tech Company, MedWand Solutions, LLC, Set to Revolutionize Telemedicine," PRWeb press release, April 28, 2014, http://www.prweb.com/releases/2014/04/prweb11799903.htm.

95b R. Matheson, "Mental-Health Monitoring Goes Mobile," *MIT News*, July 16, 2014, http://newsoffice.mit.edu/2014/mental-health-monitoring-goes-mobile-0716.

96 M. Wardrop, "Doctors Told to Prescribe Smartphone Apps to Patients," *Telegraph*, February 22, 2012, http://www.telegraph.co.uk/health/healthnews/9097647/Doctors-told-to-prescribe-smartphone-apps-to-patients.html.

97 S. Curtis, "Digital Doctors: How Mobile Apps Are Changing Healthcare," *Telegraph*, December 4, 2013, http://www.telegraph.co.uk/technology/news/10488778/Digital-doctors-how-mobile-apps-are-changing-healthcare.html.

98 "How Speech-Recognition Software Got So Good," *The Economist*, April 22, 2014, http://www.economist.com/node/216 011 75/print.

99 J. Conn, "IT Experts Push Translator Systems to Convert Doc-Speak into ICD-10 Codes," *Modern Healthcare*, May 3, 2014, http://www.modernhealthcare.com/article/20140503/MAGAZINE/305039969/1246/.

100 R. Rosenberger, "Siri, Take This Down: Will Voice Control Shape Our Writing?," *The Atlantic*, August 2012, http://www.theatlantic.com/technology/print/2012/08/siri-take-this-down-will-voice-control-shape-our-writing/259 624/.

101 E. Brynjolfsson and A. McAfee, *The Second Machine Age* (New York: W.W. Norton & Co., 2014).

102 K. Kelly, "Better Than Human: Why Robots Will—and Must—Take Our Jobs," *Wired*, December 24, 2012, http://www.wired.com/gadgetlab/2012/12/ff-robots-will-take-our-jobs/all/.

103 D. Bethel, "Doctor Dinosaur: Physicians May Not Be Exempt from Extinction," *KevinMD.com*, November 9, 2013, http://www.kevinmd.com/blog/2013/11/physicians-exempt-extinction.html.

104 E. Wicklund, "Korean Doctors Fight Back Against mHealth," *mHealth News*, November 27, 2013, http://www.mhealthnews.com/blog/korean-doctors-fight-back-against-mhealth.

105 J. D. Rockoff, "Robots vs. Anesthesiologists," *Wall Street Journal*, October 9, 2013, http://online.wsj.com/article/SB10001424052702303983904579093252573814132.html.

106a R. Bradley, "Rethinking Health Care with PatientsLikeMe," *Fortune*, April 15, 2013, http://fortune.com/2013/04/15/rethinking-health-care-with-patientslikeme/.

106b "The Computer Will See You Now," *The Economist*, August 16, 2014, http://www.economist.com/news/science-and-technology/21612114-virtual-shrink-may-sometimes-be-better-real-thing-computer-will-see.

106c G. M. Lucas, J. Gratch, A. King, and L.-P. Morency, "It's Only a Computer: Virtual Humans Increase Willingness to Disclose," *Computers in Human Behavior* 37 (2014): 94–100.

106d "Physician Shortages to Worsen Increase in Residency Training," American Association of Medical Colleges, 2014, https://www.aamc.org/download/153160/data/physician_shortages_to_worsen_without_increases_in_residency_tr.pdf.

106e J. Eden, D. Berwick, and G. Wilensky, "Graduate Medical Education That Meets the Nation's Health Needs," in *Institute of Medicine* (Washington D.C.: The National Academies Press, 2014), http://www.nap.edu/openbook.php?record_id=18754.

107   S. Gottlieb and E. J. Emanuel, "No, There Won't Be a Doctor Shortage," *New York Times*, December 5, 2013, http://www.nytimes.com/2013/12/05/opinion/no-there-wont-be-a-doctor-shortage.html.

108   J. Parkinson, "I Was Invited to a Private Breakfast with ...," *New Yorker*, November 8, 2013, http://blog.jayparkinsonmd.com/post/66394909190/i-was-invited-to-attend-a-private-breakfast-with.

109   "The Doctor Will Email You Now, and Patients Like It," *Science Blog*, August 6, 2013, http://scienceblog.com/65398/the-doctor-will-email-you-now-and-patients-like-it/.

110   "The Doctor Will E-mail You Now," *Consumer Reports*, December 2013, http://www.consumerreports.org/cro/magazine/2014/01/the-doctor-will-email-you-now/index.htm.

111   J. Bresnick, "42% of Docs Fear mHealth Will Lessen Their Power Over Patients," *EHR Intelligence*, October 23, 2013, http://ehrintelligence.com/2013/10/23/42-of-docs-fear-mhealth-will-lessen-their-power-over-patients/.

112   "The Dream of the Medical Tricorder," *The Economist*, November 29, 2012, http://www.economist.com/news/technology-quarterly/21567208-medical-technology-hand-held-diagnostic-devices-seen-star-trek-are-inspiring.

113   E. J. Topol and M. R. Splinter, "Stuck in the Past: Why Are Doctors Still Using the Stethoscope and Manila Folder?," *Medscape*, December 10, 2013, http://www.medscape.com/viewarticle/817495_print.

114   D. M. Knowlan, "Looking Back and Looking Forward: The White Coat Lecture," *Baylor University Medical Center Proceedings* 27, no. 1 (2014): 63–65.

115   "ICU Sonography Tutorial 9—Lung Ultrasound," Critical Echo, accessed August 13, 2014, http://www.criticalecho.com/content/tutorial-9-lung-ultrasound.

116   cyberPhil, "Why Not Teach Ultrasound in Medical School?," *Dr. Philip Gardiner's Blog*, January 9, 2013, http://www.philipgardiner.me.uk/2013/01/why-not-teach-medical-ultrasound-in-medical-school/.

117   J. A. Krisch, "R.I.P., Stethoscope?," *Popular Mechanics*, January 23, 2014, http://www.popularmechanics.com/science/health/med-tech/rip-stethoscope-16414909?utm_medium=referral&utm_source=pulsenews.

118   B. P. Nelson and J. Narula, "How Relevant Is Point-of-Care Ultrasound in LMIC?," *Global Heart* 8, no. 4 (2013): 287–288.

119   B. P. Nelson and A. Sanghvi, "Point-of-Care Cardiac Ultrasound: Feasibility of Performance by Noncardiologists," *Global Heart* 8, no. 4 (2013): 293–297.

120   A. Relman, "A Coming Medical Revolution," *New York Review of Books*, October 25, 2014, http://www.nybooks.com/articles/archives/2012/oct/25/coming-medical-revolution/?pagination=false&printpage=true.

121   E. Rosenthal, "Apprehensive, Many Doctors Shift to Jobs with Salaries," *New York Times*, February 14, 2014, http://www.nytimes.com/2014/02/14/us/salaried-doctors-may-not-lead-to-cheaper-health-care.html.

122   D. Drake, "The Health-Care System Is So Broken, It's Time for Doctors to Strike," *The Daily Beast*, April 29, 2014, http://www.thedailybeast.com/articles/2014/04/29/the-health-care-system-is-so-broken-it-s-time-for-doctors-to-strike.html.

123   D. Shannon, "Why I Left Medicine: A Burnt-Out Doctor's Decision To Quit," *Common Health*, October 18, 2013, http://commonhealth.wbur.org/2013/10/why-i-left-medicine-a-burnt-out-doctors-decision-to-quit.

124   D. F. Craviotto, "A Doctor's Declaration of Independence," *Wall Street Journal*, April 28, 2014, http://online.wsj.com/news/articles/SB10001424052702304279904579518273176775310.

125   D. Ofri, "The Epidemic of Disillusioned Doctors," *TIME*, July 2, 2013, http://ideas.time.com/2013/07/02/the-epidemic-of-disillusioned-doctors/print/.

126   A. W. Mathews, "Hospitals Prescribe Big Data to Track Doctors at Work," *Wall Street Journal*, July 11, 2013, http://online.wsj.com/article/SB10001424127887323551004578441154292068308.html.

127   V. McEvoy, "Why 'Metrics' Overload Is Bad Medicine," *Wall Street Journal*, February 12, 2014, http://online.wsj.com/news/articles/SB10001424052702303293604579253971350304330?mod=WSJ_Opinion_LEFTTopOpinion.

128   R. Abelson and S. Cohen, "Sliver of Medicare Doctors Get Big Share of Payouts," *New York Times*, April 9, 2014, http://www.nytimes.com/2014/04/09/business/sliver-of-medicare-doctors-get-big-share-of-payouts.html.

129   R. Gunderman, "For the Young Doctor About to Burn Out," *The Atlantic*, February 21, 2014, http://www.theatlantic.com/health/archive/2014/02/for-the-young-doctor-about-to-burn-out/284005/.

130   D. Drake, "How Being a Doctor Became the Most Miserable Profession," *The Daily Beast*, April 14, 2014,

http://www.thedailybeast.com/articles/2014/04/14/how-being-a-doctor-became-the-most-miserable-profession.html.

131 L. Radnofsky, "Medicare to Publish Trove of Data on Doctors," *Wall Street Journal*, April 2, 2014, http://online.wsj.com/news/articles/SB10001424052702303847804579477923585256790.

132 S. Dhand, "The Human Side of Medicine That No Computer Can Ever Touch," *KevinMD.com*, November 27, 2013, http://www.kevinmd.com/blog/2013/11/human-side-medicine-computer-touch.html.

133 D. Diamond, "Hospitals Lost Jobs—Again," *Advisory Board Daily Briefing*, August 2, 2013, http://www.advisory.com/Daily-Briefing/Blog/2013/08/Hospitals-lost-jobs-again.

134 J. Weiner, "What Big Data Can't Tell Us, but Kolstad's Paper Suggests," *Penn LDI*, April 24, 2014, http://ldi.upenn.edu/voices/2014/04/24/what-big-data-can-t-tell-us-but-kolstad-s-paper-suggests.

135 L. Rosenbaum, "What Big Data Can't Tell Us About Health Care," *New Yorker*, April 23, 2014, http://www.newyorker.com/online/blogs/currency/2014/04/the-medicare-data-dump-and-the-cost-of-care.html?printable=true&currentPage=all.

136 J. T. Kolstad, "Information and Quality When Motivation Is Intrinsic: Evidence from Surgeon Report Cards," National Bureau of Economic Research, February 2013, http://www.nber.org/papers/w18804.

137 C. Ornstein, "Beyond Ratings: More Tools Coming to Pick Your Doctor," *ProPublica*, April 8, 2014, http://www.propublica.org/article/beyond-ratings-more-tools-coming-to-pick-your-doctor.

138 Z. Moukheiber, "Grand Rounds Wants to Find the Right Doctor for You," *Forbes*, April 8, 2014, http://www.forbes.com/sites/zinamoukheiber/2014/04/08/grand-rounds-wants-to-find-the-right-doctor-for-you/.

139 L. Abrams, "Study: Hospitals with More Facebook 'Likes' Have Lower Mortality Rates," *The Atlantic*, March 2013, http://www.theatlantic.com/health/print/2013/03/study-hospitals-with-more-facebook-likes-have-lower-mortality-rates/273697/.

140 L. Abrams, "Why We're Still Waiting on the 'Yelpification' of Health Care," *The Atlantic*, October 2012, http://www.theatlantic.com/health/print/2012/10/why-were-still-waiting-on-the-yelpification-of-health-care/263815/.

141 D. Streitfeld, "Physician, Review Thyself," *New York Times*, March 4, 2014, http://bits.blogs.nytimes.com/2014/03/04/physician-review-thyself/?smid=tw-share.

142 "Consumer Reports Teams with Massachusetts Group to Rate Nearly 500 Primary Care Doctors' Practices," *Consumer Reports*, May 31, 2012, http://c354183.r83.cf1.rackcdn.com/MHQP%20Consumer%20Reports%20Insert%202012.pdf.

143 R. Gunderman, "Why Doctor Ratings Are Misleading," *The Atlantic*, April 2014, http://www.theatlantic.com/health/print/2014/04/why-doctor-ratings-are-misleading/360476/.

144 C. Doyle, L. Lennox, and D. Bell, "A Systematic Review of Evidence on the Links Between Patient Experience and Clinical Safety and Effectiveness," *British Medical Journal* 3 (2013): e 001 570.

145 J. Rossen, "Insult and Injury: How Doctors Are Losing the War Against Trolls," *BuzzFeed*, April 3, 2014, http://www.buzzfeed.com/jakerossen/insult-and-injury-inside-the-webs-one-sided-war-on-doctors.

146 J. J. Fenton et al., "The Cost of Satisfaction," *Archives of Internal Medicine* 172, no. 5 (2012): 405–411.

147 O. Khazan, "Why Aren't Doctors More Tech-Savvy?," *The Atlantic*, January 21, 2014, http://www.theatlantic.com/health/archive/2014/01/why-arent-doctors-more-tech-savvy/283178/.

148 J. Bendix, "Can the Doctor-Patient Relationship Survive?," *Medical Economics*, December 10, 2013, http://medicaleconomics.modernmedicine.com/medical-economics/news/can-doctor-patient-relationship-survive?page=full.

149 R. Harrell, "Why a Patient's Story Matters More Than a Computer Checklist," *NPR*, November 17, 2013, http://www.npr.org/blogs/health/2013/11/17/242366259/why-a-patient-s-story-matters-more-than-a-computer-checklist.

150 I. Bau, "Health 2.0 v.2013: Integration and Patient Outcomes Are Still Driving Health Technology—but So Should Empathy, Caring, and Communication," *Health Policy Consultation Services—Resources for Patient-Centered & Equitable Care*, October 4, 2013, http://ignatiusbau.com/?s=integration+patient+outcomes+health.

151 S. Guglani, "Compassionate Care: A Force for Change," *The Lancet* 382 (2013): 676.

152 E. Topol, "Machinations of the Machine Age," commencement address at Temple University,

2014, http://www.temple.edu/medicine/tusm_grad_speech_topol.htm.

153 "The Future of Jobs: The Onrushing Wave," *The Economist*, January 16, 2014, http://www.economist.com/news/briefing/21594264-previous-technological-innovation-has-always-delivered-more-long-run-employment-not-less.

The Urgent Need to Preserve and Enhance Physician Careers

Jack Cochran and Charles Kenny

The best work anywhere should be the standard everywhere.

Harris Interactive, one of the leading research firms in the nation, has conducted an abundance of research in health care and reached a stark conclusion: "Any discussion with physicians must begin with acknowledging the degree to which fear of liability drives their decisions about diagnostic test and interventions. ... They see tort reform as the elephant in the room that policy experts do not discuss."

The liability issue *is* the elephant in the room, and too often academics and policy experts fail to recognize this. It is one of the major underlying reasons why, as Harris Interactive has found, "the practice of medicine is ... a minefield today. ... Physicians today are very defensive—they feel under assault on all fronts."

Harris Interactive found that "the majority of physicians [54 percent] are pessimistic about the practice of medicine today." This is disturbing on many levels. When one considers the challenge ahead—achieving the Institute of Medicine's goals, reaching the Triple Aim, and implementing the Affordable Care Act—this level of pessimism is unsettling.

Transformational change in the U.S. health care system seems inevitable in the years to come, yet Harris Interactive found that "compliance with change depends on how much fight the docs have left in them. Some are still fired up to fight it, while others have already been beaten down."

This is as astonishing as it is alarming—the idea that some physicians may be too *beaten down* to lead us to a transformed health care system. This notion notwithstanding, an argument is often heard that the liability issue is exaggerated by physicians. When physician voices from the front lines of care are tuned out, as is sometimes the case, malpractice fears are dismissed. A lengthy indictment of physicians' malpractice concerns by Maggie Mahar in the HealthBeat Blog titled "Myths about Medical Malpractice: Part 2, Crisis or Hoax?" reported that "only" 42 percent of doctors are ever sued.

"Only" 42 percent? The article asserts that physicians' fears of litigation are "exaggerated." But when you dig a bit deeper into the issue—into what is on the minds of doctors—the fear of litigation is understandable and all too real.

The American Medical Association (AMA) reports that more than 60 percent of physicians over age fifty-five "have been sued at least once,"

Jack Cochran and Charles Kenny, "The Urgent Need to Preserve and Enhance Physician Careers," The Doctor Crisis: How Physicians Can, and Must, Lead the Way to Better Health Care, pp. 165-186. Copyright © 2014 by Perseus Books Group. Reprinted with permission.

according to an ABC television network report on the AMA study. The ABC report noted that "although most … claims are dropped or dismissed, the new survey from the AMA shows that most physicians will be sued for malpractice at some point in their careers" and that "the average defense costs between $22,000 for dropped or dismissed claims to more than $100,000 for cases that go to trial, according to data in the report from the Physician Insurers Association of America."

The liability crisis adversely influences the quality of patient care. When doctors overtreat as a defense mechanism—as a large percentage of physicians say they do—this is by definition less than ideal quality. Overtreatment impedes the flow of care, thus impacting access and resulting in a significant waste of dollars, as well as physician and support staff time in clinics and labs. The trauma of being accused of a harmful mistake is not fully appreciated outside the physician community. Doctors worry that if they make that one mistake—miss that one indicator or fail to order that one test—their professional lives could tumble down around them.

Part of our effort to preserve and enhance physician careers means joining together to solve the physician liability crisis. Many physicians and policy makers suggest that the answer is tort reform, and while reform of such laws deserves serious discussion, the liability crisis goes much deeper. Aaron E. Carroll, associate professor of pediatrics at Indiana University School of Medicine, has written insightfully about malpractice. He notes on his blog "The Incidental Economist" that a tiny minority of claims ever reach a courtroom. "The majority of claims [64 percent] are dropped, withdrawn, or dismissed," he wrote on April 16, 2012. Carroll writes that focusing on sensational tort claims "as a means to change the whole system (tort reform) doesn't always make a whole lot of sense."

If Carroll is correct—and we believe he is—then what should we focus on to solve the liability issue? The answer is clear: safety and transparency, which are essential elements of overall quality. Our approach to taking on the liability issue focuses first and foremost on making health care safer for all patients by spreading well-established best practices that significantly improve safety in hospitals and clinics. Second, our approach calls for following the recommendations of the Lucian Leape Institute at the National Patient Safety Foundation that calls for a series of steps, starting with transparency on any medical error.

We can create a much safer health care environment to reduce the overall threat of malpractice actions. Many outstanding facilities throughout the country have dramatically improved safety in their facilities. Among them is Virginia Mason Medical Center in Seattle, which adapted the Toyota Production System to health care more than a decade ago. This lean management approach has transformed Virginia Mason from the ground up, improving quality, safety, access, affordability, patient-centeredness, and efficiency—all the major measures.

The inspiration for the Virginia Mason safety methodology came directly from a Toyota factory floor. Dr. Gary Kaplan, the CEO of Virginia Mason, observed work on a Toyota assembly line. He and a number of his colleagues watched as a worker having trouble with a particular part pulled a cord that ground the entire assembly line to a halt. Supervisors rushed to the scene, collaborated with the worker, and quickly fixed the problem. Kaplan and his team learned that every worker on the line was empowered to stop the line to prevent a defect in a vehicle. Could a comparable system work within health care? Kaplan believed that it could. This would mean empowering every employee at Virginia Mason to pull the cord and stop the line (make a call or send a computer message) if there was any threat of harming any patient in any way. This Patient Safety Alert system has fundamentally changed the safety level at Virginia Mason.

"Patient safety is our foundation," says Cathie Furman, RN, Virginia Mason senior vice president of Quality and Compliance. "Our goal is zero defects, and all our efforts around safety are aimed at nothing less than that."

Virginia Mason has been recognized as one of the safest medical centers in the country. In 2012, HealthGrades, an online source for information about performance levels by physicians and hospitals, recognized Virginia Mason with a Patient Safety Excellence Award, and the Leapfrog Group, which conducts a highly respected national survey on the safety, efficiency, and quality of hospitals, gave Virginia Mason its highest safety rating.

Patient Safety Alerts quickly identify instances where a Virginia Mason team acknowledges an error, apologizes to the patient and the family, and assures the patient that no additional costs related to the mistake will be borne by the family.

In the years since the Patient Safety Alert system was put in place, Cathie Furman says that there is "a direct correlation between the number of [alerts] we have and our cost for liability insurance. As the number of alerts rises, the number of claims and lawsuits goes down."

Transparency is central to the Virginia Mason approach to safety and is also foundational to the approach from the Lucian Leape Institute. The institute was formed in 2007 by the National Patient Safety Foundation to provide both an overall vision and specific strategies to improve the safety of health care delivery. It is named for Dr. Lucian Leape, a Boston surgeon widely recognized as a leading expert on medical safety. Leape and his coauthors enunciated the basic approach to medical safety in a 2009 article titled "Transforming

Healthcare: A Safety Imperative" in *Quality and Safety in Health Care,* a British medical journal:

> We envision a culture that is open, transparent, supportive and committed to learning; where doctors, nurses and all health workers treat each other and their patients competently and with respect; where the patient's interest is always paramount; and where patients and families are fully engaged in their care. In a learning organisation, every voice is heard and every worker is empowered to prevent system breakdowns and correct them when they occur.

Virginia Mason is a model for this approach. When a patient is harmed at Virginia Mason, doctors immediately disclose the error to the patient and the family. The physicians apologize for the mistake and explain precisely what went wrong. The doctors explain what is being done to make sure a similar error is never repeated on any future patient. Cathie Furman notes that the attending physician—not someone from risk management—meets with the family to offer an explanation and an apology. After a complete internal investigation, the physician will go back to the family with a more detailed explanation of what happened and exactly what the protocol will be to prevent such a mistake in the future.

According to the Leape Institute, "the free, uninhibited sharing of information ... is probably the most important single attribute of a culture of safety. In complex, tightly coupled systems like healthcare, transparency is a precondition to safety. Its absence inhibits learning from mistakes, distorts collegiality and erodes patient trust." Other essential safety elements as stated by the Leape Institute include:

- Integrated care platforms;
- Consumer engagement, or "nothing about me without me";

- "Joy and meaning in work," suggesting that "caregivers cannot meet the challenge of making health-care safe unless they feel valued and find joy and meaning in their work"; and
- Restructuring of medical education "to reduce its almost exclusive focus on the acquisition of scientific and clinical facts and to emphasize the development of skills, behaviors and attitudes needed by practicing physicians. These include the ability to manage information; understanding of the basic concepts of human interaction, patient safety, healthcare quality and systems theory; and possession of management, communication and teamwork skills."

PAYMENT REFORM

Just as liability is a serious issue facing physicians today, so too is how we pay for medical care in the United States. And on the payment front, encouraging work is being done by a variety of individuals and organizations.

We hold an innate bias concerning payment, of course, believing that the Kaiser Permanente prepayment method serves patients particularly well, and it is certainly one of the options that should be considered in the discussion going forward.

The Commonwealth Fund, a private foundation based in New York, is one of the most intellectually robust health care–related organizations in the United States. The fund supports excellent research on a wide variety of health care issues with an overall goal of promoting improved quality, access, and efficiency. Some of the foundation's best work has involved studying various ideas pertaining to payment reform. *Confronting Costs: Stabilizing U.S. Health Spending While Moving toward a High Performance Health Care System*, published in early 2013, is a good example. In this report, the Commonwealth Fund Commission on a High Performance Health System recommends

a set of synergistic provider payment reforms, consumer incentives, and system wide reforms to confront costs while improving health system performance. ... Payment reforms would: provide incentives to innovate and participate in accountable care systems; strengthen primary care and patient-centered teams; and spread reforms across Medicare, Medicaid, and private insurers.

With better consumer information and incentives to choose wisely and lower provider administrative costs, incentives would be further aligned to improve population health at more affordable cost. Savings could be substantial for families, businesses, and government at all levels.

Another Commonwealth Fund report in August 2013 by Steve Guterman titled "Wielding the Carrot and the Stick: How to Move the U.S. Health Care System Away from Fee-for-Service Payment" noted that "not only does fee-for-service payment fail to provide incentives for efficiency, quality, or outcomes, it encourages the provision of unnecessary care and often discourages coordination of care and management of patients across providers and settings."

The call for a shift away from fee-for-service to payment for population health grows stronger each day. This approach is at the heart of the Alternative Quality Contract (ACC) created by Blue Cross Blue Shield of Massachusetts. Thus far, provider organizations working under the AQC report strong quality improvements. Whether the contract will prove to control costs over a sustained period of time is yet to be determined, but early indicators are promising.

A CEO Council report on payment reform in November 2012 titled "Remaking Health Care:

Change the Way Providers Are Paid" echoes the call to shift away from fee-for-service to "explicitly gear our system around population health" and to "reshape financial incentives to meet the goal of population health, and build capacity and reimbursement systems to support it." The council calls for transparency as well as "uniform standards for health-care service quality, performance and price transparency so consumers can make value choices. And it should encourage states to follow suit." In a round-table discussion about the report moderated by the *Wall Street Journal*'s Laura Landro, Mark Bertolini, CEO of Aetna, observed: "What happens in our system is if you get paid by a unit of service, you do more units of service. Our notion was to shift to population management. You assess the disease burden, the demography and the trends in the community and build a system and budget around that. You reward the system for improving the productivity and health of the population they serve."

Bertolini also invokes the transparency theme, calling for "a true market where people understand what the prices are for health care. Today, that's concealed. Imagine a supermarket where you go in with your cart and pull items off the shelf with no prices on them. You take it up to the counter. It's scanned. The clerk swipes your card and says, 'In thirty days you'll get your credit card bill, and you'll know how much your groceries cost.' Would you shop there? But that's how the health care system works. We need to create transparency in the system so people can understand how much health care costs."

One of the most powerful payment reform trends involves employers, especially large companies with significant market power, getting involved with the care of their employees—both its cost and quality—as never before.

Tom Emerick, coauthor with Al Lewis of *Cracking Health Costs*, has worked as a benefits consultant with some of the largest corporations in the country. Emerick predicts that we are "on the verge of a sea change in how employers pay for health care" and that employers are focused on moving toward paying for quality outcomes rather than procedures. Emerick says that the enormous cost burden on all corporations of employee health coverage has employers focused on benefits as never before. The old definition in the employer world was "is care delivered to a gold standard?" But Emerick says that major employers have a new definition: "First is the care needed and appropriate, then is it delivered to a gold standard?"

Having worked with many Fortune 500 employers, Emerick sees the Centers of Excellence model adopted by Walmart as an important future component of health benefits. The idea is to identify Centers of Excellence where the care is measurably excellent on quality and where price is competitive. Walmart has identified a number of such centers and will be sending tens of thousands of patients to these provider organizations in the years to come with the goal of better care at a lower cost. Emerick predicts that within no more than five years this will be the norm among Fortune 500 companies.

Paul Grundy has an interesting take on the payment reform issue, suggesting that we need "multiple dials," including a mixture of fee-for-service, capitated global payments, bundled payments, and more. "If you think about it that way and you are not afraid to put those dials in place, then you can adjust them based on what is working and what is not," says Grundy. "No matter how many dials you have, some will be gamed, and you have to have the ability to make adjustments."

The best work anywhere should be the standard everywhere.

Where does this leave us? There is so much good work being done in our country today—so many physicians who have stepped forward, worked cooperatively with others, and triggered breakthrough improvements—yet far too often these improvements fail to spread. And too many physicians are sitting on the sidelines, working in often dysfunctional organizations unable or unwilling to adopt some of the best that the Learning Coalition has to offer.

We do not minimize the challenge that spreading innovation presents. And we respect the notion that cultures are quite different in health care organizations and that adapting proven solutions often requires adjustments to fit comfortably into a particular local culture.

The aspiration to turn the best work *anywhere* into the standard *everywhere* still seems far away. Yet there is no doubt that the building blocks for a better future are out there. We see unmistakable signs of growing ranks of physicians who are adopting the healer-leader-partner approach. We see it from Christine Sinsky, Tom Bodenheimer, and their colleagues, who found not just an example or two but *twenty-three high-functioning primary care practices*. Their findings and recommendations, if spread throughout the country, could help transform primary care in our nation.

The grassroots initiative at Harvard Medical School to not only save but also greatly enhance the primary care program is encouraging, as is the healer-leader-partner approach by young physicians joining together with Andrew Morris-Singer in founding and expanding the group Primary Care Progress. National leadership by Paul Grundy and others who embody the concept of healer-leader-partner has provided inspiration and direction to thousands of physicians seeking to innovate on behalf of their patients.

And when we imagine physicians summoning their inner idealist and joining with others to dream of patient-care breakthroughs, we are captivated by the efforts of Paul Minardi, Jeff Weisz, and Mike Kanter as they brainstormed about how to better care for large populations of patients to eliminate perilous gaps in care. (We think they deserve a plaque at Paul's Cafe in Tarzana!)

Beth Averbeck and her colleagues at Health-Partners have recognized the power of physicians as healers-leaders-partners as they acknowledge their obligation to identify and eliminate significant racial disparities in care. Kate Koplan, Rick Lopez, and their colleagues at Atrius Health in Massachusetts have had the courage to explore and compare the highest and lowest performers on a variety of metrics—work that clearly subsumes physicians' egos and makes amply clear their deep commitment to the well-being of patients.

NEXT STEP: PHYSICIAN COMPACT

So the question is, what can we do to encourage more doctors to step forward as these physicians have done? We think that part of the answer might involve creating a new deal with doctors—a physician compact.

Physicians are at the heart of our health care system. The article by Rob Nesse, Gary Kaplan, and Jack Cochran asks, "Which stakeholder—physicians, hospitals, health plans, or others—will lead delivery system transformation? *We believe it must be physicians*. Among all providers, physicians have a disproportionate impact on the health care system, and therefore have a disproportionate opportunity and responsibility to lead change" (emphasis added). It is impossible to imagine solving the U.S. health care challenges of quality, safety, access, and affordability *without* physicians playing a leading role. "Physicians are ideally positioned, and in fact compelled, to take responsibility for helping shape the health care system—not just their own practice," the article states.

Jeff Weisz, one of the visionaries back at Paul's Cafe, made this observation in his book *It's a Great Time to Be a Physician*: "Sustainable healthcare systems can be built only if physicians lead the transformation, and if we are leaders in the teams and systems that deliver health care. This is really a change in our identity. We were trained to deliver health care not to lead."

Our nation urgently needs a unified effort by physicians to improve all aspects of health care. The foundational belief of this book is that fixing the physician crisis is a prerequisite to achieving access, quality, and affordability throughout the United States.

Remember those five hundred frustrated physicians interviewed during the Listening Tour in Colorado? Regrettably, that is the current state of countless doctors throughout the nation. And they need our help, just as those physicians in Colorado needed help to be liberated and supported to care for their patients. Doctors in our nation need our support to preserve and enhance their careers—*so they can do their best for patients.*

We need a new deal with physicians. Just as the doctors in Colorado needed preservation and enhancement of careers to trigger a surge in the quality of patient care, so too do we need a comparable deal now for the nation. This work to preserve and enhance physician careers is so critical that, as Bodenheimer says, "the Triple Aim should be a quadruple aim, with clinician and staff satisfaction a necessity to achieve the other three aims."

Physician compacts are deals that health care organizations make with their doctors. More and more organizations throughout the country are turning to compacts to make as explicit as possible what the organization can expect from doctors and what doctors can expect from the organization. In crass terms, the compacts are gives and gets. *We the organization will do x; we the doctors will do y.* (Compacts were originated by Jack Silversin of Amicus Consulting in Cambridge, Massachusetts.)

OUR OBLIGATION TO PHYSICIANS

If we were to sketch a compact—an agreement between physicians and *everyone else* (patients, hospitals, health plans, employers, administrators,

government, and other clinicians)—what might it look like? As stakeholders in the transformation of health care in the United States, we pledge to provide the essential elements that support physicians in their lifesaving work. Specifically, we pledge to work to

- Preserve and enhance physician careers,
- Support primary care by being sure the entire team takes responsibility for the work,
- Take on the liability crisis on behalf of all physicians in all specialties and improve safety of care to reduce the threat of malpractice actions against physicians, and
- Strengthen and expand the Learning Coalition.

Preservation and enhancement of physician careers was an important element that triggered the dramatic turnaround in quality as well as patient and provider satisfaction in Colorado. Preservation and enhancement means creating precisely the kind of systems that Sinsky, Bodenheimer, and others reported on that enable doctors to operate at the top of their license: to distribute work that can be done by others to others, to enable doctors to do what they are best at and trained for, and to do the work that brings physicians the greatest sense of professional satisfaction *and most benefits patients.* But there are also important benefits for physicians and other clinicians as well. Adopting innovative methods that exist today alleviates the unsustainable pressures that doctors face and enables primary care physicians to see all of their patients during the course of the day and complete all charting and other administrative work by early evening.

Here is what we do *not* mean by preservation and enhancement of physician careers. We do not mean returning to the good old days of physician pampering whereby doctors were autonomous and reluctant team players. It is in no way about doctors who feel victimized or entitled.

Support Primary Care

The building blocks that Bodenheimer and his colleagues identified from their study of primary care clinics are essential elements that improve the quality of care and the level of physician satisfaction. Is it too much to ask that these elements—listed above—be present in every clinic in our nation within a reasonable period of time?

The great majority of medical students are choosing to go into specialty fields that are more lucrative than primary care. This is why we should support students choosing primary care by providing substantial tuition support and loan relief. This will not only ease the burden on students but will also perhaps attract a greater number of students to select primary care.

This is in no way meant to underrate the immense importance of all of the medical and surgical specialties. Specialty care is crucial, yet experience globally indicates that higher-quality primary care leads to better care overall.

We must also take on the liability crisis to improve patient-care safety and reduce the threat of malpractice actions against physicians. The Harris Interactive analysis is instructive: "Any discussion with physicians must begin with acknowledging the degree to which fear of liability drives their decisions about diagnostic tests and interventions."

This is where the combination of profound safety improvement coupled with transparency can be a game changer. The powerful combination that we described above between the Virginia Mason Patient Safety Alert system along with the Lucian Leape Institute approach to dealing with errors can fundamentally change the nature of the liability threat to physicians.

Strengthen and Expand the Learning Coalition

The Learning Coalition aspires to become the "innovation accelerator" (in Arnie Milstein's words) that we need. There are many obstacles, but the most difficult and insidious is the large number of health care organizations that are, in the words of Maureen Bisognano, "hanging on, clinging to the status quo."

This approach is antithetical to the best interests of patients and providers. The reality is that the early adopters/innovators from the Learning Coalition have taken the risks and done the early work that shows a better way in dozens of areas within health care.

PHYSICIANS' OBLIGATIONS TO PATIENTS AND OTHER TEAM MEMBERS

In some ways, the other side of the compact—physicians' responsibilities to the patients and other team members—mirror our responsibilities to doctors. In return for the above, physicians agree to expand their horizons and recognize and acknowledge that the world is changing at a dizzying pace, and they also agree that physicians must change with it.

Physicians pledge to

- Become healers-leaders-partners and
- Become active members of the Learning Coalition.

Physicians have a disproportionate impact at the front lines of care and therefore must accept disproportionate responsibility and accountability. And when they commit to being healer-leader-partners and active Learning Coalition members, they are committing to providing better care for their patients. Physicians must accept a much broader role than ever before and engage on all issues that impact the health of their patients—whether those issues involve access, safety, quality, affordability, or anything else. It is essential that all physicians learn to become superb team members working collaboratively with *all* other care team members with a laser focus on what is best for the patient.

Join the Learning Coalition

Physicians as healer-leader-partners have a responsibility—to their colleagues and especially to their patients—to actively seek best practices and to bring those approaches home and apply them. Identifying proven practices in other organizations and applying them at the home organization to improve quality, safety, and efficiency is an effective way to shrink the chasm between the best performers in health care and the rest.

Berwick has noted that "It's not hard to describe the health care system we want; it's not even hard to find it. … Among the gems and the jewels throughout our country … lie answers; not theoretical ones, real ones, where we can go and visit these organizations and see how good they are."

Doctors have a responsibility to advocate for and lead the spread of best practices and to find innovations that impact patients and bring them home. If a physician group is having difficulty with flow in primary care, it is the doctor's job to find a place (or places) where the problem has been solved. Visit that facility, learn the solution, and bring it home. Physicians have a responsibility to know the best in any given area and to apply it in their own hospitals and clinics.

No health care organization holds a monopoly on best practices. Someone somewhere is doing something important in terms of care better than you are. We love the story of what Cincinnati Children's did to improve its cystic fibrosis program—that they identified the best and went there to learn. This search for the best should create a crisscross pattern throughout the country of provider organizations seeking out the very best performers in every area.

Here is where Arnie Milstein's analogy is so apt. As he puts it, "We need to shrink that gap between top performers and all the rest by a lot. Think about a race in the Olympics: the last sprinter in the 100-yard dash doesn't finish two or three seconds after the leader, he or she finishes two- to three-tenths of a second after the leader. All Olympic sprinters are excellent. That's what we need in medicine—everyone crossing the finish line on the heels of the winner."

Again where does this leave us? In a way, it brings us back to where we began, with physicians alleviating suffering, improving the quality of patients' lives, and even saving their lives.

If we are true to our mission to preserve and enhance physician careers so that they may provide the finest possible care, then we are drawn back to Antonio and his dad and to Lexi and Syd Stark and their parents. Antonio and the Stark twins relied on physicians who were deeply engaged in and passionate about their work and considered it as much a calling as a profession.

Too often today, however, that is not the case for countless doctors. The doctor crisis is a complex variety of forces preventing physicians of all stripes from putting their patients first at every step in the care process—forces such as regulation, bureaucracy, and insurance company interference. (The beauty of KP is that the insurance company partners with KP physicians and hospitals in an integrated system, with the patient front and center.)

We believe that there is a clear pathway to a much improved health care system characterized by access, quality, and affordability, and we believe that this pathway runs directly through the Learning Coalition. Following that pathway requires cultural change. It requires shedding the fear that comes with asking hard questions about one's hospital or practice. It requires asking the question—about every area in your hospitals, clinics, and physician practices—of who is doing what you do *but better*. Who has a much lower rate of falls with injuries than you? A lower infection rate?

A lower readmission rate? Which physician practices have the vast majority of their patients with diabetes under control on all key metrics? Which physician group has a much higher physician satisfaction rate than yours? How did they do it?

Is your organization as diligent about filling care gaps as Paul Minardi, Jeff Weisz, and Mike Kanter at Kaiser Permanente? If not, then some of your patients are going about their lives in an unsafe condition. How can you let that happen when you know that Minardi and his colleagues have a system to solve that problem?

Have you developed a marketplace of innovation/ ideas within your organization? Do you convene the highest and lowest performers on a variety of meaningful outcome measures to engage in learning, as Drs. Rick Lopez and Kate Koplan did at Atrius Health in Massachusetts? Are you engaged in "the free, uninhibited sharing of information" that the Leape Foundation says is essential for authentic transparency and safety?

What do you think patients want? Do they want a hospital or a doctor who not only isn't the best but also doesn't know who the best is? A hospital or doctor failing to look actively for other provider organizations from whom they can learn? Do patients want their providers to decide *not* to participate in the Learning Coalition?

If we are going to realize Arnie Milstein's vision of all "crossing the finish line on the heels of the winner," then health care must become a much stronger learning industry. This means that the Learning Coalition must be a marketplace where innovation and ideas are discussed and traded, where everyone teaches what they know best and everyone else learns, or as Maureen Bisognano puts it: "All teach, all learn."

Physicians as healer-leader-partner have a responsibility to their colleagues and especially to their patients to actively seek frontline best practices and to bring those approaches home and apply them. They have a responsibility to make clear that this work involves investments in physician leadership development and training that yield important dividends for patients.

Sinsky and Bodenheimer have identified twenty-three top performers in primary care. Have you sought to learn from any of them? Visited any of them? Is your answer—as is so often the case in health care—*I am too busy. We are too busy.*

Too busy is surrender to the status quo. Everyone in health care can legitimately make this claim, and yet tens of thousands of members of the Learning Coalition *make time* to go out and find ideas that improve care for their patients. Imagine saying to patients, yes, it is true we have dozens, scores, hundreds, or thousands of capable people working here in our organization, but we are unable to figure out how to spring some of these people free to scout out some of the best work in the country and bring it back so we can improve quality, safety, access, and affordability.

As a nation, as an industry, the only way we can achieve the goal of "the best work *anywhere* as the standard *everywhere*" is if provider organizations launch unending explorations for innovations and ideas—for work that is better than what they have and that will improve the quality of care.

The foundational belief of this book is that fixing the physician crisis is a prerequisite to achieving excellence in access, quality, and affordability throughout the United States, and it is impossible to imagine reaching this goal without physicians playing a leading role in making health care a far stronger learning industry than it is today. If more physicians take on the role of healer-leader-partner and actively engage with the Learning Coalition, there is no doubt that we can bring great joy to the practice of medicine—that we can enable physicians to have the resources and time they need to put patients first every time.

PART IV

Medical Sociology: An Applied Approach

Throughout this book, we have discussed the fundamental concepts of medical sociology, from understanding the upstream perspective of health to how technology can affect the delivery of health care. As we conclude this book, we wanted to provide an applied perspective for the concepts we discussed earlier. For instance, in Part I, we learned about health disparities, but in this part we will discuss how we address these disparities. In this final part, we will also go one step further and discuss the meaning of death and dying. Some people consider health care is a right. If it is, then should dying also be a right? Lastly, we will look at health care delivery: Will the increase in technology close the gaps in integrative care or widen them? This question and many more will be asked throughout this part.

The first article, "What Should We Do to Reduce Health Disparities?" discusses what the U.S. Department of Health and Human Services (DHHS) is doing to address the upstream effects on our health. In 1979, DHHS created the program Healthy People, whose main goal was improving the health of the American people. Today, Healthy People currently updates its objectives every ten years, with Healthy People 2020 being the latest. In this article Barr examines how Healthy People 2020 is doing and what could be improved. He asks the question why race is still a health disparity. Is it an unconscious bias that our society is reinforcing? How can this be prevented? Are there unknown health disparities yet to be examined? These are the questions that should be asked when applying medical sociology.

The next article, "The Affordable Care Act: Reviewing Impacts and Opportunities," takes an in-depth look at the biggest health policy reform in recent years, the Patient Protection and Affordable Care Act (ACA) of 2010. With the health care exchanges (websites that allow individuals and families to buy health insurance) now in full swing, Americans across the nation now have access to health care coverage, many with subsidies to pay for it. Theoretically, increasing access to health care should improve health outcomes and disparities. Yet, there is a still a struggle with the basic preventive health initiatives, such as motivating people to complete annual screenings. The next article, "Making a Place for Integrative Care in a Changing Health Care Environment," addresses this struggle and many other concerns such as complementary and alternative medicine (CAM). Are health care providers ready for alternative medicine as a treatment option? The ACA includes provisions that open the discussion for CAM providers to be part of the continuum of care of the patient. We shall see in the coming years how this opportunity will play out.

With the increased use of CAM and the public having access to health care at their fingertips (through technology), are patients now consumers? In Ebeling's article, "The Promotion of Marketing-Mediated Diagnosis: Turning Patients into Consumers," she asks that same question: What happens when the patient has access to the same knowledge and information as the health care provider? Does it influence clinical decision making? The key players in health care (insurance companies, providers, pharmacies, health systems, and patients) believe it does. The pharmaceutical industry spends billions on advertising to patients and teaching health care providers, which creates the perfect storm of commercialized diagnosis. Take a look at the commercials during the Super Bowl, how many of them are for pharmaceuticals? Do you think the American public has the education and the ability to make critical decisions about their health? Does medical marketing hurt or harm the relationship between patient and health care provider?

In Higgs and Jones's article they discuss anti-aging medicine and the aging body. They argue that those who search for anti-aging cures are "cultural dupes." Because of cultural norms and advertisements aging is viewed as a disease and with every disease there needs to be a cure. Is this the case? Is aging no longer part of life, but a consequence of it? Or is the fear of death driving us to find the cure for aging? In western culture, death and old age go hand in hand and have become a routine. In the hospitals, dying patients are given trajectories and health care providers try to sequester them which can lead to dying being an isolated experience.

If we agree that the public (patients) has the skills to self-diagnosis and be their own health champions, then why not allow them the right to make decisions about their own death? Seale, in his article "Death, Dying, and the Right to Die," examines the culture behind this lucrative decision, and why in wealthier countries (such as the United States) the trajectory of death is a longer process, especially in terminal patients. What do medical sociologists think about this "right" and the awareness of dying? Is there a new social movement developing in our country or has it always been there?

Our last article, "Increasing the Probability of Social Science Research Leading to Policy Implementation: Lessons Learned over Sixteen Years," examines the ability to transfer social science research into policy implementation. Social science research is critical in improving our society. Davies suggests framing social issues in ways the connect policymakers and communities. It is important to build partnerships and/or interdisciplinary relationships during the research process. Stopping the research once a journal article is published is simply not enough anymore; there needs to be follow-up and program implementation. This article looks at the research process on the subject of domestic violence involving children and how the researchers struggled to disseminate information to the community.

In conclusion, while reading this part we encourage you to question the norm, look deeper into research, see where the disconnect is between real-life, academic research, and policy then figure out how to bridge the gap. What are the impacts of our current health policies? These are just a few of the examples of applied medical sociology, but there are many more out there. We encourage you to investigate and explore the world of health care around you.

What Should We Do to Reduce Health Disparities?

Donald A. Barr

In 1979 the U.S. Department of Health and Human Services created *Healthy People 2000,* a national program with the objective of improving the health of the American people by the beginning of the twenty-first century across a range of indicators and conditions. Building on that program, in 2010 the federal government launched an updated version titled *Healthy People 2020,* described as providing "science-based, 10-year national objectives for improving the health of all Americans" (HealthyPeople.gov 2010). The first stated goal of that program is to improve the length and quality of life of the American public. Its second goal is to "Achieve health equity, eliminate disparities, and improve the health of all groups."

While this second goal has broad public and political support, it is important to understand the implications of such a sweeping objective. Consider, for example, the following facts:

- In 2011 the life expectancy for a white baby was 79.0 years, while that for a black baby was 75.3 years, a difference of 3.7 years.
- In 2011 the life expectancy for a female baby of any race was 81.1 years, while that for a male baby was 76.3 years, a difference of 4.7 years. (U.S. Department of Health And Human Services, Centers for Disease Control and Prevention, National Center for Health Statistics 2012)

Both gaps in life expectancy represent a disparity. In nearly all developed societies, girl babies live longer on average than boy babies. The principal source of this disparity is the genetic and biological differences between females and males, although gender-based behaviors also play a role. Few would argue that the goal of the federal government should be to equalize the life expectancy of males and females.

Disparities in life expectancy between white and black babies are different from those between female and male babies. [...] There are few meaningful genetic or biological differences between white babies and black babies, and certainly none that can explain a disparity of 3.7 years in life expectancy. The black/white disparity in life expectancy is instead the result of a combination of social and economic factors that affect living conditions, preferences, behaviors, and access to health care. There is broad consensus that it is the responsibility of the federal government to address these issues and, as a matter of public policy, to reduce the health disparities that they generate.

As defined by the *Oxford English Dictionary*, a *disparity* is an "inequality or dissimilarity in respect of age, amount, number, or quality; want of parity or equality." The health of an 80-year-old is, in most cases, unequal or dissimilar to the health of an eight-year-old. This difference represents a disparity, but not one that necessarily must be reduced as a matter of public policy. It is essential to identify those disparities in health status or access to health care that should, as a matter of public policy, be reduced or eliminated. To do so, I will delineate a framework by which I can separate out those disparities.

This book has, by design, not addressed the many health disparities that exist based on gender. There is substantial evidence that women receive a lower level of treatment for heart disease and other conditions in a way that is analogous to the racial differences in care we have seen. The book also has not considered disparities based on age, and issues of age in the allocation of health care resources. This is not to imply that these disparities are unimportant; rather, those issues exist in a different context, and are caused by a different combination of biologic and social factors. This book has instead focused on health disparities that can be explained by underlying disparities in SES, on one hand, and race or ethnicity, on the other. In doing so, I am adopting an approach that is consistent with the Secretary of Health and Human Services' Advisory Committee for Healthy People 2020, which defined health disparities as, "systematic, plausibly avoidable health differences adversely affecting socially disadvantaged groups" (Braveman et al. 2011, p. S149).

A central message of this book is that there is a complex relationship between SES and race/ethnicity in creating the disparities that are the focus of our concerns. Throughout history, those in a disadvantaged social or economic position have, on average, had shorter lives and lives with greater levels of illness and disability than those in a position of social advantage. Part of this difference is due to the material benefits of social and economic advantage—better nutrition, better housing, better sanitation, and better health care. An additional part is due to the deleterious effect a position of social disadvantage has on individual attitudes and behaviors, with much of that effect translating over time into illness and premature death.

Beyond the effects of a position of disadvantaged SES, there is a second effect of being a member of a racial or ethnic group that faces discrimination that extends beyond SES. The experience of discrimination, especially when accompanied by a sense of powerlessness to confront that discrimination, is associated with measurable differences in cellular and physiologic functioning that, over time, lead to increased illness in a way that is analogous to the effects of SES disadvantage. When the effects of SES disadvantage and racial/ethnic discrimination are combined—as they so often are—the inevitable result is a marked disparity in health. A black baby can expect to live 3.7 years less than a white baby not because of any inherent qualities associated with being black, but because of the different ways our social and economic system impacts babies who are black.

The first aspect, then, of my framework to assess health disparities is to separate out those that have, principally, a biologic cause from those that have a social or economic cause, and to focus my attention on the latter.

When the plague was ravaging Europe in the fourteenth century, those in a position of SES disadvantage were more likely to die. When tuberculosis was endemic in Europe at the turn of the twentieth century, a seamstress with low SES was more likely to die from it than was the son of a wealthy family […]. Throughout history, political and economic systems have struggled with the issue of economic inequality […]. The level of inequality within a society, measured in any number of ways, is strongly associated with the overall health within that society. We will not be solving any time soon the inequalities of social or economic position that have existed within societies for millennia. Nor will we be able to eliminate the disparities in health status that stem from those inequalities. We can, however, focus our attention on reducing those disparities in health that are due to a fundamental inadequacy of the social or economic resources that are necessary for human existence, resources that are well within the capability of modern, industrialized societies to provide. These resources were defined in 1948 at the time of the creation of the United Nations, as part of its Universal Declaration of Human Rights: "Everyone has the right to a standard of living adequate for the health and well-being of himself and of his family, including food, clothing, housing and medical care and necessary social services, and the right to security in the event of unemployment, sickness, disability, widowhood, old age or other lack of livelihood in circumstances beyond his control" (United Nations 1948, Article 25).

Nobel Prize–winning economist Amartya Sen describes what he refers to as the "instrumental freedoms" necessary to unfettered human existence. These include basic political freedoms, as well as social and economic freedoms, "which influence the individual's substantive freedom to live better. These freedoms are important not only for the conduct of private lives (such as living a healthy life and avoiding preventable morbidity and premature mortality), but also for more effective participation in economic and political activities" (1999, p. 39).

The second aspect of my framework to assess health disparities is to identify those disparities that are based on SES inequality and reflect the absence of the basic resources and opportunities that are fundamental to human existence—the "instrumental freedoms" described by Sen. It is well

within the capability of industrialized societies to provide the minimum level of resources required to live adequately and to pursue the opportunity for full participation in society. Health disparities that stem from a lack of these fundamental human rights and freedoms should be included within our focus.

As part of this focus, I include examination of disparities in access to health care. A basic level of health care is essential for the prevention of avoidable illness and the treatment of illness and injury when they occur. It remains the subject of intense social and political debate within this country as to what that basic level of health care is. Few, though, argue that there is no obligation for our society to provide at least a basic level of care. Federal and state programs such as Medicare, Medicaid, and the State Children's Health Insurance Program have provided for a basic level of care for our most vulnerable groups—children, the poor, and the elderly. Yet as we have seen throughout this book, there remain instances when illness is not prevented and serious medical conditions are not adequately treated due to the lack of economic resources on the part of the patient. All too often those without the resources to pay for that treatment are black, Hispanic, or of another racial/ethnic minority group.

In 1999 Congress instructed the federal Agency for Health Care Research and Quality (U.S. Department of Health and Human Resources, Agency for Health Care Research and Quality 2005, p. 13) to identify and monitor "prevailing disparities in health care delivery as it relates to racial factors and socioeconomic factors in priority populations." In establishing this political mandate, the federal government has helped us to define a third aspect of my framework to assess those disparities that are based on race or ethnicity alone, without an underlying basis in SES.

As I have discussed in this book, a principal source of health care disparities based on race/ethnicity stem from differences in the way physicians and other providers treat people from differing racial or ethnic backgrounds. The elimination of discrimination based on race or ethnicity continues to be one of the top social and political priorities of our society. There is a disturbing level of scientific evidence that our national legacy of racial and ethnic discrimination still lingers in the ways physicians incorporate race and ethnicity into their decisions, with resulting disparities in either access to care or quality of care. These disparities are not due to continued racial intolerance and explicit racism [...]. They are much more likely to be caused by unconscious responses to individuals of certain racial or ethnic groups or to the unconscious but inappropriate uses of racial stereotypes. In this context, the Institute of Medicine report on *Unequal Treatment* defined the racial or ethnic disparities we should focus on eliminating as "racial or ethnic differences in the quality of healthcare that are not due to access-related factors or clinical needs, preferences, and appropriateness of intervention" (Smedley et al. 2003, p. 3).

Based on the framework I have described, I can summarize those disparities on which we should focus our attention for reduction or elimination:

1. Those disparities that have, principally, a social or economic cause rather than a biologic cause
2. As described by the *Unequal Treatment* report, those disparities that are due to racial or ethnic differences in health care that are unrelated to access, clinical appropriateness, or patient preferences
3. Those disparities based in SES inequality that reflect the absence of the basic

resources and opportunities fundamental to human existence

It is possible to identify five basic steps we as a society can take to address and reduce these disparities:

1. Take explicit measures to eliminate unconscious race bias and ethnic bias as a cause of health disparities.
2. Monitor patterns of care to identify disparities when they exist.
3. Strengthen the physician-patient relationship, especially when physician and patient are from differing backgrounds.
4. Increase the racial and ethnic diversity of the medical profession and other health professions.
5. Assure access to care through universal health insurance.

ELIMINATE UNCONSCIOUS RACE AND ETHNIC BIAS AS A CAUSE OF HEALTH DISPARITIES

While we may never be able to eliminate all health disparities that stem from differences in SES, we certainly should be able to eliminate health disparities that are due to the way in which our system of health care responds differently to people of differing race or ethnicity. Those in minority racial or ethnic groups often face disparities caused by economic barriers to care. Those barriers, as discussed above, are primarily due to differences in SES. Beyond disparities caused by differences in SES, a disturbing pattern of disparities persists, apparently as a result of racial/ethnic biases that persist among physicians and other health care providers. [...] These residual biases are unconscious and unintended, and do not represent the type of explicit racism that characterized much of the history of our country.

How are we to consciously change psychological processes that are invoked on an unconscious level? This is a dilemma that has faced those who study the psychology of bias for years, if not decades. Piper described how unconscious race bias exists in "thoughtful, well-intentioned, and conscientious individuals who nevertheless have failed adequately to confront and work through their own prejudices. … Such individuals are being neither disingenuous nor hypocritical when they deny that a person's race … affects their judgment of her competence or worth" (1990, p. 299). Piper goes on to suggest that the only way to prevent unconscious biases from influencing our actions is to "scrutinize our social behavior even in situations in which we sincerely believe ourselves to be above … discrimination" (p. 289).

Stangor and colleagues (2001) summarized the research of others and demonstrated in their own research that openly confronting and discussing unconscious racial stereotypes can go a long way toward reducing those stereotypes. Their research showed that it is more effective for whites to discuss with other whites the effects of unconscious stereotypes of blacks, rather than for whites to discuss those stereotypes with blacks. Through a process of joint learning, those who hold negative stereotypes can safely reduce the impact of those stereotypes. As summarized by the authors, "withdrawing the social backing from an idea, in this case a social stereotype, goes a long way toward undermining the power of that idea over an individual thinker" (p. 494).

Geiger (2001, p. 1700) summarized the role of stereotyping and unconscious bias in contributing to health disparities. He emphasizes the incorrect attribution of data gathered from large epidemiologic studies to the case of an individual, […]. "It is important to note that in the vast majority of cases these documented disparities in diagnosis and treatment do not reflect conscious racial bias or calculated cultural insensitivity. Time pressure and cognitive complexity (the need to think about many tasks at once) stimulate stereotyping and what has been called 'application error,' that is, the inappropriate application of epidemiological data to every individual in a group."

Geiger goes on to suggest that cultural gaps that exist between the physician and the patient, based on either differences of SES or differences of race/ethnicity, are a major contributor to perpetuating the inappropriate use of stereotypes. To bridge this cultural gap, he recommends that physicians and other health care providers receive formal training to develop "cultural competence"—a catchphrase that has been widely adopted to describe skills in cultural awareness, sensitivity, and cross-cultural communication that are necessary to bridging the cultural gap between physician and patient. Betancourt and colleagues (2005, p. 499) described the rapid adoption of training programs in cultural competence and emphasized that "the goal of cultural competence is to create a health care system and workforce that are capable of delivering the highest-quality care to every patient regardless of race, ethnicity, culture, or language proficiency."

The Association of American Medical Colleges (AAMC), an organization that sets national standards for medical education in the United States, designed a curriculum to provide medical students and physicians with the skills of cultural competence. It defines cultural and linguistic competence as "a set of congruent behaviors, knowledge, attitudes, and policies that come together in a system, organization, or among professionals that enables effective work in cross-cultural situations. … 'Competence' implies having the capacity to function effectively as an individual or an organization within the context of the cultural beliefs, practices, and needs presented by patients and their communities" (Association of American Medical Colleges 2005, p. 1). In collaboration, the Liaison

Committee on Medical Education, the organization tasked with inspecting and certifying medical schools, established as one of its standards the following: "ED-21. The faculty and medical students of a medical education program must demonstrate an understanding of the manner in which people of diverse cultures and belief systems perceive health and illness and respond to various symptoms, diseases, and treatments. Instruction in the medical education program should stress the need for medical students to be concerned with the total medical needs of their patients and the effects that social and cultural circumstances have on patients' health" (Liaison Committee on Medical Education 2013, p. 11). The AAMC developed a "Tool for Assessing Cultural Competence Training" to assist medical schools in meeting this standard (Association of American Medical Colleges 2013).

Sociologist and ethicist Reneé Fox (2005) reemphasized that cultural competence involves more than developing an awareness of the cultural characteristics of others. Supporting the position of the AAMC, Fox emphasizes the point that physicians and other health care providers need to appreciate and accept "that their own culture also merits enlightened examination, for it is far from a neutral background against which other cultures are measured" (p. 1316). To become fully competent to work in cross-cultural situations, including the situation in which the patient grew up in the same country, speaks the same language, but comes from a different racial or ethnic background, a physician must recognize the risk that he or she may invoke unconscious stereotypes or feelings of aversion and that those unconscious biases may affect clinical decisions in ways that perpetuate unjustified health disparities.

MONITOR PATTERNS OF CARE TO IDENTIFY AND ELIMINATE

UNCONSCIOUS RACIAL/ETHNIC BIAS

Once we acknowledge that unconscious racial and ethnic bias continues to exert an influence on clinical decision making and adopt the goal of eliminating the effects of that bias through education, it becomes essential to have a means of monitoring the process of care to be able to identify the disparities that may have bias as a contributing factor. Historically, many issues pertaining to alleged racial discrimination have been addressed through the courts as possible violations of civil rights laws.

Because of discriminatory outcomes from the perspective of blacks or other minorities confronting racial/ethnic bias, it is understandable that they would feel that the manner in which they had been treated had been a violation of their civil rights. Consider the patient with bone marrow cancer […] and the patient with the sore knee […]. I spoke personally with each of them following their medical treatment. Each was understandably angry. Both had the clear sense that, had they been white instead of black, their treatment would have been different—they would have been provided rapid access to the care their clinical condition warranted. To them, they had been victims of unwarranted and illegal racial discrimination. […] It makes little difference to the victim of racial discrimination if that discrimination was enacted consciously or unconsciously.

There are two principal ways to address disparities in health care that may violate federal civil rights laws. The first is through the Office of Civil Rights of the Department of Justice. The second is through the Office of Civil Rights of the U.S. Department of Health and Human Services.

Addressing possible racial discrimination in health care as a matter to be resolved through the courts is extremely difficult, due to an interpretation of civil rights laws by the Supreme Court in the case of *Washington v. Davis* (426 U.S. 229

1974). In a case involving employment rather than health care, the Court held that, to find that an action had violated the civil rights of an individual or a group, the person or group alleging the violation must prove that the person who had acted in a discriminatory manner had intended to discriminate. Without proving the intent to discriminate, documenting a discriminatory outcome usually is not enough to prove that an action had violated federal civil rights laws.

This doctrine, often referred to as the "intent doctrine," makes it extremely difficult to approach possible civil rights violations through the courts. As described by the Equal Justice Society, a national civil rights advocacy organization, "The doctrine requires plaintiffs to prove the near-impossible: a decisionmaker's specific intent to discriminate. If a plaintiff cannot overcome this hurdle, the law will not recognize the discrimination he or she has experienced, even though some form of discrimination has come into play."

The Office of Civil Rights (OCR) of the U.S. Department of Health and Human Services addresses the issue of racial discrimination in health care from a different context, uses different remedies, and applies somewhat different standards. Rather than addressing instances of possible discrimination through the courts, OCR has the authority to recommend that a provider—either an individual, hospital, or other health care organization—be denied federal funds through programs such as Medicare and Medicaid. OCR was able to use this remedy extremely effectively in the 1960s to desegregate hospitals and health care facilities, both in the South and elsewhere in the United States. While the issue of school desegregation was often fought out in the courts, that of health care desegregation was redressed fairly smoothly, without substantial court intervention.

OCR publishes guidelines it uses in evaluating cases of possible discrimination in health care. In defining what constitutes illegal discrimination, OCR stated that health care providers who receive any federal health care funding "may not, based on race, color, or national origin: Deny services or other benefits provided as a part of health or human service programs. Provide a different service or other benefit, or provide services or benefits in a different manner from those provided to others under the program" (U.S. Department of Health and Human Services Office of Civil Rights 2013). These restrictions were reinforced with passage of the Affordable Care Act (ACA), which states that, "an individual shall not be excluded from participation in, be denied the benefits of, or be subjected to discrimination on the grounds prohibited under, among other laws, Title VI of the Civil Rights Act of 1964, under any health program or activity, any part of which is receiving federal financial assistance, or under any program or activity that is administered by an Executive Agency or any entity established under Title I of the Affordable Care Act or its amendments" (Affordable Care Act Section 1557 2010). OCR acknowledges that discrimination in health care may be intentional or unintentional, and that not all disparities in care are due to discrimination by the provider.

For the purposes of OCR enforcement, determination of a civil rights violation involves a balancing of intent and outcomes. Nonetheless, it would still be extremely difficult for individual patients such as those we have discussed here to successfully claim that their civil rights had been violated because of the care they had received.

However, there is another approach to unconscious discrimination in health care that a growing number of people support. Rather than approaching racial or ethnic discrimination in care as an issue of legal rights, it may be substantially more effective to approach it as an issue of quality. The federal government's 2005 National Health Care Disparities Report indicated that these disparities constitute disparities in quality as much as they may raise issues of civil rights. By defining care that continues to result in racial/ethnic disparities as poor quality care, it becomes possible to address those disparities without raising issues of individual blame, but rather by looking at the outcomes of care at the level of the organization or the system.

Fiscella, with a group of colleagues that included Carolyn Clancy of the U.S. Agency for Health Care Research and Quality, proposed that we address issues of socioeconomic, racial, and ethnic disparities in health care as fundamental issues of health care quality. They proposed five principles to be used in modifying quality review procedures to address disparities in care (Fiscella et al. 2000, p. 2579):

1. Disparities represent a significant quality problem.
2. Current data collection efforts are inadequate to identify and address disparities.
3. Clinical performance measures should be stratified by race/ethnicity and socioeconomic position for public reporting.
4. Population-wide monitoring should incorporate adjustment for race/ethnicity and socioeconomic position.
5. Strategies to adjust payment for race/ethnicity and socioeconomic position should be considered to reflect the known effects of both on morbidity.

Rather than racial disparities in care, consider the analogous issue of a high rate of postoperative infections occurring in a hospital. It would be possible to look at the care of each individual surgeon to determine why his or her patients were getting infections as a complication of surgery. It has proven more effective, however, to look at the entire system within the hospital, and to define key measures to monitor. By reemphasizing the need for quality care in the process of surgery, from the patient being admitted to the hospital to the patient's eventual discharge, one can often reduce infection rates. The way instruments are sterilized or bandages changed may prove to be equally important as the surgeon's technical skill in affecting the rate of infection. If, through careful scrutiny of the process, it becomes clear that an individual surgeon is contributing disproportionately to the infection rate, the peer review system within the hospital can address issues of professional competence and quality. The success or failure of the intervention will be measured by the overall infection rate for all the patients undergoing surgery at the hospital.

If a hospital or system of care were to monitor the patterns of care for racial or ethnic groups proven historically to be at risk for discrimination in care in the same way it monitored infection rates in patients undergoing surgery, it could identify disparate outcomes when they occur. By applying the same level of attention to improving the processes of care, the hospital or care system could identify what the OCR refers to as the "red flag for discrimination"—the finding that patients may not have received the same quality of care because of their race or ethnicity.

The federal government has charged the Joint Commission on Accreditation of Healthcare Organizations (JCAHO) with establishing standards of quality for hospitals and other health care organizations throughout the country, and with evaluating those hospitals and systems on a regular basis to certify that they have maintained those standards. A hospital or care system that is found to have met these standards of quality is accredited by JCAHO. In most cases, only those hospitals or care systems that have received JCAHO accreditation are eligible to receive federal health care funds. Many private insurers also used JCAHO accreditation as a standard of quality in selecting those organizations eligible for payment or participation. The specific quality requirements and standards used by JCAHO can be viewed on their Web page.

Miranda and colleagues (2003) demonstrated that addressing racial/ethnic disparities in care as an issue of quality of care can be very effective. Working with providers in 46 primary care practice groups and six managed care organizations, they used standard quality improvement methods to improve the treatment of depression among a group of 398 Hispanic, 93 black, and 778 white patients. Interestingly, they showed that focusing on improving the quality of care for racial/ethnic minority patients "can improve the quality of care for whites and underserved minorities alike, while minorities may be especially likely to benefit clinically" (p. 613).

Lavizzo-Mourey and Mackenzie (1996) argued that the issue of improving cultural competence should also be addressed as one of quality improvement. In addition to encompassing issues of access to treatment, they suggested that quality review and assessment mechanisms should include an evaluation of the cultural sensitivity and cultural appropriateness of care, in particular as those qualities affect the quality of the physician-patient interaction.

Rather than relying on courts to address the issue of health care disparities that have unintended racial or ethnic bias as a contributor, it may be preferable, as well as more effective, to work with organizations such as JCAHO to incorporate the issue of racial disparities into their assessment of the quality of care. By defining as issues of quality rather than violations of law, the presence of racial or ethnic disparities in care that are, as described above, unrelated to economic access, clinical appropriateness, or patient preferences, it becomes unnecessary to prove blame in order to redress those disparities. Congress or other governmental agencies may need to take the lead in establishing this definition, but once there is wide acceptance of approaching racial disparities in this manner, the issue of eliminating them becomes much more straightforward.

In adopting a quality-improvement approach to the elimination of racial/ethnic disparities in care, it is crucially important to point out a basic issue that must first be overcome. Lurie noted that "until very recently, the bulk of the delivery system had no data on race and ethnic background, so it has been virtually impossible to examine, let alone publicly report, data on the quality of care for various racial and ethnic groups … we cannot make progress without being able to measure and monitor that progress, which means that they need information about the race and ethnic background of enrollees" (2005, pp. 727–28). Before being able to implement a quality-improvement approach to eliminating racial/ethnic health care disparities, it will first be necessary to make universal the gathering of data about the race or ethnicity of patients treated. A study published in 2011 (Robert Wood Johnson Foundation) found that 80 percent of hospitals nationally collect data on the race and ethnicity of the patients they serve, while 60 percent collected data on language. Among health plans, however, the gathering of race/ethnicity data is less consistent, as compliance is voluntary (except in California and Massachusetts, both of which require health plans to collect and report race and ethnicity data).

STRENGTHEN THE PHYSICIAN-PATIENT RELATIONSHIP, ESPECIALLY WHEN PHYSICIAN AND PATIENT ARE FROM DIFFERING BACKGROUNDS

[…] There are numerous instances in which two principal factors contribute to patients who

FIGURE 16.1 Determinants of patient satisfaction with care. Solid arrow indicates a direct relationship; dashed arrow indicates an inverse relationship.

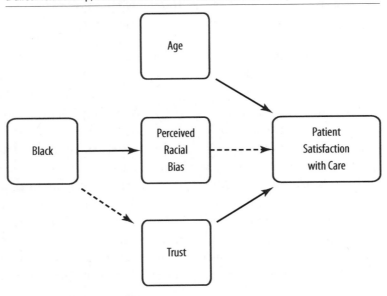

Source: Based on LaVeist et al. (2000).

otherwise are clinically appropriate for care nonetheless not receiving that care:

1. The physician recommends the care, but the patient chooses not to undergo the care.
2. The physician does not recommend the care.

The discussion so far in this chapter has focused on reducing or eliminating disparities stemming from the second reason. To fully eliminate these disparities, we must also address the causes of the first reason—racial/ethnic differences in patients' understanding of and preference for alternative treatment approaches.

Trust is central to the quality of the physician-patient interaction and is a major determinant of the treatment decisions that come out of it. As described by Hall and colleagues, "trust is the core, defining characteristic that gives the doctor-patient relationship meaning, importance, and substance" (2001, p. 613).

When seeing a physician, racial/ethnic minorities approach the encounter with lower levels of trust than whites, and come away from the encounter with lower levels of satisfaction with the care they have received. Doescher and colleagues (2000) documented this in a study of nearly 30,000 patients in a nationally representative sample. Much of the decrement in satisfaction had to do with the minorities' perceptions of the physician's thoroughness, how well the physician listened, and how well the physician explained things.

LaVeist and colleagues (2000) looked into these relationships in more depth in a study of 781 blacks and 1,003 whites with a chronic heart condition that required frequent visits to a physician. They surveyed these patients about their satisfaction with the care they received from the physicians, their perceptions of trust in the health care system, and their perceptions of racial bias inherent in the health care system. They then used multivariate analysis to determine which of the factors they measured, including the patient's age, race, gender, educational level, and type of insurance, were associated with the reported satisfaction with care. The results of their analysis are shown in Figure 16.1.

When looking only at the association between race and satisfaction, they found that blacks were significantly less satisfied with the care they received than whites. However, when they included in the analysis all measured variables, they found that only the patient's age, perceptions of racial bias, and trust in the physician were associated with the level of reported satisfaction. Understandably, the higher the level of the patient's trust in the physician, the higher the reported satisfaction. Conversely, the greater the perceived racial bias, the lower the satisfaction.

After including measures of perceived bias and trust in the analysis, race no longer had a

FIGURE 16.2 Factors that predict receiving cardiac catheterization. Solid arrow indicates a direct relationship; dashed arrow indicates an inverse relationship. The width of the line indicates the strength of the relationship.

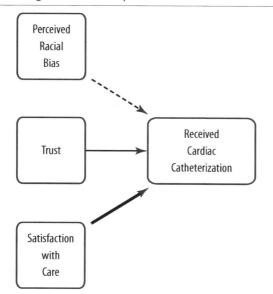

Source: Based on LaVeist et al. (2000).

significant association with satisfaction. In separate analyses, the authors were able to determine that blacks approached the physician encounter with lower levels of trust and higher levels of perceived bias. An individual's perceptions of trust and bias were associated most strongly with satisfaction, independent of race.

The authors did one final analysis: they followed the patients to see which ones actually received a referral to undergo cardiac catheterization. The results of this analysis are shown in Figure 16.2.

Patients with greater perceptions of racial bias in the health care system were less likely to end up with a referral for catheterization. Those who reported higher levels of trust in the system were more likely to end up with a referral. The strongest relationship of all involved patients' satisfaction with the care they were receiving for their heart conditions: the more satisfied the patient, the more likely the receipt of a referral. Knowing from the previous analysis that blacks report lower levels of trust and greater perceptions of bias, and as a result lower levels of satisfaction, it is understandable why blacks typically undergo cardiac catheterization less frequently than whites, other things being equal. Some of the difference can be explained by patients' preexisting perceptions of trust and racial bias in the health care system.

Communication between physician and patient seems to be a key factor in determining whether a patient refuses or avoids a treatment recommended by a physician. In a study of 1,106 adult patients from the Detroit area, Moore and colleagues found that "[patients] who felt their physicians listened more to their concerns were less likely to avoid treatment" (2004, p. 421). In support of this finding, Tucker and colleagues (2003), from the results of focus group interviews with 135 white, black, and Hispanic, low-income patients, found that all three racial/ethnic groups agreed on which factors characterized a high-quality and culturally sensitive interaction between physician and patient: good people skills, effective communication, and a sense of individualized care, in addition to evidence of technical competence.

Ashton and colleagues (2003) reviewed an extensive literature on factors that contribute to racial and ethnic disparities in health care. From this review, they developed a model of the relationship between the patient and the physician, acknowledging that both bring to the clinical encounter factors that may predispose to racial/ethnic differences in care. They suggest that communication is the linchpin in this relationship, with two key aspects to its effect (p. 146):

1. Communication during the medical interaction plays a central role in decision making about subsequent interventions and health behaviors.
2. Doctors have poorer communication with minorities than with others, but problems in doctor-patient communication have received little attention as a potential cause, a remediable one, of health disparities.

Johnson and colleagues (2004) provide support for the latter effect—that doctors tend to have worse communication with minorities. They evaluated videotapes from 458 physician-patient encounters, which included 256 blacks and 202 whites. Using standardized measurement tools to evaluate the content of these videotapes, they found that physicians tended to be more verbally dominant with their black patients, and to have more "patient-centered" communication with their white patients.

Malat (2001) suggests that minority race and lower SES combine to define a "social distance" between physician and patient, each acting independently. Patients with lower SES—independent of race—tend to feel more distant from their physician than those with higher SES. Similarly, blacks and other nonwhites tend to feel more distant from white physicians than from physicians of their own race or ethnicity. Racial/ethnic concordance—the situation in which the patient and the physician are of the same race or ethnicity—contributes substantially to reducing the sense of social distance between patient and physician, and in turn leads to higher levels of satisfaction and trust.

The opposite of a racially concordant relationship is referred to as a racially (or ethnically) discordant relationship. This term does not imply discord between physician and patient, but rather signifies simply a difference in the race or ethnicity of the dyad. Cooper and Powe (2004) reviewed the research on the implications of racial/ethnic discordance in the physician-patient relationship. They confirm that this discordance contributes to lower levels of patient satisfaction and ultimate racial/ethnic disparities in care. Cooper-Patrick and colleagues (1999) also found strong evidence for a positive effect of racial concordance between physician and patient. In a survey of 1,816 adult patients (43 percent white and 45 percent black) treated by one of 64 physicians (56 percent white and 25 percent black), they found that

- the average perceived quality of the physician-patient interaction was no different for white physicians and black physicians
- patients (white or black) in a racially concordant physician-patient relationship rated the quality of their interaction with the physician as higher than those patients in a racially discordant relationship

INCREASE DIVERSITY OF THE HEALTH PROFESSIONS AS A MEANS

FIGURE 16.3 Racial/ethnic diversity of practicing physicians, medical school graduates, and the general population, 2012. Based on population data from U.S. Census Bureau and Association of American Medical Colleges 2013.

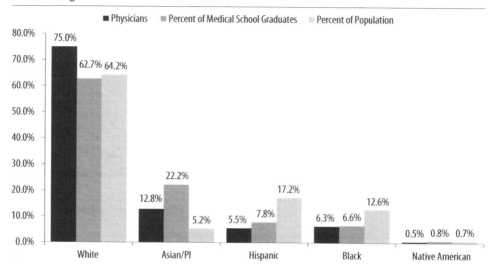

TO REDUCE DISPARITIES

It seems clear that having a medical profession with a level of racial/ethnic diversity that is similar to the racial/ethnic diversity in the general population will optimize the chances of racial/ethnic concordance between physician and patient, which in turn will increase patient satisfaction and trust. This is not to suggest that we should assign patients arbitrarily to a physician of the same race/ethnicity, but rather that we should strive to maintain a profession that reflects the racial/ethnic diversity of the general population.

The Institute of Medicine released two reports in support of this conclusion. The first, entitled *The Right Thing to Do, the Smart Thing to Do: Enhancing Diversity in Health Professions* (Smedley et al. 2001), underscored the importance of enhanced racial/ethnic diversity among physicians. The second report, issued three years later, offers an explicit acknowledgment of the importance of increasing racial/ethnic diversity among physicians as a means of reducing health disparities. "A preponderance of scientific evidence supports the importance of increasing racial and ethnic diversity among health professionals. This evidence … demonstrates that greater diversity among health professionals is associated with improved access to care for racial and ethnic minority patients, greater patient choice and satisfaction, better patient-provider communication, and better educational experiences for *all* students while in training" (Smedley et al. 2004, p. 5).

The Association of American Medical Colleges (2013) publishes data on the racial/ethnic composition of practicing physicians in the United States as well as students graduating each year from U.S. medical schools. Information about race/ethnicity is available for 471,408 physicians who graduated from a U.S. medical school between 1978 and 2008. Figure 16.3 compares the racial/ethnic diversity of those physicians, the racial/ethnic diversity of students graduating in 2012 from a U.S. medical school, and the U.S. population as a whole in 2012.

We can see that whites and Asians make up a larger share of practicing physicians than their respective share in the population. Whites make up approximately the same percentage of medical school graduates as of the population, while Asians make up a percentage of medical school graduates that is more than four times their percentage of the population. Blacks, Hispanics, and Native Americans each make up substantially smaller shares of practicing physicians and medical school graduates than their respective share in the general population. In order to attain the levels of racial/ethnic diversity in the U.S. medical profession called for in the Institute of Medicine reports and other policy documents, there will have to be a substantial increase in the number of medical students coming from the three racial/ethnic groups that are underrepresented in medicine (URM): blacks, Hispanics, and Native Americans.

In the 1960s a number of medical schools nationwide began programs of affirmative action to increase the racial/ethnic diversity of entering medical students. Within the University of California system, several medical schools adopted specific targets to increase the number of URM students in their entering class, and used the race/ethnicity of applicants, along with standard measures of academic achievement, to meet that target. Allan Bakke was a white premedical student who had applied twice for admission to the medical school at the University of California, Davis, being rejected for admission both times. In each year that he had applied, there were URM students who were admitted to Davis with lower college grades and standardized test scores than Bakke's. Bakke filed suit, asserting that his civil rights had been violated because of the racial/ethnic preference given to the URM students who were accepted. His suit was eventually heard by the U.S. Supreme Court, which ruled in 1978 (*Regents of the University of California v. Bakke*, 438 U.S. 265) that UC Davis could not use race/ethnicity as the sole or principal criterion on which to admit students. However, the Court

indicated that race/ethnicity could be used as one of a number of criteria for admissions. The constitutionality of this use of race as one factor among many was reaffirmed in 2003 in another Supreme Court case involving the University of Michigan Law School (*Grutter v. Bollinger*, 539 U.S. 306). The Court ruled that the goal of achieving diversity among students admitted to law school, and as a consequence the diversity of the legal profession, presented a "compelling interest" that permitted the use of race/ethnicity, so long as it is one of a number of factors used in the admissions process.

It seems equally compelling that the medical profession attain a substantially increased level of racial/ethnic diversity, in order to improve the quality of care and contribute to the reduction or elimination of the disparities faced by patients of minority race or ethnicity. Medical schools nationwide are taking another look at the policies they use in selecting students for admission. The predominant model of premedical education was established in 1910, as part of the Flexner Report (Flexner 1910). Writing in 2006, Emanuel suggested that much within the premedical curriculum established by Flexner in 1910 was "irrelevant to future medical education and practice" (p. 1128) and therefore no longer appropriate to select future physicians for the twenty-first century. As a principal means of reducing racial and ethnic disparities in health status and health care, medical schools and the medical profession will need to undertake a thorough reexamination of the criteria by which students are chosen for medical school. The need for increased racial and ethnic diversity within the medical profession is compelling.

The Association of American Medical Colleges has studied the issue of diversity among the students selected for admission to medical schools, and encourages medical schools to look beyond a narrow focus on grades in science classes and standardized test sores in selecting students. They have called for a "Holistic Review" process in which students are evaluated on their academic ability as well as on factors such as commitment to service, cultural sensitivity, empathy, capacity for growth, emotional resilience, strength of character, interpersonal skills, and the life choices they have made. In describing the need for a shift to Holistic Review, Witzburg and Sondheimer (2013, p. 1565) emphasize the role of diversity. "The imperative for a diverse physician workforce in an increasingly diverse society is one important driver of the move to take a more expansive view of excellence in medical student selection. This more comprehensive approach to considering a multitude of factors in evaluating all applicants provides a context for the inclusion of race, ethnic background, language, culture, and heritage, among other factors, in a way that is educationally sound and legally viable."

The need for racial and ethnic diversity goes beyond the medical profession. The same need is seen for a wide range of health professionals, including dentists, pharmacists, physician assistants, registered nurses, nurse practitioners, and licensed practical nurses (Grumbach et al. 1993). In our own research on factors affecting patients' perceptions of what constitutes culturally competent care in the primary care setting, patients from racial and ethnic minority groups cited the diversity of the nonphysician staff as equally important as (and in some cases more important than) the diversity of the physician staff (Barr and Wanat 2005).

ACCESS TO CARE AS A FIRST STEP TO REDUCING HEALTH DISPARITIES

Throughout most of the twentieth century, the United States approached the provision of medical care as largely an issue to be left to private markets. The federal government, in taking a largely hands-off approach, supported the views of Sade, published in the *New England Journal of Medicine* in 1971: "Medical care is neither a right nor a privilege: it is a service that is provided by doctors and others to people who wish to purchase it" (p. 1289). Only in the 1960s did the federal government adopt the Medicare and Medicaid programs, assuring a basic level of health care for elderly and/or poor people. While Medicare has consistently provided for a high level of care, the Medicaid program has faced continuing financial obstacles to providing a high level of care to poor families and children. As described by economist Uwe Reinhardt, "Americans have … decided to treat health care as essentially a private consumer good of which the poor might be guaranteed a basic package, but which is otherwise to be distributed more and more on the basis of ability to pay" (Reinhardt and Relman 1986, p. 23).

As a supplement to Medicare and Medicaid, in 1997 Congress passed the State Children's Health Insurance Program to provide coverage to limited numbers of children in working families earning too much to qualify for Medicaid. Together these three programs provide tax-financed health insurance for the most vulnerable segments of our society. However, a growing number of Americans who are ineligible for these programs face severely restricted access to health care as a consequence of being uninsured. They lack any form of health insurance to assist in paying for needed care. The federal government's National Health Disparities Report summarized the extensive research literature about the health effects of going without health insurance: "The uninsured are more likely to die early and have poor health status. … The uninsured report more problems getting care, are diagnosed at later disease stages, and get less therapeutic care. They are sicker when hospitalized and more likely to die during their stay" (U.S. Department of Health and Human Services, Agency for Healthcare Research and Quality 2005, p. 89).

FIGURE 16.4 Comparing the racial/ethnic composition of the U.S. population with the racial/ethnic composition of the uninsured for the four largest racial/ethnic groups, 2011.

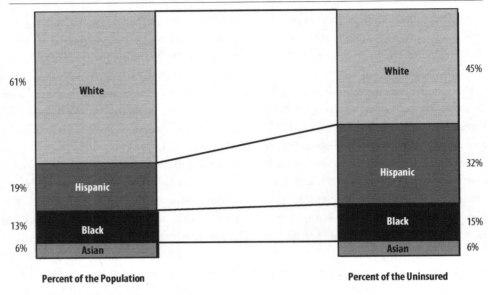

Source: Based on Kaiser Family Foundation 2013.

As the costs of health care have risen in the United States, the number of Americans who are uninsured has risen in concert. Between 1987 and 2010, the proportion of the population who were uninsured grew from just under 12 percent to about 16 percent. (U.S. Census Bureau) This increase came largely among working families. Seventy-nine percent of uninsured families had at least one adult who worked on a regular basis throughout the year. Of those who were working, 80 percent worked full-time. Sixty-two percent of uninsured adults and children lived in families with incomes greater than the federal poverty (Kaiser Family Foundation 2013). The principal cause of going without health insurance is not poverty or unemployment. It is the lack of affordable health insurance for working adults and families.

[...] We saw that nonwhite racial and ethnic groups were disproportionately represented among lower SES groups. The same is true for health insurance. Using data for 2011,

Figure 16.4 compares the racial/ethnic makeup of the U.S. population with the racial/ethnic makeup of the uninsured.

Blacks and Hispanics are overrepresented among the population of those without health insurance, compared to their percentage in the population in general. While health disparities due to economic barriers to obtaining needed health care fall disproportionately on those in lower SES groups, they also fall disproportionately on Hispanics and blacks.

Without health insurance, a low-income individual or family has available only basic health care, typically focused on emergencies. When someone places a call to 911, the paramedics will respond and treat any person with an emergency medical condition, regardless of income or ability to pay. Similarly, all hospital emergency rooms are required, as a matter of federal law, to provide care to any person with a life-threatening condition, a condition causing severe pain, or a woman who is in active labor.

Access to emergency services, while crucially important, is not the principal driver of the health disparities we have discussed. Many if not most of the those health disparities—whether for those in lower SES groups or those from minority racial/ethnic groups—are due to the effects of chronic illnesses such as heart disease, high blood pressure, or diabetes. These conditions are best treated before they have done their damage, and certainly before they have led to an emergency situation. If we are to fulfill the mandate of the Universal Declaration of Human Rights and if we are to provide all members of our society with the instrumental freedoms described by Sen, then we will need to take steps to see that all people have access to a basic level of health care that provides for the identification and treatment of chronic conditions as well as emergency conditions. Until we do so, we will have little chance of attaining a meaningful reduction in those health disparities that fall within the framework I have established.

Identifying the need to provide a basic level of health care to all people that includes prevention, health promotion, and the treatment of chronic diseases as well as emergency coverage is a task that is complicated by the intense politics surrounding health care policy. The United States has considered adopting universal health insurance at a number of times throughout its history. In the 1930s the original architects of the Social Security program had hoped to include universal health insurance as part of it, but were thwarted by the political implications of doing so. The United States again considered universal health insurance following World War II, when the United Kingdom was establishing its National Health Service and other Europe an countries were incorporating universal coverage into their reconstruction plans.

The political fear of any program that seemed to imply a movement toward socialism was sufficient to thwart that effort. Universal health insurance was again considered in the 1960s, at the time of the creation of the Medicare and Medicaid programs; in the 1970s as part of the movement to health maintenance organizations; and in the 1990s as part of President Bill Clinton's national agenda.

Each time universal health insurance was considered, the politics of special interests were able to prevent the adoption of a national program to provide the basic level of care called for by the Universal Declaration of Human Rights. In 2010 Congress passed the ACA, and in so doing took a major step in the direction of providing universal health insurance to its residents. As described by President Obama on the signing of the ACA, "We have enshrined the core principle that everybody should have some basic security when it comes to their health care" (Obama 2010). As the sometimes harsh debate following enactment of the ACA suggests, by enshrining a "core principle" we have taken a significant step toward universal coverage, but we have not gotten there yet. If we are ever to adopt the policy—previously adopted by *all* other developed countries—of providing for the basic level of care necessary to support the opportunity for all people to fully participation in society, we will have to set aside politics.

HOW FAR HAVE WE COME IN REDUCING HEALTH DISPARITIES?

The research documenting health disparities among different groups in the United States spans more than a quarter of a century. As described in this book, there have been numerous government and private reports on the progress we have made and the problems that remain. A 2011 report by the federal government on the status of efforts to reduce these inequalities offered a somewhat discouraging conclusion. "Insufficient evidence exists regarding effectiveness of particular interventions in reducing specific disparities among certain defined populations" (U.S. Department of Health And Human Services, Centers for Disease Control and Prevention 2011, p. 9).

In 2012, Prof. David R Williams of Harvard School of Public Health, one of the leading national voices in the effort to reduce health disparities, published a paper, the title of which carries a poignant message: *Miles to Go Before We Sleep: Racial Inequities in Health*. As described by Williams (p. 279), "Despite thousands of published studies, our current knowledge is limited with regard to the most effective strategies to reduce health inequities, and there is an urgent need to develop a science base to guide societal interventions." While it seems clear that we still don't know the optimal means to eliminate health disparities that are based on inequality of socioeconomic position and race/ethnicity, I hope that the material we have covered in this book will support you in your own effort to work toward attaining this important goal.

READING 17

The Affordable Care Act

Reviewing Impacts and Opportunities

Barrie Tabin Berger

The health-care exchanges required by the ACA went into effect in 2013, and many other significant provisions of the law took effect on January 1, 2014.

Since the 2010 enactment of the *Patient Protection and Affordable Care Act,* the GFOA has monitored the release of both federal regulations on implementation and Congressional initiatives to amend the law in order to determine the opportunities and impacts state and local governments face, as employers. This article summarizes recent federal activity on the ACA, discusses how it may affect state and local governments, and reviews the GFOA best practices that will help state and local governments adapt to health-care reform.

ENROLLING IN THE EXCHANGES

The ACA had a significant year in 2013. Having passed constitutional muster in 2012, a key component of the law became effective on October 1, 2013, when the state exchanges, or marketplaces, opened to provide a place for individuals and small businesses, *including smaller governments,* to purchase health-care coverage (which would begin on January 1, 2014). Sixteen states and the District of Columbia are currently operating their own exchanges, while 15 states have cooperative federal-state partnerships, and 19 have exchanges run by the U.S. Department of Health and Human

Services. Large employers—defined as those with more than 100 employees—will not be eligible to purchase coverage through the exchanges until 2017, and then only at the discretion of their state. To help communities take advantage of the new options in the health insurance marketplaces, HHS released a toolkit for local elected officials.[1] The toolkit includes an overview of the ACA, a sample outreach and enrollment plan that can be tailored to individual communities, a listing of frequently asked questions and answers, resources and information on training sessions, contacts for HHS regional offices, and sample materials that can be used for newsletters, social media, and public events.

While initial enrollment efforts were fraught with technical difficulties, the health insurance exchanges saw a surge of successful enrollments in December 2013, once all the glitches had been ironed out, pushing the number of enrollees to more than 2 million, according to HHS. Open enrollment will continue through March 31, 2014, and the Congressional Budget Office projected last year that 7 million people will have signed up by that date. (Information on enrollment can be found at www.healthcare.gov.)

The health insurance marketplaces have helped implement another of the ACA's most sweeping changes, the requirement that everyone in the

Barrie Tabin Berger, "The Affordable Care Act: Reviewing Impacts and Opportunities," Government Finance Review, vol. 30, no. 1, pp. 66-69. Copyright © 2014 by Government Finance Officers Association. Reprinted with permission. Provided by ProQuest LLC. All rights reserved.

United States, with certain exceptions, have health insurance coverage by January 1, 2014, or pay a penalty. According to HHS, starting in 2014, "the individual shared responsibility provision calls for each individual to have health insurance coverage (known as minimum essential coverage), qualify for an exemption, or make a shared responsibility payment when filing a federal income tax return. Individuals will not have to make a shared responsibility payment if coverage is unaffordable, if they spend less than three consecutive months without coverage, or if they qualify for an exemption based on hardship, religious beliefs, or certain other factors." This mandate was the chief objection to the ACA in the Supreme Court case that challenged the law's constitutionality. However, the Supreme Court upheld the constitutionality of the act, finding that the mandate to purchase health insurance was a valid exercise of Congressional power to impose taxes. The Treasury Department, the Internal Revenue Service, and HHS issued final rules on August 27, 2013, implementing the individual shared responsibility provision of the ACA.[2]

SIGNIFICANT PROVISIONS

As of January 1, 2014, many other significant provisions of the ACA also took effect. In particular, the following "essential benefits" must be included under all insurance plans with no lifetime or annual dollar limits: emergency services; hospitalizations; laboratory services; maternity care; mental health and substance abuse treatment; outpatient or ambulatory care; pediatric care, including oral and vision; prescription drugs; preventive care; and rehabilitative services. In addition, insurance companies may no longer deny coverage because of a preexisting condition; insurance coverage waiting periods of more than 90 days must be eliminated; adult children can now be covered by their parents' health insurance policy until their 26th birthday, if dependent care is offered; and wellness programs that are focused on preventing or eliminating tobacco use can provide awards of up to 50 percent of the cost of coverage, while other wellness programs can offer awards of up to 30 percent. On May 29, 2013, the Departments of Labor, Treasury, and HHS issued a final rule elaborating on the appropriate type and use of wellness programs under the ACA.[3]

While the individual mandate to purchase health insurance took effect on the first of this year, the ACA employer mandate did not. On July 2, 2013, the Obama Administration decided to delay the implementation of the ACA's employer shared responsibility and reporting requirements for one year, until January 2015. The shared responsibility provisions impose monetary assessments on employers, including governmental employers, that have more than 50 full-time employees, if they do not offer affordable health-care coverage of minimum value to employees who work an average of 30 hours per week or more. Administration officials noted that the delay would give employers more time to address the logistical challenges related to offering the appropriate level of health insurance coverage and complying with the requirements of reporting on the coverage offered to employees. On September 5, 2013, the Treasury Department and the Internal Revenue Service issued a proposed rule for health insurance information reporting by employers.[4] A final rule is likely to be issued in the near future, in preparation for the full implementation of both the reporting and shared responsibility requirements on January 1, 2015.

PROBLEMS AND CONCERNS

Despite the administration's best efforts to move forward with implementing ACA provisions and its success in resolving enrollment glitches, the act still has its detractors. Some unexpected situations in 2013 exacerbated the concerns of those who were already wary of or outright opposed to the health-care reform law.

In late November 2013, a number of concerning reports surfaced about insurance companies canceling individual policies that weren't in compliance with the requirements of the ACA. This led to considerable criticism of the president, who had maintained both before and after the ACA was enacted that any consumers who liked their insurance would be able to keep it.

In response, President Obama announced an administrative fix to the act that would allow health insurers to renew existing insurance plans in the individual market that do not meet the ACA's minimum essential health benefits requirements, if permitted by state insurance commissioners, through 2014. The House of Representatives also acted to address this problem by approving H.R. 3350, introduced by Representative Fred Upton (R-Michigan). This legislation would permit individuals to purchase policies that do not comply with the requirements of the ACA through 2014. Several similar bills are pending in the Senate, although Senate Democratic leaders have said they would like to give the president's administrative fix a chance to succeed before moving forward with legislation.

Another potential area of concern came to light in news reports that employers, including state and local governments, are reducing employee hours to avoid having to provide health insurance to employees who work 30 hours a week, which is how the ACA defines full-time employees who are eligible to receive employer-provided health insurance under the act. These reports cited the costs involved in complying with the ACA's 30-hour a week mandate as problematic.[5] On January 2, 2013, the Treasury Department issued proposed rules that address, among other issues, the definition of a full-time employee under the ACA.[6] Even though these are proposed rules, employers can rely on them until a final rule is issued, which should be before the employer mandate goes into effect in January 2015. According to several public-sector health-care consultants and attorneys, ferreting out which employees are full-time versus part-time under the ACA's definitions remains one of the biggest challenges facing the state and local government employers.

In response to the concerns expressed by both public- and private-sector employers about the 30-hour full-time employee definition, Senators Susan Collins (R-Maine) and Joe Donnelly (D-Indiana) have introduced legislation, the *Forty Hours is Full Time Act of 2013 (S. 701)*, to change the ACA's definition of full-time employee to 40 hours. The 30-hour definition, they wrote, "is inconsistent with the traditional description of a full-time 40-hour work week, and coupled with the proposed rule's application and other responsibilities, has caused significant confusion among employers who are struggling to understand and comply with the new requirements. ..." Rep. Daniel Lipinski (D-Illinois) introduced a companion bill in the House, H.R. 2988. Despite considerable discussion in both houses of Congress, this measure, like most legislative initiatives to amend the ACA, has met with considerable resistance from the Senate Democratic leadership and the White House, both unwilling to open the door to a floodgate of proposed changes to health-care reform.

LOOKING FOR OPPORTUNITIES

As regulatory efforts to implement the ACA continue and consumers become more comfortable using the marketplaces to purchase health insurance, state and local government employers continue to explore whether the Act offers opportunities for reducing costs while providing an adequate health insurance benefit to employees. One issue frequently discussed is how state and local government employers will make use of the exchanges, particularly in 2017, when the exchanges will potentially open to large employers. Some experts have suggested that increased health-care costs, particularly related to the retiree population, will require state and local governments to give greater consideration to the use of the exchanges.[7] In fact, several governments, most notably the City of Chicago, Illinois, have already expressed their intention to move their retired workers into the exchanges. The same might ultimately be true for active employees of state and local governments.

Another issue state and local governments may be forced to grapple with relatively soon is the so-called "Cadillac tax." Under that tax, adopted as part of the ACA in 2010, plans that cost more than $10,200 annually for individual plans and $27,500 for family plans in 2018 will be taxed at 40 percent of their costs above that limit—although plan amounts increase for retirees older than 55 and those engaged in high-risk professions. State and local governments are expected to be disproportionately subject to the tax because they typically offer more expensive plans than the private sector.[8] Several local governments including New York, Boston, and Orange County, California, have warned that if they cannot rein in their health-care costs or Congress does not take measures to repeal or amend the tax, it will have significant impacts. Over the years, there have been intermittent discussions about the potential effects of the Cadillac tax. As 2018 inches ever closer, interested parties, including states and localities, are likely to increase their efforts to address the tax.

Republicans in Congress are also likely to continue their slow and steady efforts to amend or repeal parts or all of the ACA. In fact, House Budget Committee Chairman Paul Ryan (R-Wisconsin) recently said he plans to spend a good deal of time in 2014 developing a plan to replace the ACA. While several measures aimed at this goal have passed the Republican-controlled House of Representatives along party lines, none have yet to pass or even be seriously entertained in the Senate, where Democrats remain in the majority. Should that balance of power shift, the ACA's future becomes a bit more uncertain.

CONCLUSIONS

To assist GFOA members with their efforts to understand how their governments may be affected by the ACA, the GFOA Committee on Retirement and Benefits Administration approved a best practice in 2011 on *Developing a Review Process for Implementing National Health-Care Reform*. In this best practice, the GFOA recommends that state and local government employers that sponsor group health plans put a process in place for regularly reviewing the requirements of the ACA to ensure cost-effective compliance balanced against the importance of offering employees and retirees an appropriate health-care benefit. The committee is currently reviewing and updating this best practice to take all newly issued federal regulations into consideration. GFOA members are encouraged to review this best practice, as well as the GFOA's other health-care related best practices, which cover health-care cost containment, health-care plan design, and other postemployment benefits.

The GFOA's Federal Liaison Center will continue to monitor Congressional and regulatory activities related to the ACA and provide members with updates regarding implications for states and local governments. GFOA members are also encouraged to attend the GFOA's upcoming annual conference in Minneapolis, Minnesota, May 18–21, 2014, where they can learn from experts around the country about how to best stay on top of ACA requirements.

NOTES

1 HHS Affordable Care Act Health Insurance Marketplace Outreach and Enrollment Toolkit for Elected Officials at http://marketplace.cms,gov.

2 Treasury/IRS/HHS Final Individual Shared Responsibility Rules at http://www.cms.gov/Newsroom/MediaReleaseDatabase.

3 Labor/Treasury/HHS Final Wellness Rule at http://www.dol.gov/ebsa/pdf/workplacewellnessstudyfinalrule.pdf.

4 Treasury/IRS Proposed rule on Employer Health Insurance Information Reporting at: https://www.federalregister.gov.

5 Caroline Cournoyer, "Is Obamacare the Reason Governments Are Scaling Back Part-Timers?" November 2013.

6 Treasury/IRS Proposed Rule on the Definition of Full Time Employee at: https://www.federal-register.gov/articles.

7 Mark Niquette and Alex Wayne, "Troubled Cities See Exchanges as a Way to Unload Retirees," July 1, 2013, Bloomberg.com.

8 Caroline Cournoyer. "Obamacare's Cadillac Tax Could Spur States & Localities to Cut Back Benefits," September 9, 2013, at governing.com.

Barrie Tabin Berger is assistant director of the GFOA's Fedral Liaison Center in Washington, D.C.

Making a Place for Integrative Care in a Changing Health Care Environment

Barbara Pacca

Over the past few years, knowledge and use of complementary and alternative medicine by health care consumers has been steadily increasing. According to information published by the National Center for Complementary and Alternative Medicine (NCCAM), 38% of adults and 12% of children in the United States have used some form of complementary therapies (NCCAM, 2007). Recent changes in our health care environment, along with increasing numbers of chronically ill patients, emphasize the need for better coordination of care and promote the patient as a partner in health care. Title IV of The Patient Protection and Affordable Care Act "directs the creation of a national prevention and health promotion strategy that incorporates the most effective and achievable methods to improve the health status of Americans and reduce the incidence of preventable illness and disability in the United States" (HealthCare.gov, 2011, 2013). The goal of the National Prevention Strategy is to improve the overall health, quality of life, and productivity of Americans across the lifespan (U.S. Department of Health and Human Services, 2011). Our focus of care is shifting to support these goals. Nurses are frequently responsible for much of the care coordination and are in a perfect position to assist patients in making safe, knowledgeable choices about their care.

When your patients ask about complimentary and alternative medicine (CAM) therapies, are you prepared to answer their questions? Do you know where to look for the appropriate answers?

Health care consumers look to CAM for many reasons. One of the primary goals for many patients is to reduce or eliminate pain. When conventional medical treatments and medication do not seem effective to patients, they frequently will begin to look at other options. Other reasons patients may look at CAM therapies include: to enhance the effectiveness of conventional therapies, improve mood and affect, enhance their sense of well-being, reduce stress, improve functionality and the ability to perform activities of daily living, and provide the patient with a better sense of control over his/her life (Hart, 2008).

Assisting patients in making decisions about the most appropriate CAM modalities can be challenging. Most literature linked to conventional medicine has not addressed the use of CAM therapies or has not supported its use. Over the past 15 years, the volume of available information supporting CAM practices has grown in order to meet the consumer demand. In October 1989, the National Institutes of Health founded the National Center for Complementary and Alternative

Barbara Pacca, "Making a Place for Integrative Care In a Changing Health Care Environment," AAACN Viewpoint, vol. 35, no. 2, pp. 4-5, 8. Copyright © 2013 by American Academy of Ambulatory Care Nursing (AAACN). Reprinted with permission.

Medicine (NCCAM, 2013) to support scientific research needed to establish the safety and efficacy of CAM therapies and their roles in health and health care. In addition to providing information on research activities, NCCAM has developed educational tools for health care providers and consumers to assist them in making the right choices for their health care needs. The NCCAM Web site (www.nccam.nih.gov) contains extensive information about CAM practices of all types (NCCAM, 2011). Other educational resources can be found through professional or specialty organizations such as the American Holistic Nurses Association (AHNA, 2013), which sponsors educational programs for nurses and the *Journal of Holistic Nursing; Journal of Complementary and Alternative Medicine;* the American Botanical Council (2013), which supports scientific research of herbal medicine; and the Healing Touch Program (2012), which supports education, research, and practice for Healing Touch Therapy. Although the term *CAM therapies* is applied to non-traditional modalities, it is more accurate to say *complementary* or *integrative* therapies. Our responsibility as traditional health care providers is to assist patients in deciding when and which non-traditional modalities will be beneficial when paired with traditional care to put the patient in the best possible position to achieve optimal health potential.

There is little documentation in the literature related to nursing scope of practice and complementary therapy modalities. The Web site of the American Holistic Nurses Association (www.ahna.org) reviews the Nurse Practice Act Project sponsored by the Nurses Service Organization; their page lists (by state) inclusion of holistic practice with links to individual state practice acts (AHNA, 2012). Nursing scope of practice in the integration of CAM therapies and conventional nursing care is governed by the same principles as traditional nursing practice. "A study conducted for the

White House Commission on Complementary and Alternative Medicine Policy in 2001 found that 47% of State Boards of Nursing had taken positions that allowed for nurses to practice CAM" (Sparber, 2001). State nurse practice acts define our roles, whether we are the CAM provider or CAM educator for the patient. In addition to nurse practice acts, CAM providers are also required to meet the credentialing specific to the modality they are practicing.

It is important to recognize that there is no standardized, national system for credentialing CAM providers. This makes it especially important for nurses to gain and maintain a strong knowledge base and appropriate skills for recommending or practicing CAM therapies.

As in nursing, licensure requirements for CAM providers are determined by state regulation. Not all modalities require licensure in order for a provider to practice. Examples of CAM modalities requiring a license to practice (in most states) would be acupuncture and chiropractic. The state of Pennsylvania recently passed a licensure requirement for massage therapists. Some modalities require certification to practice; individual programs usually determine certification requirements (e.g., training to become a Reiki Master or Healing Touch Certified Practitioner). Nurses should be familiar with state practice acts and credentialing practices prior to making recommendations.

Developing a referral network of providers in your area helps you to identify reliable options for yourself and your patients. First-hand experience with a modality will give good insight into its benefits and overall influence on health along with direct interaction with a particular provider. This can be helpful with modalities that are unfamiliar or that are not well supported in the literature. For those practices you are interested in referring patients to, you can request a professional meeting to establish a provider relationship and determine a process for accepting referrals from your practice. Another resource for finding providers of a specific modality is professional organization Web sites; many of these will provide a directory by geographic area. A good example of this can be found on the Healing Touch Web site (www. healing touchprogram.com). Many areas have annual conferences open to the public that provide education about non-traditional options for care (e.g., the Mind, Body, Spirit Expo is held in suburban Philadelphia every autumn and in New Jersey every spring). Some of your patients may be able to serve as resources for you if they already see a CAM provider. The following considerations should be made when choosing a CAM provider:

1. Education and training
2. Licensure/Certification
3. Experience in delivering care
4. Experience working with other providers, including traditional health care providers (NCCAM)

Insurance reimbursement is another consideration in choosing a modality and a provider. Licensed modalities like acupuncture or chiropractic are frequently eligible for insurance reimbursement, although not always at the same rates as conventional medical care. Modalities with certified providers may also be eligible for reimbursement.

There is wide variation on which modalities will be covered by insurance and how far that coverage extends depending on type of therapy, geographic area, and insurance company. Patients should inquire about insurance participation and coverage prior to making an appointment with a provider, as well as discuss expectations for financial arrangements so that patient and provider have clarity about this aspect of care.

As heath care reform moves us toward a more preventive model of care, complementary therapies have much to offer, providing us with care options for our patients and ourselves. Nurses and patients together, as therapeutic partners, can make informed choices about CAM therapies that could significantly impact patient care, lifestyle, and health in a positive manner. By taking the initiative to gain the appropriate knowledge, nurses can place themselves in a position to be reliable resources for patients and become experts at successfully facilitating integrative care.

REFERENCES

American Botanical Council. (2013). *Home page.* Retrieved from http://abc.herbalgram.org

American Holistic Nurses Association (AHNA). (2012). *Nurse practice acts by state.* Retrieved from http://www.ahna.org/Resources/YourPracticeCommunity/StatePracticeActs/tabid/11699/Default.aspx

American Holistic Nurses Association (AHNA). (2013). *Home page.* Retrieved from http://www.ahna.org

Hart, J. (April, 2008). Complementary therapies for chronic pain management. *Alternative and Complementary Therapies, 14*(2), 64–68.

HealthCare.gov. (2011). *Accountable care organizations: Improving care coordination for people with Medicare.* Retrieved from http://www.healthcare.gov/news/factsheets/2011/03/accountablecare03312011a.html

ADDITIONAL READINGS

Barnes, P.M., Bloom, B., & Nahin, R. (2008, December 10). Complementary and alternative medicine use among adults and children: United States 2007. *National Health Statistics Report, 12.* Hyattsville, MD: National Center for Health Statistics.

Barnes, P.M., Bloom, B., Nahin, R., & Stussman, B.J. (2009, July 30). Costs of complementary and alternative medicine (CAM) and frequency of visits to CAM practitioners: United States, 2007. *National Health Statistics Report, 18.* Hyattsville, MD: National Center for Health Statistics.

Springhouse Corporation. (2001). *Nurse's handbook of alternative & complementary therapies* (2nd ed.). Philadelphia: Lippincott, Williams & Wilkins.

The Promotion of Marketing-Mediated Diagnosis

Turning Patients into Consumers

Mary Ebeling

STARTING POINTS

- Medical marketing can influence clinical decision making.
- The pharmaceutical industry makes contact with doctors and medical students through visits, promotional events, and sponsorship of research and education.
- Insurance and publicly funded health systems shape diagnostic outcomes.

MARKETING AND DIAGNOSIS

As a student or practitioner in the medical and health-care fields, you have no doubt encountered the pervasive marketing and promotional efforts from pharmaceutical and medical device companies. If you are a medical student, depending on where you are studying, from the moment you enter the field to pursue a career in medicine, you receive visits from sales representatives who offer a range of free samples, symptom checklists, desk displays, all-expenses-paid "educational" seminars promoting a new drug or device, and script pads and pens emblazoned with a drug company's brand. A 2005 study focused on American medical students' exposure to and attitudes about drug companies on campus and found that students receive a gift or attend a sponsored event once a week on average while earning a medical degree (Sierles et al. 2005). Advertisements for a branded drug with a newly innovated formula or an implantable medical device are also common in medical and trade journals. It is possible that one of the articles you've read recently by a clinical researcher or medical practitioner was actually ghostwritten by a drug maker's public relations specialist. You may already be a well-seasoned and perhaps highly skeptical spectator of the endless parade of medical advertisements and marketing gimmicks.

As a student on the path to become a medical practitioner, you may have idealized the process of diagnosis as a relationship between a doctor and her **patient**, a social situation where your years of study, knowledge, and training come to bear on the symptoms and signs displayed in the patient. Yet you and your patient are not alone in the examination room. There are several other unseen

Mary Ebeling, "The Promotion of Marketing-Mediated Diagnosis: Turning Patients into Consumers," Social Issues in Diagnosis: An Introduction for Students and Clinicians, pp. 134-150. Copyright © 2014 by Johns Hopkins University Press. Reprinted with permission.

stakeholders who have a keen interest in influencing the outcome of that **diagnostic moment**. You are not only training to become a doctor or health-care provider, you are being socialized into a thoroughly commercialized medical industry that affects and provides the context for diagnosis. Diagnosis is ensnared in a web of contending interests from all corners of the health industry. Doctors and medical researchers increasingly have financial interests and commercial ties to any number of companies in the life sciences or in pharmaceuticals and medical devices, and these interests shape diagnosis. Directors of large hospital systems as well as managers of small clinics and private practices, concerned with the balance between what is best for their patients' health and their businesses, all strain against the demands of health insurers or nationalized health systems to cut costs or to limit resources through the diagnostic process. Patients and patient advocates increasingly have become activists around any number of diagnostic categories, from autism spectrum disorders to fibromyalgia, who collaborate with doctors and researchers to define and shape diagnosis. All of these pressures, constraints, and interests have a significant influence on how diagnostic categories are built, how diagnosis is practiced, and the medical understanding of disease and wellness more generally.

The imperatives of medical marketing increasingly have a strong sway on diagnoses. This chapter describes how medical marketing can shape, influence, construct, or disrupt diagnostic categories and relationships. It provides two cases from a selection of health and medical industrial sectors to illustrate how diagnosis is shaped and influenced by the forces of marketing. First is the construction and promotion of new diagnostic categories by pharmaceutical companies that align with a drug's approved indications and **direct-to-consumer** marketing of drugs as well as diseases.

The second case examines the marketing advancement of self-diagnosis through genetic diagnostic tests that create "patients-in-waiting" and that shape a patient's disease narratives to fit particular diagnostic categories. Specifically, by looking at these two instances, we examine in detail how medical marketing and advertising affect the diagnostic category and process.

You have already read throughout this book about how social scientists understand diagnosis as a socially mediated phenomenon that at times can be contested and controversial. Often these diagnostic controversies can include power struggles about nosology, or how a disease is defined and categorized; controversies over the very recognition of certain diagnoses, such as fibromyalgia; tensions over how much control patients should have over the diagnostic process; and the potential harmful and stigmatizing effects that certain diagnoses can have on a patient's social and working life, to name a few [...]. The aim here is to understand how powerful commercial interests shape and even dominate diagnosis, especially in the United States. Let's begin with a personal story that demonstrates how commercial forces can influence the diagnostic process.

Not long ago I was going through a period of mourning after experiencing several losses and problems with my health. At the time, I sought the support and guidance of a therapist to help me through this period of sadness. I knew that the blues I was experiencing were part of a normal and healthy response to what life had thrown at me, and that it would pass eventually, but at that moment I needed a little extra help in working through my sadness. Fortunately, I had health insurance and my plan covered six months of therapy. Because I live in the United States, my health insurer required that I be given a diagnosis, or they would not pay for treatment. As we were completing paperwork during the first session, my therapist pulled out the *Diagnostic and Statistical Manual of Mental Disorders* (DSM) and turned to the category "Depressive Disorders Not Otherwise Specified." While acknowledging that this was simply a way for us to find a diagnosis to satisfy my insurer, she explained that though it was a rather perfunctory exercise, we nonetheless had to find a diagnosis that would be convincing. She read out several disorders and asked me to choose the one I thought best described my present state. We settled on adjustment disorder with depressive mood.

This classification system my therapist was using, the DSM, was going through its fifth revision at the time, and this revision has received much criticism. The widely used diagnostic manual had come under fire when it was revealed that 70% of the panel members tasked with its revision had significant financial ties with pharmaceutical companies (Bursztajn et al. 2009). Such ties, many feared, bound these clinicians to their corporate paymasters, influencing them to define diseases not on the basis of medical and clinical evidence but by the marketing priorities of pharmaceutical companies or "marketing-based" medicine (Spielmans and Parry 2010). These priorities included expanding diagnoses of disorders and diseases in people experiencing what had previously been considered normal mood fluctuations that go with life, such as sadness during a period of loss, just as I was experiencing. This concern was so great that one member of the working group stepped down in protest, fearing that expanded categories would create "false epidemics" that could lead to the "medicalization of everyday behavior" (Urbina 2012).

I left our first appointment with mixed feelings. On the one hand, it was my first experience as a patient whose doctor collaborated so explicitly in determining what was "wrong with me." On the other, I colluded with my doctor in labeling myself as "maladjusted," and having "something wrong"

with me when all I wanted was someone to talk to. Together my doctor and I rendered what we both thought was a normal response to loss experienced in life as something "unhealthy" and abnormal in order to satisfy the demands of my insurer, the DSM, and the pharmaceutical companies that had a large role in rewriting the diagnostic categories of the manual. This diagnostic moment has come to symbolize for me how the marketing and commercial interests in medicine exert influence on diagnosis. When I chose to seek out support from a health professional, my experience became medicalized because of a range of commercial interests. The health insurance industry, the DSM, antidepressant manufacturers, and even my therapist's need to retain patients all required that I be given a diagnosis.

COMMERCIALIZING DIAGNOSIS AND MEDICINE

While many Western economies have commercialized medical systems to varying degrees, combining some amount of privatized and public health care, most countries, regardless of the tight regulations that may be in place on consumer marketing, allow for extensive and often hidden medical marketing to medical professionals. Since the focus of this chapter is how the highly consumerist and hotly contested context of the American health-care system shapes the process of diagnosis, it is important to compare the financial burden many Americans face when it comes to health costs as compared with other countries. The complex, global medical marketing regulatory field is always shifting, and since the American medical market is the largest in the world, for these reasons we focus on marketing's impact on diagnosis within the United States. In order to better understand the impact of marketing, especially direct-to-consumer (DTC) marketing, of medical goods and services on the process of diagnosis, we examine some of the history of American pharmaceutical advertising.

Americans spend more on health care than any other Organisation for Economic Co-operation and Development (OECD) country: in 2010, Americans spent on average $8,233, compared with the average for all OECD countries, $3,265 (OECD 2012). Even though many Americans have some kind of health insurance coverage or access to varying levels of health care, there are still more than forty-nine million who are uninsured, and most who have coverage overwhelmingly depend upon employer-provided private health insurance. This places the burden of financing health care squarely on the shoulders of employers and patients, with the rise in insurance premiums outpacing the average increase in earnings by roughly four times (Ginsburg 2008; Kaiser Family Foundation 2011).

The typical insured family pays more than a sixth of its annual income toward health care, yet many Americans do not experience improved health outcomes when compared with residents of other OECD countries (Sered and Fernandopulle 2005). These health-care costs are due to many factors, including private and for-profit health care and health insurance, the rise in chronic diseases as more Americans live longer, and the highly complex health system, but the high costs of medical technologies and prescription drugs cannot be minimized. Out of the total that American patients spend on health care, $792 is spent per capita on prescription drugs (almost twice the average $401 spent per capita in other OECD countries), with the United States accounting for 45% of total global drug sales, making America the world's largest pharmaceutical market (Ebeling 2011; OECD 2008). Some have argued that the cause behind the high costs of prescription medicines is largely the expenses associated with marketing and promotion. Indeed, more

financial resources are dedicated to marketing than to the research and development of new drugs (Gagnon and Lexchin 2008), and patients pay for this marketing in the high price of medicines and medical technologies that they use and consume.

The United States and New Zealand are the only countries whose regulatory bodies allow for DTC marketing of branded pharmaceuticals and medical devices. Most other countries and regions, such as the European Union, have outright bans on DTC marketing and advertising. Despite these bans, intense drug and device marketing targeting doctors and medical professionals is typical.

Marketing strategies such as "detailing" (a practice involving personal visits by pharmaceutical sales representatives to individual doctors, often accompanied by small gifts as simple as a penlight with the company's logo, trips, larger gifts and meals), promotional educational events at resorts, free samples, and institutional advertising account for the bulk of promotional budgets (Gagnon and Lexchin 2008; Greene 2005). In fact, in 2011, estimates of promotional spending by the industry globally range around $92.2 billion, of which $30.6 billion was spent in North America on total drug promotion activities. Only a fraction of that figure, $4.3 billion, was spent on DTC marketing in the United States (Arnold 2012; Mack 2012; SK&A 2012). Official estimates of spending like the ones above are notoriously underestimated, and, as Marc-André Gagnon and Joel Lexchin note, most official estimates are misleading and likely less than half of what the industry actually spends on promotional activities (Gagnon and Lexchin 2008).

The high visibility of DTC drug marketing, however, tends to attract enormous attention and concern over whether the marketing of pharmaceuticals and diseases is helping us or harming us. Still, the pharmaceutical industry deploys "hidden" marketing tactics to promote their brands. Most pharmaceutical marketing efforts aim to reach the medical practitioners who make diagnoses and write scripts: doctors and, increasingly, nurses. And there is evidence that this has an impact on how doctors diagnose.

The power of advertising to doctors in promoting simplistic *stereotypes* or misleading information about a disease, for example, can have an influence on how doctors diagnose. While there is ample clinical research demonstrating that men suffer from rates of depression on par with women, a study examining the gendering of disease in marketing showed that drug advertising that targeted doctors tended to depict depression as a disease typically afflicting women and affected the likelihood of a depression diagnosis being made for a male patient (Curry and O'Brien 2006).

All of these marketing efforts can have profound impacts on how we understand diagnosis and on the outcomes of a patient's health and treatment options. And that is the purpose of such marketing—to shape, influence, and be central to the diagnostic process. Physician and historian of medicine Jeremy Greene has noted that the diagnosis of disease "has become simultaneously an epidemiological event and a marketing event" (Greene 2007, ix). In what follows, we seek to understand how the diagnosis has become a marketing opportunity for the medical industries.

MEDICAL MARKETING IN THE UNITED STATES

American culture is a consumer culture that is often expressed through advertising. Marketing messages are so common that many times we are barely aware of them: the average city dweller in the United States sees more than five thousand advertisements every day (Story 2007). Compared to thirty years ago, when during a typical day an American could see as few as five hundred

promotional messages, it is fair to say that marketing, **branding**, and advertising is the white noise in our daily lives. And this almost-inescapable marketing environment extends to the healthcare and medical industries. Patients and medical professionals are all subjected to intense marketing. A patient may see a commercial that is tailored (and regulated) specifically for her, and her doctor might receive a visit from a sales rep. While the messages may be tweaked for each group, they are nonetheless ubiquitous and expand across virtually all media. There are advertisements for educational toys printed on the paper liners of pediatricians' examination tables; the brand names of drugs decorate the pens and charts in doctors' offices; and mobile phone applications "help" patients determine if a set of symptoms can be a sign of a disease. These messages are undoubtedly intended to shape how both patients and physicians understand health and wellness, the meaning of symptoms and diagnoses.

America's highly commercialized media environment started to take shape when the emergence of industrialized, large-scale consumer goods production in the middle to late nineteenth century created a need for manufacturers to promote these products to the new consumer classes, giving rise to mass advertising and marketing. Advertising, then as well as now, functioned to distinguish manufactured goods that often were hardly different from one another. These early advertisers paved the way for marketing messages that are now all too familiar. Advertisements, especially those for what were called "patent" medicines, often did not pitch an appeal on the discernible qualities of the product but rather strategically played on a consumer's fears of ill health; insecurities about gender roles, class status, aspirations, and, above all, the crushing guilt of not taking action. What is more, most Americans had little or no access to physicians, or did not trust some of the dangerous treatments

FIGURE 19.1 This patent medicine advertisement, which appeared in an unidentified American magazine from the 1910s, employs scare and guilt tactics to persuade potential consumers to buy the product. While today there is much legislation in place to protect patients from such blatant manipulation, many drug advertisements still use similar techniques to promote sales.

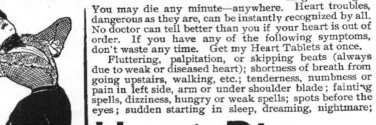

Source: MagazineArt.org

that were commonly practiced at the time, such as leeching, purging, or blistering. Access to what was called "ethical" medication, the drugs formulated by pharmacists, was even lower, and forced many to turn to self-help, self-diagnosis, and self-medication (Conrad and Leiter 2008, 826).

In an effort to distinguish their compounds from those patent medicines that were considered more nefarious and overly commercialized, several North American drug manufacturers marketed their therapeutics as "ethical" medicine, or standardized formulas that were made in accordance with the *United States Pharmacopeia* and marketed under the American Medical Association's *Code of Ethics* (Greene and Herzberg 2010, 794). Though voluntary and not required by any regulatory body, the manufacturers of ethical drugs chose not to advertise widely or directly to consumers, but rather focused on institutional advertising and marketing efforts targeted solely to medical professionals as a way to further distinguish the industry from the unsavory marketing tactics of patent medicines.

Despite their name, patent medicines were neither under patent nor had their formulas been tested for safety and efficacy; the label simply meant they were trademarked. They were the nostrums, elixirs, and potions largely associated in the public's mind with itinerant "snake oil" salesmen peddling hokum. Patent medicines were secretly formulated with either ineffective or potentially dangerous ingredients (Fox 1997, 16). Often these nostrums were labeled and promoted with misleading, wildly exaggerated, and patently false claims in regard to the symptoms treated and to the medicine's effectiveness.

This early instance of medical advertising had profound effects on the bottom lines of producers. As advertising historian Stephen Fox notes, sales of one of the era's most popular preparations, Lydia Pinkham's Vegetable Compound, a formulation purported by its makers to address all female ailments and "complaints," increased by 2500% over ten years after the company began advertising (Fox 1997, 19). At the time, the patent medicines were the first products to be advertised widely and nationally, so much so that in the public's mind the two were inextricably connected (16–19). In fact, the push to nationally advertise patent medicines helped to create not only the first advertising agencies, where more than half of agencies' revenues came from the patent medicine industry, but also helped to prompt a massive increase in magazine publishing (Goodrum and Dalrymple 1990, 29–30). By the late nineteenth century, several magazines were founded to serve solely as vehicles for advertising, and magazines quickly subverted the traditional model of advertising: they went from selling products to potential consumers to becoming instruments that collected and sold consumers to advertisers, much like what most contemporary media now do.

But it was a magazine, *Ladies' Home Journal*, that helped to blow the lid off of the unethical marketing tactics of the proprietary drug makers. In 1892, it refused to accept any more patent medicine advertising and conducted a series of investigative articles on the safety of patent medicines.

The articles in *Ladies' Home Journal* as well as similar investigative pieces that appeared in *Collier's Weekly* led directly to the passing of the 1906 Pure Food and Drug Act, legislation that instituted the U.S. Food and Drug Administration (FDA; Bok 1921). Before 1906, false and misleading labeling of patent drugs was widespread. With

the passing of the act, the accurate labeling of drugs was mandated. The regulation of drug advertising, however, especially consumer advertising, would not be regulated until 1938, when the Food, Drug and Cosmetic Act (also known as the Wheeler Lea Act) granted regulatory jurisdiction over pharmaceutical advertising to the U.S. Federal Trade Commission (Palumbo and Mullins 2002).

Soliciting highly personal letters from women as a marketing method was common for patent medicines, especially those marketed to women. A 1911 collection of "nostrums and quackery" advertisements collected by the American Medical Association includes evidence from the Mrs. Cora B. Miller Company, owned and operated by Mr. Frank D. Miller, that had their "young women clerks and stenographers" compounding the toxic formula for "female weakness" and responding to letters from unsuspecting "marks," or women seeking relief through these mail-order treatments (American Medical Association 1911, 194–201).

In an effort to eliminate the duplication of efforts as well as to tighten rules on drug marketing, the FDA took over the regulation of drug advertising in 1962 as legislated by Congress through amendments to the earlier acts. Included in these changes were the Kefauver-Harris drug amendments, which stipulated that all drugs must be proven safe and effective before being marketed to the public. During the mid-twentieth century, most pharmaceutical companies did not pursue DTC marketing and instead focused efforts on advertising directed toward medical professionals. Doctors and practitioners were reached primarily through office visits by drug company sales representatives, in trade and medical journals, and in corporately sponsored research journals—journals often published by the public relations departments of drug manufacturers. By the close of the decade, the FDA issued guidelines for pharmaceutical advertising, which required that the information in advertisements be truthful and not misleading, as well as be "material" to the approved indications for the drug; provide a "fair balance" of information on both the benefits and risks associated with a drug; and, most importantly, offer a "brief summary" on all known risks (Ventola 2011).

It wasn't until the early 1980s, when drug makers began to advertise directly and more heavily to consumers, that the FDA implemented a brief moratorium on the consumer marketing of pharmaceuticals (Palumbo and Mullins 2002). After the moratorium was lifted in 1985, the regulatory body announced that the instated regulations were sufficient, but ostensibly only allowed advertisers to directly promote their products to consumers in print, because the requirements to provide "brief summaries" on the risks, side effects, and contraindications of a drug were too cumbersome for a thirty-second broadcast spot. By 1997, however, after a series of public hearings, the FDA loosened DTC restrictions for broadcast advertising under draft guidance, which was finalized in 1999 (Palumbo and Mullins 2002, 430). In the intervening years since DTC took off in the United States, the FDA has extended DTC advertising and marketing regulations to include medical devices.

There are generally three categories of drug advertisements that are recognized by the FDA: (1) reminder ads, which are those that name a drug, and the form it takes, but not its uses; (2) help-seeking ads that don't mention a brand-named drug but focus on a disease state or categorizes symptoms, which are often called "disease-awareness" ad campaigns and often say "see your doctor if you have these symptoms"; and (3) product claim ads, which state the brand name and mention indications, efficacy, and risk information (Palumbo and Mullins 2002; Ventola 2011).

Direct-to-Consumer Drug Marketing, Disease Awareness, and Self-Diagnosis

What has been the impact of such marketing on diagnosis? To answer this question, we look at two types of marketing: disease awareness marketing and DTC pharmaceutical marketing. These two instances provide clear examples of how marketing shapes the definition of disease by influencing the construction of categories and what symptoms mean in regard to health and illness. One of the implicit aims of marketing is to encourage patients to self-diagnose, which on the face seems empowering to the patient and disruptive of traditional power relationships in medicine. But it is really a marketing strategy not unlike that seen in nineteenth-century patent medicine—to spur the sales of drugs, disease screenings, and diagnoses of diseases that are marketed by the pharmaceutical makers. These new approaches to marketing pose a new challenge in the lay-professional relationship [...].

In a little over fifteen years, the DTC marketing of medicine, pharmaceuticals, and devices has grown exponentially in the United States. Those opposed to drug advertising point to harmful health effects such as overprescribing, overdiagnosing, or increased misdiagnoses, which are all attributable to such marketing. Those in favor believe that DTC marketing provides necessary and empowering health information to patients.

Remember the television commercials for GlaxoSmithKline's (GSK) branded drug Requip (ropinirole), marketed as a treatment for restless leg syndrome (or RLS, also known as Willis-Ekbom disease), a condition rebranded by the drug manufacturer when it sought FDA premarket approval for its drug? The commercials and print ads were ubiquitous in the mid-2000s across the United States, so much so that RLS became the butt of many comedians' jokes. A neurologist at the Center for Restless Legs Syndrome at Johns Hopkins University, Dr. Christopher Jenkins, noted at the time that the condition had gained "out-of-the-blue disease" status and that RLS advertising was creating an increased consumer demand for the diagnosis, a condition with a low prevalence in the general population (Aleccia 2008). While seen as a transparent attempt on GSK's part to flog drugs by creating a disease where one didn't exist (or at least not as it was branded or at the rate suggested), the campaign quickly became symbolic of all that is harmful with consumer drug advertising.

GlaxoSmithKline's RLS campaign is an example of what is termed **disease awareness marketing**. A significant portion of industry marketing efforts across both DTC and marketing to healthcare providers involves the promotion of certain diagnoses and diseases to the public as well as to the medical profession. There are a number of features that distinguish disease awareness campaigns from other forms of health marketing. These campaigns do not explicitly promote a product; they tend to be "unbranded," which means they do not mention the name of the drug maker sponsoring the advertisement, and they can appear to be sponsored by a research foundation or patient advocacy group organized to fight for recognition or a cure for the disease.

Pharmaceutical companies expend huge financial resources to ensure that identified symptoms converge with the approved indications of the drugs that they brand and market. These disease marketing campaigns often begin years ahead of regulatory approval for a company's drug. Most promotional planning begins in the preclinical development of compounds in the laboratory, years before regulatory approval and legal marketing begins (Fugh-Berman and Dodgson 2008). American pharmacological marketing textbooks published as early as the 1950s noted that product marketing and clinical research are essentially interwoven processes, where the development of compounds and how those drugs are marketed to treat disease or symptoms are inextricably linked (Greene 2005).

In the early 1980s, in a rather blatant attempt to invent a disease to protect market interests, during FDA hearings on the safety and reclassification of silicone breast implants as Class III medical devices, the American Society of Plastic Surgeons (ASPS) created a diagnosis of "micromastia," or "small breasts," a deformity the ASPS claimed at the time had detrimental effects on women suffering from the "disease" and whose only remedy was augmentation surgery (Cohen 1994, 169). The ASPS used its power as a lobbying organization to create a definition of disease in order to protect its market interests.

In another widely discussed case, Eli Lilly's exerted strong influence on the work group responsible for the definition of premenstrual dysmorphic disorder (PMDD) in the revision of the DSM-IV. By placing clinical psychiatrists under the pay of Eli Lilly into positions of responsibility with regard to the disease categorization for the revised DSM, the pharmaceutical maker was assured that the associated symptoms of the controversial disorder neatly fit the reapproved indications of Prozac, which was rebranded as Sarafem, a treatment for PMDD (Ebeling 2011).

Conditions, diseases, and diagnoses that are now widely recognized and rarely disputed, at least publicly, are promoted in order to sell the given diseases or diagnoses to physicians, to the larger health industry (including insurers and regulators), and to the public. Commonly recognized health problems such as hypercholesterolemia or hypertension were linked to heart disease in part through the tireless marketing efforts of drug maker Merck during the middle to late twentieth century (Greene 2007). Through Merck's pursuit to build a market for its compounds, company marketers and product developers collaborated with chemical engineers and clinicians to construct a relationship between diagnostic categories, chronic diseases, and the drugs under development in order to promote both conditions as seriously underdiagnosed problems afflicting millions. Through the aggressive marketing of three drugs in particular—Diuril, a diuretic; Orinase, an antidiabetic taken orally; and Mevacor, the first statin on the American market—diagnostic screenings were extended to apparently healthy and asymptomatic patients and assured that the pharmaceutical industry, through a universe of chronic disease that could expand ad infinitum, would realize an equally expandable and profitable market (Ebeling 2011; Greene 2007).

Routine scanning even in the absence of symptoms has become part of a dominant public health discourse, at least in the highly marketing-mediated health environment of the United States. Once an individual reaches a milestone age, the American Cancer Society (and other similar organizations) promote annual screenings in otherwise healthy patients, such as mammograms for women beginning at age forty, or prostate-specific antigen tests to screen for prostate cancer in men at age fifty onward (Cassels 2012). The fact that much of this testing can lead to false positives or unnecessarily alarmist diagnoses that have profound, cascading health implications is of course not part of any of the promotional marketing of these tests or public health messages (Cassels 2012; Welch et al. 2011).

The mainstay of these campaigns, however, is to promote awareness of particular symptom clusters. These campaigns then project a specific diagnosis to these symptom clusters, one for which the drug company's branded drug is an approved treatment. This enables the pharmaceutical company to assist individuals to speak of their own symptom clusters in ways that align with the approved indications for their drugs. Patients then bring this language of marketing to discuss with their doctors. This way, a drug maker can stake a claim for a particular disease, predicate its treatment, and inextricably link the illness and the cure together in the public's mind, much like Eli Lilly did with depression and Prozac. Through marketing, Prozac defined depression.

Advancements made in diagnostic technologies, particularly "at-home" tests and diagnostic assessments administered by patients themselves, when coupled with DTC marketing of diagnoses and disease states, likewise make it easier for patients to see themselves as diseased and in need of medical or pharmaceutical intervention. More testing, and more marketing of testing, leads to more intervention, necessary or otherwise. While self-diagnosis of some illnesses may not necessarily be negative, and can be the first step for a patient to seek out support and guidance from her physician (public health disease awareness campaigns may use the same tools as commercial enterprises), the promotion of self-diagnosis by medical marketing is not designed to benefit the patient. Its purpose is to sell drugs, tests, and services that may not all benefit the patient.

Many critics argue that little has changed since the days of patent medicines and hokum, at least in regard to some of the tactics used in DTC drug advertising and disease awareness marketing. As with patent medicines of one hundred years ago, contemporary pharmaceutical marketing campaigns attempt to persuade patients to recognize symptoms or even asymptomatic conditions as disease, as well as to diagnose themselves and to self-medicate, even if indirectly by pressuring a desired diagnosis and prescription from his doctor (Conrad and Leiter 2008; Ebeling 2011).

Marketing Genetic Diagnostics and the Creation of "Patients-in-Waiting"

Direct-to-consumer genetic diagnostic tests can have an influence on diagnosis by marketing potential risks for developing a disease, even in the absence of any symptoms. In the decade since the Human Genome Project successfully completed a full map of the human genome in 2003, a new industry in personalized medicine and DTC genetic diagnostic testing has sprouted up to take advantage of the plummeting costs and streamlined processes that have made gene sequencing faster and more affordable. Generally these diagnostic tests fall into two broad categories. The first category includes tests that are regulated by the FDA as medical devices, are marketed to medical professionals, and can only be ordered and administered by a doctor or health institution to help designate a diagnosis or treatment plan. Tests that help a doctor optimize the best dosing level for the blood thinner warfarin based on a patient's genetic makeup or the controversial BRACAnalysis test are examples of tests within this class (Boddington 2009).

The second category of tests includes those that are not necessarily regulated by the FDA and are marketed and sold directly to consumers with no intervention by a physician. Some tests are used and marketed for curiosity purposes, such as to investigate genealogical history, while others claim to provide predictive information on diseases ranging from Alzheimer disease and multiple sclerosis to prostate cancer and asthma (Chapman 2008). Companies such as 23andMe Inc. (with financial backing and company leadership connected to Internet behemoth Google), Navigenetics, Pathway Genetics, and Knome market DTC tests that scan a person's genetic makeup to look for markers that purportedly indicate a risk for developing diseases (Parthasarathy 2010; Pollack 2010).

These genetic tests are not diagnostic of a disease; they test for the presence of a genetic marker on the patient's genotype. These tests do not determine how that gene may or may not be expressed in the phenotype. For most diseases, the likelihood of a patient actually developing a condition based on a genetic marker depends on many factors, meaning that a person's genes are not necessarily his destiny. Yet this is how many of the DTC genetic tests are marketed. While industry advocates argue that their tests provide crucial health information that empowers patients to make informed decisions about their health or to take preventative action, many medical professionals are deeply concerned that DTC genetic tests do not provide meaningful health information because there is still scant clinical evidence linking genetic variance and the probability of disease. These tests actually have the potential to harm patients because few individuals are equipped to interpret information about disease probabilities. At issue is that the typical odds ratio of most genome-wide association studies is so low as to be statistically and medically insignificant (Magnus et al. 2009).

A DTC test targeting a gene variant related to cardiovascular disease, for instance, may report results of an increase in risk from 1% to 1.6%. While an increase of 50% or more seems like a clear indication that the chances are high that you will develop the disease, a ratio of 1.6 is in fact inconsequential and prone to be misinterpreted by most patients without guidance (Caulfield and McGuire 2012). There is concern that do-it-yourself personalized genetic testing amplifies weak genetic associations, which may lead to unnecessary procedures or a misdiagnosis, not to mention the unnecessary increase in anxiety and worry on the part of patients. Most DTC genetic tests, however, are promoted on these low odds of genetic prevalence leading to disease.

Genetic diagnostic tests and their marketing can influence diagnosis in radical ways. Until recently, companies could "own" genes, patenting them as intellectual property. They could then develop, control, and market tests for those genes. As one example, Myriad Genetic Laboratories Inc., a Utah-based genetic diagnostics manufacturer, co-owned (with the University of Utah) patents on two genes that have been associated with certain hereditary breast and ovarian cancers, BRCA1 and BRCA2. While these forms of cancer are not as common, their detection in women with family histories of breast or ovarian cancer has clear benefits. And the commercial laboratories are understandably keen for their use to be much wider.

The diagnostic test developed and marketed as BRACAnalysis by Myriad is the only one available and accounts for more than 84% of Myriad's revenues. The marketing website for the test promotes the idea that a personal or family history of non-specific "cancer" is indication enough for suspicion of the BRCA1 or BRCA2 gene, broadening widely by such an assertion the range of individuals likely to consider themselves at risk of having the genetic mutation. Myriad's mass marketing approach targets all women, rather than the specific (and relatively small; less than 5% of breast cancers are associated with BRCA1 and BRCA2) group of women who are at risk. The marketing narrative casts women as "patients-in-waiting," requiring responsible and early testing (Rajan 2005).

The ownership of the BRCA1 and BRCA2 genes has a profound impact on doctors' ability to confirm the gene marker in patients they suspect have heredity cancer. The genetic tests that could confirm that women carry this gene are only covered by insurance policies issued by companies who have negotiated a contract with Myriad. In the absence of such a contract, or of insurance, the tests cost several thousand dollars, preventing many doctors from using the diagnostic tool their patients require. This concern over access to diagnosis is so great that the American Civil Liberties Union along with geneticists, pathologists, patients, and clinicians filed a class-action suit against Myriad, arguing in part that the patents are denying women access to potentially life-saving diagnostics (Fuchs 2013). In June 2013 the U.S. Supreme Court found in favor of the plaintiffs' claim against Myriad's ownership of BRCA1 and BRCA2, arguing that a naturally occurring human gene is not eligible for patenting (Ledford 2013).

THE CROWDED EXAMINATION ROOM

As illustrated by the cases above, when the patient arrives in the examination room, both she and the clinician have often been primed, often despite their best efforts, to understand disease in ways that have been shaped by commercial interests. The reasons for, results of, and interactions during the visit between patient and doctor are steered by much more than the health and well-being of the individual patient. The examination room is crowded with commercial and marketing interests from pharmaceutical and medical device companies, medical industries, health insurers, policy makers and regulators, health advocacy groups, and the patient.

Diagnosis is a process that does not simply begin and end with the patient but rather is a phenomenon that is shaped along the production pipeline of drugs, devices, and diseases, with each moment upstream and down proffering an opportunity for a marketing intervention. From its earliest history in the late nineteenth century to the present, medical marketing seeks to intervene its construction of diseases and attendant cures into the diagnostic relationship between doctor and patient; to promote the use of self-diagnosis among patients; and to shape the understanding and interpretation of the meaning of symptoms, disease, and how to manage health and illness. Pharmaceutical and medical device companies do this from the very beginning of the creation of a compound or the discovery of a molecule or genetic mutation. These interventions begin in the laboratory and extend recursively through the development pipeline through to the regulatory bodies and medical **institutions** responsible for overseeing the safety of medicine or the defining of diseases and to the direct marketing to consumers or medical professionals. Within this context, physicians in training need to expand their understandings of what roles they play in the diagnostic relationship. It is no longer enough for medical professionals to see themselves as arbiters of a medically understood diagnosis, they must also expand their roles to recognize and, when appropriate, act as critics of diagnosis marketing, providing alternative sources of information and treatment that result in effective patient-centered care.

TAKEAWAY POINTS

- Understanding marketing's influence on diagnosis from the perspective of doctors, patients, clinicians, and administrators is important to successful management of health problems.
- The meaning of diagnosis may be transformed by marketing influence for the individuals involved in the diagnostic process, with nonclinical meanings taking precedence.
- Insurers and other health-care managers can deny, divert, or direct diagnoses, which can determine health outcomes for patients.

DISCUSSION QUESTIONS

1. How can medical marketing serve patients while supporting the industry's interests? What are the conflicts, and how might these be managed?

2. Identify five ways in which pharmaceutical marketing has been visible in your practice, education, or health in the past year.

3. Have you ever received a gift (even a small one) from a pharmaceutical sales representative? What was the brand being promoted? How easy was it for you to recall?

4. Identify four sources of information about a disease or syndrome, a medication it is approved to treat, and how to prescribe it. Compare the information presented by these sources to the information provided in a disease awareness campaign. What are the similarities and differences? How do the sources frame the information differently?

5. Are at-home genetic diagnostic tests empowering to patients or endangering their health? What would you say to a patient who presents you with results of a test that you find of dubious use for their health or future chances of illness?

REFERENCES

Aleccia, JoNel. 2008. "Without TV Ads, Restless Legs May Take a Hike." *NBCNews*, http://www.nbcnews.com/id/24603237/ns/health-health_care/t/without-tv-ads-restless-legs-may-take-hike/, May 14.

American Medical Association. 1911. *Nostrums and Quackery: Articles on the Nostrum Evil and Quackery Reprinted from the Journal of the American Medical Association*. Chicago: American Medical Association.

Arnold, Matthew. 2012. "Pfizer, Crestor Tops for Global Promotional Spend in 2011." *Medical Marketing and Media*, http://www.mmm-online.com/pfizer-crestor-tops-for-global-promotional-spend-in-2011/article/238922/, May 1.

Boddington, Paula. 2009. "The Ethics and Regulation of Direct-to-Consumer Genetic Testing." *Genome Medicine* 1(7): 71.1–2.

Bok, Edward William. 1921. *The Americanization of Edward Bok: The Autobiography of a Dutch Boy Fifty Years After*. New York: Charles Scribner's Sons.

Bursztajn, Harold J., Lisa Cosgrove, David J. Kupfer, and Darrel A. Regier. 2009. "Toward Credible Conflict of Interest Policies in Clinical Psychiatry." *Psychiatric Times*, http://www.psychiatrictimes.com/articles/toward-credible-conflict-interest-policies-clinical-psychiatry, January 1.

Cassels, Alan. 2012. *Seeking Sickness: Medical Screening and the Misguided Hunt for Disease*. Vancouver: Greystone.

Caulfield, Timothy, and Amy L. McGuire. 2012. "Direct-to-Consumer Genetic Testing: Perceptions, Problems, and Policy Responses." *Annual Review of Medicine* 63(1): 23–33.

Chapman, Audrey. 2008. "DTC Marketing of Genetic Tests: The Perfect Storm." *American Journal of Bioethics* 8(6): 10–12.

Cohen, Kerith. 1994. "Truth & Beauty, Deception & Disfigurement: A Feminist Analysis of Breast Implant Litigation." *William and Mary Journal of Women and the Law* 1(1): 149–82.

Conrad, Peter, and Valerie Leiter. 2008. "From Lydia Pinkham to Queen Levitra: Direct-to-Consumer Advertising and Medicalisation." *Sociology of Health and Illness* 30(6): 825–38.

Curry, Phillip, and Marita O'Brien. 2006. "The Male Heart and the Female Mind: A Study in the Gendering of Antidepressants and Cardiovascular Drugs in Advertisements in Irish Medical Publication." *Social Science and Medicine* 62(8): 1970–77.

Ebeling, Mary. 2011. "'Get with the Program!': Pharmaceutical Marketing, Symptom Checklists and Self-Diagnosis." *Social Science and Medicine* 73(6): 825–32.

Fox, Stephen. 1997. *The Mirror Makers: A History of American Advertising and Its Creators*. Champaign: University of Illinois Press.

Fuchs, Erin. 2013. "Supreme Court Seems Highly Skeptical That Biotech Can 'Patent Nature.'" *Business Insider*, http://www.businessinsider.com/supreme-court-myriad-case-2013-4, April 16.

Fugh-Berman, Adriane J., and Susanna J. Dodgson. 2008. "Ethical Considerations of Publication Planning in the Pharmaceutical Industry." *Open Medicine* 2(4): http://www.openmedicine.ca/article/view/118/215.

Gagnon, Marc-André, and Joel Lexchin. 2008. "The Cost of Pushing Pills: A New Estimate of Pharmaceutical Promotion Expenditures in the United States." *PLoS Medicine* 5(1): e1, doi:10.1371/journal.pmed.0050001.

Ginsburg, Paul B. 2008. "High and Rising Health Care Costs: Demystifying U.S. Health Care Spending." In *The Synthesis Project*, 1–28. Princeton NJ: Robert Wood Johnson Foundation.

Goodrum, Charles, and Helen Dalrymple. 1990. *Advertising in America: The First 200 Years*. New York: Harry N. Abrams.

Greene, Jeremy A. 2005. "Releasing the Flood Waters: Diuril and the Reshaping of Hypertension." *Bulletin of the History of Medicine* 79(4): 749–94.

———. 2007. *Prescribing by Numbers: Drugs and the Definition of Disease*. Baltimore: Johns Hopkins University Press.

Greene, Jeremy A., and David Herzberg. 2010. "Hidden in Plain Sight." *American Journal of Public Health* 100(5): 793–803.

Kaiser Family Foundation. 2011. "The Uninsured: A Primer." In *The Kaiser Commission on Medicaid and the Uninsured*, 1–39. Washington, DC: Kaiser Family Foundation.

Ledford, Heidi. 2013. "Myriad Ruling Causes Confusion." *Nature* 498: 281–82.

Mack, John. 2012. "Lipitor Holds Key to DTC Ad Spending in 2012." *Pharma Marketing* (blog), http://pharmamkting.blogspot.com/2012/04/

lipitor-holds-key-to-dtc-ad-spending-in.html, April 15.

Magnus, David, Mildred K. Cho, and Robert Cook-Deegan. 2009. "Direct-to-Consumer Genetic Tests: Beyond Medical Regulation?" *Genome Medicine* 1(2): 17.1–3.

OECD. Organisation for Economic Co-operation and Development. 2008. "Pharmaceutical Pricing Policies in a Global Market." Paris: Organisation for Economic Cooperation and Development.

———. 2012. "OECD Health Data 2012." Paris: Organisation for Economic Co-Operation and Development.

Palumbo, Francis B., and C. Daniel Mullins. 2002. "The Development of Direct-to-Consumer Prescription Drug Advertising Regulation." *Food and Drug Law Journal* 57(3): 423–44.

Parthasarathy, S. 2010. "Assessing the Social Impact of Direct-to-Consumer Genetic Testing: Understanding Sociotechnical Architectures." *Genetics in Medicine* 12(9): 544–47.

Pollack, Andrew. 2010. "F.D.A. Faults Companies on Unapproved Genetic Tests." *New York Times*, June 12, B2.

Rajan, Kaushik Sunder. 2005. "Subjects of Speculation: Emergent Life Sciences and Market Logics in the United States and India." *American Anthropologist* 107(1): 19–30.

Sered, Susan Starr, and Rushika J. Fernandopulle. 2005. *Uninsured in America: Life and Death in the Land of Opportunity*. Berkeley: University of California Press.

Sierles, F. S., A. C. Brodkey, L. M. Cleary, F. A. McCurdy, M. Mintz, J. Frank, D. J. Lynn, J. Chao, B. Z. Morgenstern, W. Shore, and J. L. Woodard. 2005. "Medical Students' Exposure to and Attitudes about Drug Company Interactions: A National Survey." *JAMA* 294(9): 1034–42.

SK&A. 2012. "One Key Market Insights." Irvine, CA: SK&A.

Spielmans, Glen, and Peter Parry. 2010. "From Evidence-Based Medicine to Marketing-Based Medicine: Evidence from Internal Industry Documents." *Journal of Bioethical Inquiry* 7(1): 13–29.

Story, L. 2007. "Anywhere the Eye Can See, It's Likely to See an Ad." *New York Times*, http://www.nytimes.com/2007/01/15/business/media/15everywhere.html?pagewanted=all&_r=0, January 15.

Urbina, Ian. 2012. "DSM Revisions May Sharply Increase Addiction Diagnoses." *New York Times*, May 12, A11.

Ventola, C. Lee. 2011. "Direct-to-Consumer Pharmaceutical Advertising: Therapeutic or Toxic?" *Pharmacy and Therapeutics* 36(10): 681–84.

Welch, H. Gilbert, Lisa M. Schwartz, and Steven Woloshin. 2011. *Overdiagnosed: Making People Sick in the Pursuit of Health*. Boston: Beacon Press.

COPYRIGHTED MATERIAL — DO NOT DUPLICATE, DISTRIBUTE, OR POST

READING 20

The Aging Body
Towards a Sociology of Health in Later Life

Paul Higgs and Ian Rees Jones

The association between the physical appearance of the aging body and notions of tragedy can be traced back to ancient Greece (Fox 2006) suggesting that negative attitudes to bodily aging are not just a consequence of the youth-based obsessions of modern societies. In this context the aging body is interpreted as a sign of failure. As Sennett (2006) argues, old age brings with it the specter of uselessness. This syndrome is closely related to the rise of the 'somatic society' dominated by the 'will to health' (Rose 2001). In this society the body becomes a concern which preoccupies people of all ages and all walks of life. Body maintenance and body image move to the center of social life and social relations.

The very success of modern capitalist welfare states has led to longevity becoming a normal expectation. The normal human lifespan has been expanded and older individuals are findings ways to extend their physical and mental capabilities into their later years. As a consequence, experience of aging is accompanied by an increase in uncertainty and insecurity about what later life entails and what constitutes appropriate age-related health. At the same time, social and cultural norms of youth and youthfulness have become ever more strongly entrenched. Because of these norms, the ideal of actively pursuing body maintenance deep into later life has a hold over large numbers of individuals (Katz 2005).

Historical changes in bodily regime mark a move from standardized bodies defined around military and industrial needs to bodies defined by the needs of a consumer society. While health concerns become increasingly privatized, welfare systems more and more see their objective as the regulation of populations (Lupton 1995). Differences in forms of bodily maintenance and bodily appearance in this context become key markers of inequality. Just as Bourdieu charted the role of bodily aesthetics as markers of distinction in French society (Bourdieu 1984), Bauman sees bodily regimes and bodily obsession as key markers of an increasingly polarized consumer society. The capacity to resist both the appearance of aging and bodily decline in later life becomes a form of distinction in itself. When Bourdieu referred to the process of social aging as 'nothing other than the slow renunciation or disinvestment (socially assisted and encouraged) which leads agents to adjust their aspirations to their objective chances, to espouse their condition, become what they are and make do with what they have' (Bourdieu 1984; 110–11) he was outlining the effect of time and structure on individual trajectories. But in consumer society, despite ample evidence of inequality and

Paul Higgs and Ian Rees Jones, "The Aging Body: Towards a Sociology of Health Later in Life," Medical Sociology and Old Age: Towards a Sociology of Health in Later Life, pp. 34-35, 86-99. Copyright © 2008 by Taylor & Francis Group. Reprinted with permission restricted social mobility, these trajectories are seen to be matters of individual aspirations and choice.

THE CONFLICT BETWEEN ANTI-AGING MEDICINE AND GERONOTOLOGY

As we have noted […] the sociology of the body has not really paid sufficient attention to the aging body and as a consequence has been unprepared for many of the issues thrown up by anti-aging medicine and new medical technologies. More familiar with ideas of body modification as transgressive rather than age-related (Pitts 2003) sociologists of the body now find themselves in overlapping positions with social gerontologists who, as we saw earlier, are also grappling with the phenomenon. The rise of the somatic society has focused attention on the aging body in ways that previously have been seen as the province of gender (Davis 1995). The cosmaceutical industry markets greater numbers of anti-aging products to men as well as women (Dychtwald 1999). These developments affect the middle classes in a particularly visible way (Featherstone and Hepworth 1991). For them, attempts to delay the onset of the negative aspects of aging take on ever more active and self-conscious cast. Gullette (2004) sees this in terms of cultural life being saturated by the cult of youth. It is in this space that anti-aging medicine finds its willing subjects and exerts its influence on the meaning of health.

The rise of anti-aging medicine reflects the capacity of markets to capitalize on the youth orientation of consumer culture and to promote anti-aging as a solution to the 'natural' aging trajectory. The pursuit of desires expressed as new needs is a key part of this in that many anti-aging treatments can be viewed as being responses to the construction of desires that are doomed to be forever unsated. One can become, to borrow a

term, age-orexic (D'Souza 2007) and addicted to anti-aging interventions (Singh and Kelly 2003). Anti-aging medicine operates at the boundaries of both conventional medicine and biogerontology and has been condemned for it (Butler et al. 2002). For some, its view of aging as treatable is a welcome challenge to mainstream gerontology (de Grey 2003; Mykytyn 2006). Obviously, as we have seen, one of the major problems with the term is that it encapsulates such a wide variety of treatments from cosmetic surgery to telomere cellular shortening (Katz, 2005). It is this broadness, we would argue, that makes the area as important for medical sociologists as it does for social gerontologists. Given the rise of new medical technologies, bio-medicine and commercialization of anti-aging products the boundaries between medical treatment and beauty treatment become blurred. Geronotological approaches tend to see aging as a failure to repair defects at the molecular level. In contrast the work of anti-aging scientists and practitioners seeks to promote the extension of human life span by introducing techniques that prevent many of the conditions that accompany aging. While gerontologists highlight the quackery of much anti-aging medicine, and draw an important distinction between legitimate and illegitimate attempts to treat old age and the diseases of later life, their distinction between medically necessary and 'cosmetic' interventions is not as clearcut as they would like to believe.

Vincent (1999) argues that contested scientific discourses on aging reflect the dominant cultural discourse in the West that denigrates old age and dying. In doing so he identifies four types of anti-aging science. The first, 'symptom alleviation', is appearance based and can take cosmetic, prophylactic and compensatory forms. This type of antiaging is very strongly linked to changing notions of the body and identity. Bauman talks about the importance of 'fitness' in contemporary society. However this is not a benign focus on health promotion. Rather, it marks one of the chief characteristics of the relationship between the self and society; namely, constant change and movement. For Bauman, bodily fitness is pursued as the supreme goal by many. But it is a state that can never be truly achieved. Relating this back to aging, it would seem that the practices that we have been discussing fit very well into this indeterminate notion of fitness and therefore much of the value of investigating how they redefine aging as well as notions of health is lost if the debate is confined to naturalistic understandings of the body. Rather than pursuing moral arguments about the rights and wrongs of anti-aging medicine, a sociology of health in later life needs to address the causes and consequences of anti-aging practices. Such a field needs to explore the lived experience of those who engage, refuse to engage or find themselves unable to engage witnn these practices.

The second, 'life expectancy extension,' is disease based and addresses 'diseases of aging,' including cancer and heart disease. The third, 'lifespan extension,' is dominated by research at the genetic and molecular level. Here old age is equated with cellular senescence. Finally, 'abolition' refers to the wilder shores of anti-aging that seek immortality or its equivalent. [...] There are strong moral judgements associated with the anti-aging debate and Vincent is explicit in his attempts to bring back notions of a worthy acceptance of biological limits and human finitude. In a similar vein Moody (1995) draws on Habermas to call for resistance to the medicalization of old age and for a restoration of meaning to old age and death. The recourse to Habermas should perhaps be expected. It suggests that these developments are being viewed through the prism of ethics, rather than in terms of a transformation of the relations of health and healing in modern society (Scambler 2002). In the discussion of anti-aging medicine we can hear the echo of Ivan Illich's view of medicalization (Illich 1976) where those who seek out anti-aging medicine are rendered cultural dupes. They fall prey to a cult of youth and youthfulness in their desire to access anti-aging treatments. If people turn towards anti-aging products and technologies they are viewed as somehow suffering from a form of false consciousness, whereas the adoption of seemingly 'natural' pursuits in later life is valued as appropriate and morally worthy. Clearly technology offers new ways of pushing the boundaries of the human body but as Habermas (2003) argues our response to these challenges should transcend notions of nature versus scientific progress. The ambiguity and complexity that is present within anti-aging medicine is a useful development in allowing us to see to what extent our views of the relationship between the body and health need to change.

THE AGING PROCESS IN CONTEMPORARY SOCIETY

Aging opens up certain possibilities for new lifestyles, activities and meanings, while at the same time closing down other opportunities (Gilleard and Higgs 2000, 2005). With regard to later life therefore we propose that a useful metaphor for understanding individual and group trajectories of aging is that of the 'arc of acquiescence.' This arc traces the decline associated with a gradual withdrawal from successful body maintenance and the greater acceptance of bodily limits.

One of the key aspects of the changing nature of aging is the distinction between the third and fourth ages. While principally conceptual in nature the division between these two categories carries with it very different experiences of aging (Twigg 2004). It is towards the complex boundary work between the third and fourth ages that we now turn. As we have previously noted, Peter Laslett's vision of the third age suggested the emergence of a 'new' period in the lifecourse standing between middle age concerned with the responsibilities of work and child-raising and a fourth age of decline and ultimately death (Laslett 1996 [1989]). Differences between Laslett's conceptualisation of the third age and other European and North American understandings of the term were recognised early on by Laslett. In the second edition of *A fresh map of life* (Laslett 1996) he was particularly critical of attempts such as those by the Carnegie Enquiry (1993, 2000) to define the third age in terms of chronological age. These criticisms have been echoed in a recent attempt by Midwinter (2005) to replace approaches to the third age based on ages or birth dates with a 'stages of life' approach based on the economic status of the citizenry (drawing on engagement in paid work). Midwinter argues that his approach gives a more accurate picture of the relative size of first, second and third ages in the UK over the last 150 years. It seems clear from this discussion that the fourth age is not simply a life stage development from the third age. While the fourth age has become associated with the dependency and decline of 'very old age' and fourth agers are often identified as the 'oldest old' there is considerable confusion and dispute about definitions of the fourth age which depend on whether it is being approached from demographic, biological, psychological or quality of life perspectives. Certainly attempts to use chronological age as a marker appear too rigid in the face of the considerable variation in the age of onset of the fourth age. Results from the Berlin aging study (BASE) suggest that life in the fourth age is a very negative experience (Baltes and Meyer 1999).

The fourth age therefore presents particular difficulties because the oldest old are at the limits of their functional capacity. The pessimistic scenario is that the capacity to intervene successfully in the fourth age is limited with the additional unintended consequence that extending the life span may have the effect of reducing the opportunities of many older people to live and die in dignity. But this still does not answer the question of precisely how the fourth age is constituted other than through being defined as the physical and mental decline of deep old age. Gilleard and Higgs (2007a) see it as a much more significant category in the articulation of aging, a category that plays a role for others as much as it defines the predicament of the oldest old. They argue that it is when people are incorporated as third persons in other people's age-based discourse, that they become subjects of a fourth age. This might occur because of a public failure of self-management as much as a specific physiological or psychological symptom. The failure prompts the need to secure the failure by some institutional form of care. Gilleard and Higgs suggest that the failure exists as an 'event horizon' which once passed allows the older person to become the subject of other 'competent' people's decisions. The use of the event horizon metaphor is designed to indicate that a qualitative break in the older person's competence has occurred and that while it might not be catastrophic it does suggest a point of no return. From this point on the pursuit of agency becomes conditional if not redundant. It is in this way that the fourth age is related to the third age. Moreover, unlike the habitus associated with the third age, the fourth age cannot sustain a set of its own dispositions or support forms of symbolic differentiation. Instead, for Gilleard and Higgs, the fourth age acts as a metaphorical 'black hole' of aging creating fear among those outside its reach, reminding them that deep old age means passing beyond the social world. For observers, influenced in varying degrees by the commodification of consumer society, there appears neither opportunity to articulate a lifestyle within this agency-free environment nor any reason to trust that previous choices will be honoured or acted upon. The fourth age therefore becomes the sum of all the fears lying under the surface of the third age. As such, it is more than a synonym for the oldest old. In seeing the third age as defined by a cultural rejection of old age, we are better positioned to see the deeper connections between the somatic society and aging.

DEATH AND IMMORTALITY

Our increasing longevity and knowledge of the underlying genetics of disease has stimulated an increasing obsession with the calculability and predictability of disease and ultimately death. On the internet one can find numerous sites such as 'death clock' and 'death date' that promise to predict our personal demise. Within the field of Public Health, deaths prior to a certain defined cut-off are referred to as avoidable deaths and a good deal of research into the 'old old' is based around predicting functional deterioration and calculating contributions to healthy life expectancy. Bauman (1992) argues that the fact of human mortality and our awareness of it is the basis for social institutions and behavioural patterns that reproduce the society of the living. Extending healthy life-expectancy and the life span has many profound consequences for human relations including marriage and inter-generational transfers. What does living a healthy active life into one's 90s mean in terms of living in the same marriage? How do inter-generational relationships based on love and reciprocity adjust to both increasing longevity and increasing calculability of life expectancy?

Peter Berger (1967) argued that death was a fundamental feature of all societies. His ideas have been taken up by a number of writers, including Giddens (1990). Giddens suggests that the conditions of late modernity have precipitated an increase in anxieties about death. These sociological approaches have emphasized the developments which have made untimely death a less common occurrence, and indelibly associated with aging and later life.

Within western culture, death and old age are closely tied in the popular consciousness. Not only is death associated with old age but also from the mid-twentieth century onwards death became increasingly medicalised (Illich 1976). Sociological studies of the impact of medical science on the experience of death highlighted how the organization of death in the USA's healthcare system resulted in death becoming routinized and bureaucratized (Sudnow 1967). Other studies showed how hospital staff categorized dying patients at different points along 'dying trajectories' and how this extended clinical control over what is considered a 'good death'(Glaser and Strauss 1968). The sequestration of the dying (Mellor and Shilling 1993) has made it an increasingly lonely, isolated experience (Elias 1985) and the individualized, private and clinically controlled process of dying has become the source of many people's difficulty in coming to terms with their mortality (Mellor 1993).

Advances in medical science and in material affluence have destabilised received wisdom about the biological limits of aging. Gilleard and Higgs (2000) highlight the blurring of boundaries and the extension of limits through cyber-technology and bio-technologies. On the face of it, therefore, the technological advances of second modernity appear to place immortality at the centre of human concerns. Paradoxically Bauman (2001) offers an alternative view suggesting that the imperatives of the consumer society mean that we have entered an entirely new phase where immortality is of no consequence. Instead, it is the throw away, disposable, short-term, impermanence of life that is valued; 'the "long term" is but a package of short-term experiences amenable to endless reshuffling and with no privileged order of succession' (Bauman

2001: 250). Does this therefore mean that death has lost its meaning in the same way that aging seems to have?

As Thomas Cole puts it in The Journey of Life (1992), if the lifecourse is seen as flexible and fluid does this mean that the finitude of life becomes just another demarcation which should be approached in the same ways as other lifestyle options? This brings us back to the territory of naturalistic views of aging and death. Should we see a good death as not constructed in the right dosage of medication but rather constructed out of 'human relationships and symbols that transcend individuals and their bodies?' Should this be our aim? Or are we once again returning to a long departed lifeworld where aging and death have significance precisely because they are not subject to individual choice?

DISCUSSION QUESTIONS

1. Why is growing old(er) in our youth-oriented, medicalized, and less consumerist society so complex and challenging?

2. What is the "cult of youth" and how does it affect the experiences of individuals as they grow into their "third" and "fourth" ages?

3. What is the conflict between anti-aging medicine and gerontology all about? Why does it raise fundamental questions about the nature of aging and the way in which contemporary societies?

4. What does it mean that the process of dying has been institutionalized and medicalized? What does this mean for the dying person and his or her loved ones? What does this mean for society as a whole?

REFERENCES

Baltes, P.B. and Smith, J. (2003). "New Frontiers in the Future of Aging: From Successful Aging of the Young Old to the Dilemmas of the Fourth Age." *Gerontology*, 49 (2): 123–35.

Bauman, Z. 2000. Liquid Modernity. Cambridge, UK: Polity.

———. 1992. Mortality, Immortality and Other Life Strategies. Cambridge, UK: Polity Press.

Beck, U. 2000. The Brave New World of Work, Cambridge, UK: Polity

———. 1992. Risk Society, Towards a New Modernity, London: Sage.

Beck, U., Giddens, A. and Lash, S. 1994. *Reflexive Modernization: Politics, Tradition and Aesthetics in the Modern Social Order*. Oxford, UK: Blackwell.

Berger, P. 1967. *The Sacred Canopy*. New York: Anchor Books.

Bourdieu, Pierre. 1984. *Distinction: A Social Critique of the Judgement of Taste*. London: Routledge.

Butler, R., (2002) "The study of productive aging." Journals of Gerontology B Psychological Sciences and Social Sciences, 57: 323.

Davis, K. 1995. *Reshaping the Female Body: The dilemma of Cosmetic Surgery*. New York: Routledge.

D'Souza, C. (2007). "My name is Christa. I'm an age-orexic," *Observer Woman*, May 2007: 21–25.

Dychtwald, K. 1999. *Age power: How the 21st Century will be Ruled by the New Old*, New York: Tarcher.

Elias, N. 1978. *The History of Manners. The Civilizing Process; Volume I*. New York: Urizen Books.

Elliott, C. 2003. *Better than Well, American Medicine meets the American Dream*, London: W.W. Norton & Co.

Featherstone, M. and Hepworth, M. 1991. "The mask of Aging and the Post-modern Lifecourse." in M. Featherstone, M. Hepworth and B.S. Turner (Eds.) *The Body: Social Processes and Cultural Theory*. London: Sage.

Fox, N.J. 1999. *Beyond Health: Postmodernism and Embodiment*. London: Free Association Books.

Giddens, Anthony. 1990. *The Consequences of Modernity*. Cambridge, UK: Polity Press.

———. 1991. *Modernity and Self-Identity: Self and Society in the Late Modern Age*. Cambridge, UK: Polity Press.

Gilleard, C., Higgs, P., Hyde, M., Wiggins, R. and Blane, D. 2007. "The third age and the baby boomers: two approaches to the structuring of later life." *International Journal of Aging and Later Life*, 2 (2): 13–30.

———. (2005b). "Class, Cohort and Consumption: the British experience of the third age," *Journal of Gerontology*: Social Sciences, 60B: 305–10.

Gullette, M.M. 2004. *Aged by Culture*. Chicago, IL: University of Chicago Press.

Habermas, J. 2003. *The Future of Human Nature*. Cambridge, UK: Polity.

Illich, I. 1976. *Limits to Medicine: Medical Nemesis: The Expropriation of Health*, Harmondsworth, UK: Pelican.

Katz, S. 1996. *Disciplining Old Age: TheFformation of Gerontological Knowledge*, London: University Press of Virginia.

———. 2005. *Cultural Aging: Lifecourse, lifestyle and Senior Worlds*, Peterborough, Canada: Broadview Press.

Laslett, P. 1996, 1989. *A fresh Map of Life: The Emergence of the Third Age*, 2nd edition, Basingstoke, UK: Macmillan Press Ltd. Latour, B. (2003)

Lupton, D. 1995. *The Imperative of Health: Public Health and the Regulated Body*. London: Sage.

Mellor, P. 1993. "Death in High Modernity." in D. Clarke (Ed.) *The Sociology of Death*, Oxford: Blackwell

Mellor, P. and Shilling, P. (1993). "Modernity, Self-Identity and the Sequestration of Death." *Sociology*, 27 (3): 411–31.

Midwinter, E. (2005). "How many people are there in the third age?" *Aging and Society*, 25: 9–18.

Moody, H.R. (1993) Overview: What is Critical Gerontology and Why is it important? in T.R. Cole, W.A. Achenbaum, P.L. Jakobi and R. Kastenbaum (Eds.) *Voices and Visions of Aging: Toward a Critical Gerontology*, New York: Springer.

Mykytyn, C. (2006). "Anti-aging medicine: A Patient/practitioner Movement to Redefine aging." *Social Science and Medicine*, 62: 643–53.

Neugarten, B.L. (1974). "Age-groups in American Society and the rise of the young-old." *Annals of the American Academy of Politics and Social Sciences*, 9: 187–98.

Pitts, V. 2003. *In the Flesh: The Cultural Politics of Body Modification*, New York: Palgrave.

Rose, Nikolas. 2007. *The Politics of Life Itself: Biomedicine, Power and Subjectivity in the Twenty-First Century*. Princeton NJ: Princeton University Press.

Scambler, G. 2002. *Health and Social Change: A Critical Theory*. Buckingham, UK: Open University Press.

Sennett, R. (1994). *Flesh and Stone, The Body and the City in Western Civilization*, London: Faber and Faber.

Singh, C. and Kelly, M. (2003). "Botox: an 'elixir of youth'?" *European Journal of Plastic Surgery*, 26 (5): 273–74.

Sudnow, D. 1967. *Passing On: The Social Organization of Dying*. Englewood Cliffs, New Jersey: Prentice Hall.

Twigg, J. (2000). "Carework as Bodywork." *Aging and Society*, (20): 389–411.

Vincent, J. (1999). *Politics, Power and Old Age*. Buckingham, UK: Open University Press.

READING 21

Death, Dying, and the Right to Die

Clive Seale

Death in late-modern mass societies has a particular character which sociological analysis, informed by historical, anthropological, and demographic studies, is well suited to bring out. Such analysis exposes the underlying dynamics of common ethical dilemmas in end-of-life care, showing that subjective experiences otherwise thought to be purely psychological in origin—dying, grief, care provision—are shaped by historical and social forces. This chapter reviews some important features of modern societies that influence and explain our experience of death, focusing on the desire of many modern individuals—manifest in the growth of right-to-die social movements—to benefit from an open awareness of dying and to control the manner in which death is experienced.

There is considerable cross-cultural variation in the degree to which personal control of the dying process is seen to be desirable, partly influenced by level of affluence, education, and religiosity, as well as cultural patterns associated with race or ethnicity. For example, the right-to-die movement largely prospers in wealthier societies and appeals most to educated sections of the population that have good access to health care. The desire to benefit psychologically from awareness of dying has particular appeal in cultural groups where freedom of choice is embraced as a duty of citizenship, and

self-identity is taken to be a personal, worked-upon project. Much of the detailed empirical work reviewed in this chapter describes such variation.

DEATH IN MODERN SOCIETIES

The modern experience of dying is highly influenced by a transformation in life expectancy and in the pattern of disease in modern societies. In 2006 the average life expectancy at birth worldwide was sixty-seven years, having risen from just forty-eight years in 1955 (WHO 1988, 2008). Historical data for England going back to 1541 (Wrigley and Schofield 1981) show life expectancy fluctuating below forty years until the 1830s, after which it began a steady rise to the 2006 averages of seventy-seven for men and eighty-one for women (WHO 2008). The drop in the infant and child mortality rates and decline of deaths in middle-aged groups that has accompanied raised life expectancy means that in the wealthier countries of the world, death is typically experienced at the end of a long life. Thus the experience of dying is increasingly linked to the more general experience of being old (Seale 2000).

Again in wealthier countries in particular, changing patterns of disease also influence the experience of dying. Broadly speaking, death from

Clive Seale, "Death, Dying, and the Right to Die," Handbook of Medical Sociology, pp. 210-225. Copyright © 2010 by Vanderbilt University Press. Reprinted with permission.

infectious disease, epidemics, and malnutrition has largely been replaced by death from cancer, heart disease, and stroke. A rising incidence of dementia in later life adds to the social care needs of people approaching death. The position of elderly women in terms of access to informal care and financial resources is more difficult than that of elderly men (Arber and Ginn 1991). Kellehear (2007) argues that, increasingly, people are living longer than they want to, so the social exclusion of elderly people and their placement in care homes where many experience a "shameful" death is an unwelcome feature of contemporary societies. He relates a relatively high rate of suicide among elderly people to the desire to avoid such circumstances.

Additionally, the management of death has become increasingly subject to professional management and sequestration in institutions, reflected most obviously in the rising proportion of deaths that occur within hospitals and the decline in home deaths in wealthier countries. This has led to a common perception, often aired in mass media discourse, that modern society is "death denying," by which is usually meant that modern individuals rarely encounter dying people and are relatively unskilled in managing the realities of death, both in terms of responding to the emotions of dying and bereavement and in dealing with the physical aspects of dying and dead bodies. This denial-of-death thesis has attracted careful critical examination by sociologists, including Talcott Parsons (1978; Parsons and Lidz 1967), who argues that in an important sense modern societies are remarkably death affirming, being effectively organized to control death as part of a primary cultural pattern of activism. This involves the use of health care to resist premature death and alleviate the physical suffering of dying, and the control of deliberately imposed death by state management of warfare, violence, and capital punishment.

Premature death has thus come to be regarded as an unnatural violation of a normal lifespan.

The concept of "death brokering" (Timmermans 2005) has been helpful in understanding the contemporary medical role in the management of dying and the construction of meaning around death. Timmermans argues that medical authorities, through clinical and forensic activities, are dominant in providing acceptable explanations for death, thus rendering it "culturally manageable and understandable" (2005, 1005). Forensic medical investigation, by ensuring that the cause of each death is securely located within an explanatory system for bodily events, renders even the most mysterious type of death understandable. Clinical activities involve an active approach to the management of the physiological aspects of dying, as well as the expectations of patients and relatives. Thus they enable the pursuit of an ideal death (for example, one that is explainable as the result of a physical disease process, free of uncontrolled physical suffering, predictable so that it is preceded by the right amount of time spent "dying," and accompanied by an appropriate degree of emotion). Sometimes, of course, efforts to provide for such a death fail, but, argues Timmermans, these serve only to mark out a realm for further activity by medical authorities, maintaining the continuing cultural authority of medicine over the meaning of modern dying.

More broadly, as Blauner (1966) pointed out, the retirement and replacement of older people ensures the continuity of modern institutions. Specialized professions and institutions—health-care staff, hospitals and other places of care—complete the sequestration of dying people from mainstream social life, ensuring the minimum of disruption to the smooth functioning of social institutions. All this might be regarded, as in Parsons, as part of facing up to the reality of death rather than denying it. Nevertheless, such sequestration means that many people lack personal familiarity with death when compared with individual experience in smaller, premodern social groups, where the end of a life is generally witnessed and, in many cases, experienced as very disruptive to the continuity of group social life. Funerals in such groups are then rituals to revive community spirit as well as to address personal grief (Hertz 1960). There is a greater focus on mourning rather than on the emotions of dying in such pre-modern societies because of the unpredictability of death, which means "dying" people cannot readily be labeled as such (Kellehear 2007).

The growth in popularity of life insurance, overcoming religious objections, is an indicator of the acknowledgment of the reality of death that is typical of modern mass societies. Zelizer (1978), who studied its introduction in the nineteenth-century United States, demonstrates that the ministry initially opposed life insurance, viewing it as a gamble on the outcome of the divine will. But families living in urban conditions without the safety net of a supportive local community increasingly experienced destitution on the death of a breadwinner. Taking out life insurance was gradually reinterpreted as the moral duty of responsible fatherhood, eventually becoming an aspect of the risk planning that characterizes a modern approach to life (Beck 1992; Giddens 1990, 1991). By this means modern individuals take charge of their destinies and attempt to control the effects of adverse life events.

But the insurance industry is just one example of a broad range of social institutions that contribute to this sense of control. The chief institution is, of course, medicine and the health care system, including public health and associated state sponsorship of health-promoting (and therefore death-avoiding) lifestyles. The works of Arney and Bergen (1984), Armstrong (1987), and Prior (1989), examples of sociological work informed by Foucauldian theory, bring out this particular character of modern societies. These authors show that the most basic contribution of the medical perspective is to locate death in the body as the natural outcome of disease, so that medical endeavors in combating disease then become part of the "sheltering canopy" (Berger and Luckmann 1971) constructed by human activity as a shield against death. As the technical efficacy of medical science has improved, this contribution has largely substituted for religious defenses against death, or adds to them for individuals able to hold on to both scientific and religious understandings of life. There is a sense, then, in which health promotion is a religion, and the zeal with which some people devote themselves to health and fitness regimes is considerable (Glassner 1989).

Death certification is an important social instrument for locating death in the body. Bloor's (1991) study shows that doctors in Scotland, whose training in the practice is minimal, experience it as a minor routine. This means that certification is done in sometimes idiosyncratic ways by doctors whose main concern may be to fulfill the legal requirement of ruling out such "unnatural" causes as murder or accident (Bloor 1994). Yet, in spite of its limitations as an accurate description of bodily processes, certification follows certain principles. Prior (1989) observes that we no longer find "intemperate living," "want," or "cold and whiskey" written on certificates, or "poverty," "bad luck," or "the will of God." Instead, a causally linked chain of bodily processes resulting in death is required. Certification rules out understandings of death, social causes, and human agency and is a pure assertion of the bodily containment of death, a ritualized identification of the workings of natural disease within the body. As medicine holds out the possibility of successful intervention into the course of natural disease, so the death certificate is an indirect promise to the living that death can be controlled.

Interactions between medical staff and relatives at the time of death continue to describe death as the outcome of bodily events, as medical sociologists studying observations of death announcements by hospital staff (Sudnow 1967) and coroners' officials (Charmaz 1976) show. Charmaz notes that key tasks which must be achieved by coroners' deputies in notifying relatives of a sudden unexpected death (apart from preserving composure and ensuring acceptance of burial costs by relatives) are to make the death credible, accountable, and "acceptable" to relatives. A common strategy is to delay announcing a death until details of an accident or collapse have been given as "cues," which ideally prompt the relative to jump to the conclusion that a death has occurred. For example: "I tell them that he collapsed today while at work. They asked if he is all right now. I say slowly, 'Well, no, but they took him to the hospital.' They ask if he is there now. I say, 'They did all they could do—the doctors tried very hard.' They say, 'He is dead at the hospital?' Then I tell them he's at the coroner's office" (Charmaz 1976, 78).

To the question that then follows—What must I do?—the deputy points the shocked recipient toward activity to deal with the death. Sudnow (1967) notes that in every such hospital announcement scene he witnessed, a "historical reference" was made to a medically relevant antecedent "cause of death" such as a heart attack. Talk then proceeds to further elaboration on this cause, to a discussion of whether the person had "suffered," and to assurances that all that could have been done was done. On this last matter, Sudnow records occasions where this impression was made easier to sustain by artificially delaying the appearance of the medical announcer to suggest that heroic but futile rescue attempts were made. On the matter of suffering, Sudnow notes that "doctors …

routinely lie in their characterizations of death as painless" (1967, 146), an impression that relatives are often equally keen to sustain. In these various ways people learn about deaths and participate in the confirmation of death as the outcome of bodily processes.

Practices such as these can be understood as similar in their function to the mortuary rites described by anthropologists studying tribal or traditional societies (Bloch and Parry 1982). The task of the living is to enclose and explain death, reduce its polluting effects, and symbolically place individual deaths in a context that helps survivors turn away from death and toward continuing life. In other words, medicine writes a cultural script that enables participants to engage in a resurrective practice (Seale 1998).

Palliative Care

On the whole, the demographic transition means that dying trajectories for those in wealthier countries tend to be longer and, particularly in the case of cancer, more predictably threatening to life. A form of terminal care has emerged that is largely predicated on the existence of cancer, finding its expression in the hospice and palliative care movement. In many respects this movement has promoted a model for what dying should be like: something that involves emotional accompaniment, awareness of oncoming death, and psychological and relationship development during the final phase of last farewells, coupled with expert medical and nursing care devoted to the alleviation of suffering (Kubler-Ross 1969; Saunders and Baines 1983). As Kellehear (2007) argues, this continues conceptions of the "good death" that were developed when societies changed from hunter-gatherer to pastoral modes of life.

Walter (1994) has described the ideas promoted by the hospice and palliative care movement as "revivalist," incorporating a critique of the "modern" way of death that had developed in Western societies up until the mid-twentieth century, which influential commentators such as Gorer (1965) perceived as involving a taboo. The revivalist alternative that developed and gathered strength through the 1960s and continues to the present day resists the consequences of sequestration, or the hiding away of dying and bereavement, so that these are subject to greater public attention as well as psychological and medical expertise. Revivalism enables people encountering bereavement and death to engage in institutionalized practices (such as hospice care or grief counseling) that include their experience in a publicly available discourse or cultural script, providing a sense of community membership that combats the isolation and abandonment otherwise experienced by dying and bereaved people. Drawing on this perspective, Arnarson (2007) argues that bereavement counseling serves to regenerate the sense of autonomy that drives a modern image of self-identity.

The microinteractions involved in providing a sense of membership have been studied by a number of sociologists, including Hunt (1991a, b) whose ethnomethodological account of home palliative care nurses "being friendly and informal" describes processes reminiscent of Hochschild's (1983) account of the emotional labor of flight attendants. Hunt (1991b) describes nurses performing their tasks informally, wearing non-uniform clothing, and beginning a home visit with small talk that continues, interspersed with clinical questioning, as the visit proceeds. Professional friendliness is distinguished from friendship by the degree to which self-disclosure is reciprocal, and Hunt shows that nurses only rarely make such disclosures, though families often do. At the same time, such nurses are carrying out important tasks such as identifying who in the family might be expected to provide care and indeed who might

be constituted as "family" (Hunt 1991a). Perakyla (1991), in similar vein, has brought an ethnomethodological perspective to bear on the "hope work" done in care settings for the terminally ill.

The hospice and palliative care social movement that began in the 1960s and rapidly spread through the UK, North America, and other Anglophone countries in the 1970s, subsequently influencing terminal care worldwide, is subject to certain tensions which sociologists have documented. Early work by Abel (1986) and Paradis and Cummings (1986) argued that U.S. hospice care, initially the product of grassroots activism to rehumanize dying, had rapidly moved toward organizational homogeneity through a process of institutionalization. In part this was due to the narrow vision of health-insurance agencies, which could not incorporate a service with diffuse aims, intangible psychosocial interventions, and unquantifiable gains in their reimbursement systems. Abel echoes the concern of Dooley (1982, 37), who observed the danger that care then came increasingly to look like "traditional health care service with hospice overtones." Paradis and Cummings identify the "normative" influence exercised by the influx of staff from orthodox care settings who were not fully acculturated into hospice ways. The professionalization of hospice nursing was also a sign of encroachment and corruption of the ideal.

In the United Kingdom, James and Field (1992) put forth a similar argument, drawing some of their empirical data from James's experiences as a participant observer in a palliative care unit within the NHS (James 1986), where James identified a dilution of hospice ideals that led to an emphasis on physical rather than psychosocial care. James and Field (1992) draw on Weberian ideas to describe the routinization of hospice care, the reestablishment of interprofessional hierarchies that the early hospice movement had challenged, and a resurgence in rule-bound behavior, rationalization, and the commodification of humanitarian values through processes of audit, measurement, and marketing.

There is no doubt that palliative care as a nursing and medical specialty is now securely established within the health-care systems of many developed countries and is beginning to be taken up in different forms in developing regions where terminal care has become more relevant with the changing patterns of disease that accompany growing wealth and better health (Wright et al. 2008). With institutional success comes an input of resources, so the decline in the initial idealism of the movement may be no bad thing. Additionally, as Giddens (1990) has observed about the assumption that bureaucratization is restrictive, "rather than tending inevitably towards rigidity, [such] organisations [can] produce areas of autonomy and spontaneity which are actually often less easy to achieve in smaller groups" (1990, 138). The extent to which this is true of modern palliative care requires further empirical sociological work.

Hospice and palliative care services largely provide for people with cancer; for many in Western societies, this provides a model of what it is like to die. However, cancer causes a minority of deaths, albeit a fairly large minority, in the societies where hospice and palliative care services have developed, with heart disease, strokes, old age, and other conditions eventually carrying off the majority of the population. These conditions have somewhat different trajectories from cancer and different degrees of predictability that they will end in death (Kellehear 2007; Seale 1991, 2000). Indeed, Logue (1994) points out the limitations of hospice-style care for elderly people with dementia or for those experiencing social care needs rather than terminal illness, who are not seen to be appropriate clients of palliative care

services. This author has noted elsewhere that the demographic profile of the elderly population, coupled with the disadvantages experienced by elderly women, means that the quality of care provision for very elderly women is a "women's issue" (Logue 1991, 97). Indeed, as we will see, gender is also an important consideration in relation to the right-to-die social movement, which represents an alternative method to that of hospice care in influencing the timing and manner of death.

AWARENESS OF DYING

No account of the sociology of dying can avoid the conclusion that the work of Glaser and Strauss (Glaser and Strauss, 1965, 1968; Strauss and Glaser 1977) for the project that also saw the launch of grounded theory (Glaser and Strauss 1967) represents a foundational moment. Their account of "awareness contexts" in *Awareness of Dying* (Glaser and Strauss 1965) deserves particular attention in this review, because it permits a reevaluation and reinterpretation of that work from the perspective of contemporary sociological thinking. Broadly speaking, this involves looking back from a sociological viewpoint that is somewhat influenced by poststructuralism and postscientism to see that this seminal work which presents itself as an objective and scientific account is in fact very much a product of its time and culture—a "story" about dying, in fact. This perspective is consistent with a view that sees research reporting in the human sciences as an artful practice whose texts may be deconstructed in that light (Clifford and Marcus 1986; Atkinson 1990). I will contrast *Awareness of Dying* with later work in institutional ethnography by Lawton (1998, 2000) that reflects a more contemporary but nevertheless realist perspective that draws on the sociology of the body.

The main purpose of *Awareness of Dying* is to describe four "awareness contexts"—closed, suspicion, pretense, and open—in which dying can occur. In the first of these, the dying person is unaware that they are dying but relatives and caregivers are aware; in the last of these all openly acknowledge the person's terminal disease. The other two contexts represent stages between these points. The typology is based on observations across a range of institutional settings in which people die. Much of the book explores the conditions under which movement from one context to another occurs, as well as the consequences of each context for interaction between the parties involved. Glaser and Strauss are critical of the sociologist who develops a theory "that embodies, without his realization, the sociologist's ideals, the values of his occupation and social class, as well as popular views and myths" (260). The contrast to this is the systematic induction of theory grounded in data, which ensures both objectivity and practical relevance to a broad variety of situations.

Yet, read as a literary production, *Awareness of Dying* reveals itself as a dramatic parable of revivalism (Walter 1994), in which dying people are portrayed as romantic heroes struggling with diminishing resources against an iron cage of modernist bureaucracy. Doctors, as chief system representatives, call the shots, and in a subdrama to the main plot, nurses stressfully vacillate between the roles of patient advocate and the instrument of doctors' will. As a "side interest," relatives hover in the background, occupying a role whose tensions resemble those of nurses.

The main plot concerns the dying patient versus the impersonal forces of the hospital, a "single individual ... who is pitted against" staff (Glaser and Strauss 1965, 12). Suspicion awareness is a "contest" or a "fencing match" (47) or a matter of "tactics" (53), in which "the patient's actual resources are exceedingly slim" (51). Unlike wives who suspect a cheating husband, say the authors, patients do not have intimate knowledge of their

opponent, are physically somewhat immobile, and cannot pay private detectives. Unlike spies, the patient has no team but "faces an organized team" (52) that is unlikely to contain any allies.

Doctors in *Awareness of Dying* behave like tricksters or con men when a patient is in closed awareness. Possessing the advantage of membership on an experienced team they will, for example, "make meaningless trips" (186) to the bedside to maintain an illusion of a commitment to cure. More worrying, they may add to this a layer of inhumanity, discounting dying patients' requests to withdraw from clinical trials and restricting levels of analgesic medications in case they become confounded with the effects of the experimental treatment. Doctors may keep patients alive "for the rest of the semester" if they present "interesting" teaching material, forcing a patient to "have to ask for his own death" (186). Little evidence is provided for these claims in the text; we do not know how the authors determined whether particular visits to the bedside were "meaningless" in medical terms, or how many (and why) terminal patients were or were not allowed to withdraw from trials, or how they came to the view that particular patients were kept alive for teaching purposes. In Baruch's (1981) terms, these are "atrocity stories" which align the reader with the authors' judgments through an appeal to emotion. Additionally, the depiction of doctors is striking for what it omits. We are not told how things seem from their point of view (unlike nurses, whose position is explored in more sympathetic terms). The effect is to present doctors as impersonal system representatives, without humanity.

Glaser and Strauss promote in this book a particular model for desirable dying. First, there is the rhetorical strategy of inciting talk about death by claiming the existence of a widespread culture of death denial: "typical Americans ... are unlikely to initiate ... a conversation [about a patient's impending death]" (1965, 67), and "Americans are characteristically unwilling to talk openly about the process of dying" (3). As the Foucauldian sociologist Armstrong (1987) has pointed out, such silence about death has been constituted as a "lie," and therefore to be condemned, only since the late 1950s. Up until that point, "to keep death a secret was justifiable because patients inevitably feared death and relied on the hope which the secret gave them" (1987, 653). After this point, a new regime of truth emerged, which meant that the announcement by Glaser and Strauss of a prohibition against talking about death was an invitation to break the taboo. The new system prioritized the subjective experience of the dying person, so that in Armstrong's words, "the chief mourners become the dying themselves" (654).

Glaser and Strauss's open awareness context provides for this self-mourning role. The authors point out that "there is much to recommend giving the patient an opportunity actively to manage his own dying" (1965, 135), including the chance for all concerned to prepare themselves, say good-byes and "close their lives with proper rituals" (43). These psychological benefits are "of course not available to unaware patients in the closed awareness situation" (43). Such patients fail to prioritize important things, make unrealistic plans, and may even hasten their deaths by not realizing why they should cooperate with treatment (43–44). Thus these sociologists are fully aligned with the ideals of the nascent hospice movement of the time, itself informed by a philosophy expressed by the humanist physician Kübler-Ross, whose account of the psychological and spiritual benefits of acceptance of death in *On Death and Dying* (1969) became an international best seller. The emerging psychosocial discipline of thanatology was informed by such ideals, prompting the observation from one enthusiast: "We begin to live the moment we begin to die" (Kalish 1980, 7).

We can see now, with the benefit of more than forty years' hindsight, that *Awareness of Dying* presents a particularly culture-bound portrayal of dying. That it does this under the cloak of a supposedly objective, scientific methodology should prompt reflection on broader issues of method in sociological research. Evidence from cultures where personal projects of self identity are less intense and care of the self is more readily given over to others contribute to the view that open awareness of dying is evaluated in more widely varying ways than Glaser and Strauss acknowledged. What in Anglophone culture may be seen as a conspiracy of silence that abandons the patient may in other societies be regarded as an appropriate way of protecting dying persons by allowing others to shoulder the responsibility of decision making on their behalf (see studies reviewed in Seale 1998, 110–12).

Sociology of the Body

All sociological writing relies on rhetorical devices that construct realities reflecting the times in which the writer lives. This does not necessarily entail dismissal of the insights contained in such work. The work of Glaser and Strauss continues to be highly influential, prompting further modifications to the theory of awareness contexts. Mamo (1999), for example, is critical of the emphasis placed on information and cognition in the work of Glaser and Strauss, proposing that the role of emotional work done by both care providers and patients should be recognized as a part of the maintenance and negotiation of awareness contexts. Lawton's (1998, 2000) ethnography of care of dying people in a hospice setting is of particular note in its explicit contrast with the work of Glaser and Strauss; Lawton places the deteriorating body, and its consequences for social interaction and selfhood, at the center of the analysis. In so doing, she provides an implied critique of the impetus toward death awareness to which the work of Glaser and Strauss contributes.

Lawton draws on the historical work of Elias (1978, 1982) concerning the civilizing process, whereby the physical and animal aspects of human life—bodily functions, illness, death—have become increasingly regulated and controlled. In modern European societies, Elias argues, the growth of "manners" means that we no longer blow our noses on our sleeves, eat from communal bowls with our fingers, or urinate in full view of others. Hygiene as a rationale for the decline of these practices masks their relation to social practices that developed in courtly European society in response to the political needs of a central royal authority, and thereafter spread through the bourgeoisie as markers of social distinction. Lawton interprets the sequestration of the dying in hospice care as a part of the "civilized" hiding away of bodily decay that has become increasingly disturbing to modern sensibilities and is now regarded as unmanageable in family settings. She presents particularly harrowing case studies of bodily deterioration and "unboundedness" that involve the leakage of bodily fluids and associated smells to demonstrate her thesis that the experience of dying from advanced cancer often included a loss of personhood, a state in which benefiting from awareness and acceptance of dying appears impossible.

A number of patients observed by Lawton withdrew socially before their deaths in response to the experience of their deteriorating bodies. They also sometimes asked for euthanasia, as in the case of "Dolly":

> Dolly … had cancer of the colon and was admitted after becoming chronically incontinent at home. Her husband informed me that every time she had a severe bout of diarrhoea she begged him to help her take her own life. Dolly's requests for euthanasia continued during the first week of her stay in hospice. The staff were unable to get her diarrhoea under control. In addition, she went into obstruction. The tumour mass expanded and blocked her colon and, as a consequence, digested food would reach her lower gut and then come back up as faecal vomit. Around the time Dolly went into total obstruction staff observed a notable change in her behaviour. Dolly stopped requesting euthanasia; in fact she stopped talking altogether. When the nurses came to turn her in bed or to attend to her care she would close her eyes and totally ignore them. As one nurse observed: "it's as if she's shut the outside world out and herself off in the process." (Lawton 1998, 129–30)

Through such case studies Lawton's work demonstrates the body's central role in enabling a performance of self through social interaction, reflecting the growing interest of sociologists in embodiment that has occurred since Glaser and Strauss (Malacrida and Low 2008). Reading Lawton, it becomes difficult to regard with equanimity statements like Kalish's, just quoted, about dying being an opportunity for new life: these are people who are experiencing "social death" (Sudnow 1967) before they die, as their bodies cease to provide them with possibilities for meaningful existence.

THE RIGHT-TO-DIE MOVEMENT

The desire to control the timing and manner of death before the experience of such assaults on self-identity is a particular aim of the right-to-die movement, represented by such organizations as the Hemlock Society (United States until 2003), Compassion and Choices (United States), Dignity in Dying (UK), and the World Federation of Right to Die Societies. This new social movement has the particular political agenda of overturning legal prohibitions against assisted dying (euthanasia and physician-assisted suicide), and an educational agenda in arguing for the need to exercise a right to die; more controversially in some jurisdictions, it disseminates information on practical methods for ending life (McInerney 2000; Fox, Kamakahi, and Capek 1999).

The movement is particularly developed in North America, several European countries including the UK, and Australia and New Zealand, consistent with the view that it is a phenomenon of wealthier countries with extensive health-care coverage. Additionally, the members of right-to-die movements tend to be more affluent and educated than the general population (Fox, Kamakahi, and Capek 1999). Studies of euthanasia movements in the UK (Kemp 2002) and the United States (Emanuel 1994) show that in their early history (the late Victorian period and first half of the twentieth century), eugenicist ideas about improving population health and aspirations to conserve scarce societal resources provided an impetus—termed "social Darwinism" by Emanuel (1994). Though somewhat controversial even before the Second World War, these arguments were later downplayed in the light of the horrors of the Nazi euthanasia program. Members of the right-to-die movement now stress the humanitarian goal of relieving suffering that is intractable by other means. Sociologically it is clear, then, that the claim for a right to die in such countries is an expression of the individualism that pervades Western nations, representing resistance to using readily available medical technology to preserve life at the expense of its quality. By contrast, opposition to the right to die stems at least in part from a religious and communitarian conception of human existence, which downplays individual needs in favor of a divine will or the needs of the community at large.

A familiar communitarian argument against the legalization of euthanasia is that of the "slippery slope," which claims pressure will be brought to bear on vulnerable people who will interpret the "right to die" as a "duty to die" (Saunders 1992). In particular, elderly people without resources, who feel themselves to be a burden on others, are likely to feel an obligation to opt for assisted dying. As Logue (1991) points out, elderly women are likely to feel this because of their multiple disadvantages in later life. Some empirical support for this view has been provided in a survey of relatives of people who die, where elderly women with no family members with an emotional investment in the continuation of their lives were shown to be more likely than others to feel that they were better off dead (Seale and Addington-Hall 1995).

The slippery-slope argument, though, also alerts us to a particular feature of the assisted dying debate: it arises in wealthier countries with relatively good health-care coverage and, as we shall see, is supported by people in countries with particularly good access to health care who fear excessive provision of life-sustaining care at a time when it will damage quality of life. Where people are poor and have inadequate access to health care, there is far less concern about the dangers of excessive medical care being provided. King and Wolf (1997–1998) document the long history of discrimination and disadvantage experienced by African Americans whose autonomy of decision making is compromised because of their race. Noting that U.S. opinion polls show greater support among the white than among the black population for legalizing euthanasia, they suggest that African Americans see legalization of physician-assisted suicide not as the opening up of an opportunity, but merely as permission for another way of ending black lives. They quote the account of an elderly black woman from Dula's (1994) report: "Look like every time I turn on the TV, somebody's talking about euthanasia, and doctors helping kill off old and sick folks. Well, I ain't seen them ask nary a elderly black on none of them TV shows and news programs what they thought about euthanasia. I believe the Lord will take me away when it's time to go" (King and Wolf 1997–1998, 1022).

Sleeboom-Faulkner's account of death and health care in China provides a further twist. She notes that surveys show a majority of the Chinese population to be in favor of allowing euthanasia, but not for the same reasons as in the individualistic West, where the specter of Nazi eugenics rules out any appeal to societal betterment through disposing of people who are a drain on scarce resources. It is clear that Chinese support for euthanasia involves a communitarian justification of self-sacrifice in the interests of society. Thus party secretary comrade Deng Yingchao was reported in 1989 to have stated: "A Communist Party member before death faces a revolution once more. When I am about to pass away, by all means do not try to save me by applying medication. It would be a waste of effort and resources. Please organize criteria for legalising euthanasia" (Sleebohm-Faulkner 2006, 207). Other statements on euthanasia in China, occurring for example in the medical textbooks surveyed by Sleebohm-Faulkner, involve the view that relatives should have the right to ask for euthanasia for a patient and the idea that people with Alzheimer's are suitable candidates. She points out that this situation contrasts markedly with that in the Netherlands and warns against any assumption that the Dutch example can be easily transferred to a country with such a different history and culture.

Opinion polls in Western countries where the right-to-die movement is strong show widespread public support for the legalization of assisted dying. This support has grown since the mid-twentieth century (Emanuel 2002; Seale 2009b) as consumerism in health care and more general societal stress on a way of life that requires people "to understand and enact their lives in terms of choice" (Rose 1999, 87) has gained ground. The mass media of these countries are in general sympathetic to cases of "mercy killing" because these provide opportunities to tell human-interest stories of individuals battling for the right to die against tragic circumstances and apparently unsympathetic legislators or medical authorities (Clarke 2005–2006; Hausmann 2004; McInerney 2006, 2007; Pollock and Yulis 2004). It is perhaps more difficult to construct attractive human-interest stories that oppose euthanasia, as there are no evident "victims" of a pro-euthanasia policy that has not yet been implemented. Emanuel (1994) also relates rising support for assisted dying in these countries to increasing willingness to question the cultural authority of doctors: "The interest in euthanasia may be the culmination of the 20-year effort to curtail physician authority over end-of-life decisions" (1994, 800).

Perhaps understandably, doctors are on the whole less likely than the public to endorse the idea that medically assisted dying should be sanctioned by law (Seale 2009b). Where there are exceptions to this rule, the law can change as a result. The passage of legislation permitting physician-assisted suicide in Oregon in the United States was made easier when the Oregon Medical Association adopted a formal position of neutrality on the bill, in spite of pressure from the American Medical Association to oppose it (Fox, Kamakahi, and Capek 1999). In the Netherlands too, a country with a long history of a permissive approach to euthanasia, the support of the Royal Dutch Medical Association has been crucial in implementing the practice and eventually in passing a permissive law. In the UK, changing the briefly held neutral policy of the British Medical Association to restore its formal opposition to euthanasia became a focus for campaigners in a failed 2004 attempt to pass permissive legislation (Sommerville 2005).

Assisted dying presents a dilemma for doctors, whose professional ethics commit them to providing patients with comfort yet enshrine the historical role of medicine as a defense against death. The majority of deaths do not require doctors to confront the possibility of actively assisting in dying, and withdrawing or withholding treatment or providing medications that may shorten life as a secondary effect have increasingly become normal parts of end-of-life care (Seale 2006, 2009a). Yet some deaths cannot be managed by these means and continue to present doctors with the dilemma of how to help. Individual doctors solve this in a variety of ways in jurisdictions where euthanasia and physician-assisted dying is illegal, and studies have demonstrated that medical assistance is responsible for a small proportion of deaths in many countries where these actions are against the law (van der Heide et al. 2003; Kuhse et al. 1997; Emanuel 2002; Seale 2006). Research also shows that some doctors, as well as other health-care providers, became involved in covert acts of assisting dying in deaths from AIDS for a brief period in the 1980s and 1990s, providing fertile ground for sociologists exploring covert euthanasia.

AIDS and the Euthanasia Underground

In the 1980s and 1990s the high AIDS mortality in wealthier countries such as Australia, Canada, and the United States included younger people who would not otherwise have expected to confront death until later in life. Additionally, AIDS mortality disproportionately included people who by virtue of their social identity as urban-dwelling gay men tended to be marginalized, somewhat critical of mainstream social norms, and particularly used to formulating their own meanings for life events. They faced the prospect of a distressing death, often already witnessed in others, which could involve a variety of wasting syndromes, cancers, infections of the central nervous system, AIDS-related dementia, and the like. All these assaulted the capacity of individuals to maintain control over both body and self-identity, leading many HIV-infected individuals to consider the prospects for influencing the manner and timing of their death in a way that was consistent with their hard-won image of who they were and how they wanted to appear to others. Now that HAART (highly active antiretroviral [anti-HIV]) therapy has transformed the picture for mortality from AIDS for those with good access to it (Bhaskaran et al. 2008), it can be assumed that this demand for control over dying will have declined. This was therefore a time-limited social and medical phenomenon that provides revealing insights into the sociological basis of the desire for assisted dying.

Lavery and colleagues interviewed thirty-two people with HIV in Toronto, Canada, showing that the desire for an assisted death arose from an anticipation of personal disintegration and loss of community, resulting in a loss of self. One person who had also acted as a caregiver expressed personal disintegration:

> You turn them over, they're in pain. They're going to shit themselves, they're going to piss themselves, they're going to lie there and have someone do all their bodily functions and just, there's going to be no happiness, they're going to go down to 60–70 pounds, they're just going to, their whole last weeks of life is just going to be pain and agony and people coming in, people being upset, them being upset. (Lavery et al. 2001, 363–64)

Such indignities could be accompanied by dependency on others that the dying person experienced as intolerable. Loss of community, for these authors, described a progressive diminishment in the capacity to maintain social relationships. This could arise from stigmatization by others who rejected the person with AIDS, as well as from a declining inner desire to maintain contacts with others, associated with lowered levels of energy or loss of function. The resultant loss of self led to the perception that euthanasia could both limit the experience of decline and restore a sense of mastery over events, as in the following account:

> If I'm going to be rolling around in my own faeces because I have no control, then forget it. ... It's the dignity and wholeness of my body, as well as spirit. And, it is, it's cruel too for others to have to do this when there's no end in sight, other than death. To just, to clean me up. I just don't want that ... Dignity is that I have control over my body, when, when, not, not a virus that is going to take my life. I'm the one who is going to decide when my life will end, not a virus, and not with great pain. Not anything else other than in, in my control. It is my control, my choice to do. (365)

Magnusson's (2002) study of the "euthanasia underground" in San Francisco, Sydney, and Melbourne makes a persuasive case for understanding opposing views in the euthanasia debate as a clash of worldviews. On the one hand, those opposed to legalization are likely to draw on religious justifications about the sanctity of life, or to uphold communitarian values through arguments such as the "slippery slope." Those in favor of legislation, on the other hand, tend to espouse liberal rather than conservative values, emphasize individual needs, and reject religion as a basis for moral choices.

Magnusson explores the fine detail of individual cases with considerable sensitivity, exposing dilemmas that are experienced when particular circumstances cannot easily be fitted to the preexisting categories made available by the conflicting cultural scripts for thinking about assisted dying. For example, interviewees told him that some individuals experience "shifting goalposts" whereby they enter states of being which previously they had thought would be intolerable, yet seem to manage: "it's sort of snuck up on them," one interviewee said, "and it's not as bad as they thought it was going to be" (2002, 82). Another interviewee recalled a man who had earlier asked friends to "take him home and kill him" (83) but later experienced ambivalence, finding it difficult to confess that he now wanted to live. Yet sometimes the request for euthanasia is persistent and the goalposts do not shift. It appears that many in the euthanasia underground are then ready to help out.

A diversity of attitudes by members of the euthanasia underground—many of whom were doctors and other health-care workers—toward assisting in a death was evident in this study, ranging from outright opposition through ambivalence to radical pro-euthanasia activism. The ambivalent were people who were willing to help individuals to die but felt uncomfortable with breaking the law. The radicals were often themselves gay men who felt alienated from the values of the mainstream medical establishment. Some radicals resisted the proposal that euthanasia be legalized because they felt this would result in unwelcome regulation of their activities. Magnusson describes a number of disturbing features of the illegal practice of euthanasia, some of which are reminiscent of the scenarios painted by those warning of slippery-slope consequences of legalization. These include sometimes ill-considered decisions to go ahead with euthanasia after the most superficial of explorations of the desire for an assisted death, occasional cases of a lack of professional distance that led to considerable distress and dubious ethical decision making, and an arbitrarily variable level of access to skilled assistance, meaning that there were botched attempts at both assisted suicide and euthanasia. These led Magnusson to argue that legalization might result in "harm reduction" by exposing these practices to quality control.

The Slippery Slope? Euthanasia in Practice

Another case that has been intensively observed by researchers is the Netherlands, where euthanasia has been permitted since the early 1990s. Study of assisted dying in this country has been supplemented by studies of Switzerland and Oregon, in both of which jurisdictions forms of assisted dying are permitted. They provide a good opportunity to explore the view that legalization of assisted dying results in a slide down the slippery slope, whereby vulnerable people come under pressure to end their lives, or whether Magnusson's "harm reduction" argument has some force.

Statistical reports from the Netherlands (van der Heide et al. 2007) show that the proportion of Dutch deaths from euthanasia has varied between 1.7 percent and 2.6 percent between 1991 and 2005. A much smaller percentage of deaths are physician-assisted suicides, and from 0.4 percent to 0.8 percent involve people whose lives are ended without an explicit request, usually because they were unable to communicate but had requested this in the past and were hours from death, which was judged clinically beneficial because of signs of unrelieved distress. In addition, much higher proportions of deaths were cases where a person's death may have been hastened by a decision to withhold or withdraw treatment, or involved giving medication such as morphine in doses that doctors estimated might have contributed to the end of life. A particular phenomenon of the Dutch situation is a growing recognition that continuous deep sedation until death occurs in a high proportion of deaths—8.2 percent in 2005—meaning that doctors can often avoid becoming involved in actions deliberately designed to end life.

If evidence for the slippery slope were to be derived from such studies, one might expect to see disproportionately higher rates of assisted dying, or perhaps of continuous deep sedation, among very elderly people, women, or noncancer deaths, but data presented by van der Heide et al. (2007) do not show this, instead demonstrating that these acts are more common in younger dying people, men, and cancer deaths.

Ganzini (2004) reports the characteristics of people who carried out physician-assisted suicide under the Oregon Death with Dignity Act over a period of six years (1998–2003), showing that these did not include any African Americans, were almost all covered by health insurance, were largely affected by cancer, were either enrolled in hospice programs or had declined enrollment, were slightly more likely to be men, and had a higher than average level of education. Although the interpretation of the Oregon figures is not uncontroversial (Foley and Hendin 2002), these do not on the surface appear to provide evidence of a slippery slope.

Bosshard, Ulrich, and Bar (2003) report on 748 cases of suicide assisted by the main Swiss right-to-die association during a ten-year period (1990–2000) and reveal a picture that is somewhat more disturbing for those concerned with the slippery-slope argument. Unlike the Netherlands or Oregon, such deaths were more likely to involve women, particularly where older groups were involved, and 21 percent of the dying suffered from nonfatal conditions such as rheumatoid arthritis, osteoporosis, chronic pain syndrome, or blindness. In this last group, 76 percent were women and tended to be of higher mean age. In a few cases the wish to die was related to depression or another mental illness, with no concomitant disease. Over the study period the number of such deaths per year rose threefold. On the surface, then, it appears that the Swiss situation may have slid down the slippery slope for those who believe assisted dying ought to be confined to clear cases of terminal illness.

Swiss regulations concerning assisted dying are more open than those of Oregon and the Netherlands, where medical second opinions are required. In Oregon a terminal illness must be present and in the Netherlands, where the medical profession has been intimately involved in drawing up guidelines for euthanasia practice, doctors must be convinced that the patient is facing unremitting and unbearable suffering. Exit, the Swiss organization responsible for assisting the 748 deaths reported by Bosshard, Ulrich, and Bar (2003), by contrast has a history of conflict with the Swiss medical association (Bosshard, Fischer, and Bar 2002) and is a citizen organization with some involvement of sympathetic doctors.

The evidence of these statistical studies in Switzerland, the Netherlands, and Oregon and the earlier evidence about underground euthanasia suggests that an approach which permits but firmly regulates the practice of medically assisted dying is more likely to protect the socially disadvantaged and is a strategy described by Magnusson (2002) as a "harm reduction" approach, drawing on a vocabulary developed for dealing with illegal drug usage. Clearly the evidence base for such policies remains somewhat thin and there remain many opportunities for policy-oriented sociologists and social researchers to explore and illuminate this important issue.

CONCLUSION

The research highlighted in this chapter provides evidence supporting the view that the experience of dying is determined by social, historical, and cultural conditions, as well as by physical events in the body. Historically and cross-culturally informed medical sociology is well placed to bring this evidence out. At various points medical sociology diverges from psychologically informed ideas about dying, most obviously in relation to views about the "denial of death," which many psychologists as well as cultural commentators in the mass media perceive to be a widespread feature of modern life. As this chapter has shown, Parsons's view that modern society is a particularly death-affirming one is supported by sociological investigation and appropriate theoretical reflection.

This chapter has reported that in a great variety of ways, members of modern societies are organized to manage the problem of dying people, with medical endeavors and health-care institutions providing for their specialist treatment, as well as being part of the larger medical system for the avoidance of illness and death. Because of the demographic transition undergone by developed countries, dying is largely confined to the elderly in modern societies, and the pattern of disease results in different dying trajectories, notably a rise in the incidence of cancer as a terminal illness. Specialized services to manage the dying process for people with cancer have been associated with the promotion of the benefits of "death awareness," a phenomenon documented by sociologists, whose culture-bound character has also been made clear through study of dying in several cultures.

More recent medical sociology has brought the life (and death) of the body to center stage, demonstrating through the study of dying how central the body is for adequate social interaction. Much care of the dying can be interpreted as managing the boundary between social and bodily existence. It is clear, too, that the activist orientation of many people in developed countries expresses itself in movements that argue for the right to die. This chapter has reported that such movements draw support from more affluent sectors of the population whose access to health care is such that they fear an excessive application of life-sustaining technology. Such fears are less likely to be shared by the more disadvantaged. Additionally, like the "death awareness" movement, which similarly seeks to influence the manner of dying, the right to die is conceived of as an individual matter. Studies have been reviewed which show that in societies that place individual needs second to the good of the community, the call for euthanasia has a complexion that many Western supporters would find unacceptable.

Sociologists have much to contribute in future research to the important field of end-of-life decision making. For example, continuous deep sedation is increasingly common in the care of dying people and in some respects may have become an alternative to euthanasia. The circumstances that lead to the decision to use this medication and the communication and ethical issues that this procedure involves are topics that deserve further investigation. Additionally, there is a widespread belief that people prefer, where possible, to die at home rather than in institutions. To some extent this belief may be fueled by the negative imagery of institutional dying associated with the "denial of death" thesis. Empirical investigation of preferences and factors associated with place of death, particularly for people dying with nonmalignant diseases such as heart failure, stroke, or respiratory conditions, offers many opportunities for sociologists to make original contributions. In general, the investigation of care of the dying allows for the empirical investigation of ethical dilemmas, and nowhere is this more evident than in the debate over the legalization of euthanasia. The tension here between the rights of individuals and the concerns of the community is classic sociological territory, and we may look forward to studies that illuminate and inform ethical and policy debates in this important area.

REFERENCES

Abel, Emily K. 1986. "The Hospice Movement: Institutionalising Innovation." *International Journal of Health Services* 16:71–85.

Arber, Sara, and Jay Ginn. 1991. *Gender and Later Life: A Sociological Analysis of Resources and Constraints.* London: Sage.

Armstrong, David. 1987. "Silence and Truth in Death and Dying." *Social Science and Medicine* 24(8): 651–57.

Arnarson, Arnar. 2007. "'Fall Apart and Put Yourself Together Again': The Anthropology of Death and Bereavement Counselling in Britain." *Mortality* 12:48–65.

Arney, William R., and Bernard J. Bergen. 1984. *Medicine and the Management of Living: Taming the Last Great Beast.* Chicago: University of Chicago Press.

Atkinson, Paul. 1990. *The Ethnographic Imagination: Textual Constructions of Reality.* London: Routledge.

Baruch, Geoffrey. 1981. "Moral Tales: Parents' Stories of Encounters with the Health Profession." *Sociology of Health and Illness* 3(3): 275–96.

Beck, Ulrich. 1992. *Risk Society: Towards a New Modernity.* London: Sage.

Berger, Peter L., and Thomas Luckmann. 1971. *The Social Construction of Reality.* Harmondsworth, Eng.: Penguin.

Bhaskaran, Krishnan, Osamah Hamouda, Mette Sannes, Faroudy Boufassa, Anne M. Johnson, Paul C. Lambert, and Kholoud Porter. 2008. "Changes in the Risk of Death after HIV Seroconversion Compared with Mortality in the General Population." *Journal of the American Medical Association* 300(1): 51–59.

Blauner, Robert. 1966. "Death and Social Structure." *Psychiatry* 29:378–94.

Bloch, Maurice, and Jonathan Parry, eds. 1982. *Death and the Regeneration of Life.* Cambridge: Cambridge University Press.

Bloor, Michael. 1991. "A Minor Office: The Variable and Socially Constructed Character of Death Certification in a Scottish City." *Journal of Health and Social Behavior* 32:273–87.

———. 1994. "On the Conceptualisation of Routine Medical Decision-Making: Death Certification as an Habitual Activity." In *Qualitative Studies in Health and Medicine,* ed. Michael Bloor and Patricia Taraborelli, 96–109. Aldershot, Eng.: Avebury.

Bosshard, Georg, Stephen Fischer, and Walter Bar. 2002. "Open Regulation and Practice in Assisted Dying: How Switzerland Compares with the Netherlands and Oregon." *Swiss Medical Weekly* 132:527–34.

Bosshard, Georg, Esther Ulrich, and Walter Bar. 2003. "748 Cases of Suicide Assisted by a Swiss Right-to-Die Organisation." *Swiss Medical Weekly* 133:310–17.

Charmaz, Kathy C. 1976. "The Coroner's Strategies for Announcing Death." In *Toward a Sociology of Death and Dying*, ed. Lyn Lofland, 61–81. Beverly Hills: Sage.

Clarke, Juanne N. 2005–2006. "Death under Control: The Portrayal of Death in Mass Print English Language Magazines in Canada." *Omega: Journal of Death and Dying* 52(2): 153–67.

Clifford, James, and George E. Marcus, eds. 1986. *Writing Culture: The Poetics and Politics of Ethnography*. Berkeley: University of California Press.

Dooley, J. 1982. "The Corruption of Hospice." *Public Welfare*, spring, 35–39.

Dula, Annette. 1994. "The Life and Death of Miss Mildred. … The Life Story of an Elderly Black Woman in the Rural South." *Clinics in Geriatric Medicine* 10(3): 419–30.

Elias, Norbert. 1978. *The History of Manners*. Vol. 1 of *The Civilizing Process*. Oxford: Blackwell.

———. 1982. *State Formation and Civilization*. Vol. 2 of *The Civilizing Process*. Oxford: Blackwell.

Emanuel, Ezekiel J. 1994. "The History of Euthanasia Debates in the United States and Britain." *Annals of Internal Medicine* 121:793–802.

———. 2002. "Euthanasia and Physician-Assisted Suicide: A Review of the Empirical Data from the United States." *Archives of Internal Medicine* 162:142–52.

Foley, Kathleen, and Herbert Hendin. 2002. "The Oregon Experiment." In *The Case against Assisted Suicide: For the Right to End-of-Life Care*, ed. Kathleen Foley and Herbert Hendin, 144–74. Baltimore: Johns Hopkins University Press.

Fox, Elaine, Jeffrey J. Kamakahi, and Stella M. Capek. 1999. *Come Lovely and Soothing Death: The Right-to-Die Movement in the United States*. New York: Twayne.

Ganzini, Linda. 2004. "The Oregon Experience." In *Physician-Assisted Dying: The Case for Palliative Care and Patient Choice*, ed. Timothy E. Quill and Margaret P. Battin, 165–83. Baltimore: Johns Hopkins University Press.

Giddens, Anthony. 1990. *The Consequences of Modernity*. Cambridge: Polity Press.

———. 1991. *Modernity and Self-Identity: Self and Society in the Late Modern Age*. Cambridge: Polity Press.

Glaser, Barney G., and Anselm L. Strauss. 1965. *Awareness of Dying*. Chicago: Aldine.

———. 1967. *The Discovery of Grounded Theory: Strategies for Qualitative Research*. Chicago: Aldine.

———. 1968. *Time for Dying*. Chicago: Aldine.

Glassner, Barry. 1989. "Fitness and the Postmodern Self." *Journal of Health and Social Behavior* 30(2): 180–91.

Gorer, Geoffrey. 1965. *Death, Grief and Mourning*. London: Cresset.

Hausmann, Elke. 2004. "How Press Discourse Justifies Euthanasia." *Mortality* 9(3): 206–22.

Hertz, Robert. 1960. *Death and the Right Hand: A Contribution to the Study of the Collective Representation of Death*. Translated by Rodney Needham and Claudia Needham. First published 1907. Glencoe, Ill.: Free Press

Hochschild, Arlie R. 1983. *The Managed Heart: Commercialisation of Human Feeling*. Berkeley: University of California Press.

Hunt, Maura W. 1991a. "Being Friendly and Informal: Reflected in Nurses', Terminally Ill Patients', and Relatives' Conversations at Home." *Journal of Advanced Nursing* 16:929–38.

———. 1991b. "The Identification and Provision of Care for the Terminally Ill at Home by 'Family' Members." *Sociology of Health and Illness* 13(3): 375–95.

James, Veronica. 1986 "Care and Work in Nursing the Dying: A Participant Study of a Continuing Care Unit." PhD thesis, University of Aberdeen.

———. 1989. "Emotional Labour: Skill and Work in the Social Regulation of Feelings." *Sociological Review* 37:15–42.

James, Veronica, and David Field. 1992. "The Routinization of Hospice: Charisma and Bureaucratization." *Social Science and Medicine* 34(12): 1363–75.

Kalish, Robert A., ed. 1980. *Caring Relationships: The Dying and the Bereaved*. Farmingdale, N.Y.: Baywood.

Kellehear, Alan. 2007. *A Social History of Dying*. New York: Cambridge University Press.

Kemp, Nick D. A. 2002. *Merciful Release: The History of the British Euthanasia Movement*. Manchester, Eng.: Manchester University Press.

King, Patricia A., and Leslie E. Wolf. 1997–1998. "Empowering and Protecting Patients: Lessons for Physician-Assisted Suicide from the

African-American Experience." *Minnesota Law Review* 82:1015–43.

Kubler-Ross, Elisabeth. 1969. *On Death and Dying*. New York: Macmillan.

Kuhse, Helga, Peter Singer, Peter Baume, Malcolm Clark, and Maurice Rickard. 1997. "End-of-Life Decisions in Australian Medical Practice." *Medical Journal of Australia* 166:191–96.

Lavery, James V., Joseph Boyle, Bernard D. Dickens, Heather Maclean, and Peter A. Singer. 2001. "Origins of the Desire for Euthanasia and Assisted Suicide in People with HIV-1 or AIDS: A Qualitative Study." *Lancet* 358:362–67.

Lawton, Julia. 1998. "Contemporary Hospice Care: The Sequestration of the Unbounded Body and 'Dirty Dying.'" *Sociology of Health and Illness* 20:121–43.

———. 2000. *The Dying Process*. London: Routledge.

Logue, Barbara. J. 1991. "Taking Charge: Death Control as an Emergent Women's Issue." *Women and Health* 17(4): 97–121.

———. 1994. "When Hospice Fails: The Limits of Palliative Care." *Omega—Journal of Death and Dying* 29(4): 291–301.

Magnusson, Roger S. 2002. *Angels of Death: Exploring the Euthanasia Underground*. New Haven, Conn.: Yale University Press.

Malacrida, Claudia, and Jacqueline Low. 2008. *Sociology of the Body: A Reader*. Oxford: Oxford University Press.

Mamo, Laura. 1999. "Death and Dying: Confluences of Emotion and Awareness." *Sociology of Health and Illness* 21(1): 13–36.

McInerney, Fran. 2000. "'Requested Death': A New Social Movement." *Social Science and Medicine* 50:137–54.

———. 2006. "Heroic Frames: Discursive Constructions around the Requested Death Movement in Australia in the Late 1990s." *Social Science and Medicine* 62:654–67.

———. 2007. "Death and the Body Beautiful: Aesthetics and Embodiment in Press Portrayals of Requested Death in Australia on the Edge of the 21st Century." *Health Sociology Review* 16(5): 384–96.

Paradis, Leonora Finn, and Scott B. Cummings. 1986. "The Evolution of Hospice in America toward Organizational Homogeneity." *Journal of Health and Social Behavior* 27:370–86.

Parsons, Talcott. 1978. "Death in the Western World." *Action Theory and the Human Condition*, 331–51. New York: Free Press.

Parsons, Talcott, and Victor Lidz. 1967. "Death in American Society." In *Essays in Self Destruction*, ed. Edwin S. Shneidman, 133–70. New York: Science House.

Perakyla, Anssi. 1991. "Hope Work in the Care of Seriously Ill Patients." *Qualitative Health Research* 1(4): 407–33.

Pollock, John C., and Spiro G. Yulis. 2004. "Nationwide Newspaper Coverage of Physician-Assisted Suicide: A Community Structure Approach." *Journal of Health Communication* 9(4): 281–307.

Prior, Lindsay. 1989. *The Social Organization of Death*. Basingstoke and London: Macmillan.

Rose, Nikolas. 1999. *Powers of Freedom: Reframing Political Thought*. Cambridge: Cambridge University Press.

Saunders, Cicely. 1992. "Voluntary Euthanasia." *Palliative Medicine* 6:1–5.

Saunders, Cicely, and Mary Baines. 1983. *Living with Dying: The Management of Terminal Disease*. Oxford: Oxford University Press.

Seale, Clive. 1991. "Death from Cancer and Death from Other Causes: The Relevance of the Hospice Approach." *Palliative Medicine* 5:12–19.

———. 1998. *Constructing Death: The Sociology of Dying and Bereavement*. Cambridge: Cambridge University Press.

———. 2000. "Changing Patterns of Death and Dying." *Social Science and Medicine* 51:917–30.

———. 2006. "National Survey of End-of-Life Decisions Made by UK Medical Practitioners." *Palliative Medicine* 20(1): 3–10.

———. 2009a. "End-of-Life Decisions in the UK Involving Medical Practitioners." *Palliative Medicine* 23(3): 198–204.

———. 2009b. "Legalisation of Euthanasia or Physician-Assisted Suicide: Survey of Doctors' Attitudes." *Palliative Medicine* 23(3): 205–12.

Seale, Clive, and Julia Addington-Hall. 1995. "Dying at the Best Time." *Social Science and Medicine* 40(5): 589–95.

Sleeboom-Faulkner, Margaret. 2006. "Chinese Concepts of Euthanasia and Health Care." *Bioethics* 20(4): 203–12.

Sommerville, Ann. 2005. "Changes in BMA Policy on Assisted Dying." *British Medical Journal* 331:686–88.

Strauss, Anselm L., and Barney G. Glaser. 1977. *Anguish: A Case Study of a Dying Trajectory.* London: Martin Robertson.

Sudnow, David. 1967. *Passing On: The Social Organization of Dying.* Englewood Cliffs, N.J.: Prentice Hall.

Timmermans, Stefan. 2005. "Death Brokering: Constructing Culturally Appropriate Deaths." *Sociology of Health and Illness* 27(7): 993–1013.

van der Heide, Agnes, Luc Deliens, Karin Faisst, Tore Nilstun, Michael Norup, Eugenio Paci, Gerrit van der Wal, and Paul J. van der Maas. 2003. "End-of-Life Decision-Making in Six European Countries: Descriptive Study." *Lancet* 362:345–50.

van der Heide, Agnes, Bregie D. Onwuteaka-Philipsen, Mette L. Rurup, Hilde M. Buiting, Johannes J. M. van Delden, Hanssen-Johanna E. de Wolf, Anke G. J. M. Janssen, Roeline W. Pasman, Judith A. C. Rietjens, Cornelis J. M. Prins, Ingeborg M. Deerenberg, Joseph K. M. Gevers, Paul J. van der Maas, and Gerrit van der Wal.

2007. "End-of-Life Practices in the Netherlands under the Euthanasia Act." *New England Journal of Medicine* 356(19): 1957–65.

Walter, Tony. 1994. *The Revival of Death.* London: Routledge.

WHO [World Health Organisation]. 1988. *World Health Statistics.* Geneva: WHO.

———. 2008. *World Health Statistics.* Geneva: WHO. who.int/whosis/whostat/2008/en/index.html.

Wright, Michael, Justin Wood, Tom Lynch, and David Clark. 2008. "Mapping Levels of Palliative Care Development: A Global View." *Journal of Pain and Symptom Management* 35(5): 469–85.

Wrigley, Edward A., and Roger S. Schofield. 1981. *The Population History of England, 1541–1871: A Reconstruction.* London: Edward Arnold.

Zelizer, Viviana A. 1978. "Human Values and the Market: The Case of Life Insurance and Death in 19th Century America." *American Journal of Sociology* 84(3): 591–610.

Increasing the Probability of Social Science Research Leading to Policy Implementation

Lessons Learned over Sixteen Years

Emma Davies

ABSTRACT

This article tells a story about research and development, drawing on eight projects concerning child witnesses and complainants in New Zealand's child abuse investigation and criminal justice systems. It identifies triggers to changes in policy and practice and concludes with five ideas for social scientists who wish to create more evidence-informed action: Developing a multi-disciplinary professional advisory group from the start of the research, seizing opportunities in the wider environment, considering a secondment into the public service, carefully planning dissemination of research findings and incorporating a plan for the evaluation of any programme implemented.

INTRODUCTION AND OVERVIEW OF PROJECTS

This story evolved from 1996 to 2012. It is about research and policy on child complainants and witnesses in the investigation and criminal justice systems. Most of these children allege abuse from adults. They do a community service by giving evidence in the criminal court. It is important that the systems in place are appropriate for children.

Table 22.1 outlines the projects upon which this story is based. Some of the research and programme development was commissioned by the Ministry of Justice (MoJ). However the majority of the project funding was independent of the government, coming primarily from the Health Research Council (HRC) and the New Zealand Law Foundation (NZLF). All the projects were supported by an advisory group of senior practitioners. It is not the results of the research per se that are important in this article (see references for a partial list of published articles), but the research and development *process*. This article identifies triggers to changes in policy and practice and ideas for researchers who want to generate more evidence-informed action.

1996–2008

This research involved an analysis of 26 criminal court transcripts of children's evidence, examining the language and tactics used during cross-examination. Interviews were also conducted with 51 children and 145 primary carers of children alleging sexual abuse, about their experiences of the investigation and, when relevant, of giving evidence

in the criminal court. Children and primary carers reported poor interagency coordination in investigations and received no information about what was expected of them at court.

1999–2003

This project involved the development of multi-agency child abuse investigation centres in Auckland to improve inter-agency co-ordination, and a *Court Education for Young Witnesses* programme to inform children and their carers what would happen at court. The first multi-agency centre opened in 2002. The pilot court education programme was evaluated in 2002/3 and was implemented nationally in 2003/4.

TABLE 22.1 Projects

Projects	Year	Researchers	Funders	Contract/ grant
Literature review for the Courts Consultative Committee Working Party on Child Witnesses	1996	Davies	MoJ	Contract
Analysis of transcripts of children's evidence and interviewing children and families	1996–1998	Davies, Seymour, Pasese	HRC	Grant
Development of court education	1999	Davies, Seymour, Ronald	MoJ	Contract
Development of multi-agency centres	2000	Davies, Seymour, Cooke, Bidois	NZLF	Grant
Evaluation of pilot court education programme	2003	Davies, Fortune, Verbitsky, Seymour, Devere, Smith	MoJ	Contract
Analysis of delays in court system, transcripts of children's evidence, and best practice in comparable jurisdictions	2007–2010	Hanna, Davies, Henderson, Crothers, Rotherham	NZLF, MoJ MSD NZ Police	Grant
Mock trials of intermediaries	2011	Davies, Hanna, Henderson, Hand	NZLF, JR McKenzie Trust	Grant
Lawyers' and victim advisors' experiences of nine cases of prerecorded cross-examination	2012	Davies, Hanna	MoJ	Contract

2007–2010

This research involved questionnaires with police to access information about criminal court cases involving child witnesses (e.g. delays, modes of evidence used) and a replication of the 1997 court transcript analysis of the language used during cross-examination. The key findings included long delays through the court system and poor questioning of children during cross-examination. There was also a review of special measures used with children in other countries to address these problems. This research led to recommendations for prerecording cross-examination and the introduction of intermediaries. Some child witnesses' testimony was pre-recorded from December 2010 to June 2011 in the Auckland District Court. In 2011, the New Zealand Government proposed legislative reforms to facilitate pre-recorded testimony for children under 12 and intermediaries for all child witnesses.

2011–2012

Research in 2011 involved mock trials of different models of intermediaries to improve court communication with children. Research in 2012 examined victim advisors' and lawyers' experiences of nine pre-recorded hearings in the Auckland District Court.

Embarking on Doctoral Research 1996–1999

Having found a compatible supervisor who had good relationships with senior practitioners who work with abused children, I consulted these professionals and those they recommended. In groups and individually, I asked statutory social workers, psychologists, lawyers and forensic interviewers what research they would find helpful. Most of the practitioners expressed surprise at being asked and most did not know how to respond. From the ideas that emerged from a few early in the process,

I started to narrow the parameters of the research and form the research questions.

Interested senior practitioners were then invited to comment on the methodology, research tools and conclusion of the work. They formed a multidisciplinary Advisory Group alongside two mothers of abused children. Members gave their time freely and valued discussing issues with their colleagues, some of whom they had not met before. Others had worked on cases together but had not had the opportunity to discuss systemic issues with service users and colleagues from other services and disciplines.

Coincidentally, in 1996 the Courts Consultative Committee, a judicial body, established a Working Party on Child Witnesses because they had received a number of complaints from parents of child witnesses. Members of the Advisory Group had been consulted by the Committee. As a result, the Committee became aware of the research and commissioned me to write a literature review for them. This was partly fortuitous timing but it is also a good example of why establishing relationships in the field matter. The connections between the Working Party and the Advisory Group facilitated the commissioning of the literature review. The review was one building block of information upon which to base professional conversations about this vulnerable group of children.

The research proposal involved interviews with children and their primary carers on child sexual abuse investigation and criminal justice processes. Clearance from the New Zealand Police and the Courts was straightforward. However, despite senior practitioners from the statutory child protection agency (CYFS) being on the Advisory Group, it proved difficult to get clearance from CYFS head office because there were no processes in place in the 1990s for consideration of research proposals submitted by outsiders. After six months, I coincidentally met a Principal

Policy Advisor (Research) from a related agency at a conference and sought her advice. She took up the case. Her active engagement led to permission from the Chief Social Worker for me to conduct the research and, moreover, the establishment of a *Research Access Committee* so that other researchers would not have similar problems in the future. In 2012, this Committee indicates a six-week time-frame for consideration of research proposals requesting access to staff or clients of the Ministry of Social Development (now includes CYFS).

The university's Ethics Committee process was equally time-consuming. The proposal to interview children who had alleged abuse was seen as very risky. The university Ethics Committee sought views from New Zealand's Chief Social Worker and two academic experts. A year after the proposal was submitted to CYF and the Ethics Committee, the project was cleared to proceed.

In the meantime, the Advisory Group suggested analysing the language used to question children in the forensic interview and in cross-examination at court. This study, initiated by a prosecutor, proved to be a useful line of inquiry. The Chief Judge enabled access to transcripts for research purposes. The findings, based on a sample of trials held in 1994, confirmed practitioners' concerns about the types of questions posed to child witnesses, their complexity, and the tactics of cross-examination (Davies, Henderson and Seymour, 1997; Davies and Seymour, 1998). Similar research on questioning practice has since been replicated twice, with comparable results. All these studies reported age-inappropriate questioning of children during cross-examination (Hanna, Davies, Crothers and Henderson, 2011; Zajac and Hayne 2003).

Children and their primary carers were interviewed about their experiences of the system. They talked about poor interagency collaboration and not understanding what is expected of them at court (Davies, Seymour and Read, 2000). Having been involved from the beginning in developing the methodology and the questions asked of children and their families, the Advisory Group was invested in the results. The practitioners were keen to see better structures and processes that would enable them to address the problems identified in the research, particularly those that resonated with their experiences.

RESEARCH, POLICY AND PRACTICE 1999–2004

The Ministry of Justice acted on the findings that child complainants and their families were poorly informed about court processes. In 1999, they commissioned the researcher and an amended Advisory Group to develop child-friendly programmes for child complainants and child defendants about what happens in court. Although the then National government rejected the proposal, a limited version of the programme was funded by a new Labour government two years later. Court education was funded for child complainants, but not for child defendants. It is possible that child defendants do not need such a programme because they go through the Youth Court, but practitioners at the time considered that the need was equal to child complainants. While child defendants have equal rights to information, the politics are quite different. The high-profile victims' rights agenda renders more public sympathy for poorly informed child witnesses than poorly informed child defendants. It is easier for politicians to be seen to be attending to the needs of victims. And so they did.

The *Court Education for Young Witnesses* Programme (excluding child defendants) was evaluated and rolled out nationally in 2003 (Davies, DeVere and Verbitsky, 2004). In 2009, approximately two-thirds of eligible children in New Zealand's four largest centres received the programme (Hanna et al., 2010: p. 28). Policy, however, does not guarantee *full* implementation.

Practitioners were keen to see action on children's and primary carers' experiences of poor coordination between agencies. They became interested in *Child Advocacy Centres* in the United States. These are centres designed to increase coordination between agencies involved in child abuse investigation processes, namely police investigators, forensic interviewers, paediatricians and allied health professionals, psychologists, child protection social workers and prosecutors. The New Zealand Law Foundation funded us, a group of similar professionals, to develop a proposal for multi-agency centres in Auckland and Manukau, learning from the research participants and *Child Advocacy Centres* in the United States. A long journey to generate policy interest ensued.

Decision-making was centralised in CYFS (Wellington), and regionalised in the police and health agencies. The boundaries of the police and health regions differed. It appeared to be hardest for practitioners in the child protection agency to be heard on their views on policy in their head offices. Many years later, I learned that Child Youth and Family policy advisors had heard the practitioners. They had decided not to engage with the development team because they did not believe that a centre was the best way to improve coordination. Avoidance of conflict does not create good policy. It probably would have been wiser for government policy advisors to engage in discussions with the multi-disciplinary team of researchers and practitioners about how to improve inter-agency coordination. Policy advisors may have been fearful of engaging in dialogue because journalists often sought comment on child abuse from the practitioners and researchers involved. They may have been concerned that frank discussions would have ended up in the media. Discussions with 'outsiders' will often hold some risks for government

agencies and their Ministers. However, robust discussions on policy ideas with diverse views are critical dimensions of a thoughtful policy making process. Fears can be partially allayed through holding discussions under the Chatham House Rule:

> When a meeting, or part thereof, is held under the Chatham House Rule, participants are free to use the information received, but neither the identity nor the affiliation of the speaker(s), nor that of any other participant, may be revealed (www.chathamhouse.org/about-us/chathamhouserule).

It did not prove possible, initially, to develop a multi-agency centre in South Auckland, for many practical reasons, including lack of funding and lack of support for the police from health and child protection agencies. In central Auckland, it was a high profile media campaign and the practicalities of leases in government agency buildings expiring that prompted the opening of Puawaitahi, a multi-agency child abuse assessment and investigation centre, in 2002:

> Puawaitahi was established in November 2002 as a multi-agency, one-service centre for investigating alleged abuse of children and young people and to ensure that victims of abuse—and their families—can easily access the best possible services to help with treatment after abuse (www.police.govt.nz/district/aucklandcity/puawaitahi.html.)

This centre includes police, health and CYFS staff. The initial plan to also include space for community agencies (Davies, Seymour, Cooke and Bidois, 2000) had been abandoned in part through lack of funding. This multi-agency centre was not evaluated before similar centres opened in Manukau in 2010 and in Wellington in 2011; both initiatives driven by the Police.

At the time of writing, none of these centres have been evaluated. No evaluation plan was built in from the start. With hindsight, there also wasn't sufficient engagement between researchers, practitioners and policy advisors to work out the best ways to improve interagency communication and coordination before developing a physical centre. Through constructive dialogue within and between agencies, better use of research findings and agency could have been made. Moreover, a better monitoring system could perhaps have been created from multiple agencies' judicious use of their own data.

Child Witnesses Research and Policy 2006–2012

In 2006, we approached an independent legal trust for research funding for a follow-up study on child witnesses to include an analysis of court transcripts, administrative data and measures for child witnesses in other countries. The Trust thought that some of this work should be funded by government, so they awarded half of the funding pending an equal contribution from government. Their grant helped us to secure the remaining funding from the New Zealand Police, Ministry of Justice (MoJ) and Ministry of Social Development (MSD). My relationships in MSD, developed from a recent secondment in MSD, also helped the research team to secure government funding.

Agency data on child witnesses was as elusive in 2007 as it had been in the 1990s. It wasn't even possible to determine how many child witnesses give evidence in the courts. Our initial proposal to work off administrative data was thwarted by different agencies' data coded in ways that anonymous cases could not be related to one another, so we had to develop primary sources of data collection. Setting up the research involved navigating a range

of relationships at different levels of the organisations. The Principal Investigator's tenacity and the Advisory Group of senior practitioners made it feasible. Once again, the group's commitment to the results and their implications was facilitated by their involvement in setting the questions. This time, at the instruction of the newly formed Judicial Research Committee, the Advisory Group included a Judge and defence counsel.

The research found that delays between forensic interviews and trials involving child witnesses averaged fifteen months in the main centres (Hanna, et al., 2010: p. 13), and that the questioning of children during cross-examination had changed little in fourteen years (Hanna, et al., 2011). Other countries processes for dealing with these issues were documented (Henderson, 2010) and the Advisory Group then processed this information in the light of their professional experiences. While the resulting recommendations were the view of the authors (Davies, Henderson and Hanna, 2010), the discussions led to much common ground, particularly in relation to pre-recording cross-examination prior to trial and the importance of training lawyers and judges on questioning children. The Advisory Group also promoted dissemination of the research findings through their communities.

2010 was coincidentally a year in which the National-led government's Minister of Justice was actively interested in how to improve responses to child complainants in the criminal courts, yet his proposals were not yet developed. He raised concerns about the way that children were treated in court in a media interview. The Advisory Group wrote to the Minister informing him of the research and inviting him to a meeting to discuss the issues. He attended two meetings for discussions in confidence. The Minister would not have attended or listened if he hadn't been informed of Advisory Group members' expertise and then, on receiving the report, been informed by advisors that there had been a careful contextualising of New Zealand's practice against research and practice internationally.

The government funders had given comments, a condition of their funding, on the draft report: *Child Witnesses in the New Zealand Courts: A review of Practice and Implications for Policy* (Hanna et al., 2010). The Minister was also sent an embargoed final copy prior to release. The main opposition party was sent a copy after a briefing. Their Justice spokesperson then asked the Minister a sympathetic question in the House to encourage the Minister to act. Likewise, the research team's briefing of non-government organisations encouraged community organisations to show support for the proposals through press releases.

Public release of the research report and active engagement with the mainstream and professional media was like a trial run for Ministers in the public arena, with others taking the heat at first. A thoughtful investigative journalist, with time and space to write a feature article, also informed the public by reading the research, interviewing researchers, and defence and prosecution lawyers from the Advisory Group (Masters, 2010). The Minister's engagement on the issues increased the visibility of the research findings in the mainstream news. The Ministry of Justice then developed interagency guidelines on working with child witnesses (Ministry of Justice, 2011) and an Issues Paper on pre-trial and trial processes child witnesses in New Zealand's criminal justice system, for consultation with government and non-government agencies (Ministry of Justice, 2010). This revealed legal support for the changes to legislation and practice as well as support from non-government organisations working with child victims.

Many judges in the Auckland District Court supported pre-recorded cross-examination of child witnesses by the end of 2010. Despite legislative provision to pre-record children's testimony in New Zealand (The Evidence Act 2006 ss103–107),

it was not until December 2010 that the first application to pre-record children's entire testimony was approved (*R v Sadlier*, 2010). Since then, there have been a number of hearings completed in the Auckland District Court, operating according to established processes for pre-recording evidence developed by the Ministry in the first half of 2011 (Ministry of Justice, June 2011).

In late June 2011, the Court of Appeal heard two appeals in relation to pre-trial cross-examination: *M v R* (CA 335/2011) and *R v E* (CA 339/2011). Although the Court of Appeal was satisfied that pre-recording children's entire testimony is within jurisdiction (para 28), they restricted its use to rare circumstances (para 41). While awaiting the Court's findings and reasons for those findings, 17 planned pre-recorded hearings were frozen (Davies, Hanna, Henderson and White, 2011). After the Court's judgement none of these prerecorded hearings scheduled for later than June 2011 went ahead. However some of the trials, involving pre-recorded hearings conducted before the Court's findings, went ahead by consent. The research team approached the Ministry of Justice in 2011 with a proposal to learn from the first pre-recorded hearings with child witnesses. A scaled-down version of this research project was funded by the Ministry in 2012 in order to inform the planned implementation of pre-recorded testimony for children under 12 (DOM Min (11) 10/1).

With many questions about how to improve the language used in court, the research team accessed independent funding in 2011 to explore three models of intermediaries in a simulated 'trial'. It is not the methodology or results that are important here (Davies, Hanna, Henderson and Hand, 2011; Hanna, Davies, Henderson and Hand, in press), but the process of engagement between researchers, senior practitioners and the Ministry of Justice. A Senior Policy Analyst from the Ministry of Justice observed a simulated cross-examination and heard the multi-disciplinary professional discussion that ensued. She developed relationships with some of these practitioners and the policy team discussed the findings with the research team.

The Cabinet minute released in 2011 included the intent to introduce a legislative presumption in favour of pre-recording all of some children's testimony and proposals to improve the court's communication with children (DOM Min (11) 10/1). (See www.justice.govt.nz/publications/global-publications/c/child-witnesses-in-the-criminal-courts-proposed-reforms/child-witnesses-in-the-criminal-courts-proposed-reforms.) Fortuitous timing sparked research into informing the 2010 discussion paper (Ministry of Justice, 2010) and this subsequent 2011 Cabinet Minute. As a result, there was a policy team with similar questions keen to engage with the multi-disciplinary team of researchers and members of the Advisory Group on improving how children are addressed in court in 2011/12. The research amplified judicial concern about child witnesses. Dialogue throughout the research, with disagreements and unintended consequences discussed, contributed to a learning culture.

CONCLUSION: FIVE IDEAS FOR SOCIAL SCIENTISTS

1. Develop a multidisciplinary professional advisory group. Involving practitioners early in the research process secures commitment to the questions asked. This means they are more invested in seeing the results put into practice. The role of the Advisory Groups extended beyond improving the relevancy of the research. Through successive projects, they helped to ensure knowledge diffusion through their communities, formally through seminars and conferences, and informally through conversations with colleagues. Of primary importance, the Advisory Groups created spaces in which

ideas for improving practice and policy could be debated on the basis of their experiences alongside systematic information they had not had before. Researchers can encourage policy analysts, advisors and politicians to engage in such discussions by helping to create safe spaces for them to explore options. This needs to be carefully planned and held under the Chatham House rule.

2. Seize opportunities to facilitate dialogue through the research process. Politicians operate in three year government cycles in New Zealand. They need to see action in the short-term. Social science researchers do themselves no service by ignoring the constraints upon politicians and public servants. In 2010, the research team seized opportunities that were created by the Minister of Justice. This was unusual and fortuitous. Nevertheless, it is incumbent on researchers seeking action on their findings to look for these opportunities in the wider environment and carefully consider the best ways to frame the issues under discussion.

3. Consider a secondment in the public service. In my secondment, I learned something of how policy is made and the importance of framing issues in ways that connect with decision-makers. Relationships developed in the public and judicial sectors also helped to draw attention to the research proposal, thereby securing research funding years later. Furthermore, understanding the roles of policy analysts and advisors, including the constraints upon them, renders it easier to use research findings to develop recommendations that have more chance of being implemented.

4. Carefully plan dissemination of research findings. The mainstream media is an important component of the path from research to politics and policy. Constructive engagement in disseminating research findings with NGOs and other political parties as well as mainstream media, probably helped the government to realise that there would be public support for proposals, or at least no public backlash. Short news stories on the day of release of reports were assisted by professional media and thoughtful background pieces in newspapers. One 'feature' article eventuated in 2010 because of connections with journalists developed a decade earlier. Of equal importance, one of these journalists had a few days to read and reflect on research, and time to interview a number of people to get different perspectives. Even this limited amount of time is all too rare. Researchers can assist by lining up other people, with divergent opinions, willing to talk to a journalist at short notice.

5. *Build in a plan for the evaluation of the programme implemented.* When research leads to development, it is important that the programme developed is evaluated. In this story, the multi-agency centre wasn't evaluated but the court education programme was. Developing an evaluation plan at the start of implementation of a programme might increase the chances of it happening.

Social science research can be a complex, and often arduous, process. For some social scientists, the research process ends with the report or journal article. For others, to successfully reach the end of your project, but see no recommendations implemented, can be soul-destroying. I hope that my story, and the lessons learnt along the way, may help to reduce the frequency of that oft heard complaint 'But they didn't act on our findings!' I hope, too, that my suggestions may increase the chances that all your hard work will make a positive impact on the people and systems you have studied, which may be why you chose to be a social scientist in the first place.

REFERENCES

Davies, E., DeVere, H. and Verbitsky, J. (2004) Court education for young witnesses: Evaluation of the pilot service in Aoteoroa New Zealand. *Psychiatry, Psychology and Law*, 11 (2): 226–235.

Davies, E., Hanna, K., Henderson, E. and Hand, L. (2011) *Questioning child witnesses: Exploring the benefits and risks of intermediary models.* Auckland: Institute of Public Policy at AUT University. Available at: www.ipp.aut.ac.nz/publications/all-publications

Davies, E., Hanna, K., Henderson, E. and White, M. (2011) Prerecording children's entire testimony: Benefits and risks. *New Zealand Law Journal*, November: 335–338.

Davies, E., Henderson, E. and Hanna, K., 2010. Facilitating children to give best evidence: Are there better ways to challenge children's evidence? *Criminal Law Journal*, 34: 347–362.

Davies, E., Henderson, E. and Seymour, F.W. (1997) In the interests of justice? The cross-examination of child complainants in criminal proceedings. *Psychiatry, Psychology and Law*, 2: 1–13.

Davies, E. and Seymour, F.W. (1998) Questioning child complainants of sexual abuse: Analysis of criminal court transcripts in New Zealand. *Psychiatry, Psychology and Law*, 5(1): 47–61.

Davies, E., Seymour, F.W., Cooke, A., and Bidois, C. (2000) Developing multi-agency centres for child abuse investigation and treatment: A collaborative approach to developing centres of excellence. Unpublished report.

Davies, E., Seymour, F.W. & Read, J. (2000) Children's and primary carers' perceptions of the sexual abuse investigation process in Auckland, New Zealand. *Journal of Child Sexual Abuse*, 9: 41–56.

Hanna, K., Davies, E., Crothers, C. and Henderson, E. (2011) Questioning child witnesses in New Zealand's criminal justice system. Is cross-examination fair? *Psychiatry, Psychology and Law:* 1–11. First published on May 24th October, 2011. DOI:10.1080/13218719.2011.615813.

Hanna, K., Davies, E., Henderson, E., Crothers, C. and Rotherham, C. (2010) Child *Witnesses in the New Zealand Courts: A review of Practice and Implications for Policy.* Auckland: Institute of Public Policy at AUT University. Available at: www.ipp.aut.ac.nz/publications/all-publications.

Hanna, K., Davies, E., Henderson, E. and Hand, L. (in press) Questioning child witnesses: Exploring the benefits and risks of intermediary models. *Psychiatry, Psychology and Law*

Henderson, E. (2010) Innovative practices in other juris-dictions. In K. Hanna, E. Henderson, C. Crothers and C. Rotherham. *Child witnesses in the New Zealand criminal courts: A review of practice and implications for policy.* Auckland: Institute of Public Policy at AUT University. pp. 117–168 Available at: www.ipp.aut.ac.nz/publications/all-publications

Masters, C. (2010) Small *bodies of evidence.* New Zealand Herald. 24th April 2010. http://www.nzherald.co.nz/nz/news/article.cfm?c_id=1&objectid=10640468

Ministry of Justice. (2010) Alternative pre-trial and trial processes for child witnesses in New Zealand's criminal justice system: Issues Paper. Wellington: Ministry of Justice.

Ministry of Justice (2011a) Operational *Circular for Pre-recording Evidence.* Wellington: Ministry of Justice.

Ministry of Justice (2011b) National *guidelines for agencies working with child witnesses.* Wellington: Ministry of Justice.

Zajac, R. and Hayne, H. (2003) I don't think that's what really happened: The effect of cross-examination on the accuracy of children's reports. *Journal of Experimental Psychology: Applied,* 9(3): 187–195.

Dr. Emma Davies was a Principal Analyst in the Ministry of Social Development in 2006 and had worked as a Researcher at AUT over the last decade. At the time of writing she is a Partner in Rowe Davies Research Ltd. She takes up a position at Liverpool John Moores University Law School in June 2013. Email: emma@rowedaviesresearch.co.nz